NEW MEDIA INSTALLATION

INSTALLATION

TECHNOLOGY IN PUBLIC ART

GINGKO PRESS

NEW MEDIA INSTALLATION

TECHNOLOGY IN PUBLIC ART

First Published in the USA by
Gingko Press by arrangement with
Sandu Publishing Co., Ltd.

Gingko Press, Inc.
1321 Fifth Street
Berkeley, CA 94710 USA
Tel: (510) 898 1195
Fax: (510) 898 1196
Email: books@gingkopress.com
www.gingkopress.com

ISBN 978-1-58423-718-1

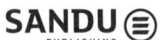

Sponsored by Design 360°
– Concept and Design Magazine

Edited and produced by
Sandu Publishing Co., Ltd.

Book design, concepts & art direction by
Sandu Publishing Co., Ltd.
Chief Editor: Wang Shaoqiang
Design Director: Niu Huizhen
Copy Editor: Jason Buchholz

Cover project by Kuflex

info@sandupublishing.com
www.sandupublishing.com

Printed and bound in China

CONTENTS

PREFACE

—

*By **David Torrents***

—

Humanity believes in progressing. But at the same time, we need to hold on to what we already know to continue developing new works. And this is the spirit we intend to convey through this book—to display the innovative techniques and technological breakthroughs that many artists and designers have recently developed in their new media projects.

Throughout the twentieth century, artists and designers in all fields have sought new forms of expression. A constant searching has brought us to a crossroads where new technologies have become protagonists of the first order, and have spawned the birth of many innovative artistic disciplines. It is important for people to be aware that this replanting of new languages and codes goes beyond a merely formal and intrinsically visual game. The changes urge us to discover the aspects of life that are not banal and to consider our future development, and in doing so they help us to understand the reality we live in.

Perhaps contemporary new media designers and artists have provided an opportunity to break the physical dimensions of space, and move into absolutely unknown worlds. It is a privilege to live as spectators among these new media facilities and to feel ourselves as travelers to the near future, beyond impossible landscapes and reality. This exploration impacts our whole sensory system, and at the same time, our perception towards the varying moments.

Working with new media also involves the determination of new content. We cannot just explore radical codes and leave the public indifferent with simple speeches. The new platforms invite us to narrate stories and get closer to the audience. Perhaps these stories have been the same throughout history and the only thing that has changed is the way they have been presented to us. It is difficult to escape from the known discourse, but the form invites us to explain different contents and to break free of the well-known and banal discourses. This book shows the rising trends of new media art—not only the styles, but also a whole new type of speech. In this book the reader will encounter many amazing works and come to understand something of the complexity of the process behind them.

Undoubtedly, light is the basis of many technological installations. Light converts the static into magic forms—it illuminates and personalizes the dark. Technology often presents through light while darkness becomes its stage. Technology and light come together to transform both public and private spaces into mysterious and poetic zones. Light invites us to step into our fantasies and embrace our dreams. Light is the virtue and essence of new media which transforms perceptions into mystery.

Moreover, interactivity is an essential element in many projects. This interaction brings the cold, dull, and digital closer to us. In short, to discuss the human roles in technology is to talk about interactivity. The coldness of programming has some deeper meanings, which lead us to another aspect: to be able to decide when and how we want to interconnect with art and design.

In recent years, we have witnessed the new media development and its implementation in public art including video installations, mapping projections, the internet, geolocation devices, and all kinds of novelties, from small projects to large-scale interventions, from optical games to interactive games. This book guides us to discover the power of new media and its profound influence on the culture, and the transformation it entails in our lives. Enjoy it!

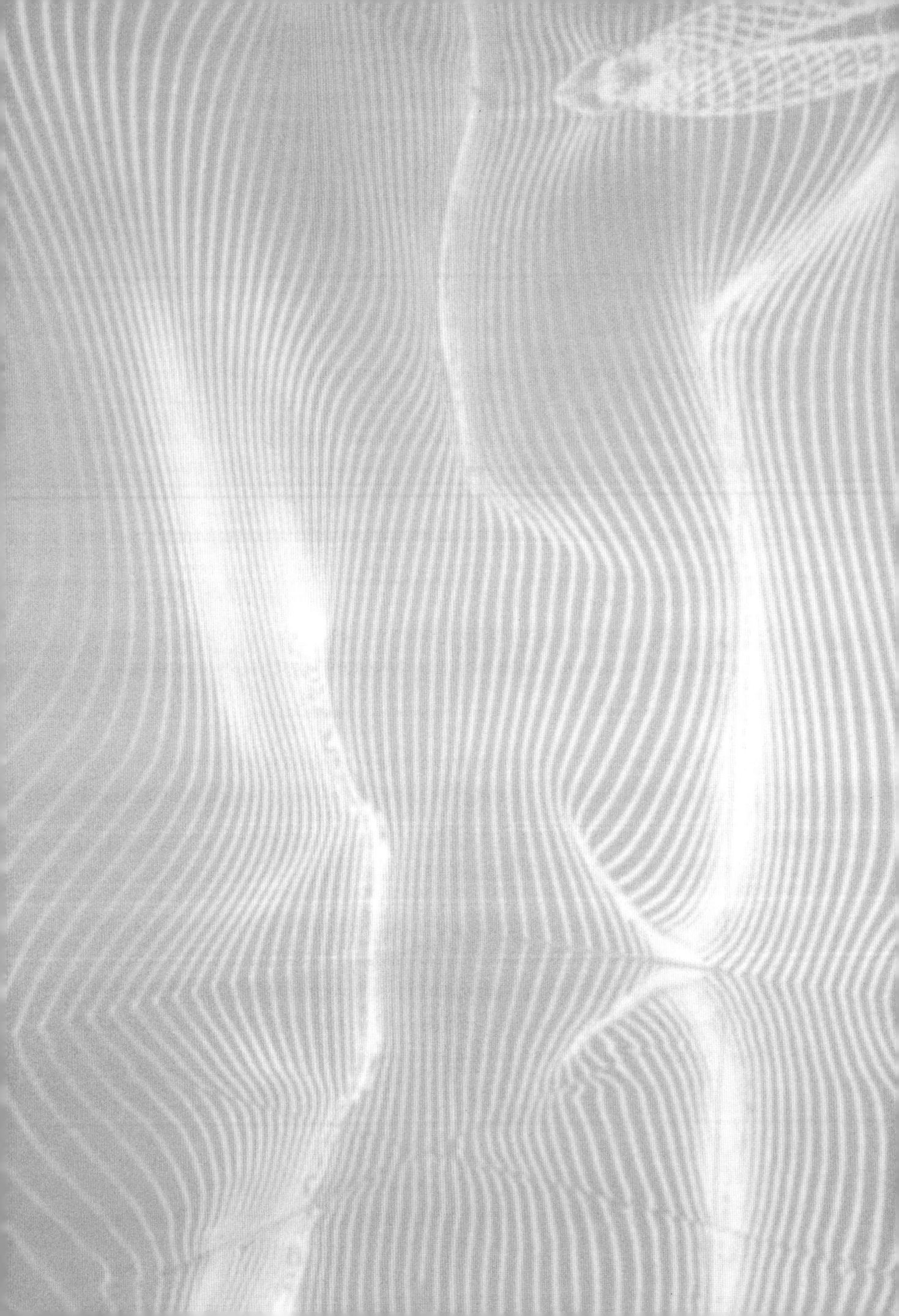

"Light converts the static into magic forms—it illuminates and personalizes the dark. Technology often presents through light while darkness becomes its stage."

—David Torrents

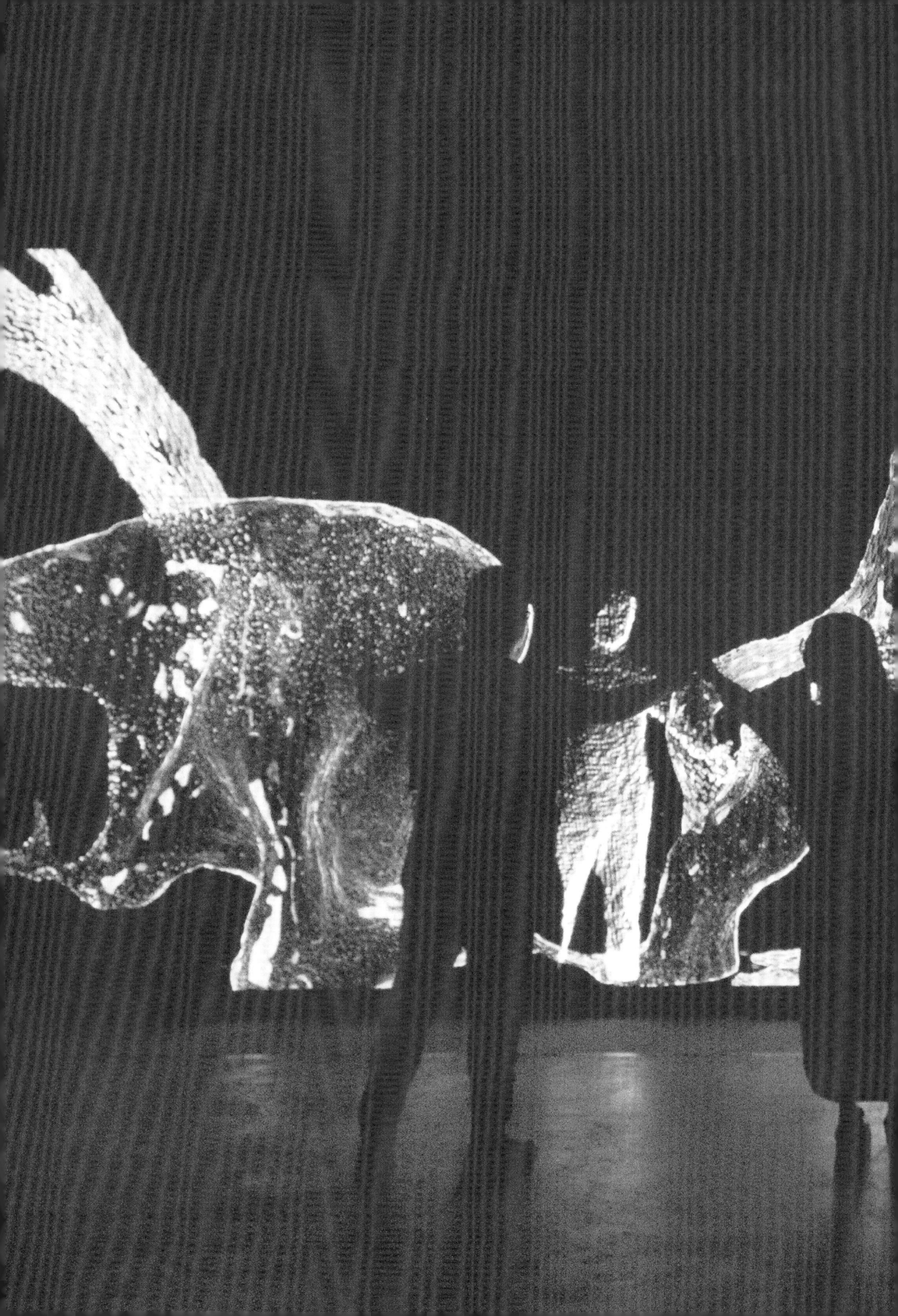

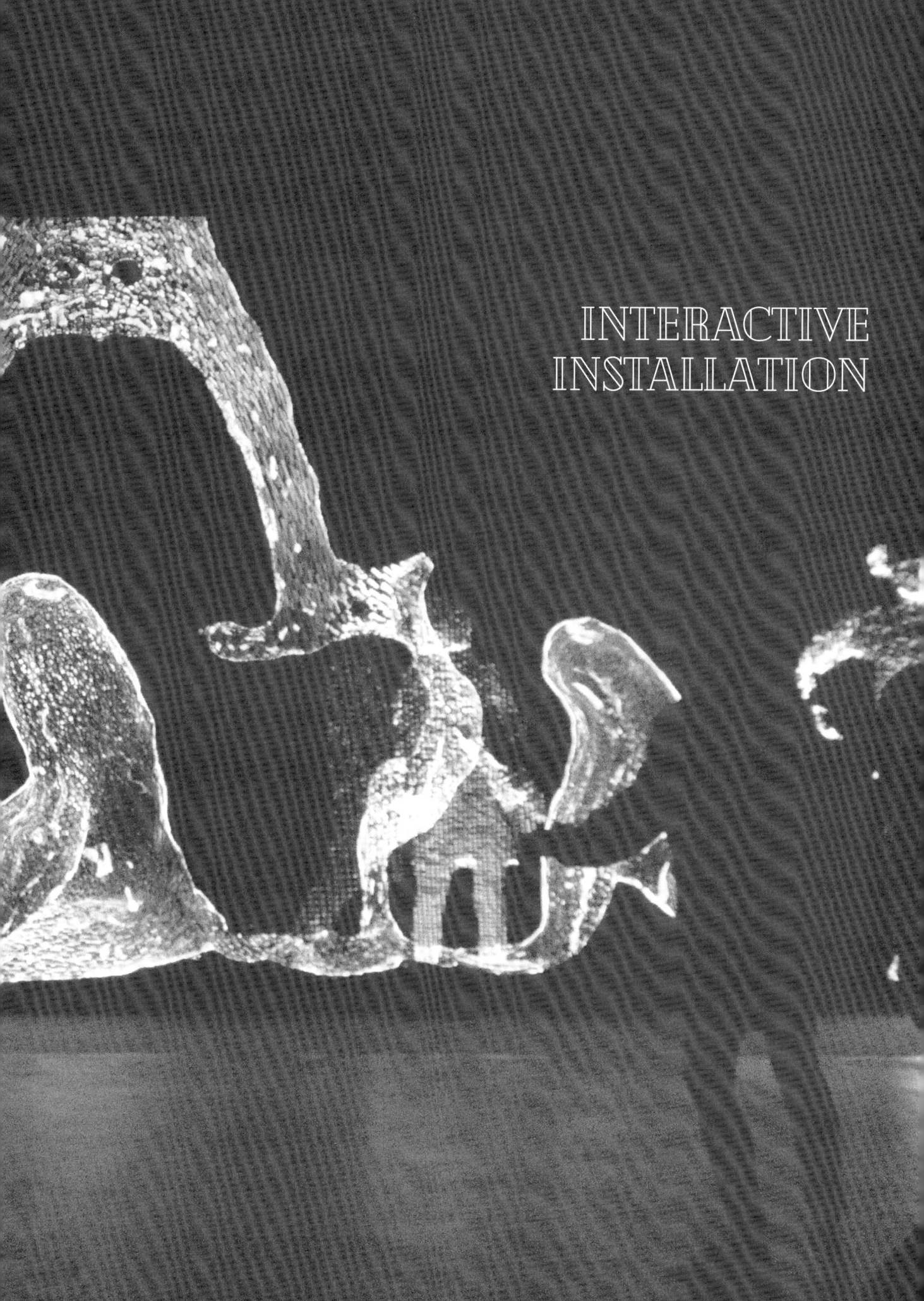

INTERACTIVE
INSTALLATION

LIQUID LIGHT

—

Design: **Malin Bobeck Tadaa**
Photography: **Jan Berg**

—

Liquid Light is a series of experimental optical fiber textiles inspired by the interaction between water and light.

Droplet is a jacquard woven fabric that lights up through optical fibers. The idea was to create a fabric with many dimensions and where the light is partly hidden in the fabric. The inspiration comes from raindrops forming a pattern on a smooth surface.

Flow is a translucent fabric woven on a shaft loom. Optical fibers run through the fabric. They are cut to different lengths, creating varied light points. The inspiration comes from water that flows down a window.

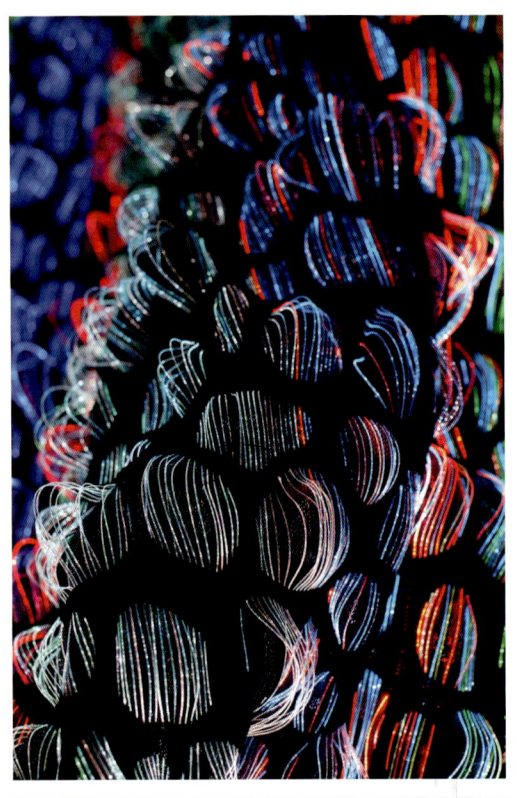

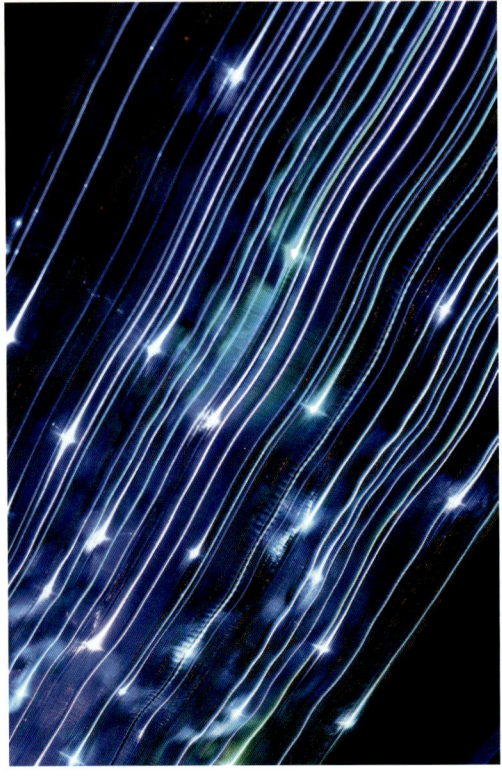

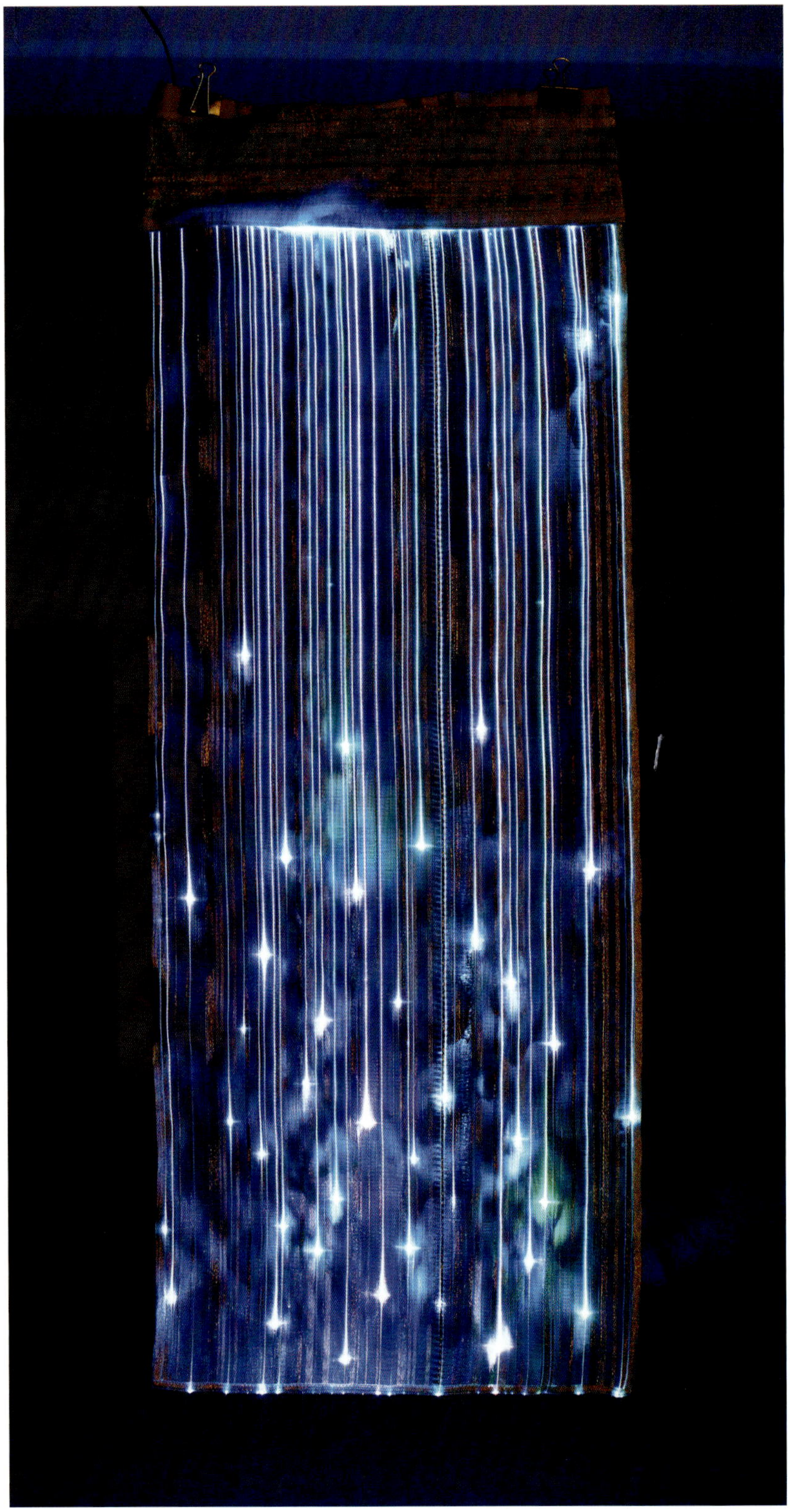

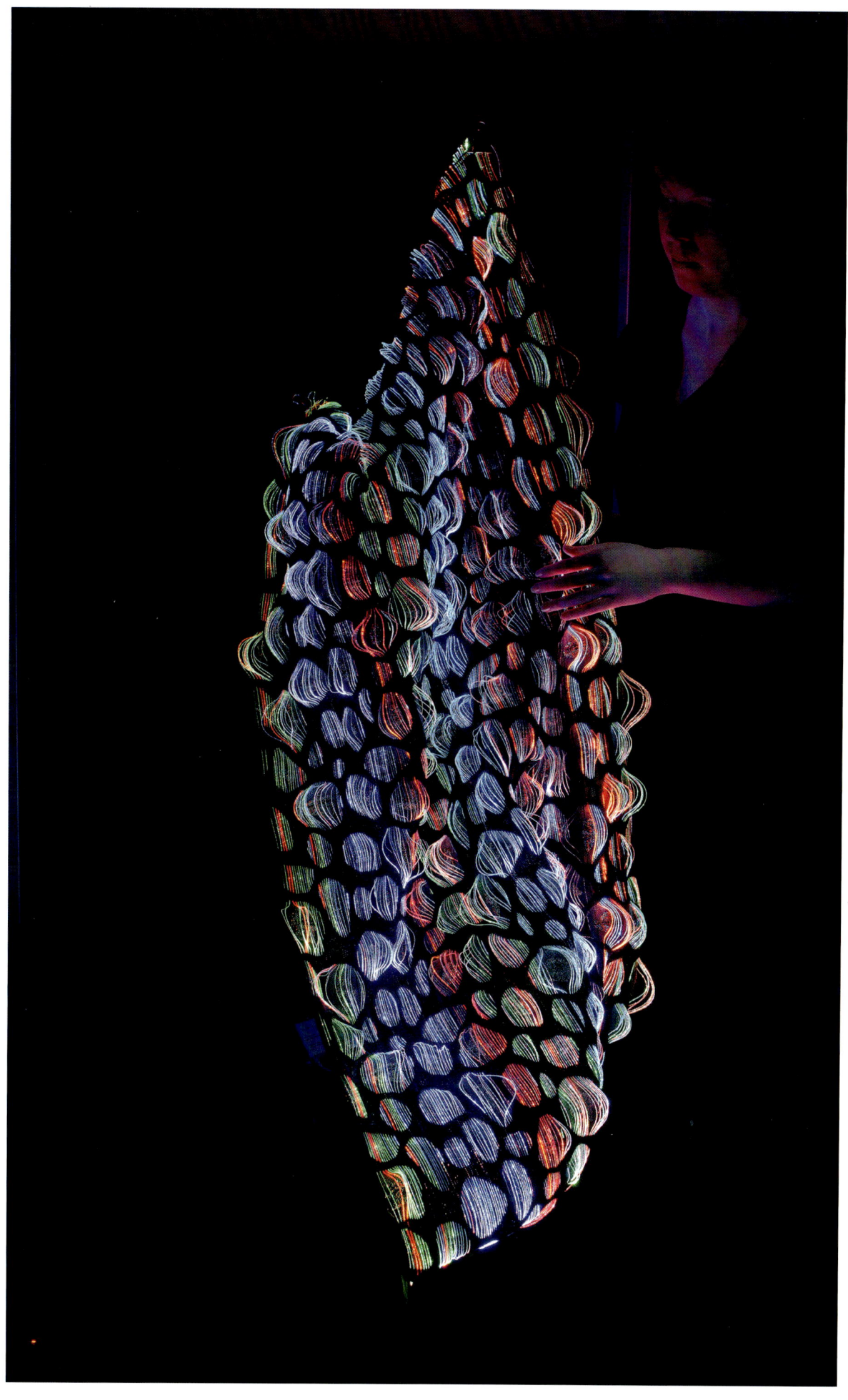

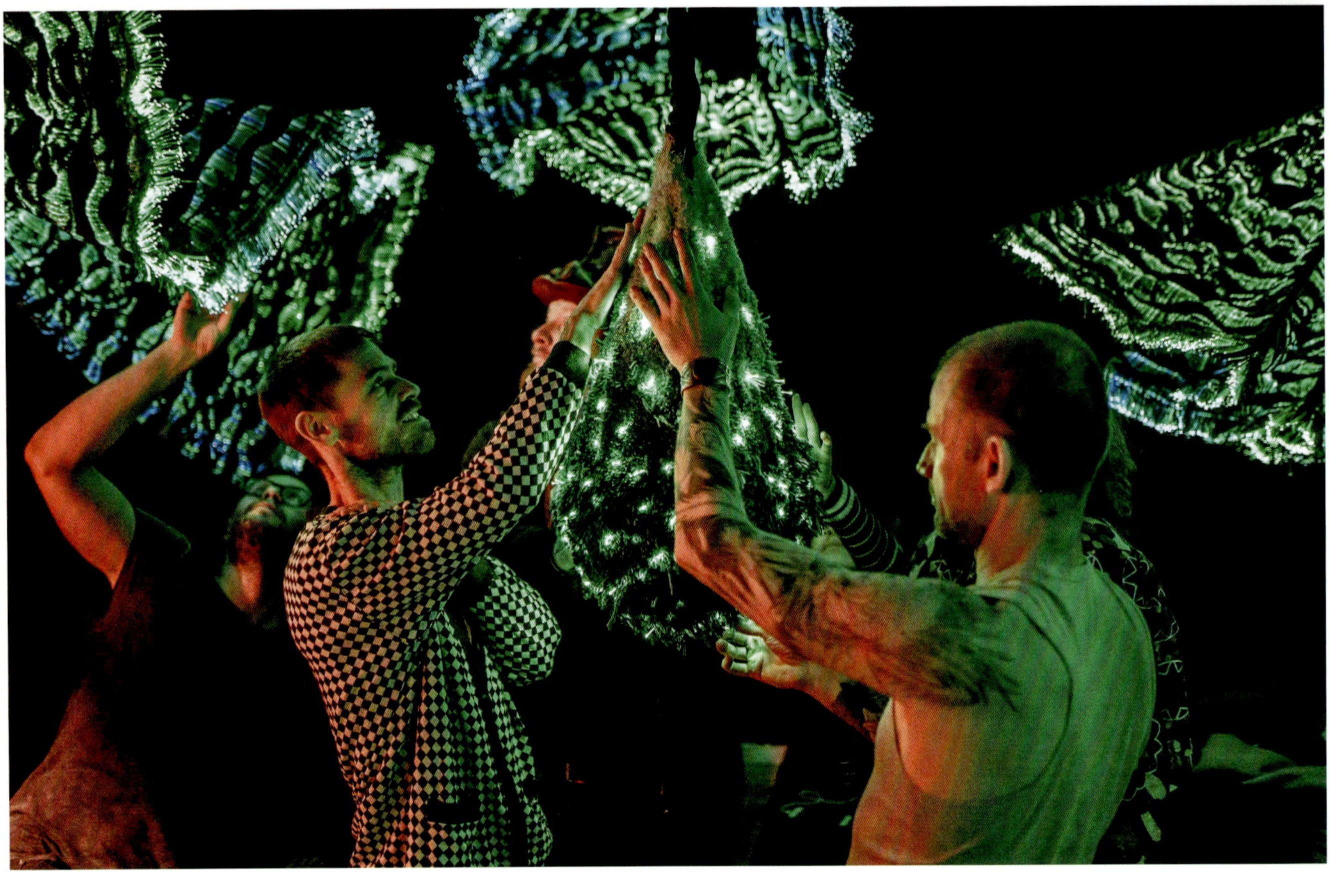

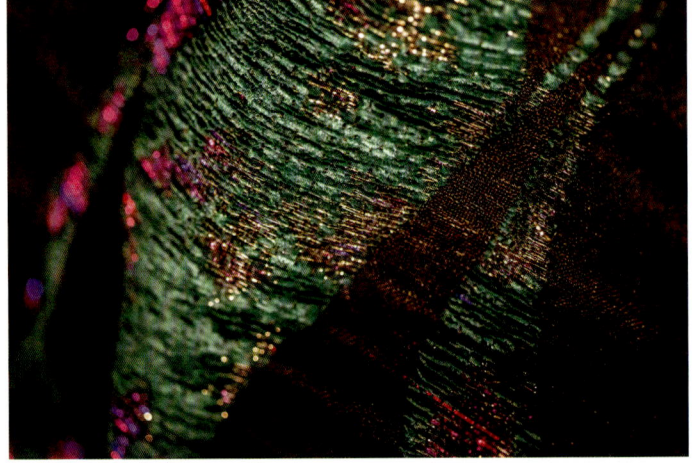

TACTILE REFUGE

—

Design: **Malin Bobeck Tadaa**
Photography: **Yann Houlberg Andersen**

—

Tactile Refuge is an interactive, light-emitting, textile installation in which the viewer creates the environment. The piece consists of six fabric wings, woven with optical fibers that are lit from within, and a hanging centerpiece, hand-tufted and implanted with optical fibers and LEDs. The installation is seemingly floating in a sheltered, dark space.

The centerpiece sculpture registers human touch and reacts by changing color. It affects the entire installation and intensifies the immersive light patterns in the fabric of the wings. Collaborating makes the reaction even stronger, changing the atmosphere of the entire space.

Tactile Refuge, originally inspired by the curious worlds under the Earth's waters, provides a space in which participants can submerge themselves in a calm and curious tranquility, under the glow of glimmering LED lights.

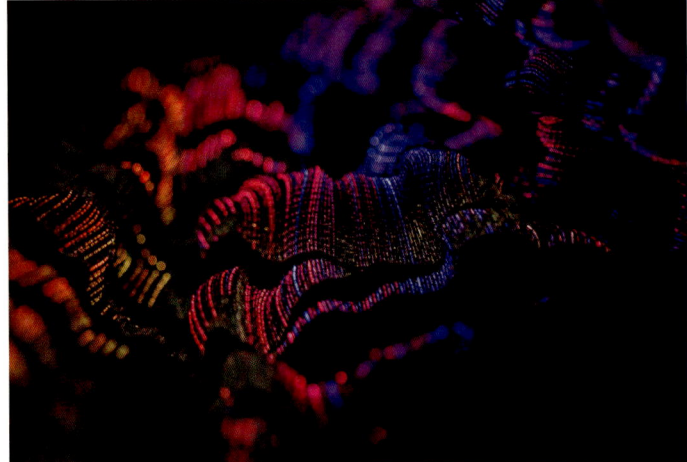

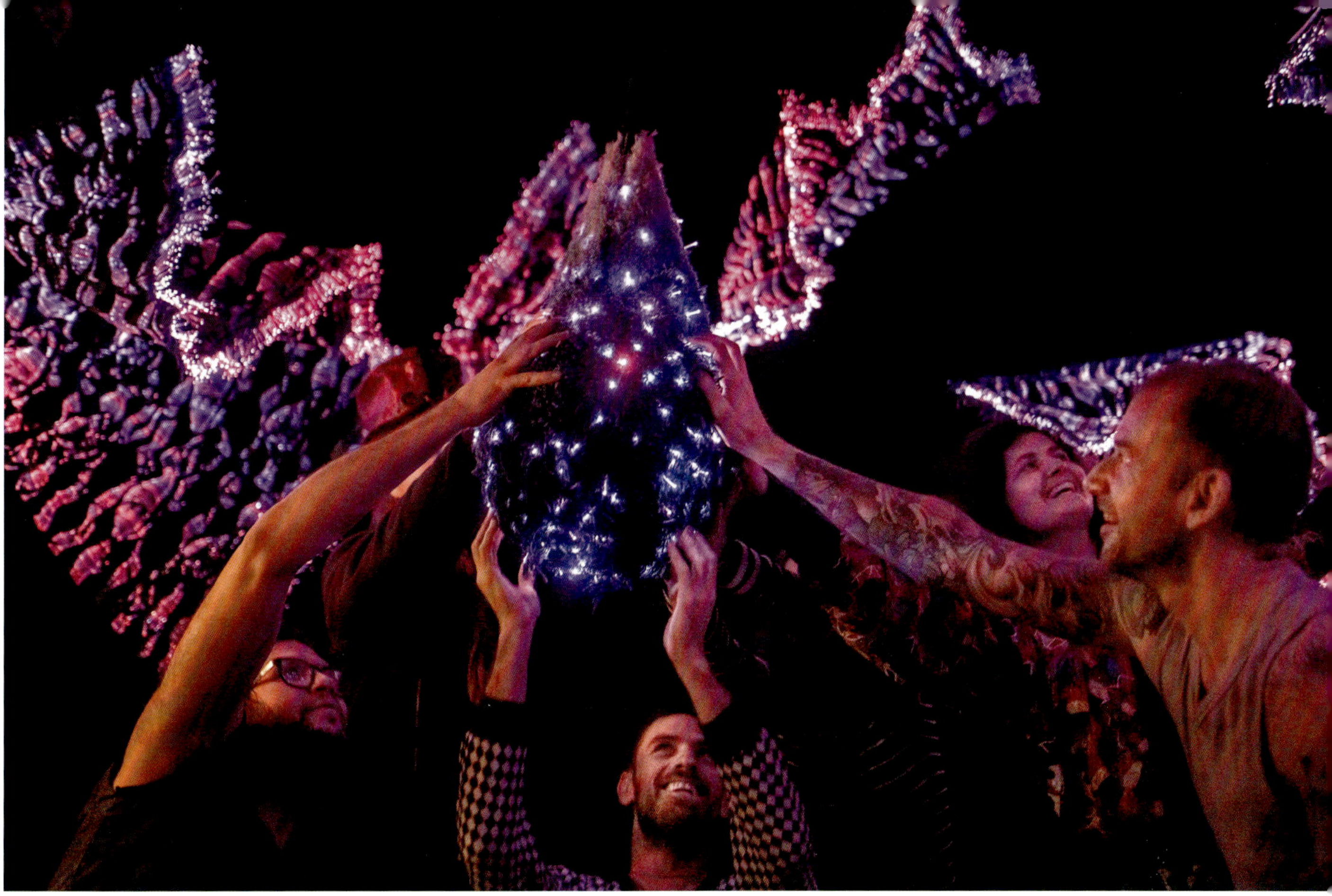

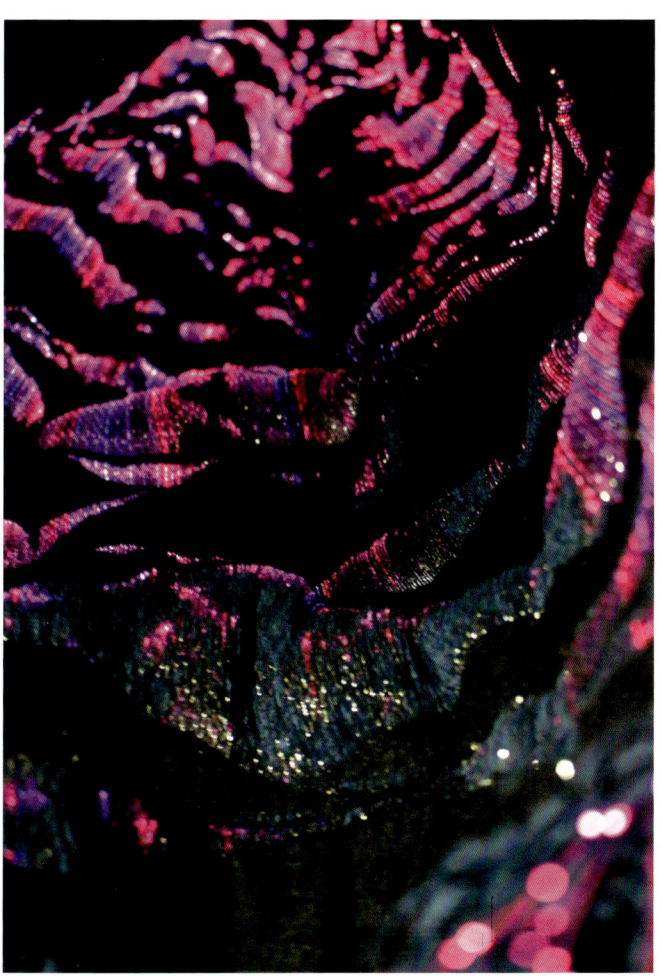

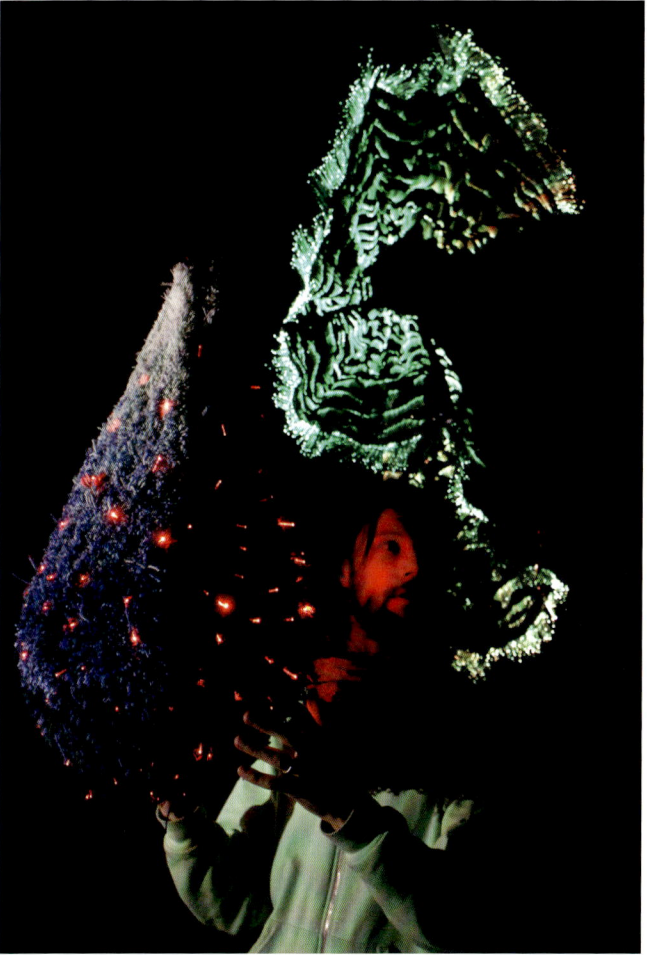

THOSE WHO AFFECTED ME

Design: **Malin Bobeck Tadaa**
Photography: **Yann Houlberg Andersen**

—

Those Who Affected Me is an interactive light-emitting textile art installation. Suspended in midair, over 1.5 meters tall and 2.5 meters in diameter, the four-winged structure invites the audience to gently touch the textile and reacts by sending colorful ripples up and down the intricate fabric.

The custom-designed jacquard textile uses optical fibers connected to about 500 individually programmable color LEDs, connected to a microcomputer. Thin, electrically conducting copper threads are woven in to create touch-sensitive areas inside the fabric. The 11 meters of fabric are mounted with steel rods around a steel cylinder.

The sculpture is exhibited in a small room with tilted mirror walls, creating a distorted universe where the sculpture is multiplied in infinity.

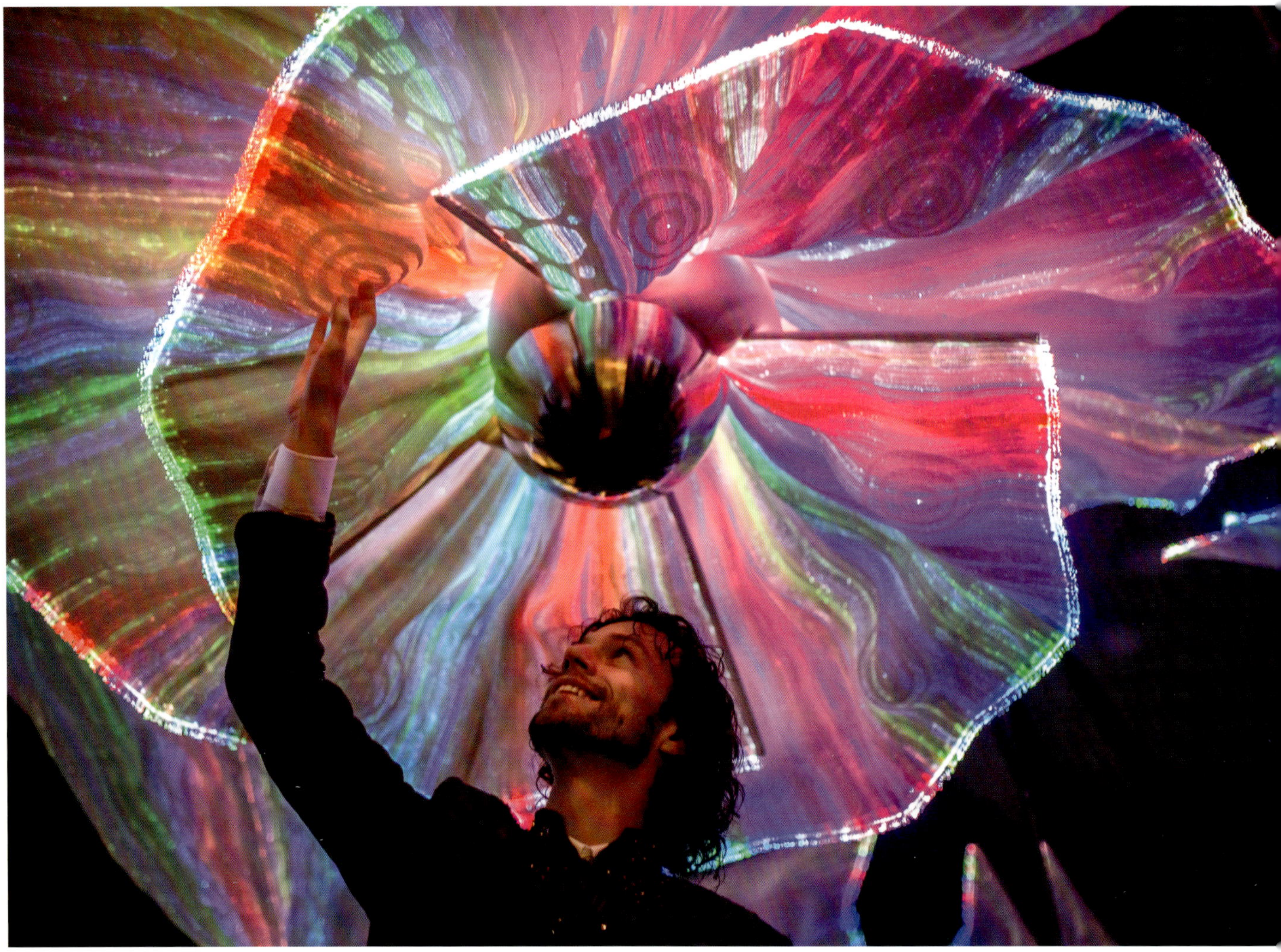

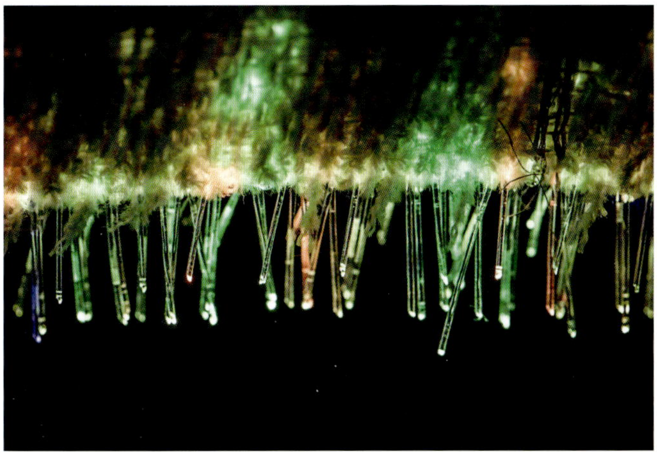

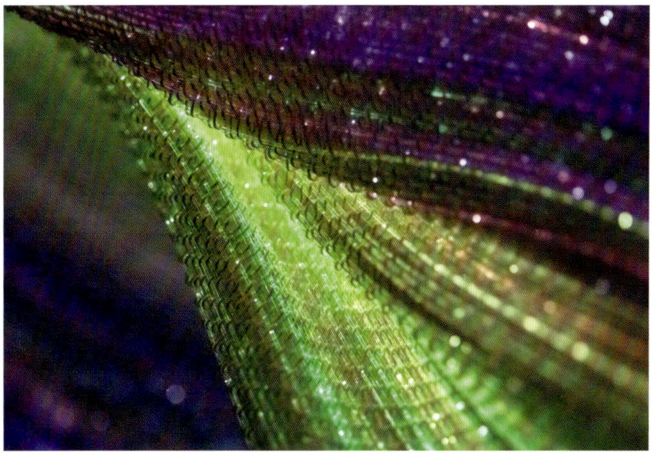

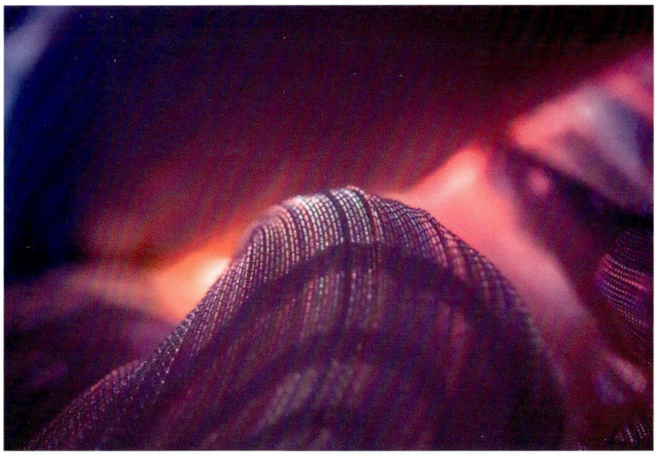

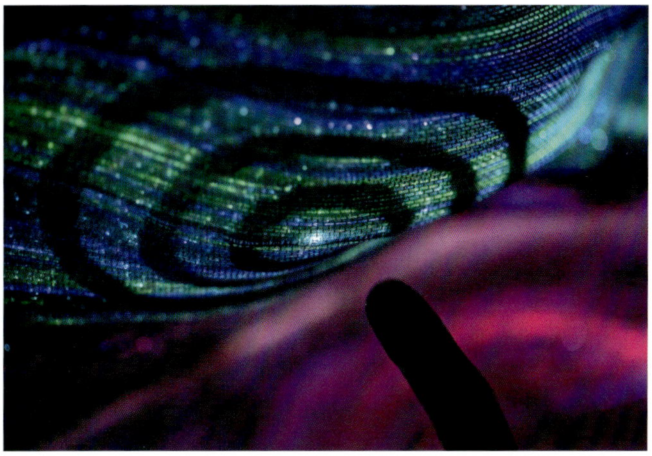

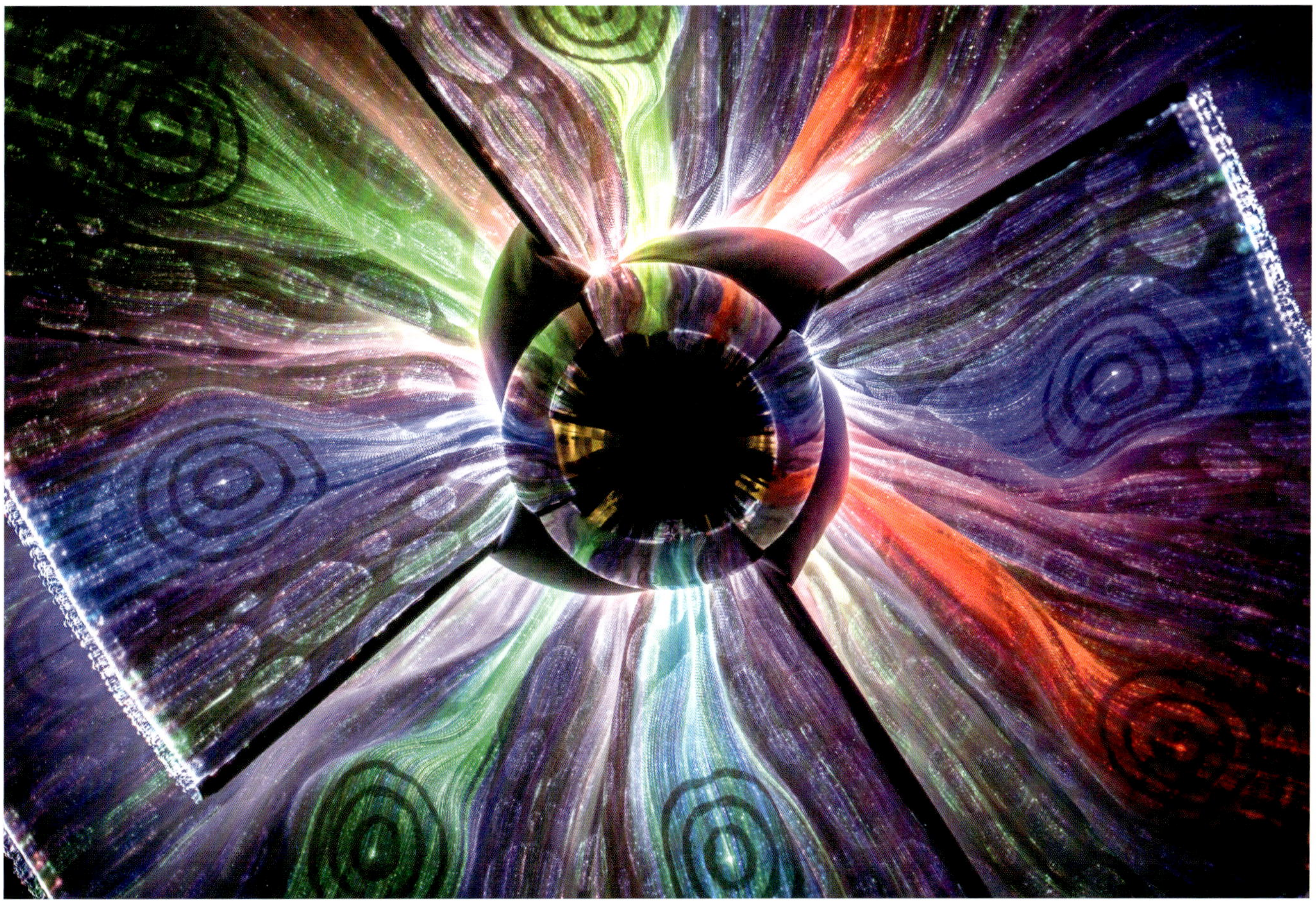

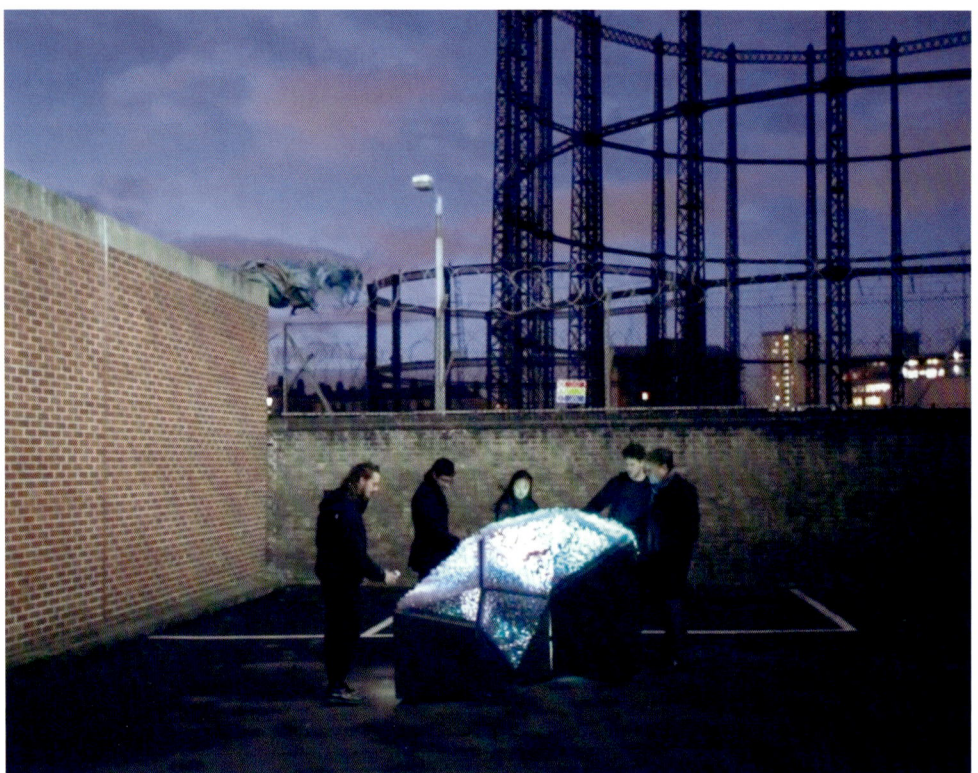

LIGHT POLLINATION

—

Design: **UniversalAssemblyUnit**
Client: **iGuzzini**
Photography: **Amandine Alessandra, UniversalAssemblyUnit**

—

Light Pollination seeks to spread the word about light, and in doing so, it explores the strong links between light and communication. Optical fiber, the primary material used to create the artwork, is a vehicle for light through which high-speed communication is facilitated. Thus, the art installation is both an expression and a prototype of this, albeit on a smaller scale. Rather than addressing a particular function, it imagines an alternative way of interacting with artificial light that is playful and social.

Powered by love of playful light, this installation features around 20,000 individual points of LED light brought to the surface through fiber optics, and is dotted with sensors measuring light intensity. By shining a light onto these "pollination" points, the artwork responds with bursts of illumination resembling a kind of bioluminescent coral reef. This effect is created in real-time using the game engine Unity3D to simulate the swarming effect of fireflies. The interaction is similar to turbulence fields that disturb the trails of light across the surface.

The piece was inspired by animals that use bioluminescence for methods of communication or warning signals.

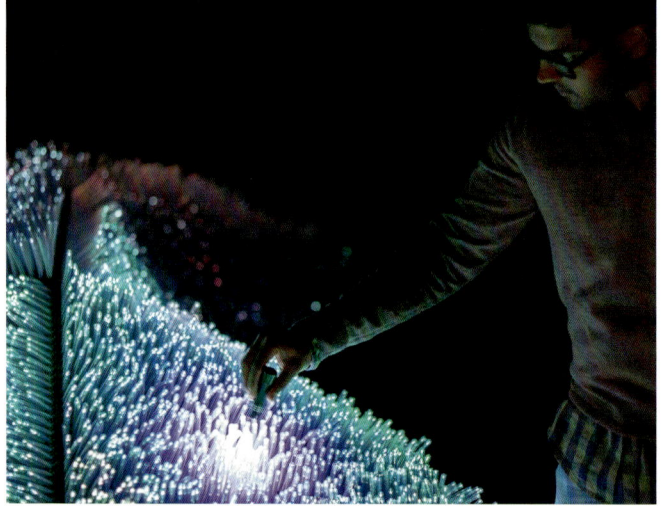

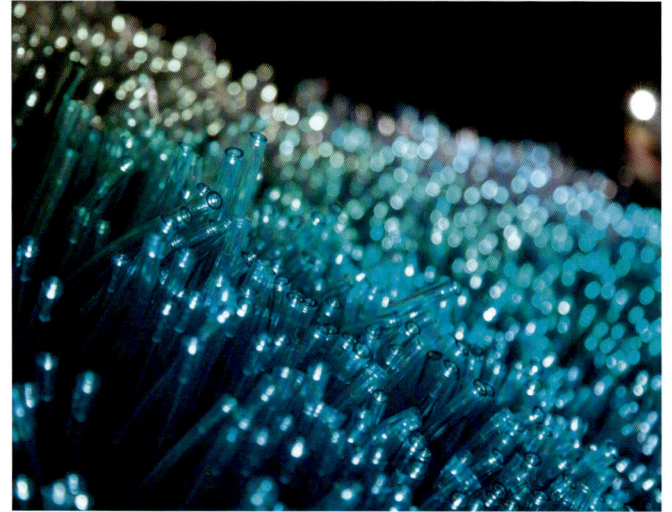

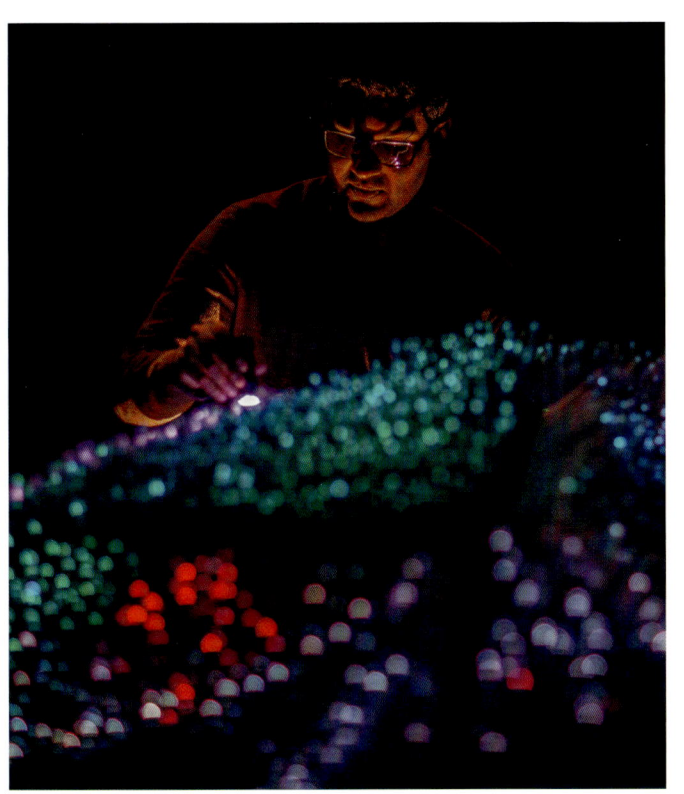
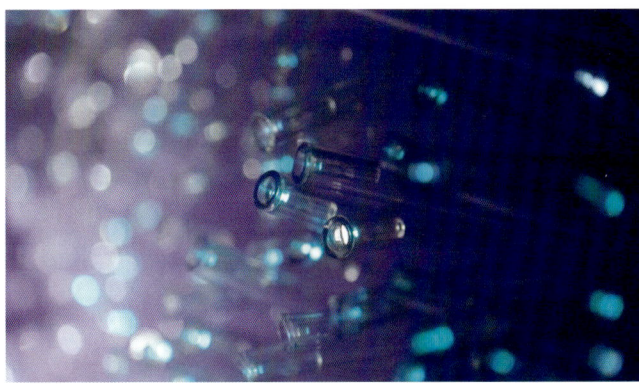
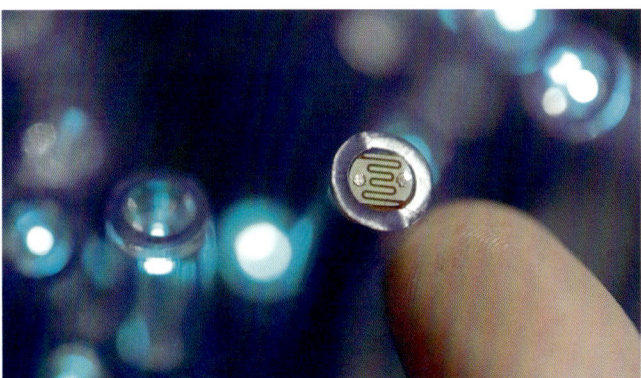

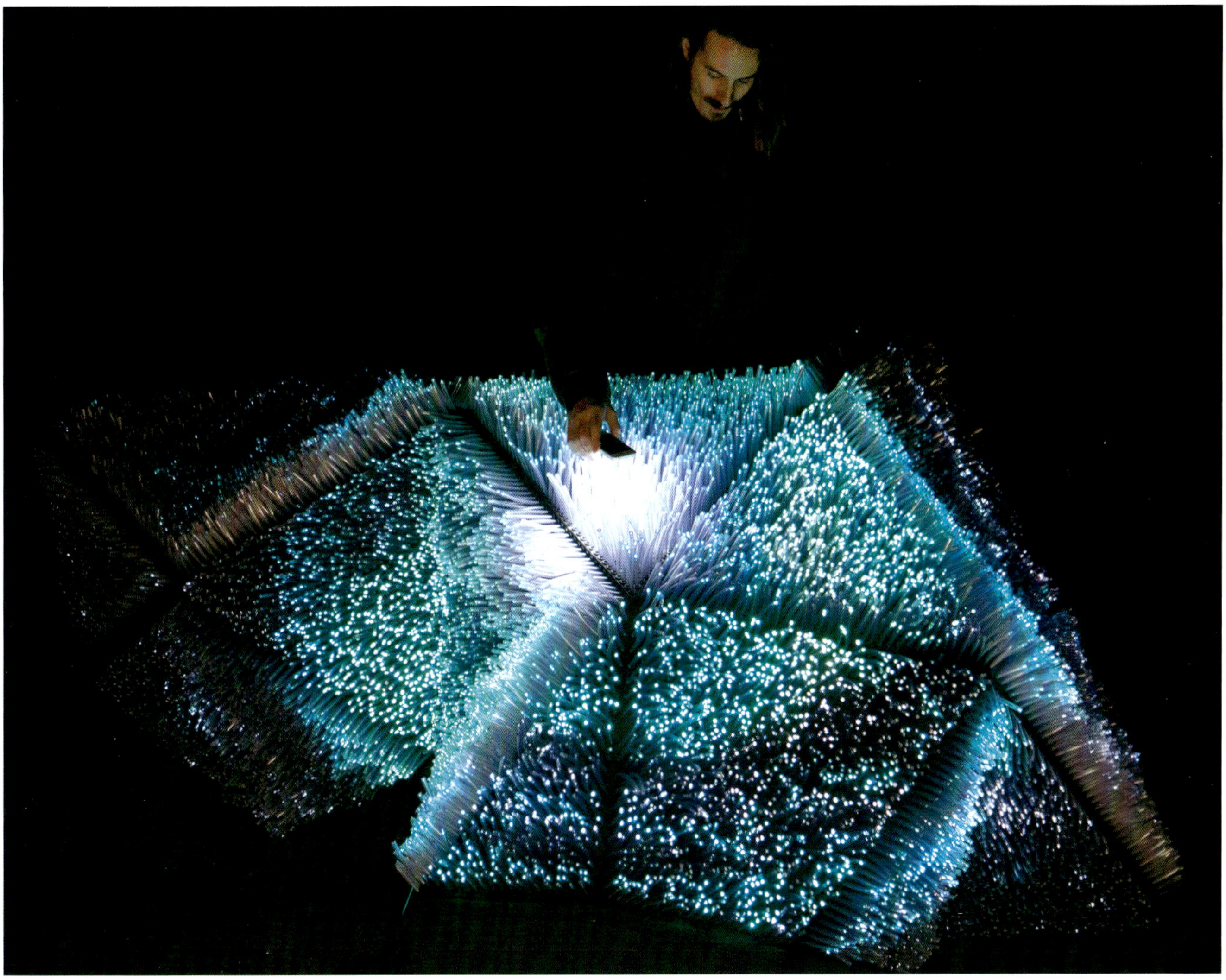

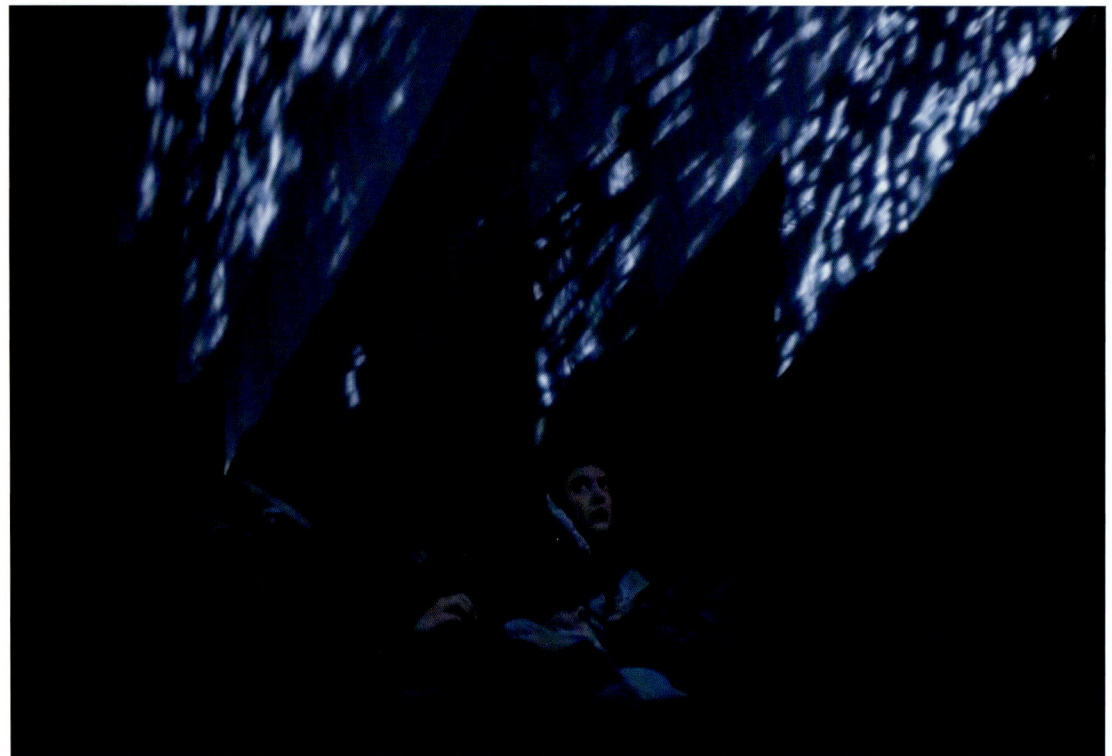

65°-75°

—

Design: **Bertrand Lanthiez**

—

65°-75° is an interactive installation in which the audience is invited to a quest for the Northern Lights. Striving to share the sense of mystery of tracking these lights in northern Scandinavia, the artist presents an almost indecipherable map. If audience members find the correct path, they can trigger light and sound pulses projected on the curtains around them.

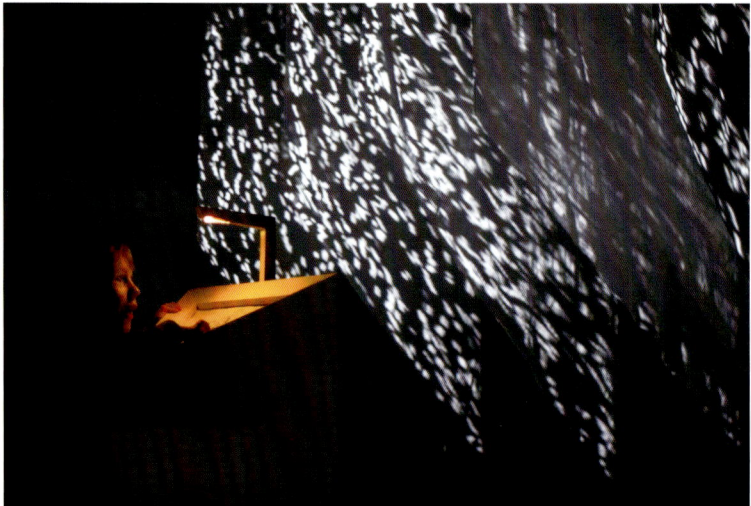

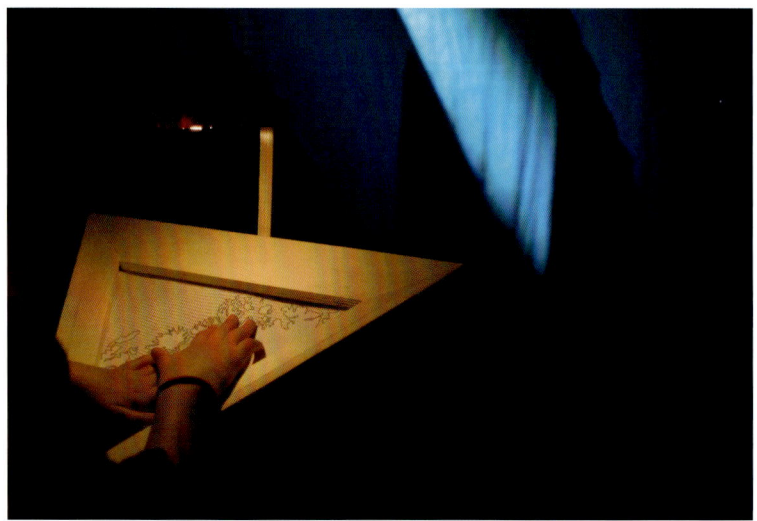

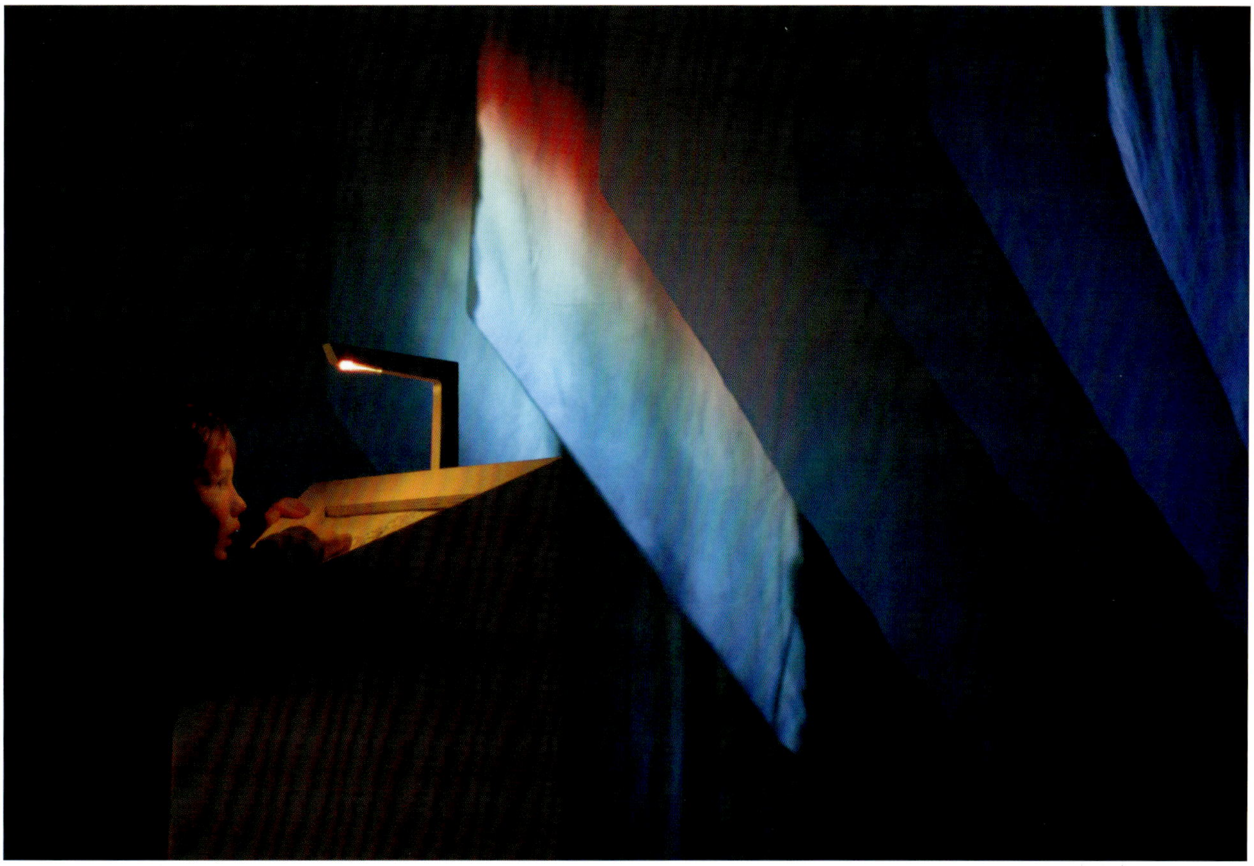

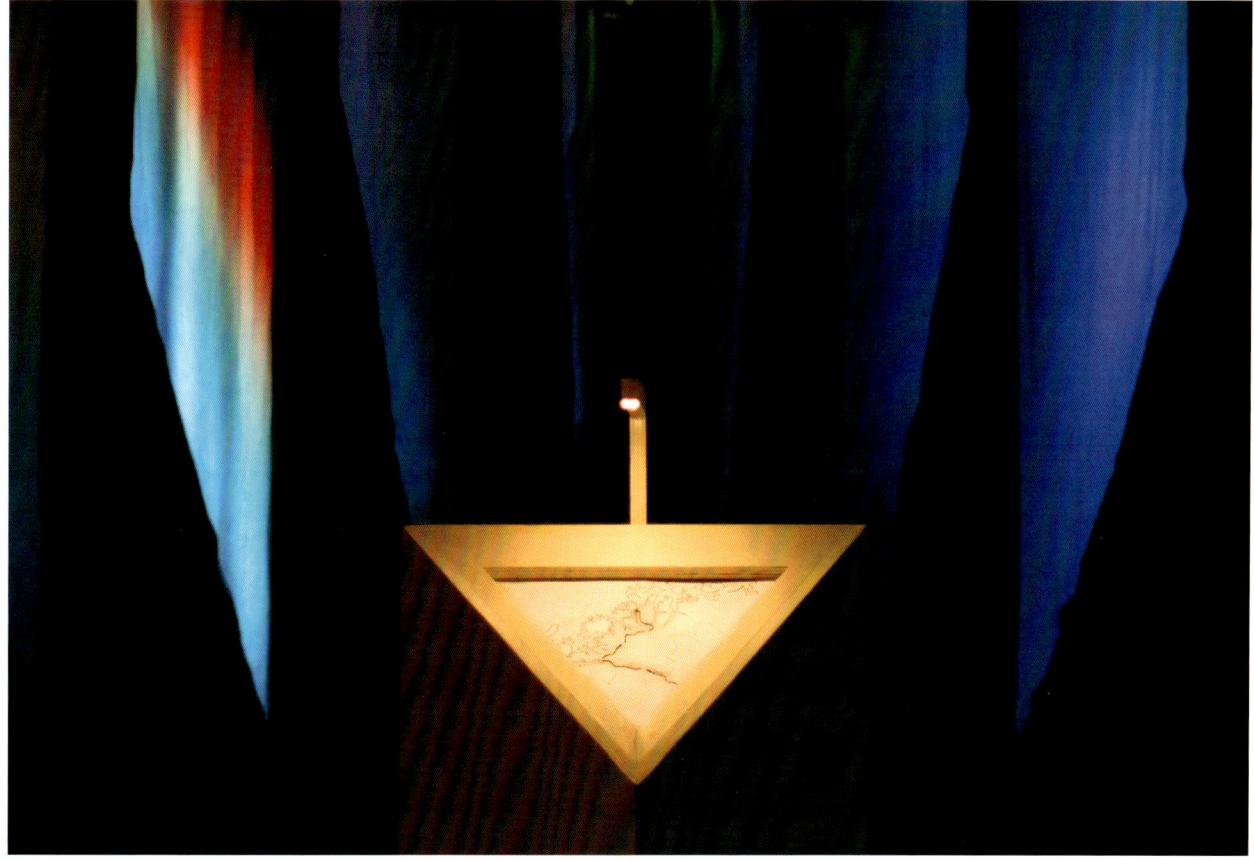

GLOWING NATURE

—

Design: **Studio Roosegaarde**

—

Glowing Nature expresses the beauty of nature
on the Afsluitdijk (a causeway in the Netherlands)
through a unique encounter between man, biology
and technology. This interactive, mysterious
exhibit features live bioluminescent algae, one
of the oldest microorganisms in the world. Only
under the perfect conditions and with the right
amount of maintenance and care do these single-
cell algae give off a prolonged natural light when
they are touched. The algae are also a possible
component of emerging circular economic
models, teaching audience members about new
energy and light solutions drawn from nature.
The exhibit is presented exclusively in the historic
bunkers on the Afsluitdijk.

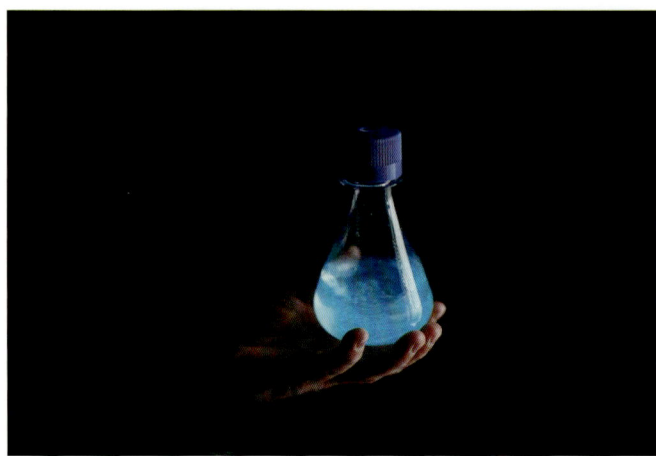

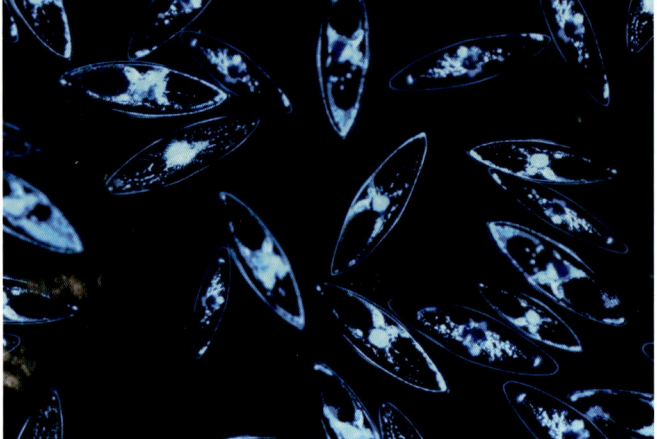

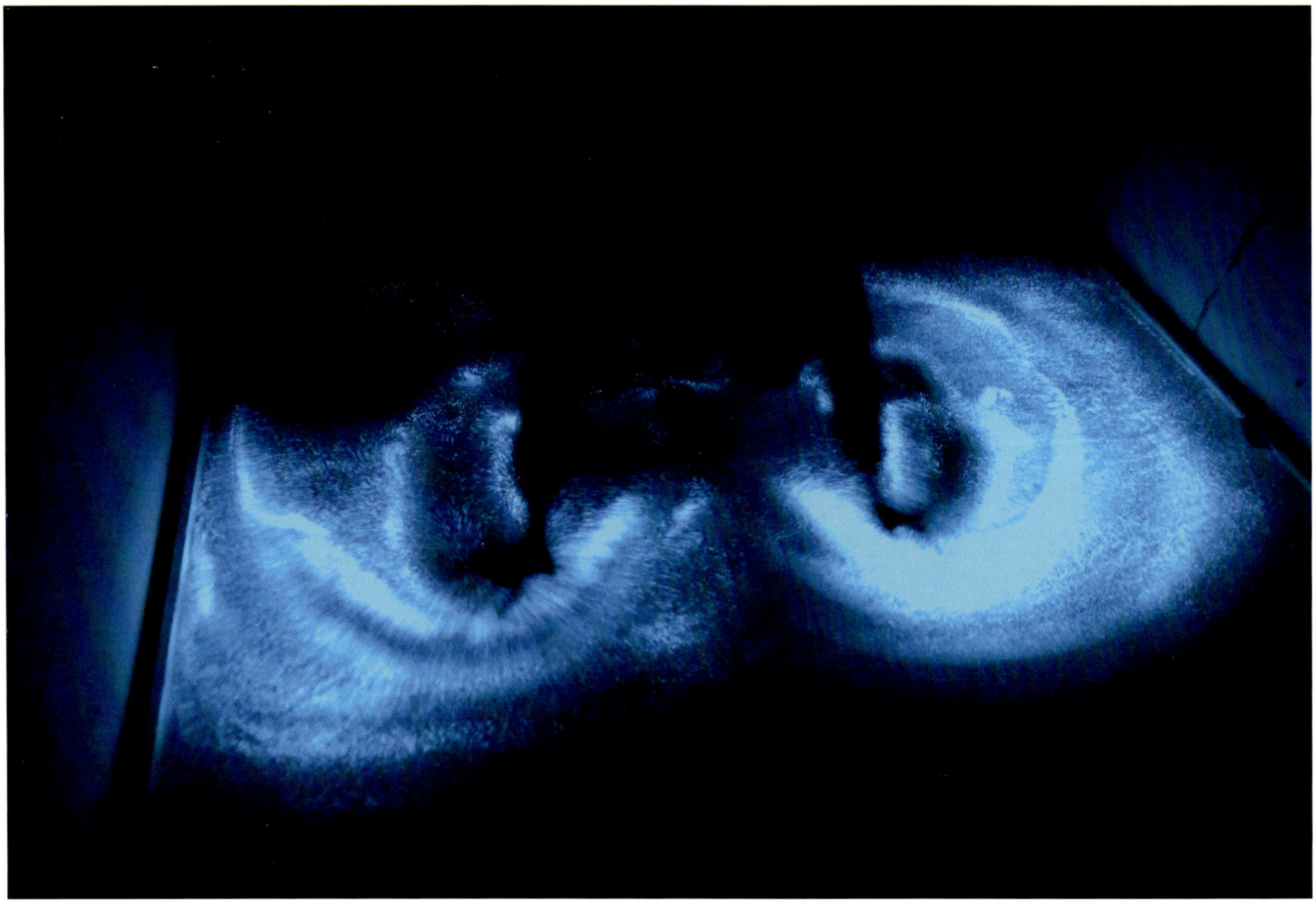

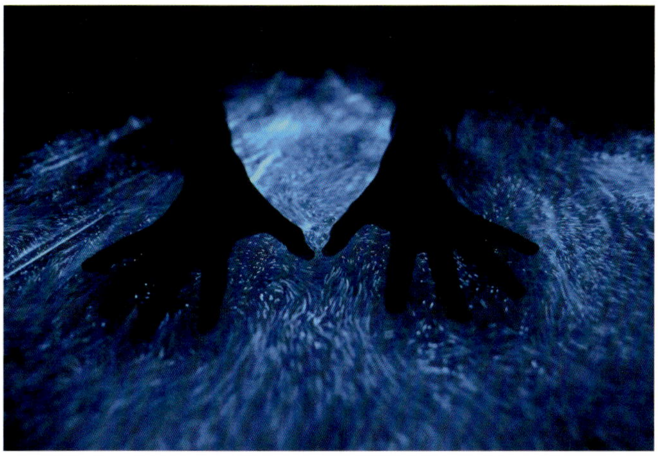

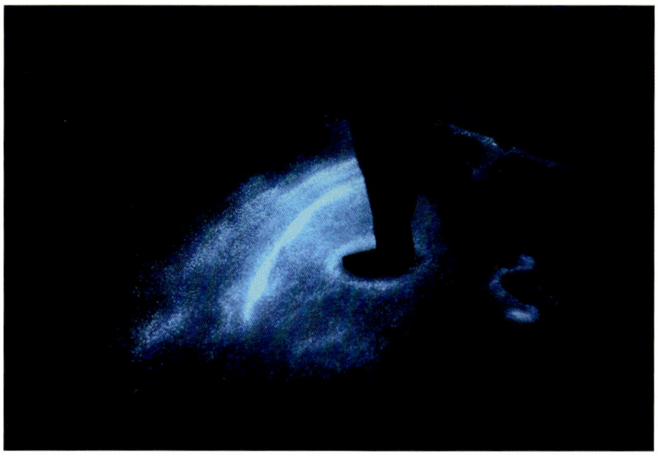

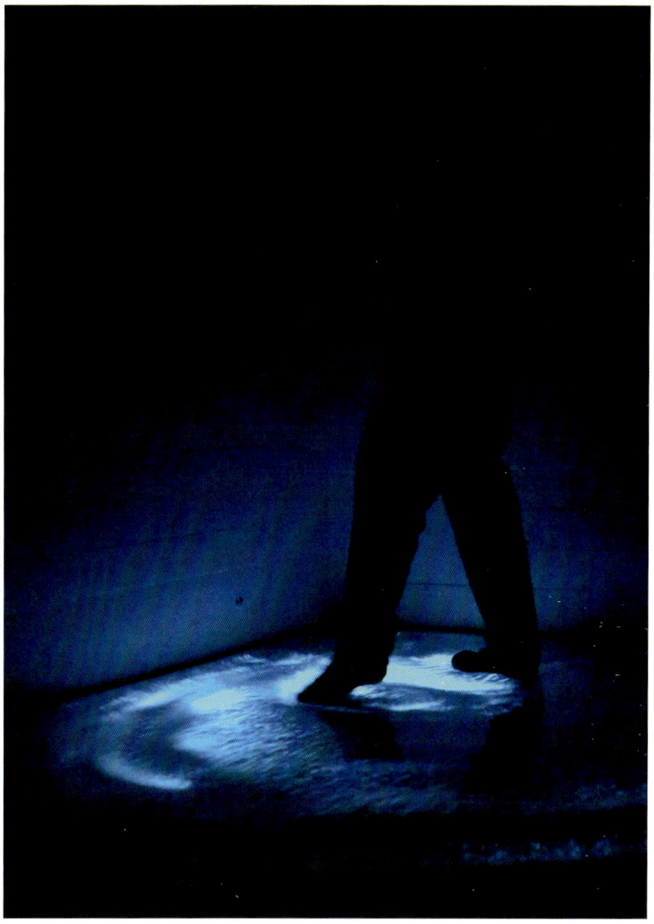

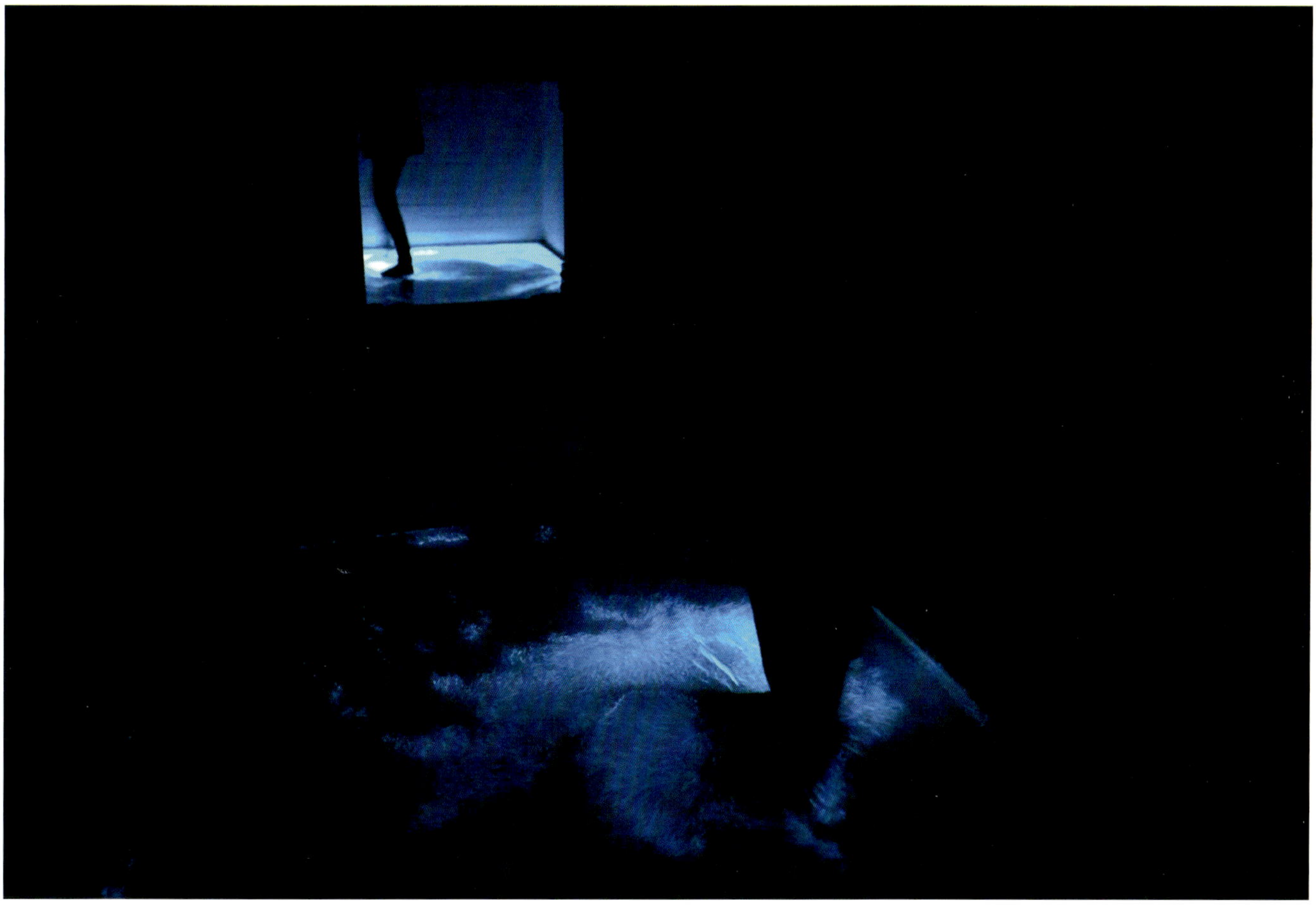

KALEIDOSCOPE

—

Concept Design & Art Direction: **Karina Smigla-Bobinski**
Photography: **FILE Festival, Dominik Schumacher**

—

KALEIDOSCOPE is an analog interactive installation that functions as a very large lightbox. Red, green, and blue inks float in separate layers beneath a touch-sensitive surface, and pressure from the viewer—whether with a finger, the feet, or the entire body—displaces and shifts the inks, creating new colors and shapes. These changes are picked up by cameras and projected onto other surfaces at the exhibition space. In one case, at the FILE festival in Brazil, the installation's output appeared on the huge LED facade of the festival building.

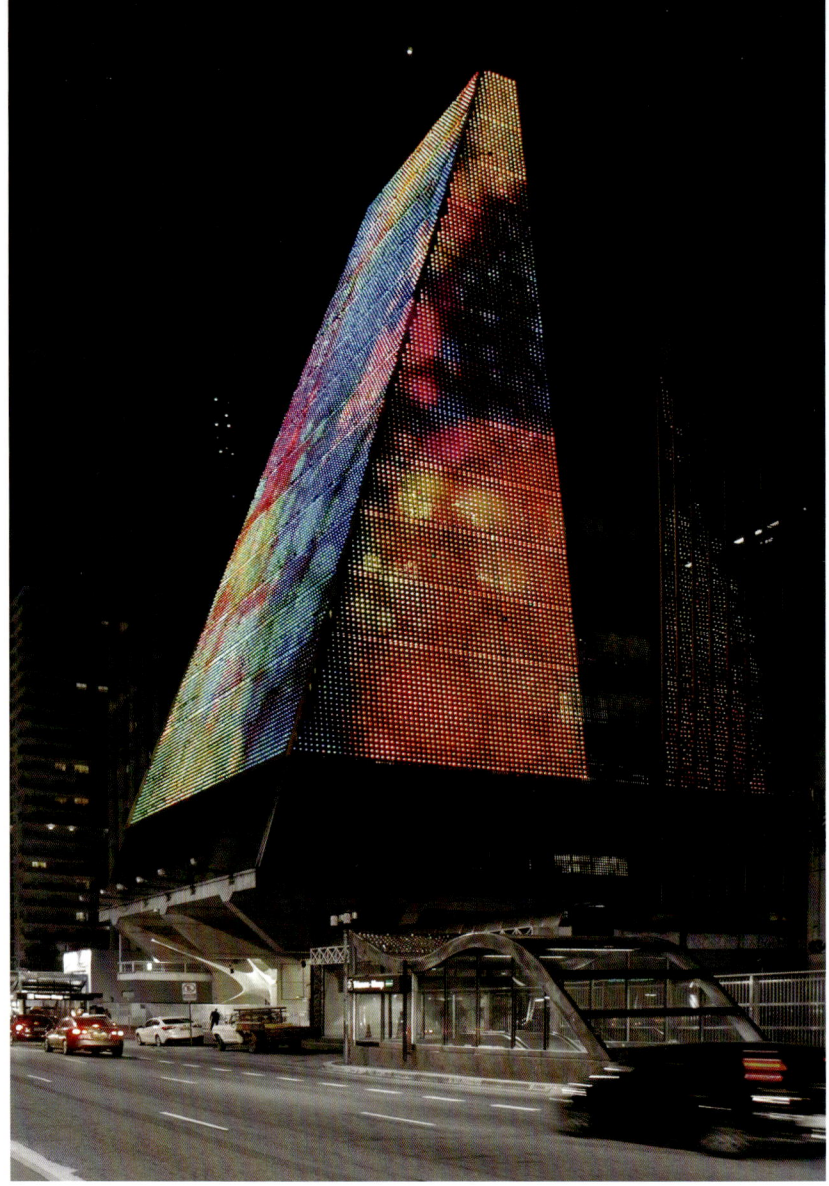

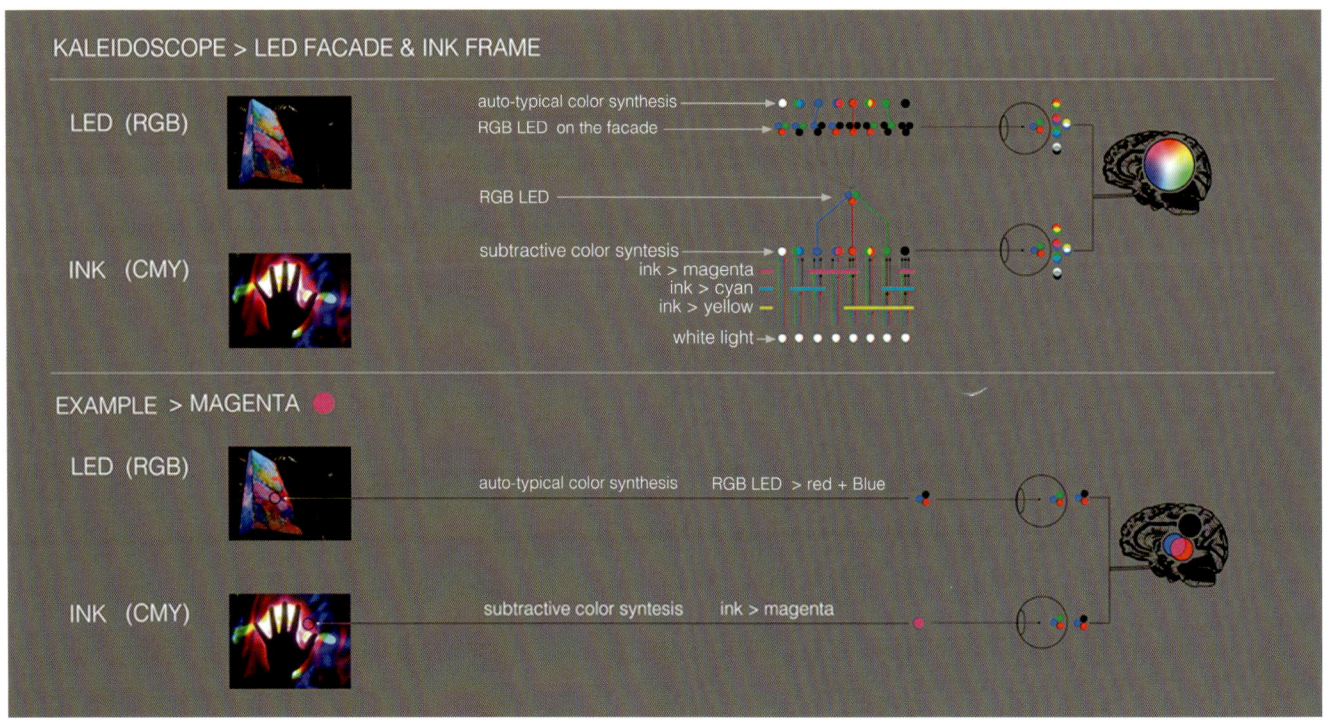

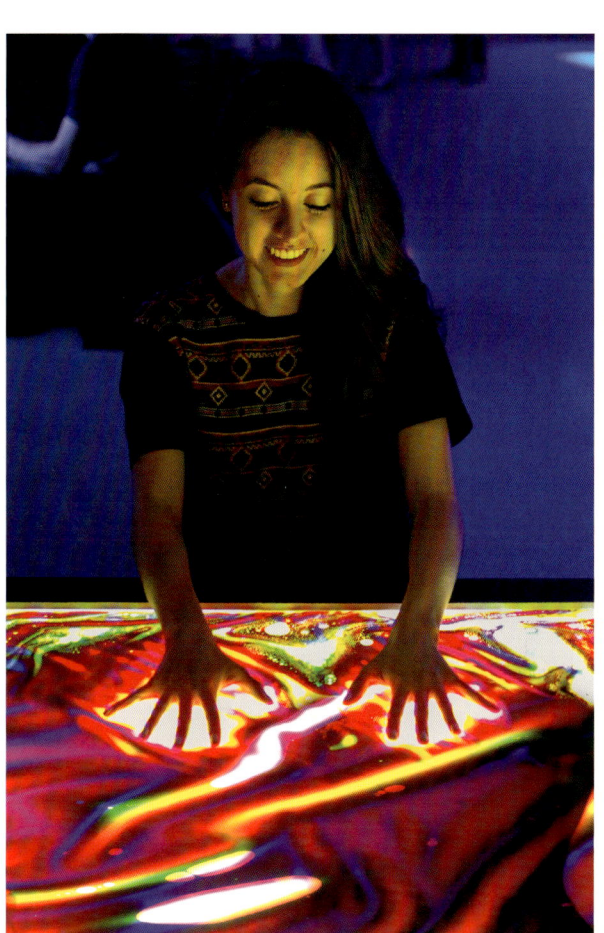
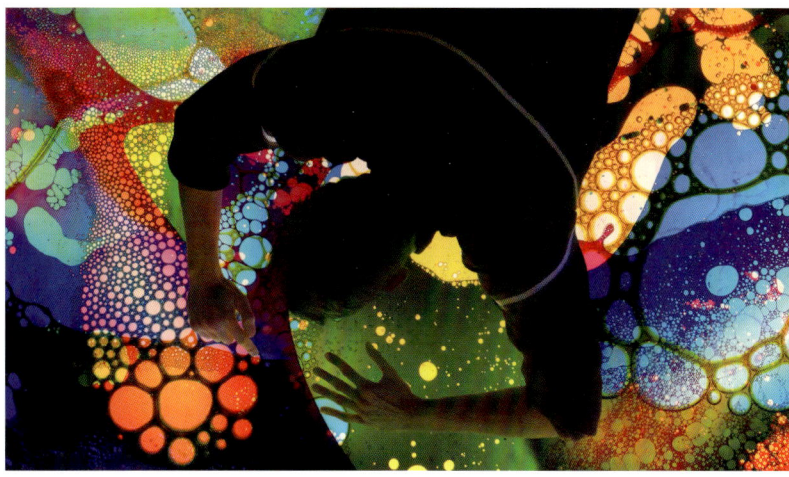
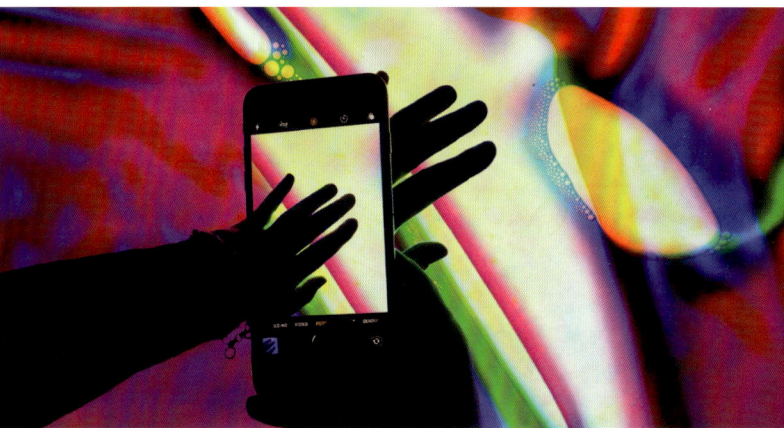

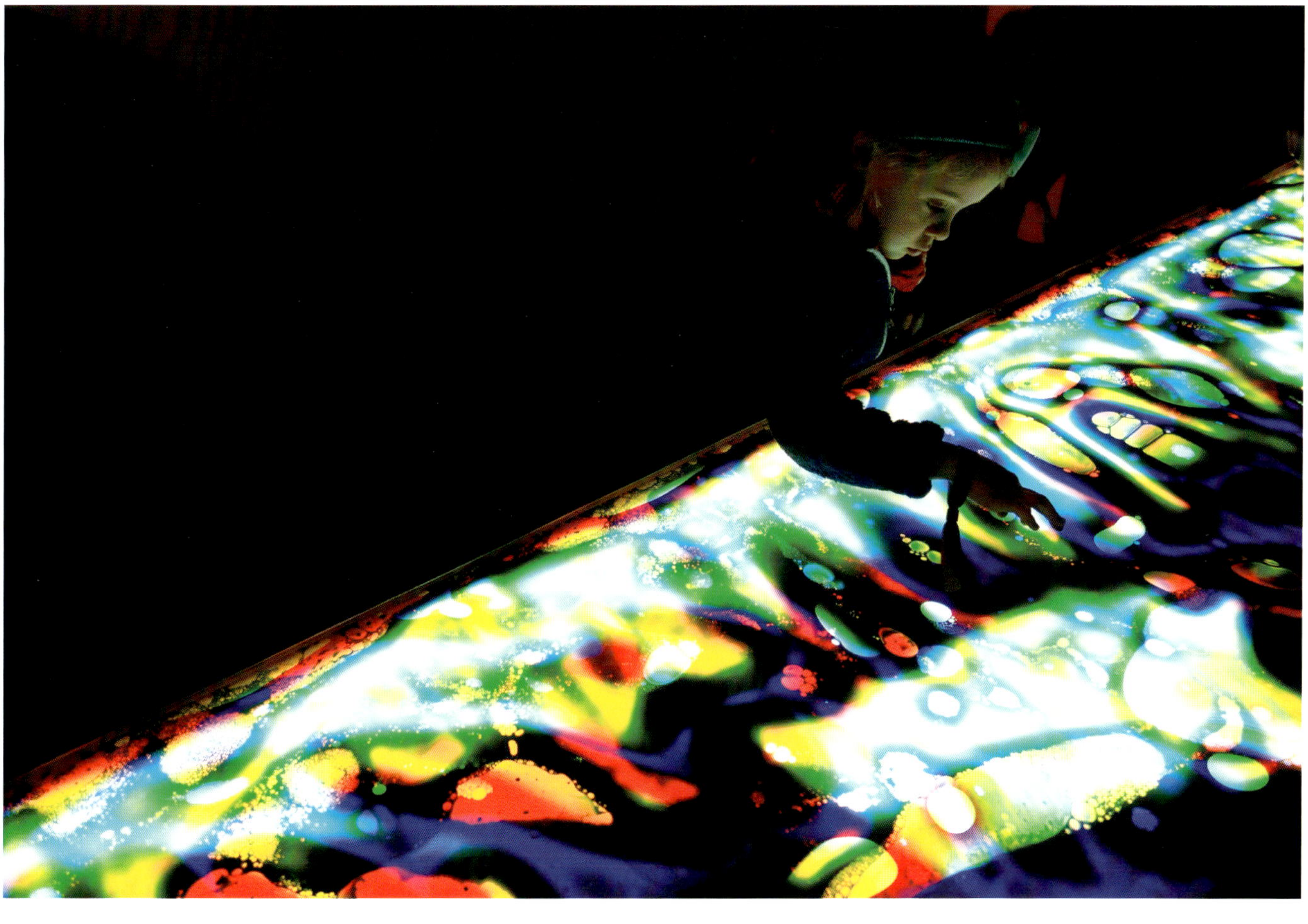

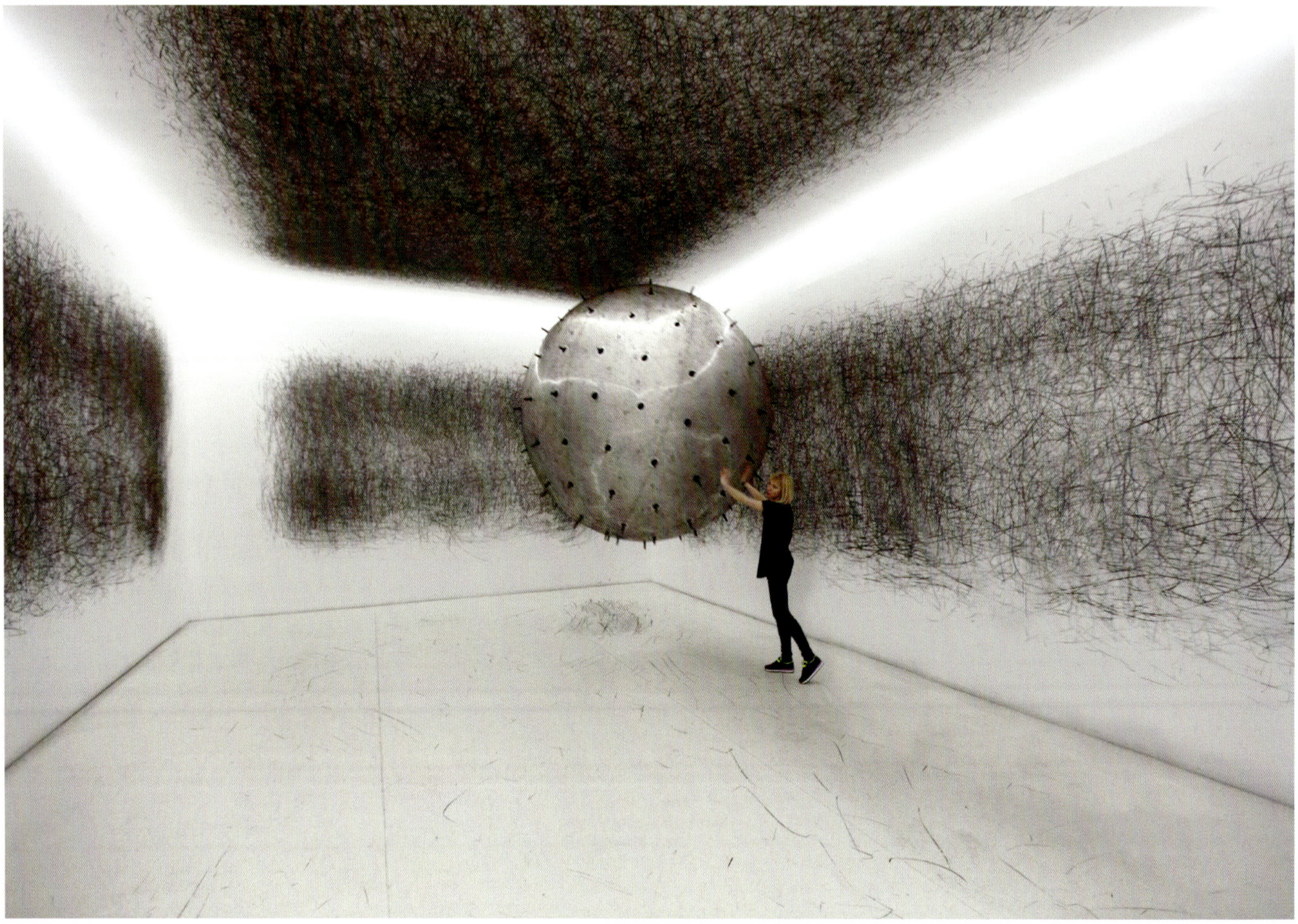

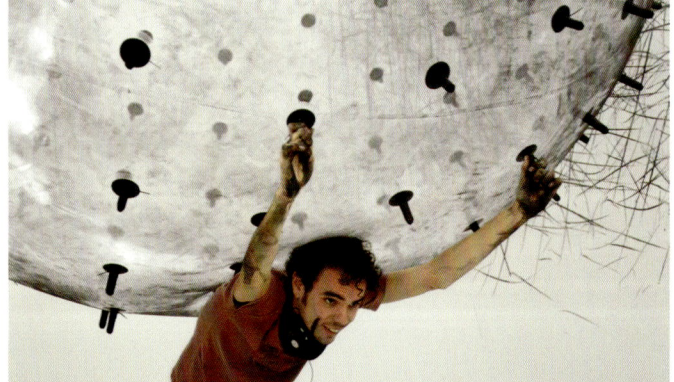

ADA

—

Concept Design & Art Direction: **Karina Smigla-Bobinski**
Photography: **Caitlind r.c. Brown**

—

ADA is an interactive art-making machine. Filled with helium and floating freely in a room, a transparent, membrane-like globe, spiked with charcoal, leaves marks on the walls, ceilings and floors.

ADA produces these marks quite autonomously, although moved by visitors. The globe has an aura of liveliness and its black coal traces create a composition of lines and points that remain incalculable in their intensity, expression, and form, however hard the visitor tries to control *ADA*. Whatever he tries, he finds soon that *ADA* is an independent performer, studding the originally white walls with drawings and signs. More and more complicated, fabric-like structures arise. The interaction is comparable to a computer that makes an unforeseeable output after a user enters a command.

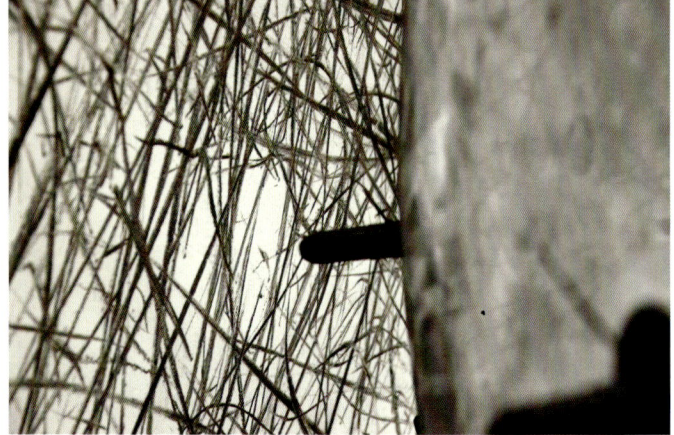

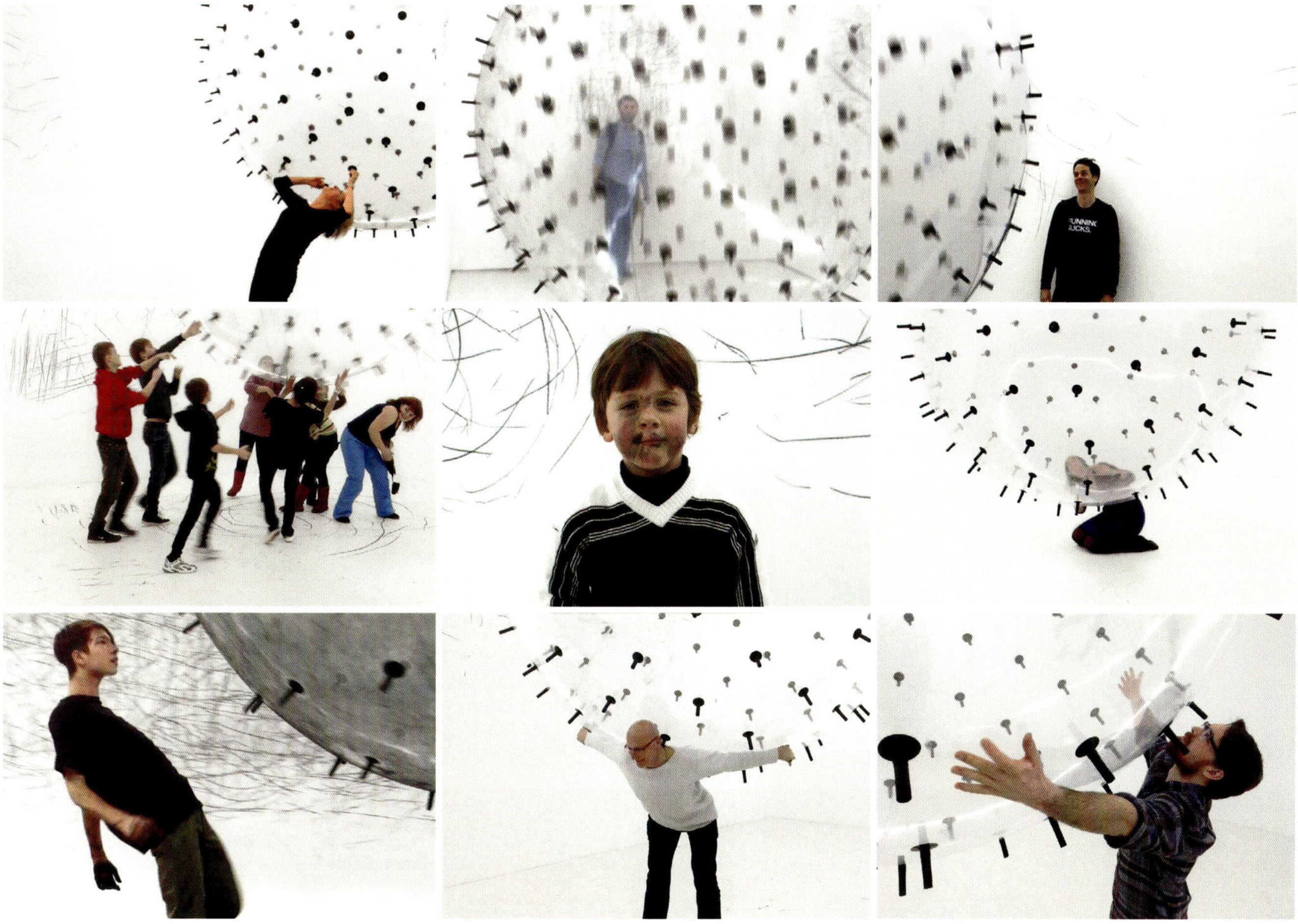

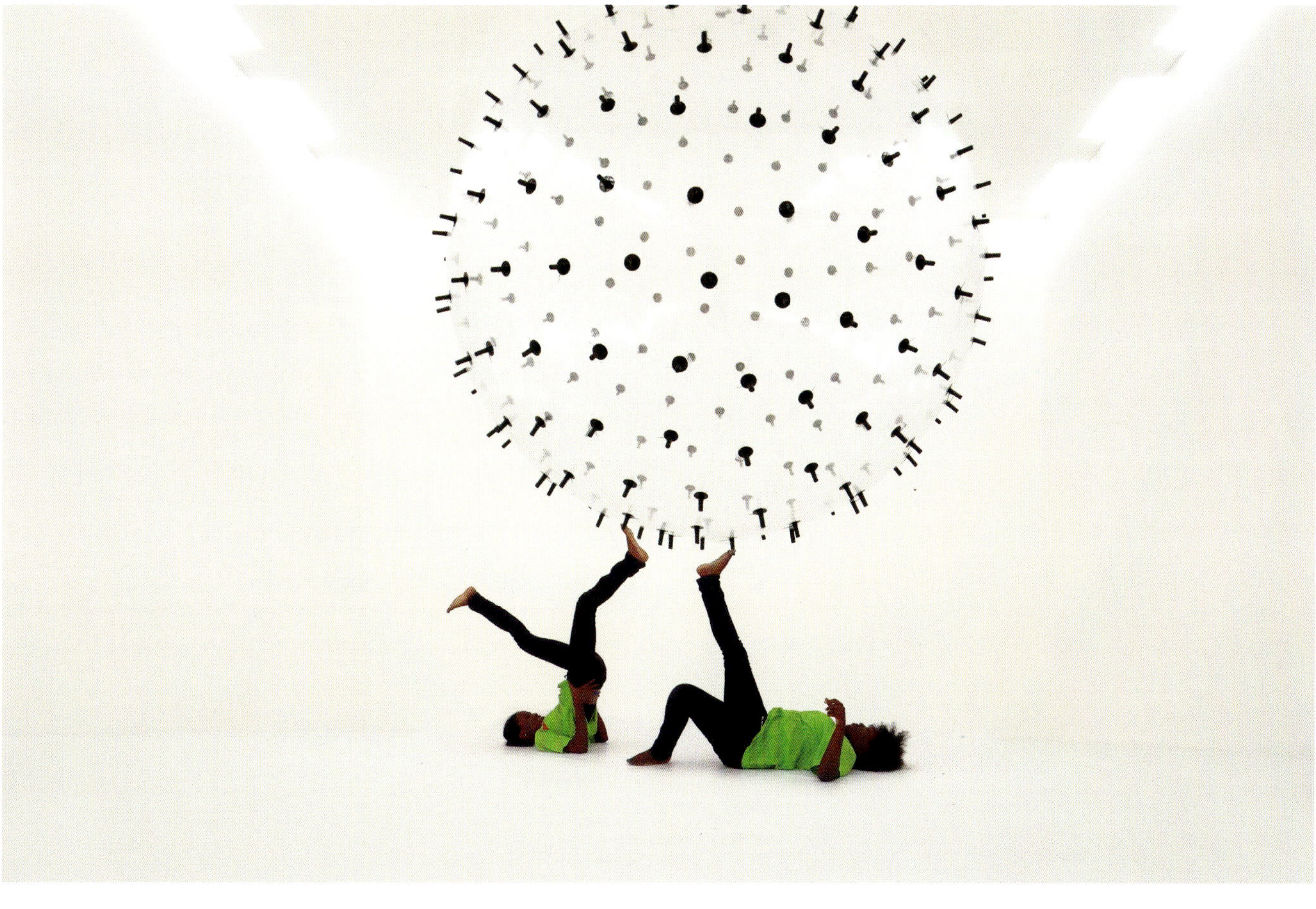

INTERFERENCE

—

Design: **Daria Jelonek**

—

Interference is an interactive light installation that deals with the complexity and interconnectivity of light pollution and air pollution using the model of the Bloch sphere. The installation consists of two physical elements to make the different interactions of light pollution and air pollution understandable: a 1m circular light sculpture and a related respiration point for the audience. When the circular light sculpture is lit up, the color and timing of the light change according to the breath of the participant, representing the different interconnections of light pollution and air pollution. As soon as it reaches a point of over-production of light and air it changes from appealing light to deterrent light, signaling over-pollution.

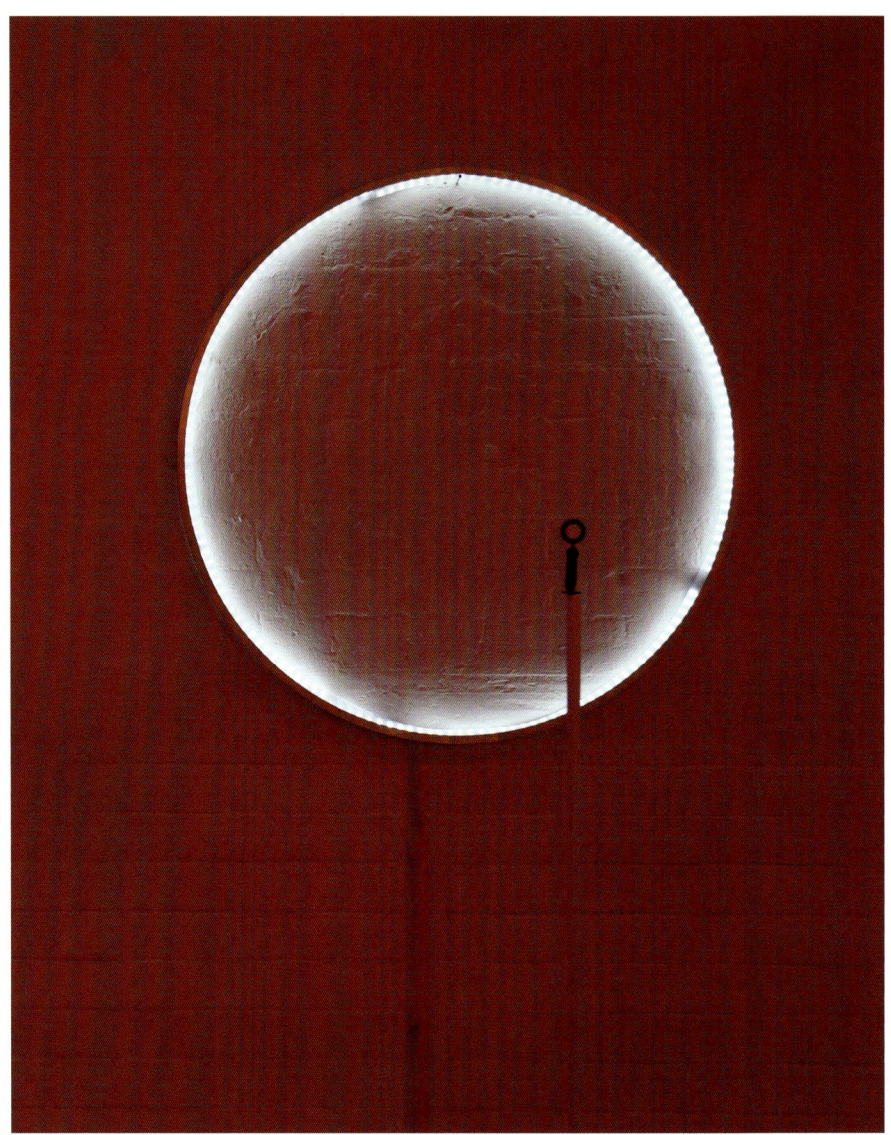

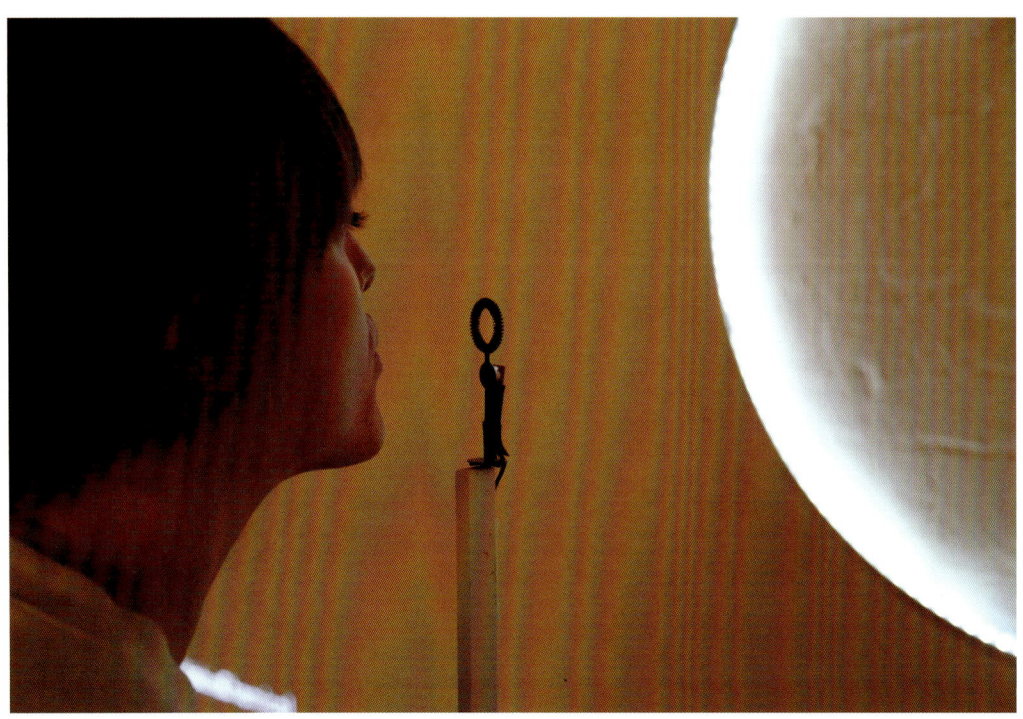

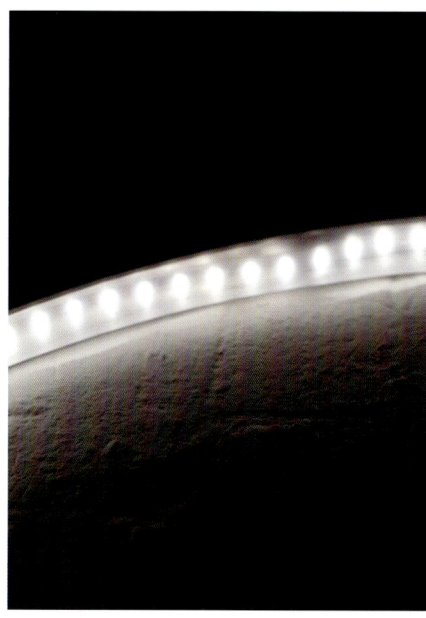
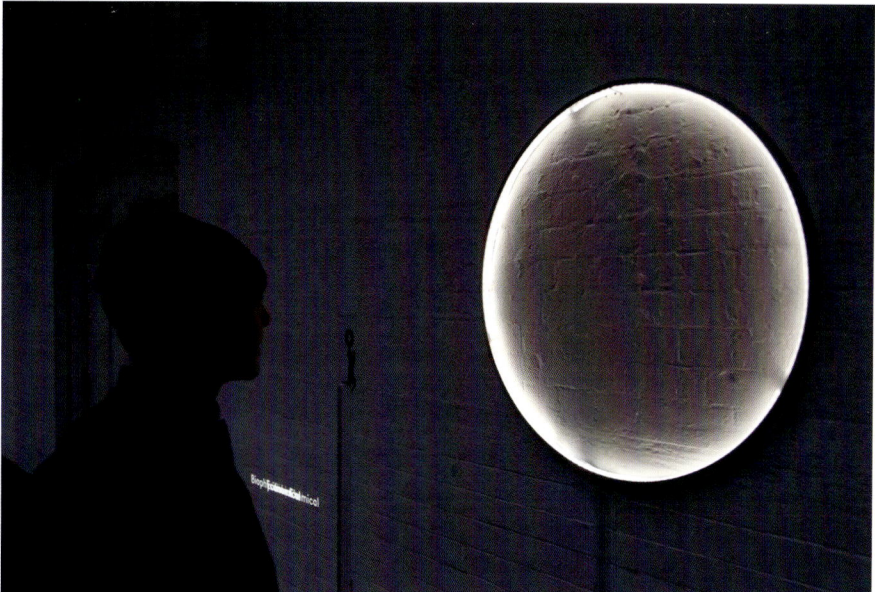

The phenomenon of light pollution is a result of human society using a large amount of artificial light. It has reached a harmful point now throughout the world as the natural circadian rhythms of plants, animals and humans are being affected through this unnatural extension of the day.

Just like light, air is an essential matter for life on our planet. However, the mixture of gases that form our breathable air is out of balance. Air pollution, caused by the introduction of human-made particles and substances into our atmosphere, has risen rapidly in recent years, causing alteration and damage to living organisms.

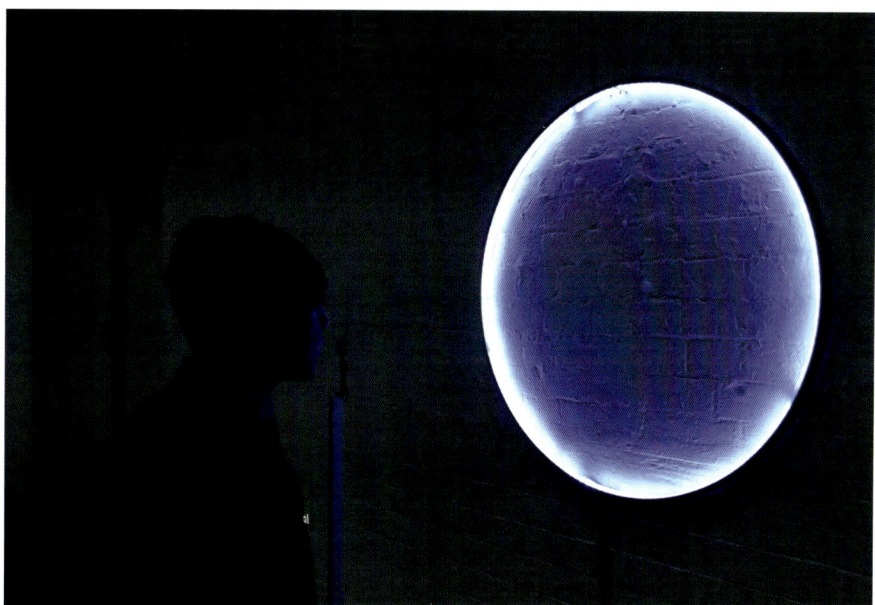

Both light pollution and air pollution are results of capitalism, which leads to a 24/7 society with habits of constant production and consumption. This leads to air pollution which is caused mainly by exhaust from automobiles and emissions from factories which require permanent industrial productions, causing light pollution. Light pollution additionally comes from private light clutter for airports, shopping malls, households and factories. The extreme and ultimate superposition between light pollution and air pollution is revealed by studies by the American Geophysical Union in San Francisco: Light pollution inhibits particles called nitrate radicals, which naturally clear the harmful smog during the night. But living without real night and darkness consequently increases atmospheric pollution and contributes to the rise of global warming—harmful long-term changes on Earth.

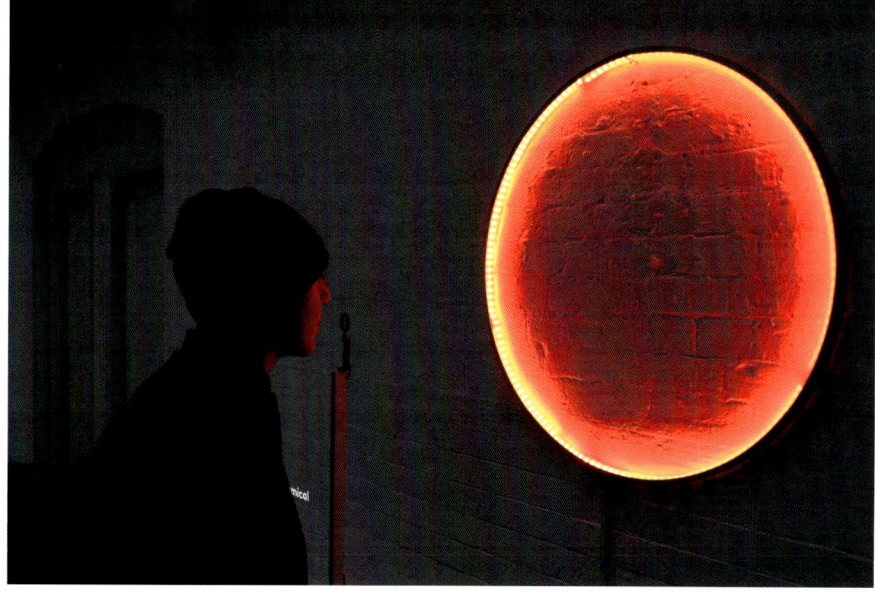

WONDER MOMENTS

Agency: **LUCENT**
Design: **Takahiro Matsuo**
Photography: **Nacasa and partners**

—

WONDER MOMENTS is an interactive light installation capturing impressive, beautiful and spellbinding moments found in nature with the aid of spherical images and music suspended in time and space. The experience is like looking at a star from far across the universe. The themes are drawn from natural phenomena, color itself, and the mind forever dreaming of the beauty and wonder of nature.

A five-meter diameter sphere, which morphs into different scenes (WATER / Sense of Nature / UNIVERSE), synchronizes with the projections on the floor, while occasionally reacting to viewers' movements.

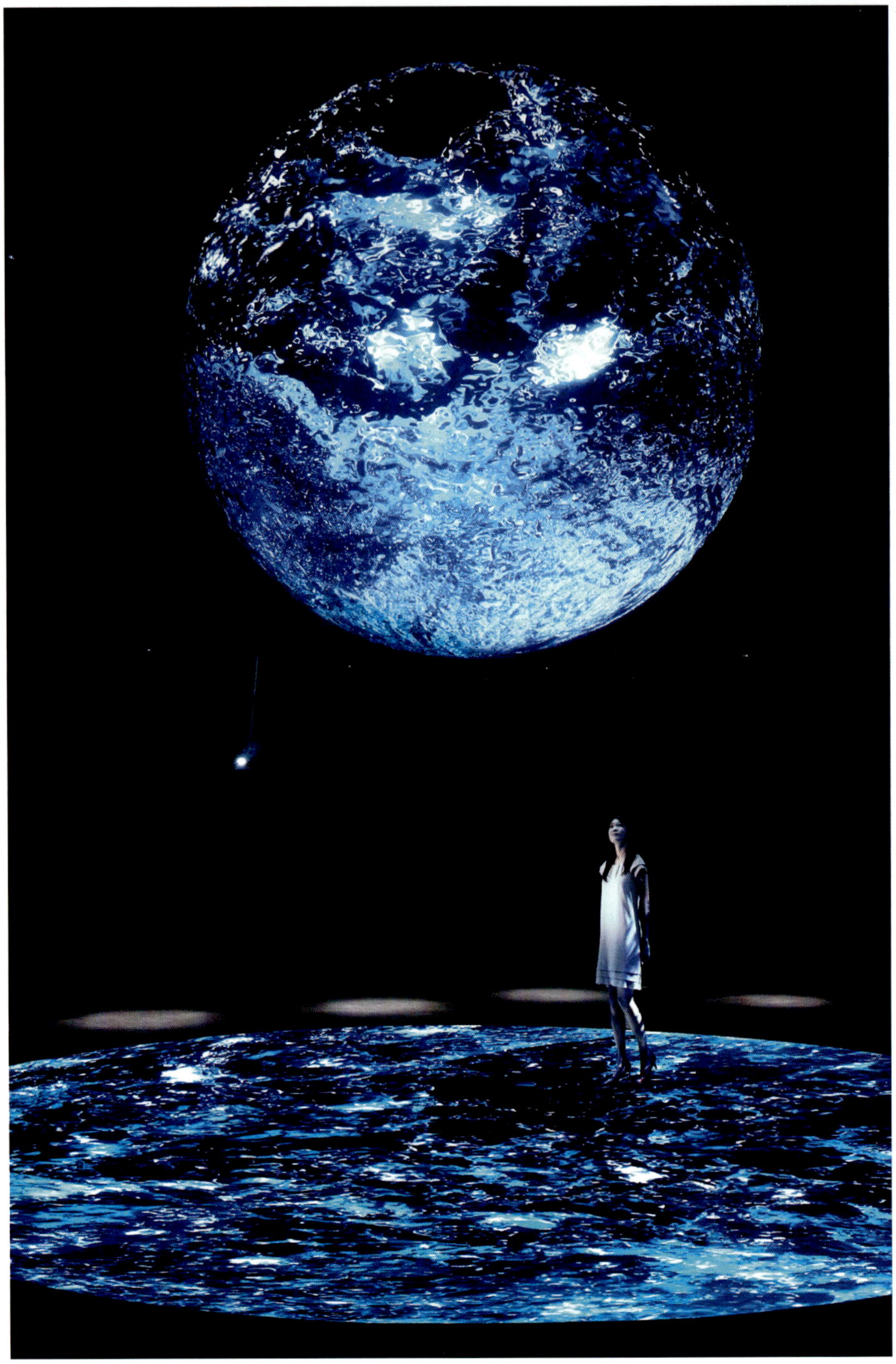

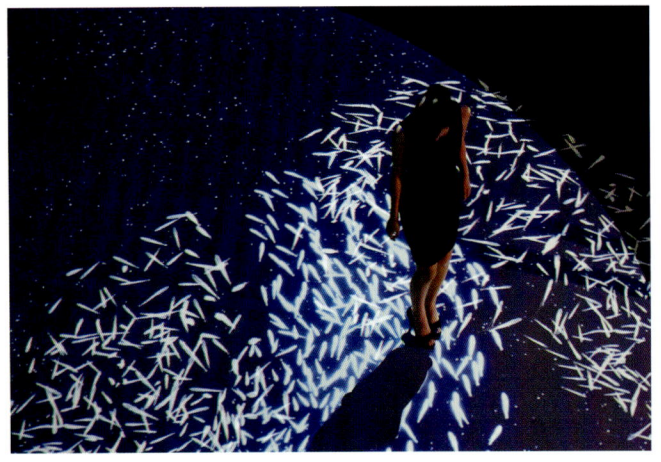

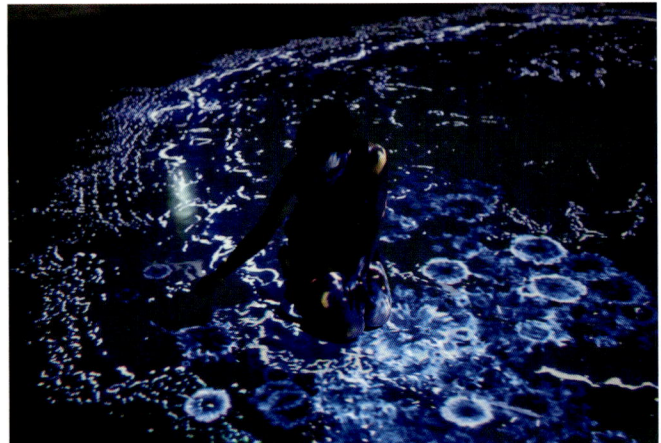

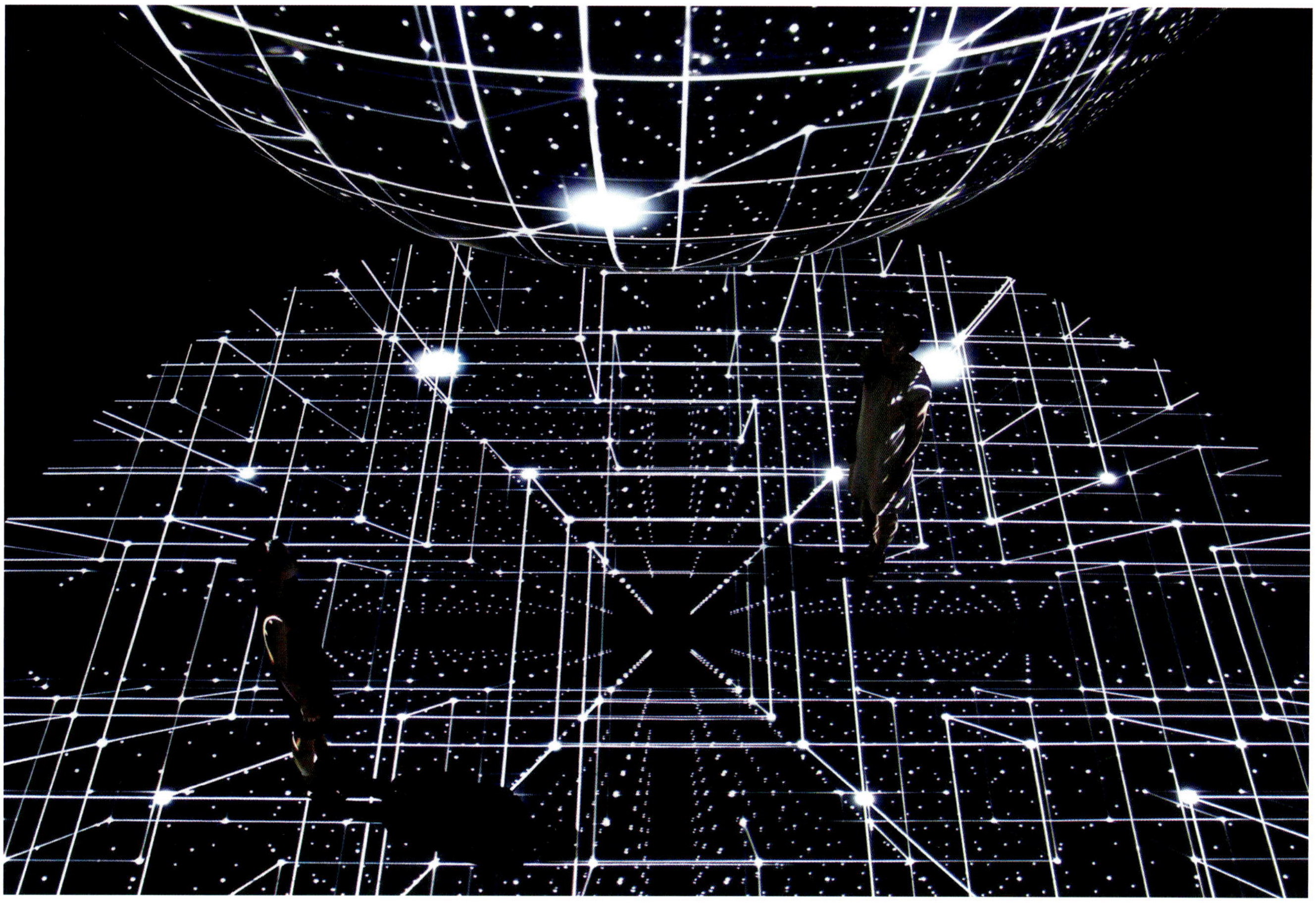

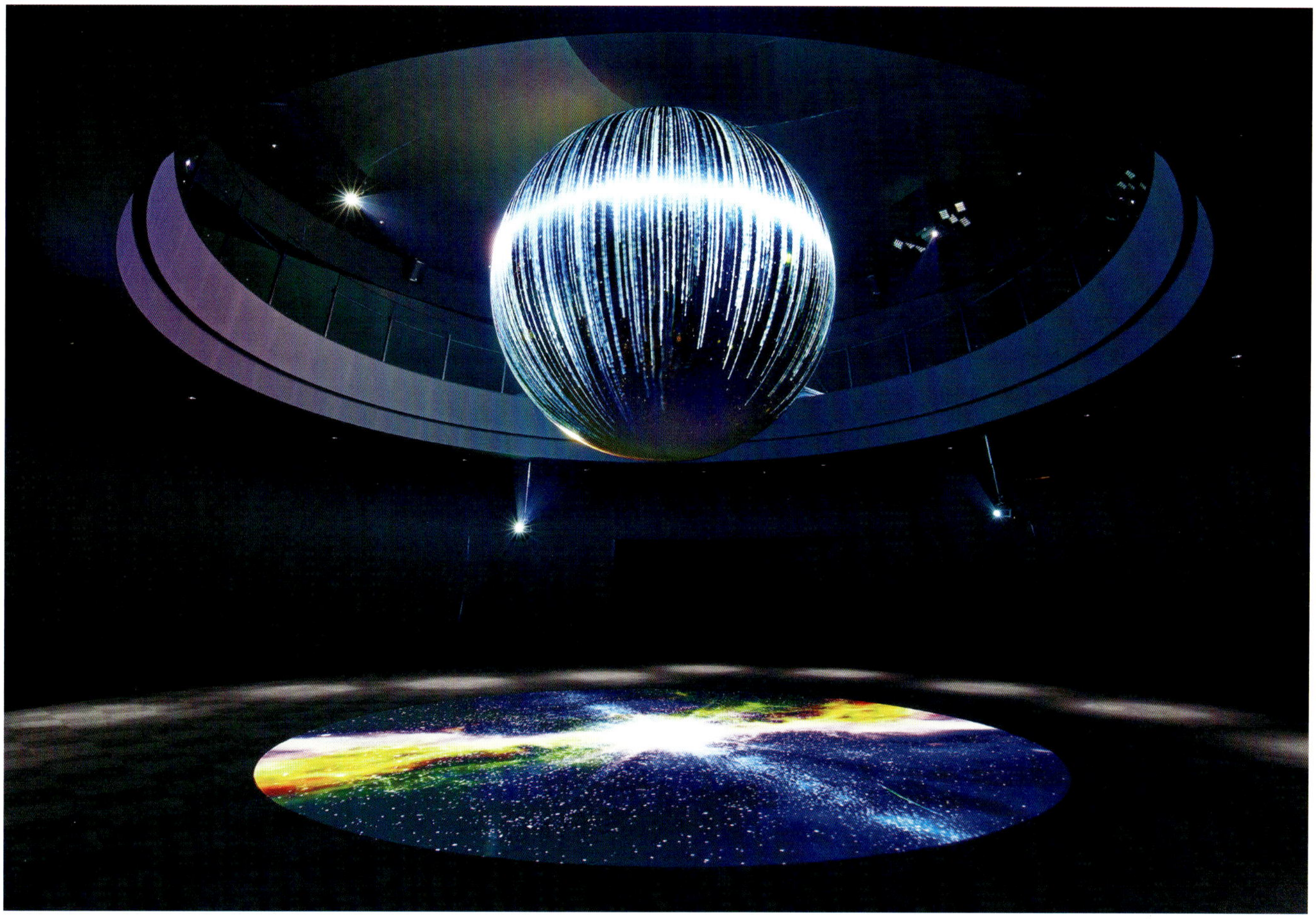

ARCHIVE DREAMING

Design: **Refik Anadol**

—

Commissioned to work with SALT Research collections, artist Refik Anadol employed machine-learning algorithms to search and sort relationships among 1,700,000 documents.

In this project, a temporary immersive architectural space was created as a canvas with light and data applied as materials. This radical effort to deconstruct the framework of an illusory space transgresses the normal boundaries of the viewing experience of a library and the conventional flat cinema projection screen into a three-dimensional kinetic and architectonic space of an archive visualized with machine learning algorithms. By training a neural network with images of 1,700,000 documents at SALT Research the main idea was to create an immersive installation with architectural intelligence to reframe memory, history and culture in museum perception for the 21st century through the lens of machine intelligence.

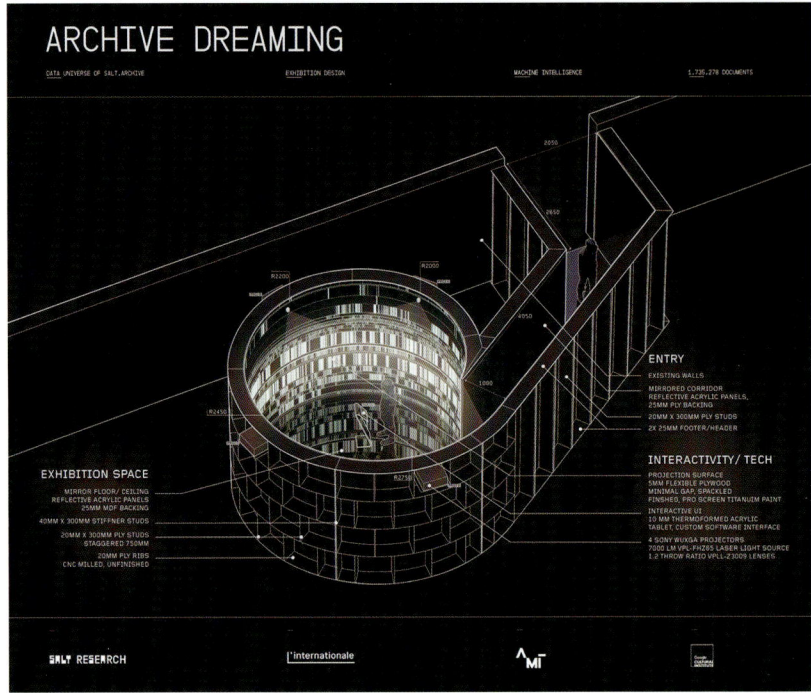

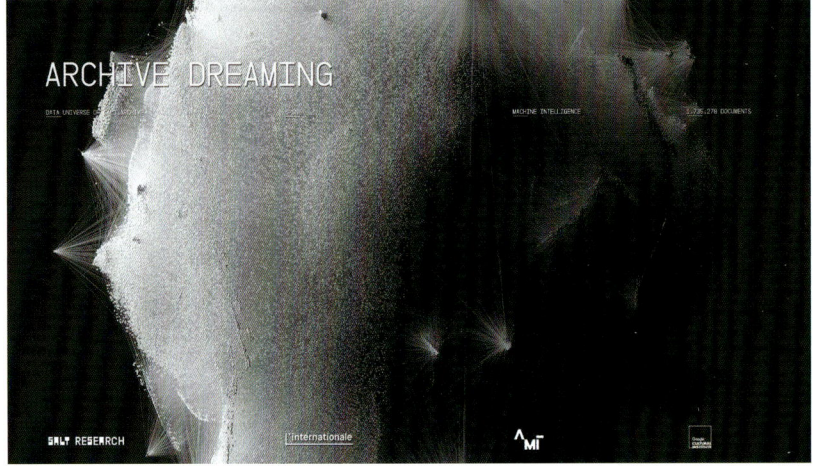

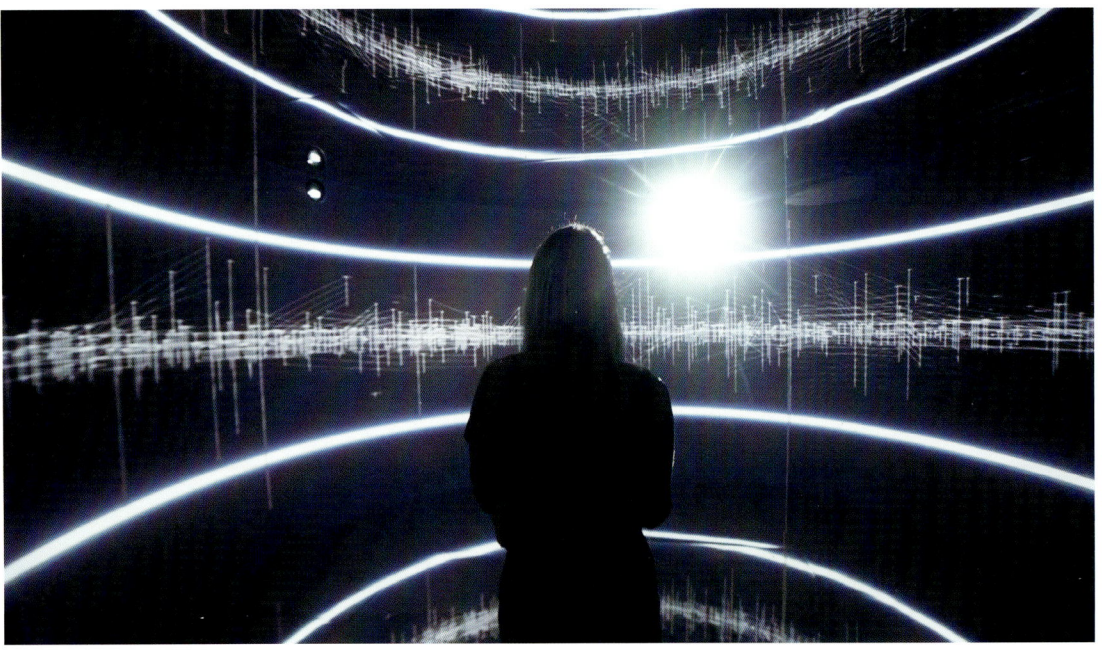

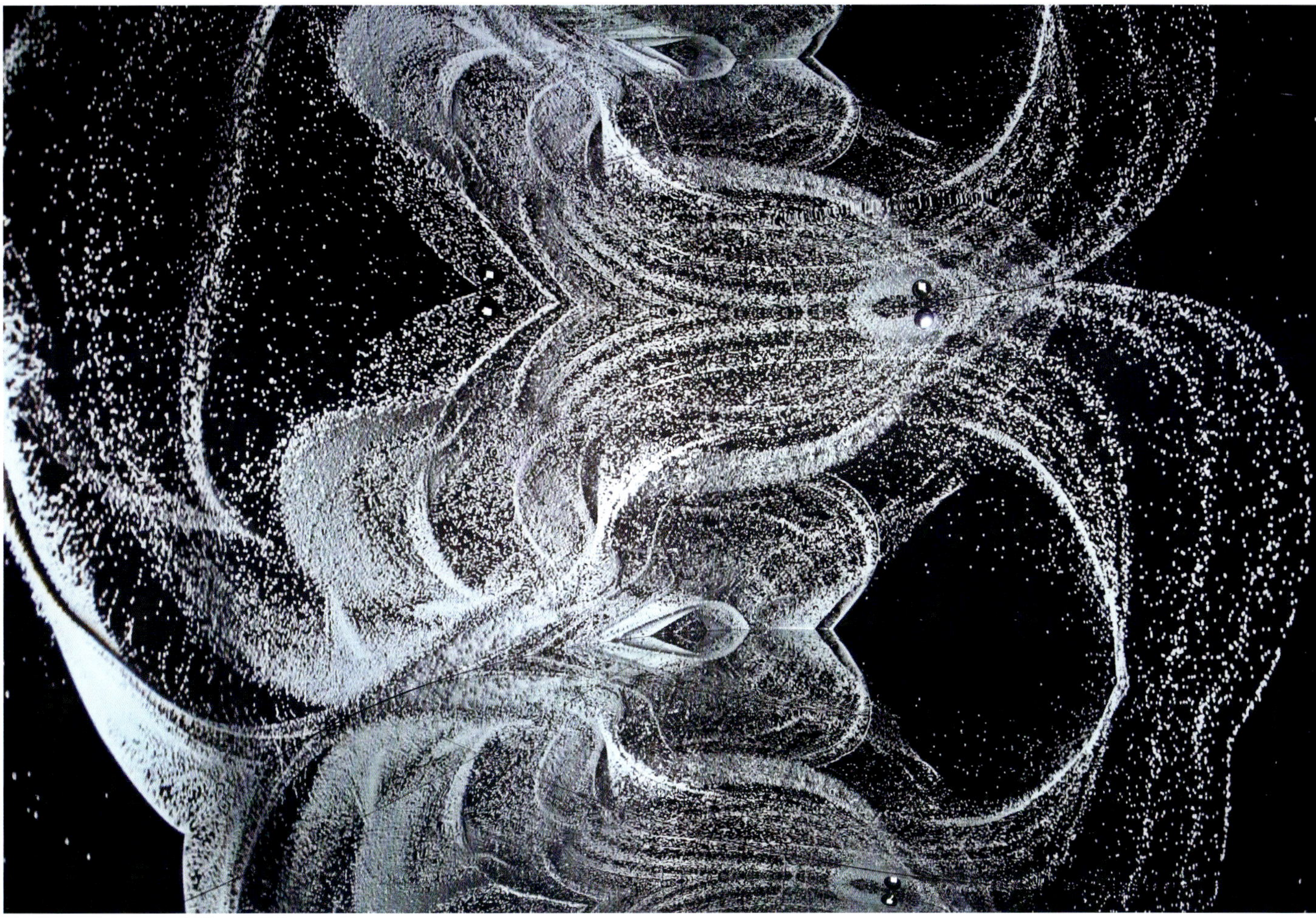

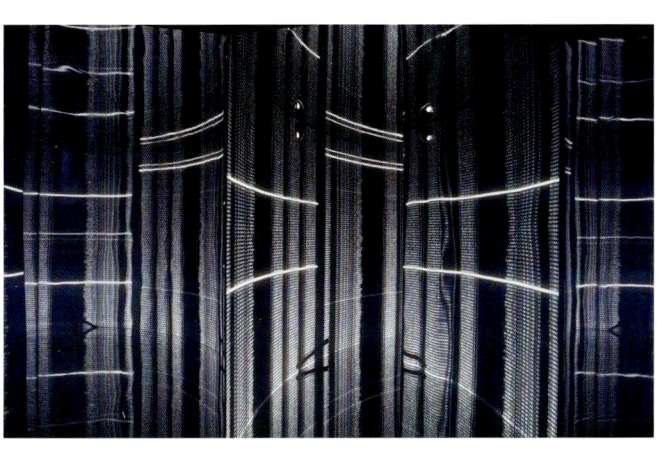

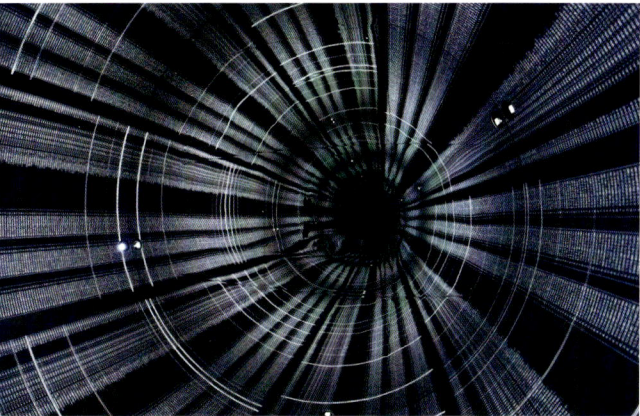

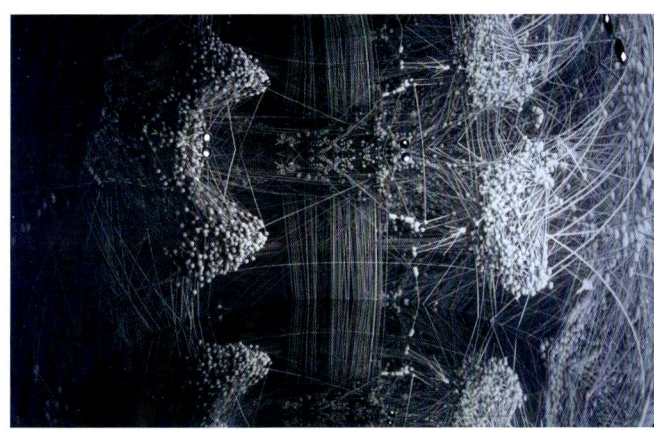

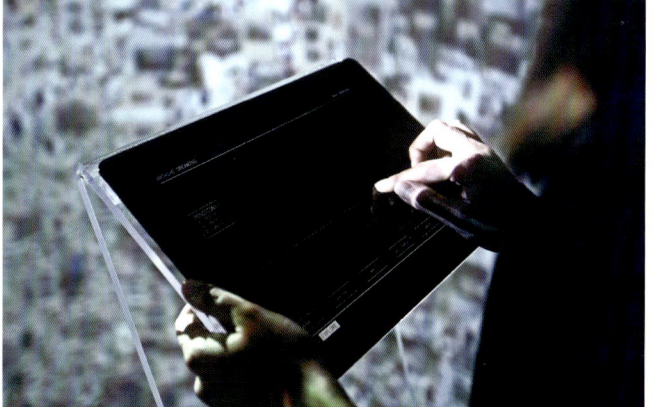

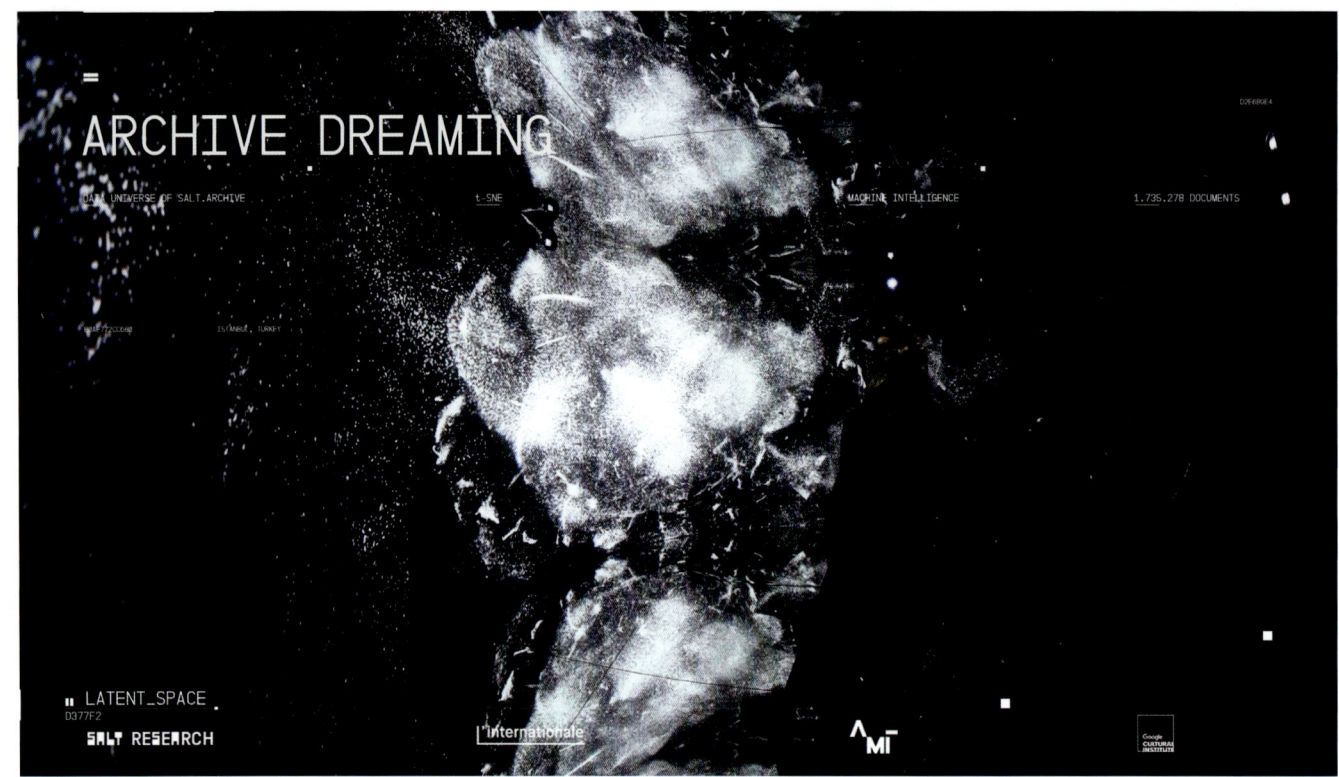

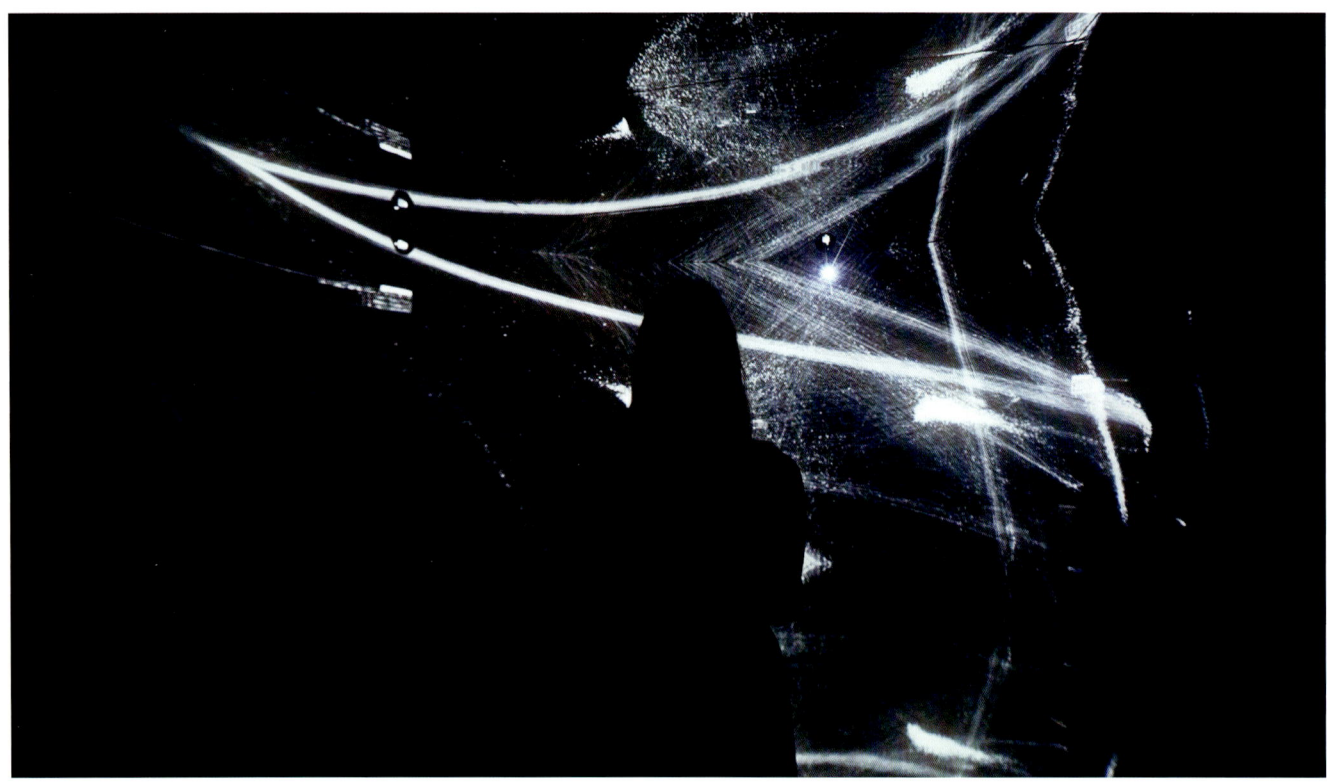

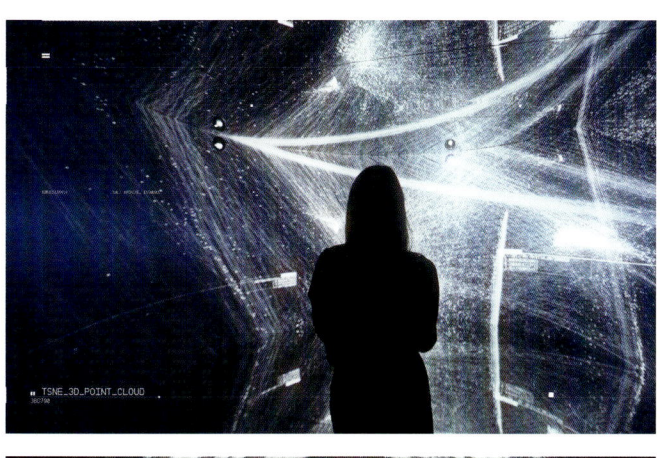
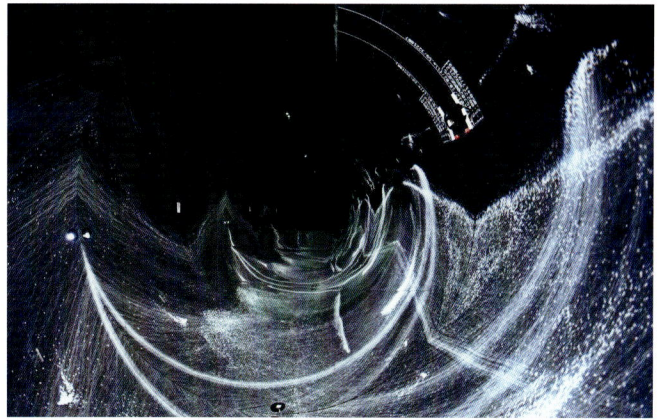
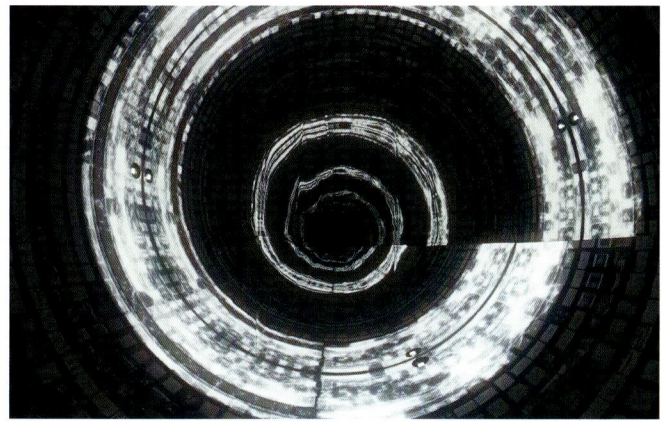
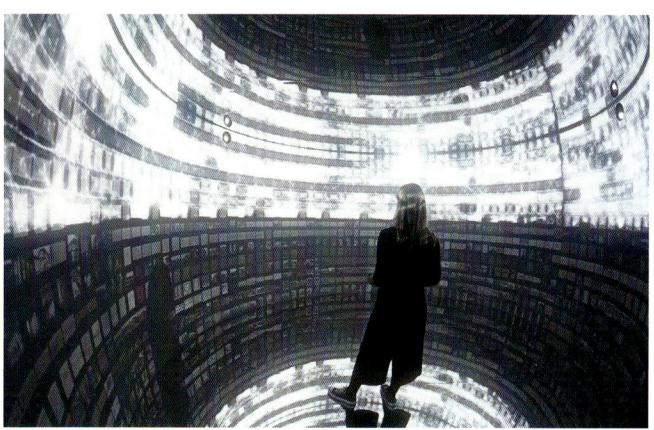

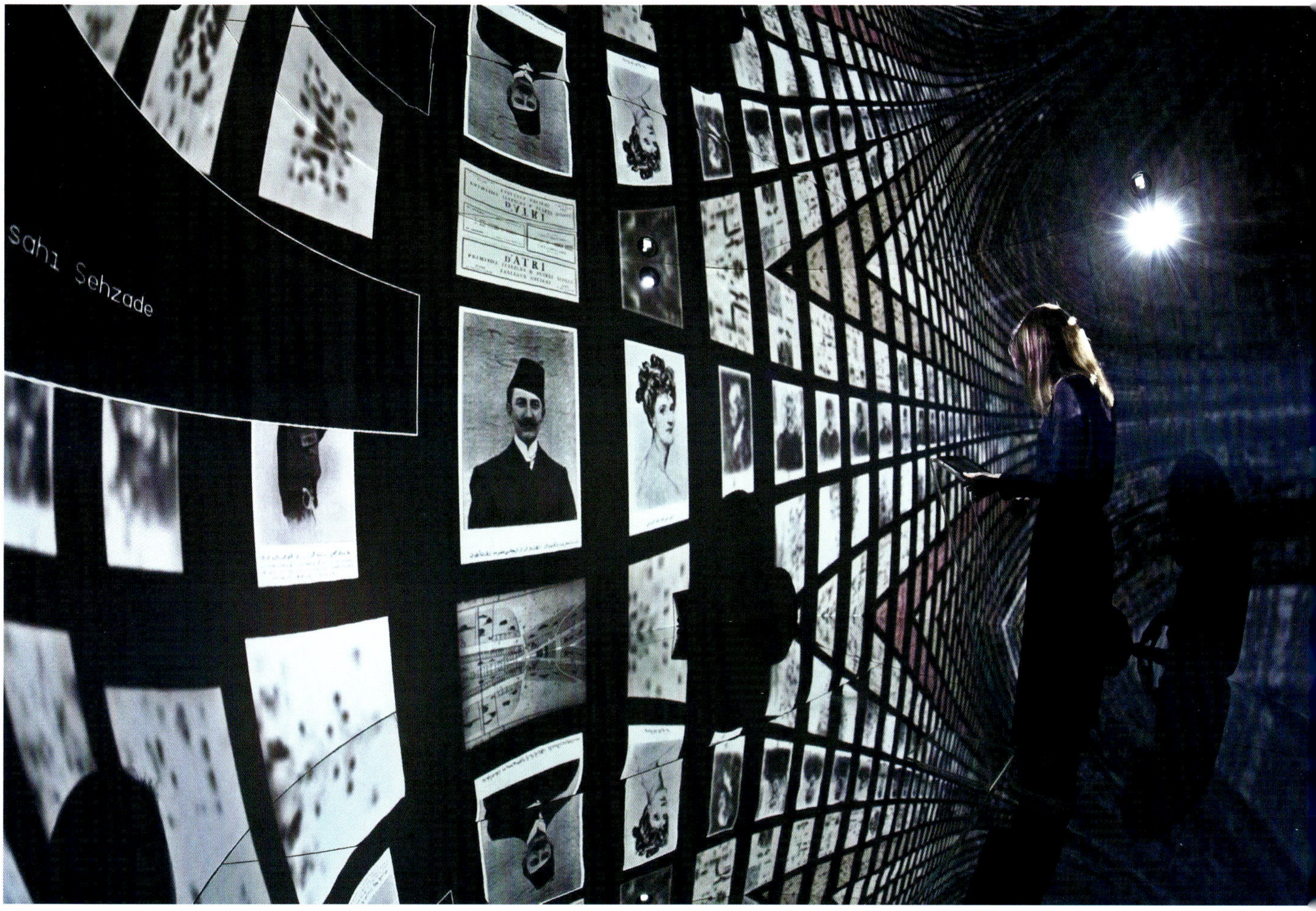

MURMUR

—

Agency: **Chevalvert**
Design: **Stéphane Buellet, Patrick Paleta, Julia Puyo Calvo**
Sound Design: **Splank Studio**
Development: **2roqs**

—

Murmur is an architectural prosthesis that enables communication between passers-by and the wall upon which it is connected. The installation simulates the movement of sound waves, building a luminous bridge between the physical and the virtual worlds. There is a magical effect, a mystery in the way that sound waves move. *Murmur* focuses on this movement, thus creating an unconventional dialogue between the public and the wall.

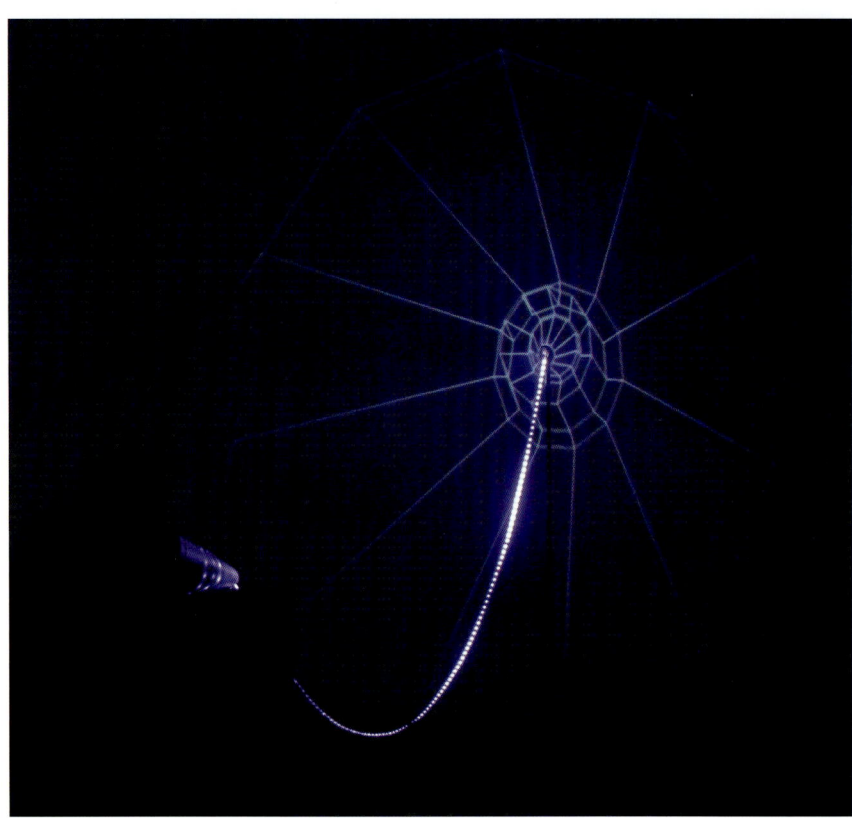

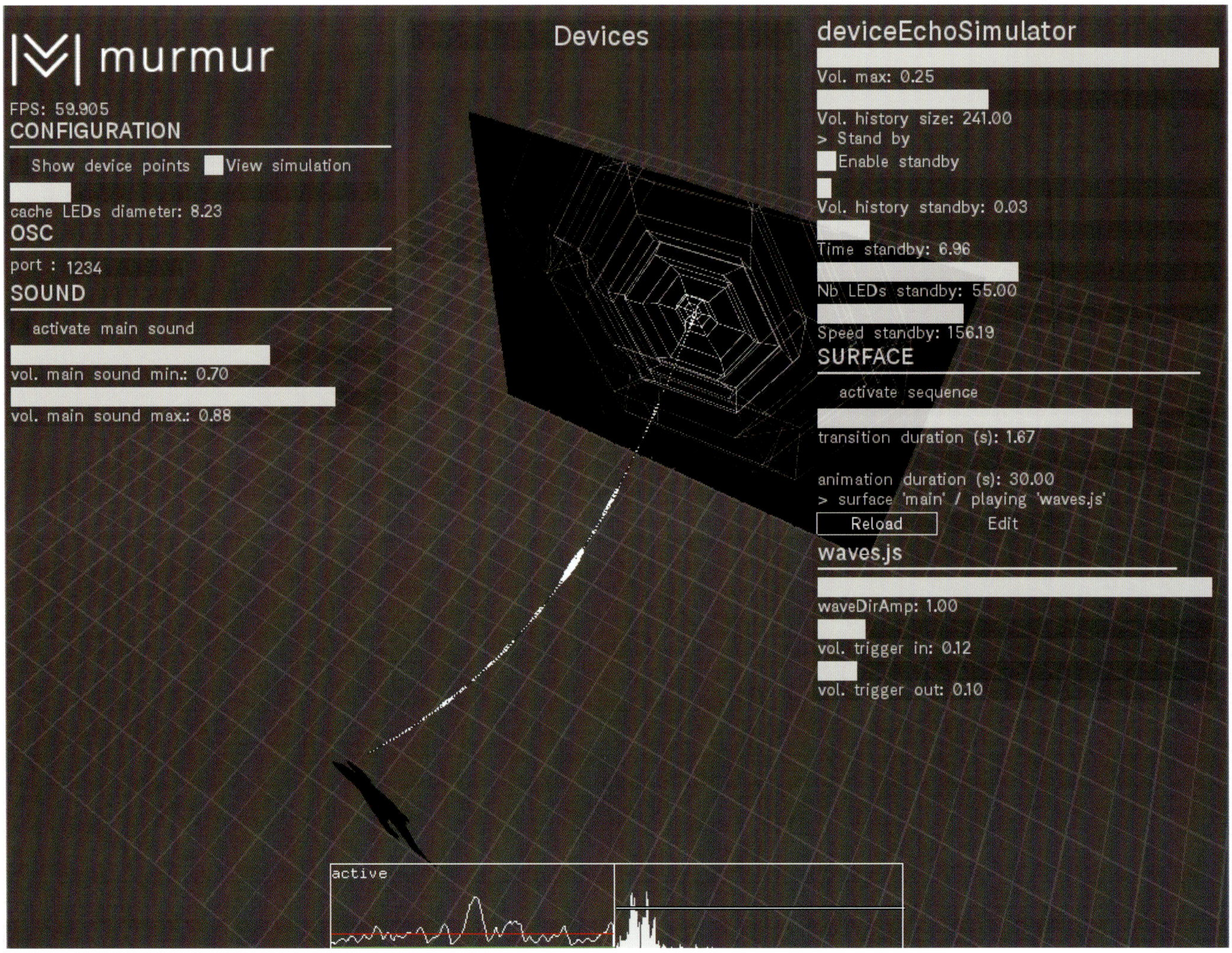

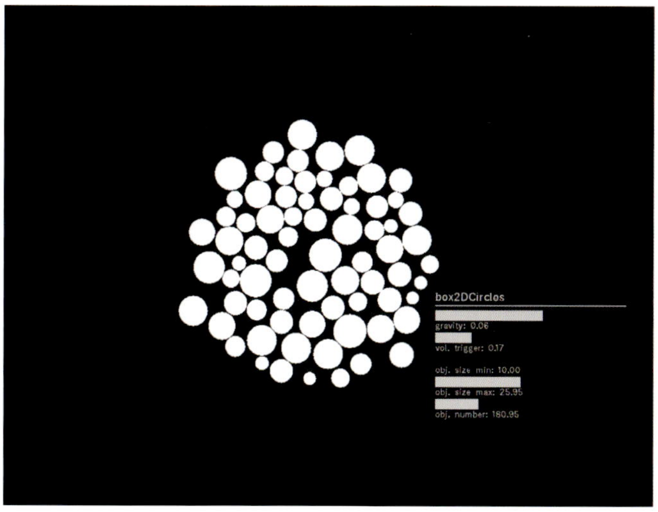

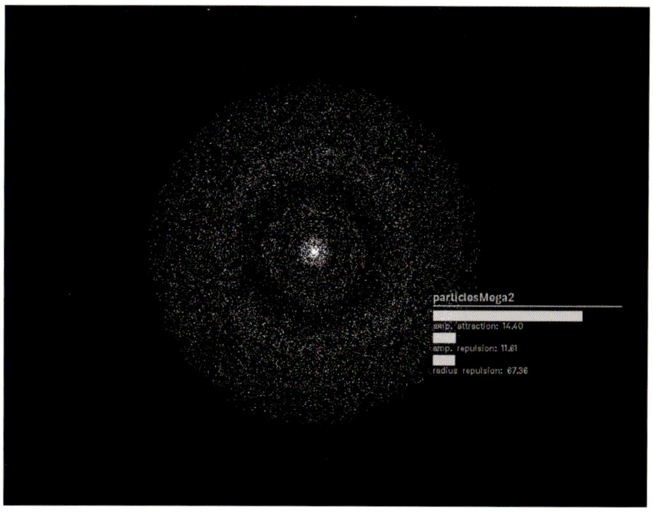

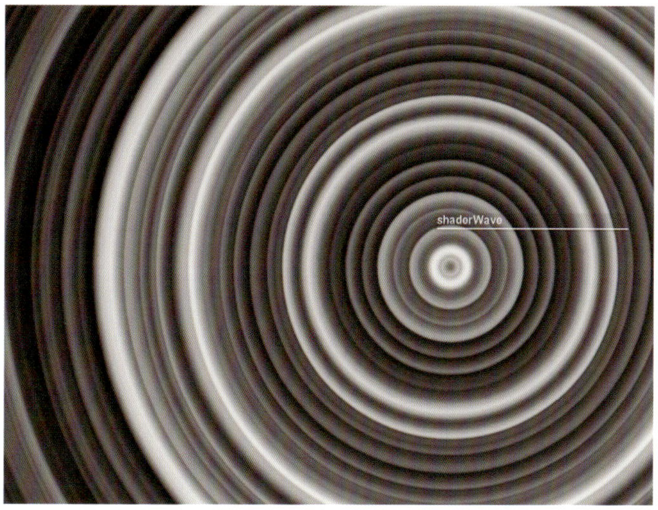

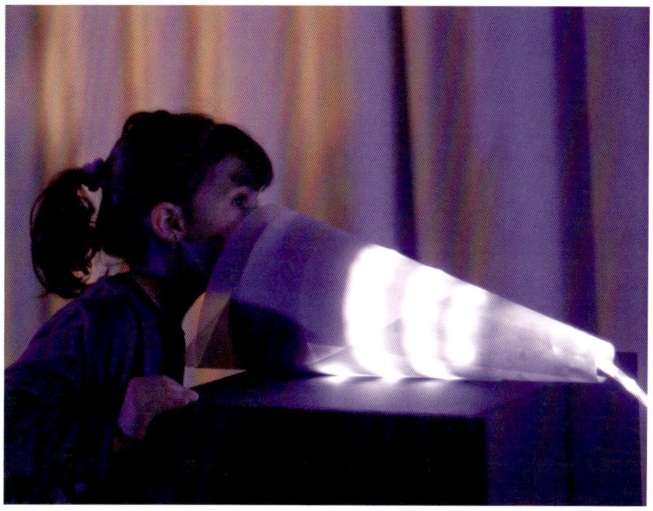

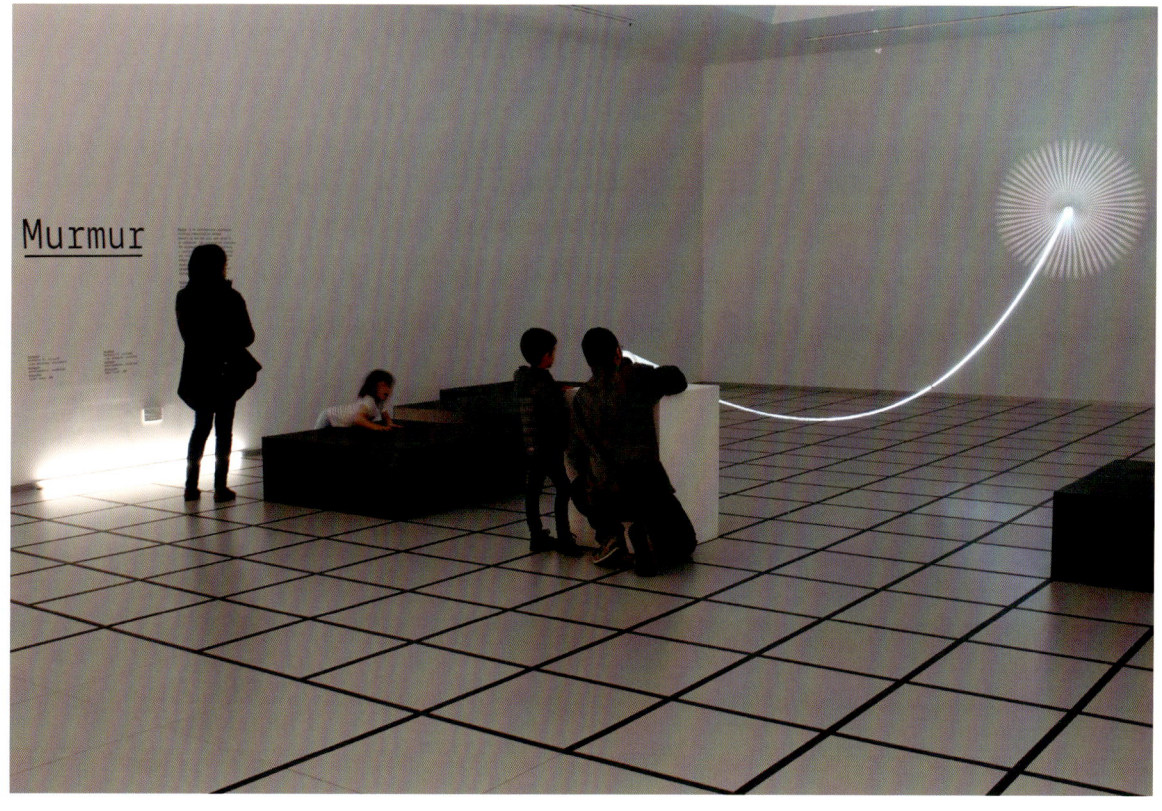

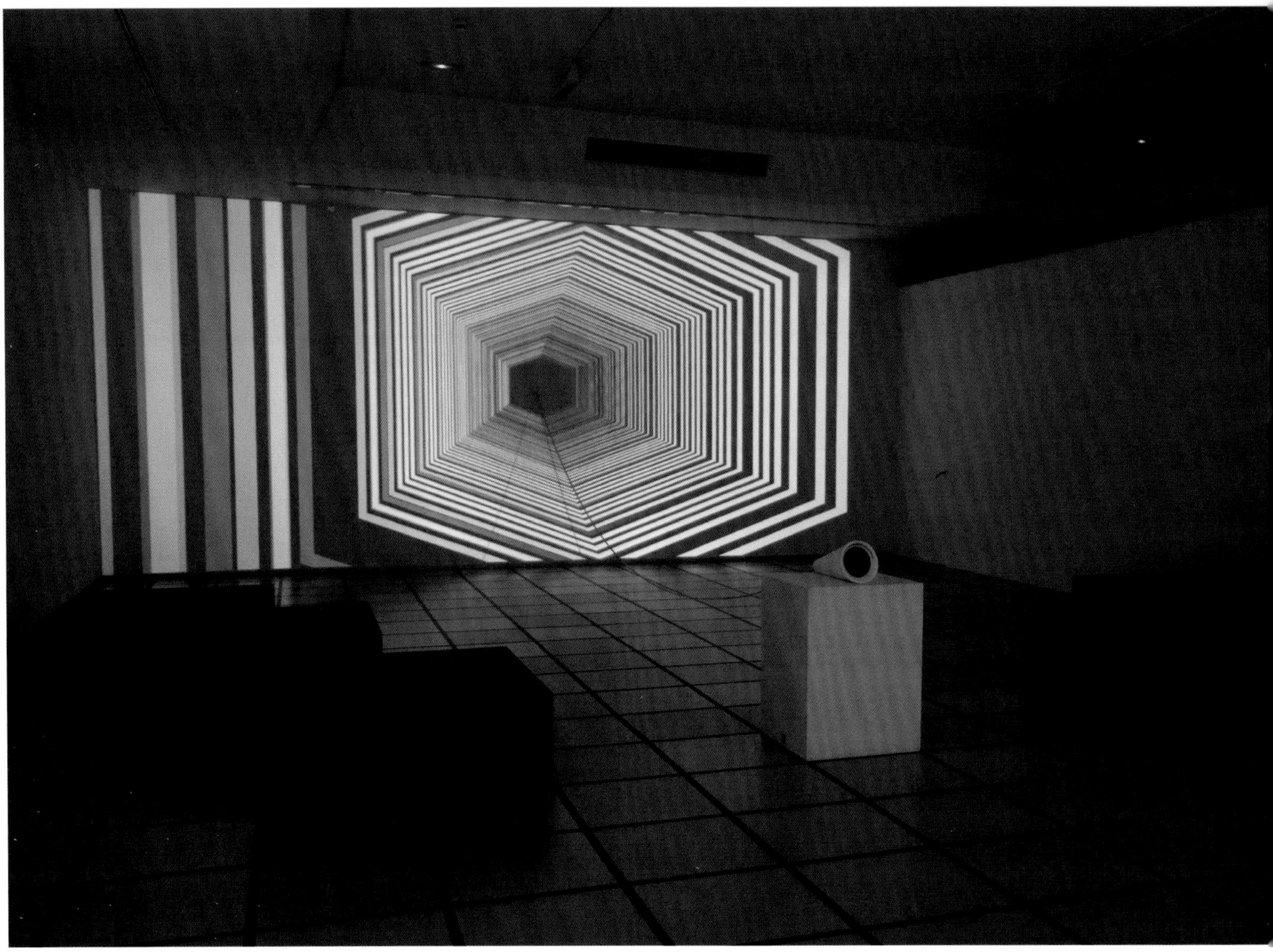

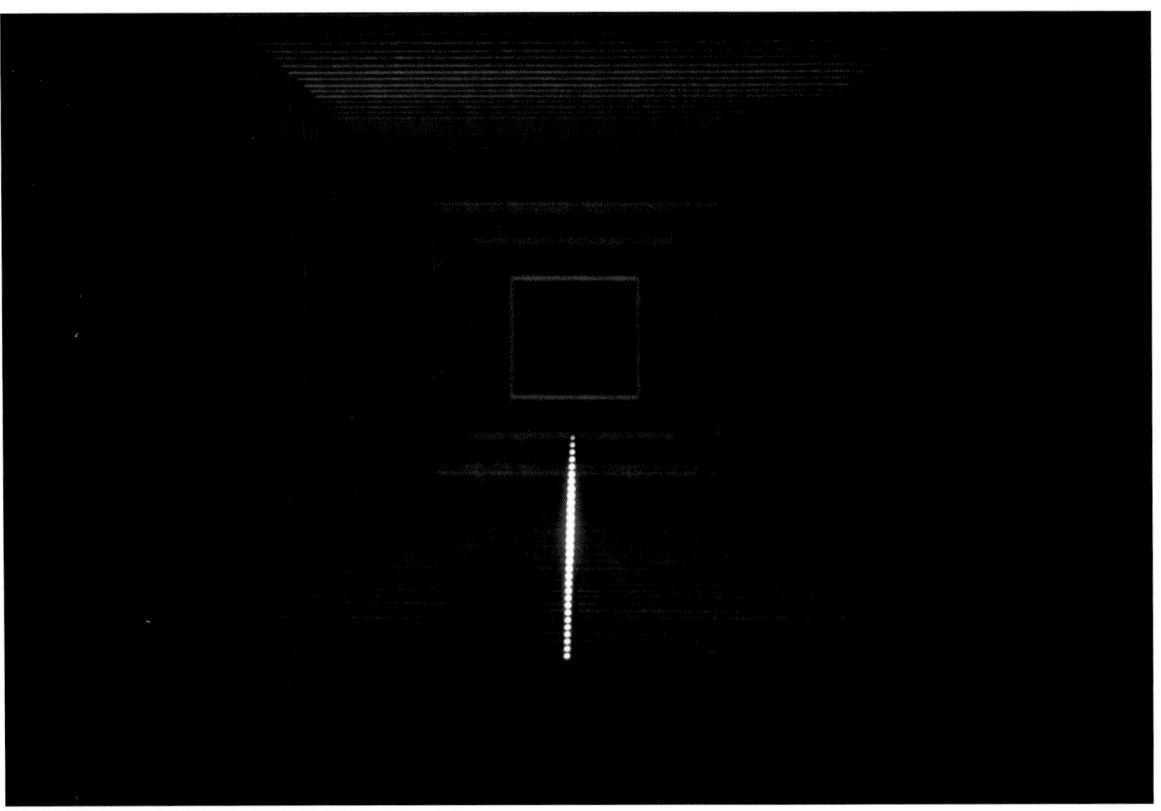

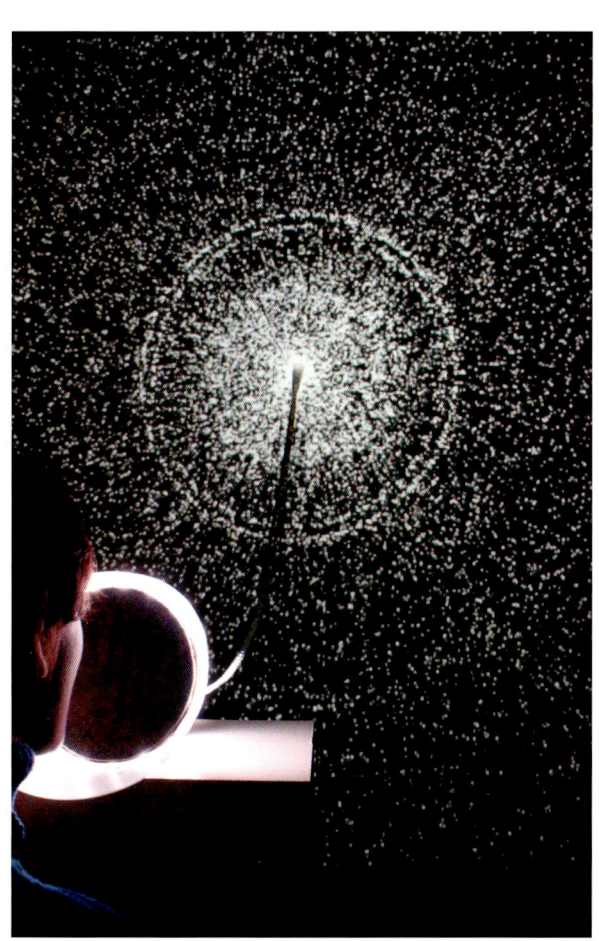
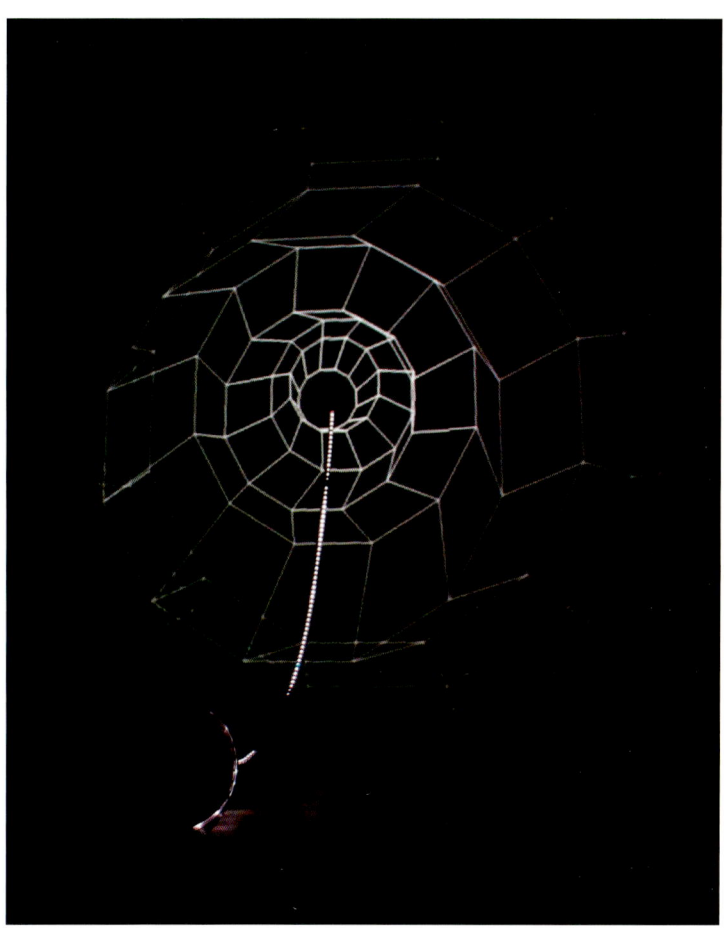

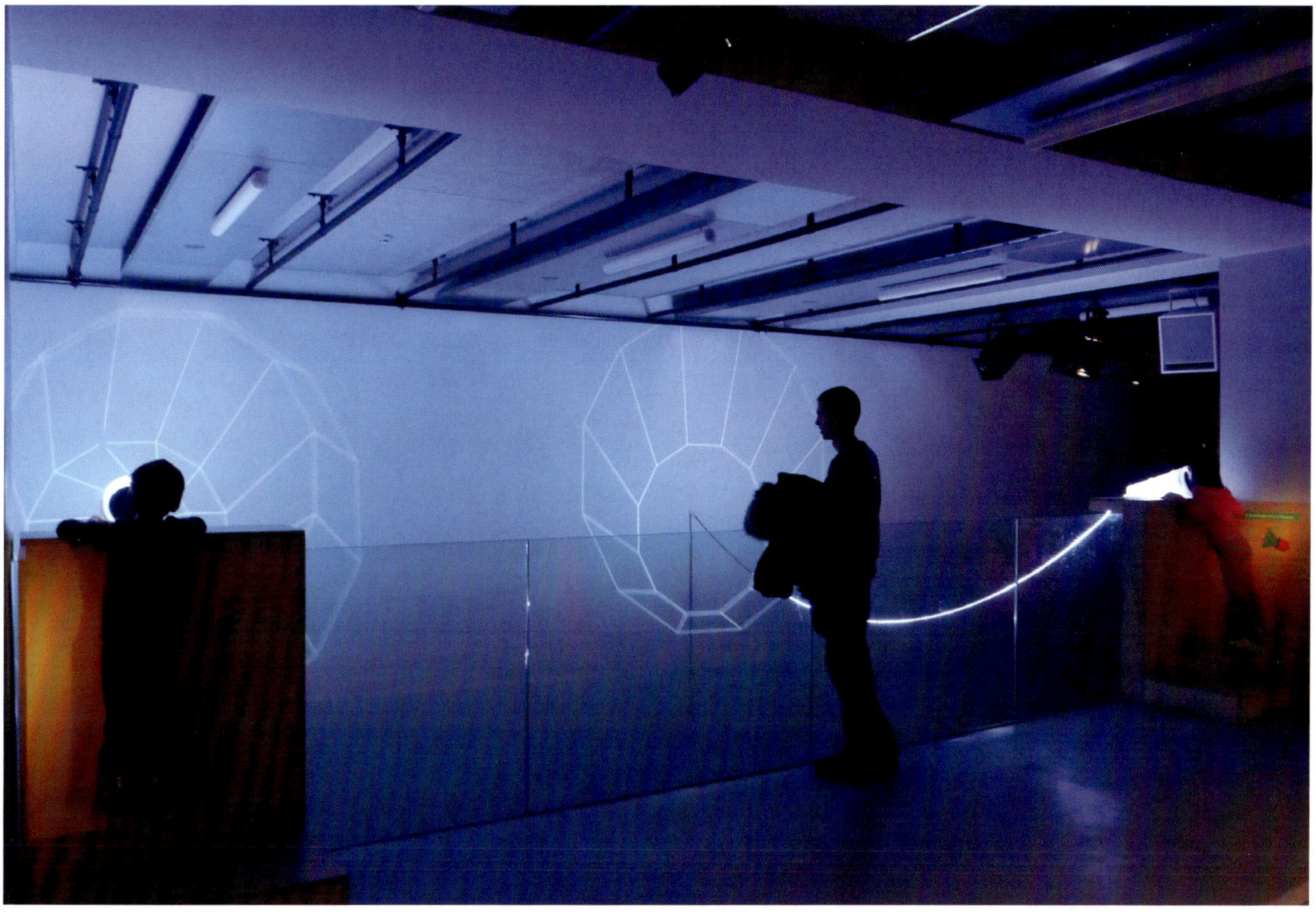

RENCONTRES RÉELLES ET IMAGINAIRES

—

Design: **Scenocosme**

—

This installation offers an interactive walking, visual and sonic exhibition space. When a visitor enters the room he finds his face projected on a mosaic of screens throughout the exhibition space, growing in size as the video projection increases.

In the images, virtual hands try to touch him, to catch him. These varied gestures suggest a range of interactions and relationships with the participant. When the visitor leaves, the hands do, too, until the next visitor arrives, when the hands reappear, with a different set of behaviors.

The light and sound in the room pulse according to the rhythm and interactions between the visitors.

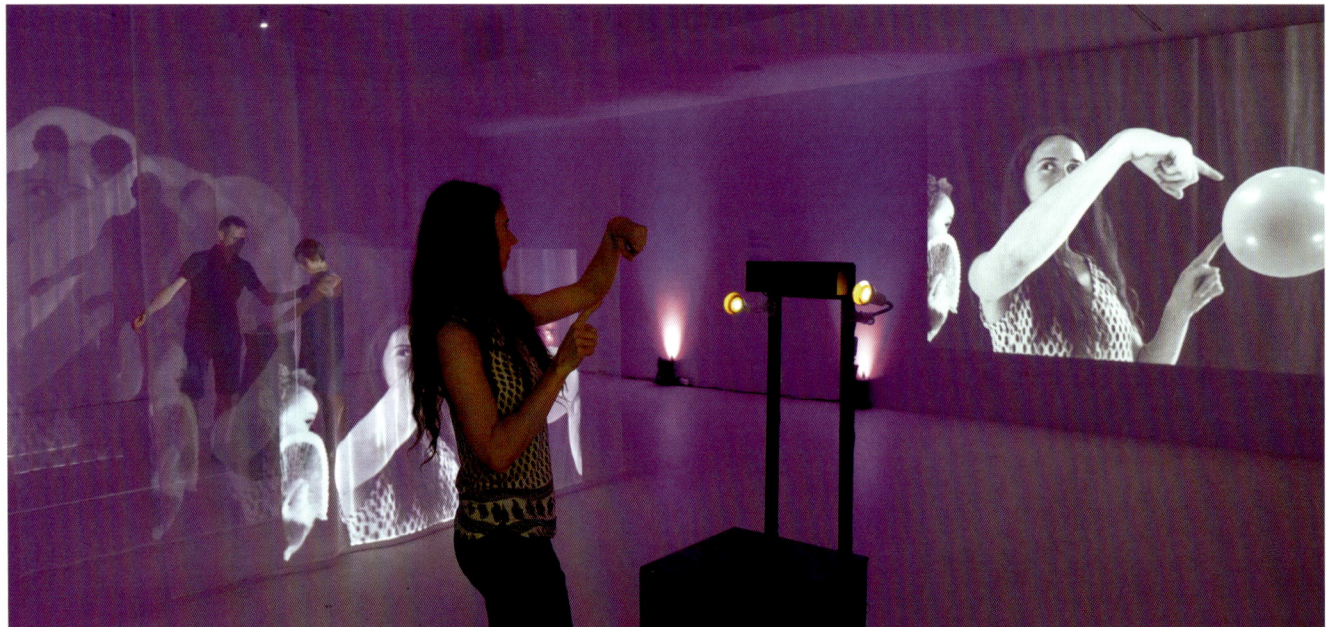

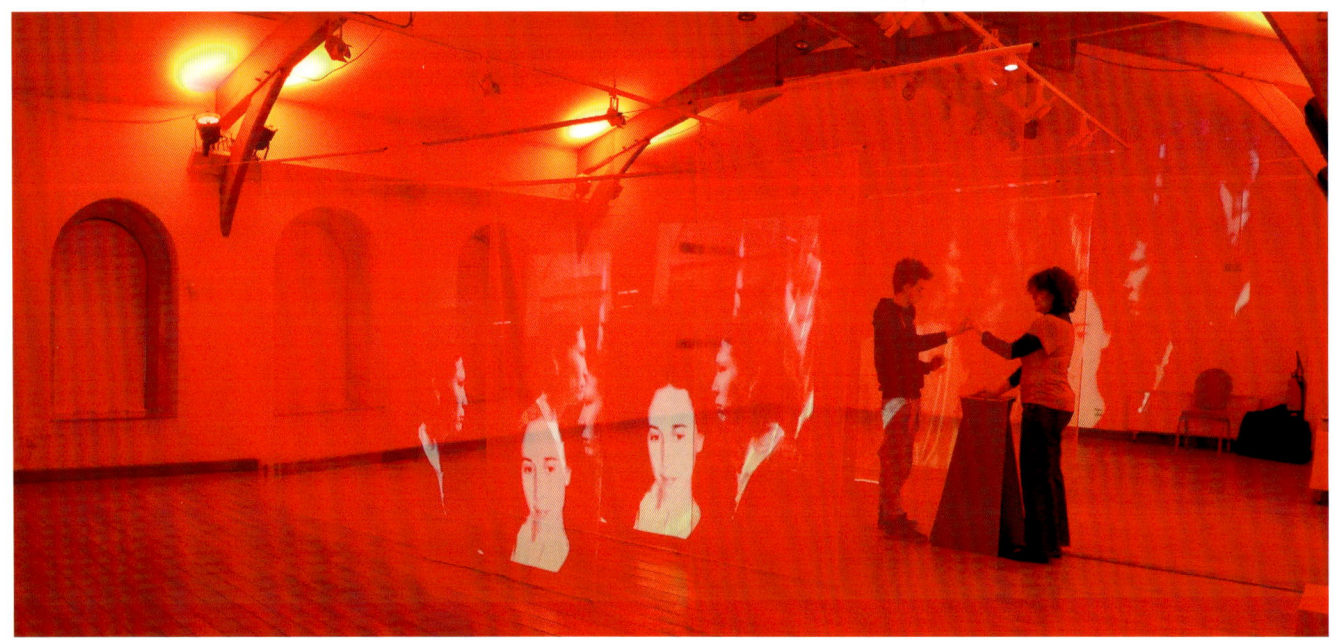

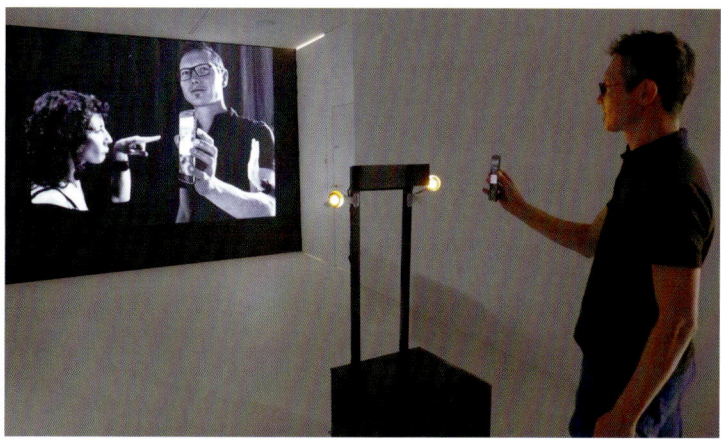

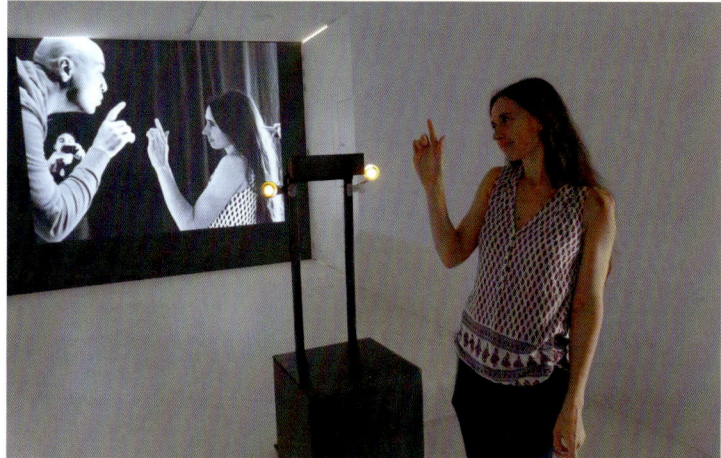

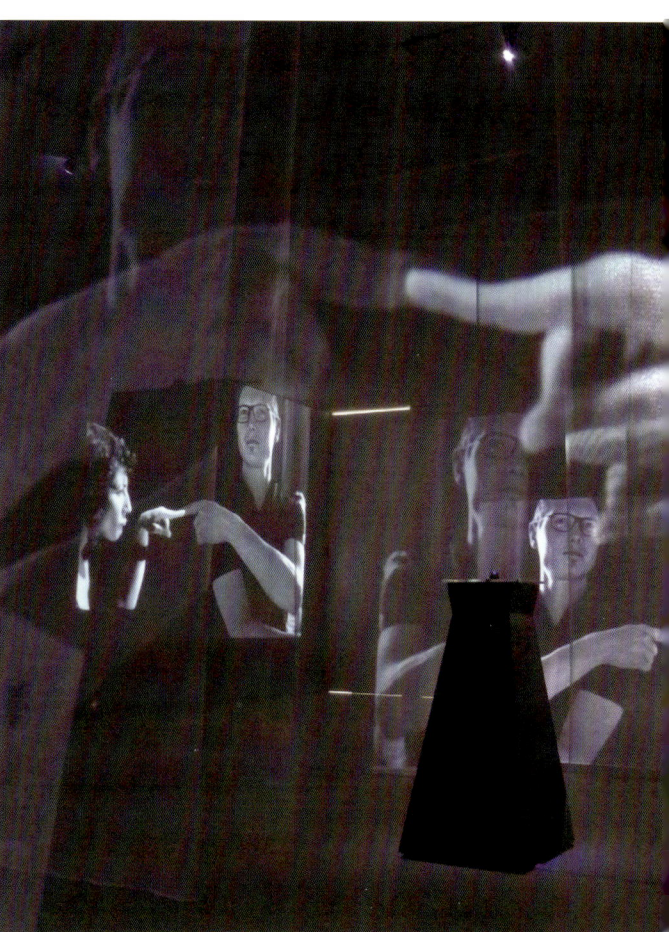

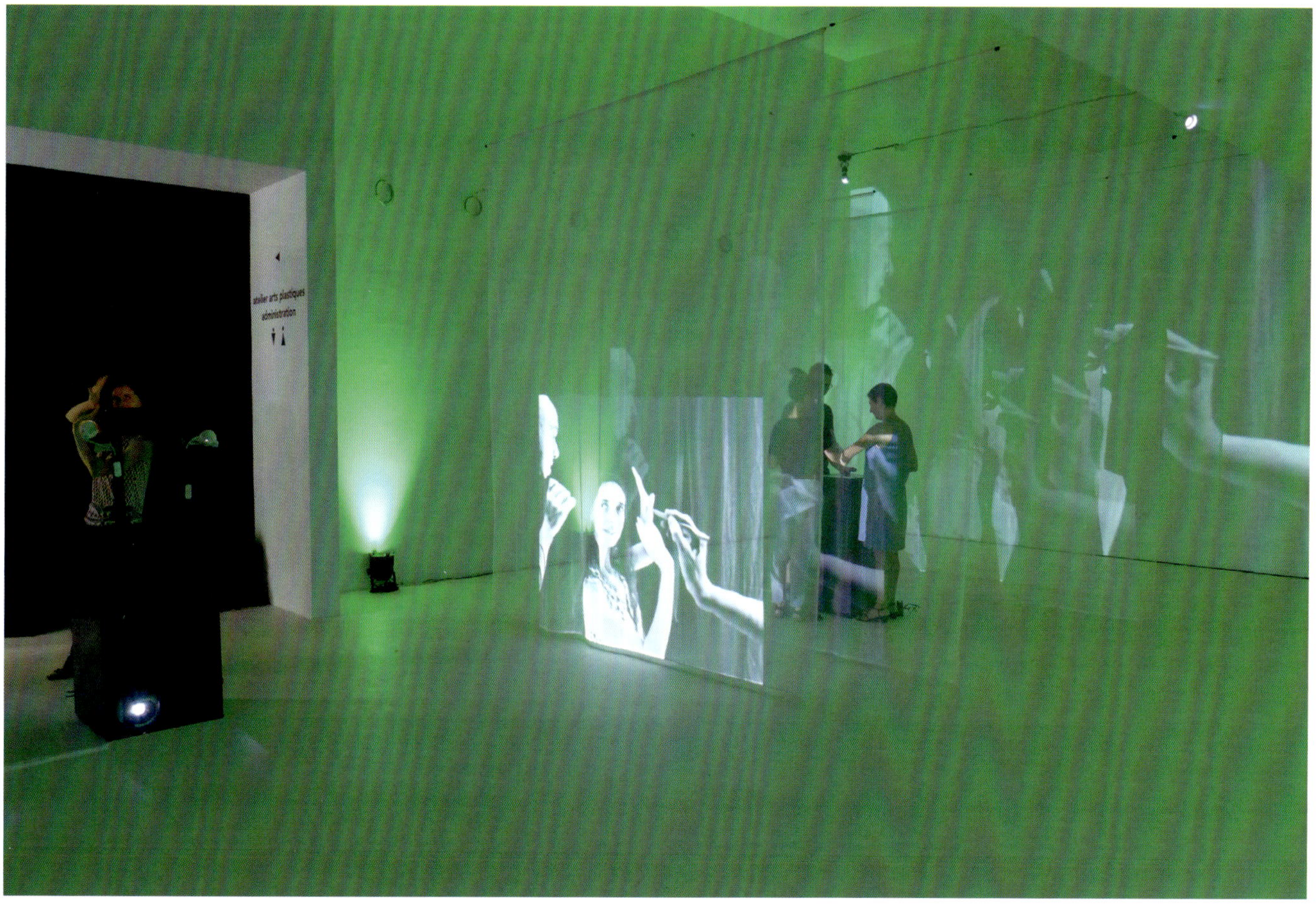

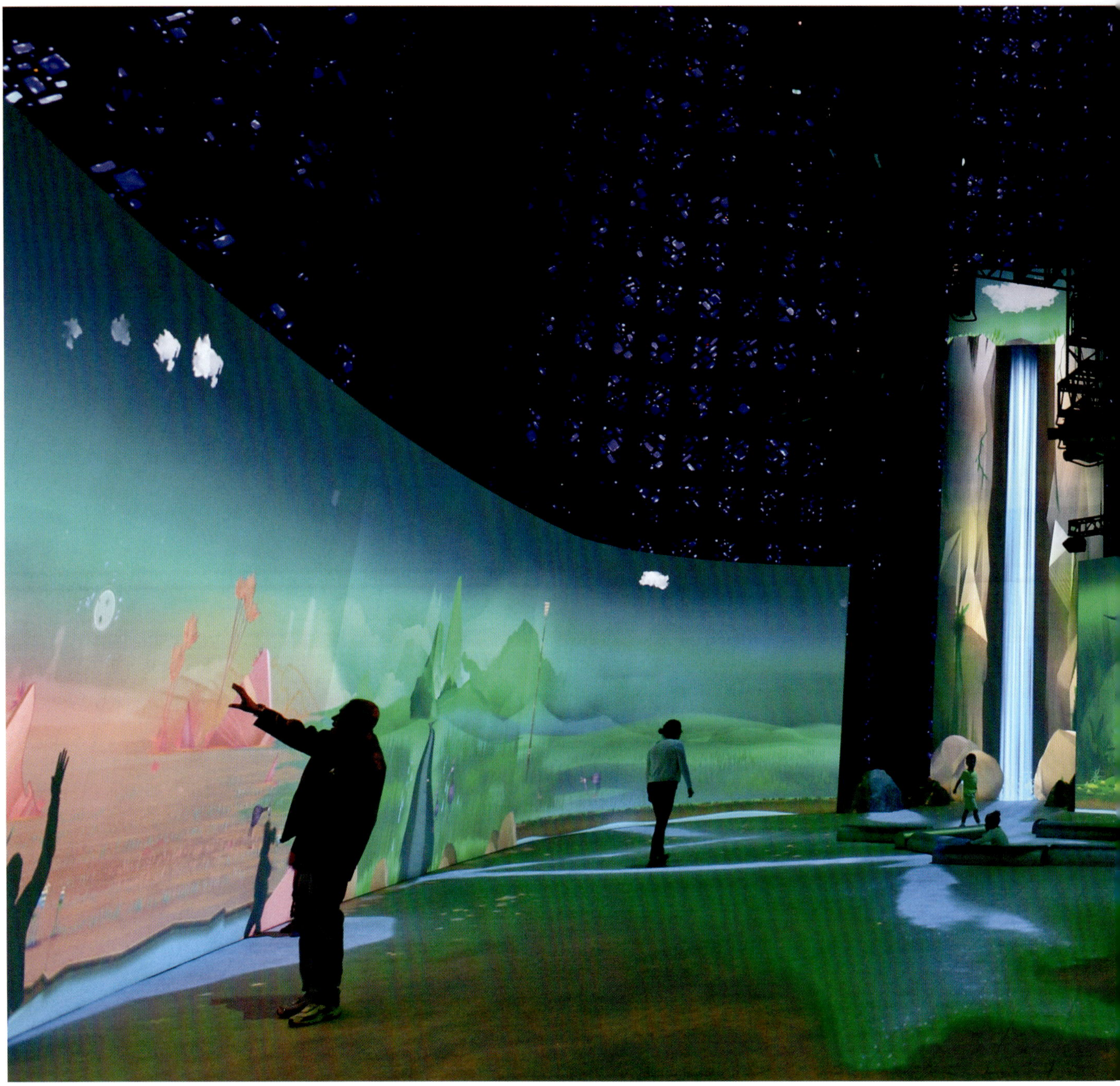

CONNECTED WORLDS

—

Design: **Design I/O**

—

Connected Worlds is a large-scale immersive and interactive ecosystem developed for the New York Hall of Science. The installation is composed of six interactive biomes spread out across the walls of the Great Hall, connected together by a 3000-square-foot interactive floor and a 45-foot-high virtual waterfall. Visitors can use physical logs to divert water flowing across the floor from the waterfall into the different habitats, where they can then use their hands to plant seeds of their choice. As the habitats bloom, creatures appear based on the health of the environment and the type of plants growing within it. If multiple habitats are healthy,

creatures will migrate between them, causing interesting chain reactions of behaviors.

Connected Worlds is designed to encourage a systems-thinking approach to sustainability where local actions in one environment may have global consequences. Visitors work with a fixed amount of water in the system, and have to collaborate to manage and distribute the water across the different environments. Clouds return water from the environments to the waterfall, completing the cycle.

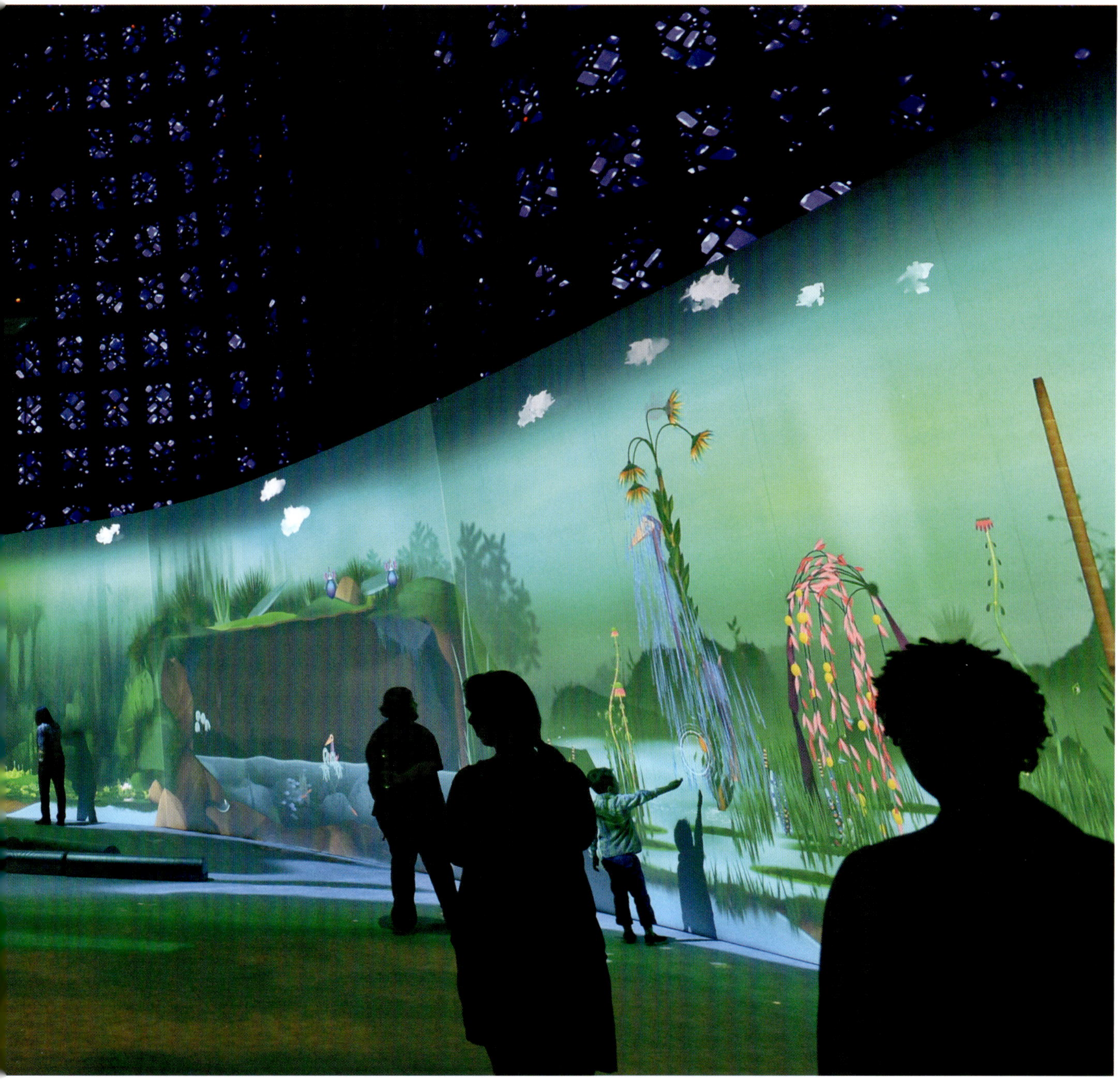

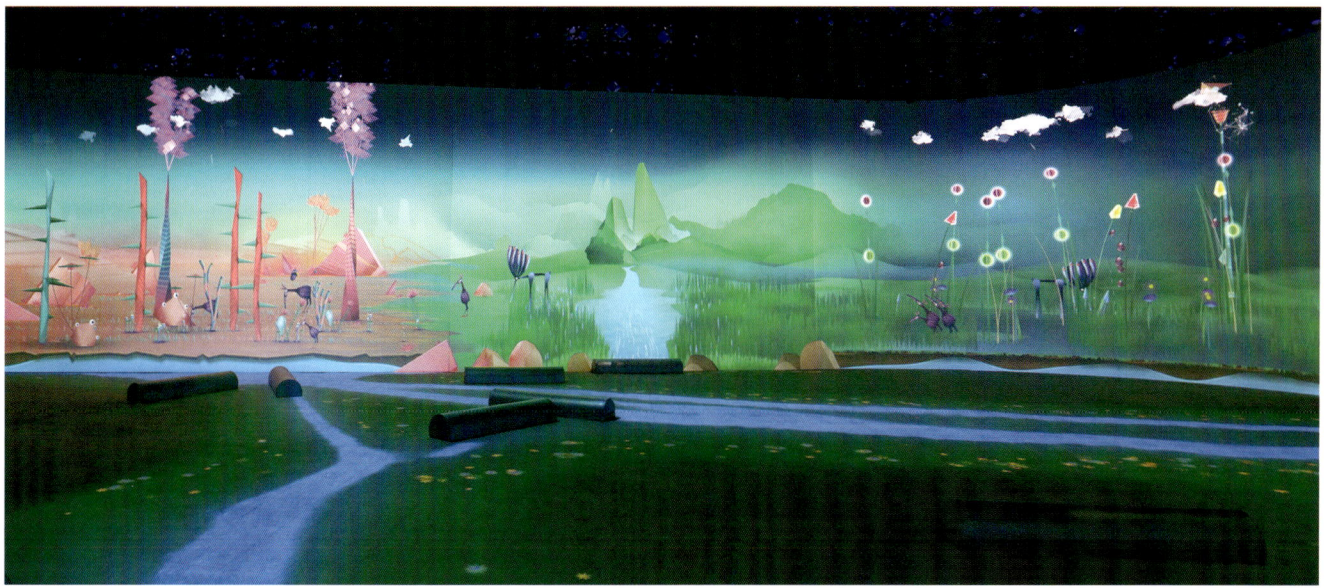

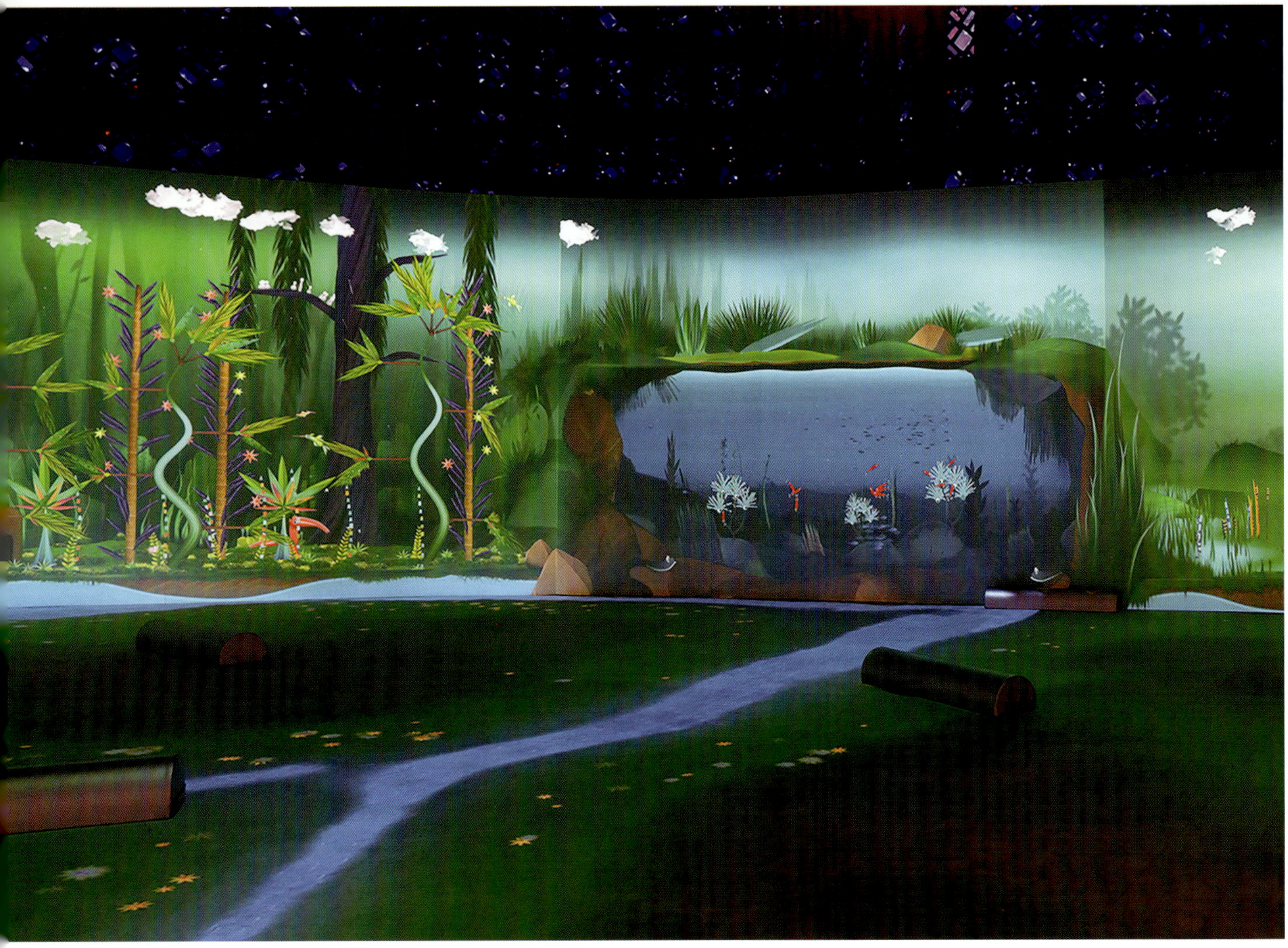

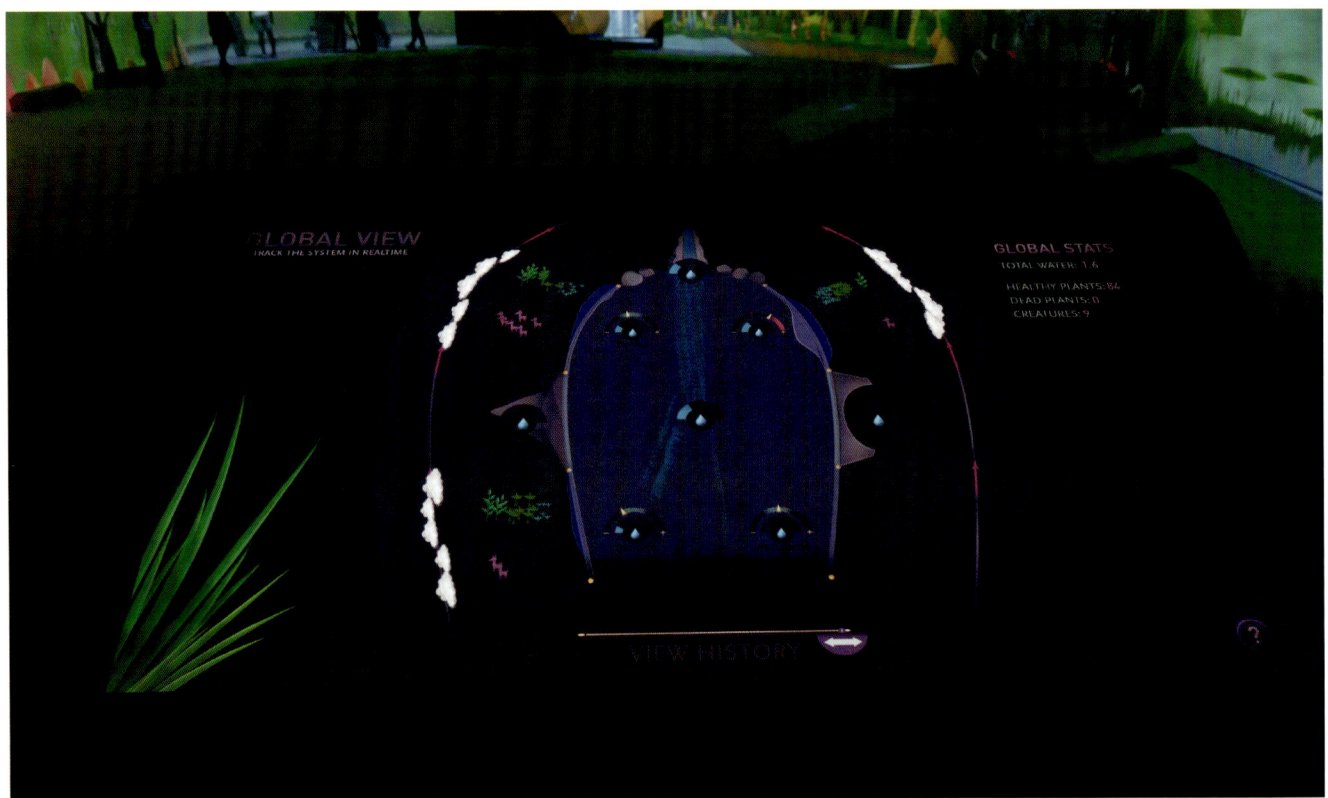

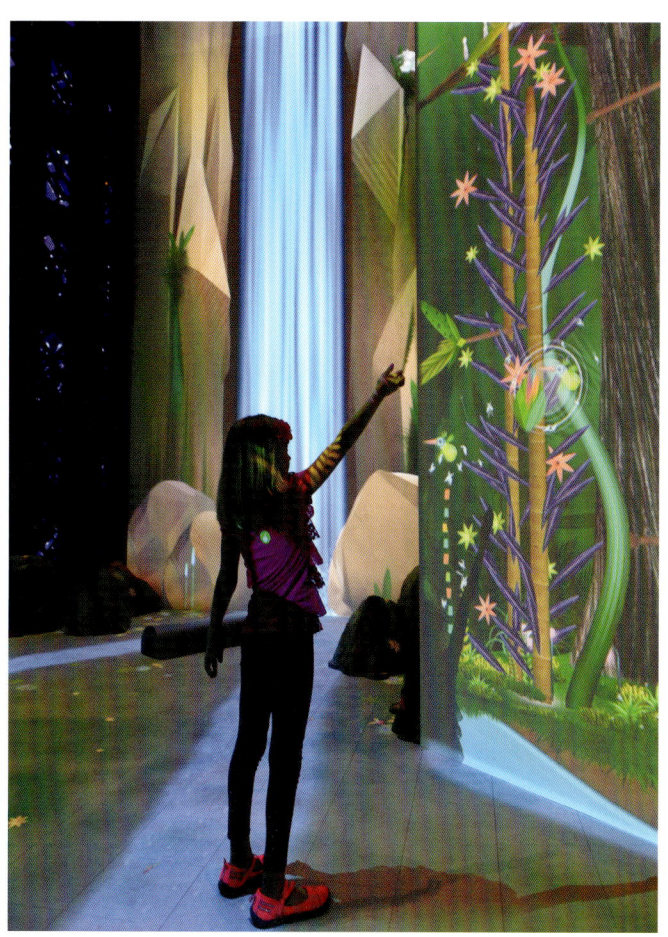

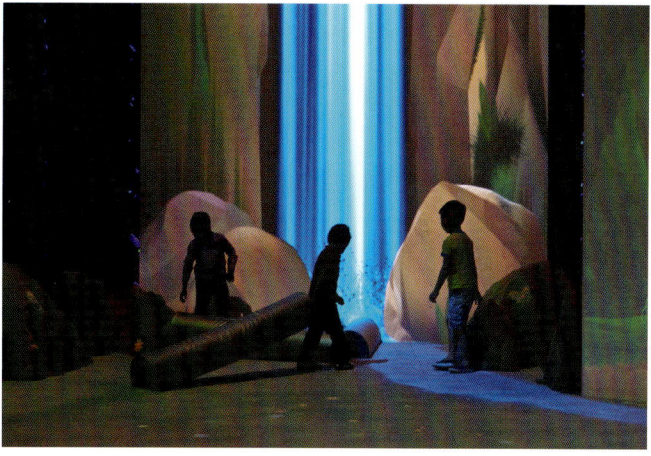

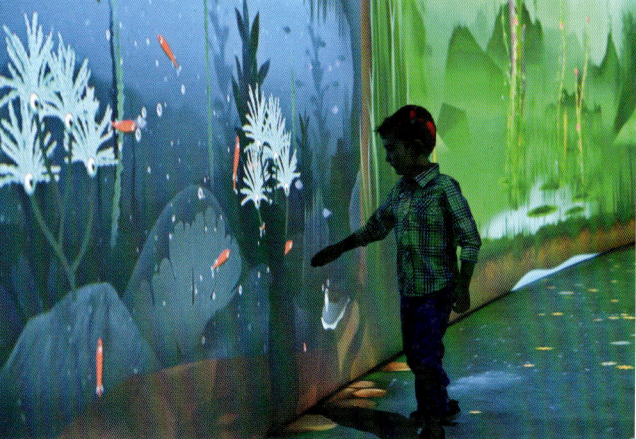

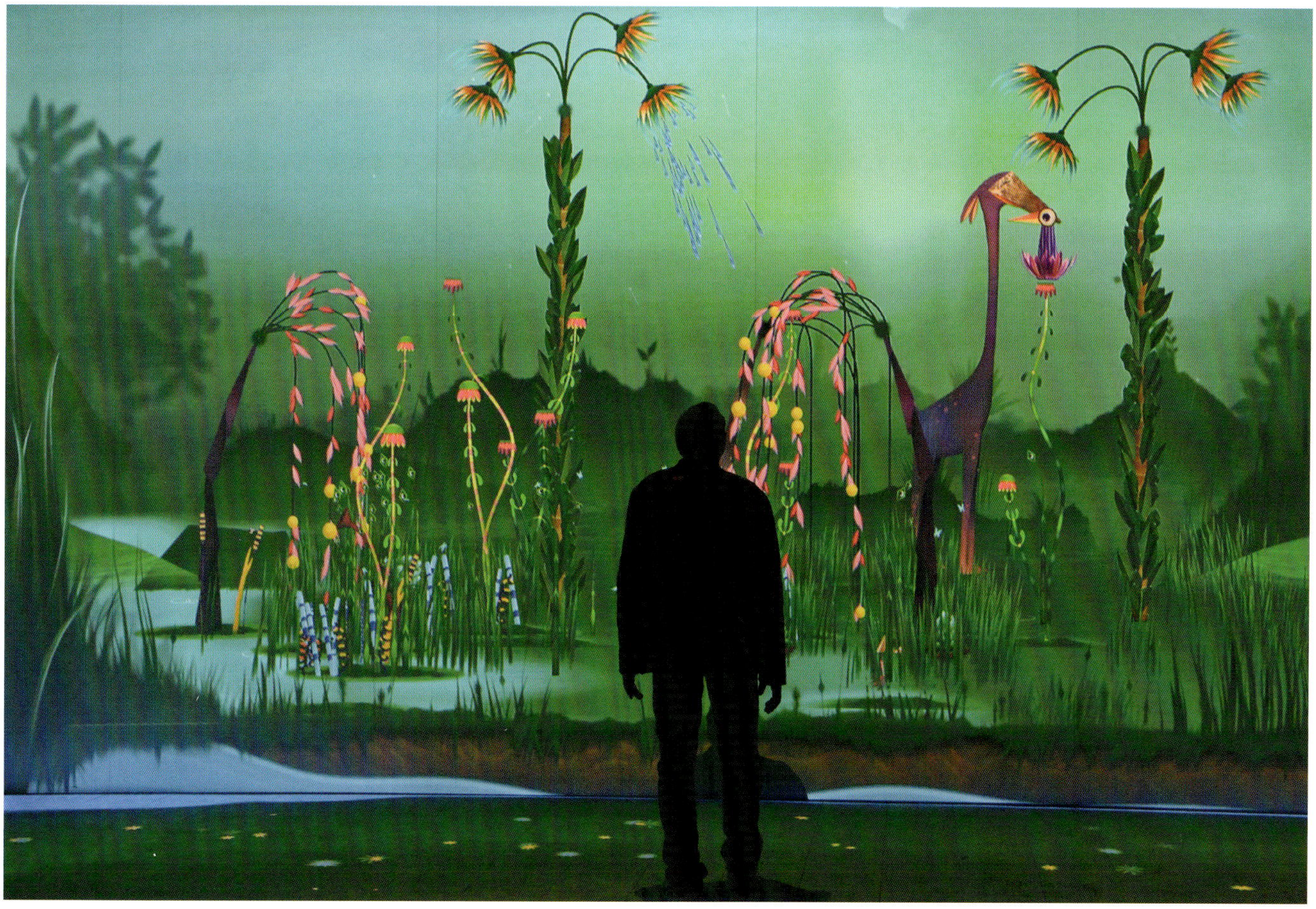

ANOTHER LAND

—

Design: **Kuflex**
Photography: **Maria Yastrebova**

—

Another Land is an interactive video installation—part magical game and part fairy tale. The luminous forest is inhabited by amiable flying jellyfish, soft spiked balls (pointy sea urchin-type creatures) and giant live flowers. It's quite easy to make contact with them—come to the screen, and the silhouette of visitors will turn into a light wave.

Silhouettes of people are read with depth cameras located along the wall. Silhouettes and the flight paths of the balls are processed using a program written in openFrameworks. The original algorithm, developed by Kuflex, provides for natural interactions. The three-dimensional scene is rendered by Unreal Engine (a graphics engine) using custom Kuflex plug-ins. The project is realized in cooperation with 7CG Studio.

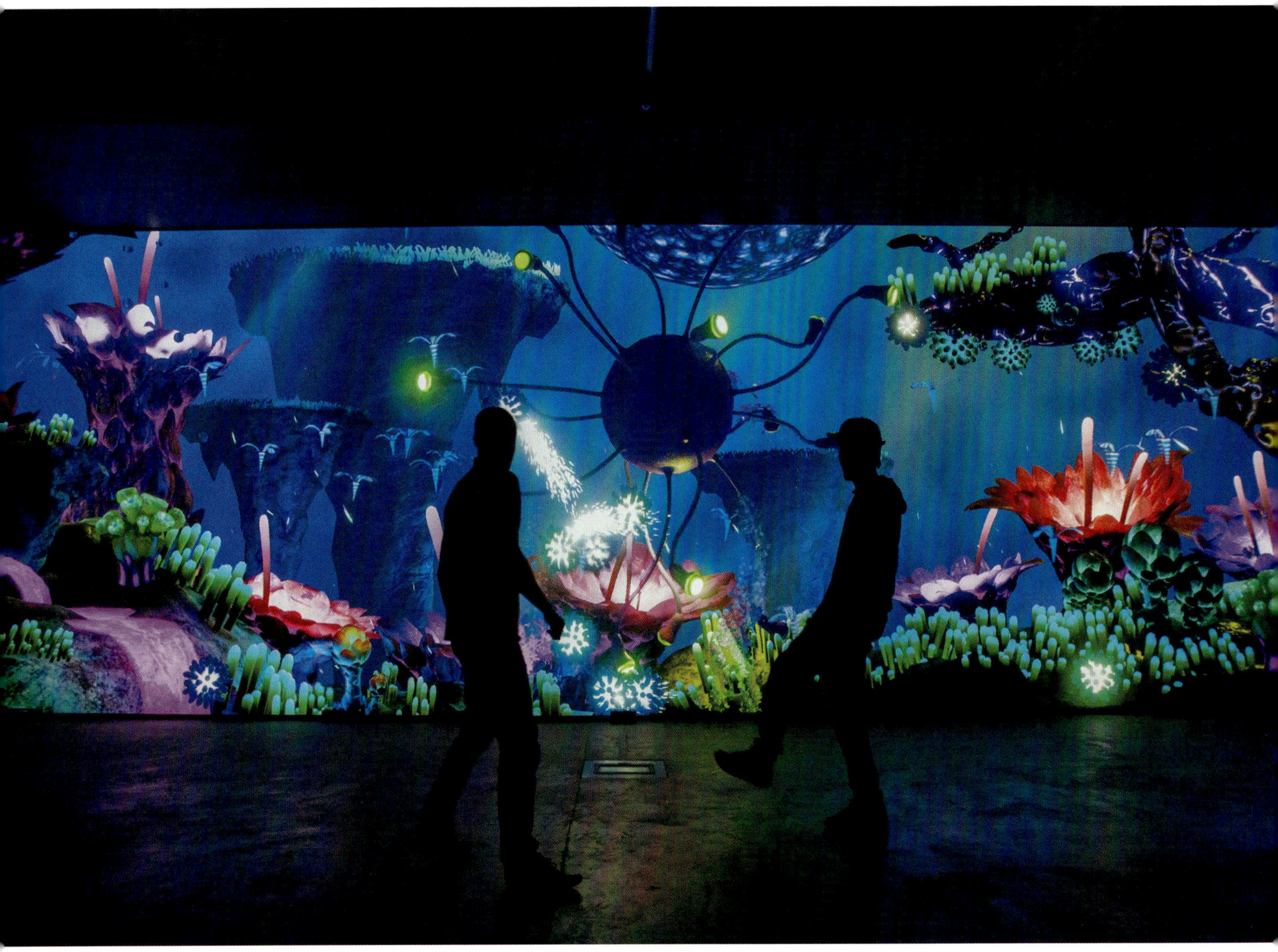

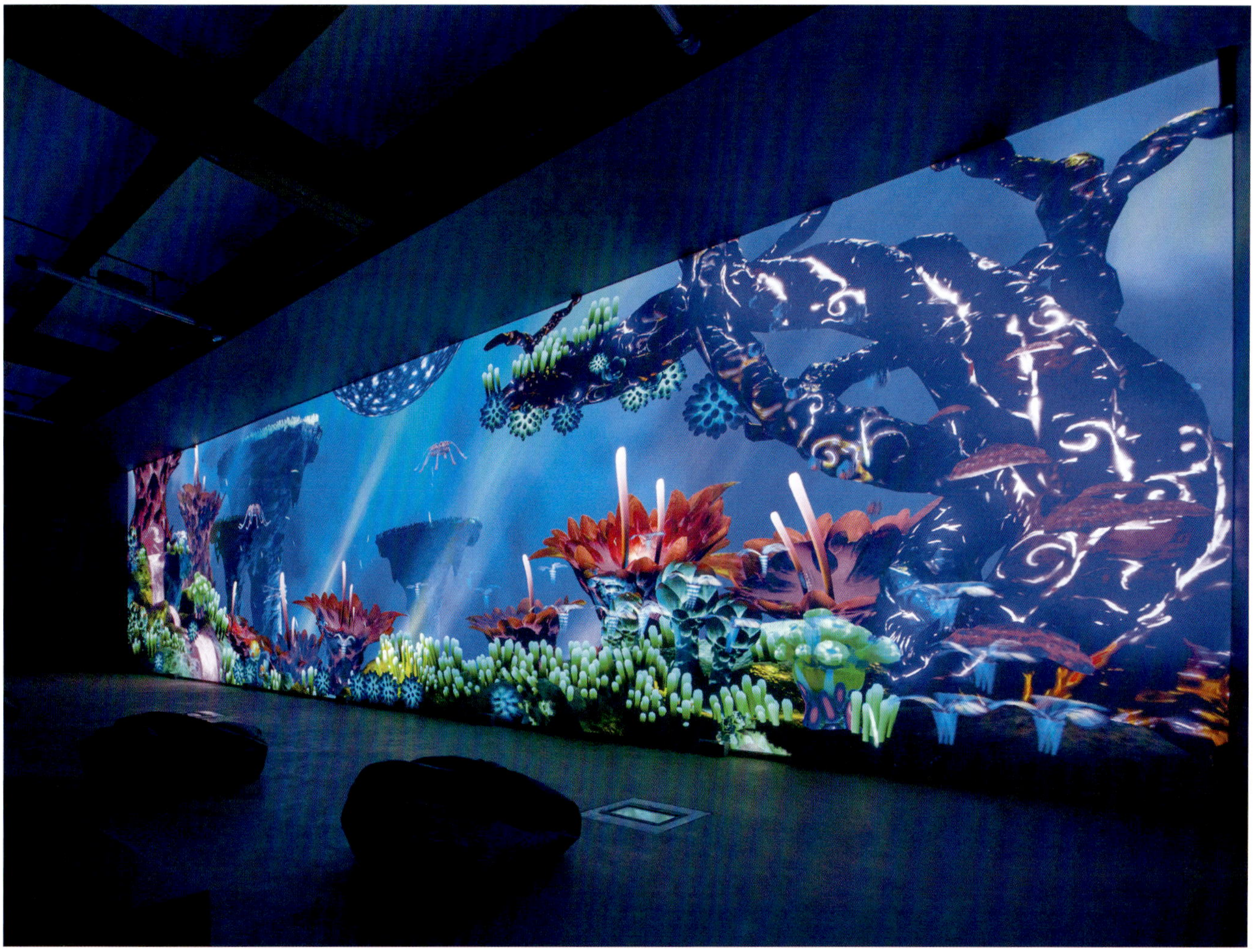

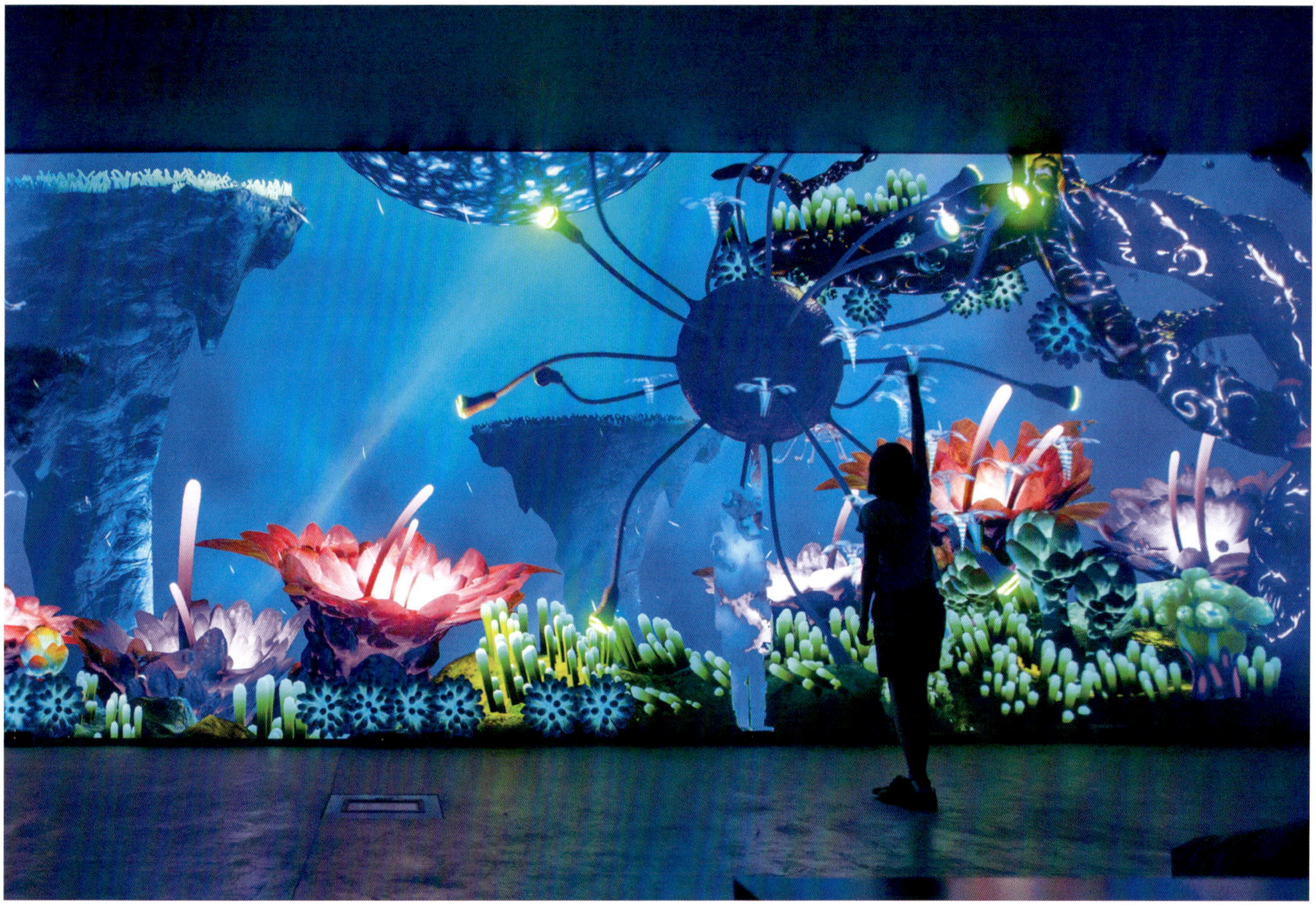

SYMBIOISIS

—

Design: **Kuflex**
Photography: **Maria Yastrebova**

—

In this installation, the human body is augmented
with projected virtual images, bringing the
participant and technology together in a symbiotic
relationship and bringing to life wonderful
biomorphic creatures. They change constantly—
reacting to every movement and turning into new
and unique forms each time. The installation was
inspired by the symmetry of living organisms,
the structure of exotic insects, and reflections on
extraterrestrial life forms.

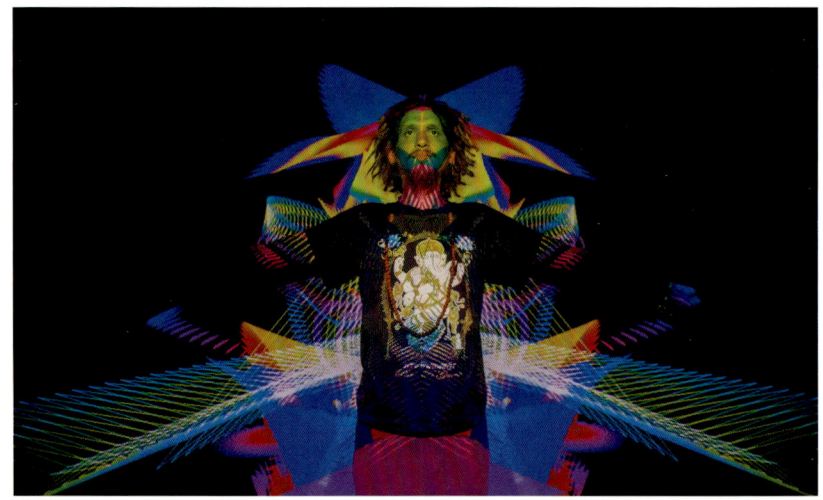

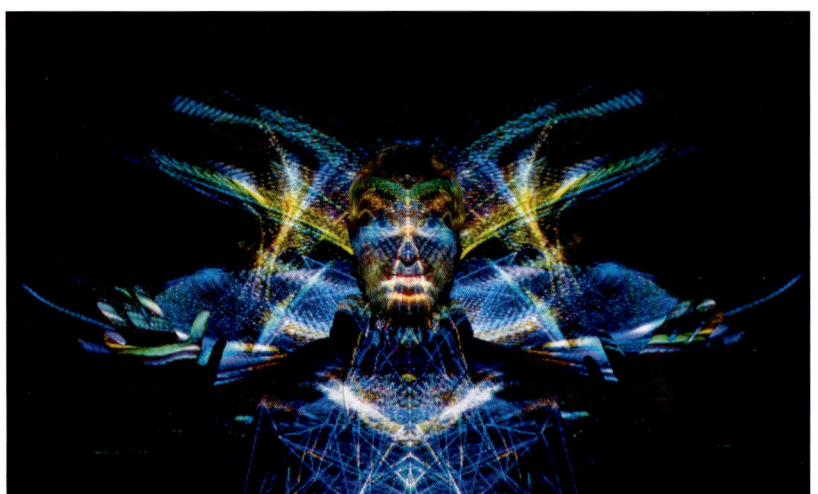

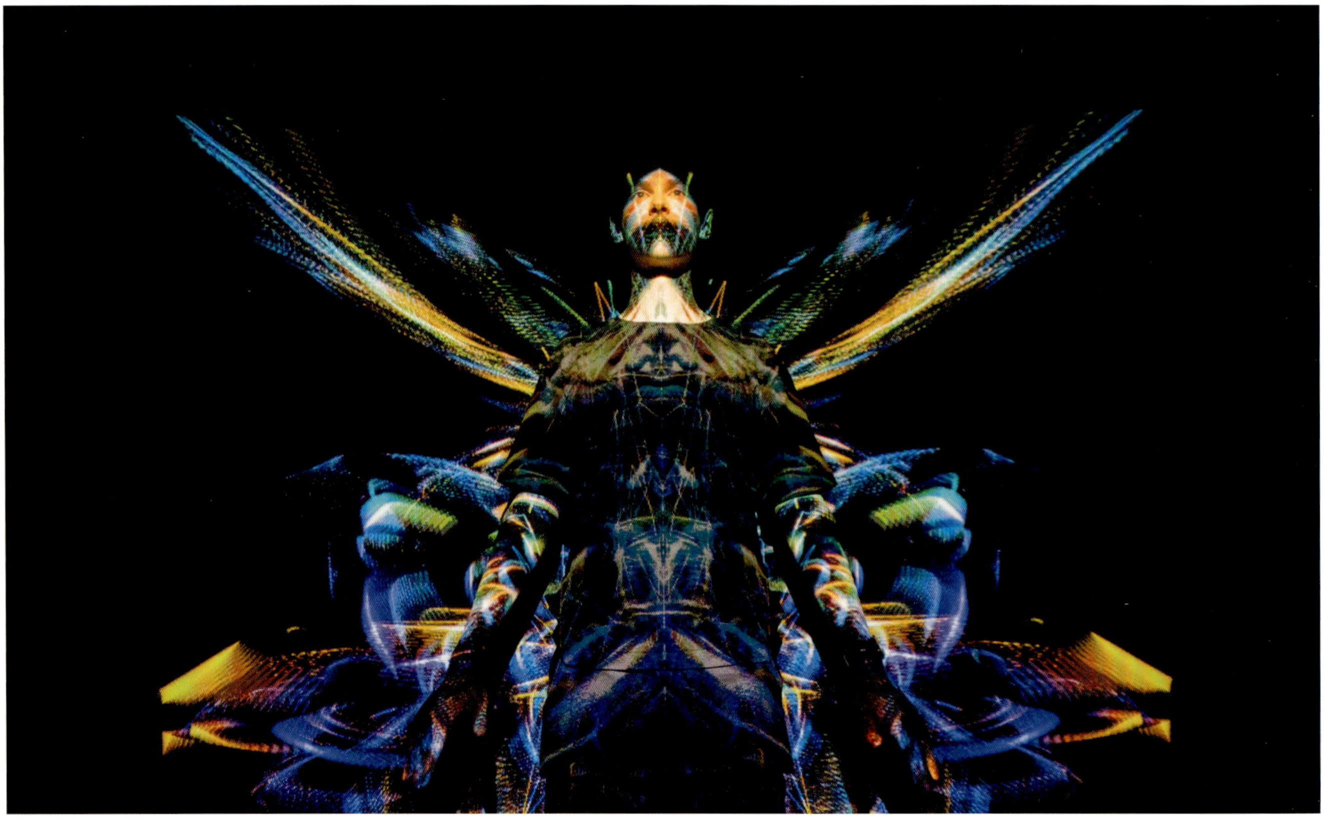

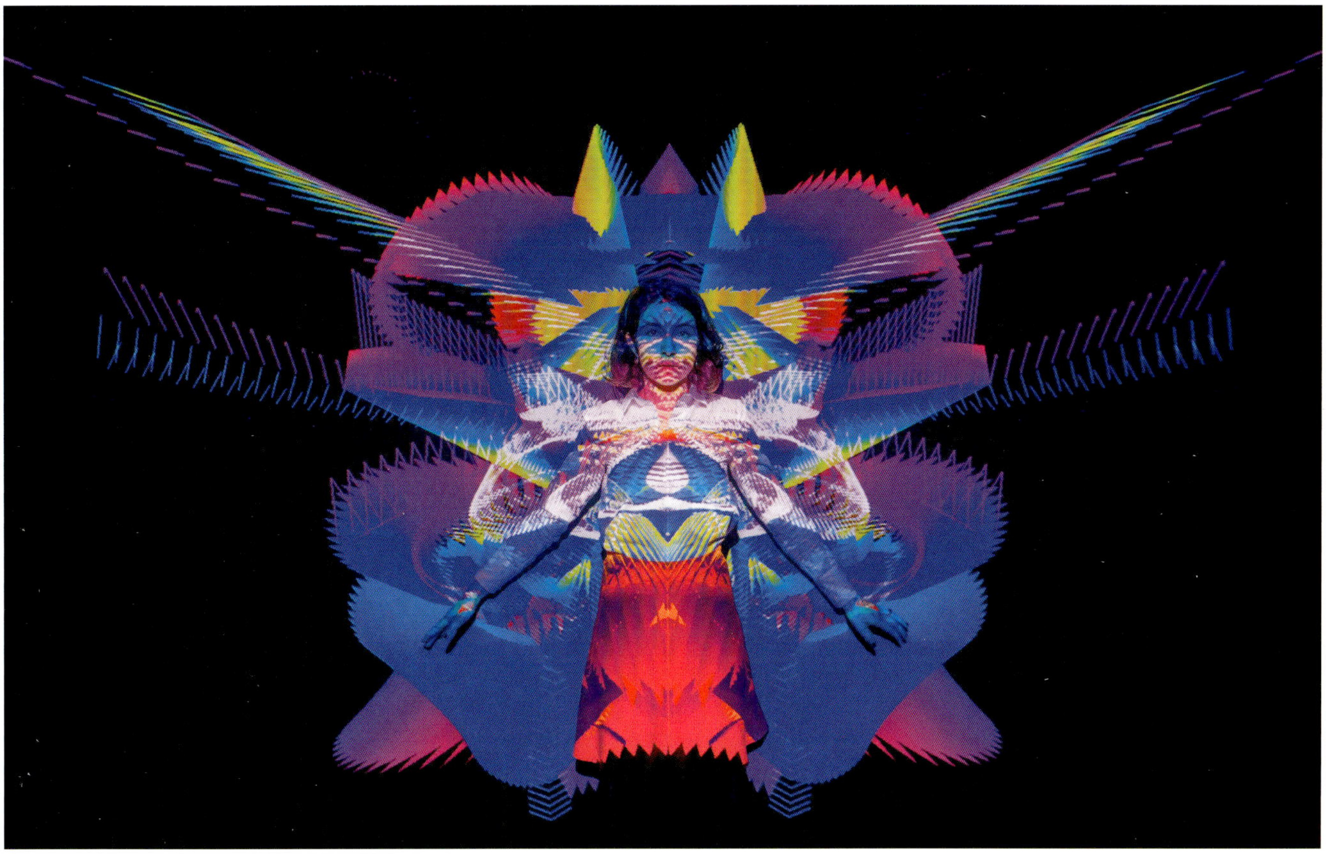

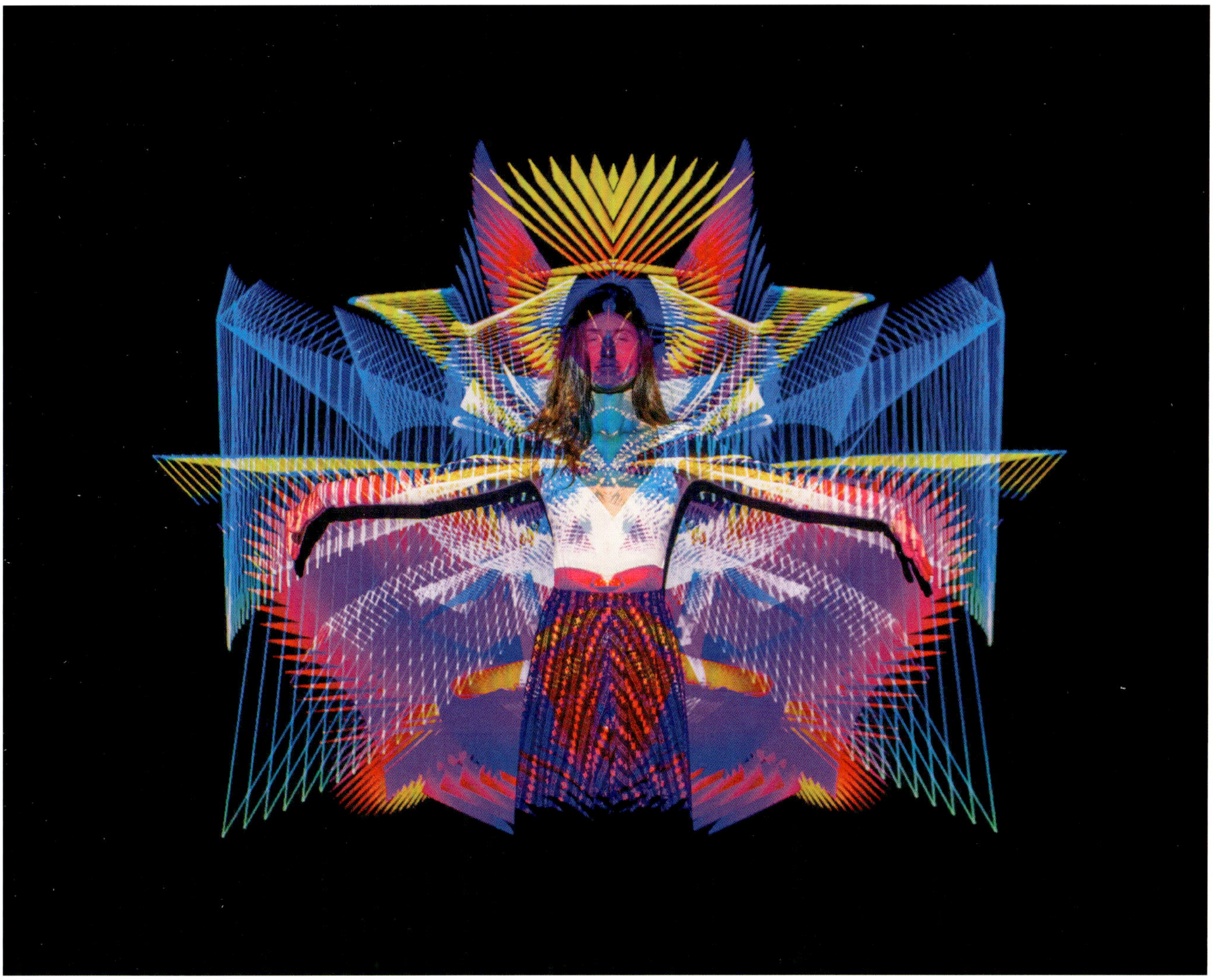

SPEED OF COLOR

—

Design: **Kuflex**

—

No one really knows what extraterrestrial life looks like. But what if it exists in the form of a color or a sound wave? This installation offers viewers the opportunity to communicate with such waves.

With their movements, spectators generate space-color waves of digital liquid that appear on a large projection screen of the video installation. The screen is similar to a digital pool filled with a virtual colorful liquid, the physical model of which is different from the real one. It slowly pulsates and changes color over time and reacts to any number of people in front of the screen.

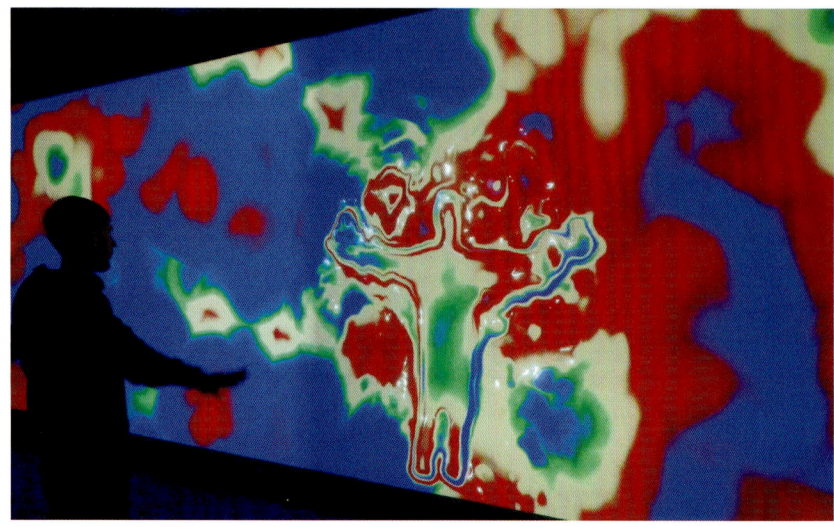

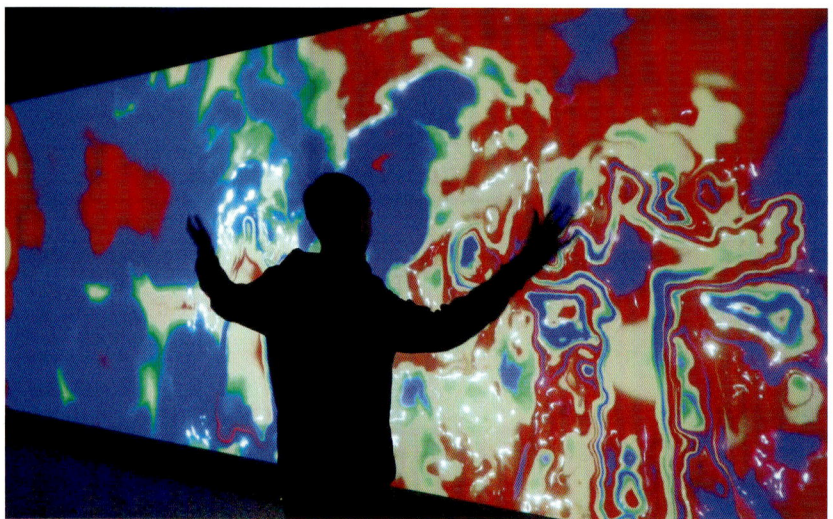

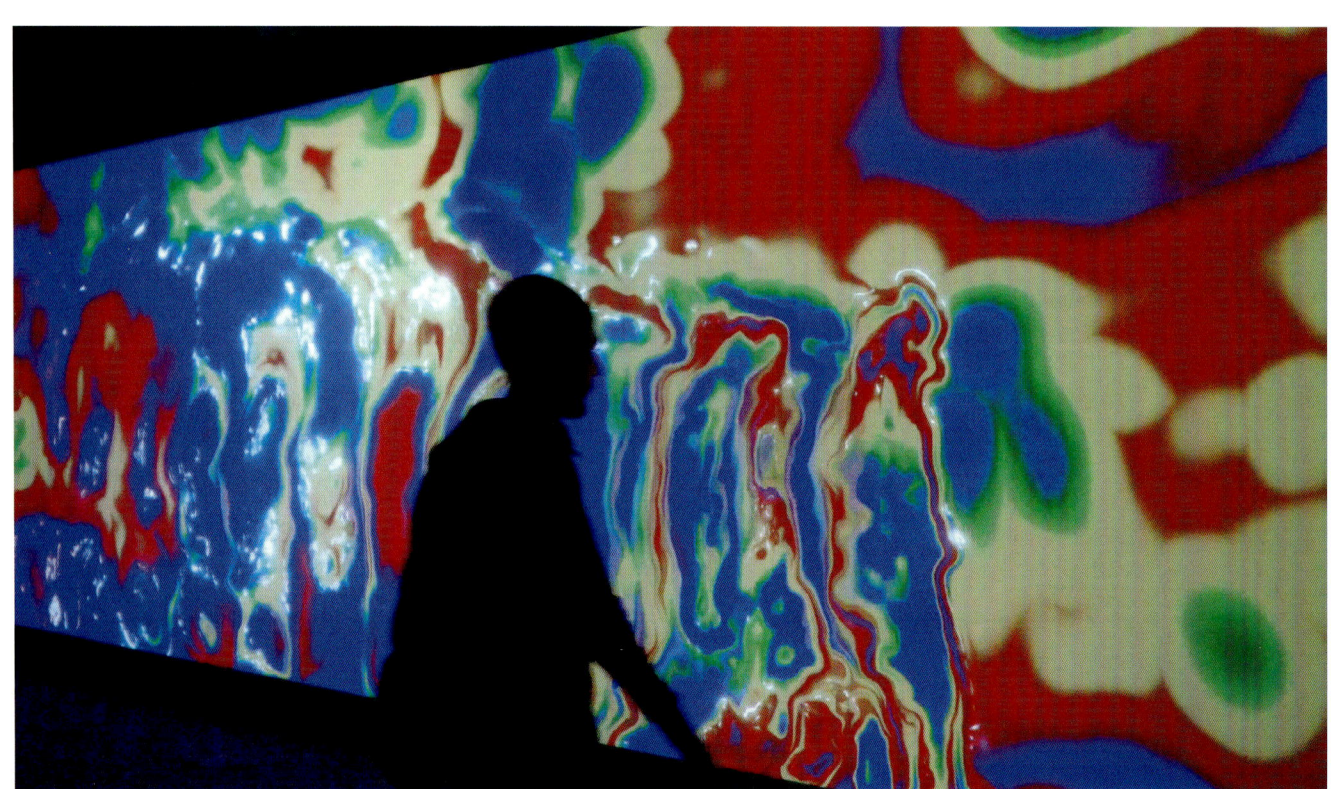

METAMORPHY

—

Design: **Scenocosme**

—

Metamorphy is a visual and sonic interactive artwork. Spectators are invited to touch and explore the depth of a semi-transparent veil. This symbolic skin is elastic—it stretches when the spectator pushes against it, and becomes flat again when the spectator releases the pressure.

The exploration of the veil's depths reveals various meditative universes, through the projection of organic, liquid or incandescent substances.

Metamorphy creates an ambiguity between a real physical space, a virtual space materialized by the reflection of a mirror, and a virtual space generated by the video projections. In this sensory artwork, real reflections and virtual images get mixed up, giving the illusion of a distorted reality. Each interaction zone on the fabric creates sound effects when the spectator pushes on it with his hand. Then, when nobody interacts with the veil, it becomes flat and empty again. Only the spectator's reflection remains.

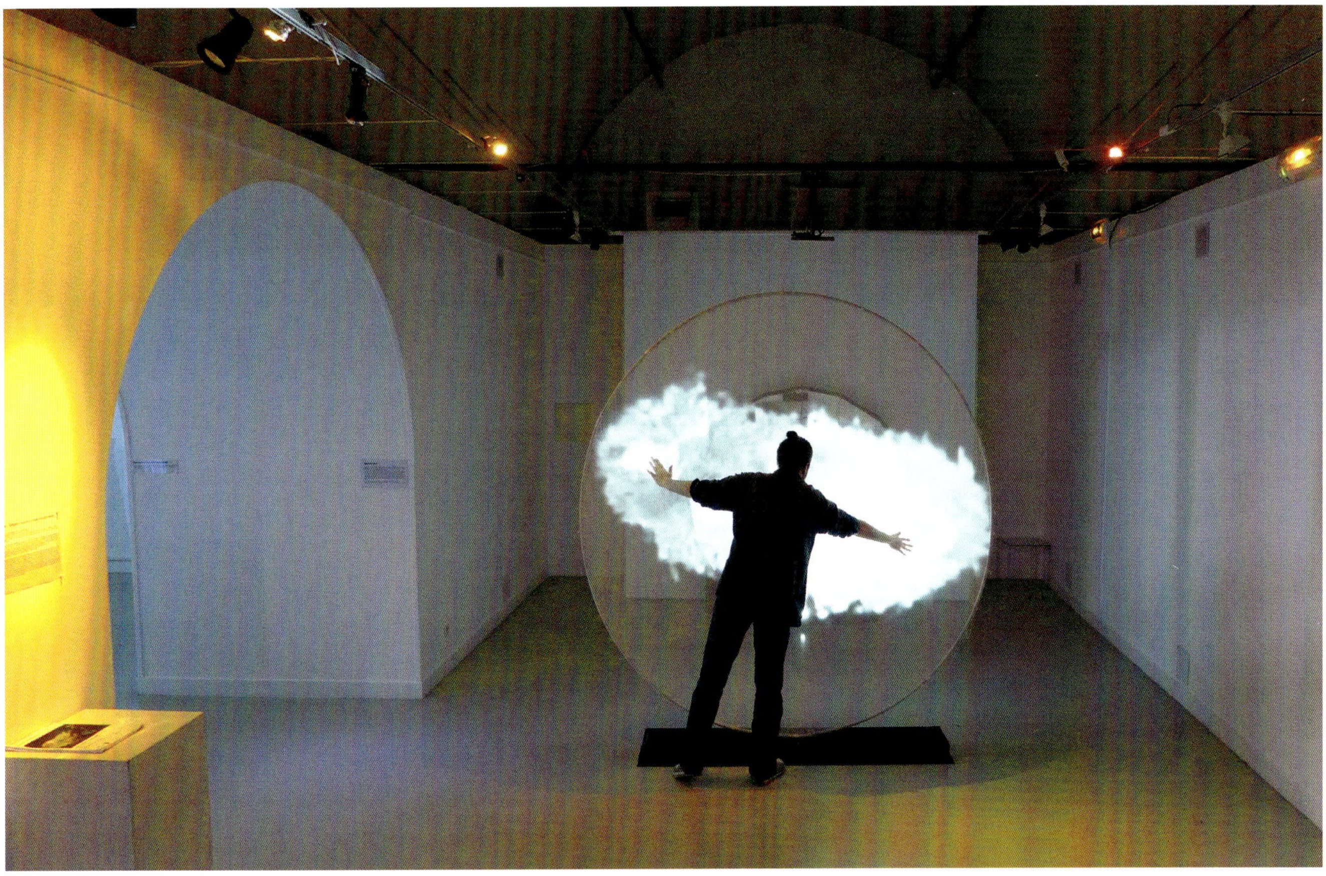

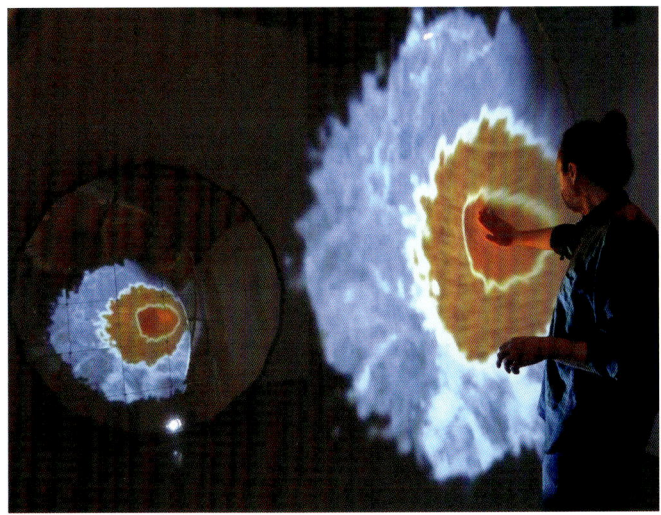

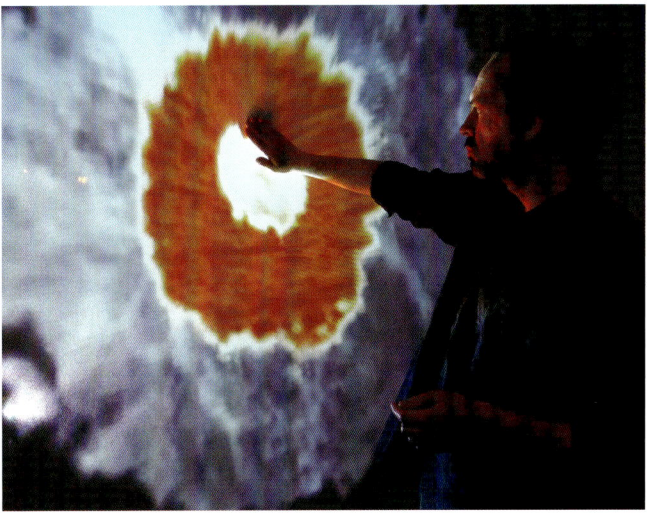

LA MAISON SENSIBLE (THE SENSITIVE HOUSE)

—

Design: **Scenocosme**

—

La maison sensible is an interactive installation artwork that augments the physical space and the relationship between an onlooker and a fragile and subtle environment. The idea was to create a work that emerges when the viewer enters the space with attention and sensitivity. It develops into a visual and auditory environment that mirrors the body by revealing an interactive audiovisual organic space on which spectators leave traces experienced as scars by the physical room.

The various behaviors of spectators cause changes in the visual and sonic environment. A sensitive table reveals shades and sound environments that evolve with the qualities of interactions.

If visitors interact with sensitivity and gentleness, the room responds by engaging in respectful dialogue through harmonious sounds. If the activity becomes too noisy, the room reaches the limits of its empathic behavior, and the sound withdraws and fades.

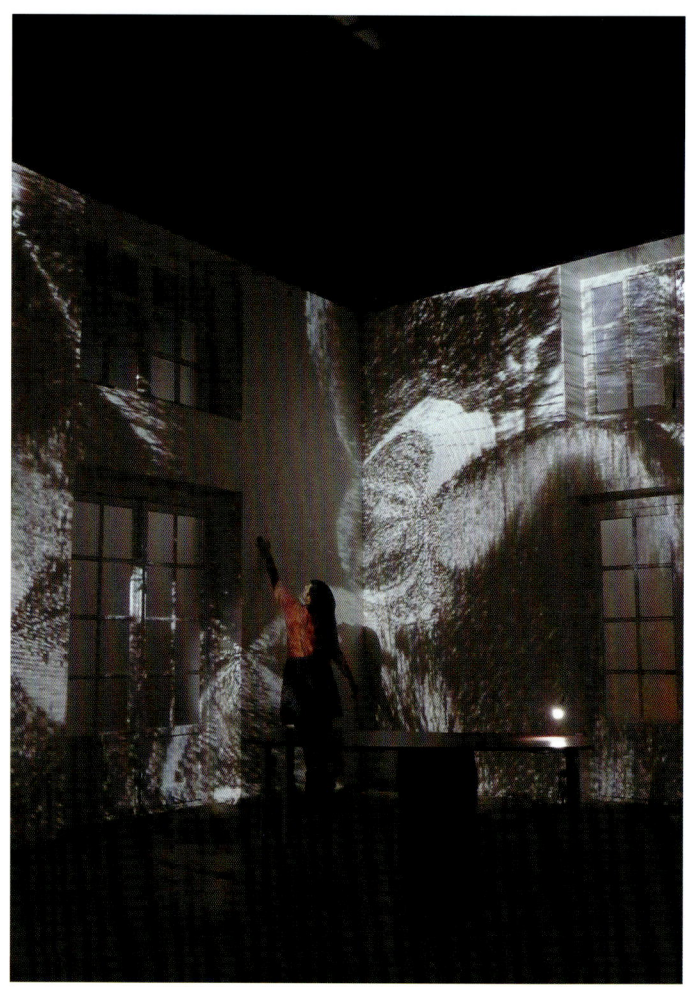

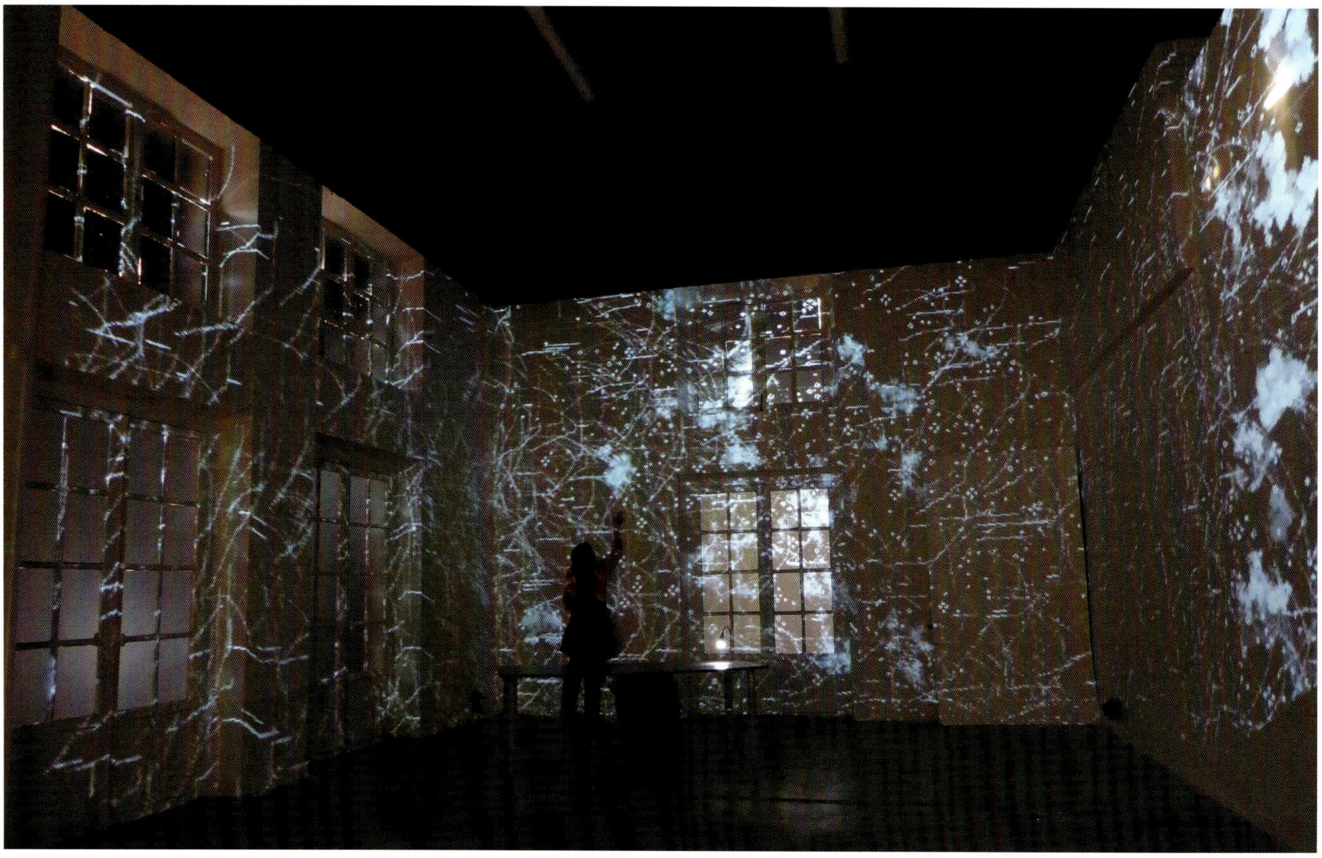

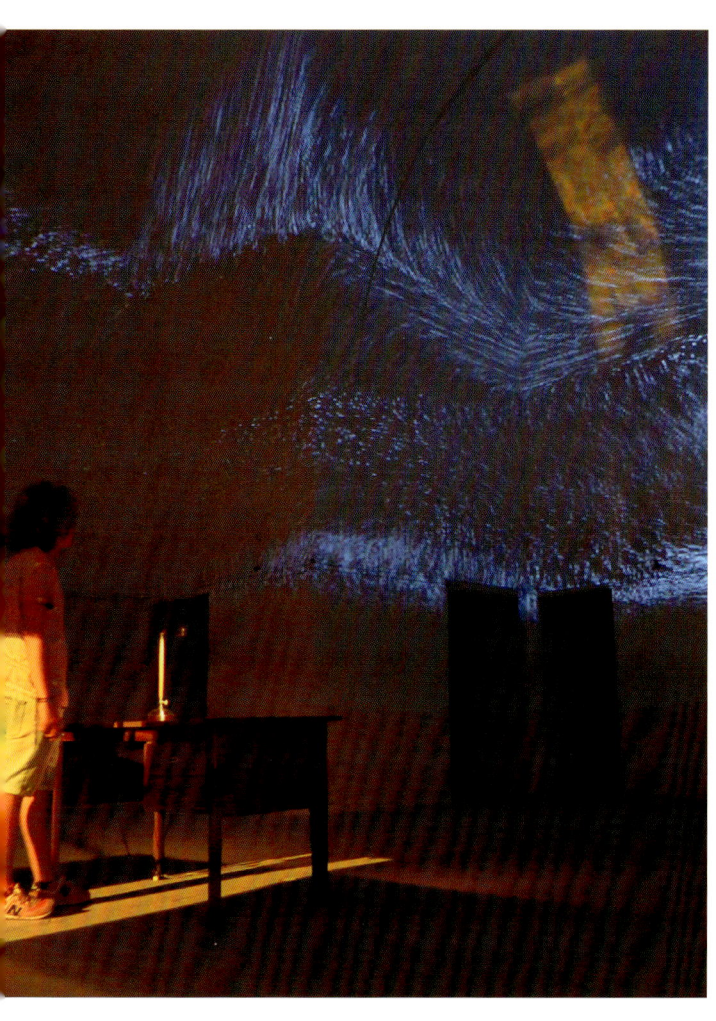

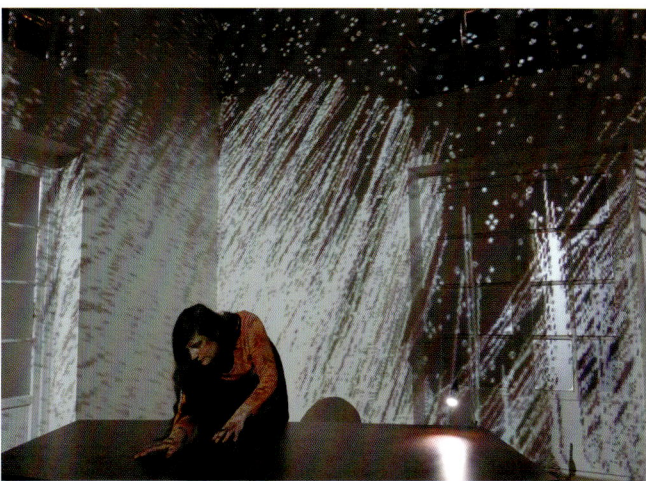

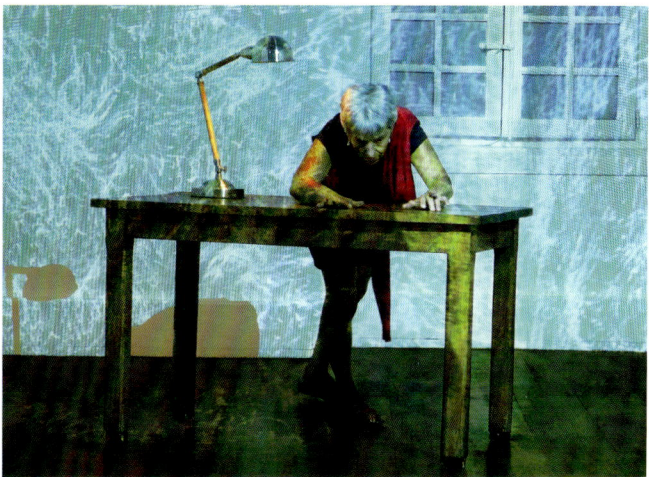

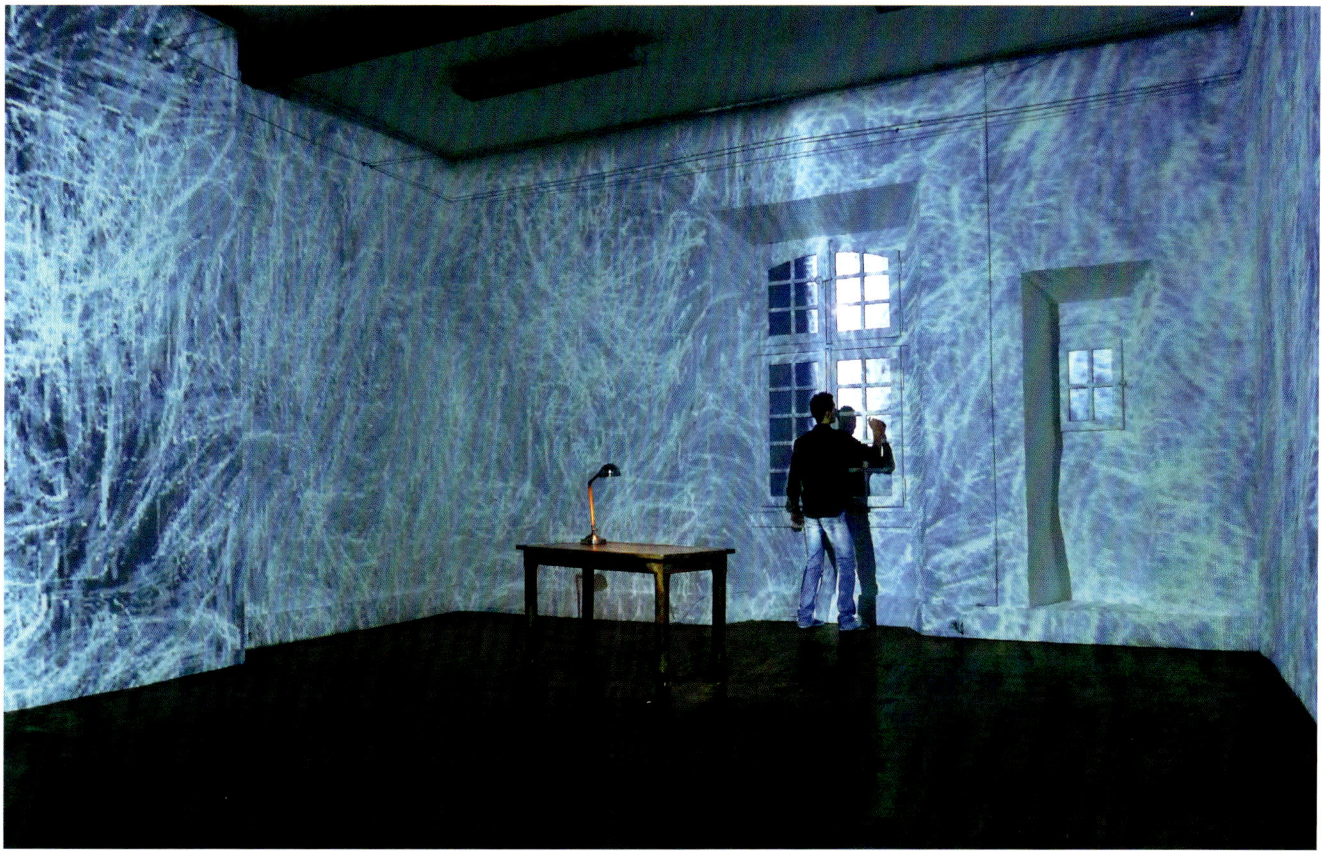

QUANTUM SPACE

—

Design: **Kuflex**
Photography: **Maria Yastrebova**

—

Quantum Space is a large-scale interactive video projection that takes the viewer to the abstract world of quanta. Here, everyone can become a particle of light and the maker, creating harmony from cosmic chaos—at the same time. Being "in sight" of the installation, the viewer sees his digital reflection, consisting of particles. All the particles are in constant motion and every action of the viewer affects their parameters: trajectory, time of life, color, gravity. Familiar phenomena can be seen in abstract images: fires, auroras, meteor showers, or streams of fluid. In this space, barriers to self-expression and spontaneous creativity disappear. Here you can become a stream of light or a particle of the infinite cosmos.

The installation automatically switches various visual modes of particle generation. Silhouettes of spectators are detected by depth cameras. Specific algorithms transform these silhouettes and their movements into new particles and forces acting on them.

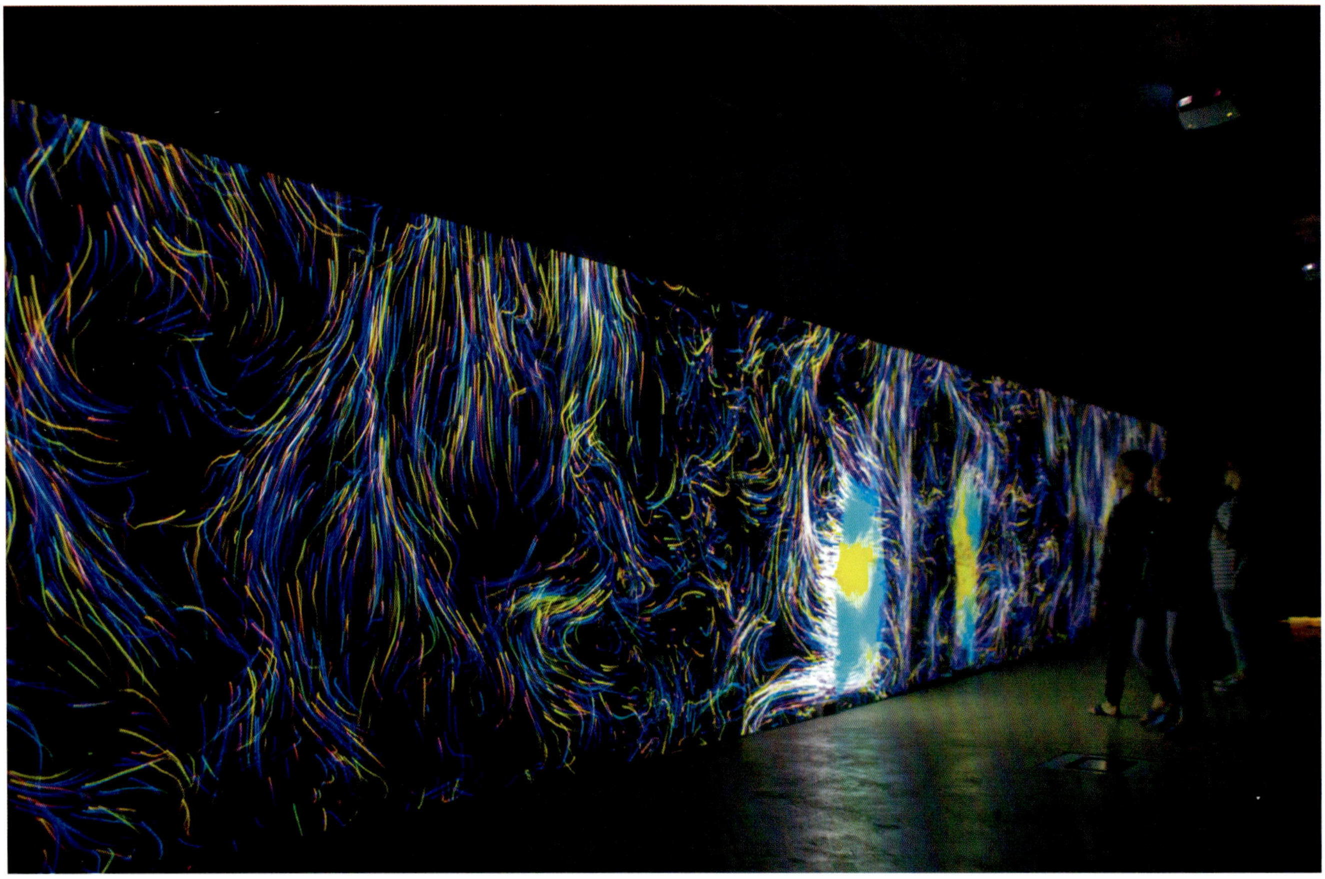

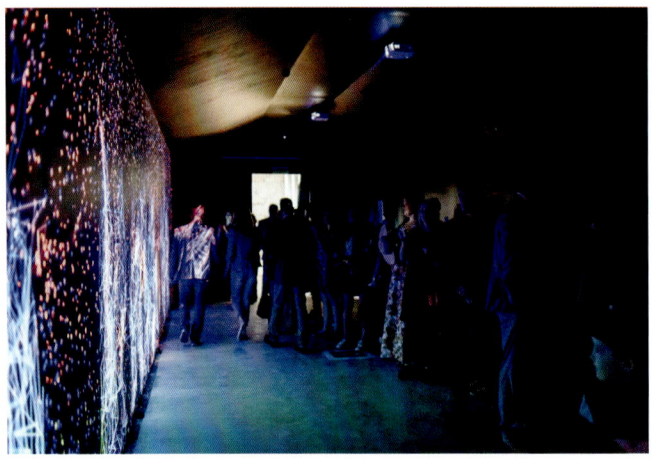

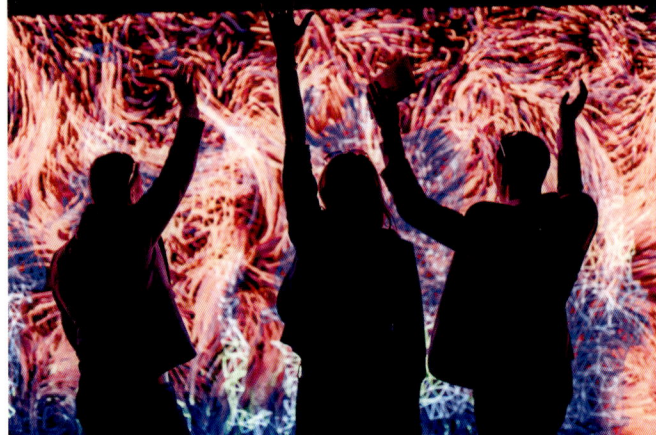

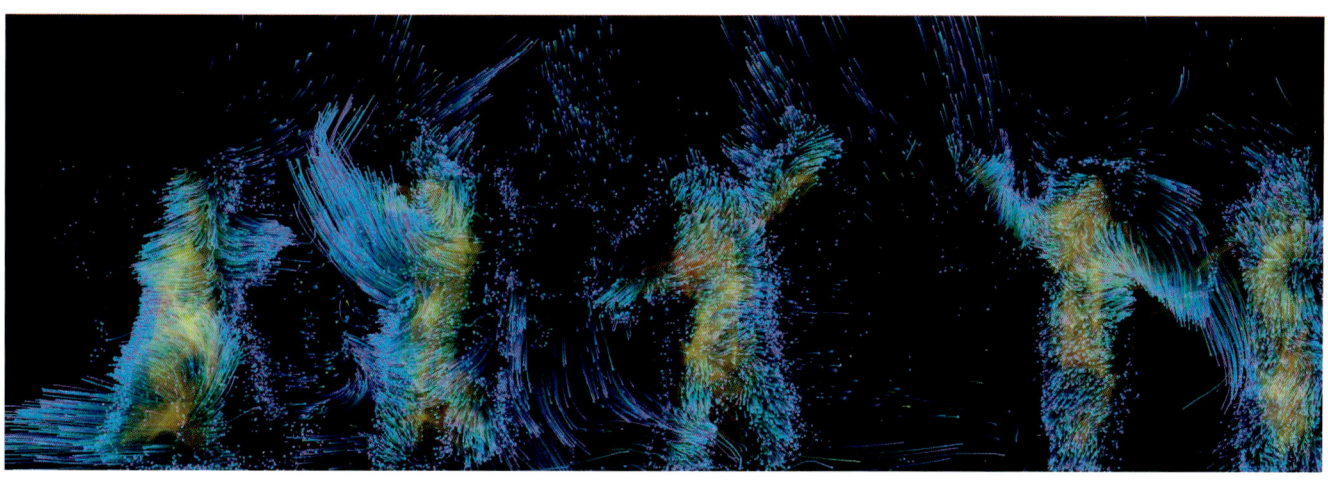

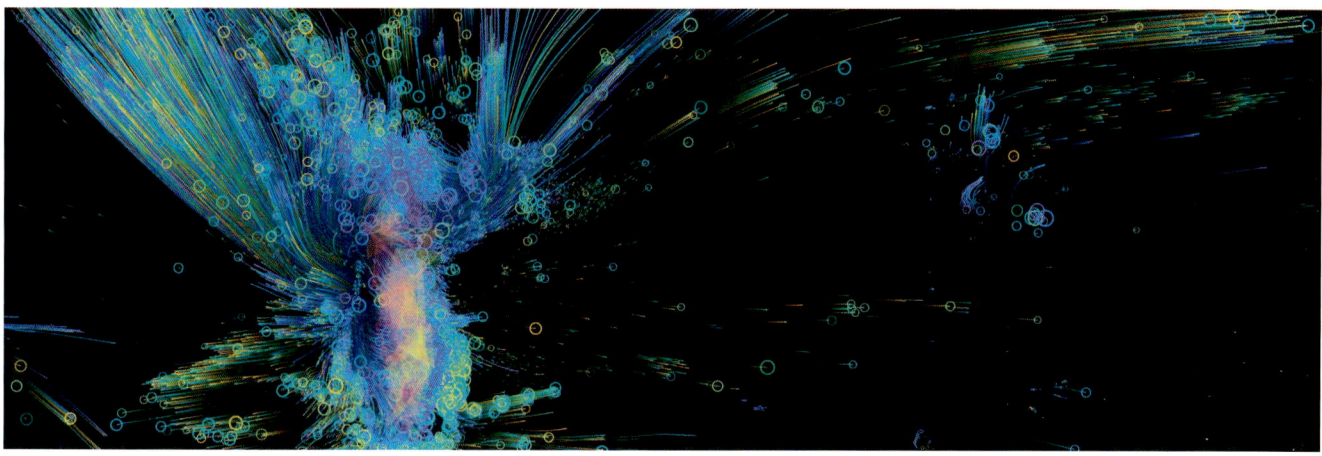

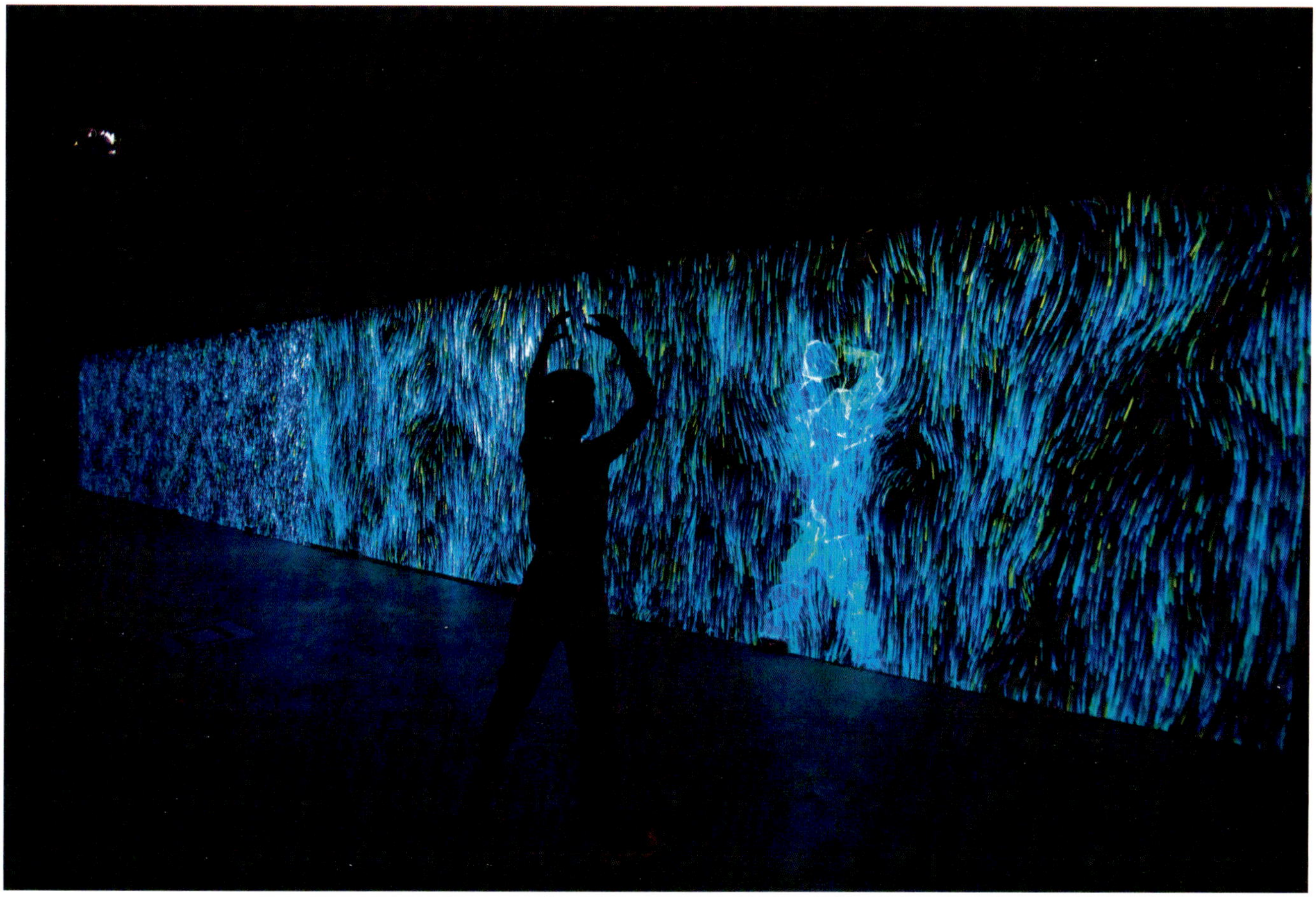

COLLIDE

—

Design: **onformative**

—

Collide explores the senses by transforming recorded motion data into abstract visuals and sound. By mixing, reversing and eliminating restrictions of time and space, a new vision of the human body and mind is discovered. The work is a multisensory experience that explores its subjects from an emotional perspective.

Collide was inspired by the phenomenon of synaesthesia, the union of senses. The digital art installation combines original chamber music and painterly visuals to reinterpret recorded motion data and to act as a conductor for the musical score composed for the installation.

The 62-foot-long digital ribbon screen acts as a window into a dream-like and abstract creative world. Ephemeral figures emerge out of a colorful void and fade into a surreal environment where movements appear in an abstract landscape of shape and color. Using the onsite 54-channel speaker system, sound travels through the space, immersing visitors as they become part of the experience.

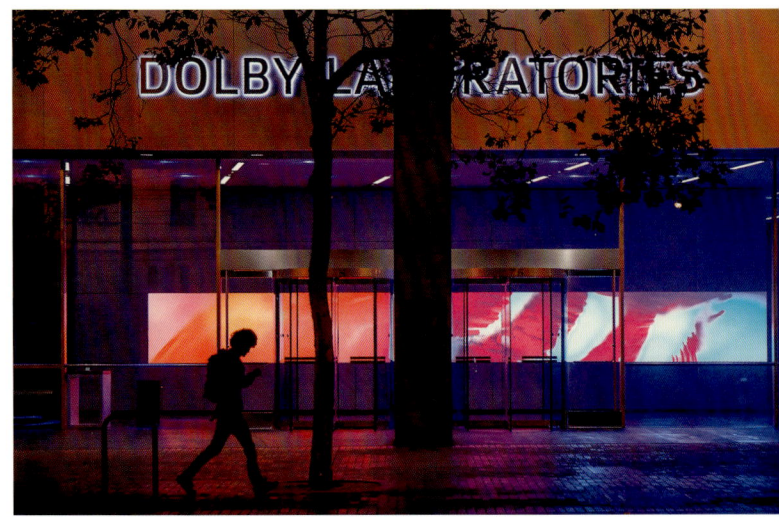

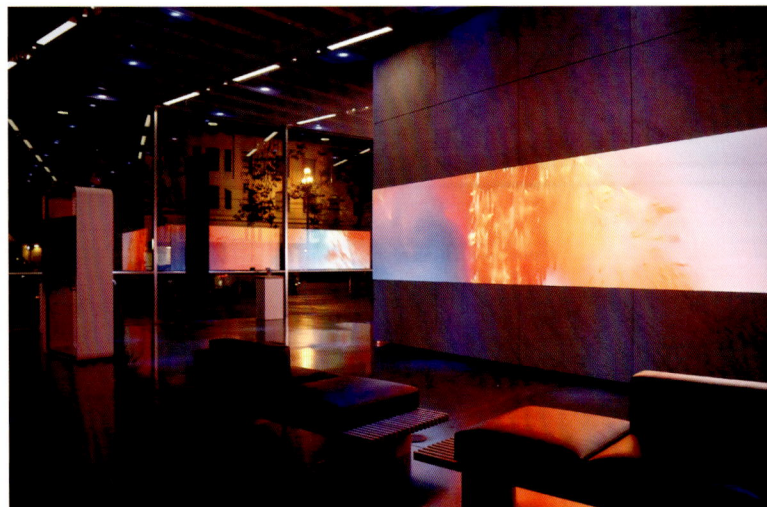

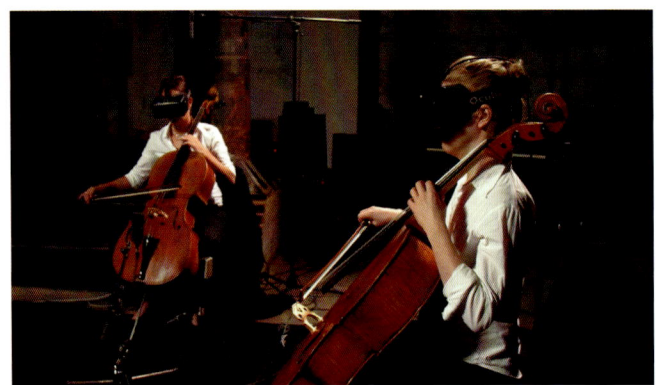

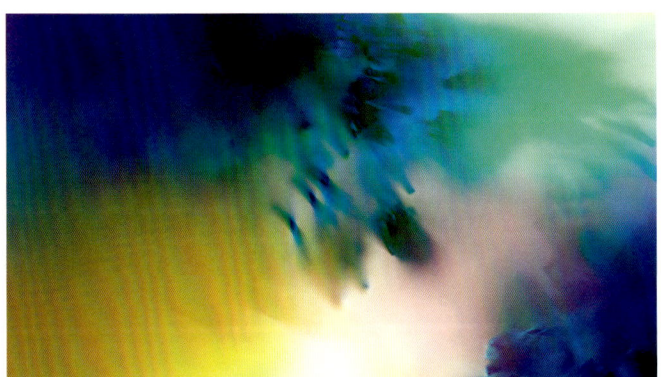

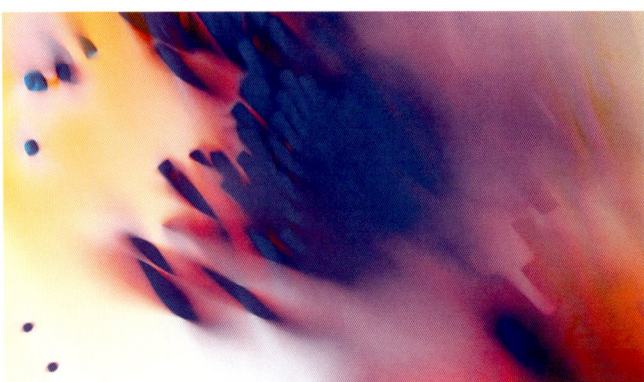

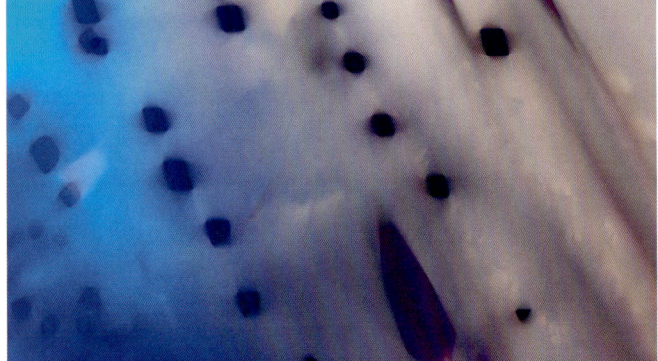

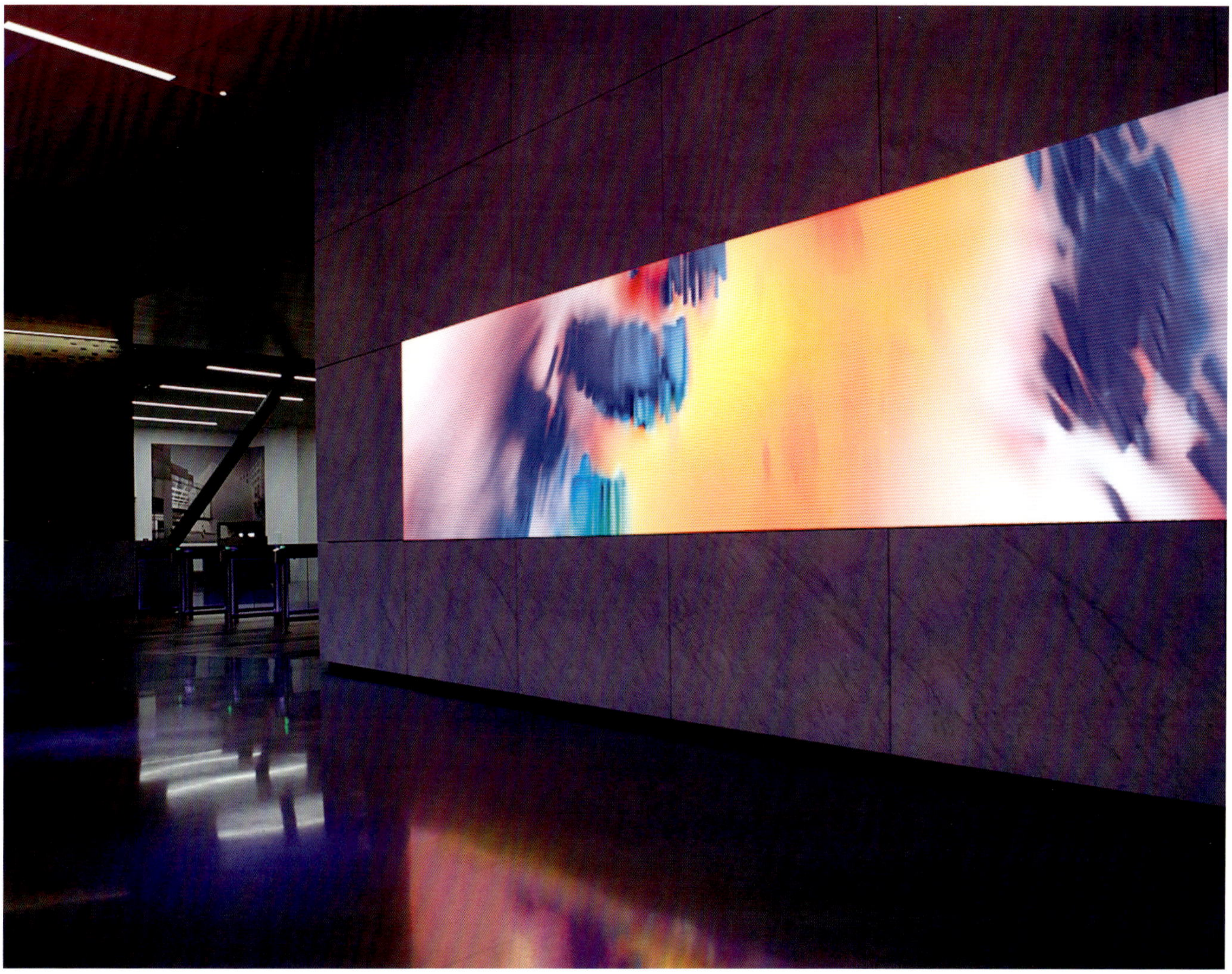

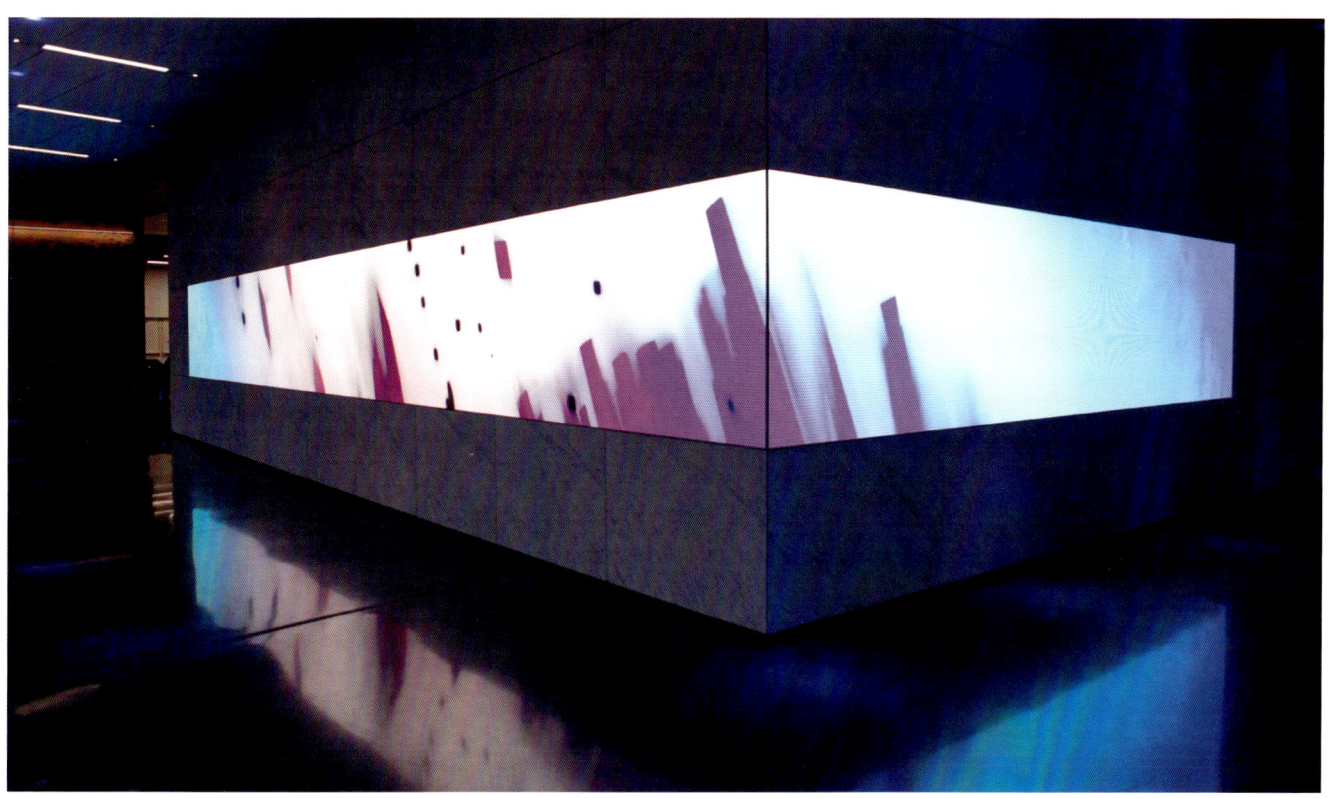

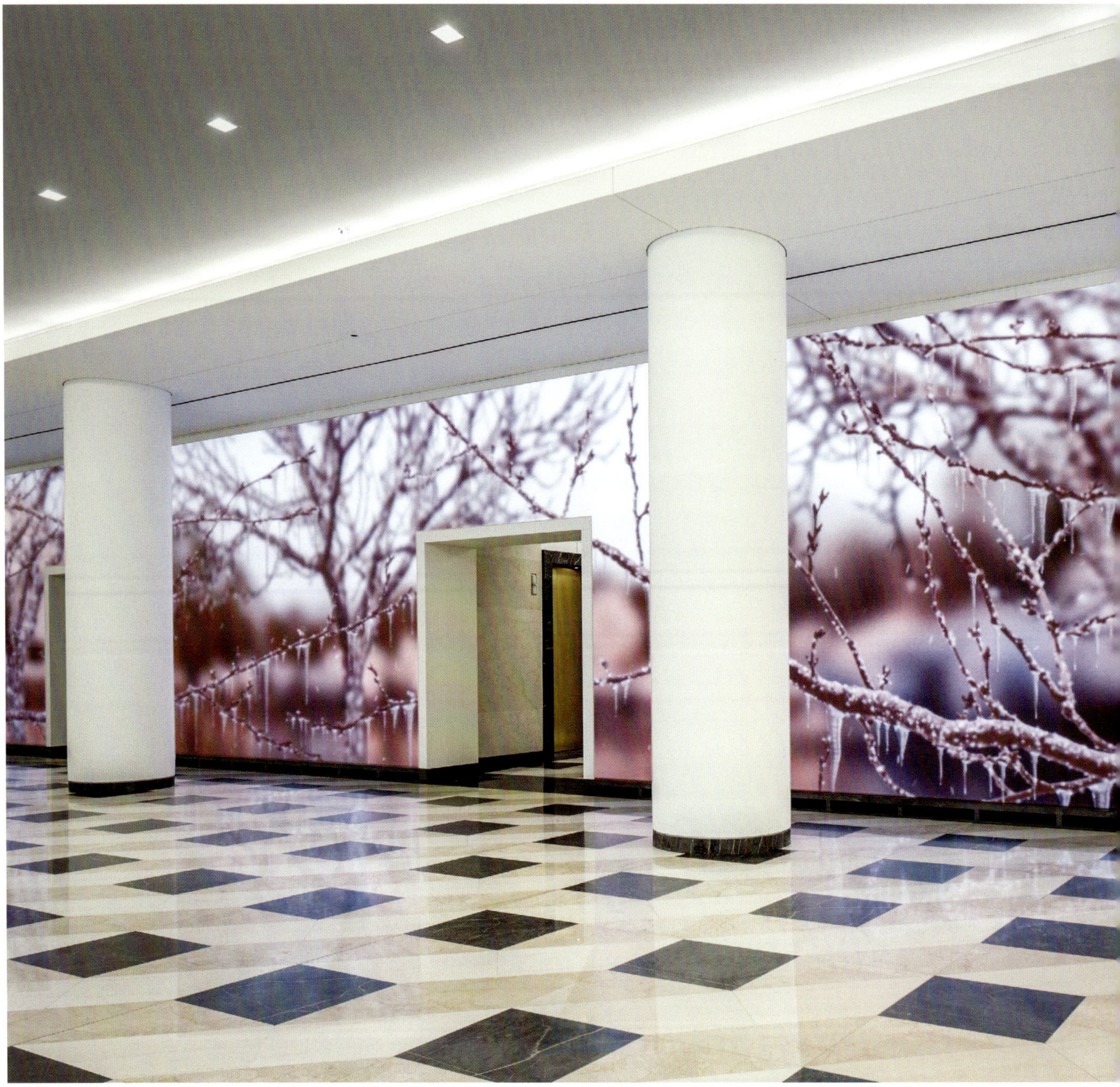

TERRELL PLACE

—

Design: **ESI Design**
Photography: **Caleb Tkach, AIAP**

—

At Terrell Place in Washington, D.C., ESI Design seamlessly integrated 1,700 square feet of diffused LED displays into the architectural surfaces of this Washington D.C building, creating an ever-evolving artwork that transforms the environment into a unique experience. The motion-activated media environment responds to people through an infrared camera system, creating beautiful scenes that ebb and flow with the morning rush and the afternoon lull.

ESI designed custom lighting, audio and media content to deliver a cohesive multi-modal experience. Three custom content modes are programmed with varying durations and sequences, ensuring that visitors never have the same experience twice. The "Seasons" mode connects Terrell Place with its Washington, D.C. neighborhood, including the lifecycle of its iconic cherry trees, from spring blossoms to snow-covered branches.

The environment is further enhanced by ambient sounds emerging from invisible speakers in the walls and ceiling, creating a fully immersive environment for visitors.

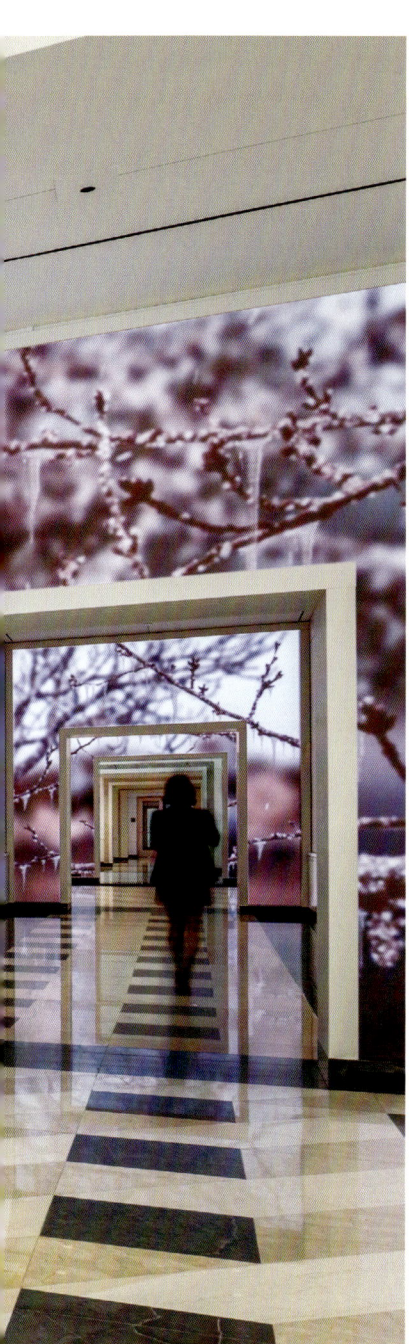
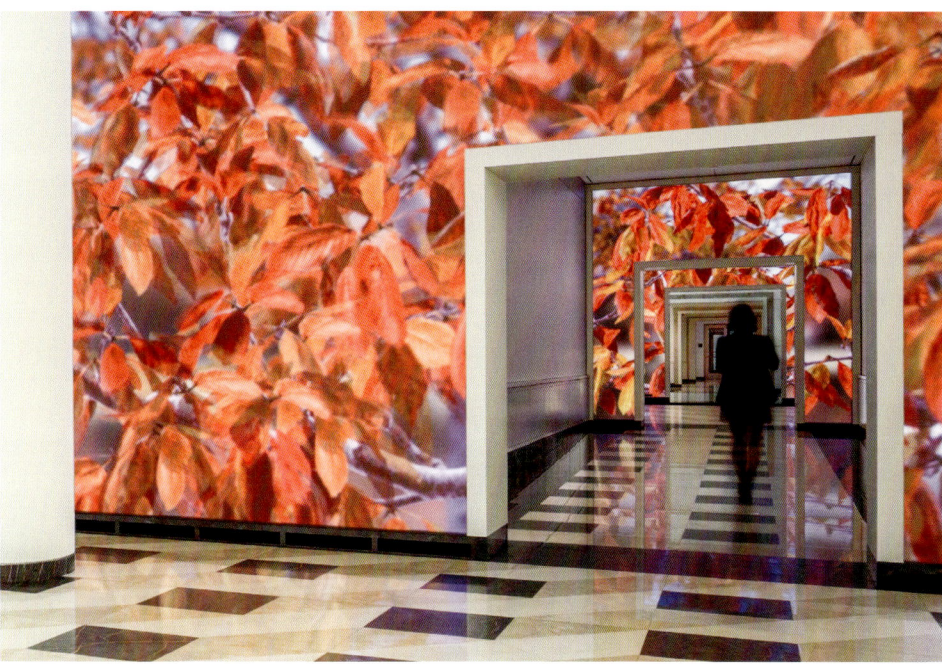
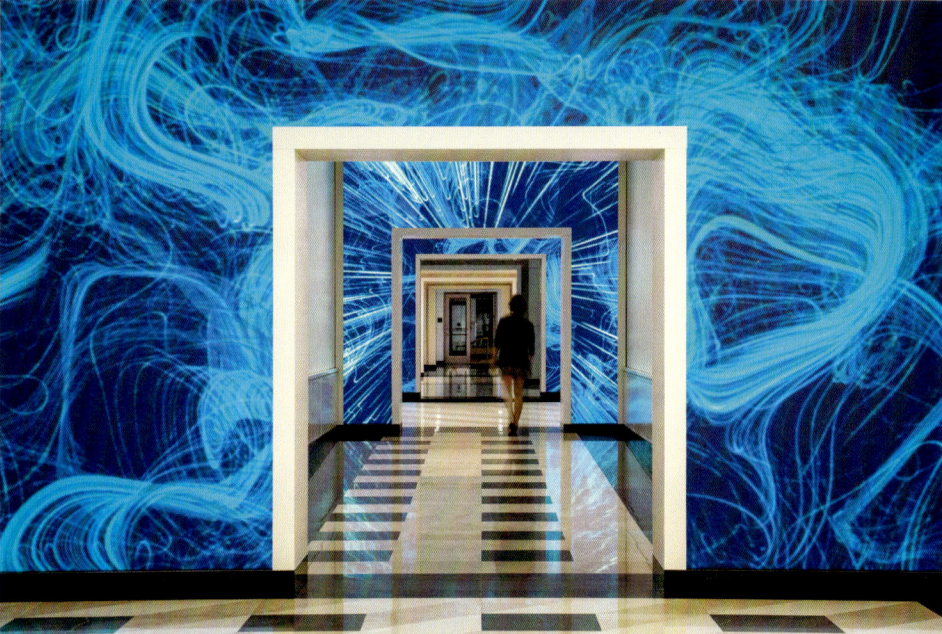
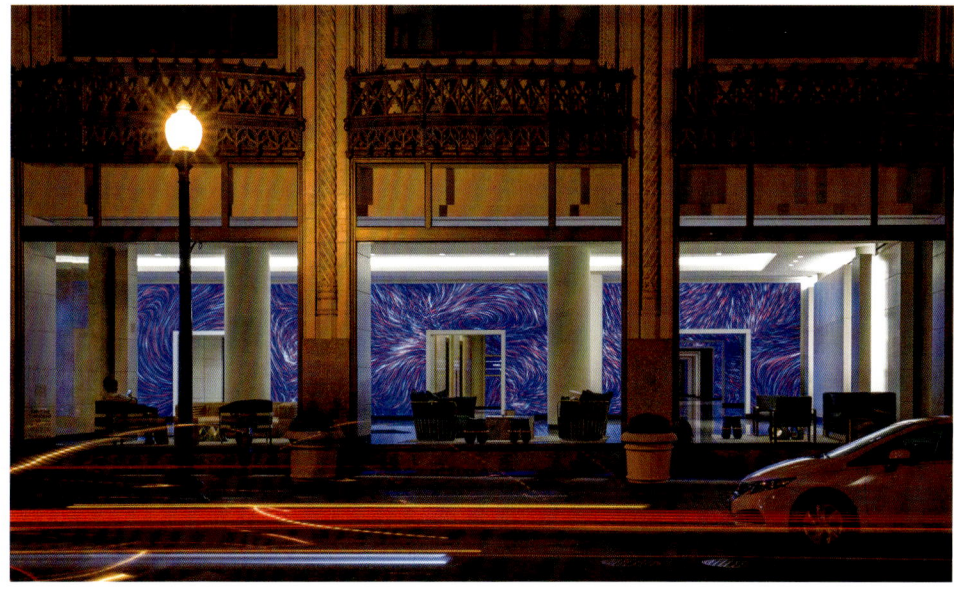

SAMSUNG GALAXY S8 LAUNCH

Design: **Universal Everything**
Photography: **James Medcraft**

—

The Galaxy S8 Design was an immersive, interactive installation open exclusively during Milan Design Week 2017, inspired by the new Samsung Galaxy design.

Together, Universal Everything and the bold, forward-looking studio of the late Zaha Hadid explored the infinite possibilities created when design and technology are seamlessly unified. Visitors were invited to journey through the installation, creating mesmerizing digital installations and bringing to life the Galaxy design philosophy of "no borders, no boundaries."

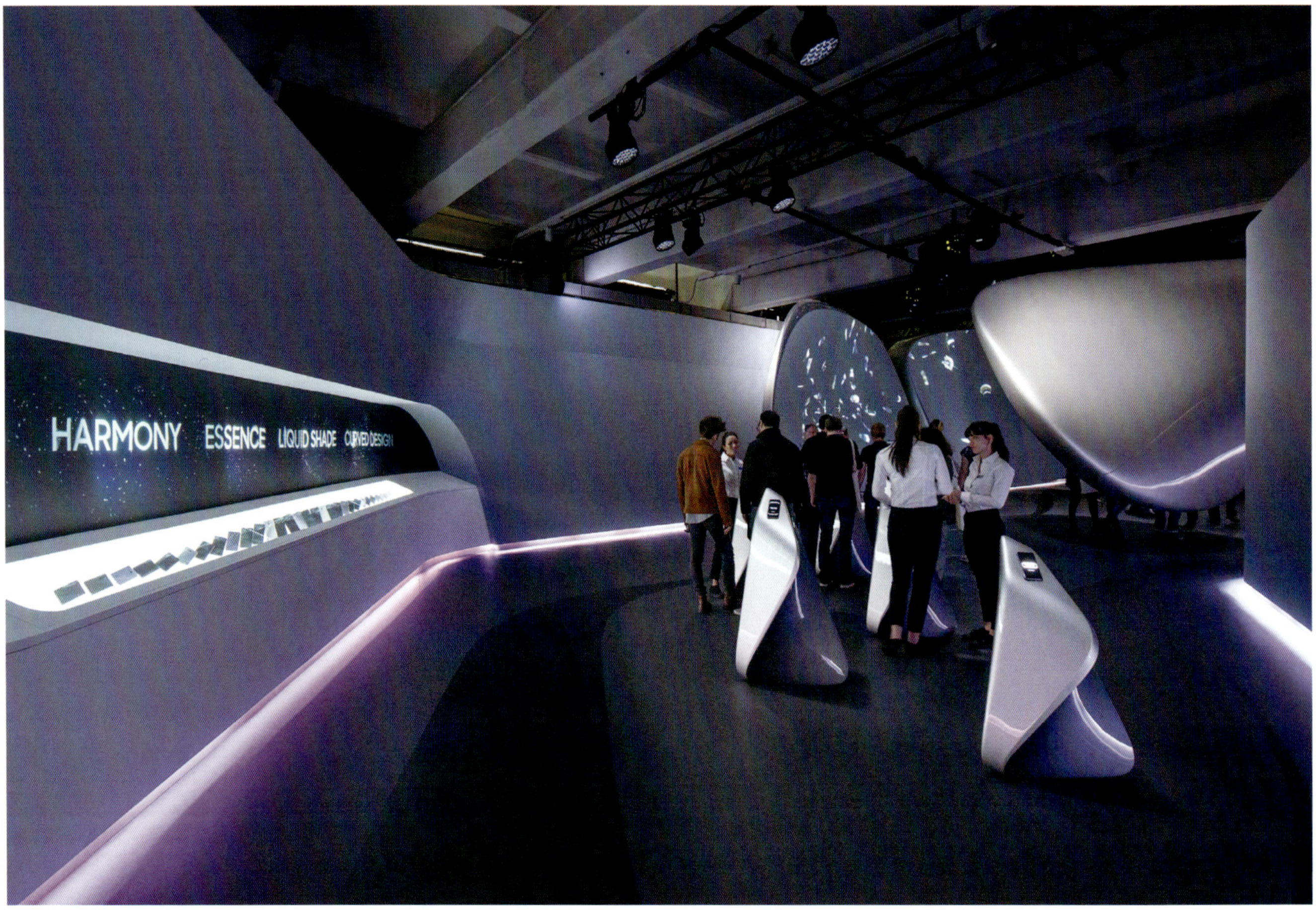

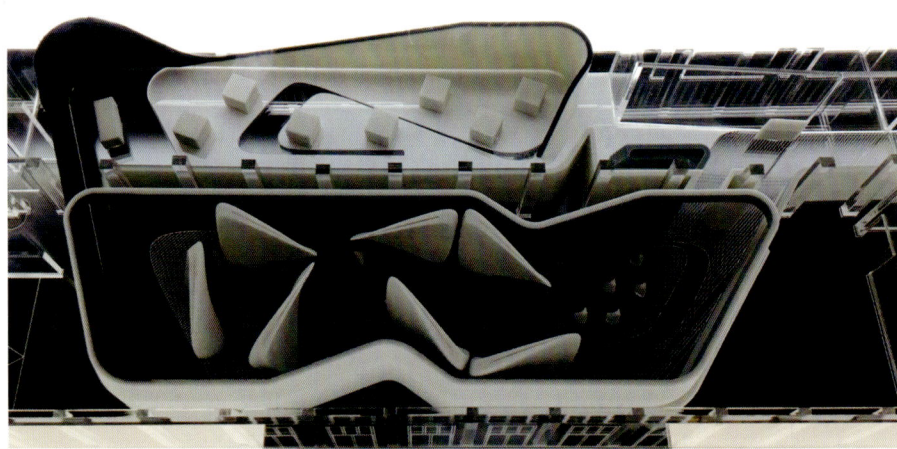

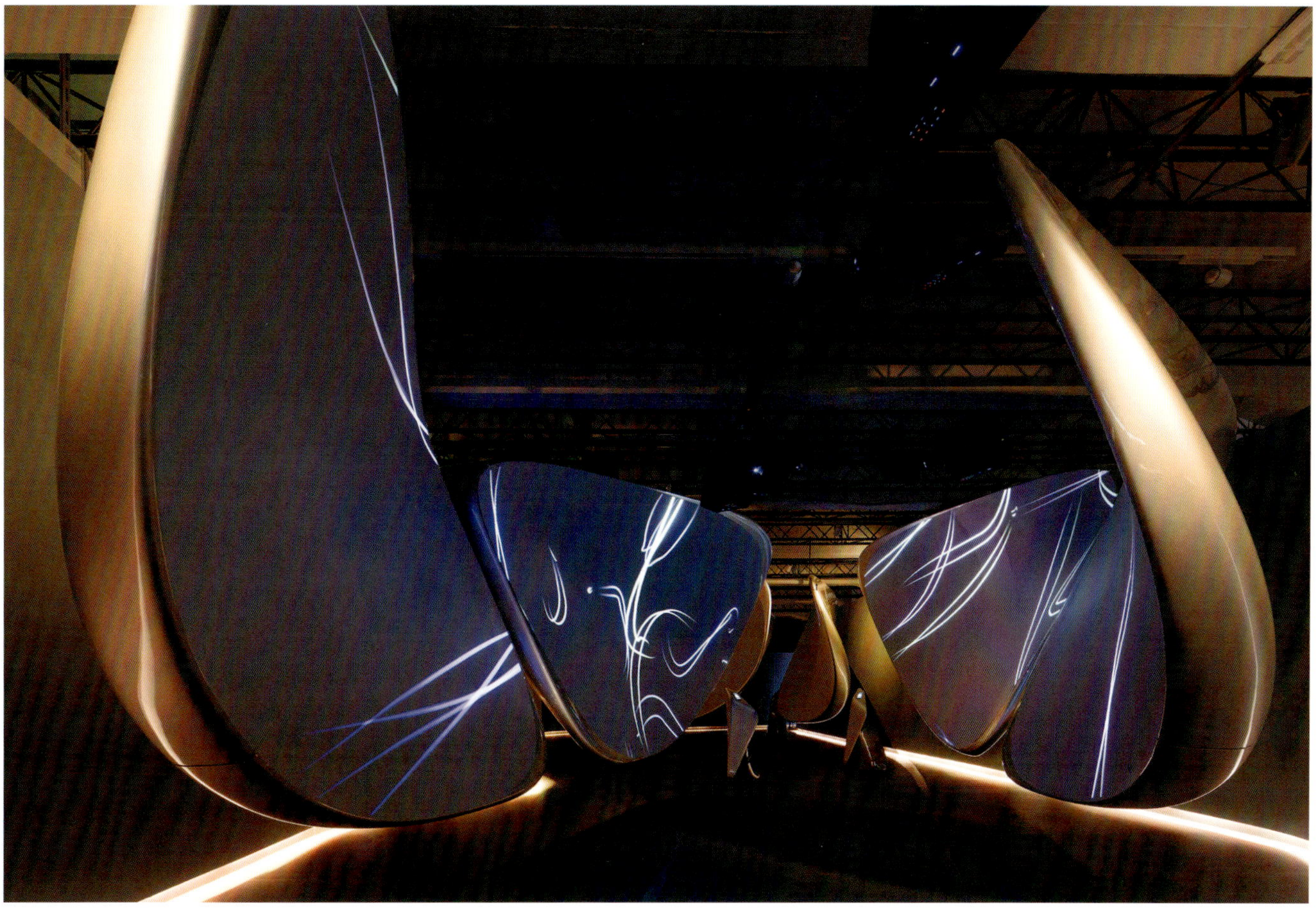

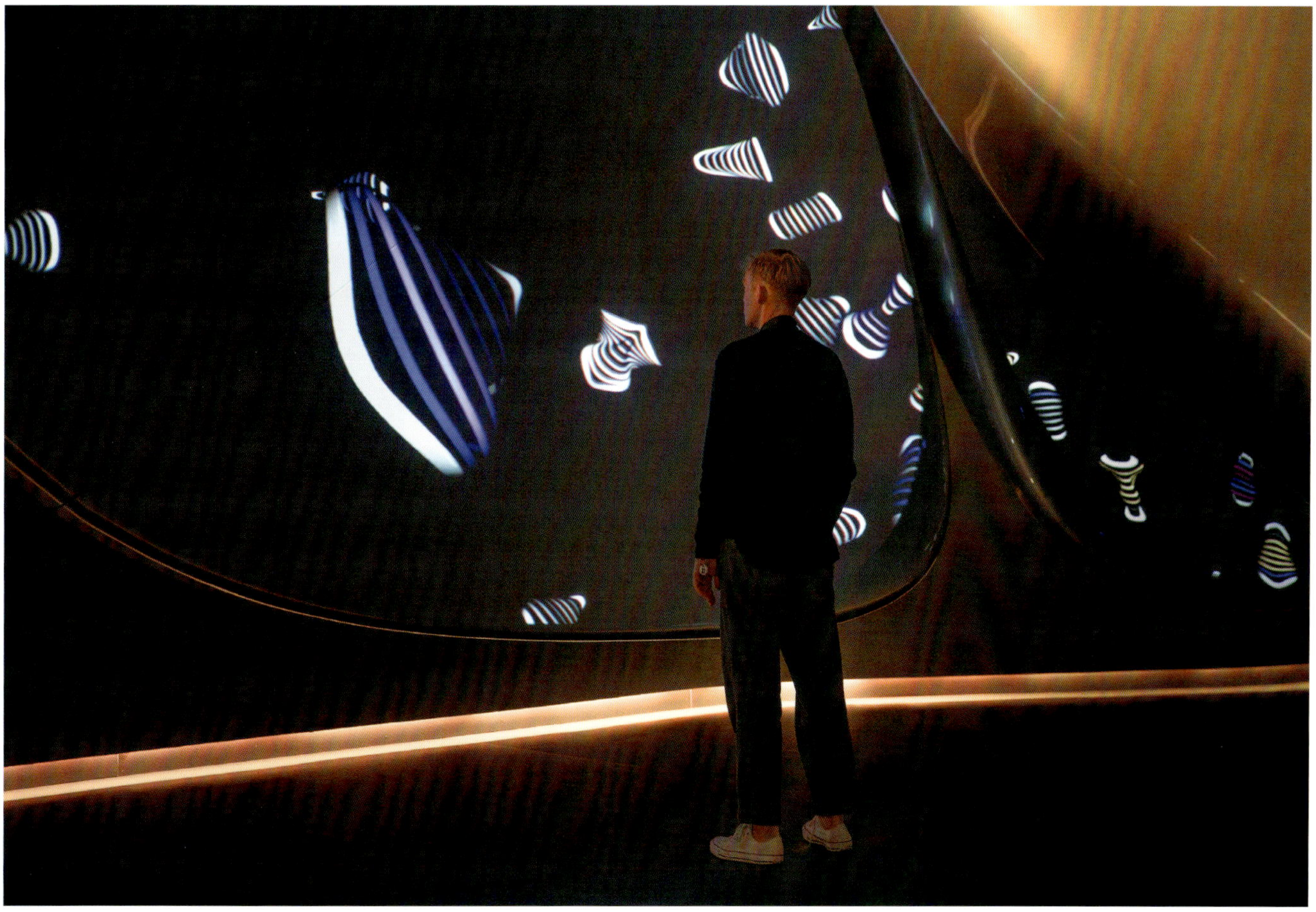

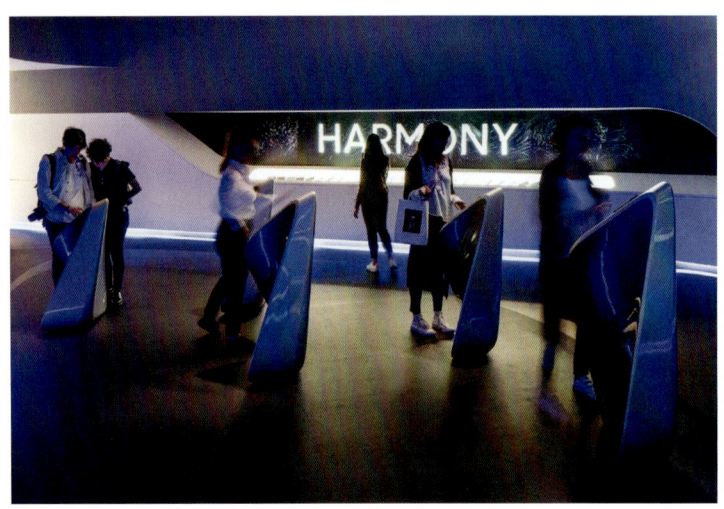
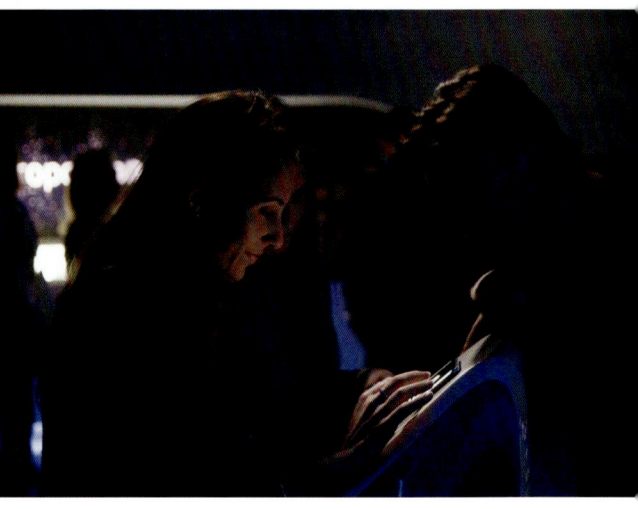

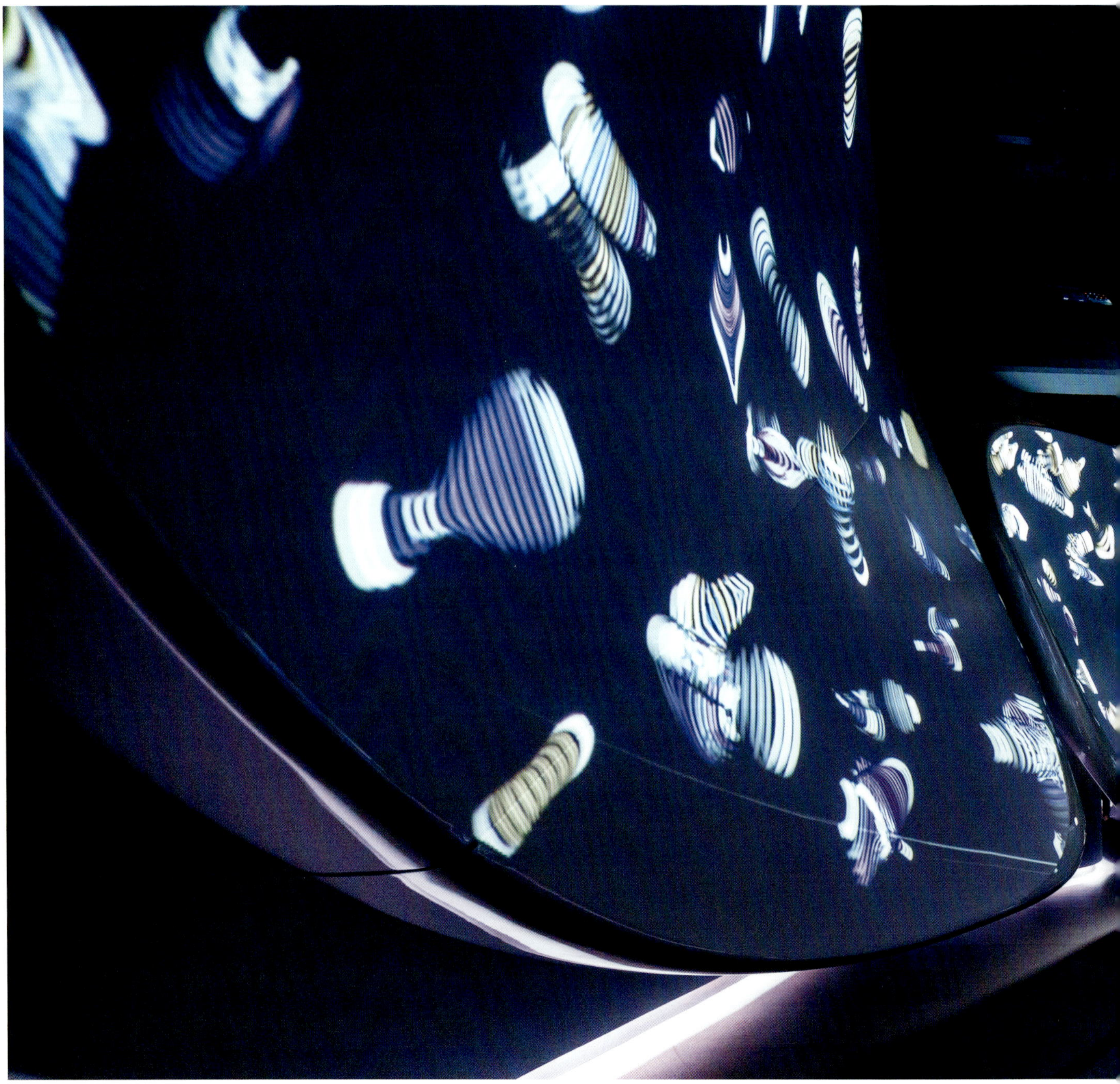

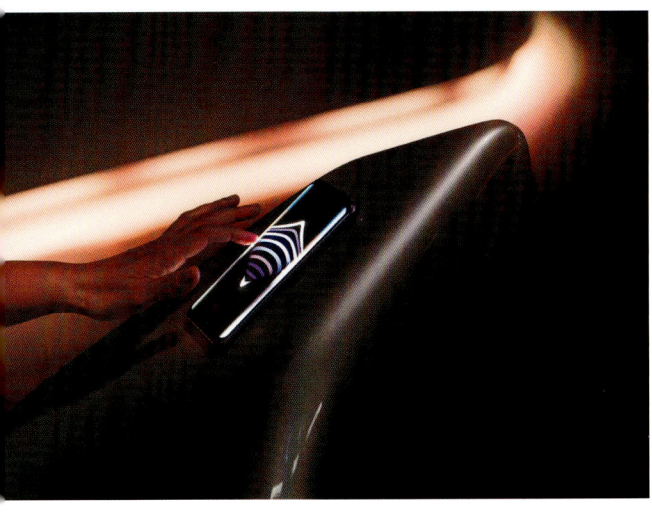
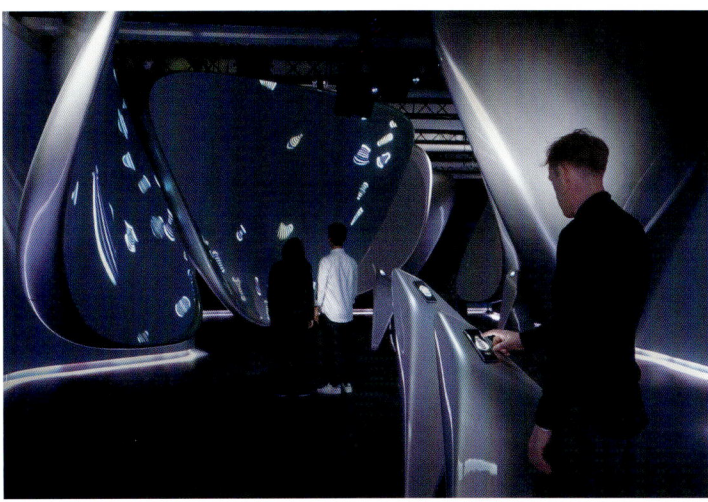

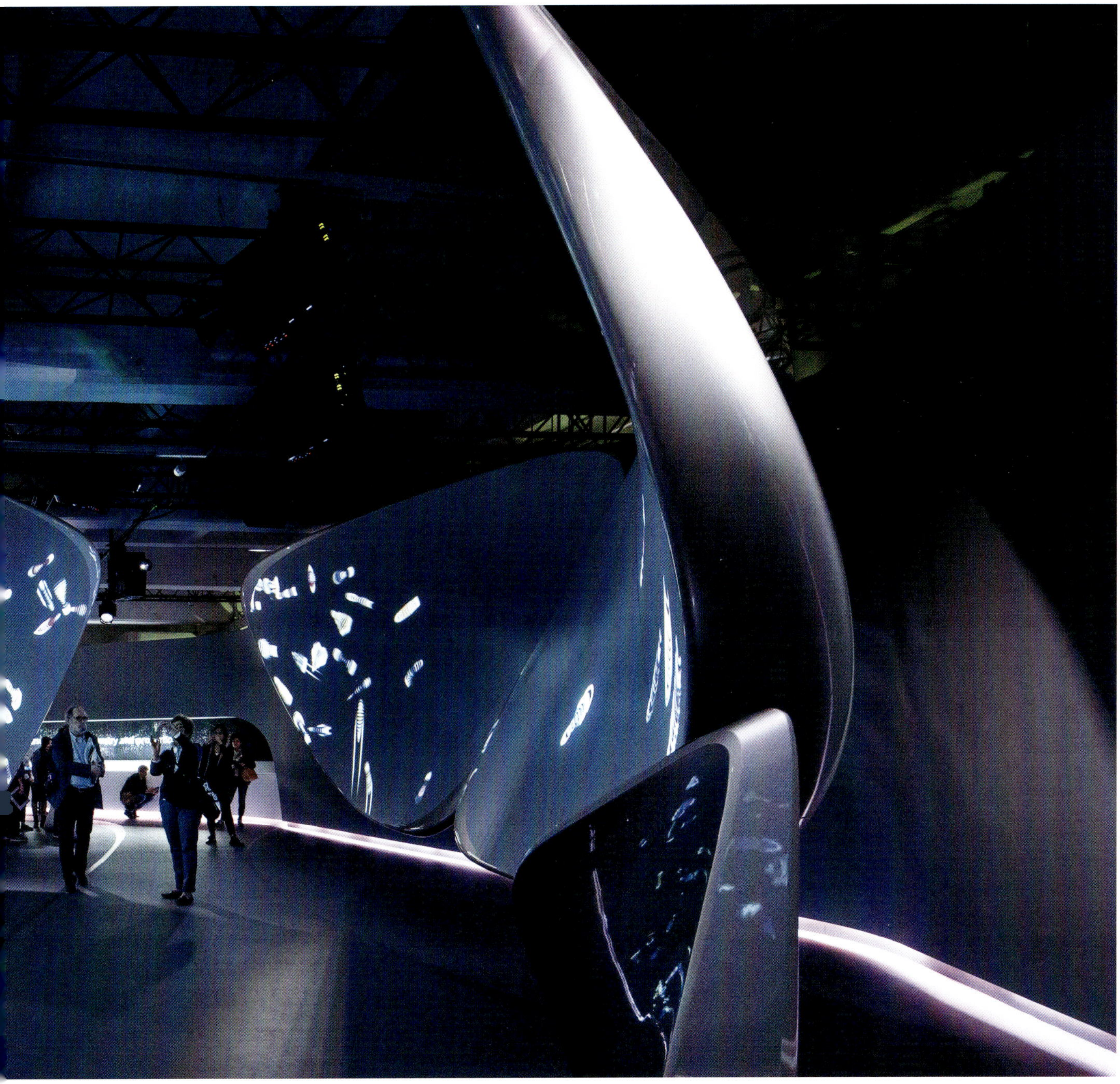

LULL

—

Design: **Vincent Houzé, AV&C**

—

This is an immersive and contemplative installation that explores the liminal state between consciousness and unconsciousness.

In the center of an unlit 6,000-square-foot warehouse, waves of liquid light undulate wistfully across the walls of a semitransparent triangular structure. Simple rules shape this ever-evolving animation, giving rise to organic abstract patterns with complex behaviors that teeter between order and chaos. Immersed in layers of distant melodies that reverberate in sync with the surging fluid, as well as in a dense plume of fog that extends and blurs the light within, visitors dip in and out of the sculpture as if in a dream.

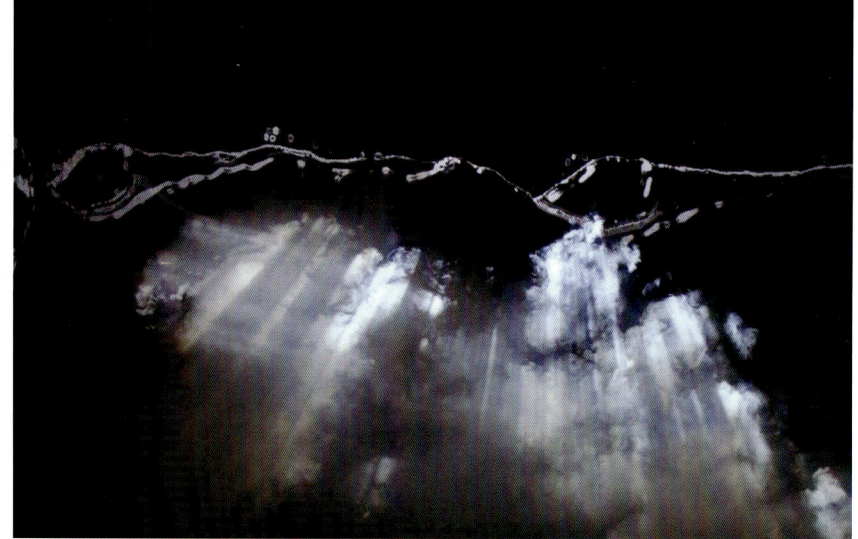

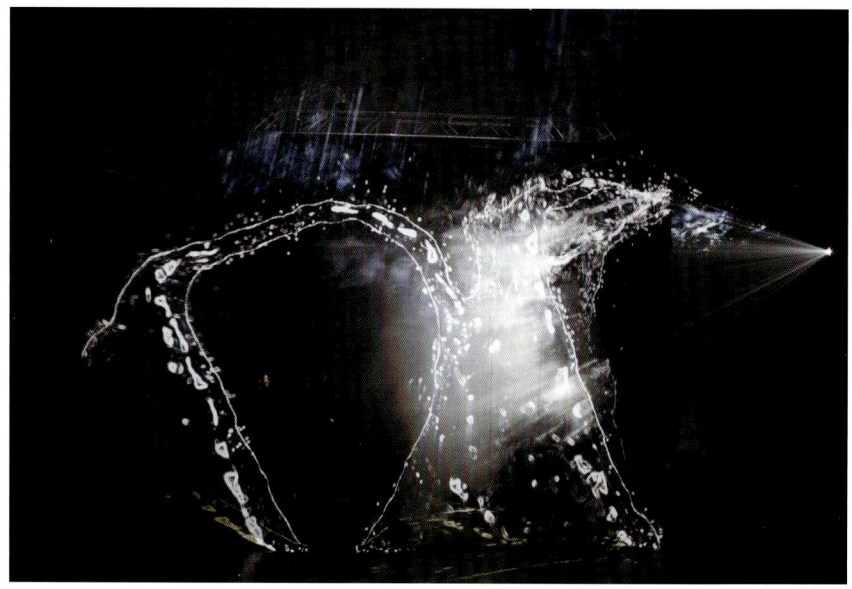

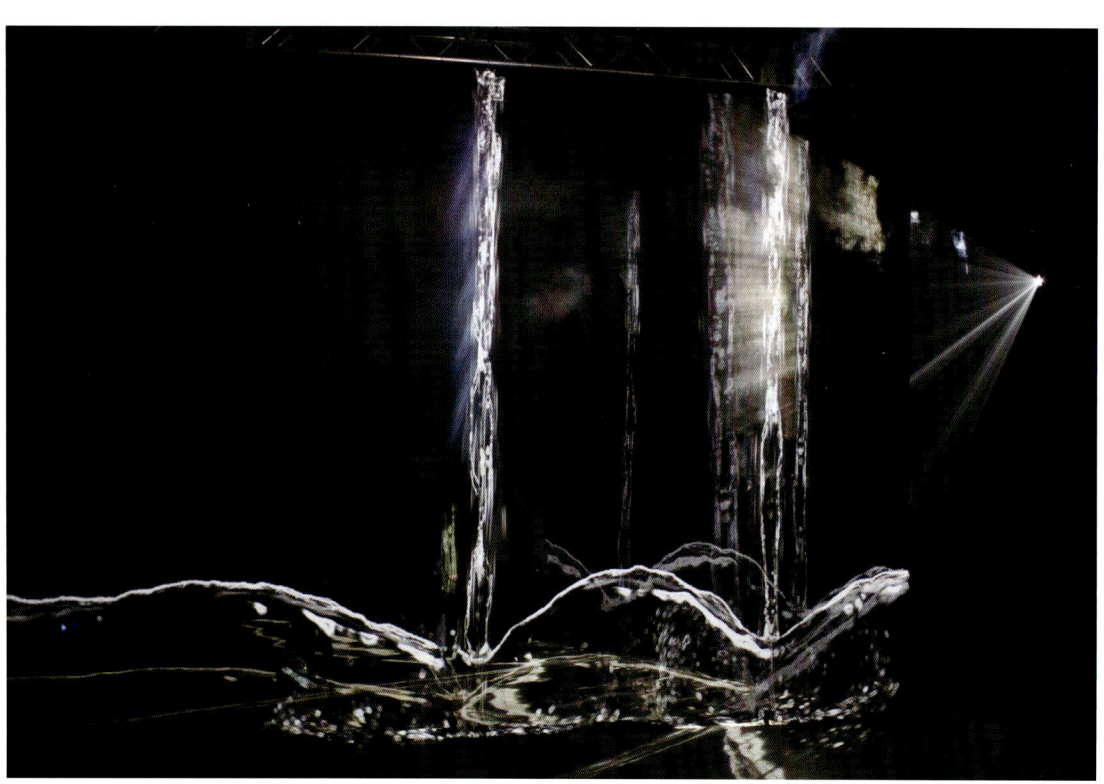

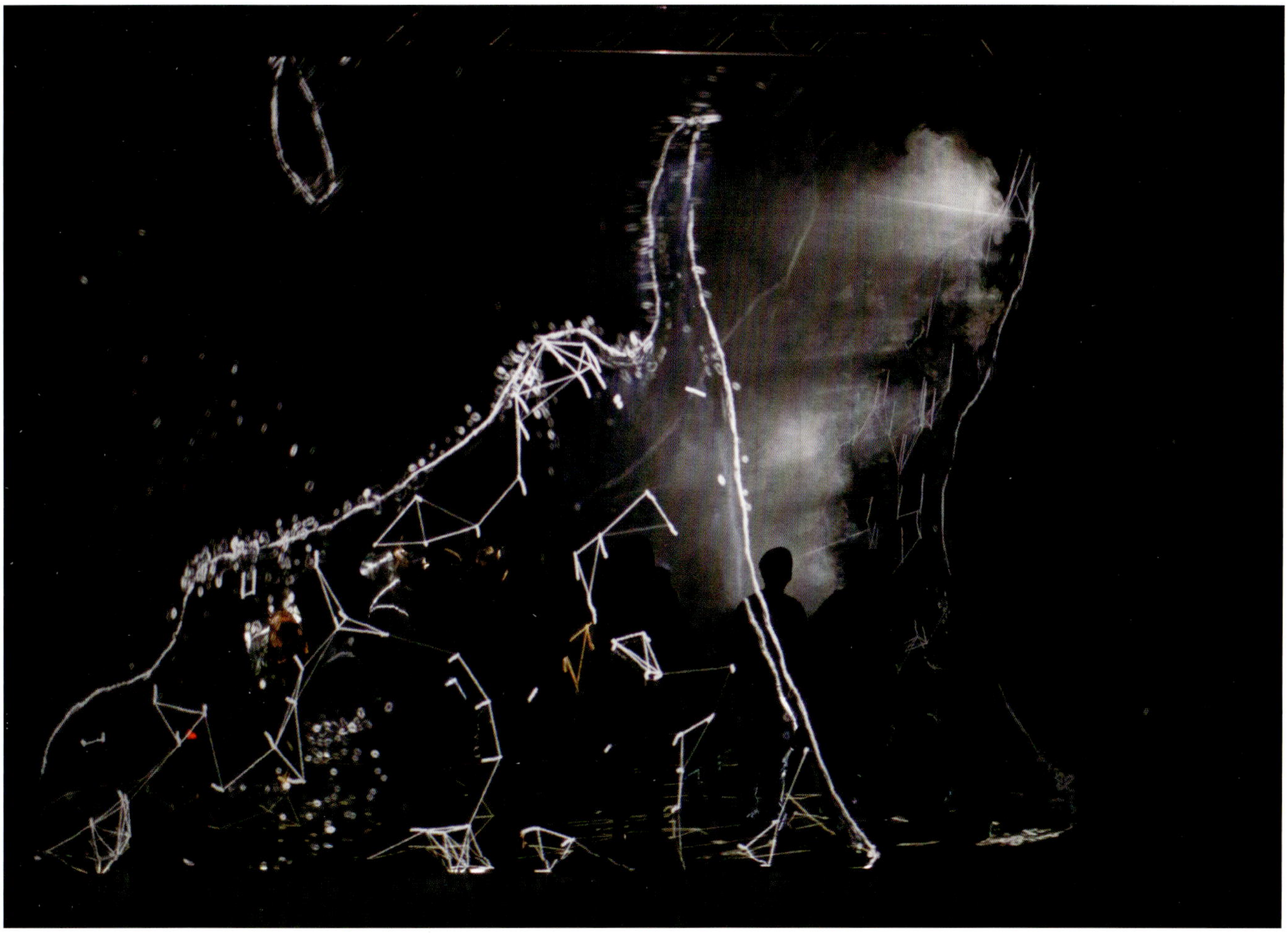

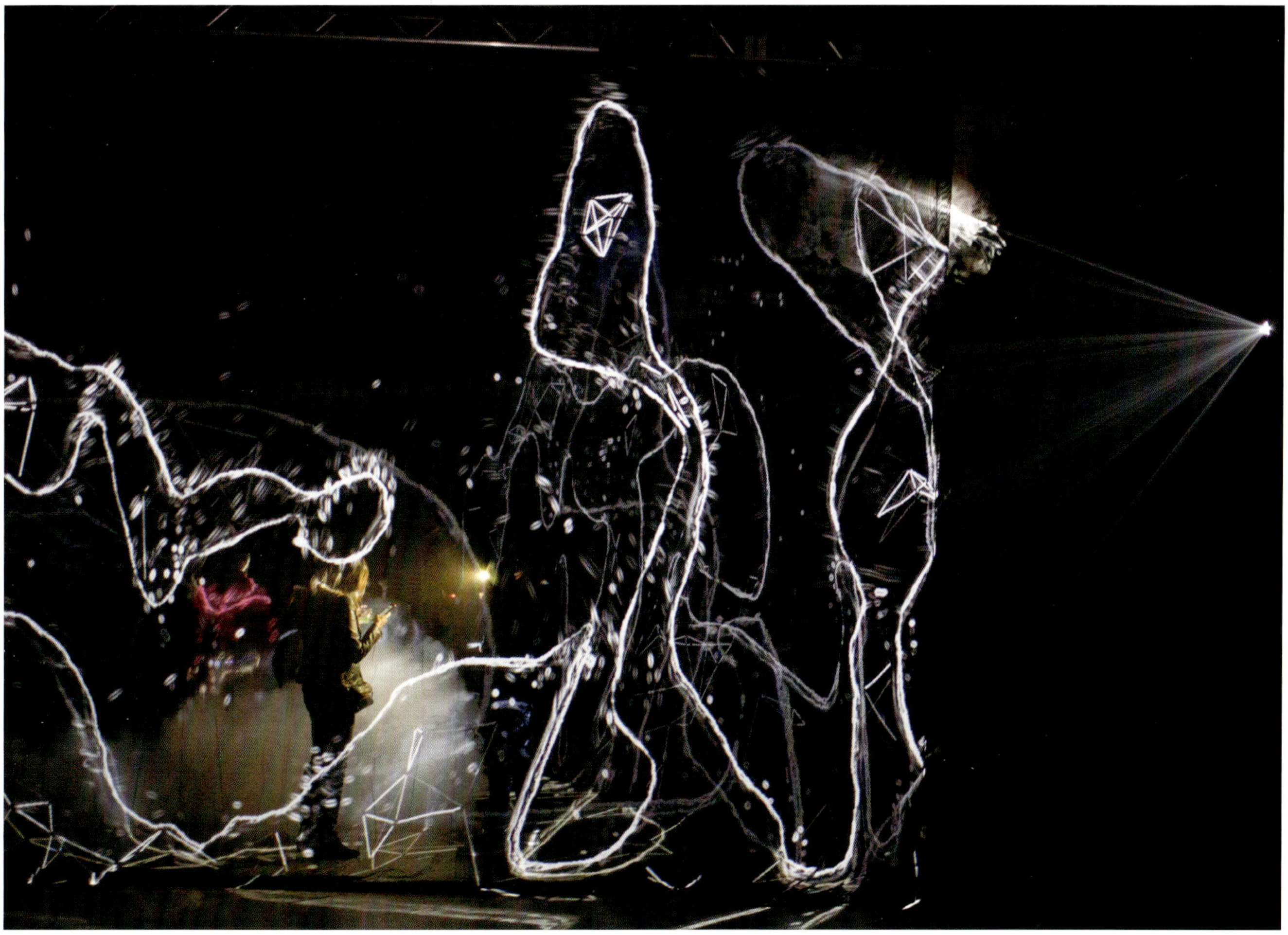

FLUID STRUCTURE

—

Design: **Vincent Houzé**

—

Fluid Structure is an immersive interactive installation which explores how an ephemeral and amorphous shape reacts under various stimuli, internal and external. Forces and collisions bend the shape until it breaks, recombining it into new aggregates. The result is an ever-changing landscape, mysterious yet familiar. A dramatic data-like visualization emphasizes the internal structure of the shape and its motion. Using computer vision the audience is made an integral part of the process, leaving its temporary physical mark, always bound to eventually to disappear. The system is driven by a state-of-the-art fluid solver able to process in real-time the forces and constraints the shape is subjected to.

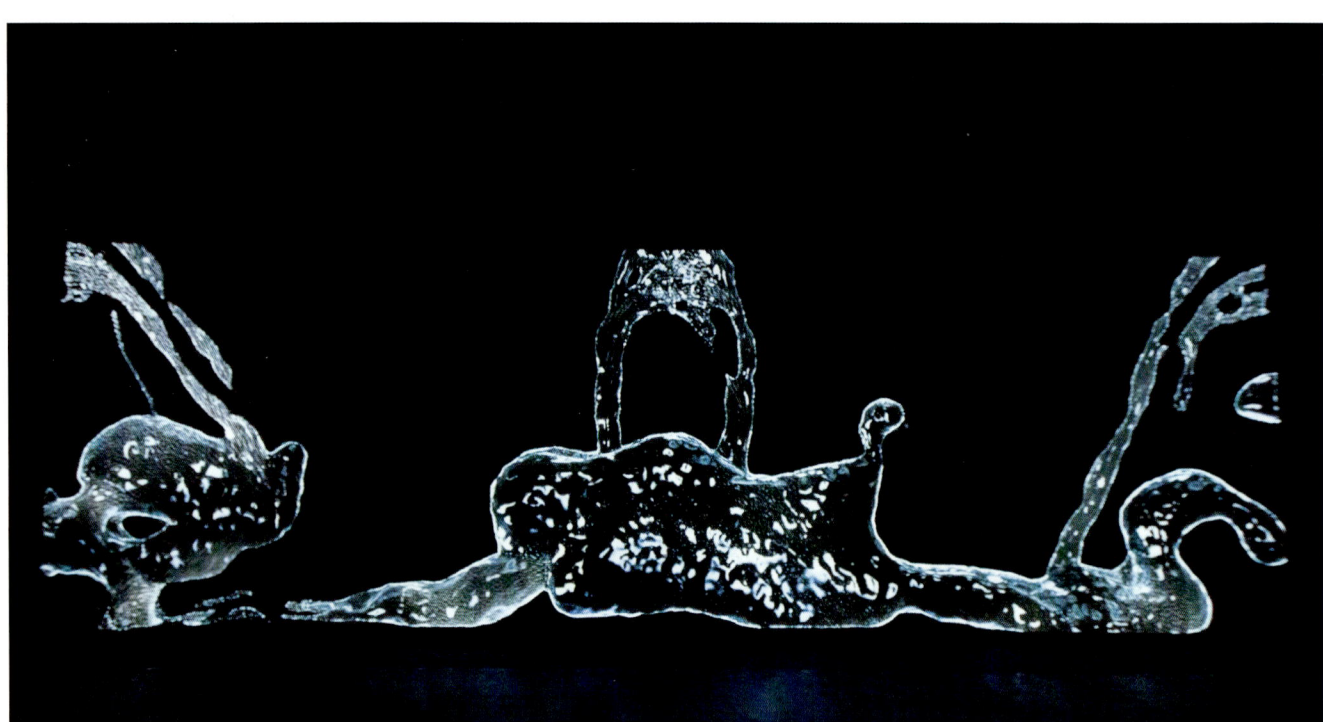

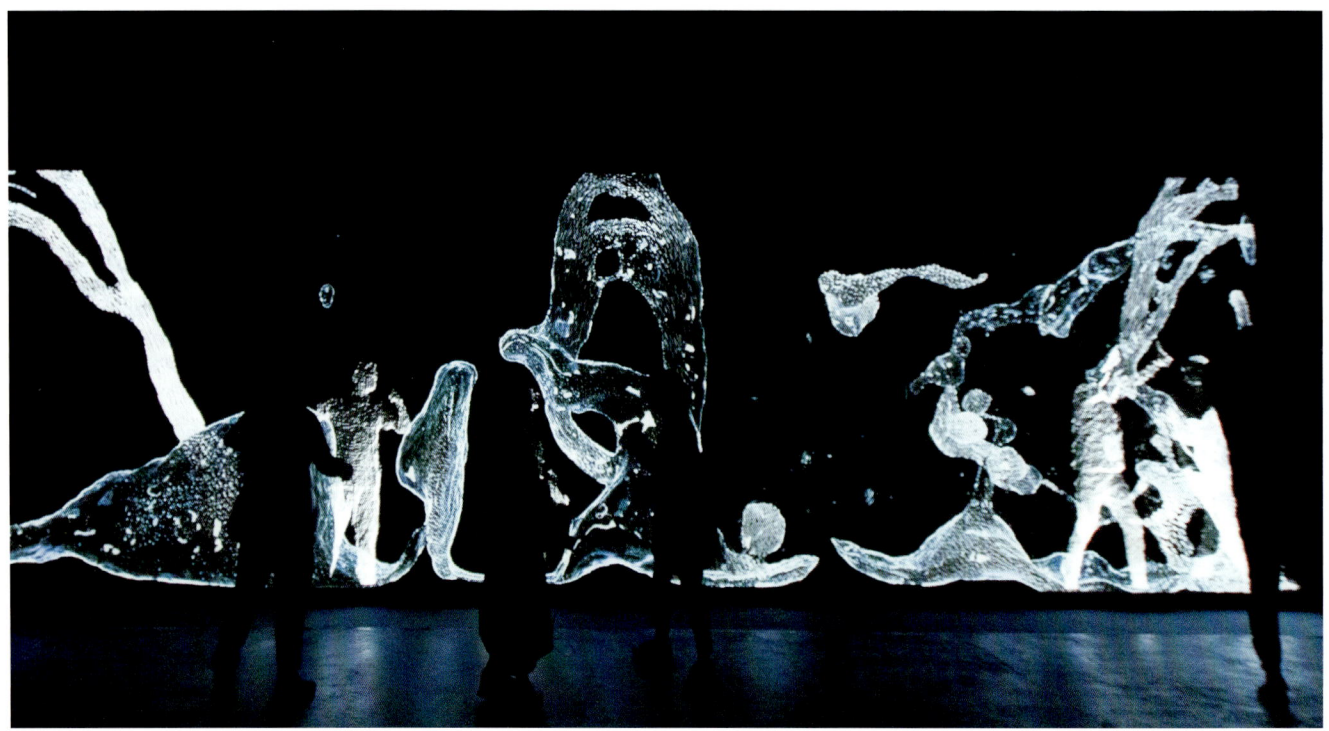

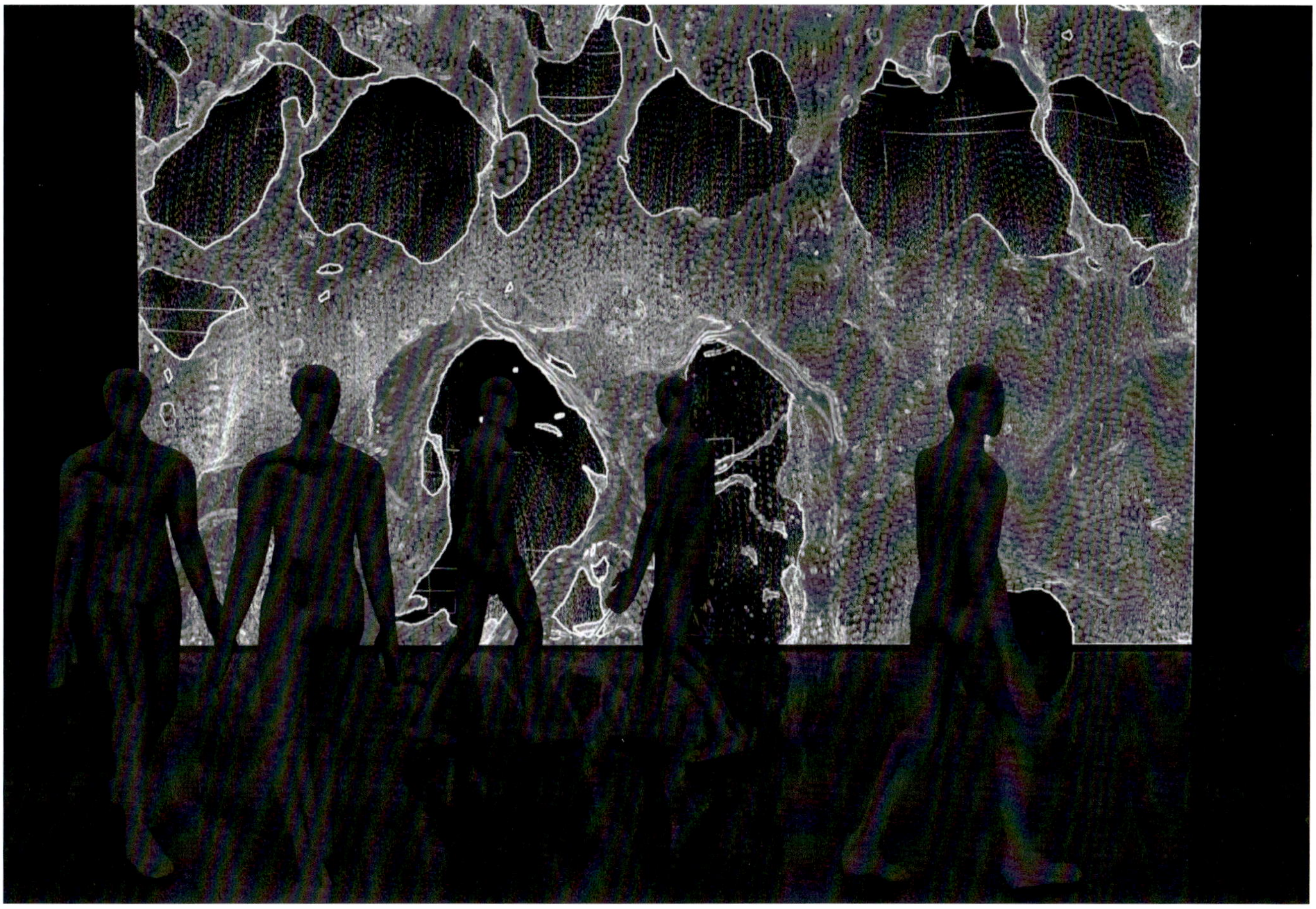

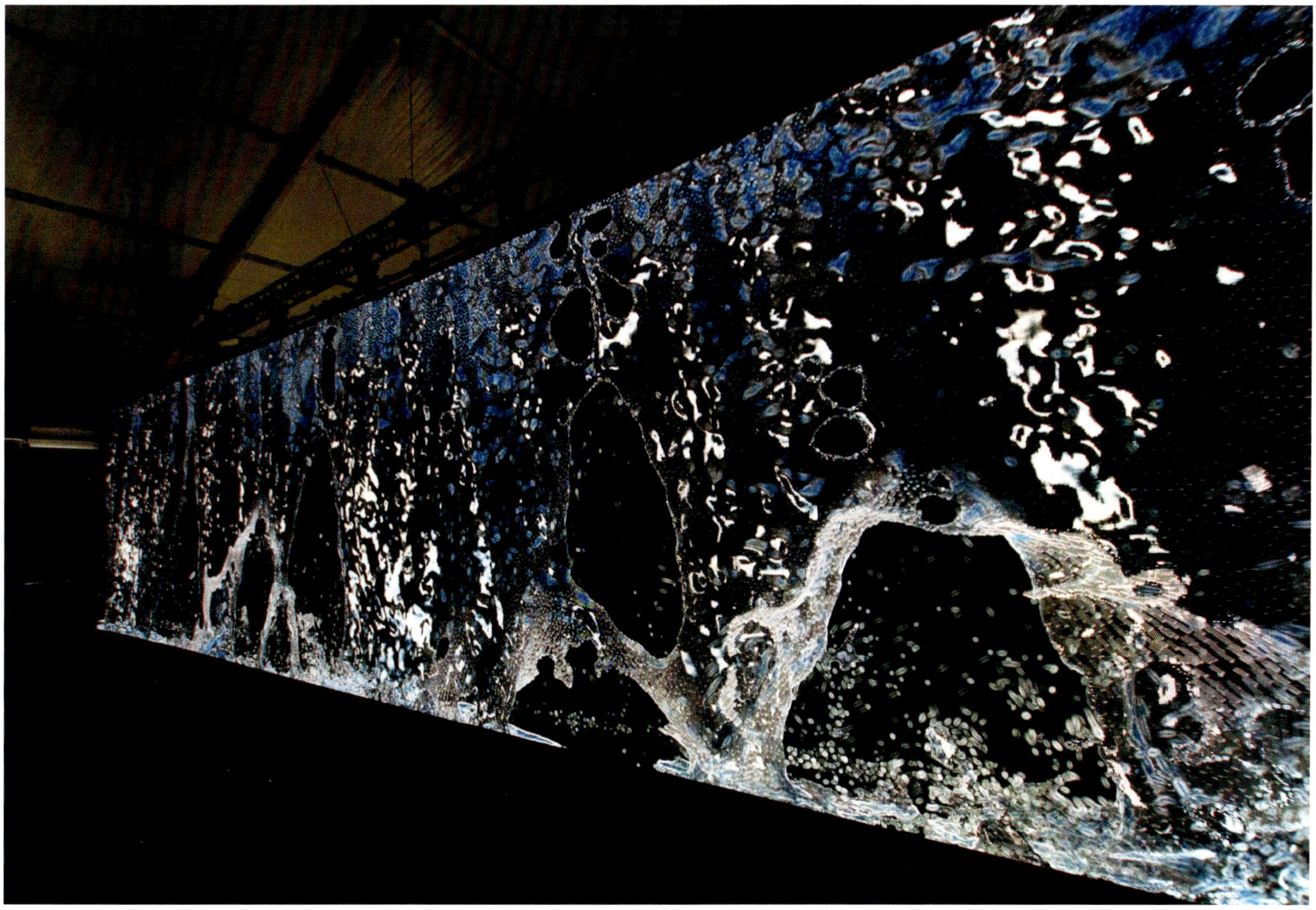

PASSAGE

—

Design: **Bonjour, interactive Lab**
Photography: **Julya Baisson**

—

Data defines our new digital life. Everything we do—surfing the Internet, using geolocation services, streaming media—leaves a trail of data, a digital image that reflects our behaviors, feelings, and thoughts. Each new digital activity overrides this image with new data, creating a representation of an instant of our lives, over and over again.

Passage is a sensitive setup that uses a digital scanner in an immersive dark environment to decrypt the visual and sound imprint of those who step near it, representing them as data. Each time someone steps into its field of detection, he is scanned by the installation, leaving a frozen three-dimensional pixelated image and a unique sound imprint of himself. This image and sound stand briefly before they collapse, leaving an empty canvas for future imprints.

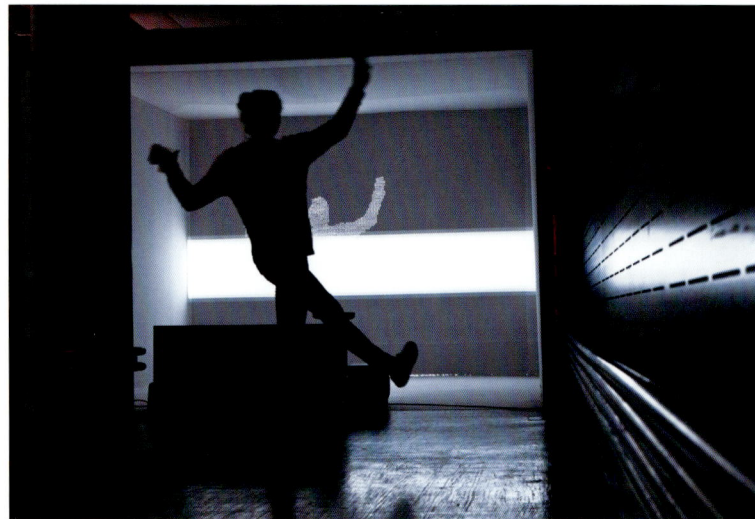

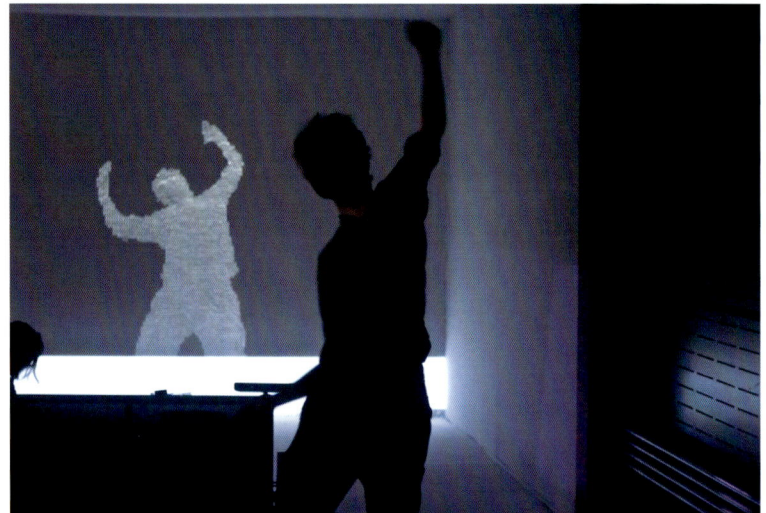

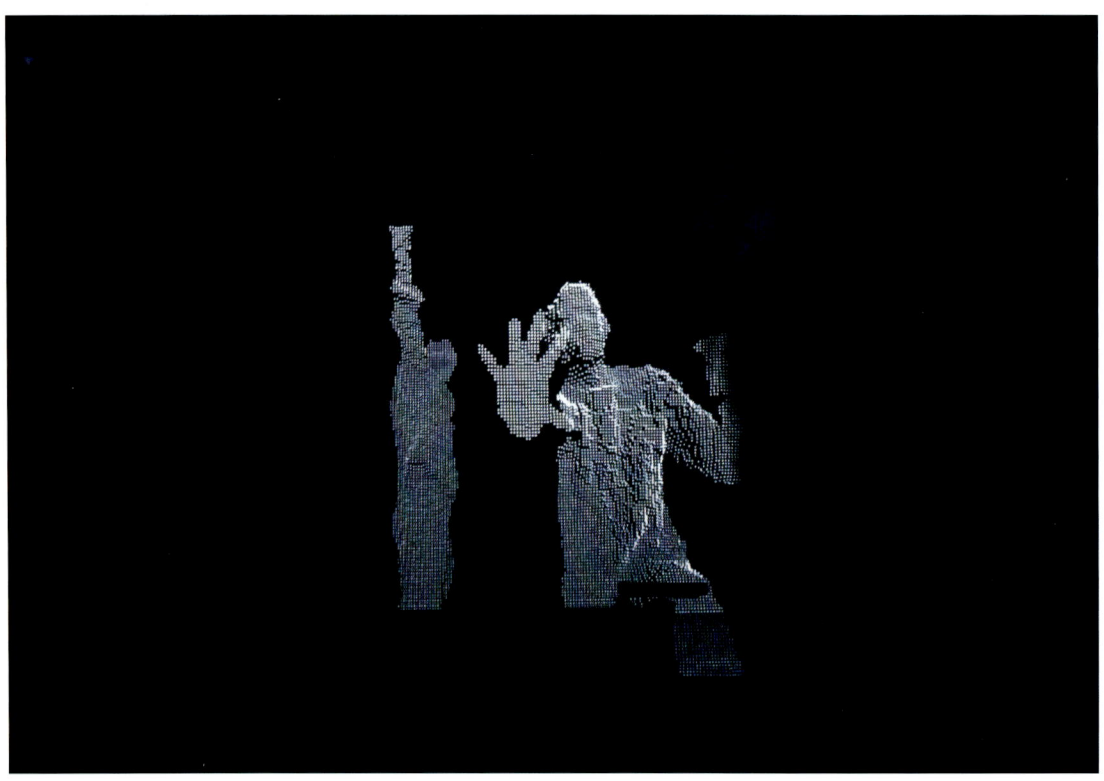

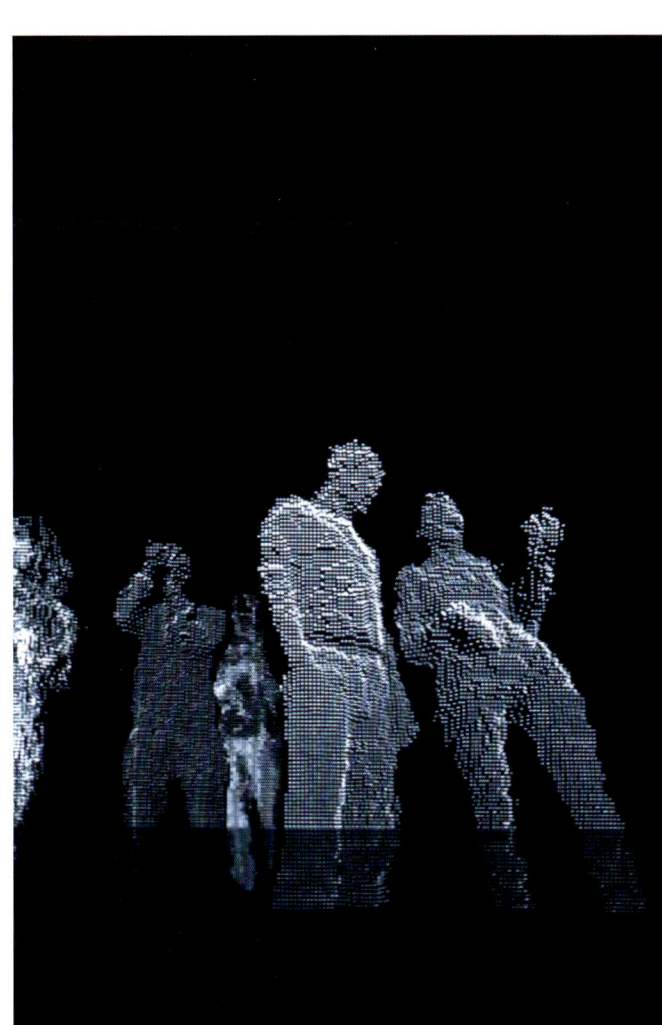
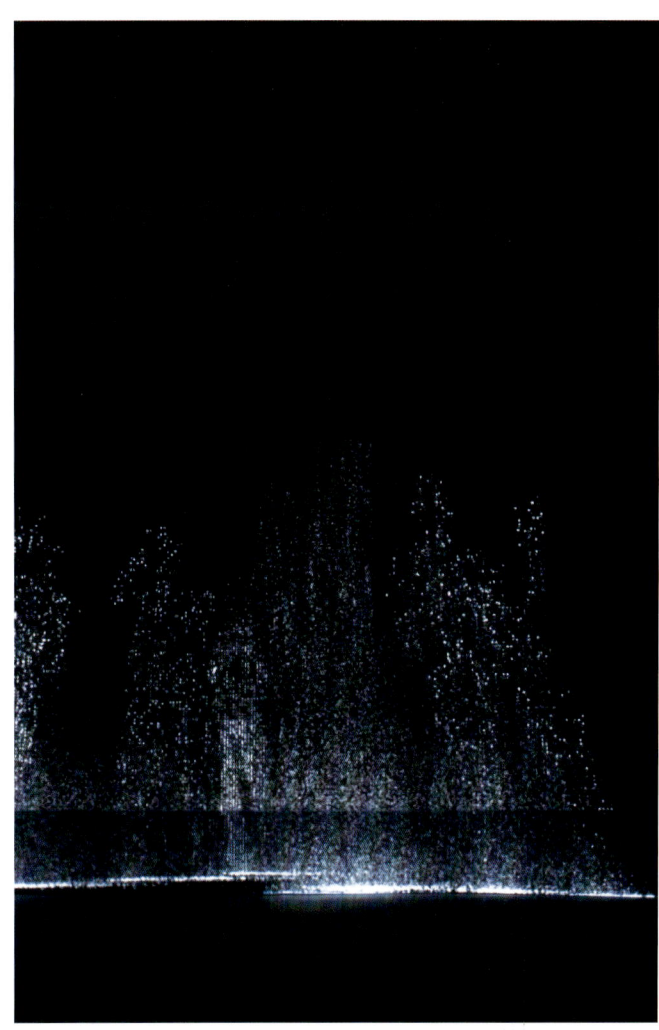

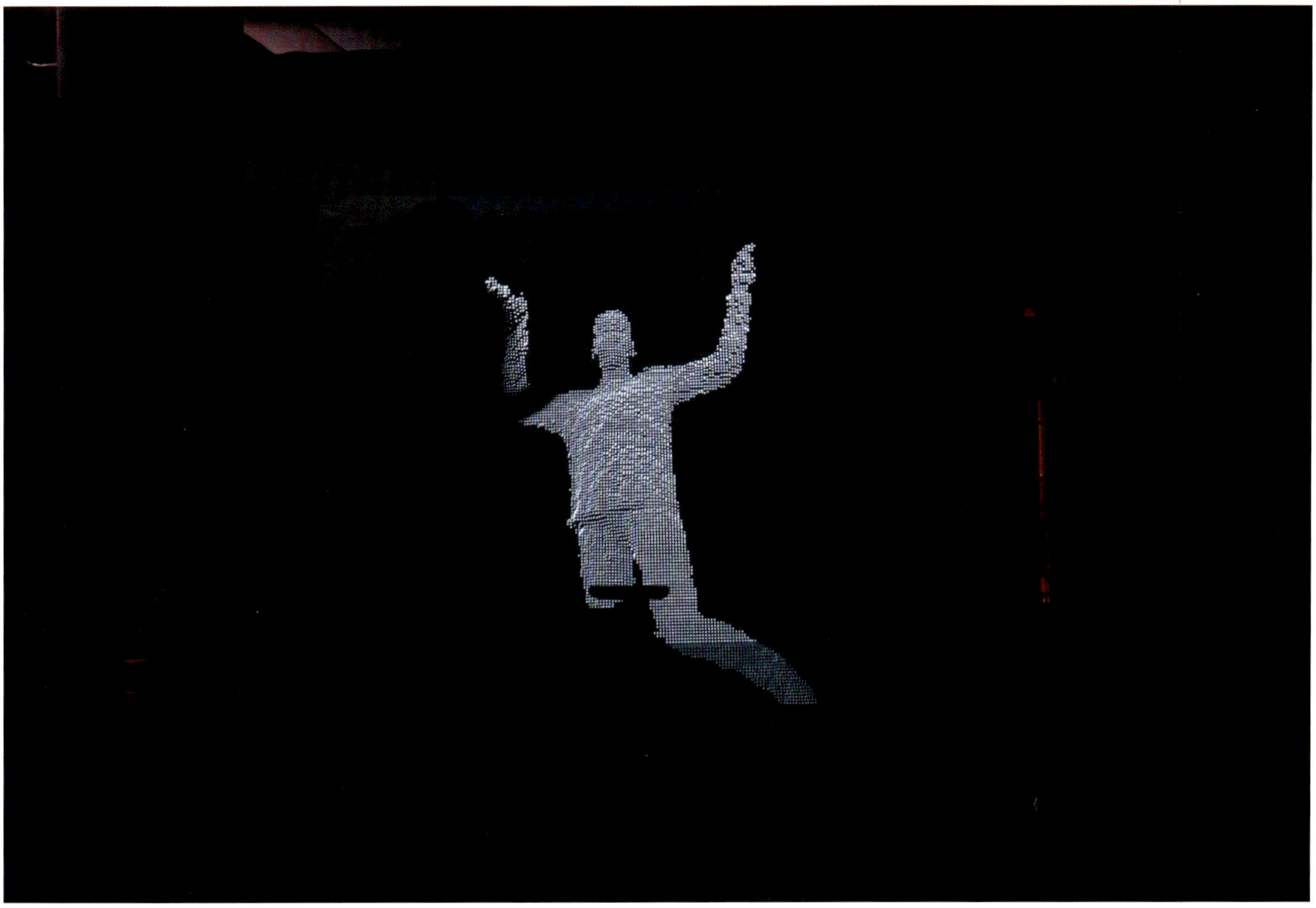

BOUNDING MAIN

—

Design: **ecco screen**

—

Bounding Main is an interactive installation featuring a vertically standing ocean displayed via projected light. As visitors approach, their reflections begin to emerge from the depths, refracting and distorting their bodily images as each wave and crest passes. Wakes and whirlpools emanate from their bodies as they glide their arms across the space in front of them, as if they were swimming underneath the surface.

It's chaotic in the interaction, but serene in the visual aesthetic. Users can either be frantic in their movement or they can peacefully watch the waves make their way across the surface in a soothing meditative experience. Sunlight produces continuous, changing showers of glittering light.

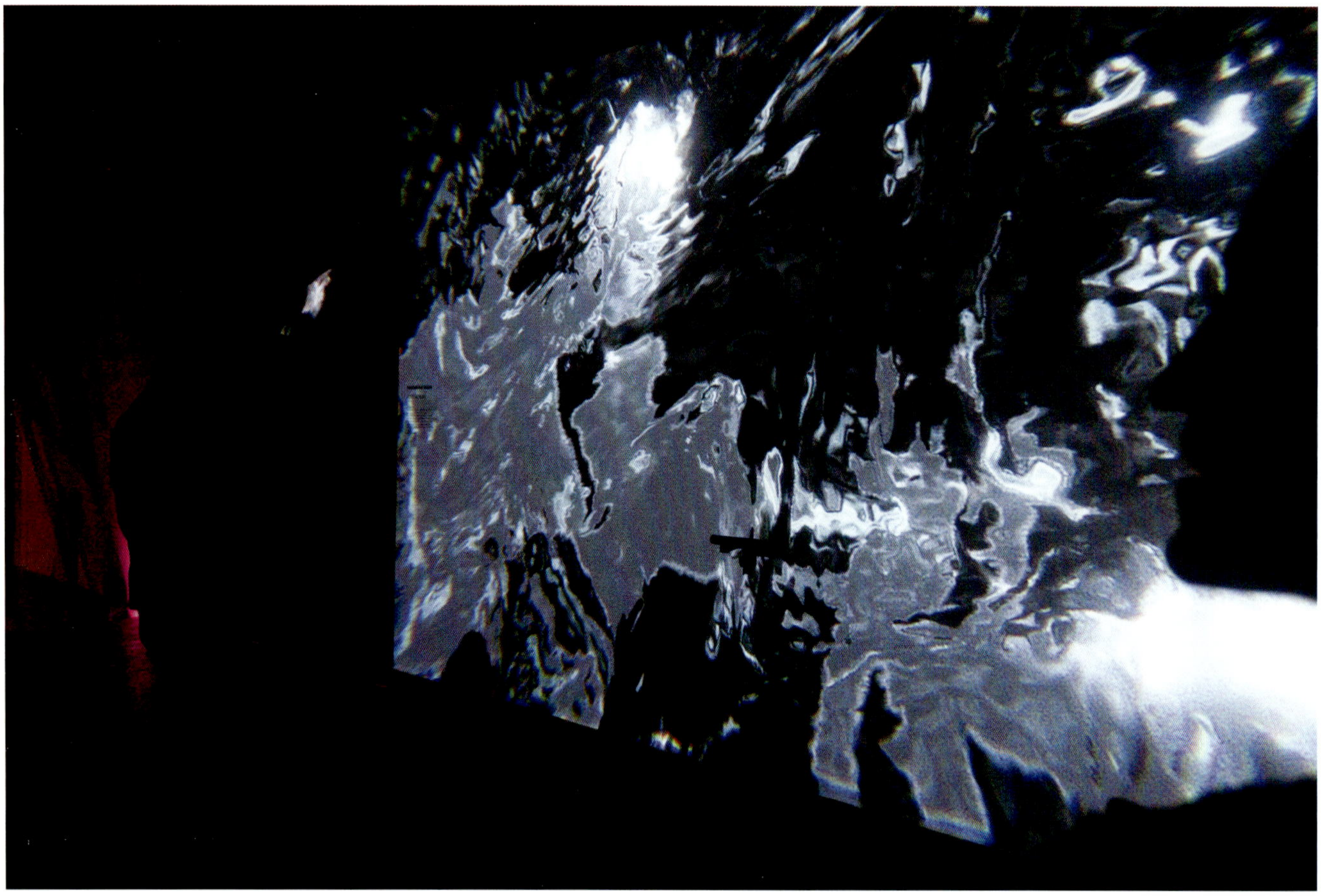

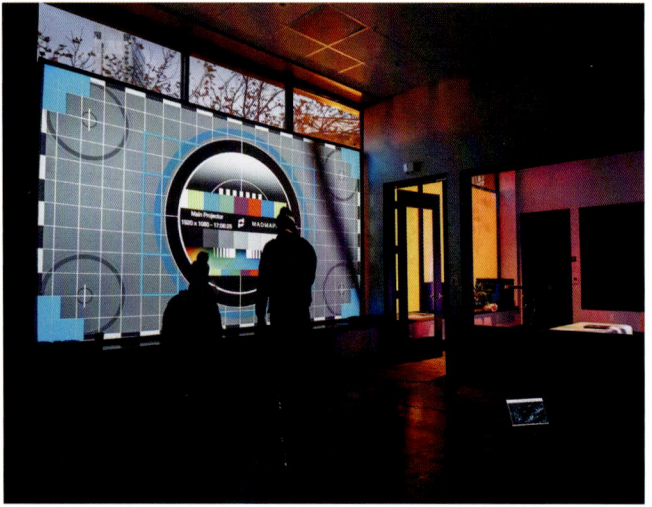

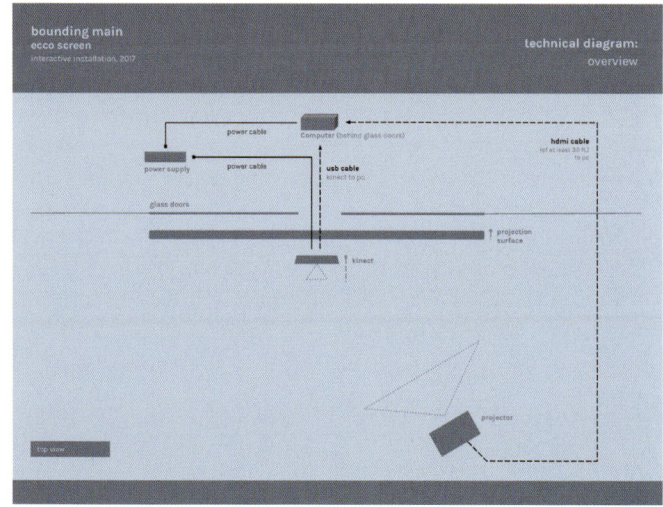

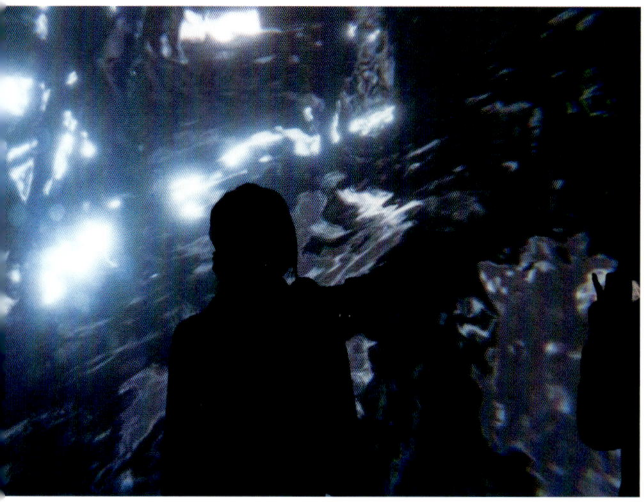

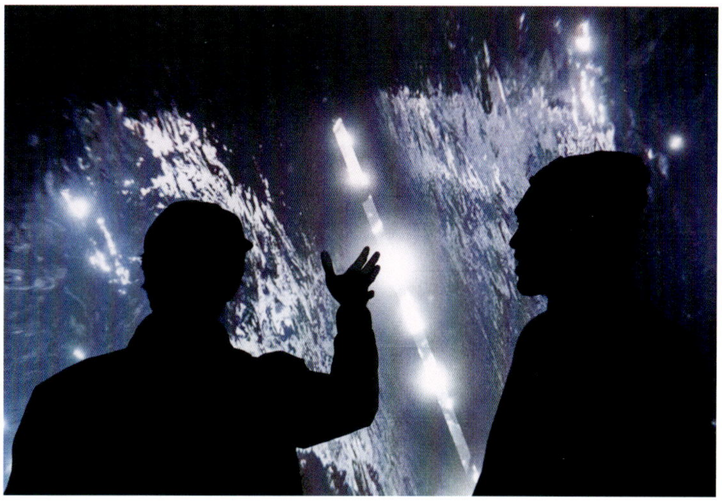

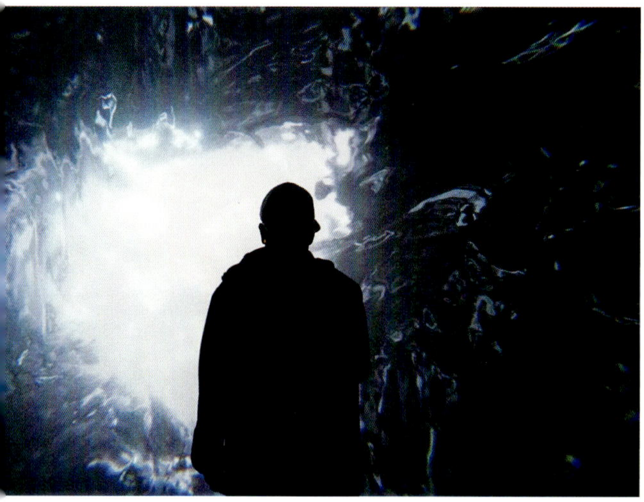

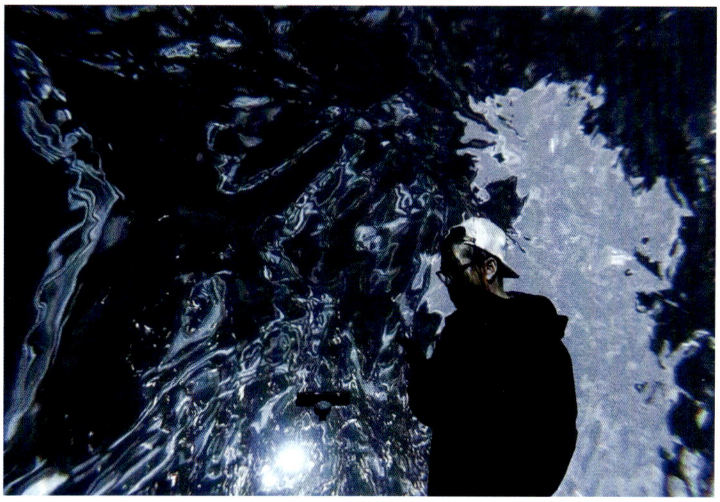

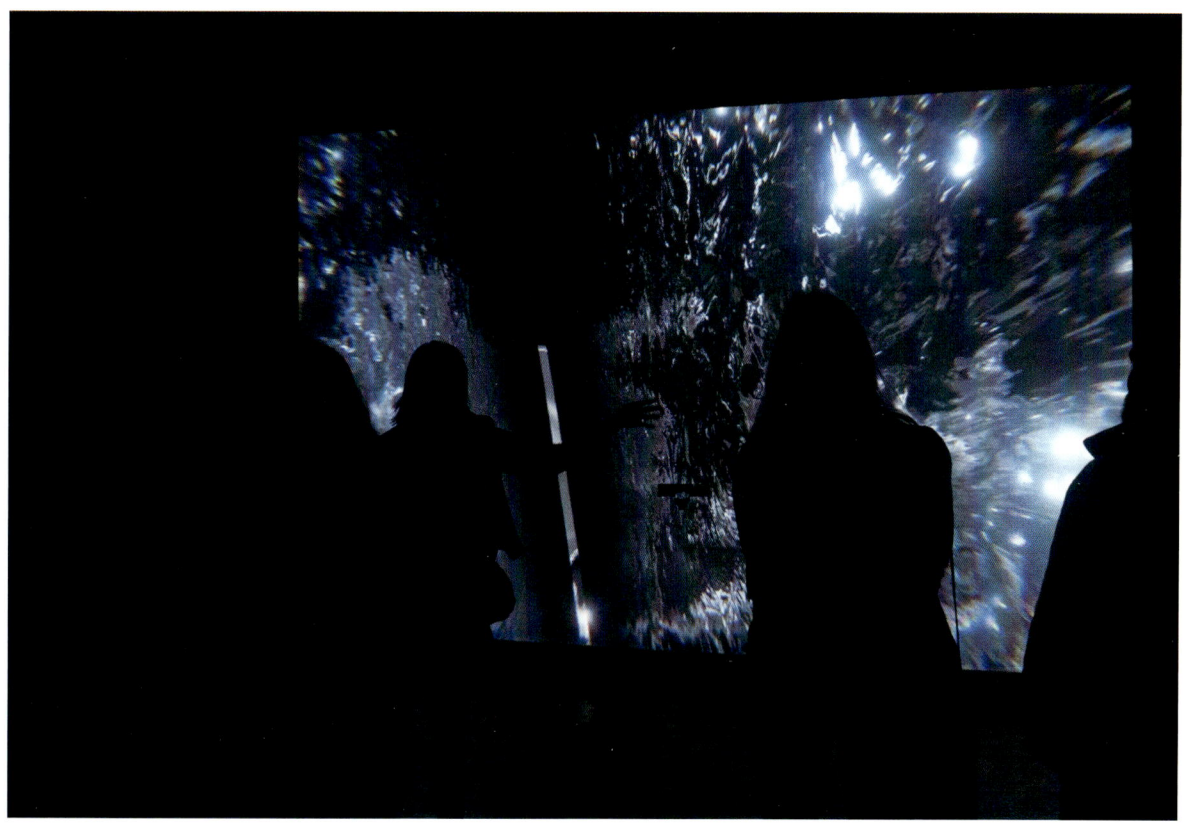

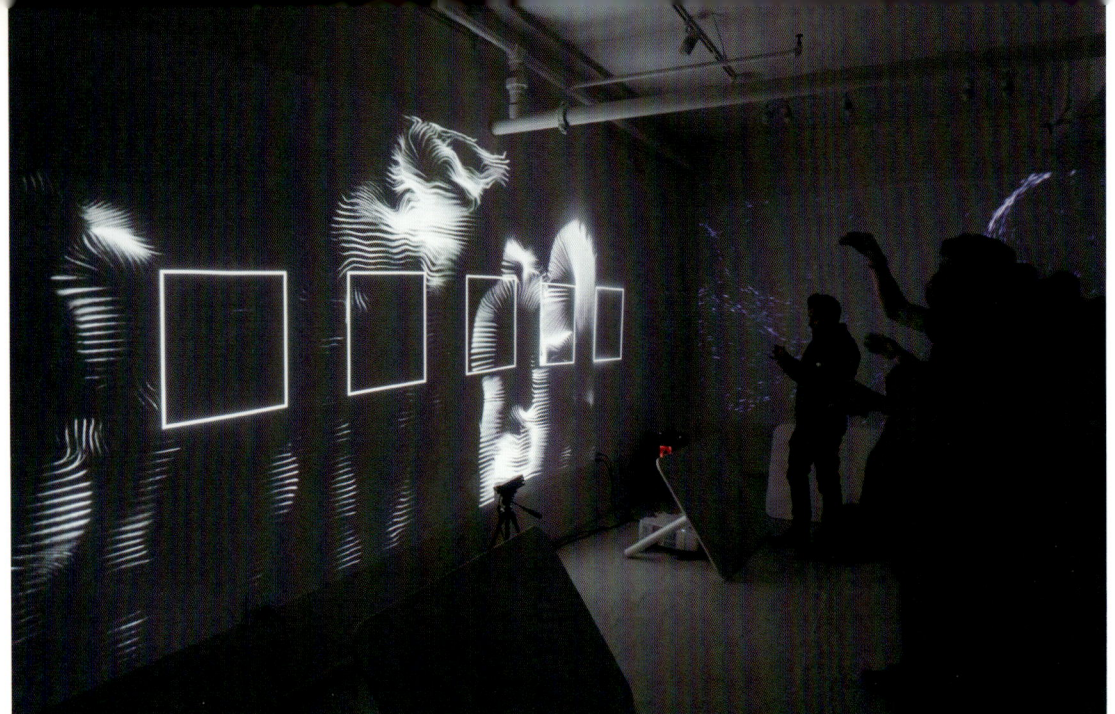

FADE

—

Design: **ecco screen**

—

Fade is a panoramic interactive installation featuring fluid-like streams of monochromatic wires that ebb and flow with the motion of its users. Each wave of the viewers' arms produce a current that aesthetically resembles electricity, but behaves in the way of a fluid. The slightest movement can produce a calm motion you'd find in a lake, while larger, more chaotic movements create the turbulent effects found in thunderstorms.

A second iteration called *Fade+* debuted at the historical Brooklyn Academy of Music (New York) in early 2018. It features a custom-built room with an interactive floor projection that allows users to walk across a pond of electricity, mixing the hot and cold colors of red and blue as they make their way through.

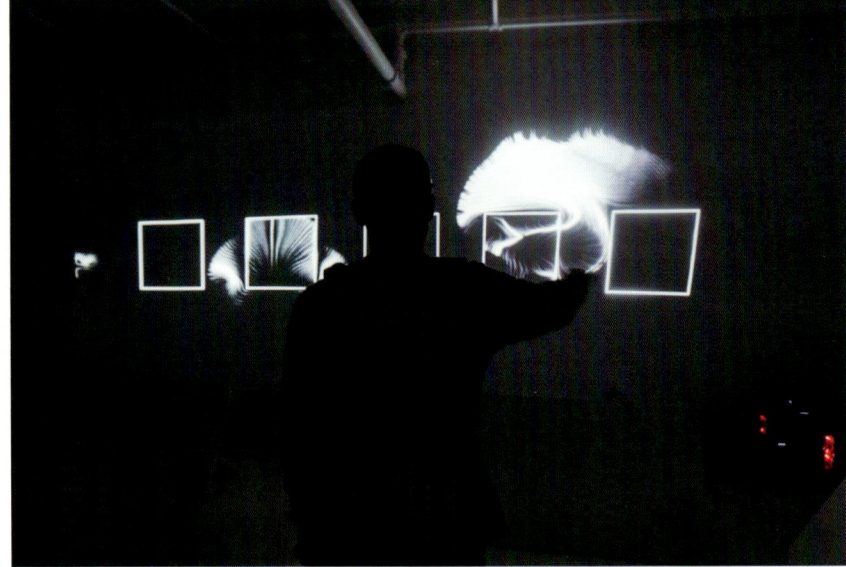

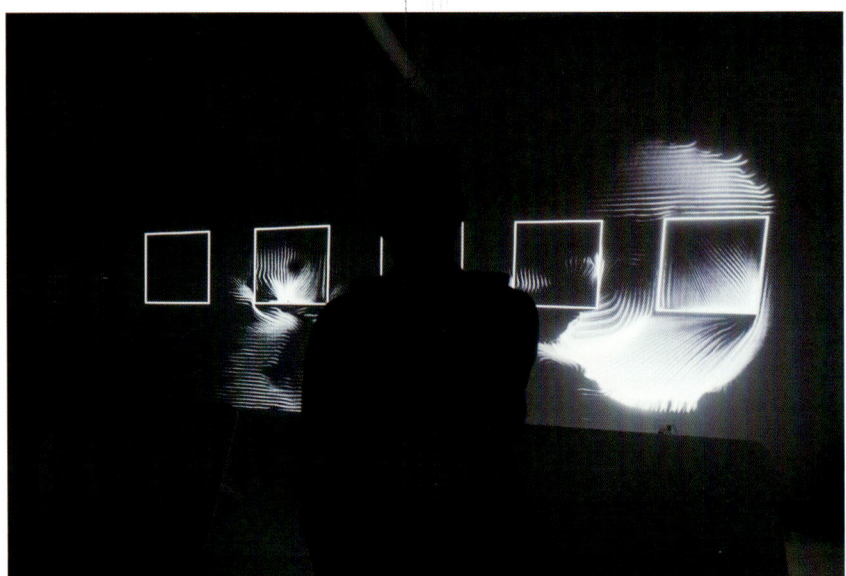

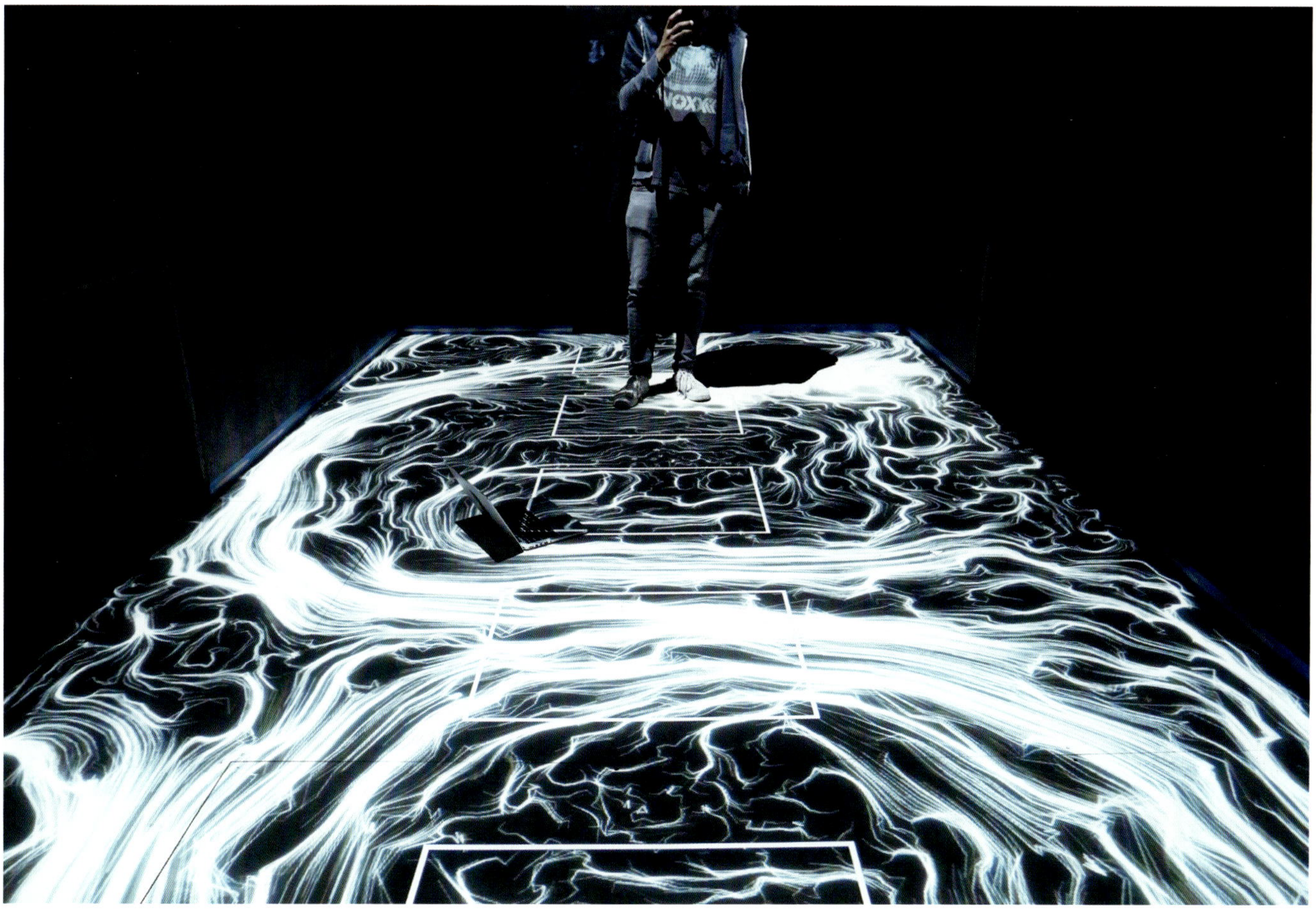

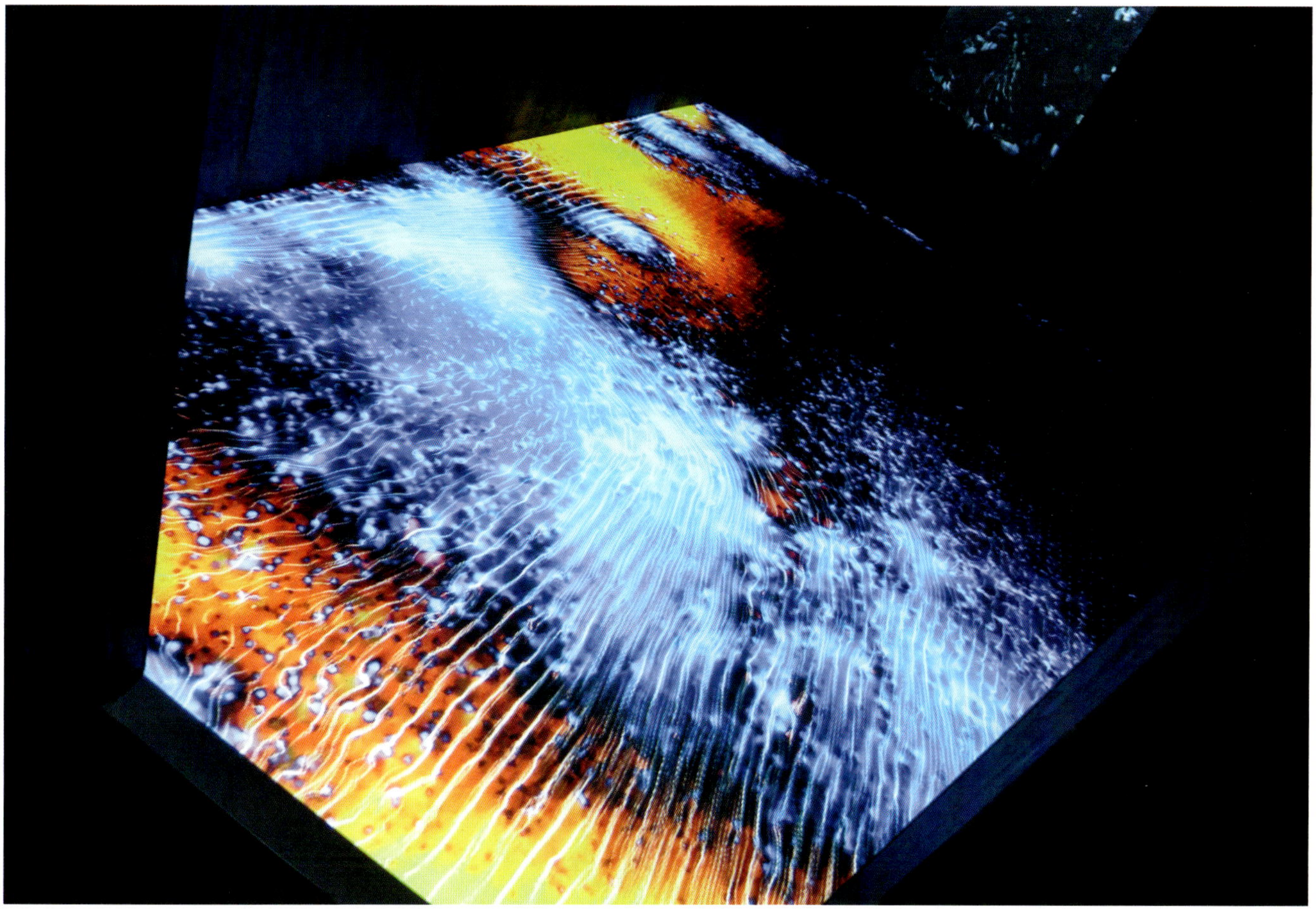

STRANDS

—

Design: **ecco screen**

—

Strands is an interactive installation consisting of an array of computer-generated strings projected onto an irregular surface which rapidly pull and push away with human interaction.

It features a monochromatic aesthetic and a metallic texture that morphs to resemble narrow strips of tape, web-like strands, or smoke trails in wind.

The behavior and physics of each strand change of their own accord, sometimes taking on the characteristics of tight harp strings and sometimes the buoyant weightlessness of aquatic plants. The strands have a lifelike, organic feel, but possess an alien nature. The ever-evolving image never repeats itself.

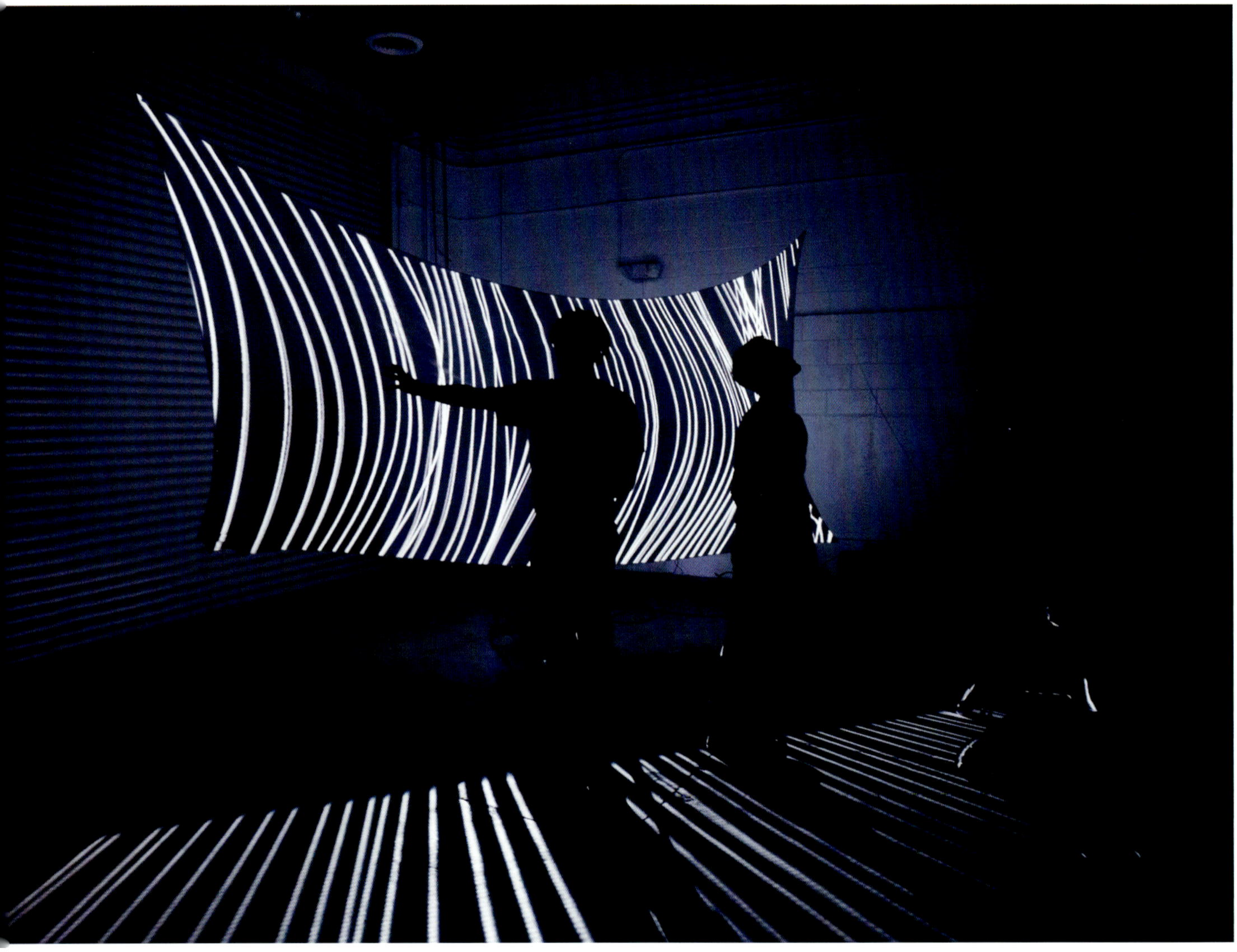

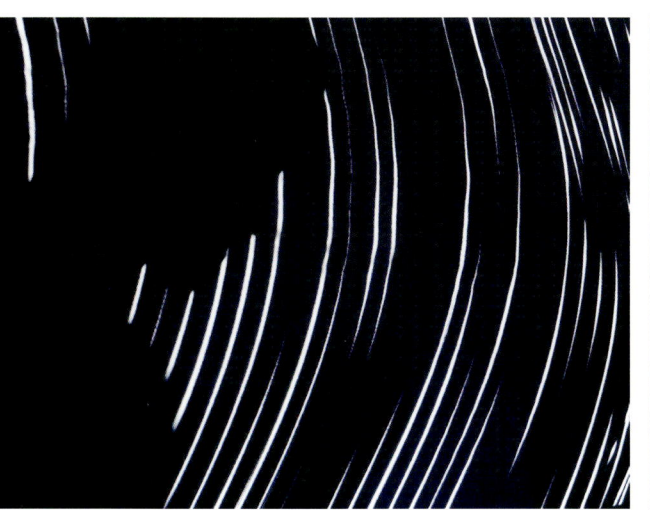
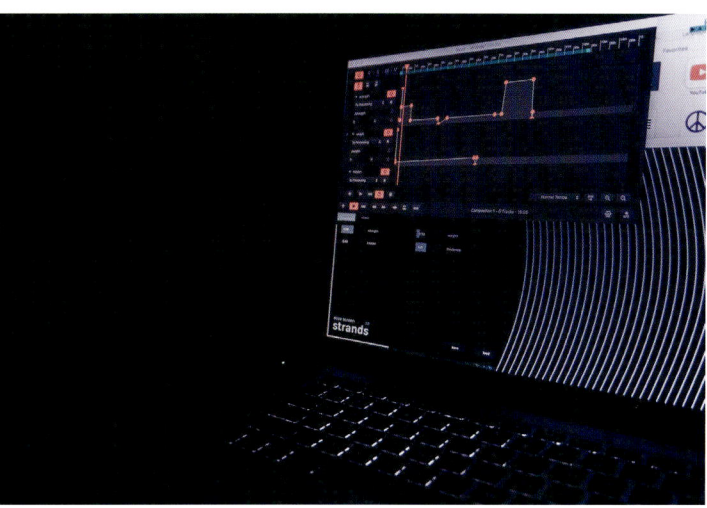
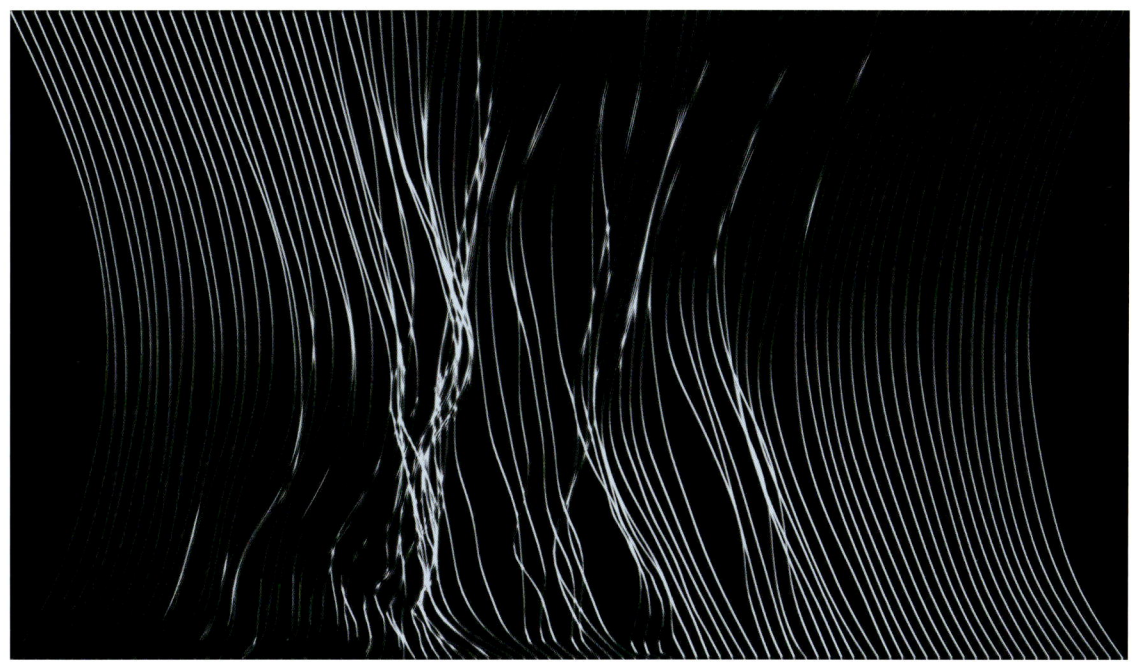
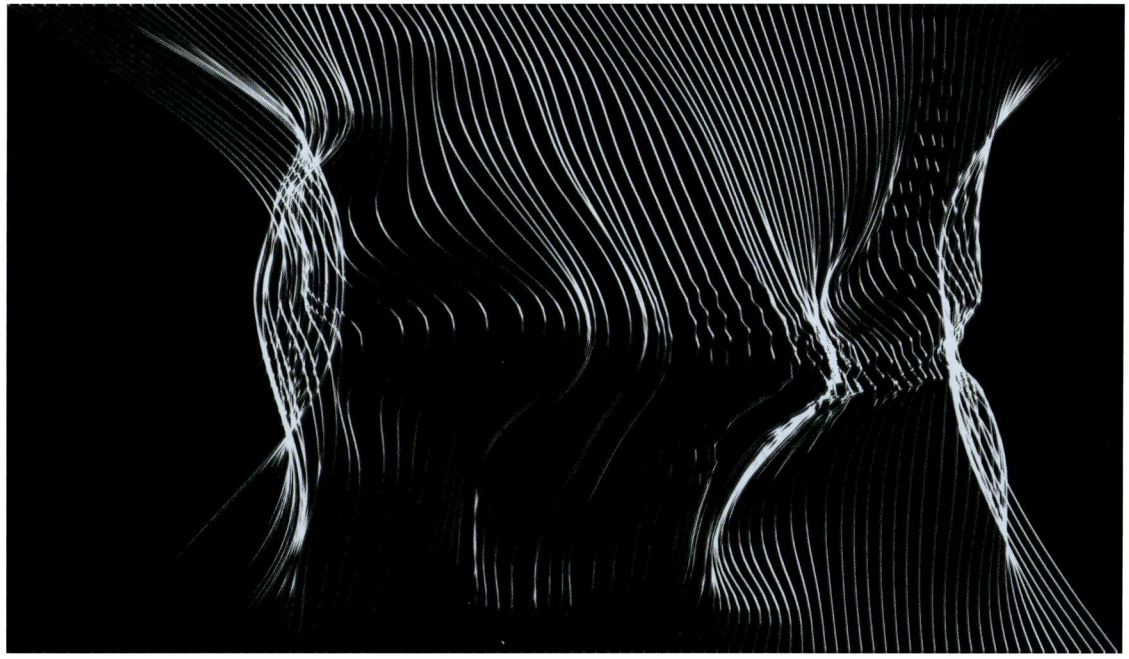

ARTIFICIAL SKY

Design: **NutBrother**

—

The first exhibition of *Artificial Sky* launched in Shenzhen, China. The whole "sky" spans 700 square meters with a dome of 9 meters in height. The layout of the "sky" is based on the star map of the Northern Hemisphere. More than 3500 LED lights are layered on the semi-elliptical dome, creating more than 7000 images of "stars" with the use of a black mirror on the ground. Combined with intelligent interactive devices, the exhibition integrates light, shadow, color, and sound, creating an immersive experience for the participants.

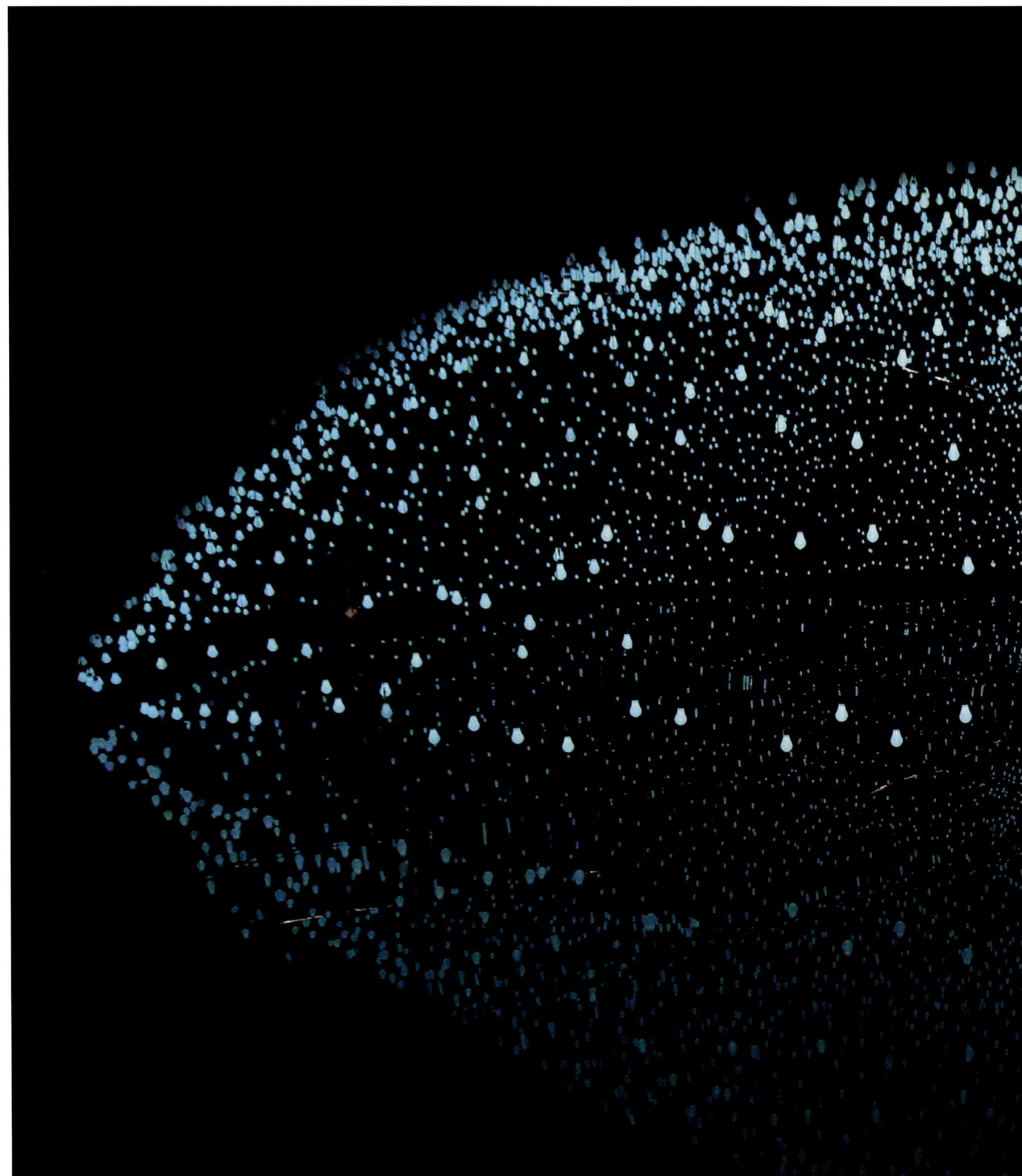

Participants had to be couples, with no restriction on gender. Entering a pitch black, quiet night, they slowly spoke out the "magic codes" which could be positive or negative to switch the "stars" on or off. There were 1,001 "magic codes" to create different skies. All the "stars" would be on once the critical "magic code" was spoken, leading the participants to the center of the galaxy. The installation was designed to take the couple through a series of feelings—loneliness, quiet, surprise, reflection, romance, and rebirth—during a ten-minute period.

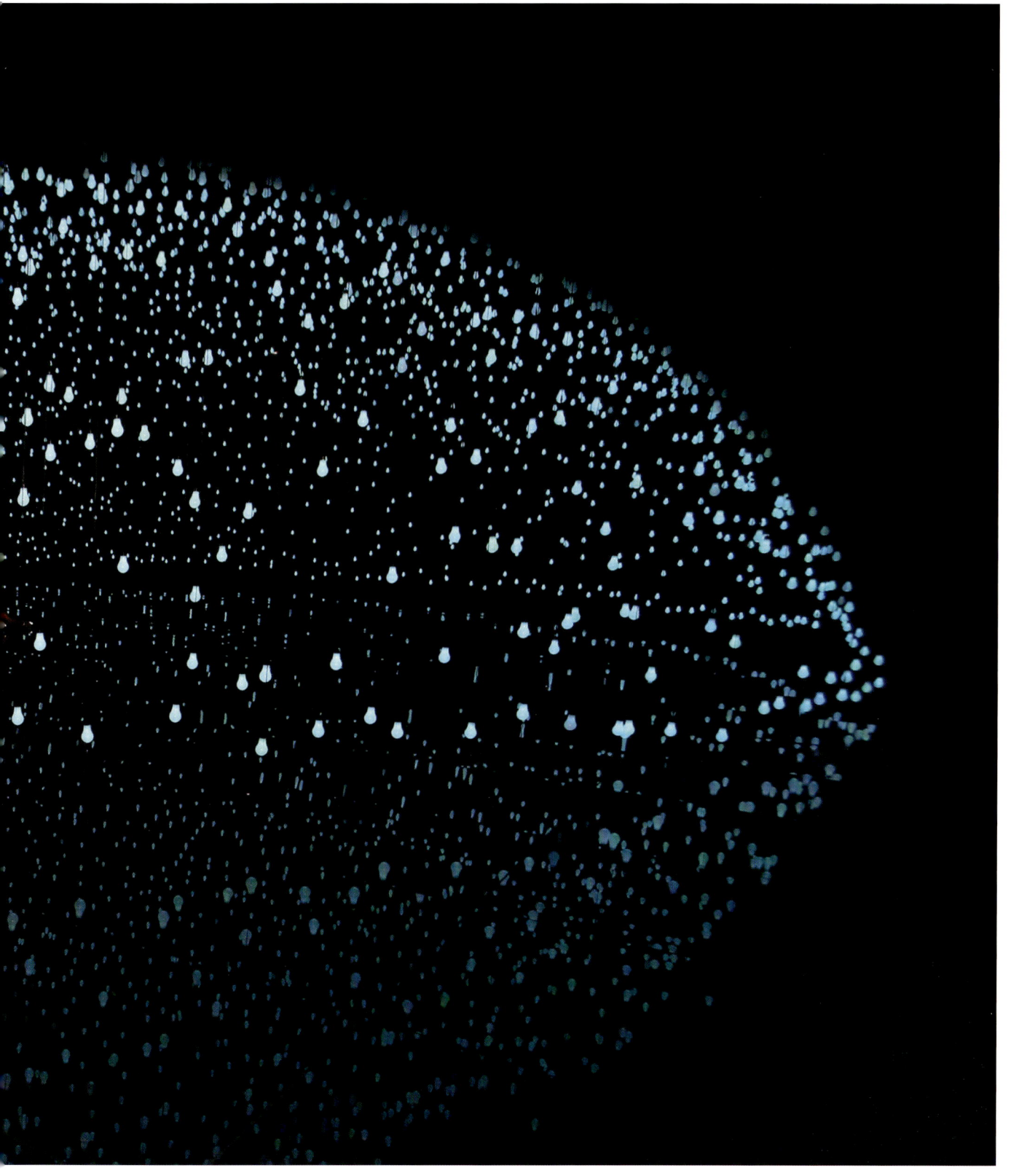

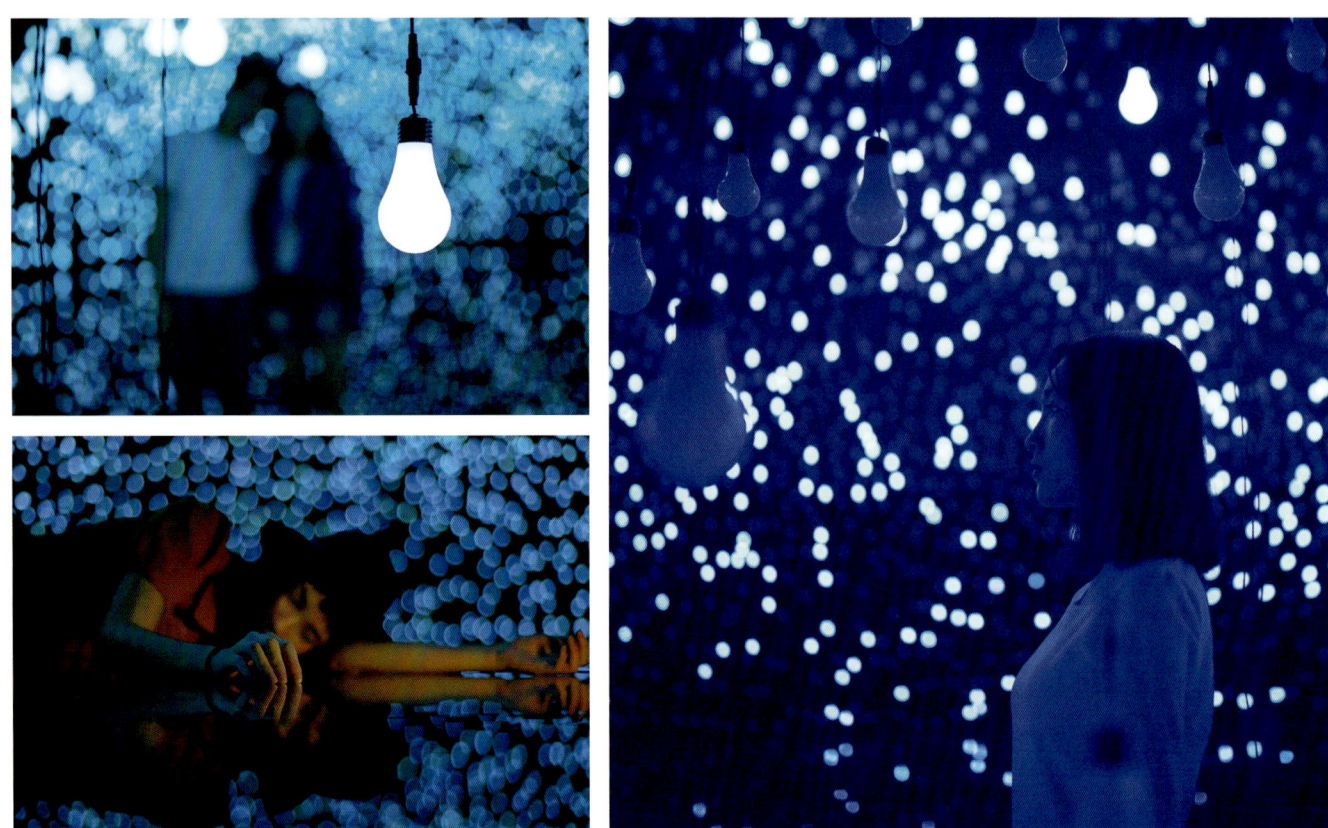

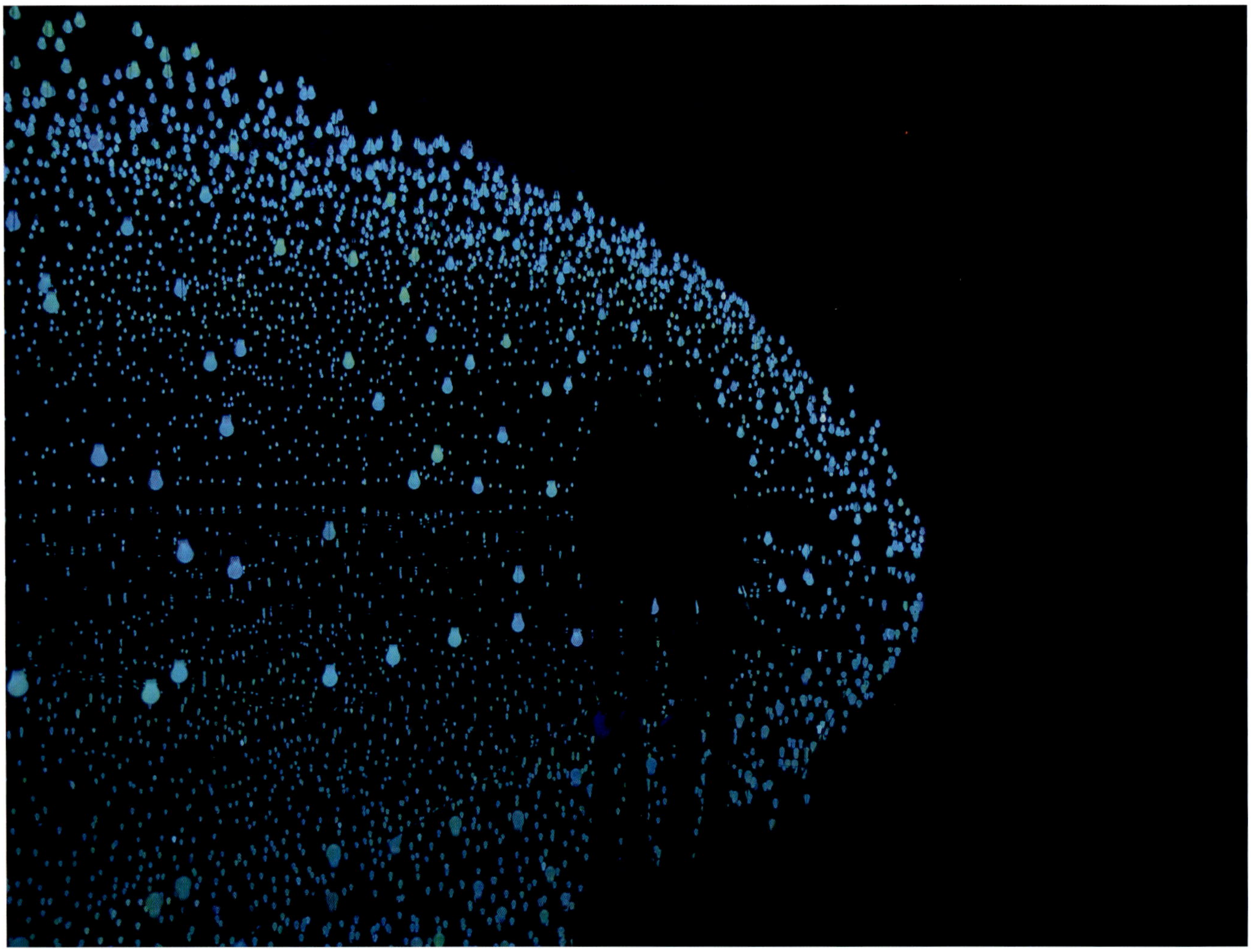

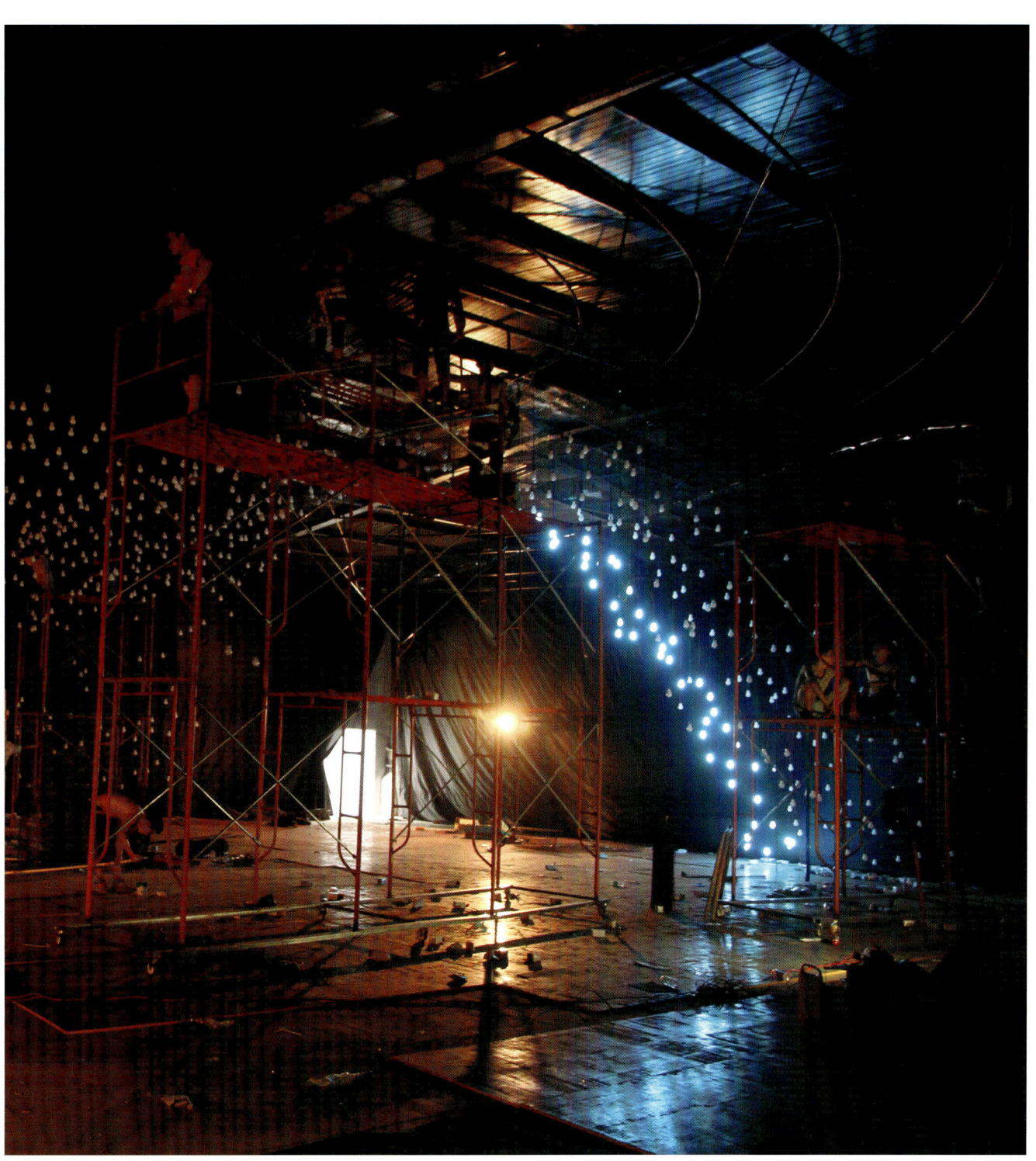

MY WHALE

—

Design: **TUNDRA**

—

This is a re-imagined and bigger-scale version of the interactive hexagonal installation *My Whale*, which was originally produced as a site-specific interactive installation by TUNDRA for "Brusov," a renovated ship, which is docked on the river in Moscow and has become a community space for art.

This version of *My Whale* was made for the exhibition "9 Lights in 9 Rooms," held at the D Museum in Seoul, Korea, and was visited by more than 200,000 visitors during the period of exhibition.

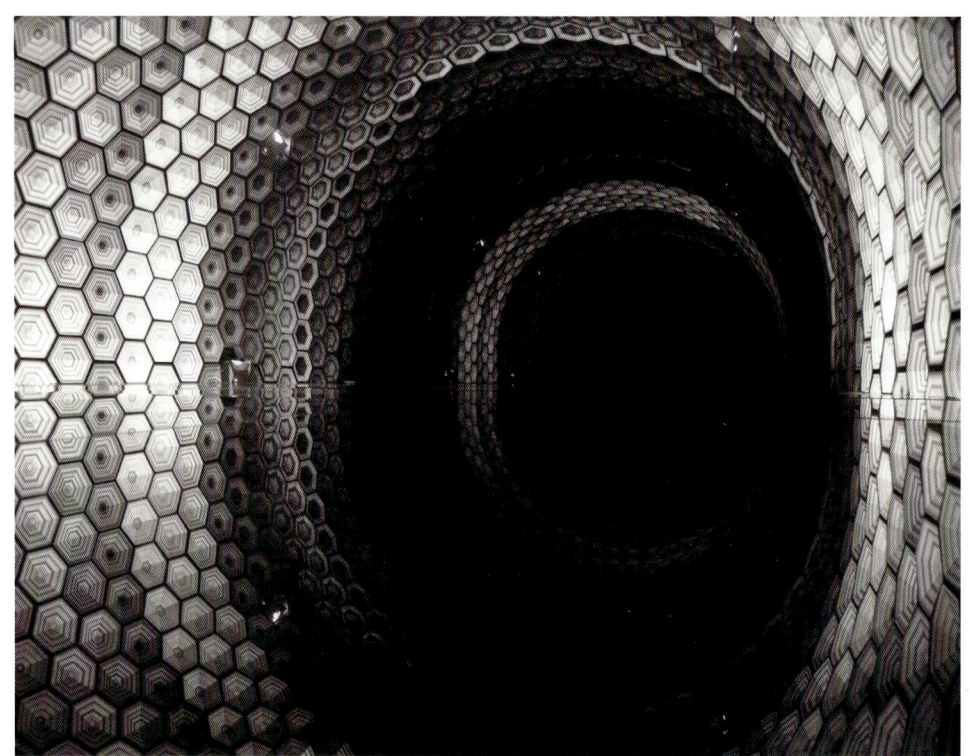

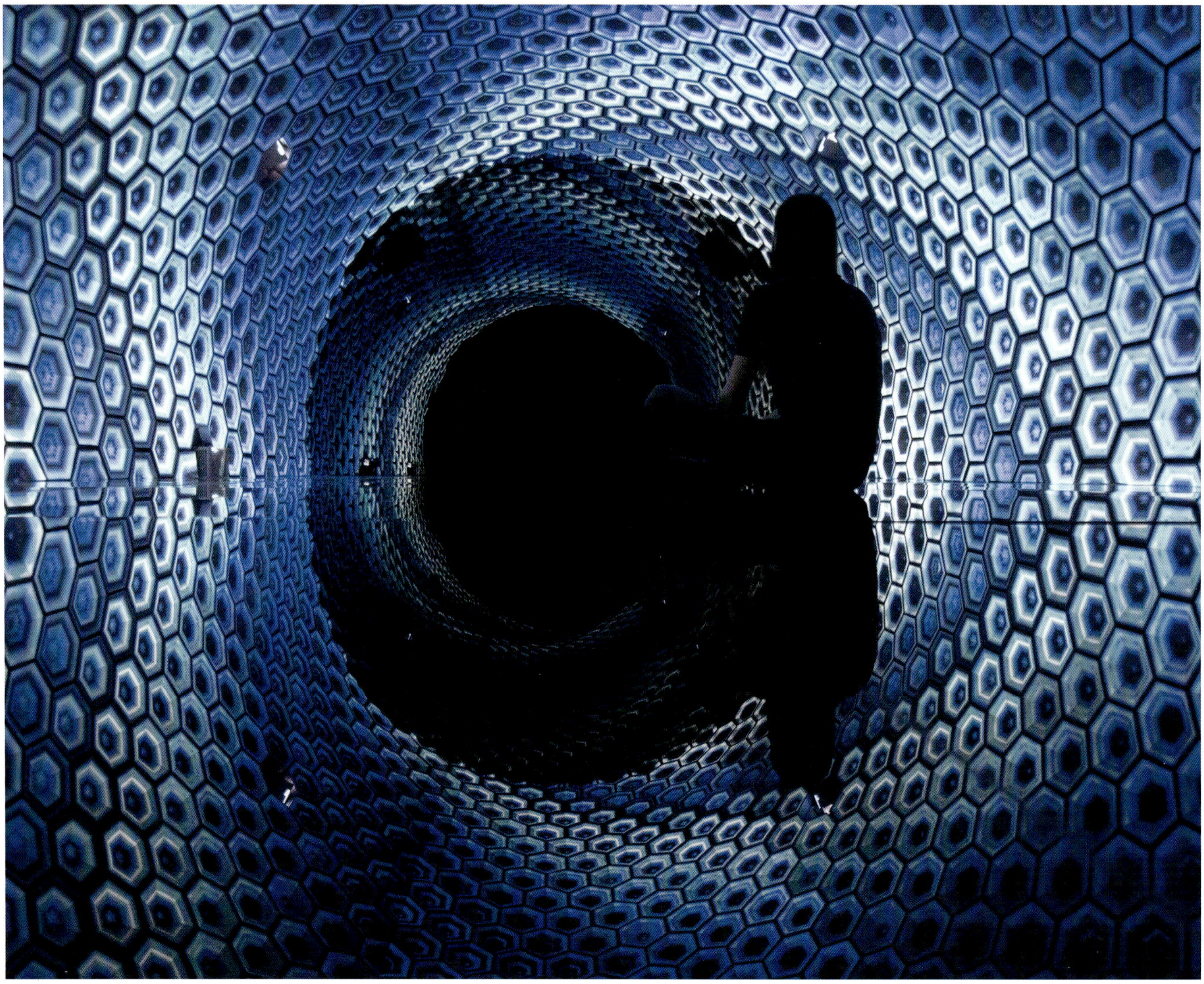

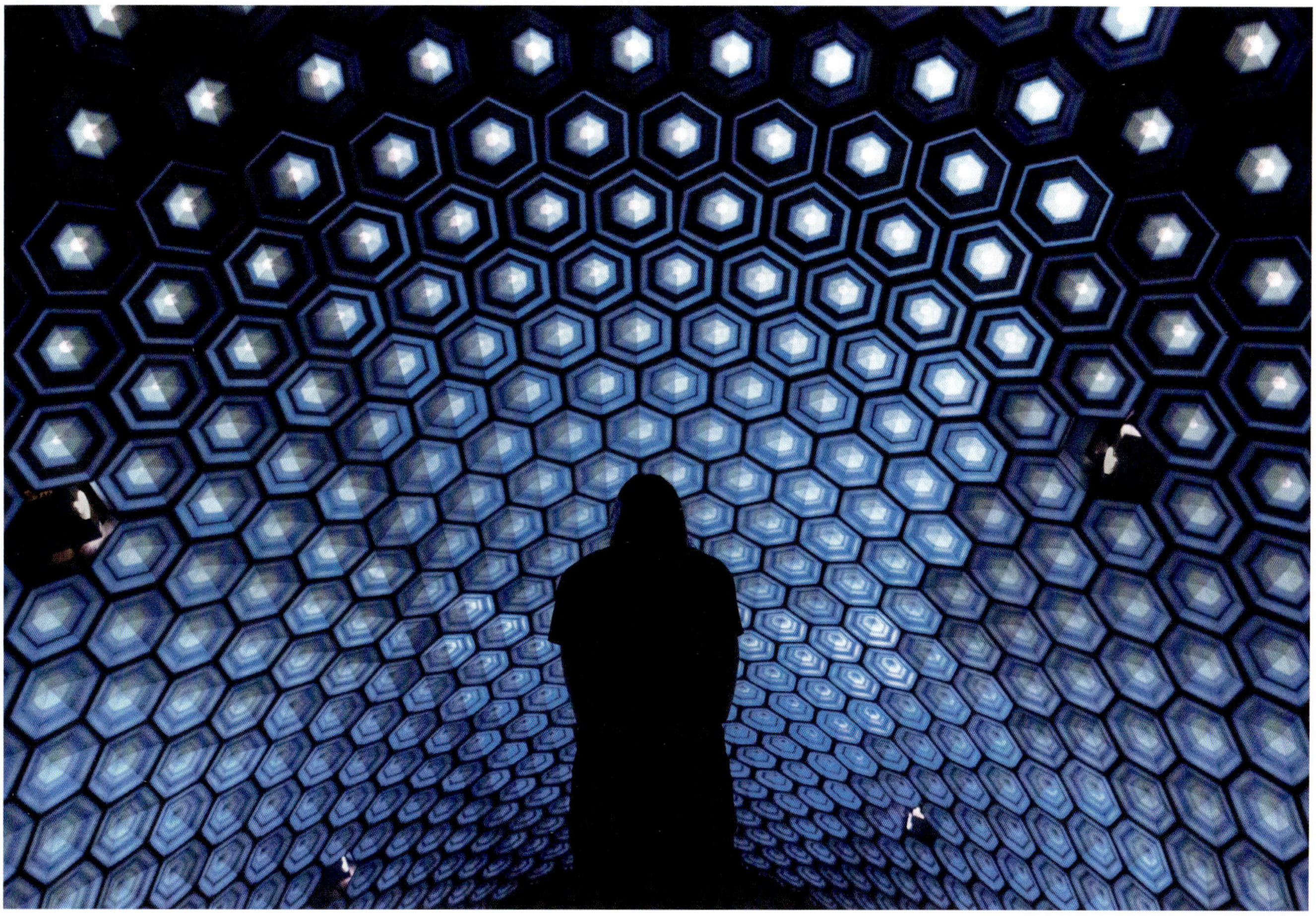

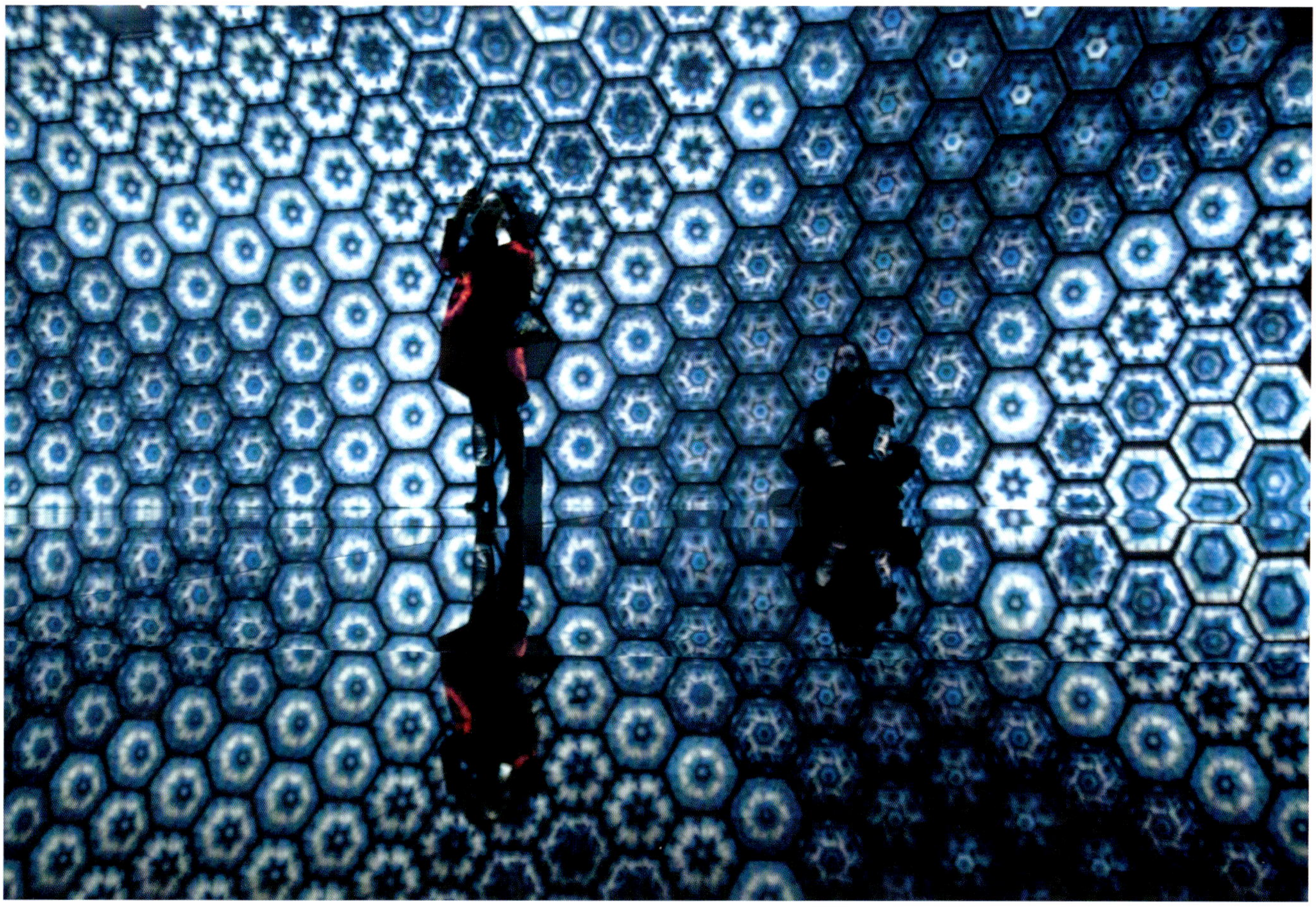

DELETE

—

Design: **Iregular**

—

DELETE is an immersive, site-specific, interactive experience for young audiences. In six phases—two websites and four rooms—*DELETE* takes the audience into a world where the line between the virtual and the real disappears. Each part explores the way we experience the digital world, like the consumption of information, our contributions, the creation of our virtual personas and the traces we leave.

SUBMIT (Part 1)
Everyone who confirms his participation in *DELETE* receives a link to SUBMIT, the first part of the experience. A profile opens and the participant answers personal questions.

EMERGE (Part 2)
"Everything you put in the virtual world makes the virtual world more real."
This room creates the image of a new being by combining all the faces in the audience.

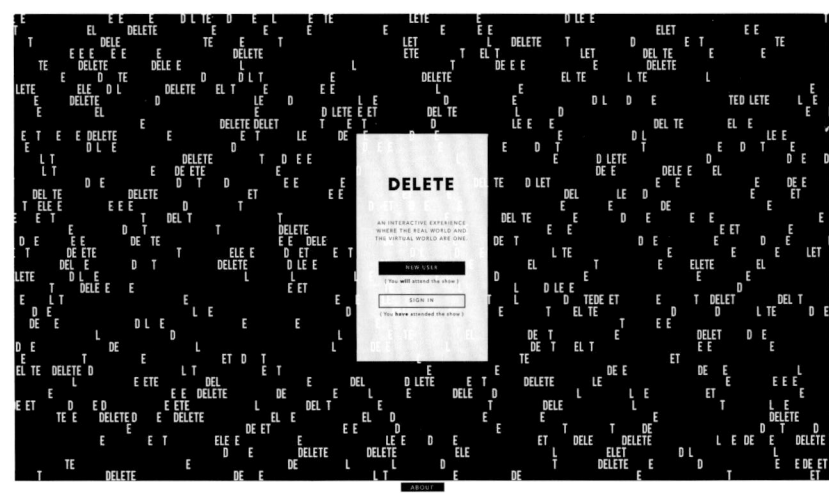

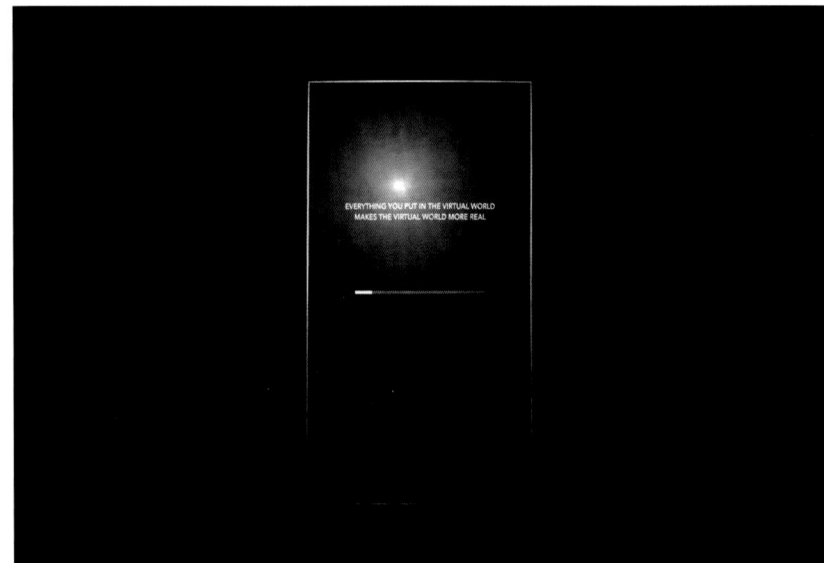

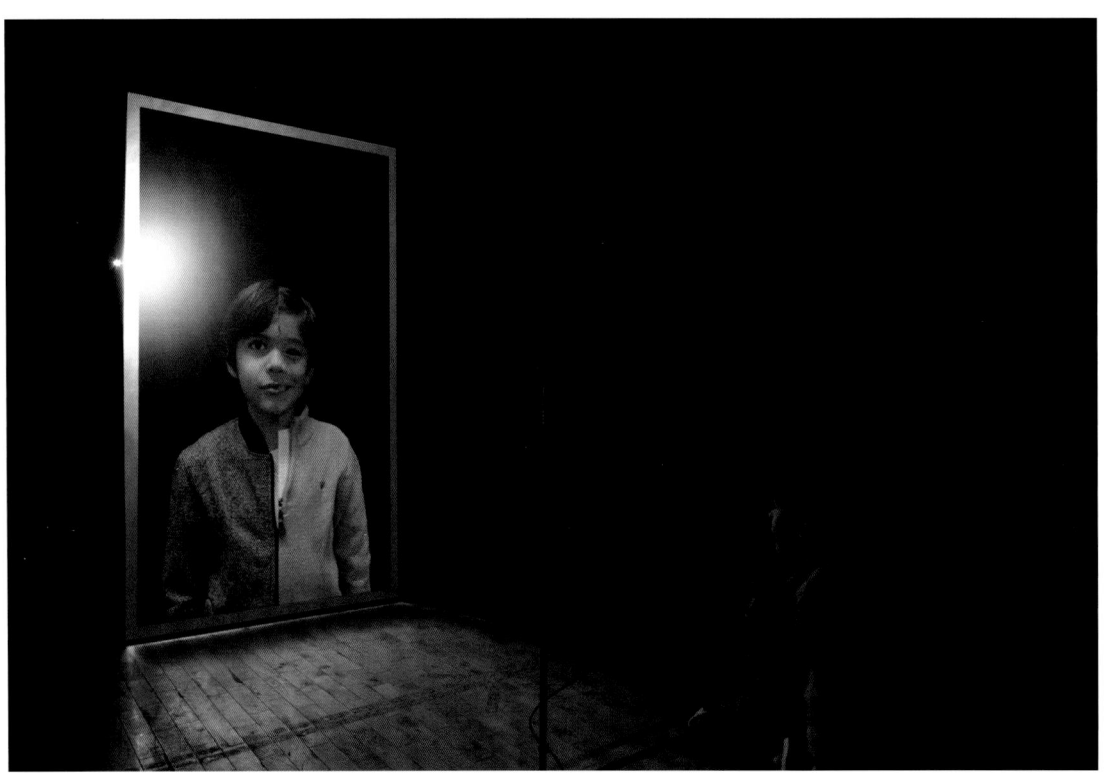

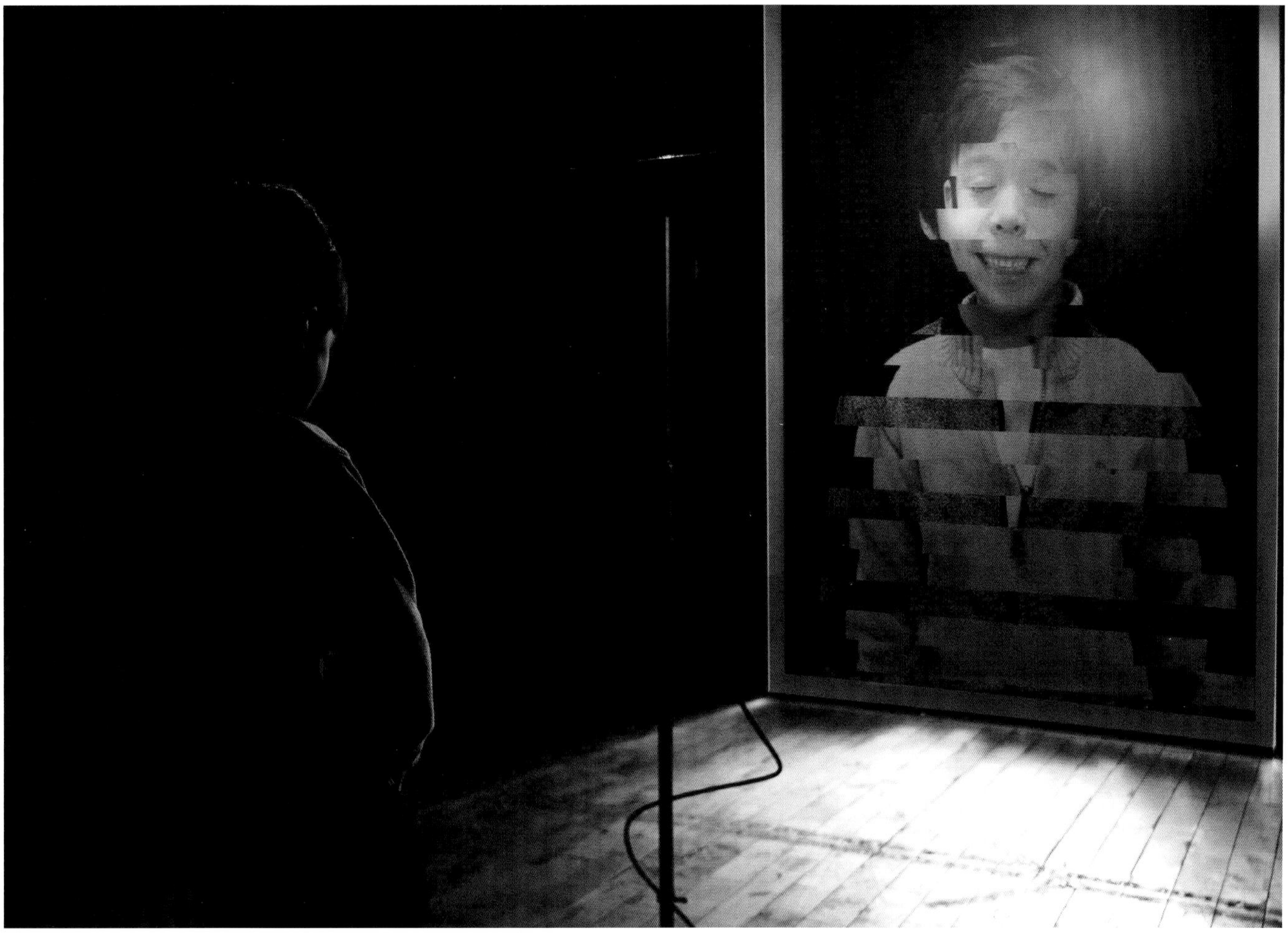

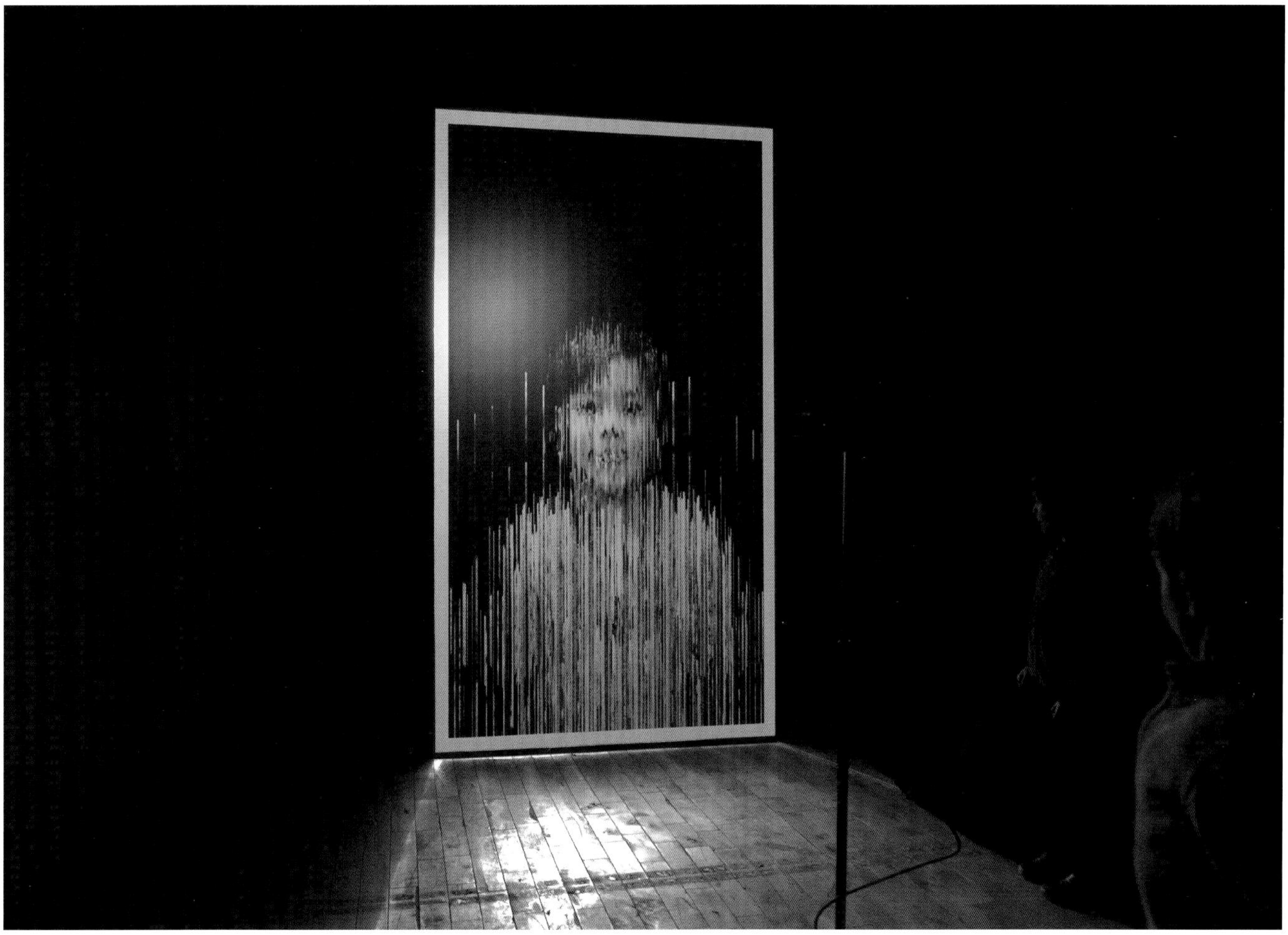

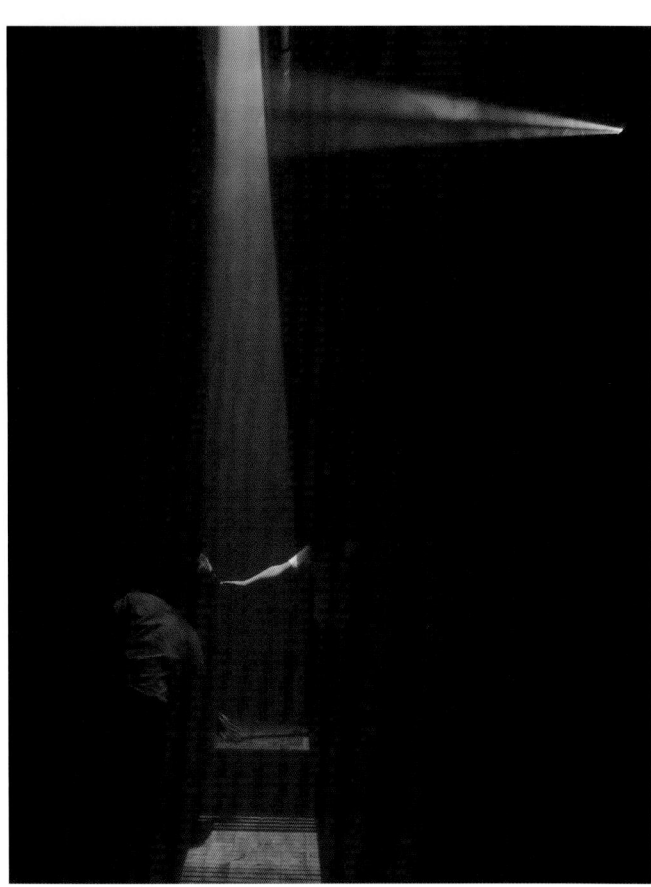 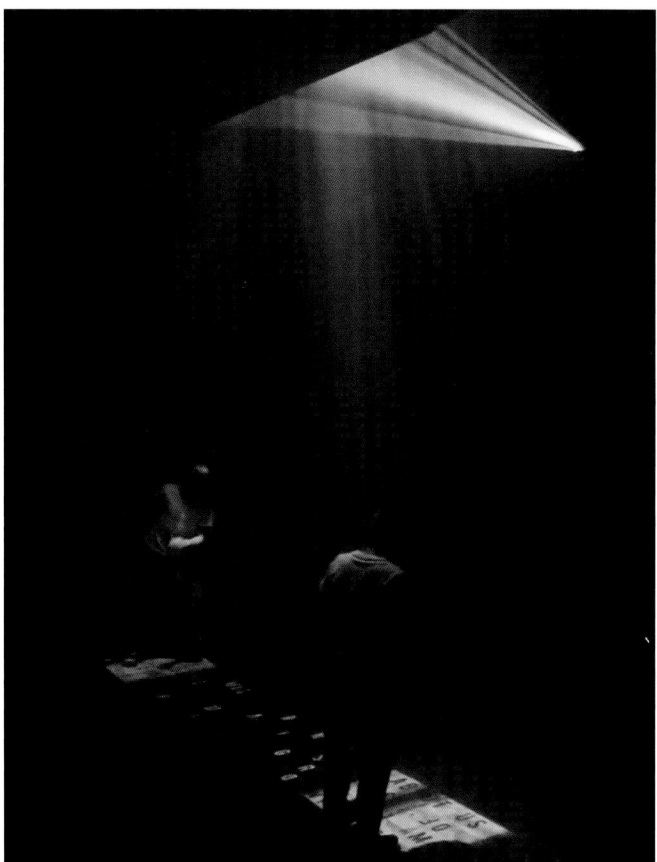

COLLECT (Part 3)
"We know more and understand less."
This room is about the overwhelming amount of information we deal
with every day and questions how much of it we are able to process or
understand.

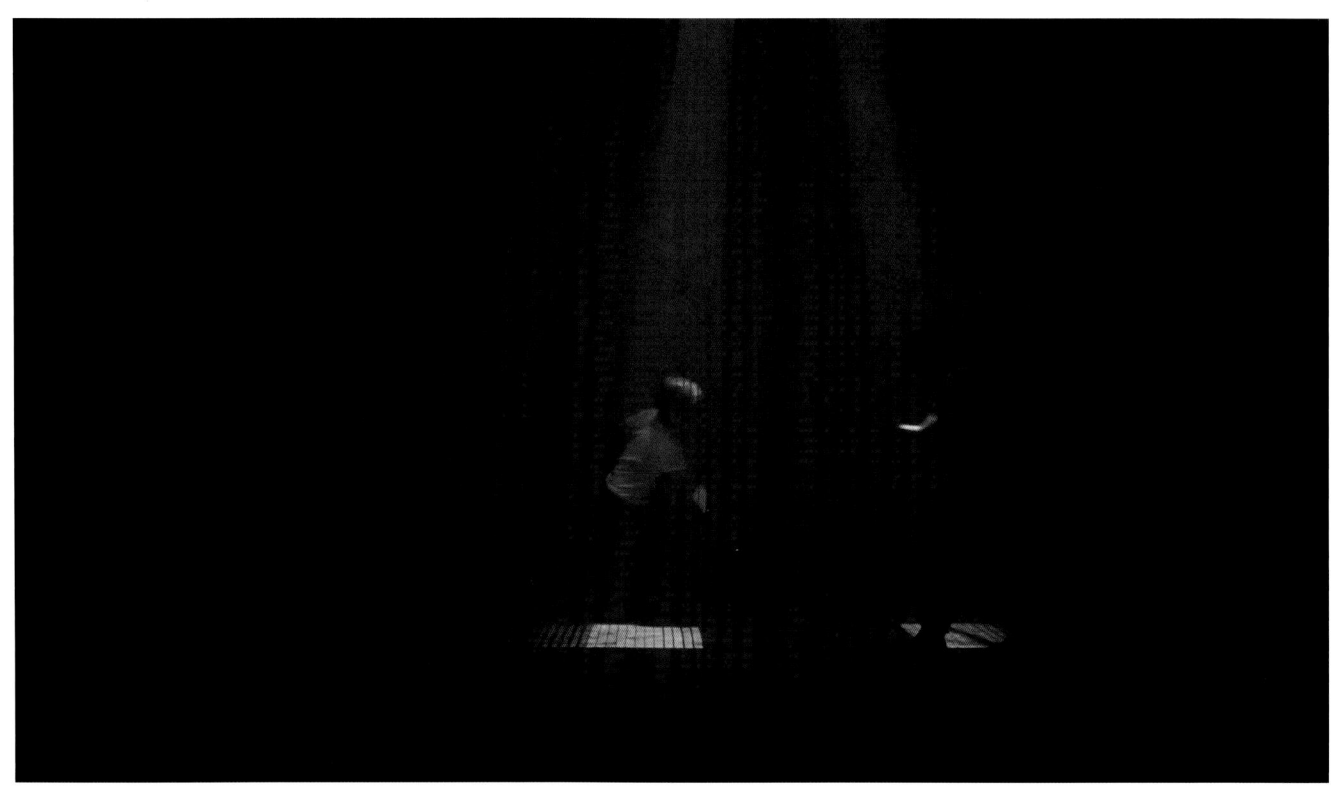

SELECT (Part 4)
"Choices construct my world."
This room is about creating new meaning by
deconstructing and combining answers provided
by the audience. In Part 1, the audience is asked:
"If you wanted to confirm if someone was a
human what would you ask?"
In this room, a disembodied character asks the
submitted questions to the audience, and uses
their answers to construct new phrases.

IDENTIFY (Part 5)
"The virtual version of you is you."
A mirror in front of a mirror in front of a mirror.
This room is about looking at your virtual self,
one of the multiple profiles you create online and
questions if that is really you or someone else.

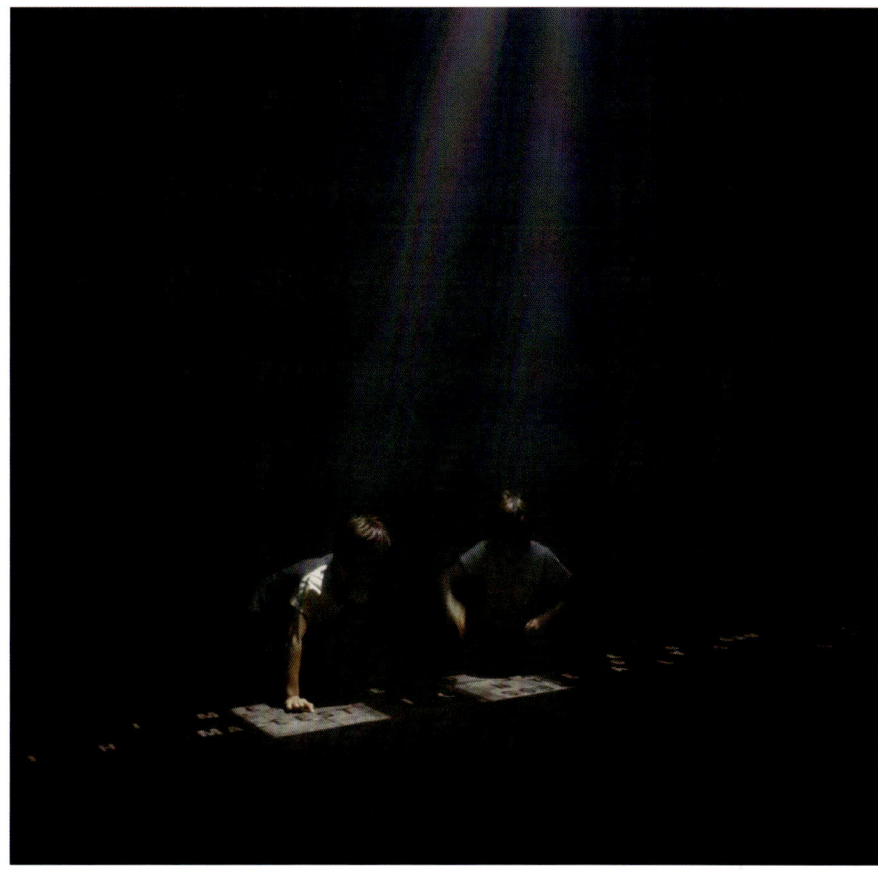

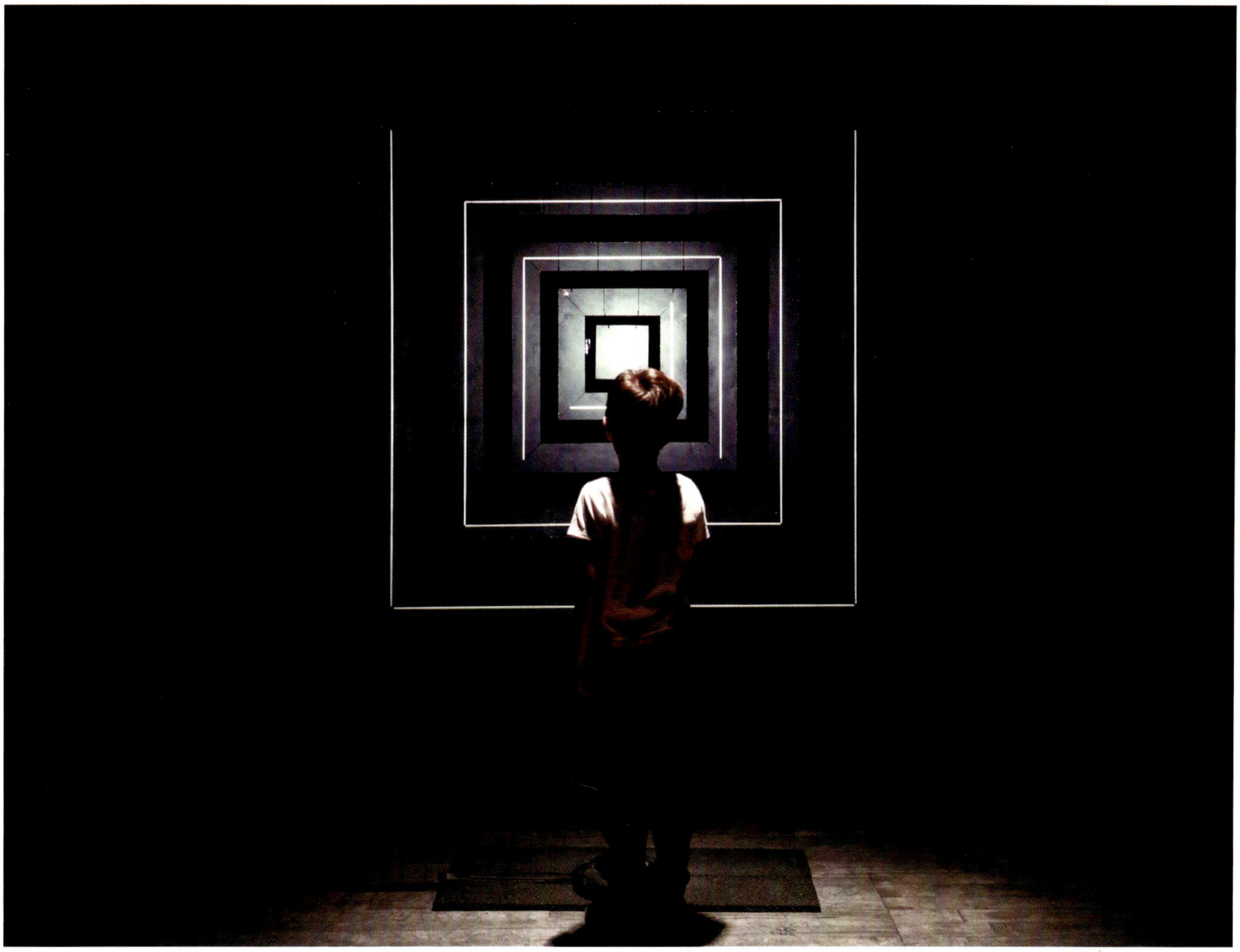

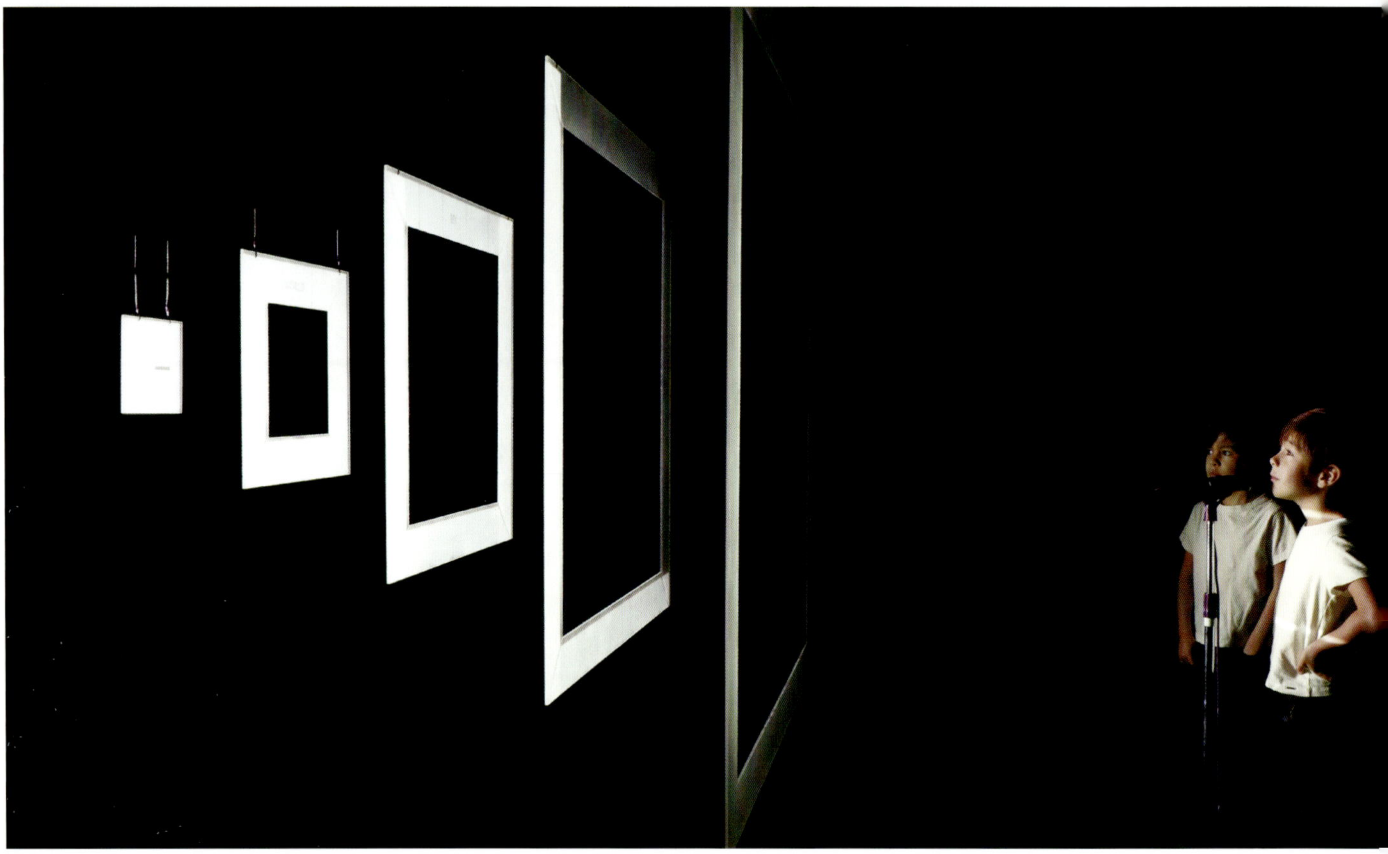

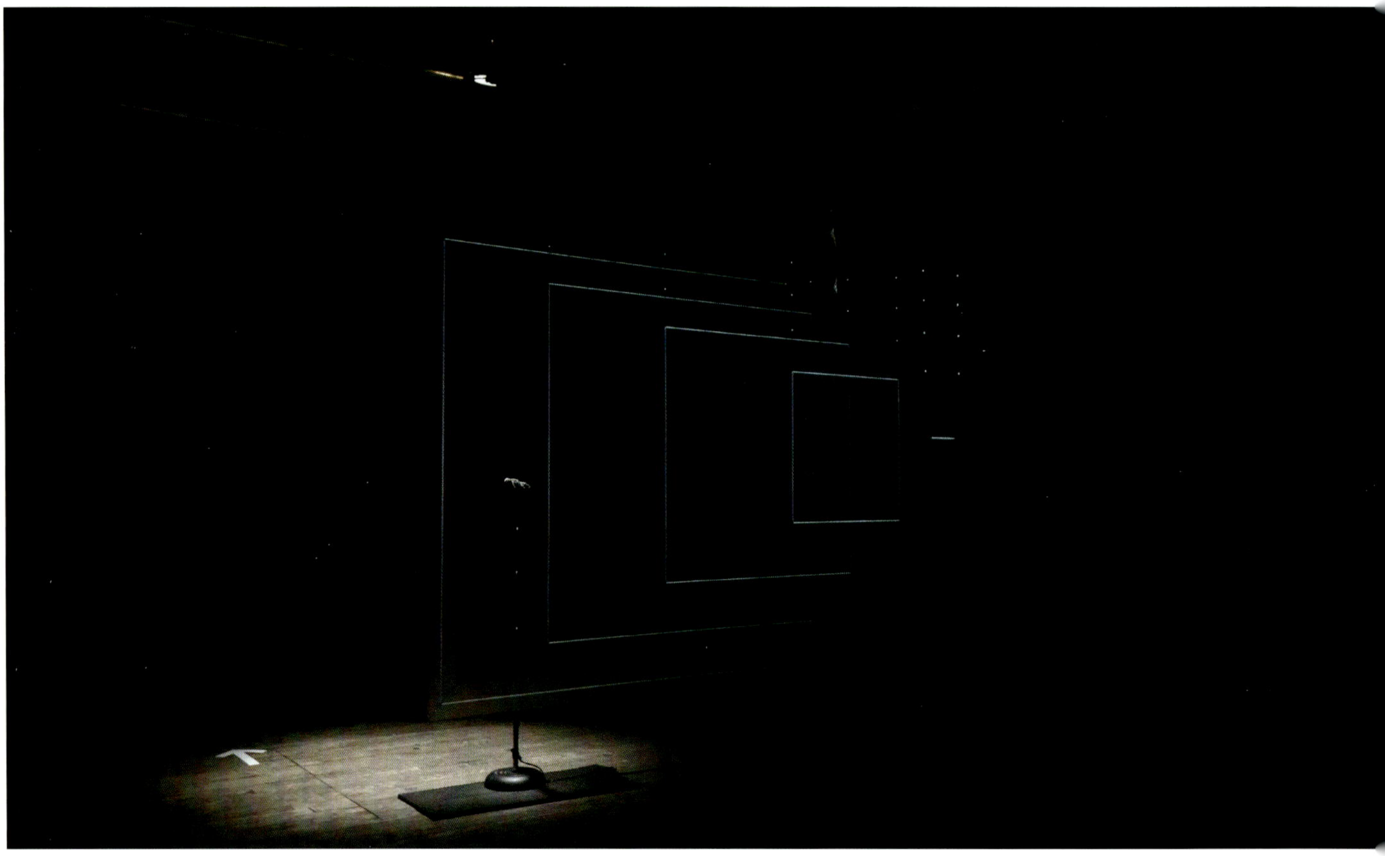

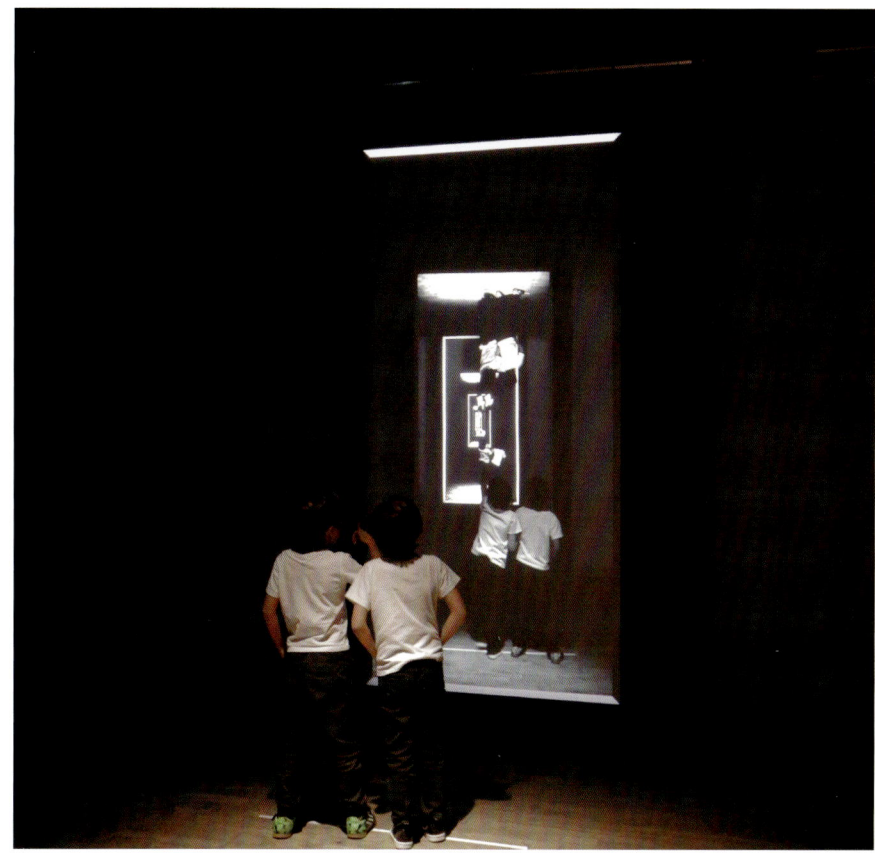

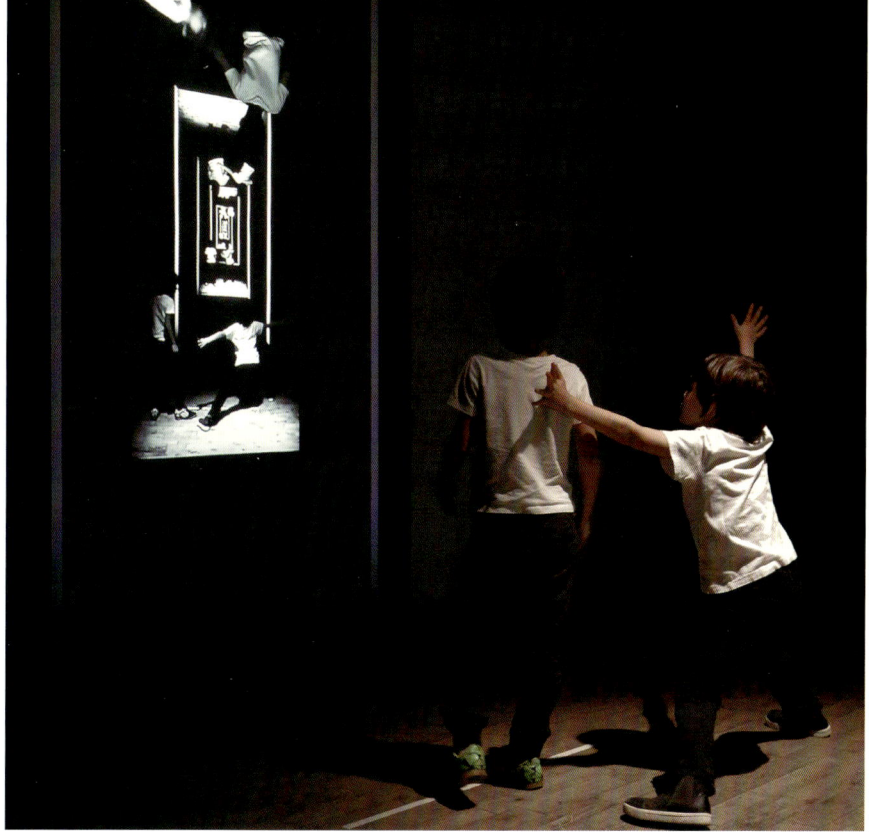

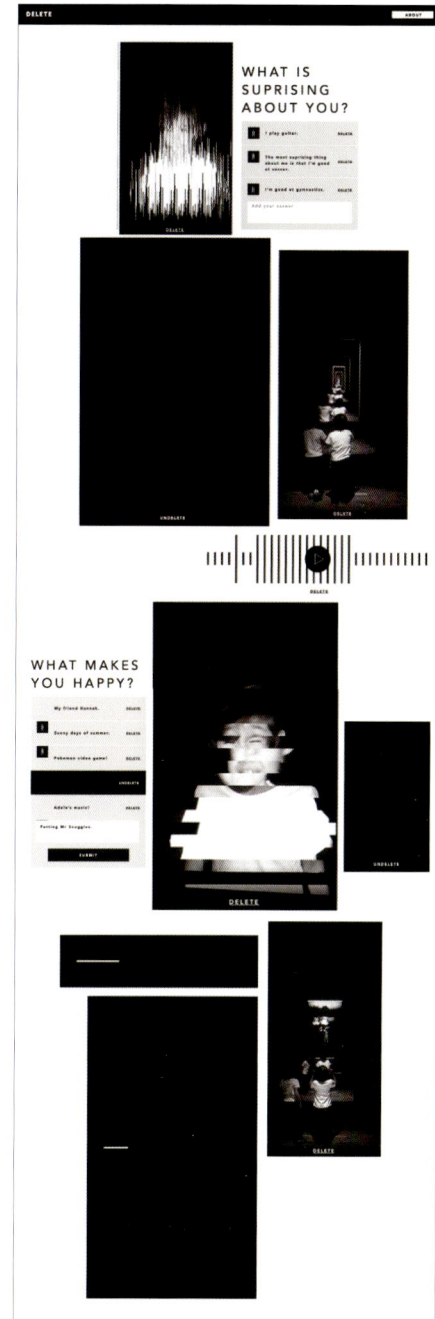

DELETE (Part 6)

After the experience, every visitor receives a link to DELETE, the final part of the experience.

Everything generated by their experience is displayed on an infinite feed. Anyone can decide to delete what they want. Anyone can also decide to undelete it.

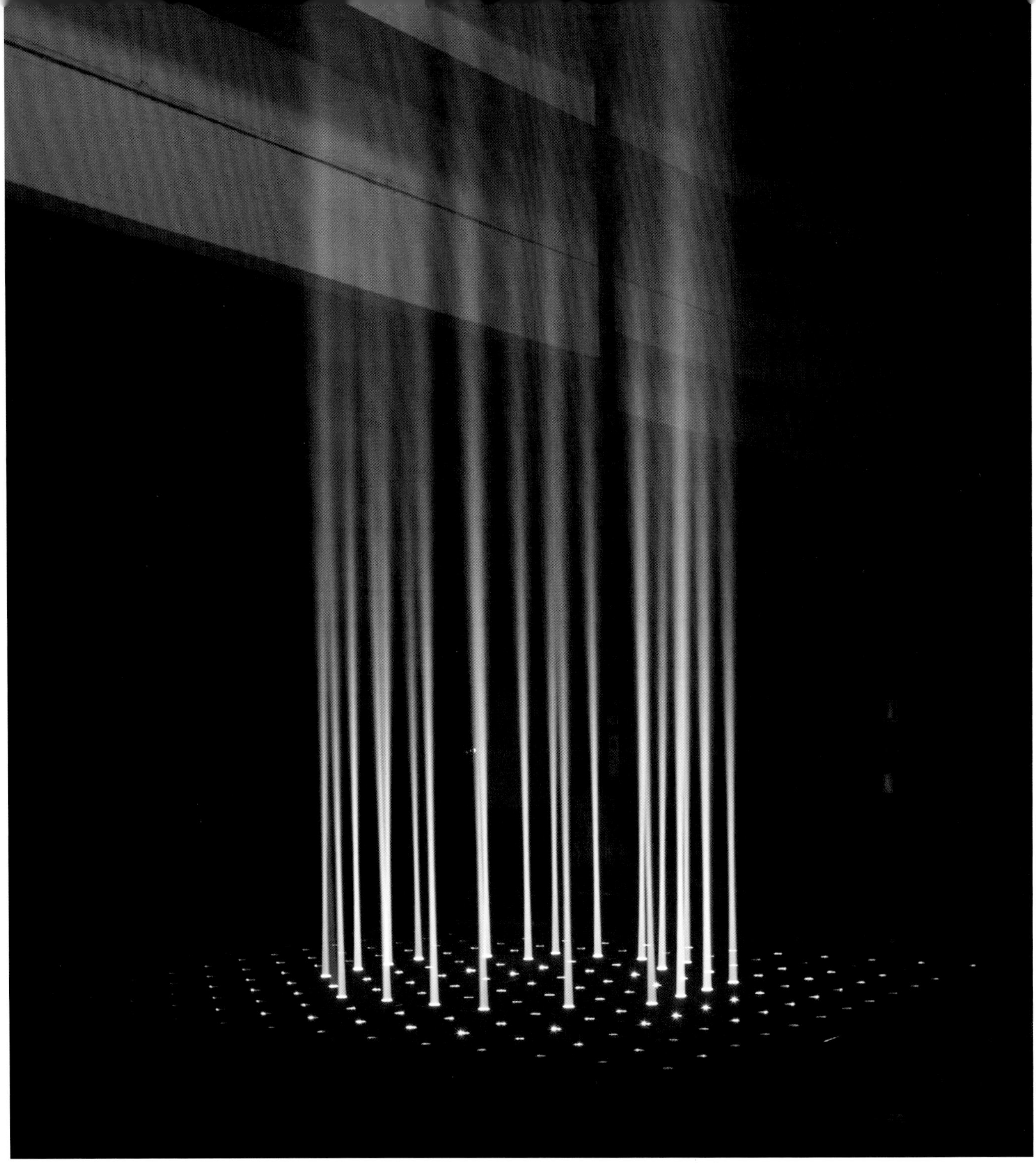

KONSTRUKTUR

—

Design: **YOKE**
Photography: **YOKE**

—

Konstruktur is an immersive light experience that explores light as material for creating temporary structures in urban space. The installation explores the fleeting urban spaces of tomorrow.

Konstruktur challenges the human perception of space. Placed directly onto the floor, the installation appears as a minimalist sculpture without a pedestal. The rhythmic movements of the light beams thus create a volatile architecture that for a while changes the space.

By adding smoke, the light beams are made visible to the human eye. This transforms an otherwise intangible form into a physical object and creates a temporary cubic form. Here the light beams appear almost like solid columns in the space.

Each light beam operates individually and reacts to movement. A camera detects bodies moving in front of the installation, which creates a temporary dialogue between the light architecture and the visitors.

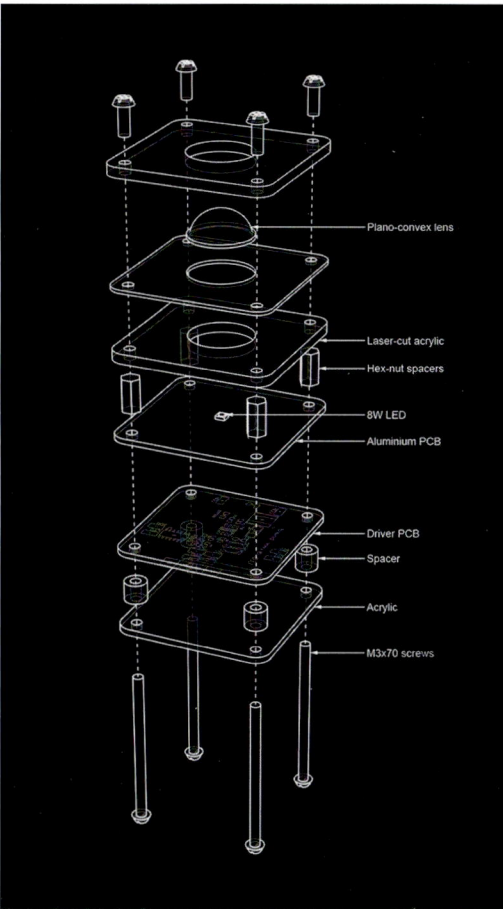

Plano-convex lens

Laser-cut acrylic

Hex-nut spacers

8W LED
Aluminium PCB

Driver PCB

Spacer

Acrylic

M3x70 screws

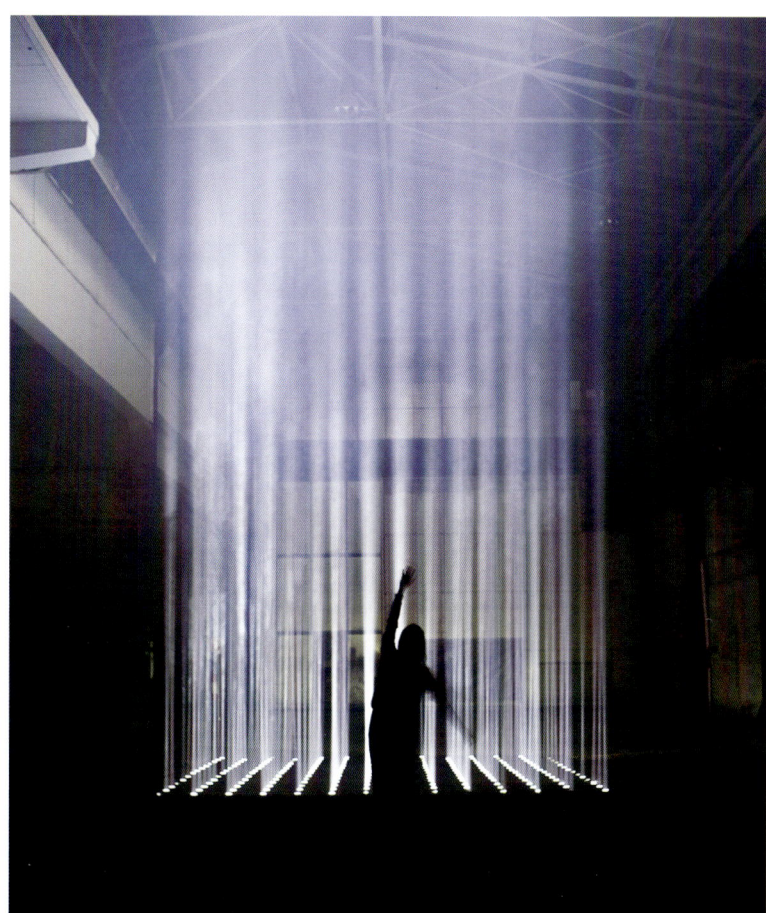

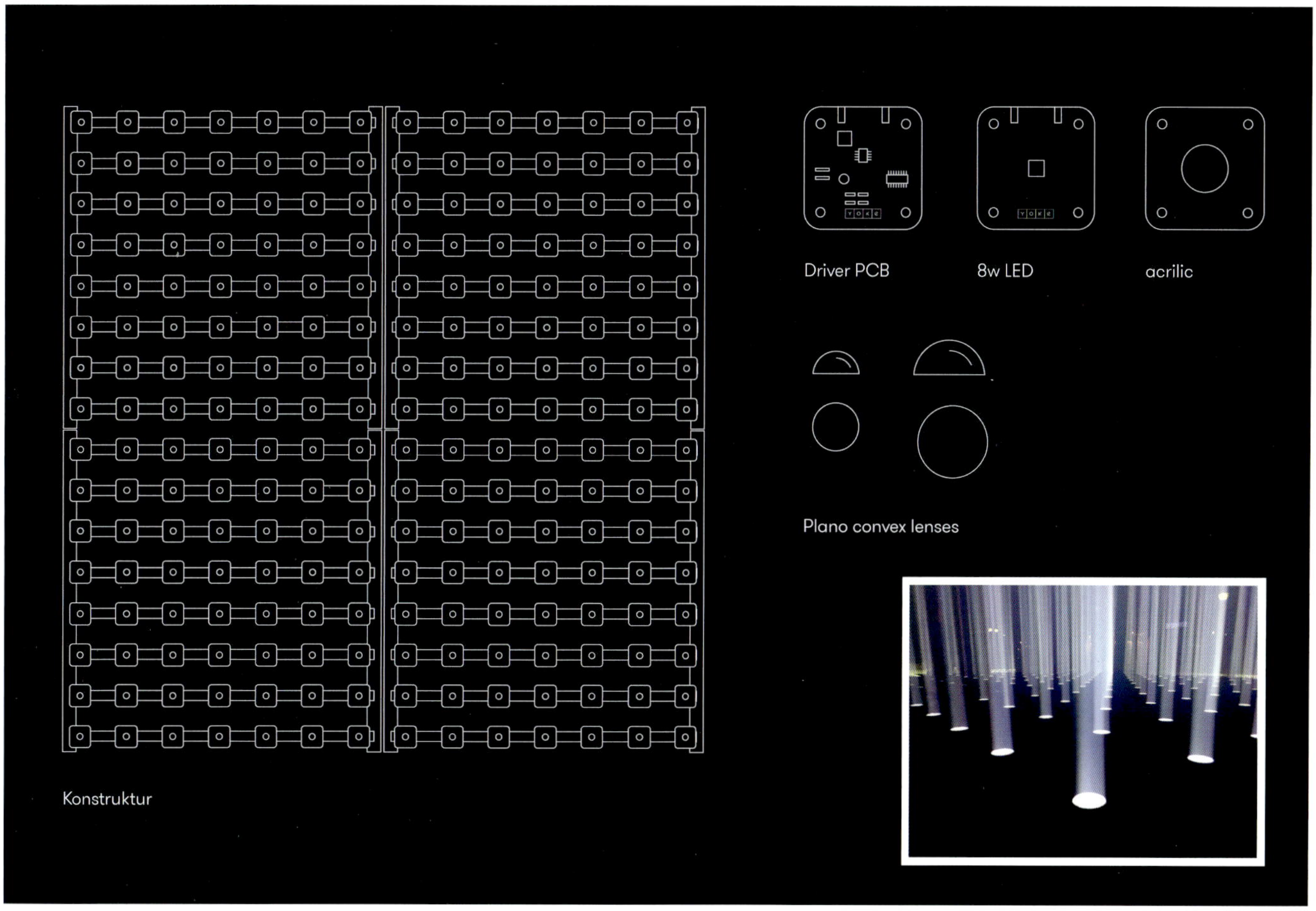

Konstruktur

Driver PCB   8w LED   acrilic

Plano convex lenses

WATERLIGHT GRAFFITI

—

Design: **Antonin Fourneau**

—

Waterlight Graffiti employs a high-resolution material, made of thousands of water-reactive LEDs. When applied to the frame of any individual LED, water creates an electrical bridge that provides the power required to light up the LED embedded under the surface. The quantity of water causes the LEDs' brightness to vary.

Inspired by the popular retro children's toy Lite-Brite, *Waterlight Graffiti*'s purpose is to be a new kind of reactive material on which users can draw or write ephemeral messages made of light. This project enables anyone to write on the wall of LEDs with a basic environment-friendly atomizer. Using water, which has neither shape nor color, to draw light is a magical experience, regardless of the participant's age or artistic sensibility.

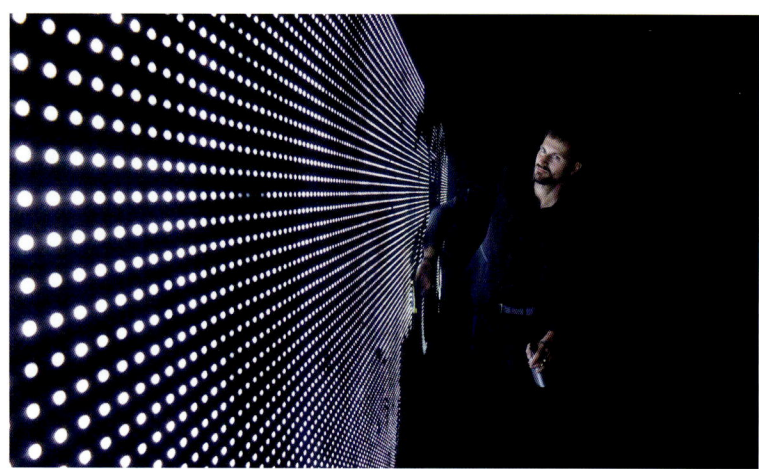

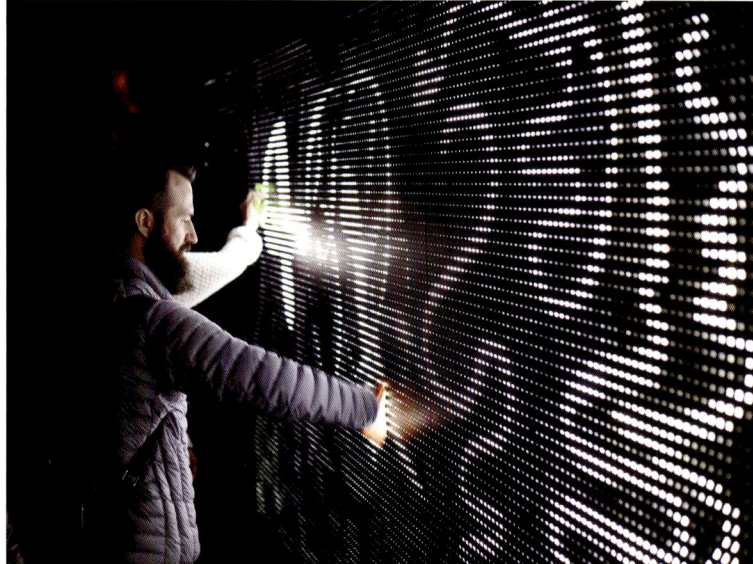

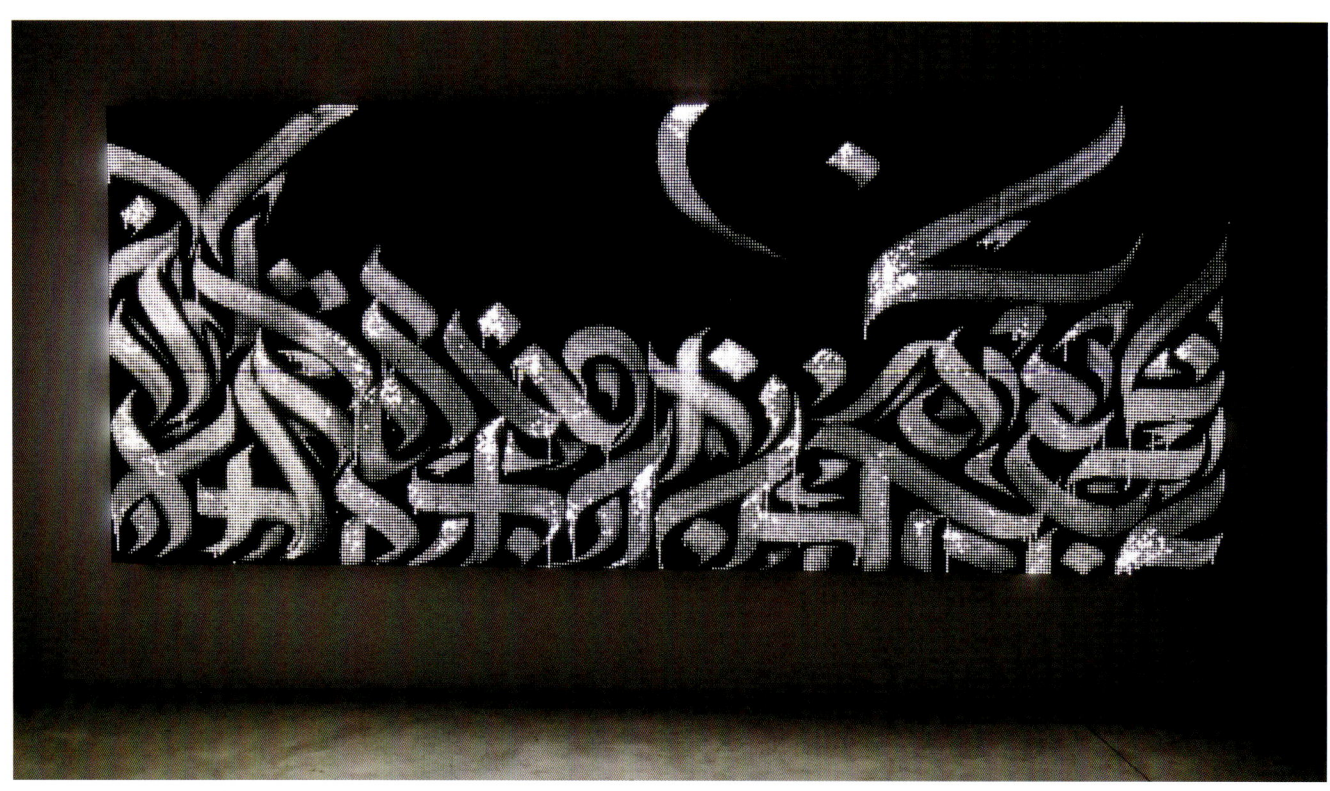

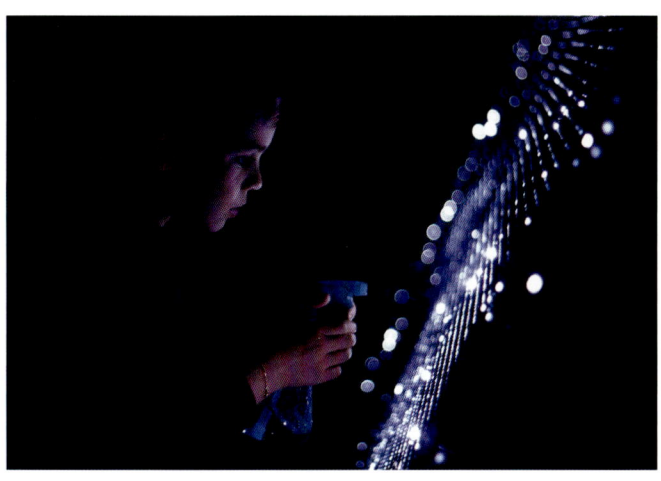
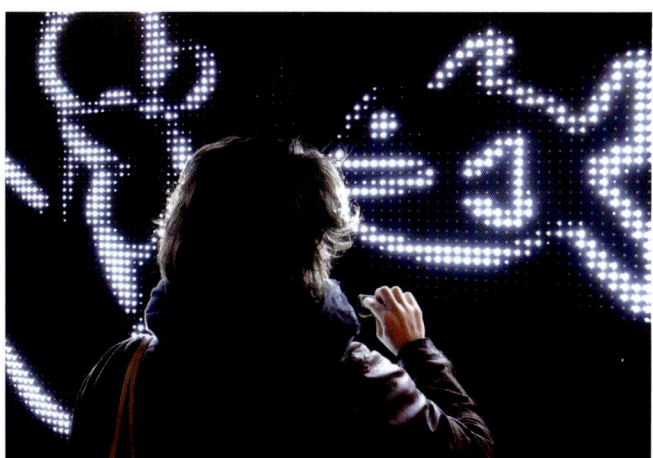
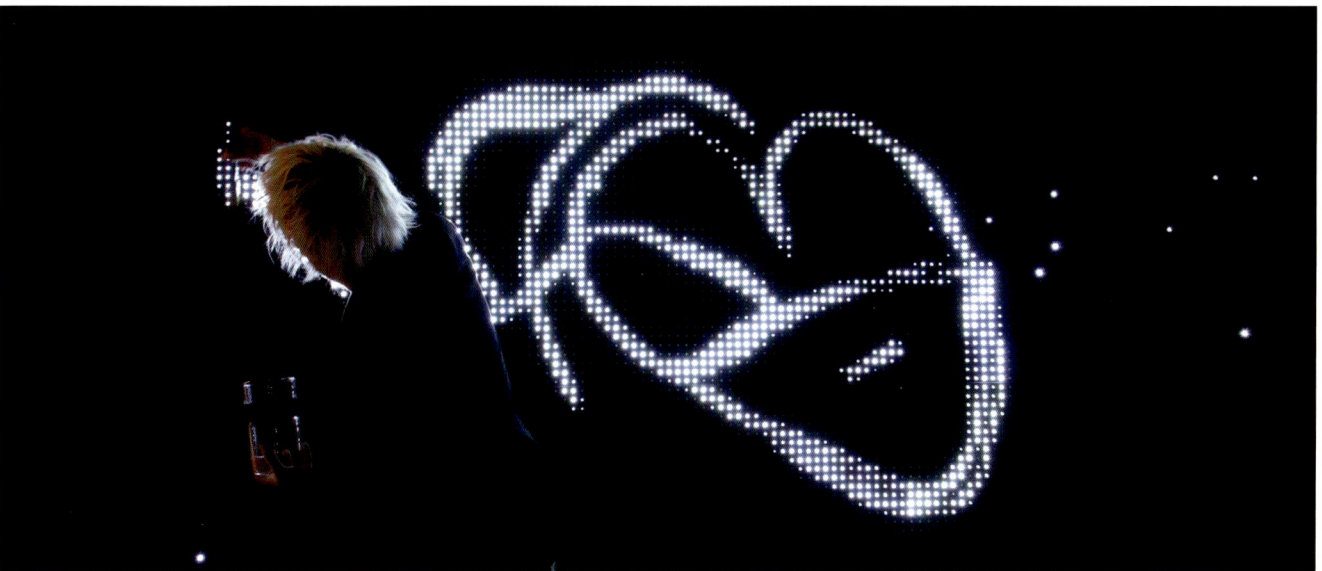
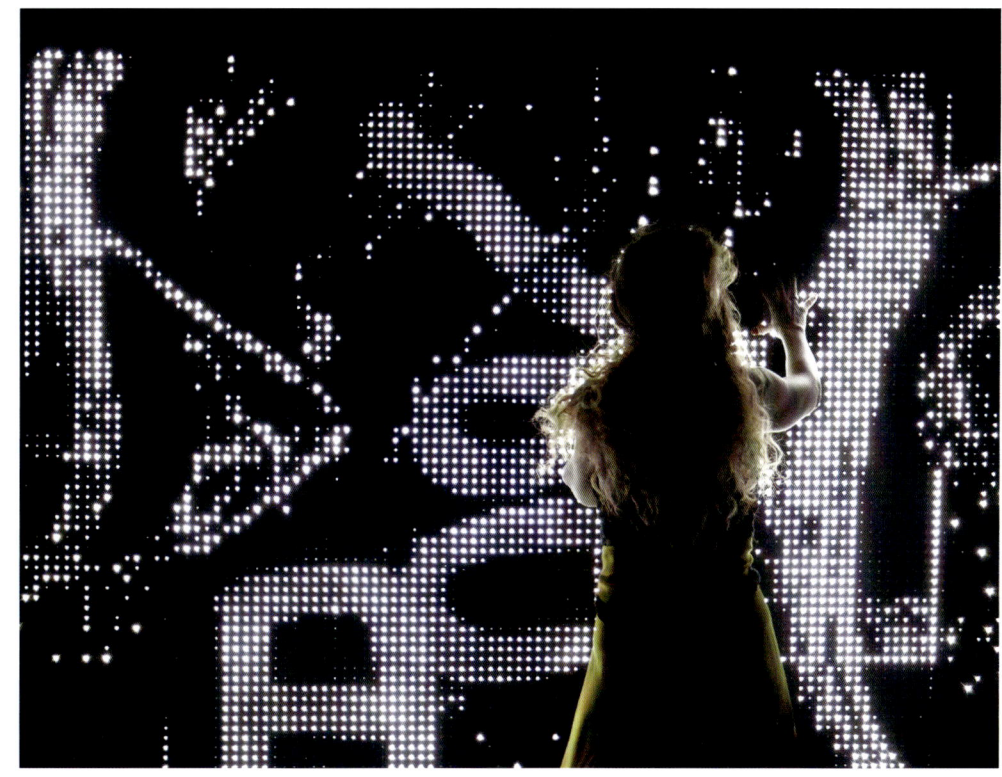

NOR MIND

—

Design: **Iregular**

—

NOR MIND is an interactive sculpture that reacts to the touch of the audience. Geometric patterns cover its surface and evolve constantly. With interaction, the random movement of the patterns is disrupted and follows the hand and body movements of the participant.

With geometric shapes, natural movements, and synthetic sounds inspired by nature, the experience aims to evoke emotions. The whole experience evolves in four phases.

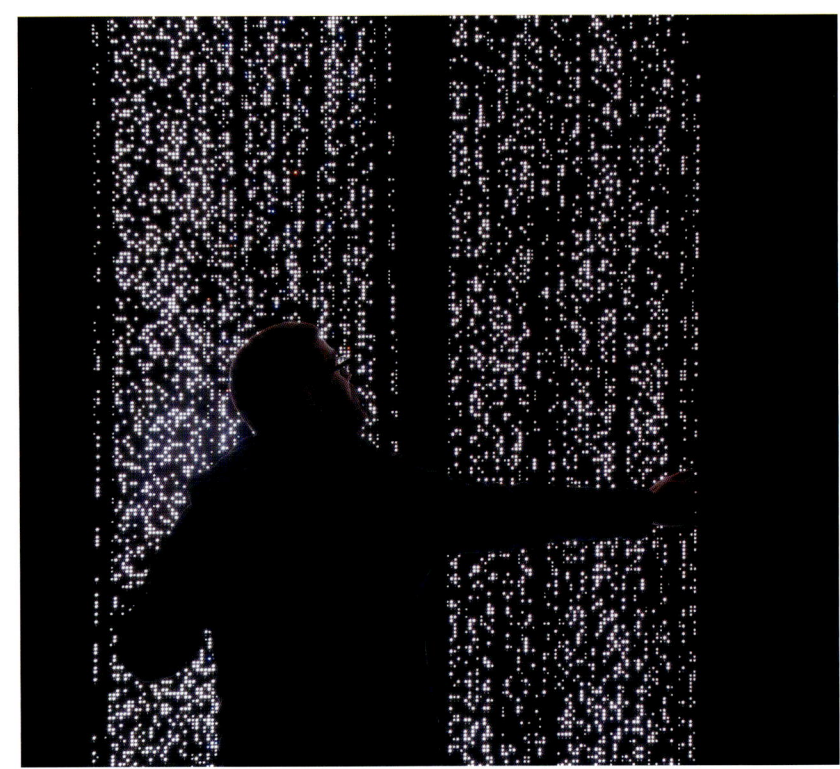

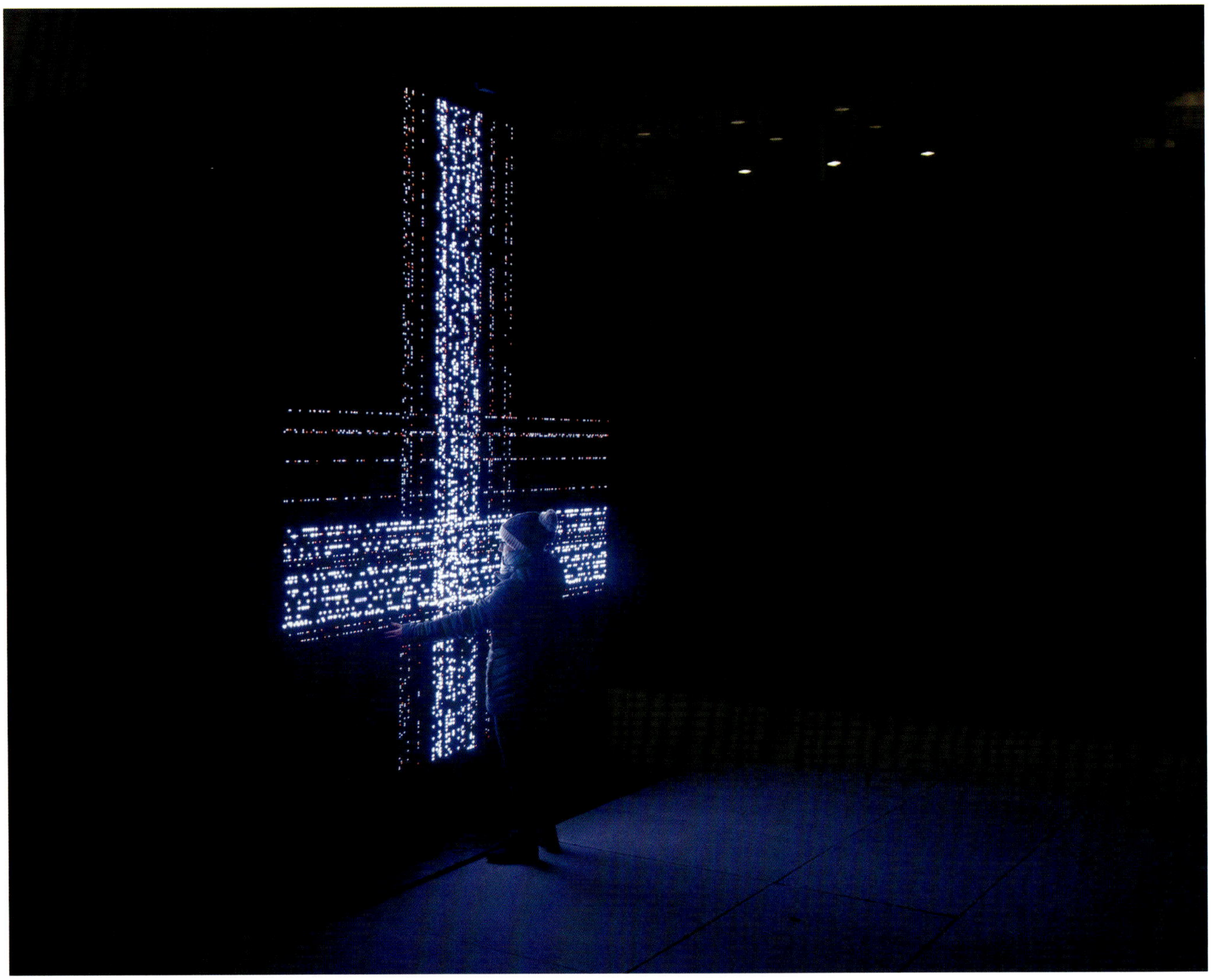

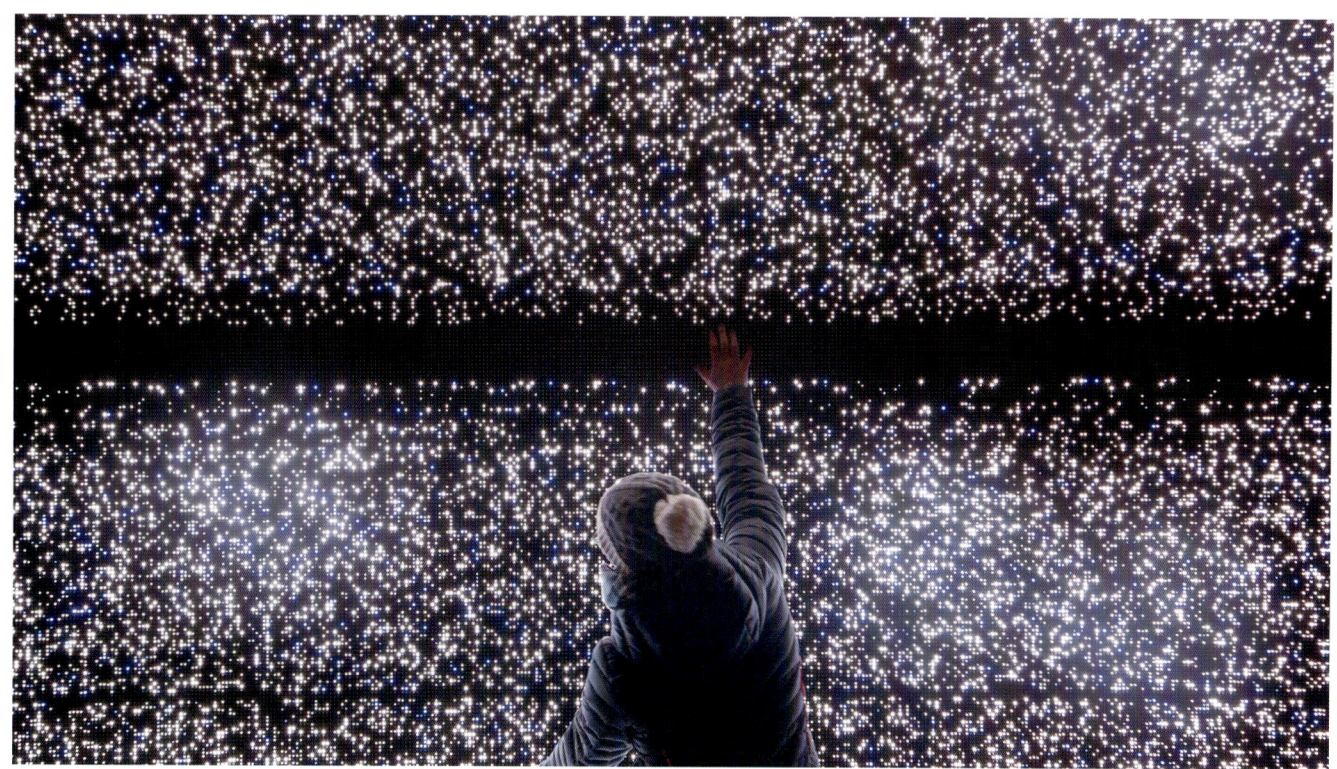

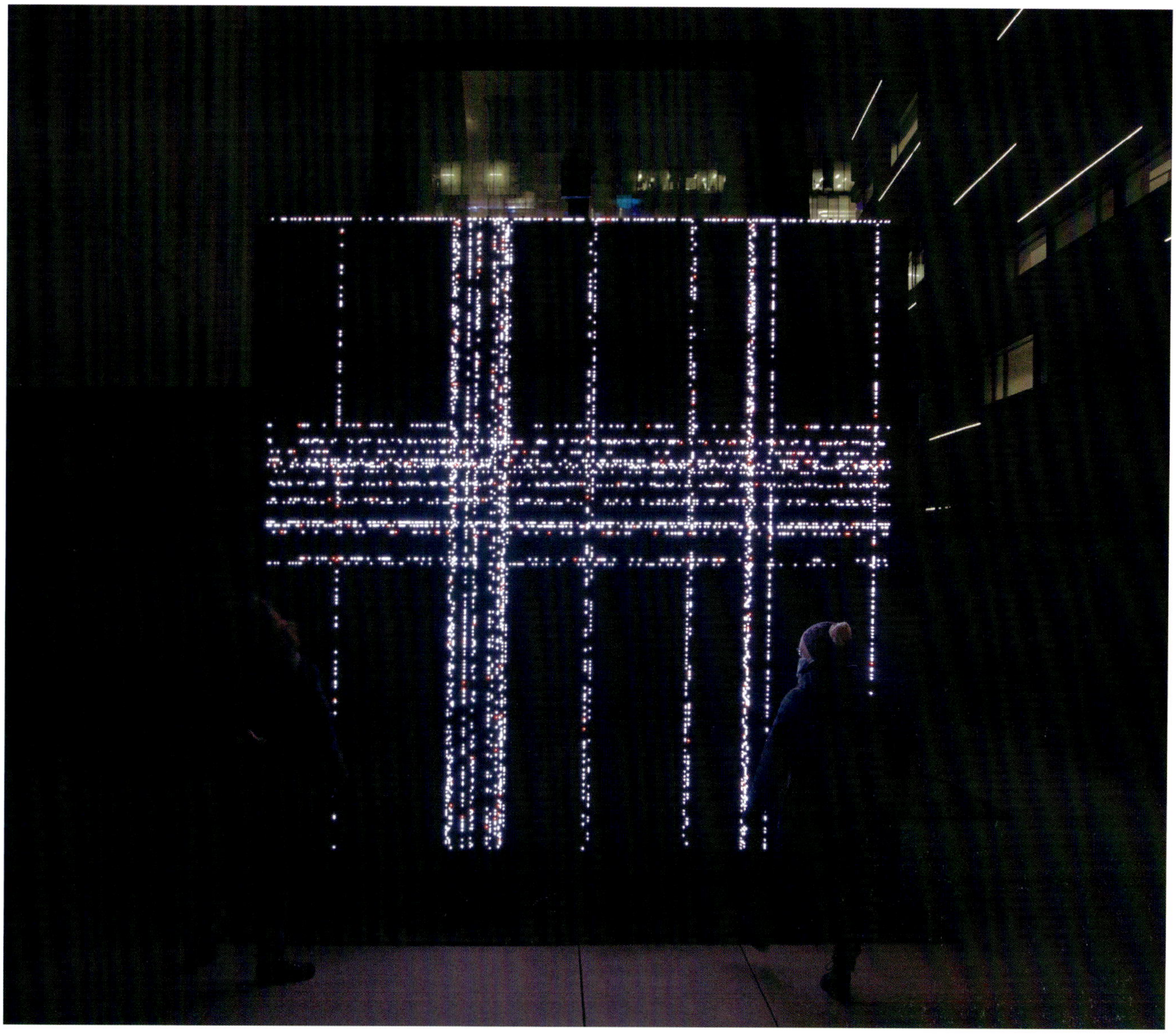

FLUX

—

Design: **YPL**

Creative & Code Development: **John Carpenter, Justin Shrake**

Photography: **Wolfgang Stahl**

—

FLUX is part of a recent series of installations that explores the spatial ambiguity of visually dense forms in space. This site-specific installation was designed for INHORGENTA MUNICH, an international tradeshow for jewelry and timepieces.

The software-based artwork visualizes real-time 3D sensor data of viewers, while several underlying algorithms constantly shift and distort the data into new configurations. The built-in processing software calculates and draws close to 200K triangles per frame at 60 fps.

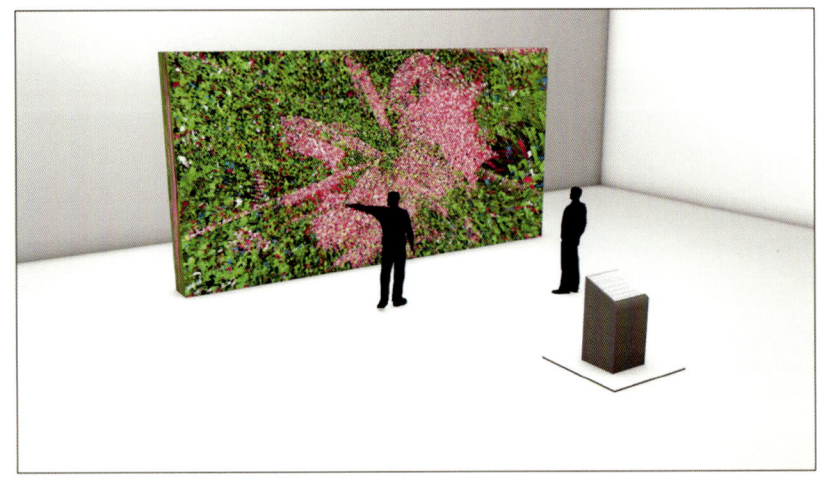

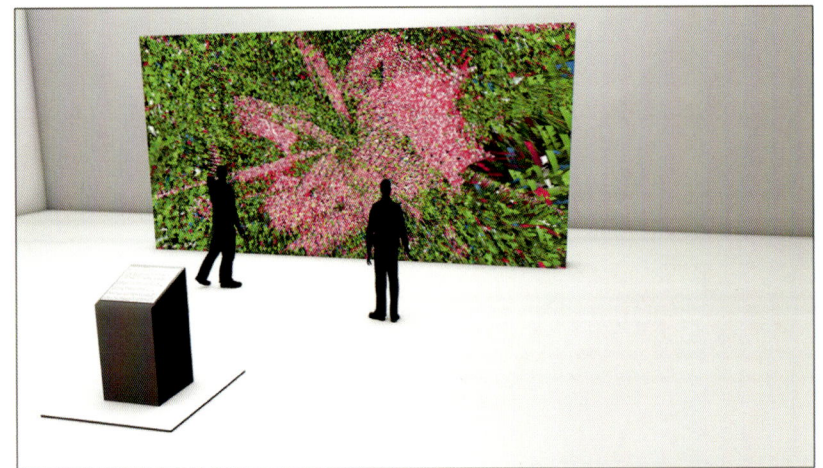

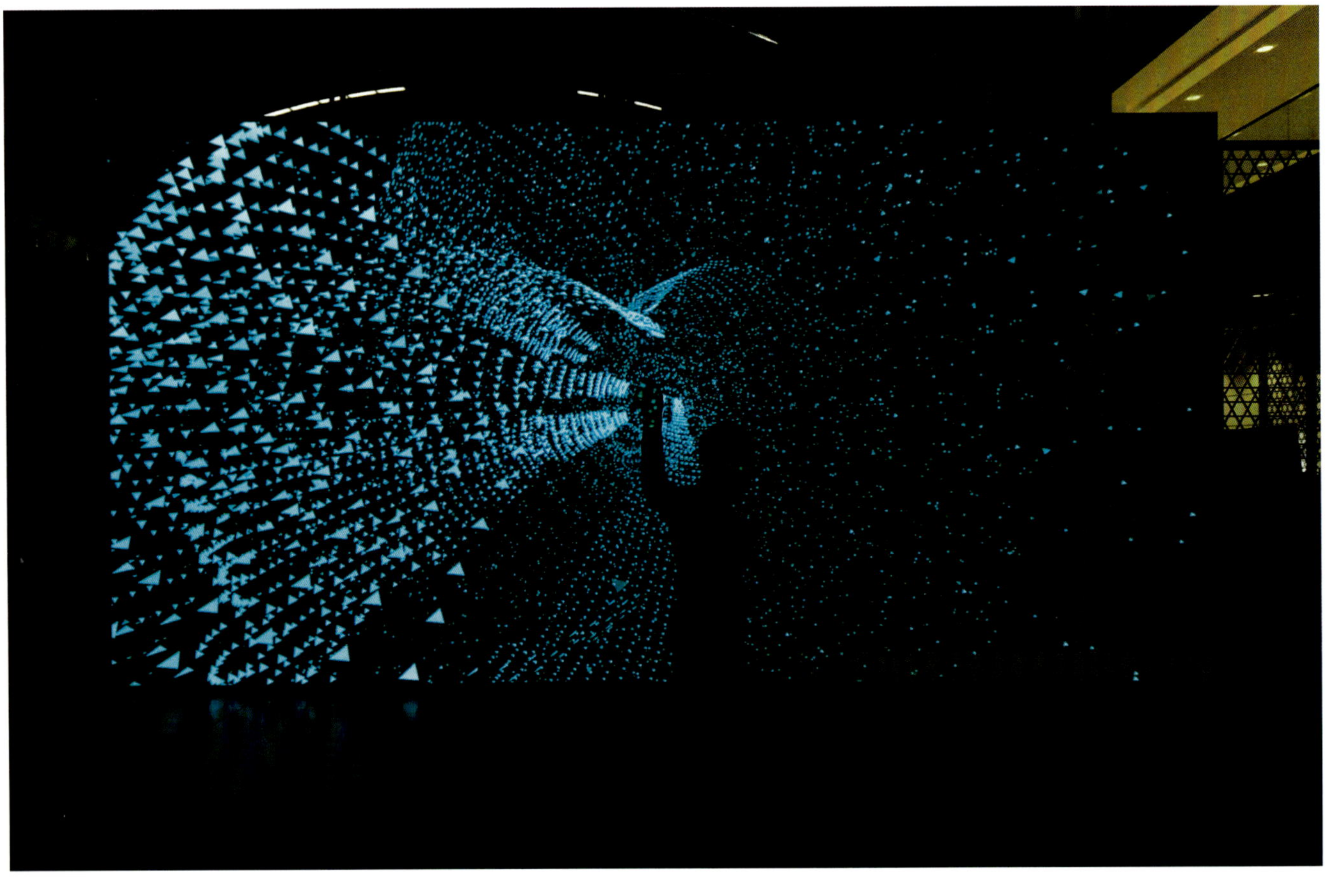

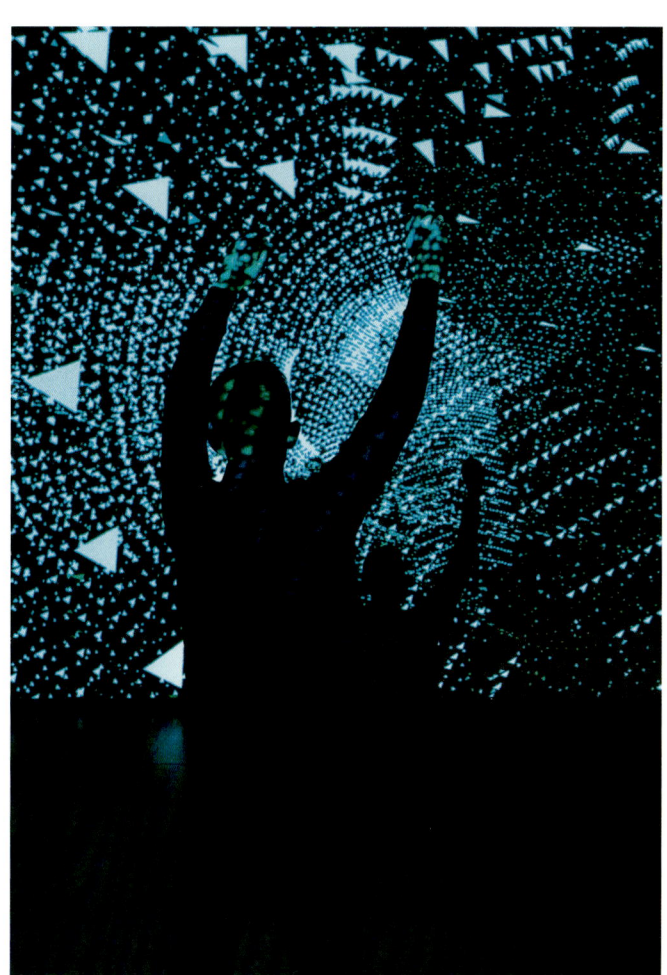
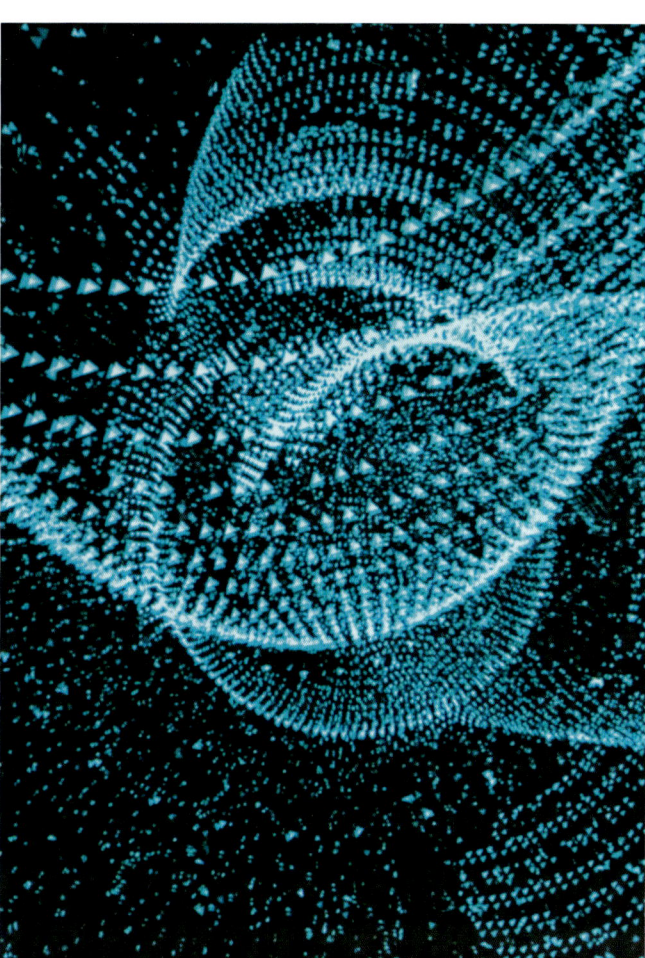

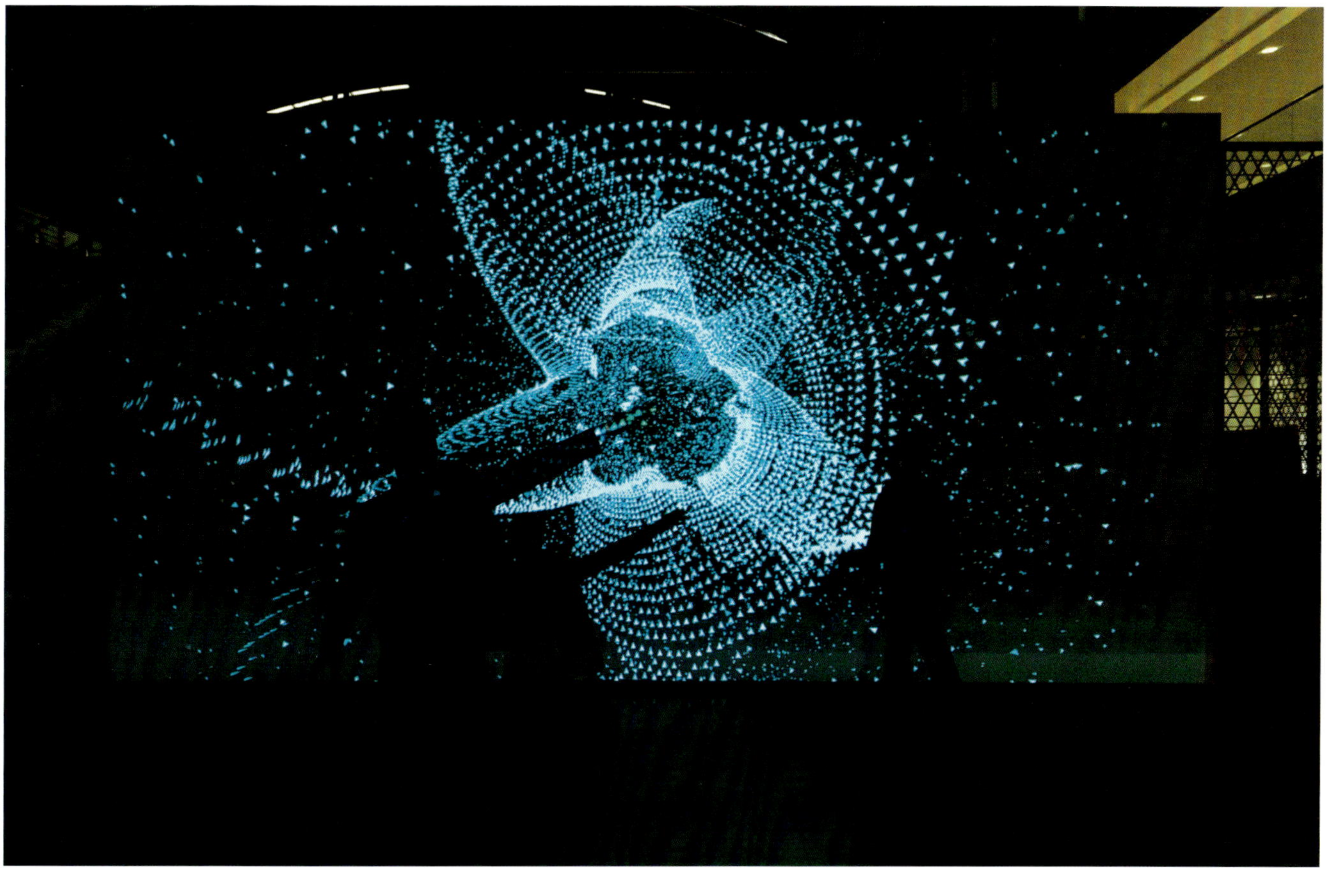

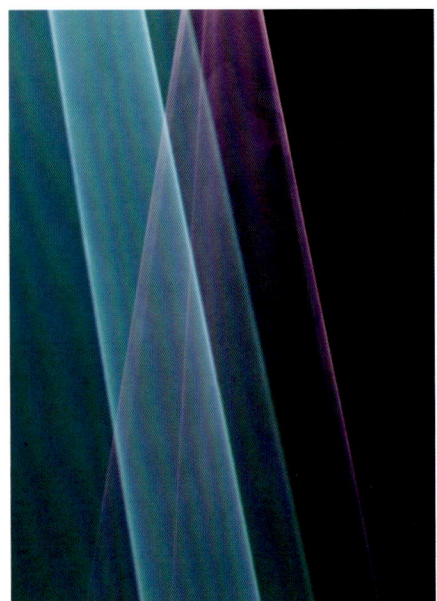

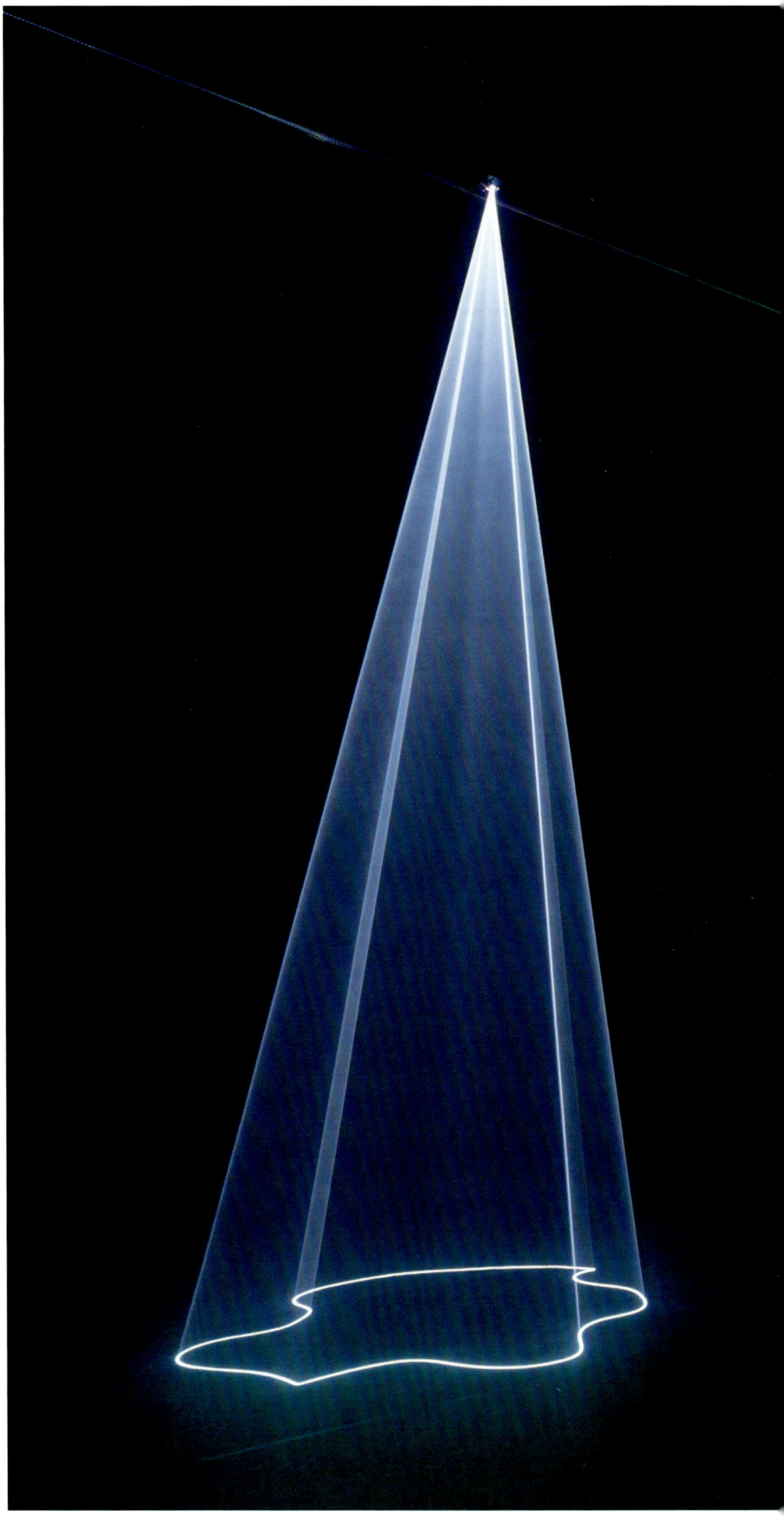

AURA

—

Design: **Studio Nick Verstand**

—

AURA is an audiovisual installation that materializes emotions into a perceptible, physical form. The audience's own emotional experience manifests as organic, pulsing light compositions of various forms, colors, and intensities. The installation pays tribute to *Solid Light Works* by artist Anthony McCall, further exploring light as a medium.

The transformation of emotions into light is accomplished by a scientific system, developed in collaboration with the Netherlands Organisation for Applied Scientific Research. Using multiple wearable biosensors, the system registers brainwaves, heartrate variability, and galvanic skin response. From the sensors, emotional "data" is analysed and metamorphosed into a symbolic representation as light. The differences in individuals' emotional responses, as influenced by a musical composition, become visible to all who are present.

AURA explores how this perceptual process influences our understanding of ourselves and of each other. The installation symbolizes the materialization of (internal) metaphysical space into (external) physical space.

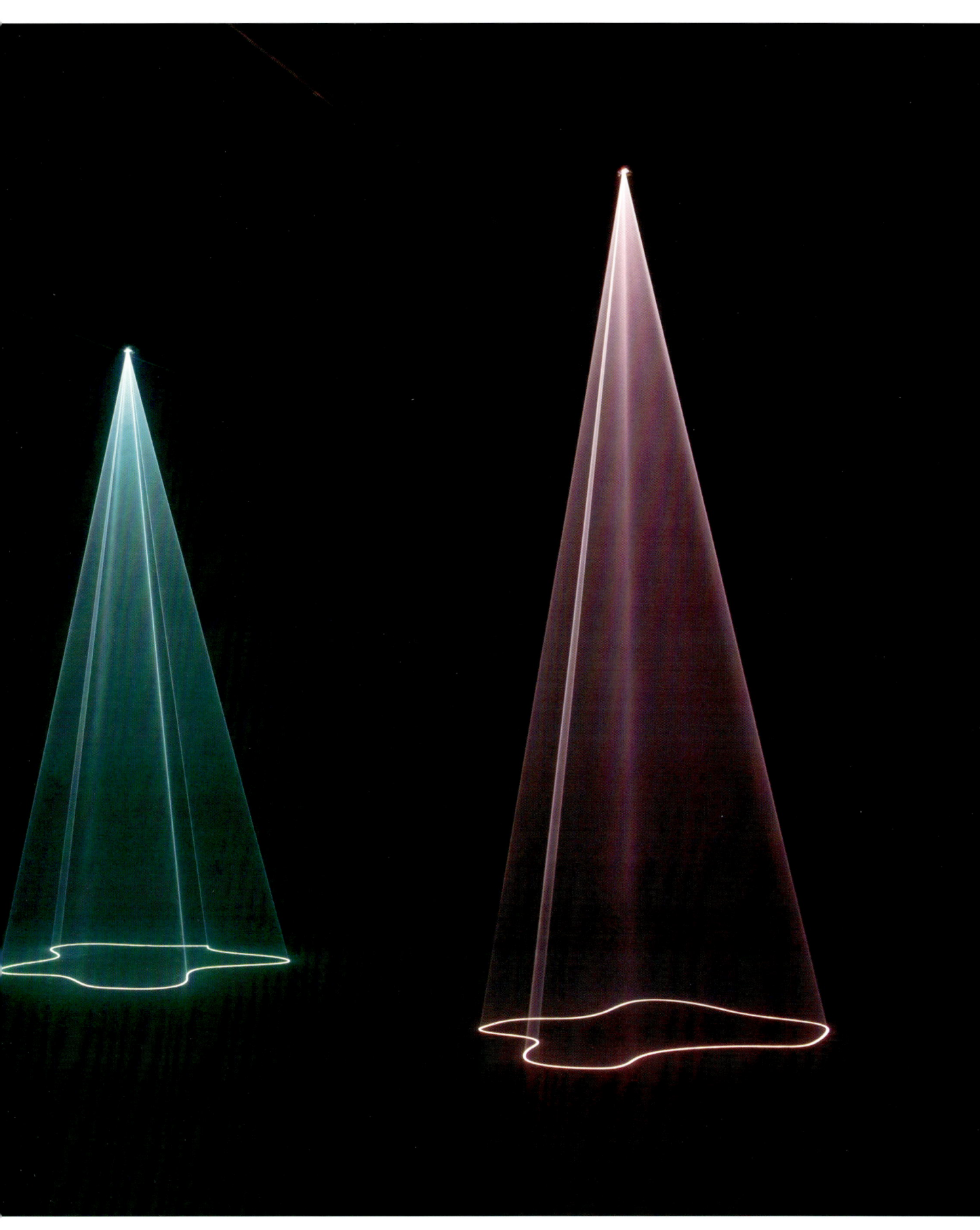

UNPAINTED

—

Design: **YPL, mayer+empl**
Photography: **YPL**

—

This room was transformed into a cathedral of light, allowing the visitor to become the focus and protagonist of the installation. Within the space, the participant was transported from reality into a digital self, and dramatized as repeating artwork on the walls. At the same time, the projections were distorted, reacting to individual sound waves.

Created by Yves Peitzner and mayer+empl for the *UNPAINTED* art fair in Munich, the installation was a digital interpretation of analog art, based on the works of pop art icon Andy Warhol.

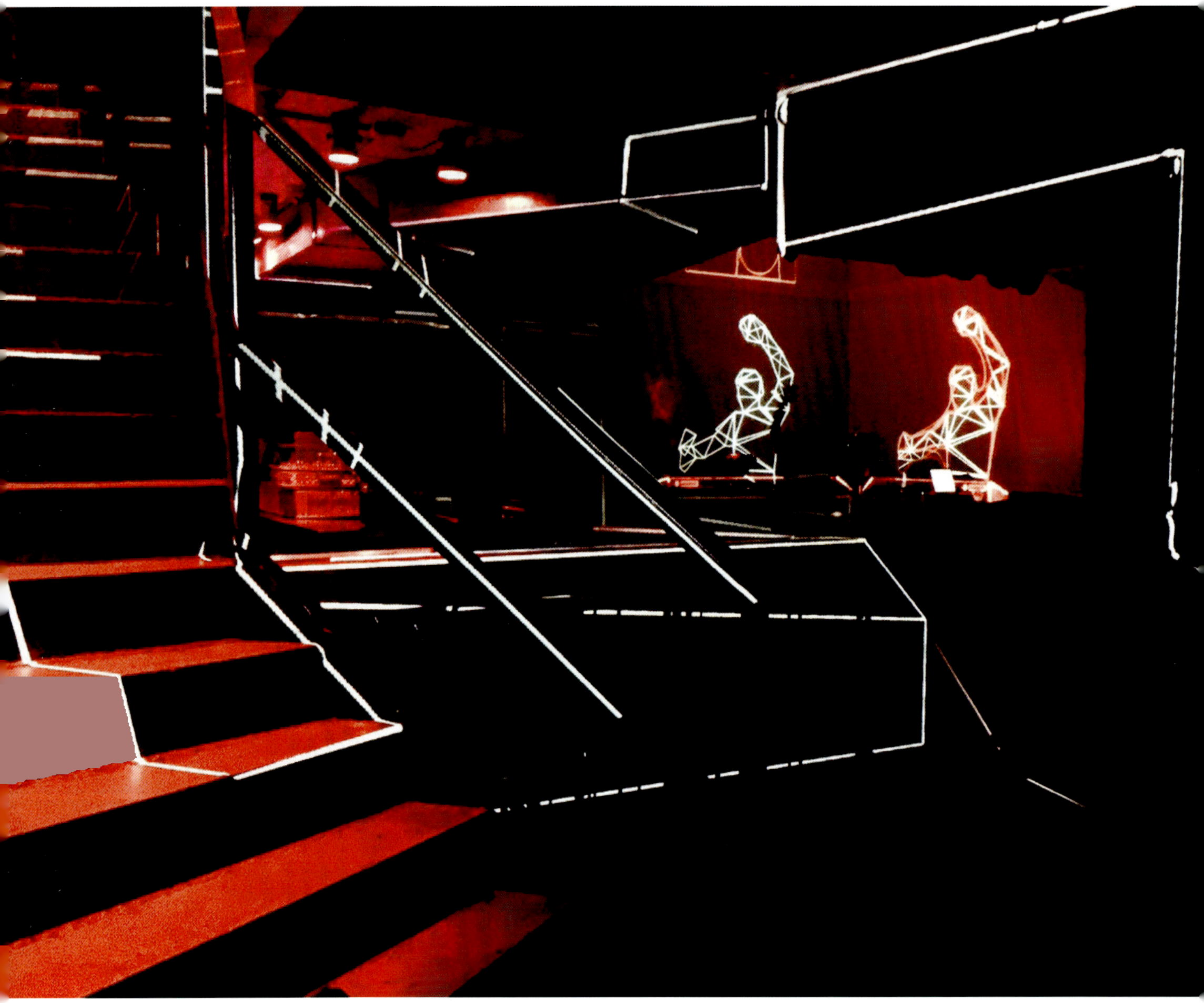

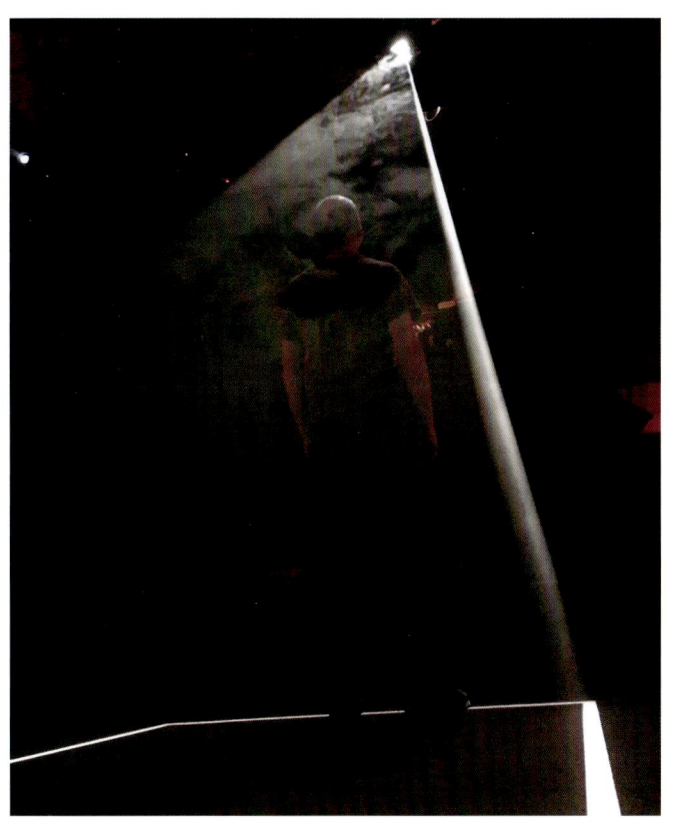
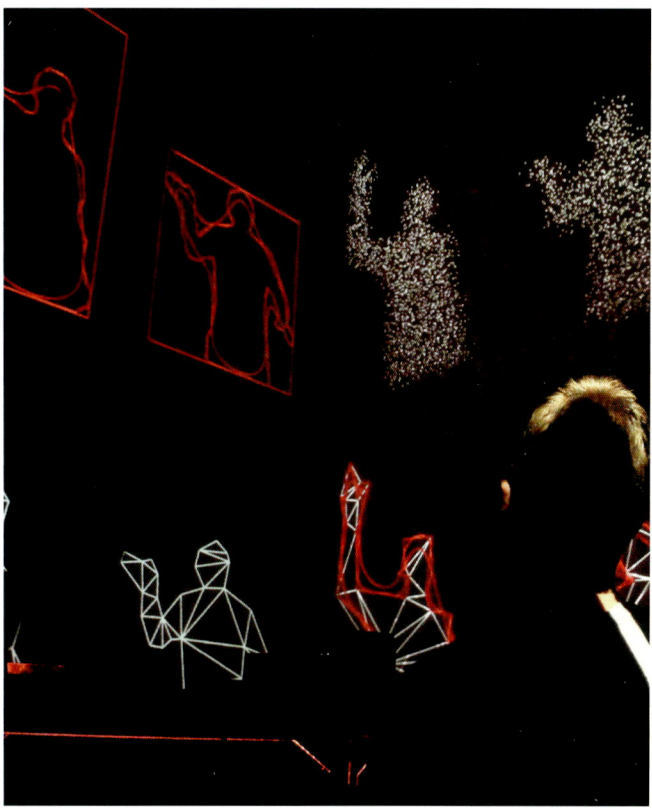

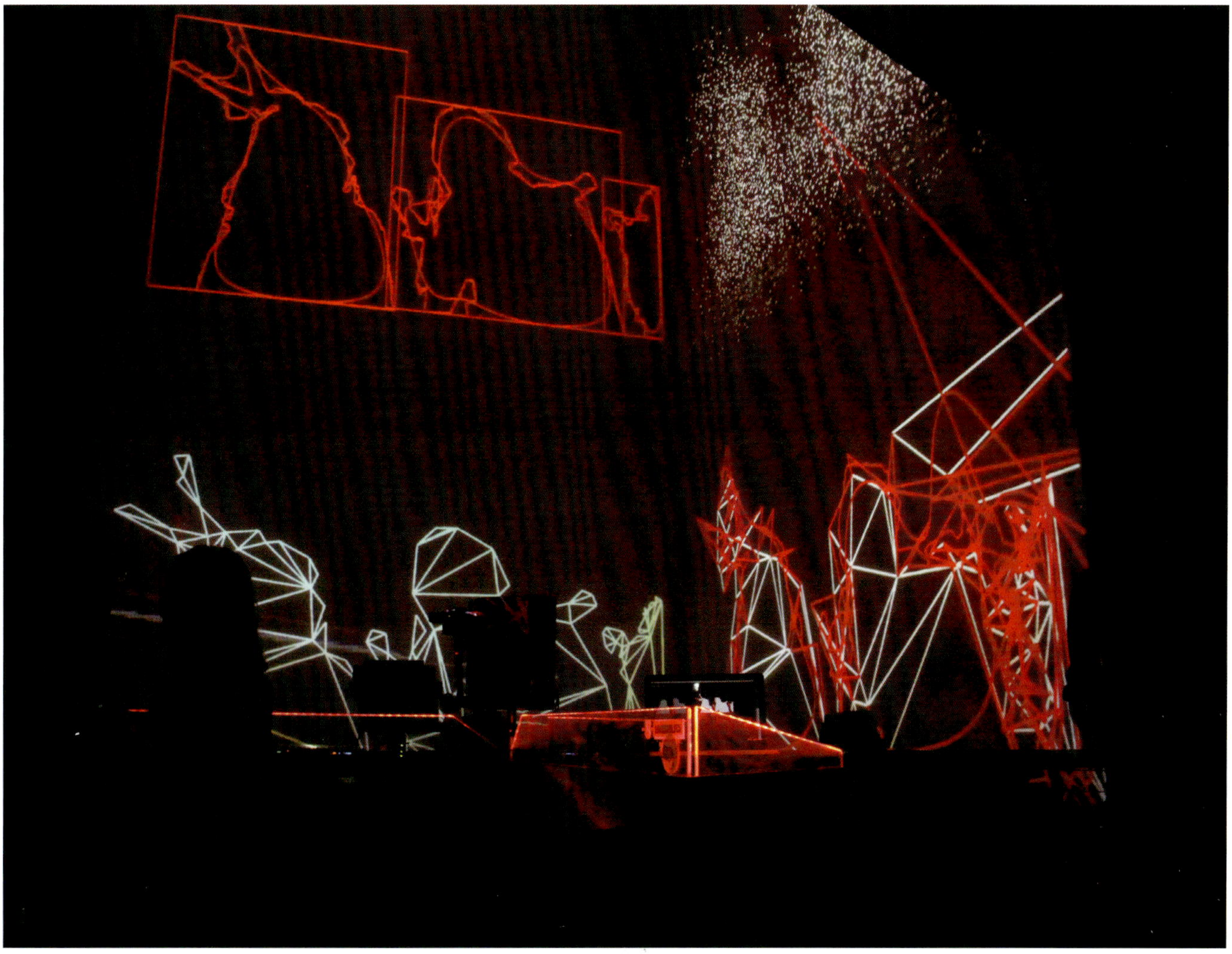

LIGHT PARTICLES

—

Agency: **Claudia Paz Lighting Studio**
Concept Design & Art Direction: **Claudia Paz**
Technology Design: **Cesar Castro**
Interactive Programming: **Chris Plant**
Sound Design: **Neil Spragg**

—

Light Particles is an awe-inspiring experience of light, sound, speed and generative content that uses visitors' body movements as input. The installation offers the visitor a canvas to display their free expression, and acts as a mirror to their emotions.

Eight scenarios were created—some related to natural phenomena, others to "magic" to pull out the child inside all of us, and others are auto-generated organic content that echo the movements of participants.

Visitors interact with the screen using a touch panel connected to the server. This panel also allows users to turn the screen on and off and to change scenarios.

The sound was designed to immerse visitors in each of the scenes, with a multi-layered soundtrack that creates depth and emotion.

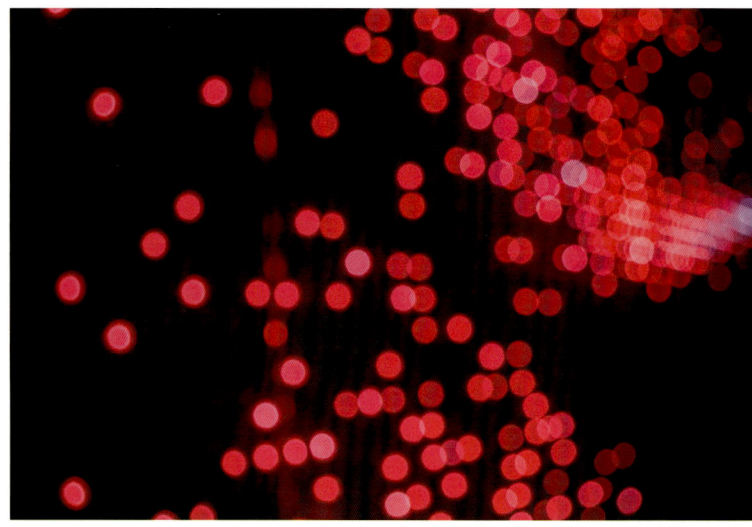

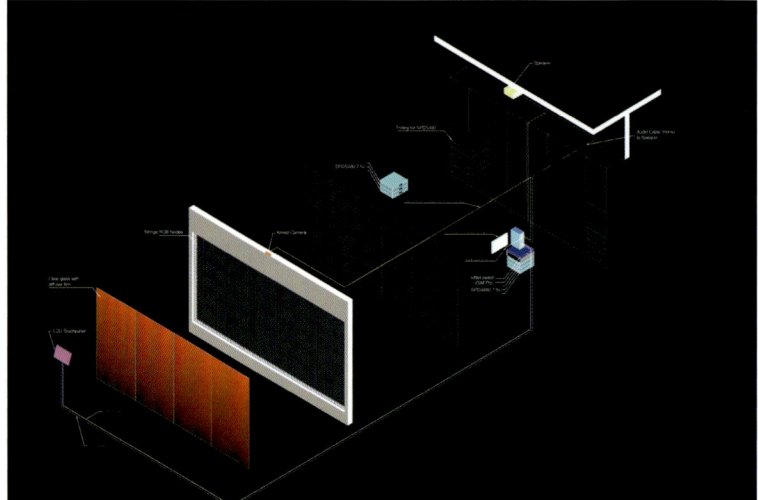

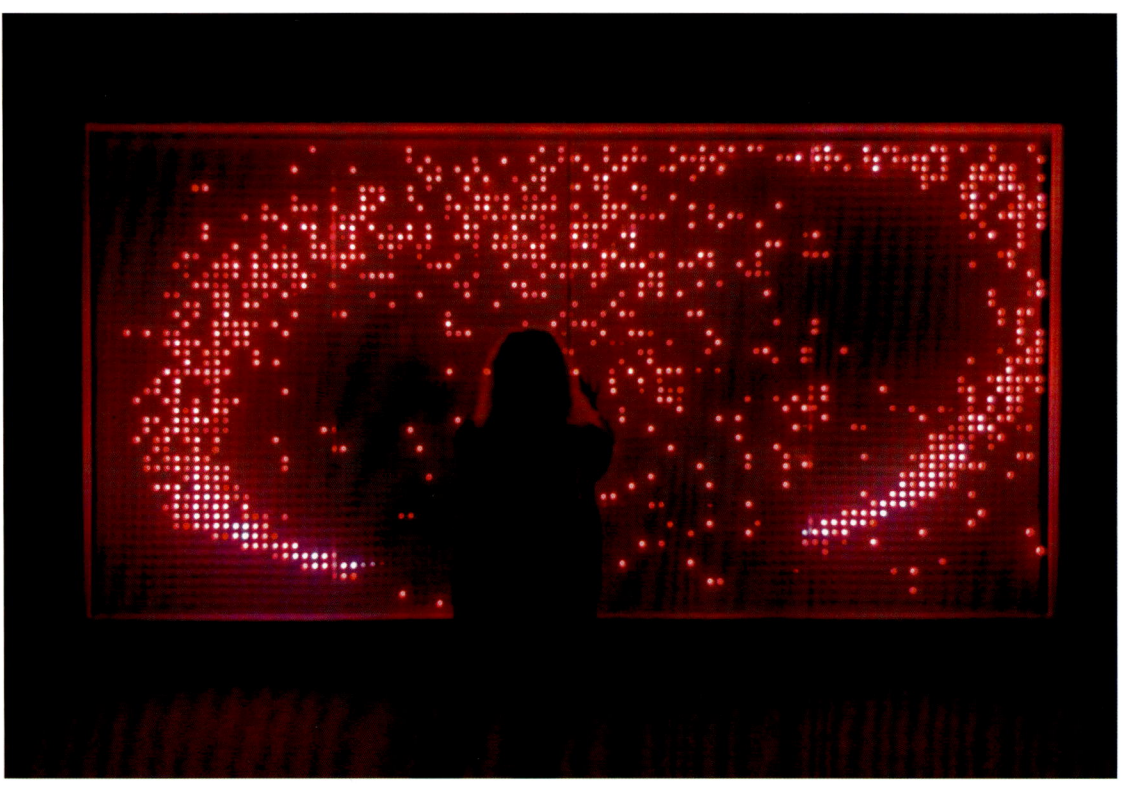

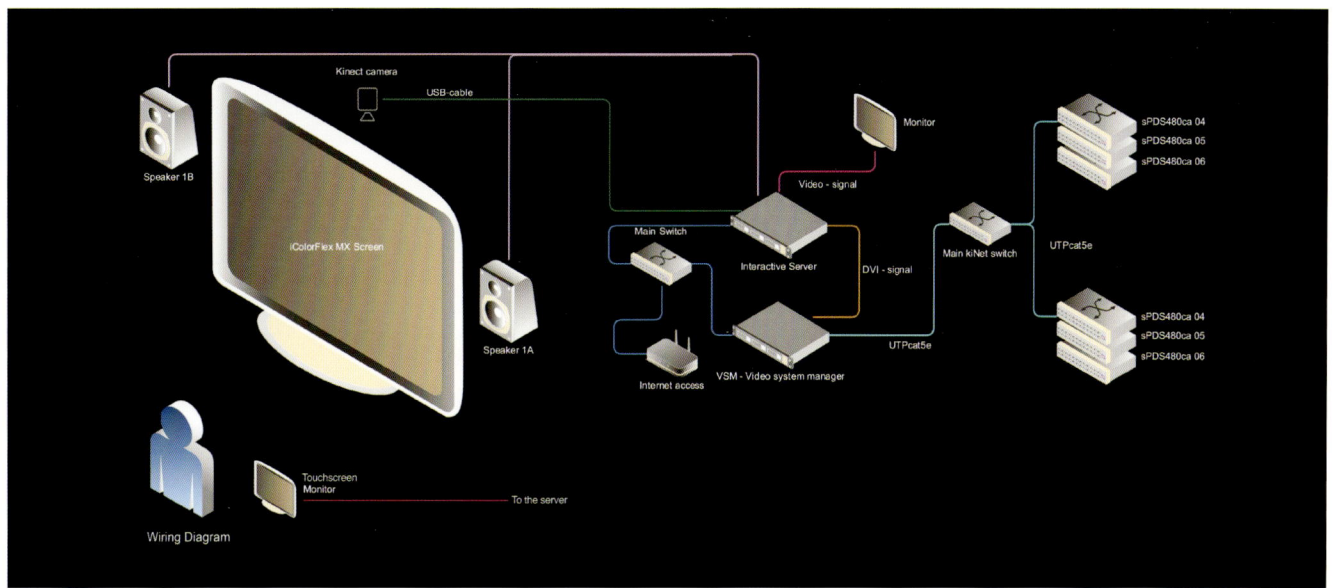

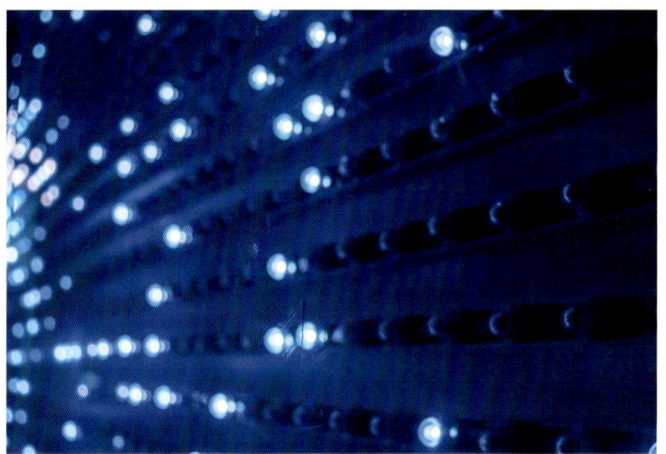

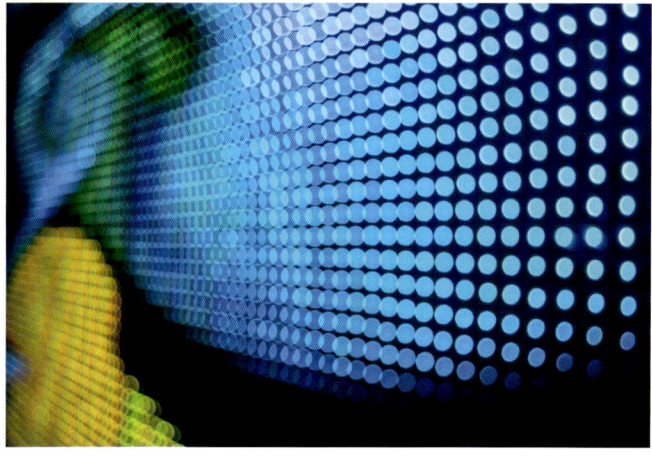

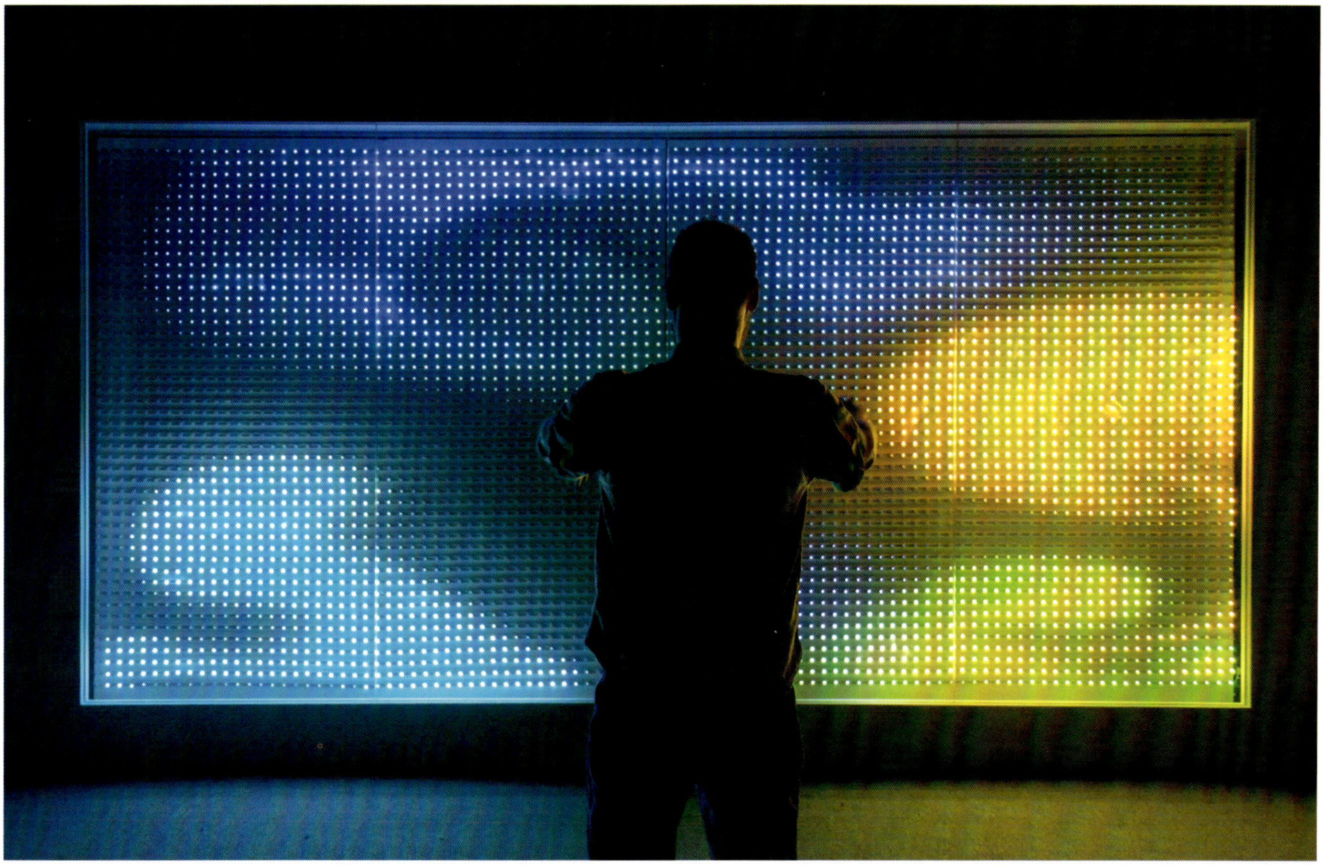

FIRE & ICE

—

Design: **Cinimod Studio**
Photography: **Cinimod Studio**

—

Inspired by Robert Frost's famous poem, *Fire & Ice*, Cinimod Studio produced an interactive art installation at WestQuay Shopping Centre in Southampton. The installation provides the viewing public with the unique opportunity to assume the personified role of either "fire" or "ice," making them integral performers within the piece.

Presented in a magnificent landscape format, the two opposing elements react to viewers' gestures. With increased movement, the ferocity of the fire and the glacial blizzard of the ice become more pronounced, thus triggering an explosive real-time transition of elemental particle simulations. Displayed on a monolithic LED video wall, the volume of light emanating from the piece further fills the public realm, encapsulating all passers-by in its glow. The aesthetic remains simple, yet powerful, and the interactions of fluctuating movements creates an artistic and visually compelling reinterpretation of the beloved Frost poem.

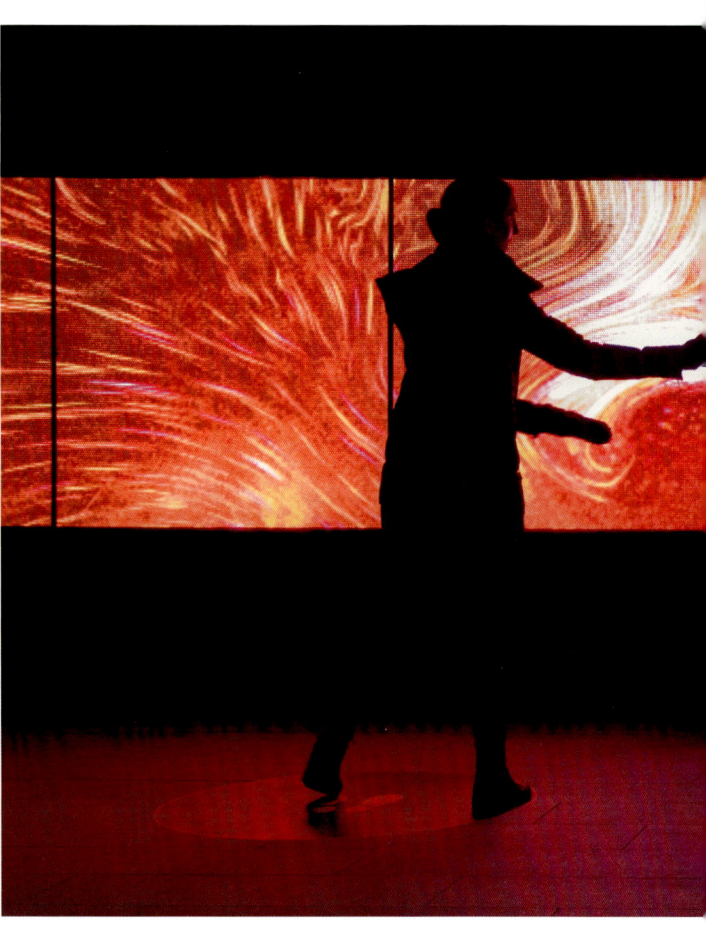

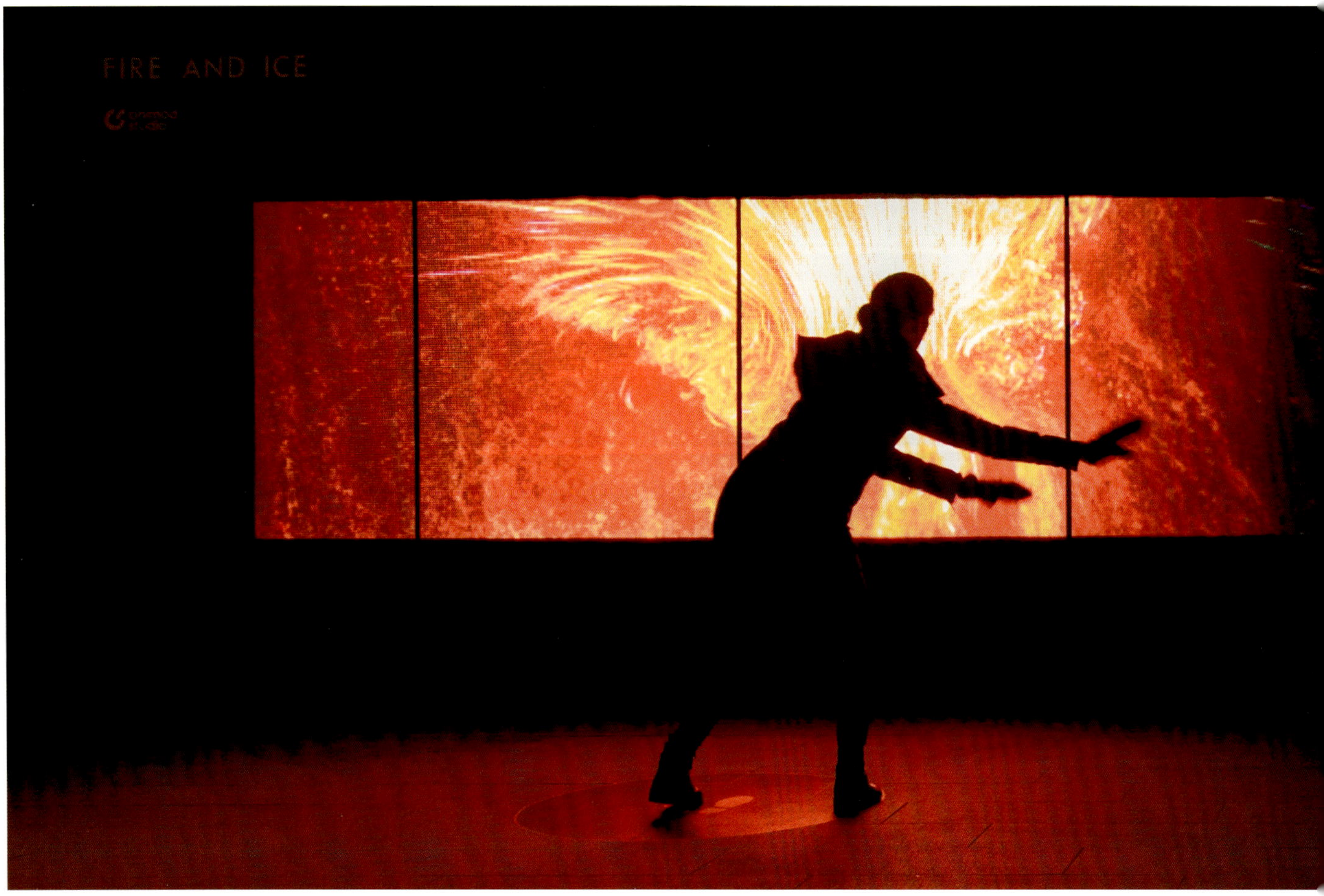

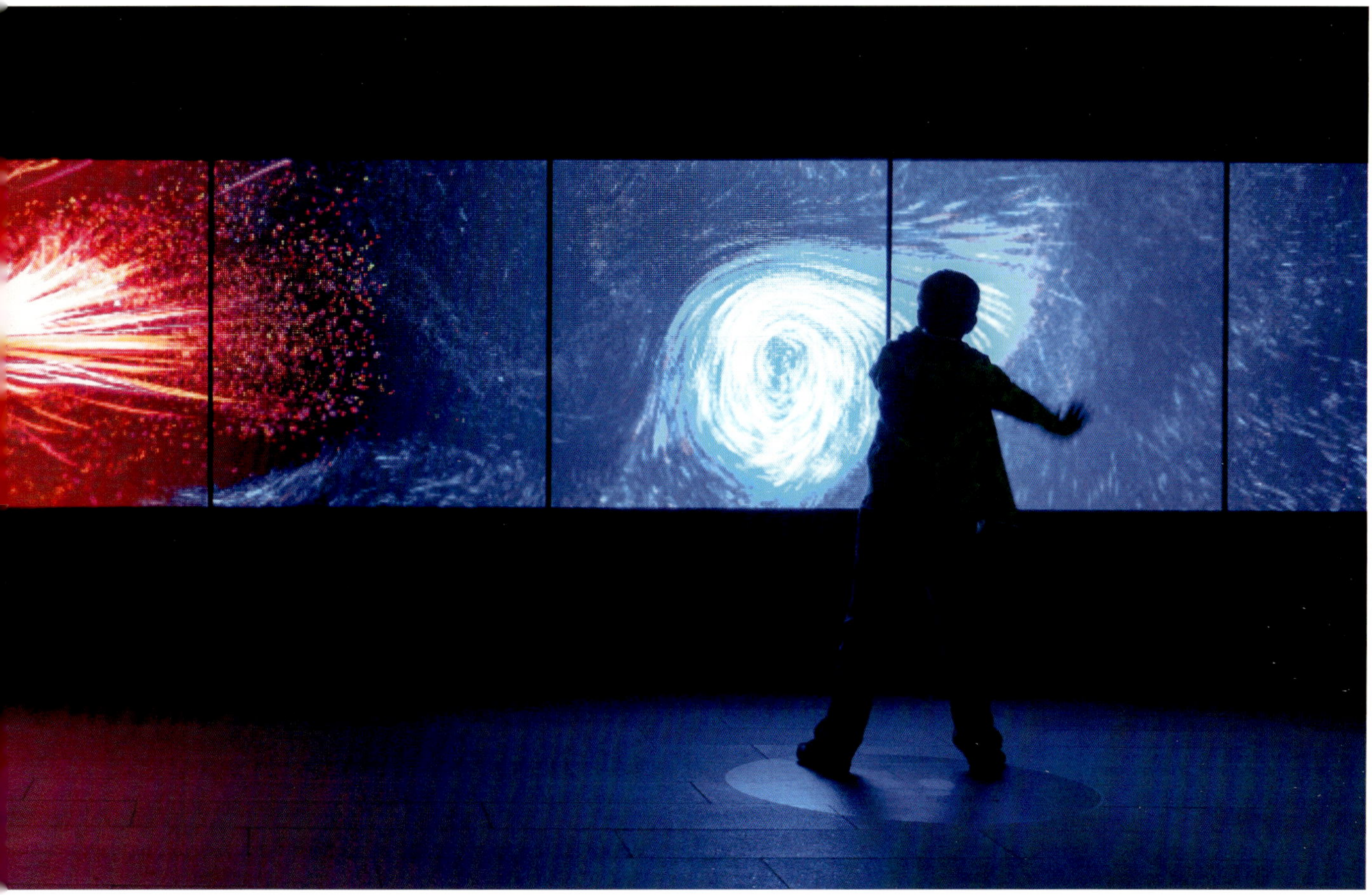

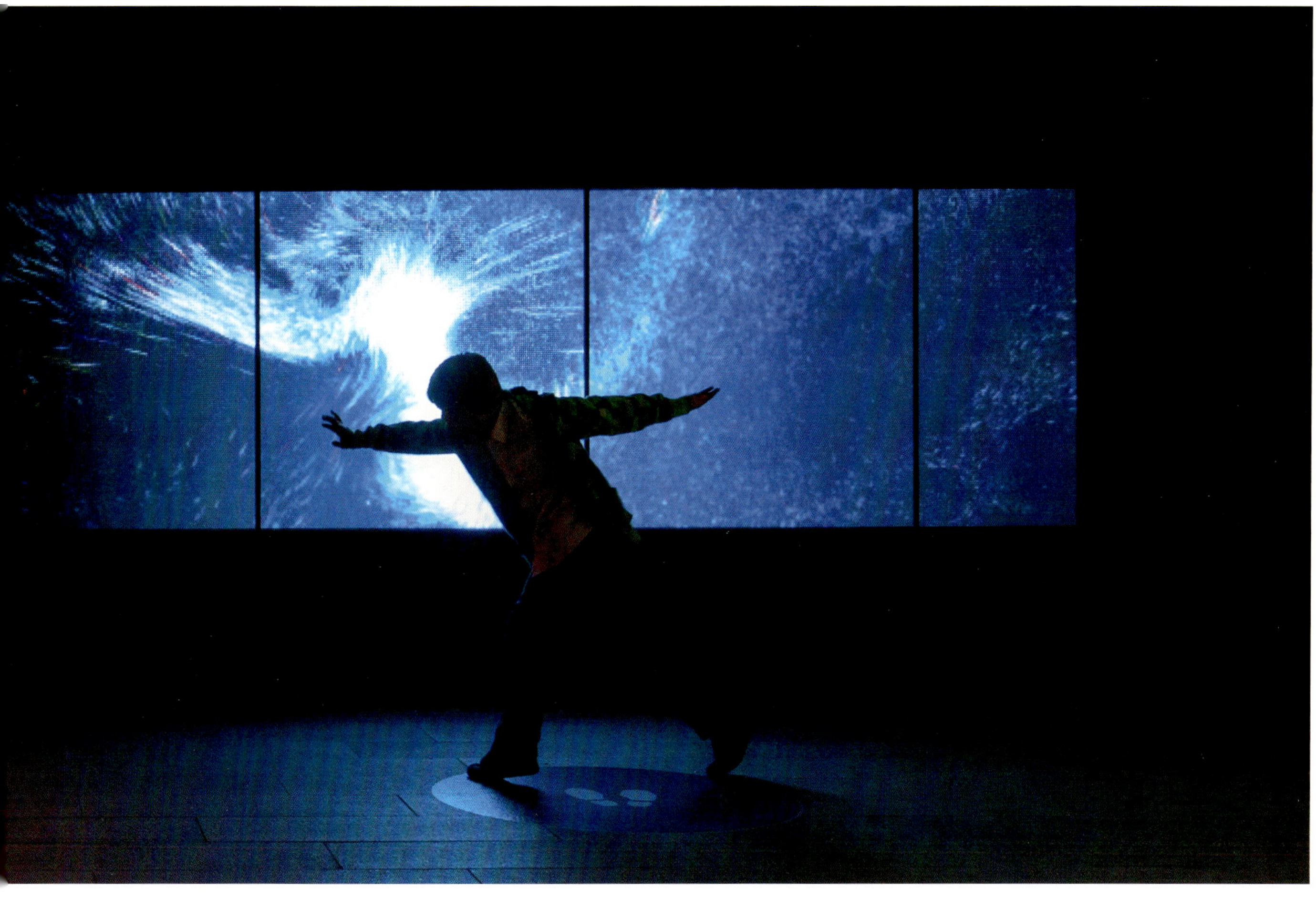

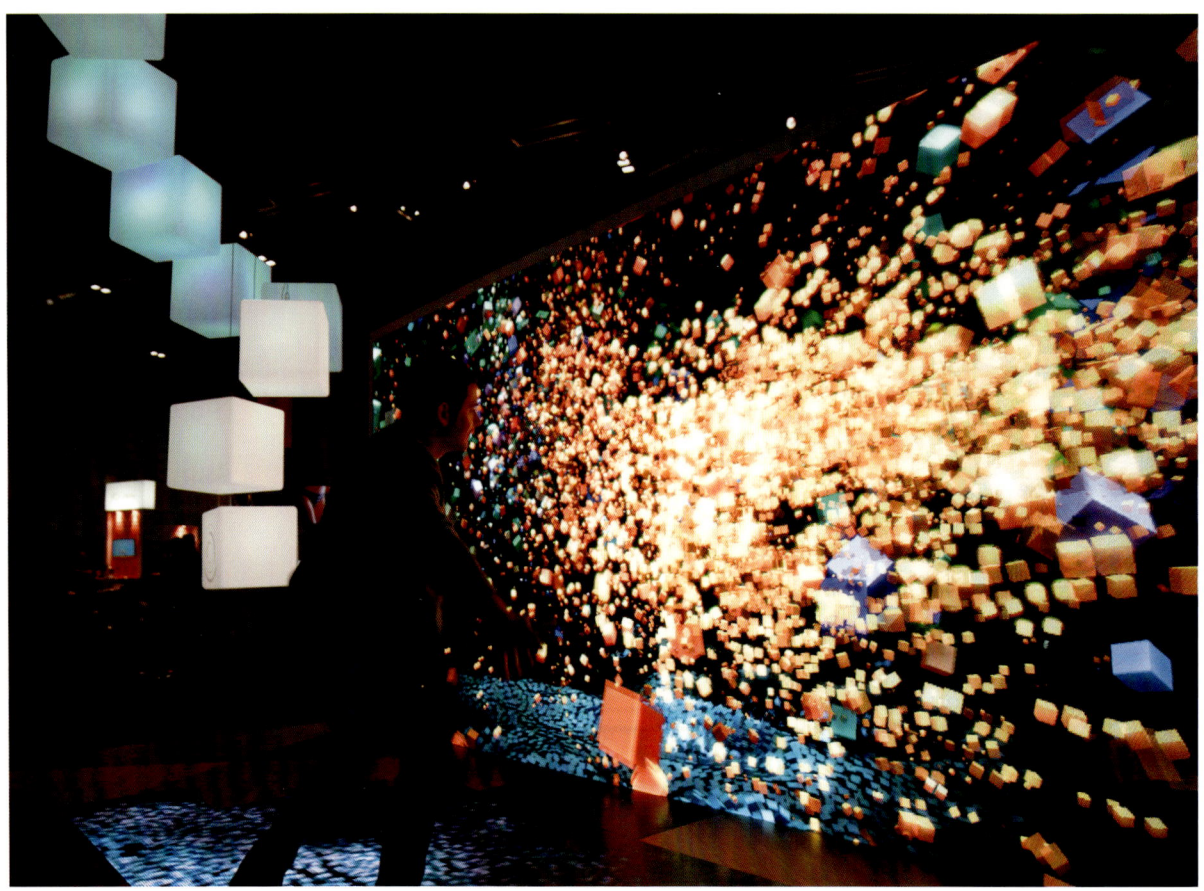

ADOBE EMEA SUMMIT
DIGITAL INSTALLATION

—

Design: **Cinimod Studio**
Photography: **Cinimod Studio**

—

This installation allowed users to use body movements to create colors on a large video canvas, and then to send them upwards across an expansive array of suspended LED cubes that meandered through the exhibition halls.

The high-resolution LED video wall and the video tiles within the floor were driven by real-time particle simulations and shader programming controlled by a 3D camera. A further 2,500 channels of Arnet-DMX and 610 RGBW cubes were driven by a notional color bleed of the screen content.

A multi-layered musical score, which was driven in real-time by the viewers' movements and the resultant on-screen colorful graphics, provided added dimension to the experience.

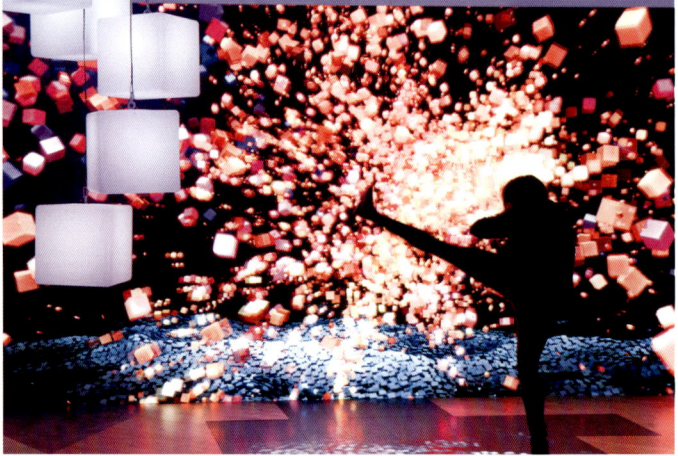

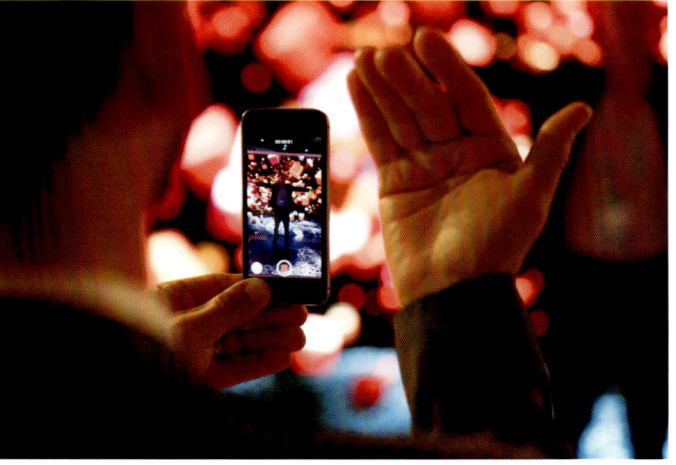

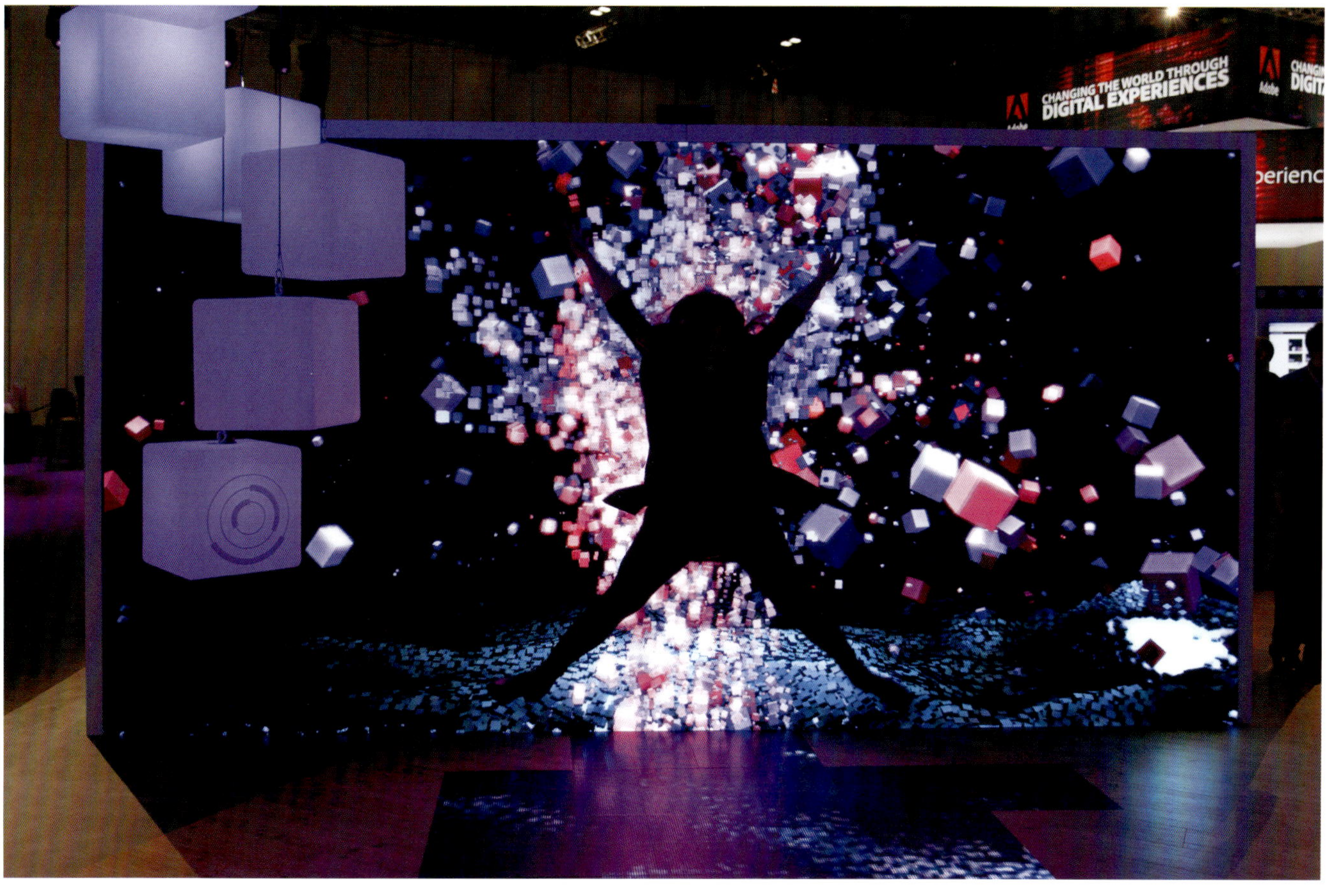
Adobe
CHANGING THE WORLD THROUGH
DIGITAL EXPERIENCES

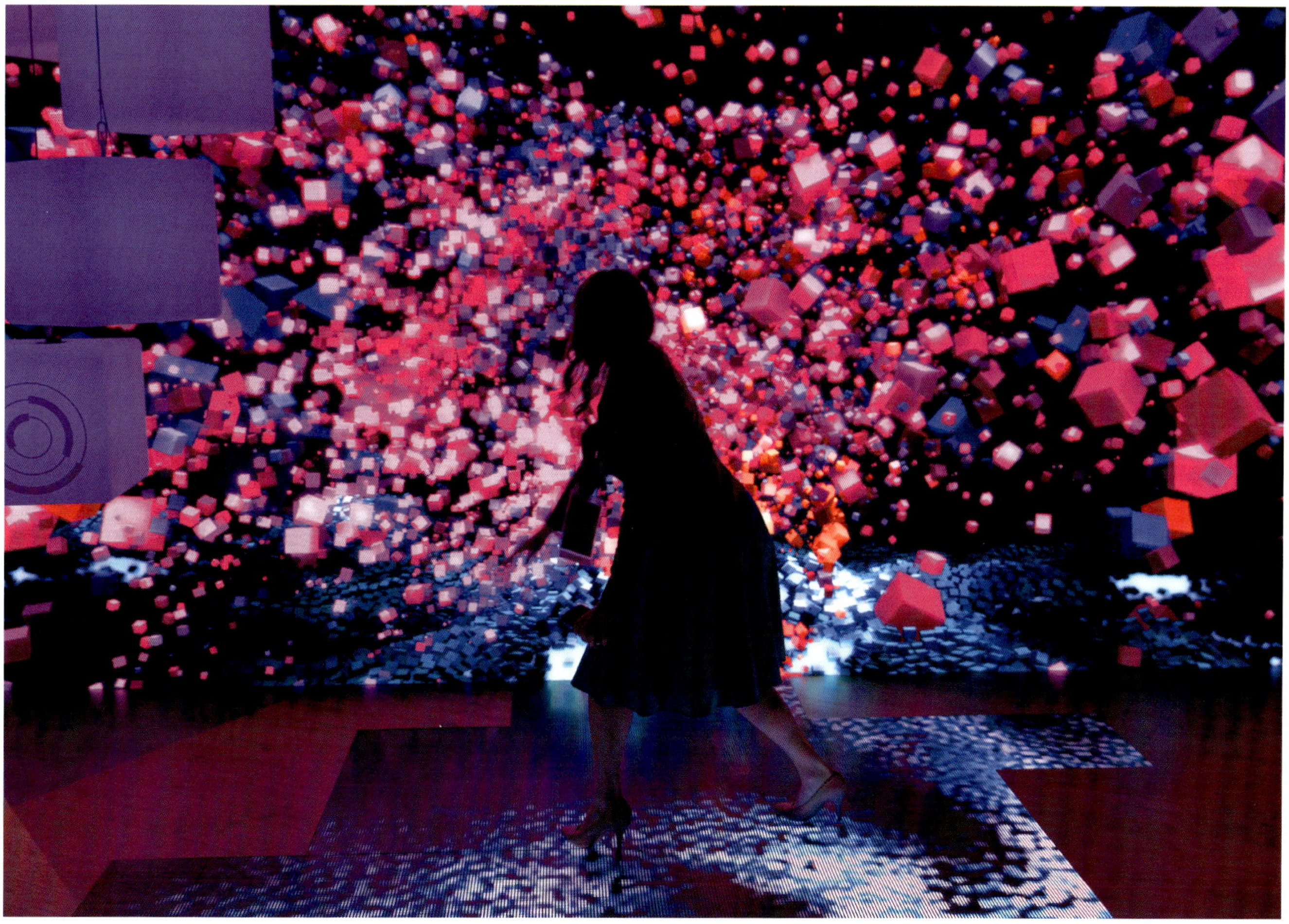

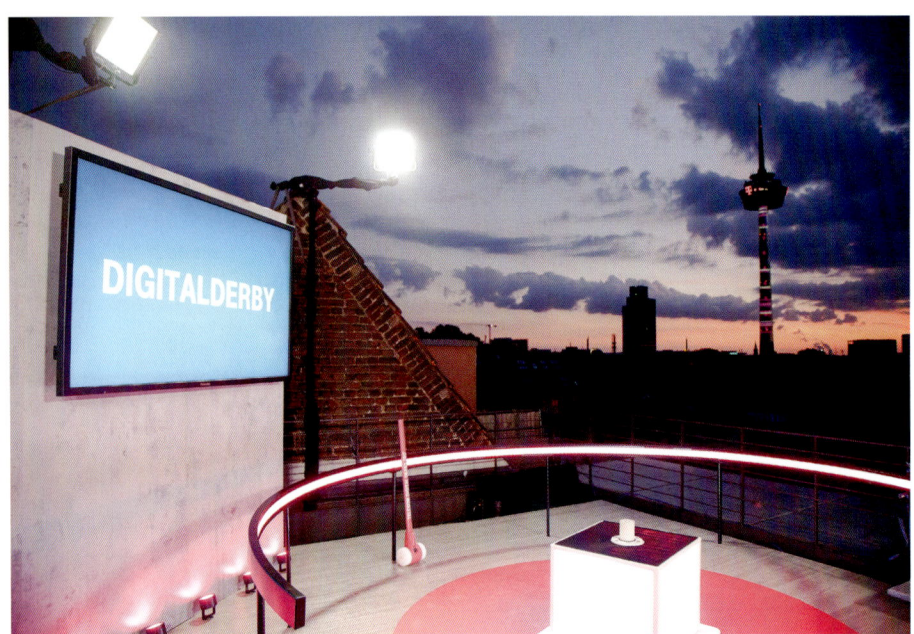

DIGITAL DERBY

—

Design: **URBANSCREEN**

—

Taking up a tempting challenge posed by the German division of Saatchi & Saatchi, URBANSCREEN developed and realized an extra-large-scale interactive game for an unusual PR event. The idea was to let the neighboring cities of Cologne and Düsseldorf compete in an epic battle of strength. With 36 projectors, they turned two telecommunication towers, the Colonius and the Rheinturm, into giant high strikers. Local companies and school classes from both cities were invited to participate in the *Digital Derby*. The impact of each hammer strike was translated into vibrant 3D animations in real time.

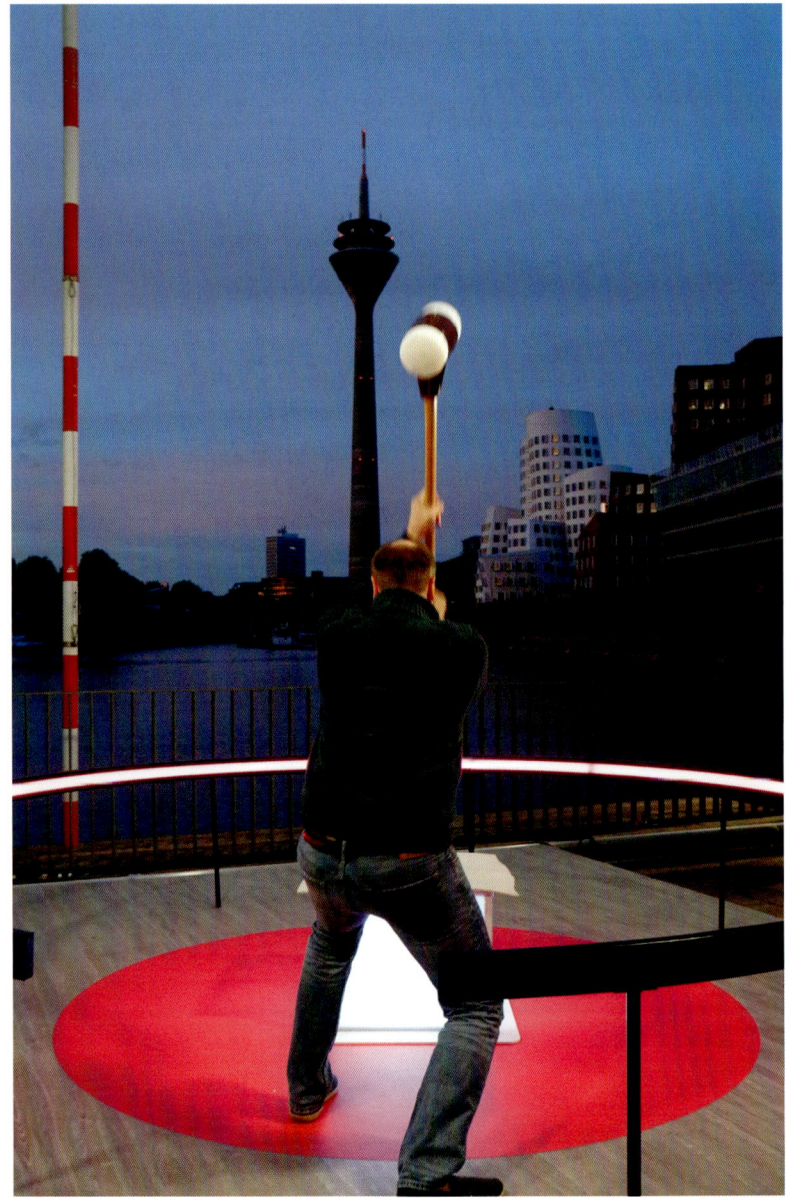

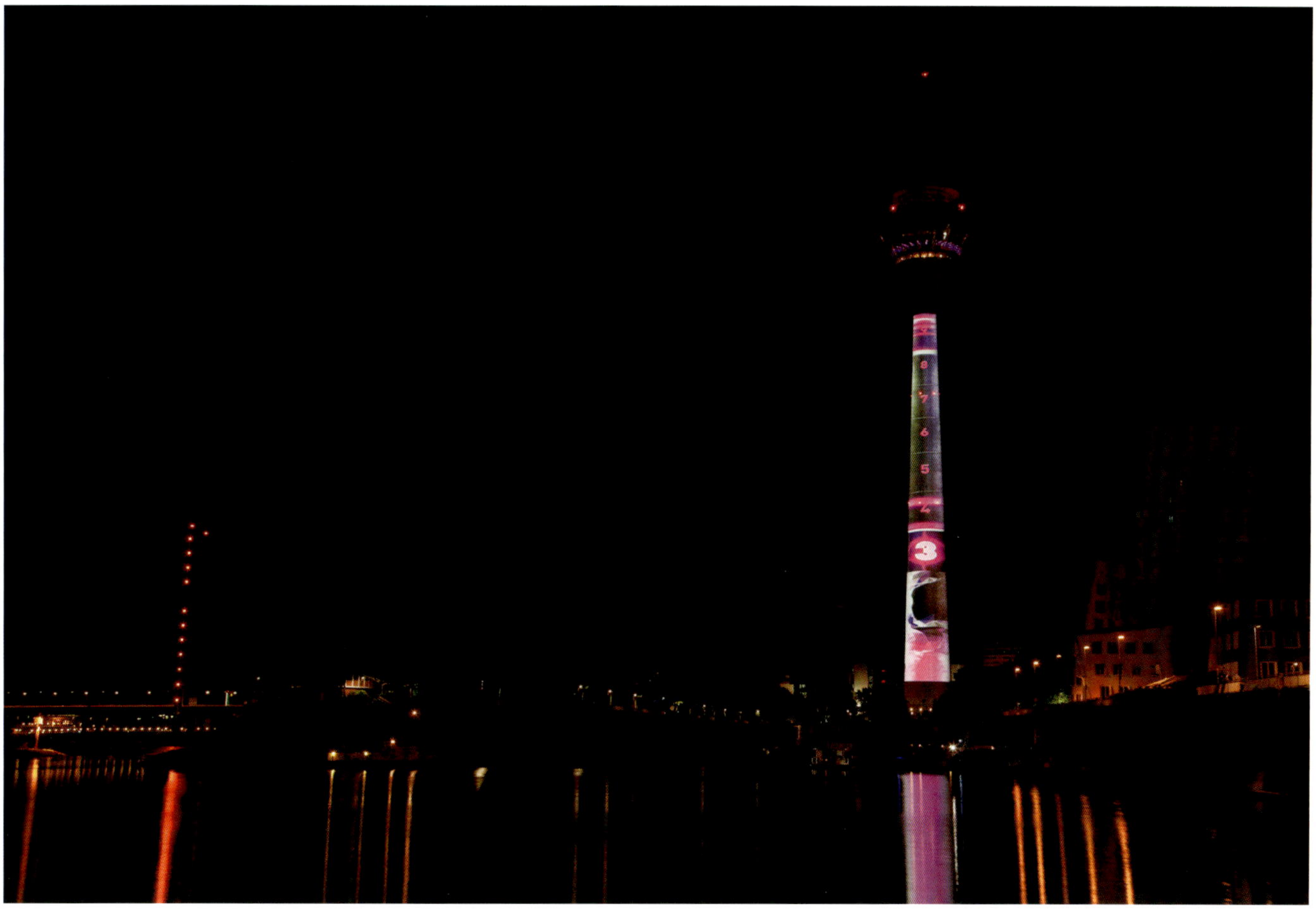

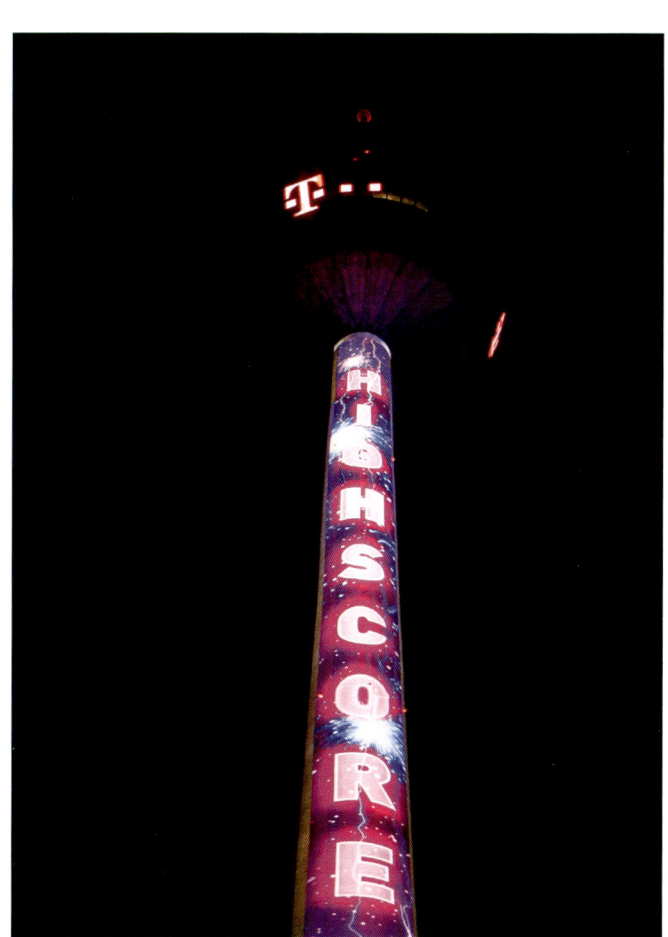
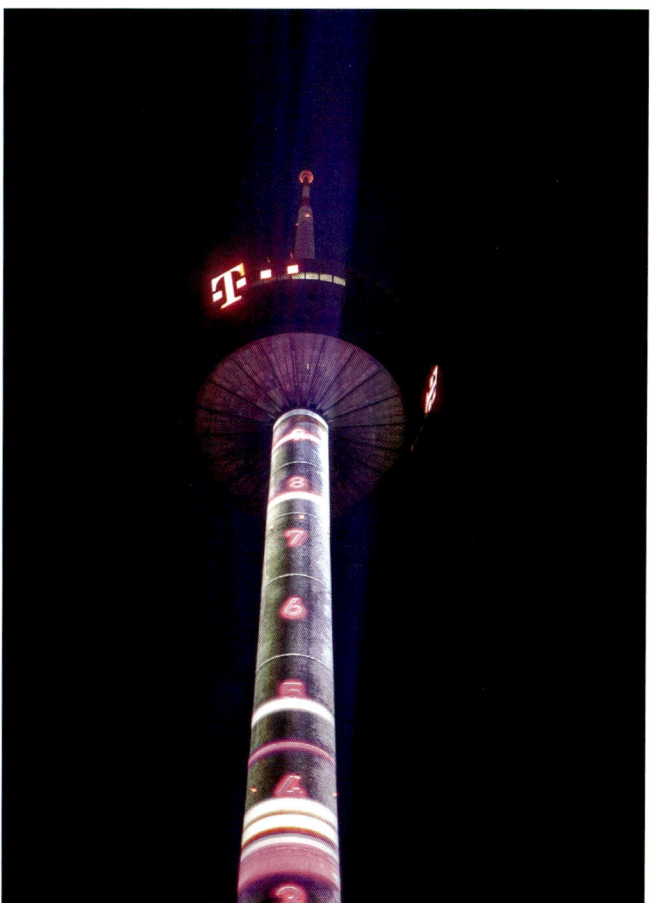

BY:LARM FESTIVAL

Design: **Oslo School of Architecture and Design**
Photography: **Irén Skjelbostad Andresen**

—

This project was a festive, inviting visual focus for "by:Larm," a three-day, multivenue music festival held annually in Oslo. It consisted of two components: a field of pulsing light boxes, lighting the space in front of the main venue, Jakob Kulturkirke, and projections of geometric forms and colors on the church wall.

It was the main project of the master's elective course "Interactive Spaces and Environments" at the Oslo School of Architecture and Design, held in the spring semester. There were two student teams, one responsible for the projection on the church and the other for the light boxes, both coordinated by professor Ståle Stenslie.

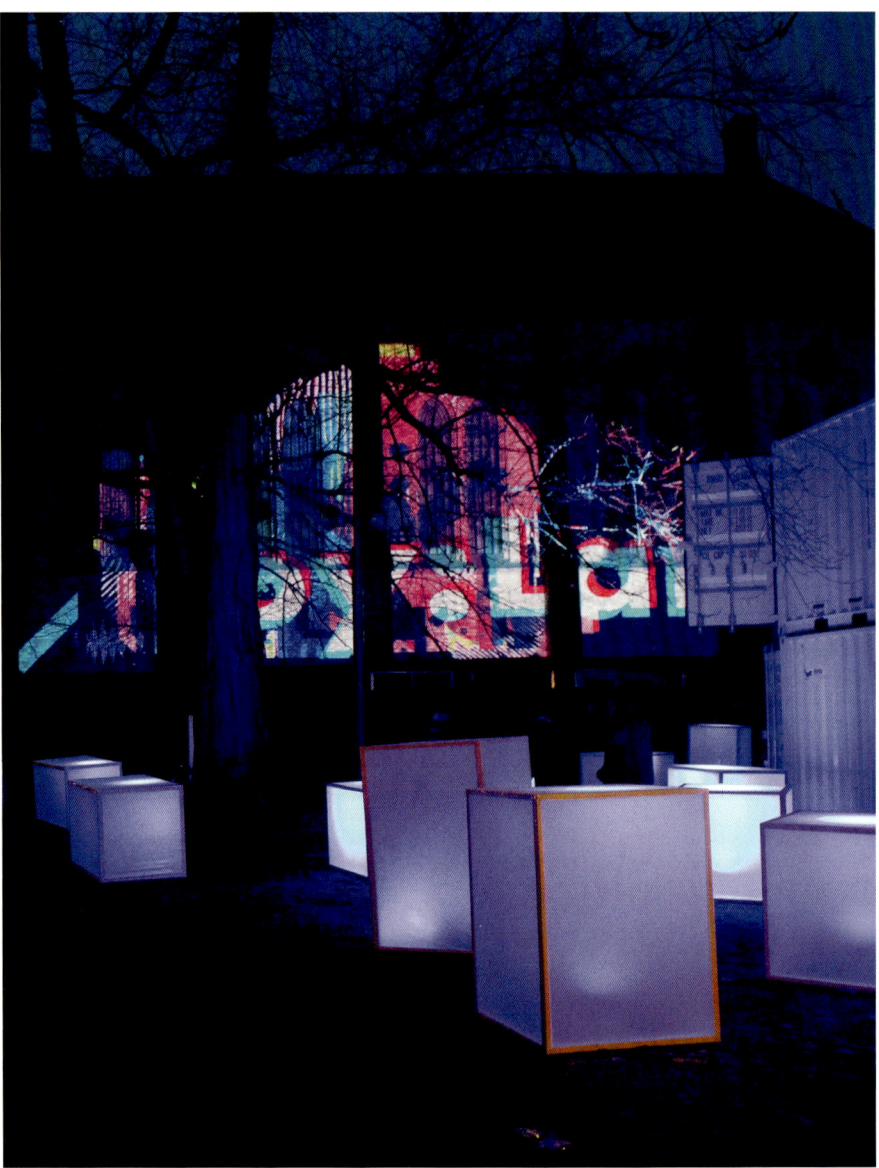

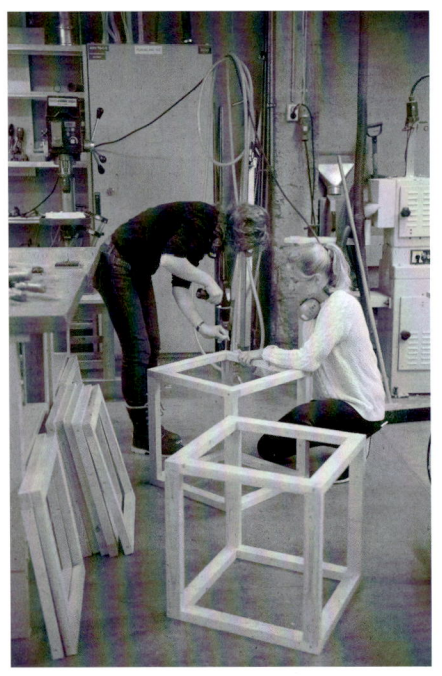

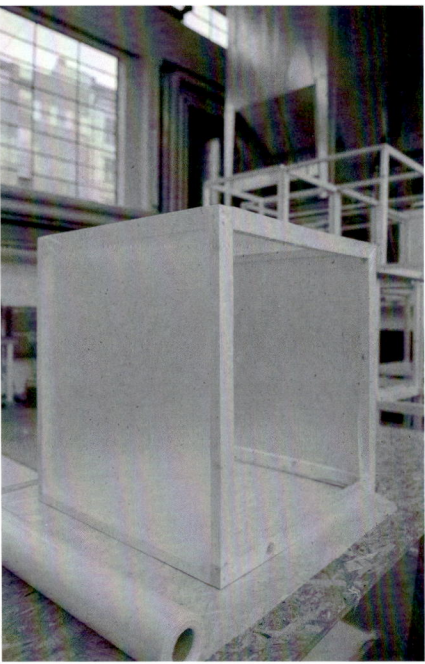

Projection team:
Amalie Skrede, Ole-Birger Neergård,
Diana Jamoido, Michelle Chow, Jialing Li,
Martin Brændhaugen, Xuan Guo, Shirui Zhuang

Box team:
Anniken Sunde Frich, Ariadne Androulaki,
Caroline Guilvard, Christopher Pearsell-Ross,
Irén Skjelbostad Andresen, Ivy Ferguson,
Izelin Tujunen, Laura Purlytė,
Ragnhild Frøyen Milter, Thea Tollefsbøl Jegerud

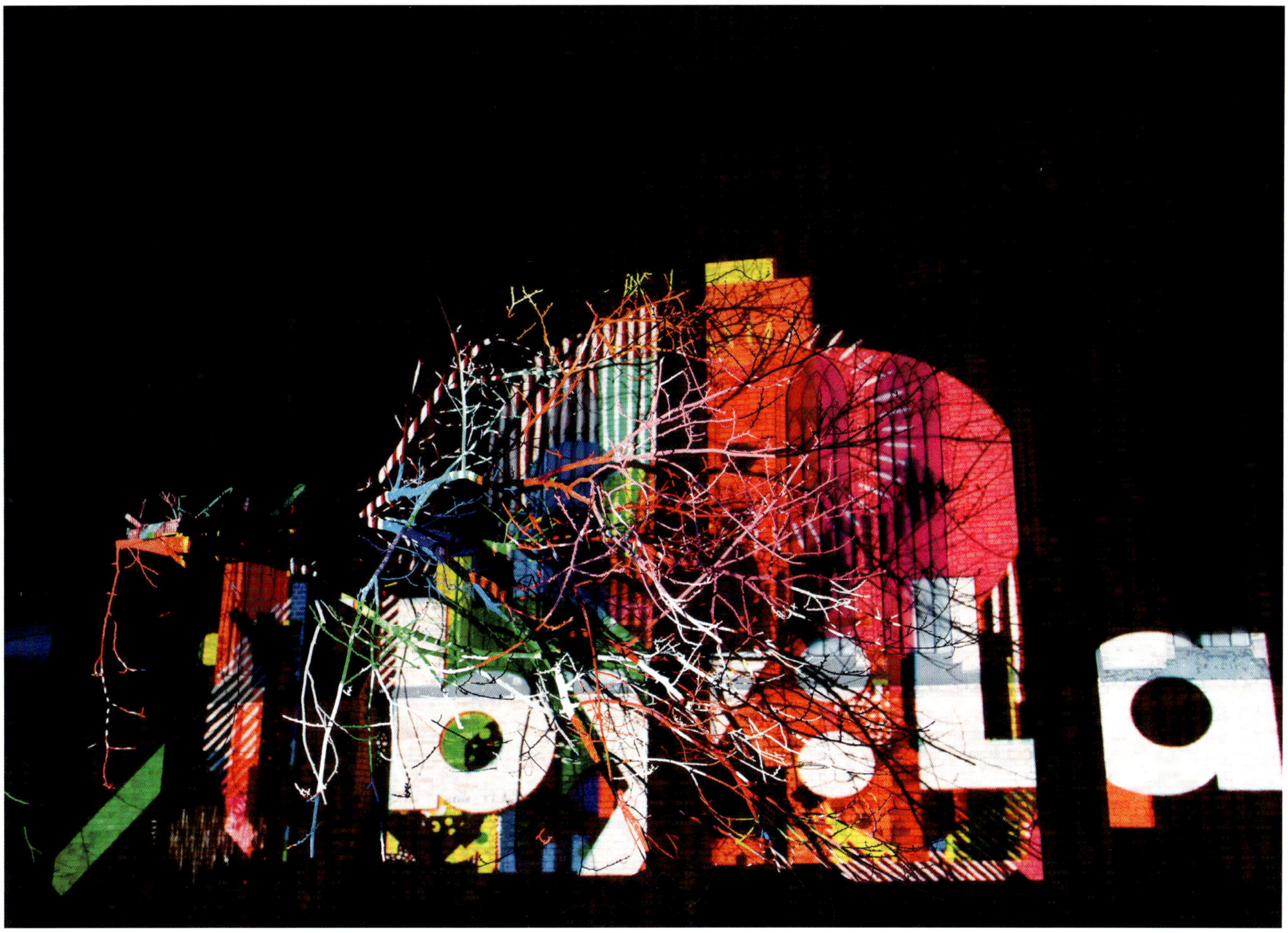

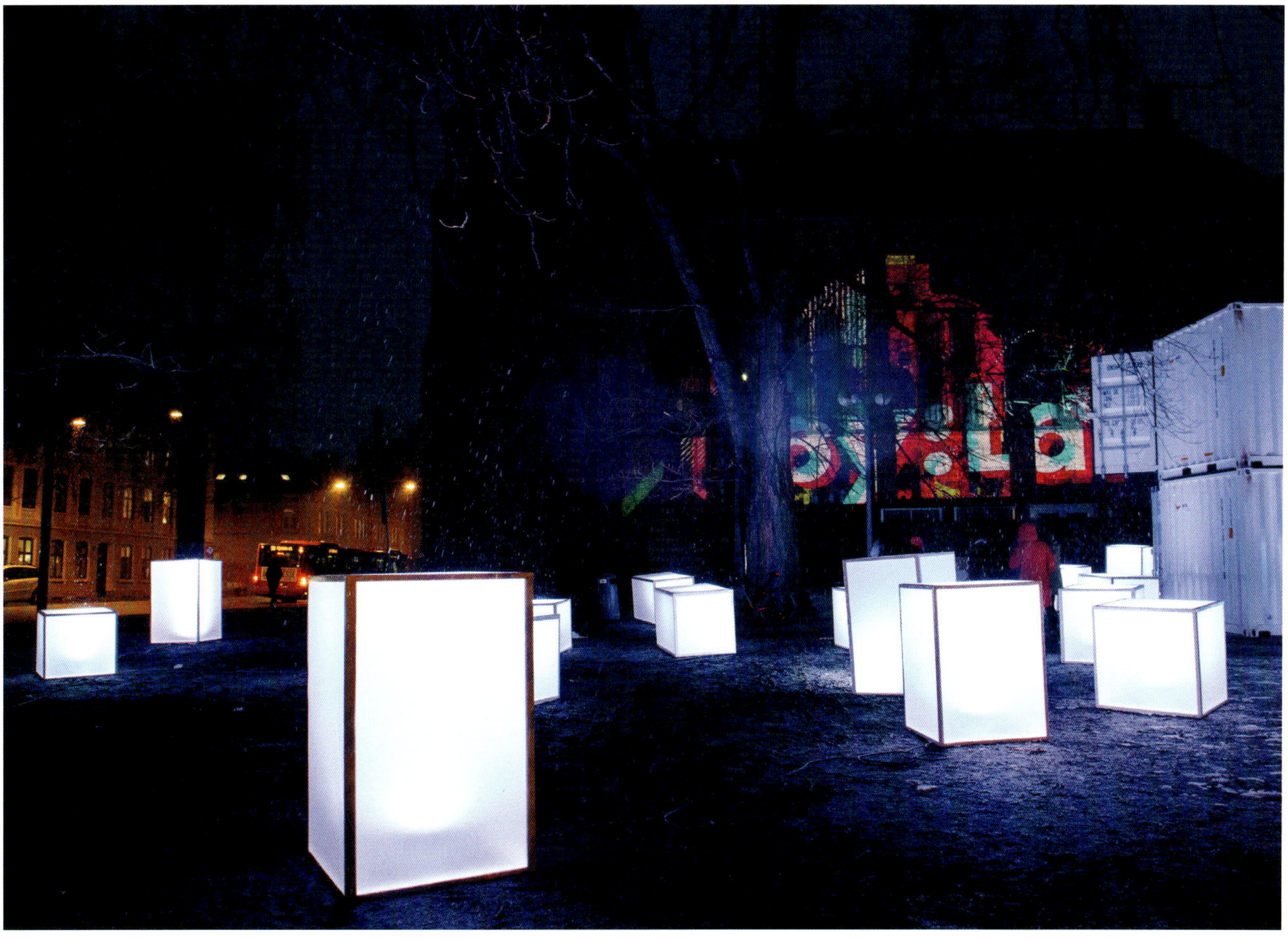

COLORFUL TALKS

—

Design: **Punto.Lab**
Photography: **Punto.Lab**

—

Colorful Talks is an interactive light installation that responds to the voices of the participants. The urban intervention, created by Group Punto.Lab, debuted in Bogotá, Colombia, where it transformed a park into a large-scale game.

A net made of lights and colors creates a challenge for the participants; they have to cross it in order to get to one of the six modules where they are asked to sing, talk, whisper, scream, blow off steam or whistle.

As its own creation process, the artwork requires the collaborative work of the participants who, located on the modules, must play with their voices to activate the whole installation. The modules use microphones and process the amplitude and frequency of the voices to transform the data into power and diverse colors.

Colorful Talks is an homage to diversity, a game that takes the public space and gathers its inhabitants and reminds them how relevant their participation is for their environment.

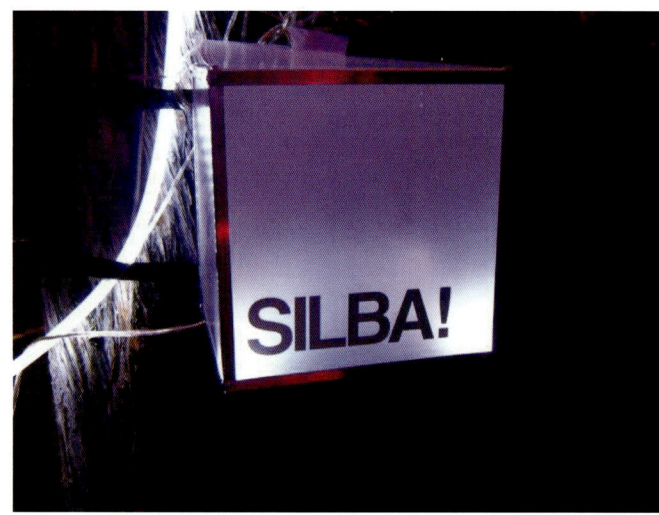

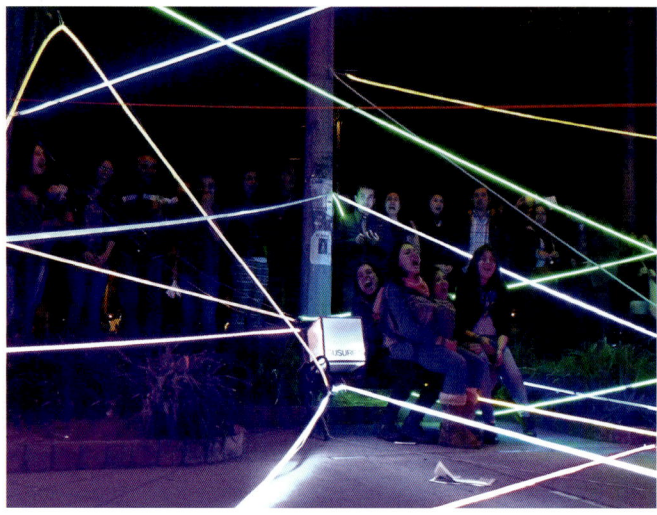

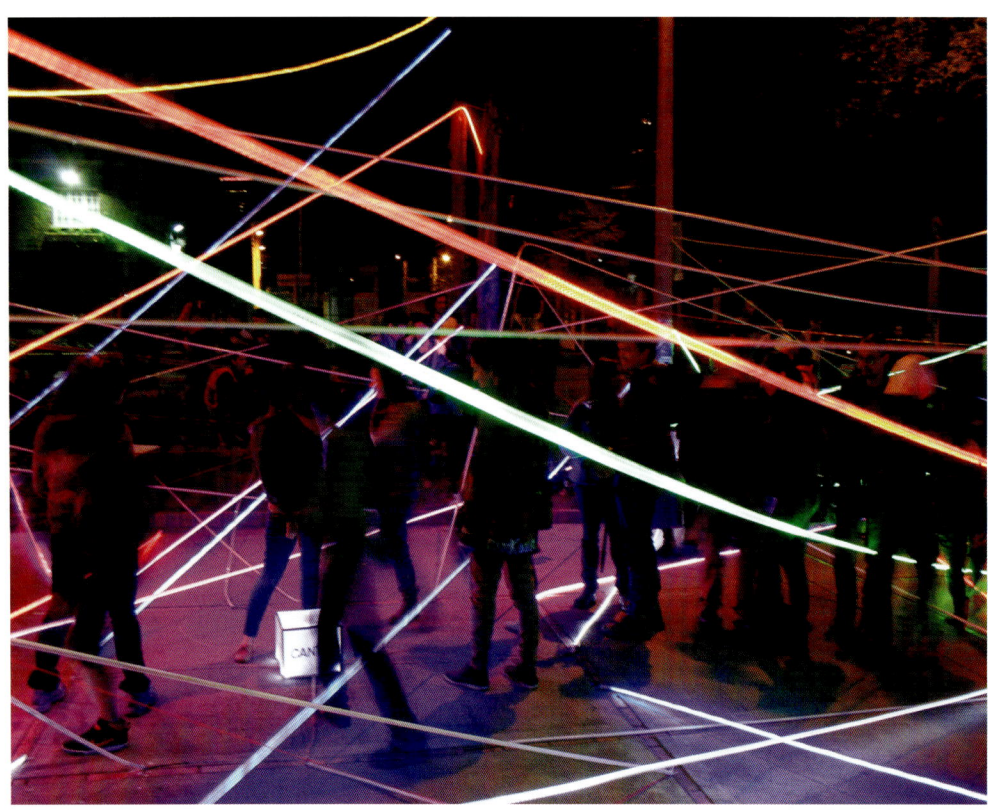

Team:
Natalia Rivera, Margarita González, Juan José Díaz, Pedro Mendoza, Juan Camilo Torres, Sergio Navas

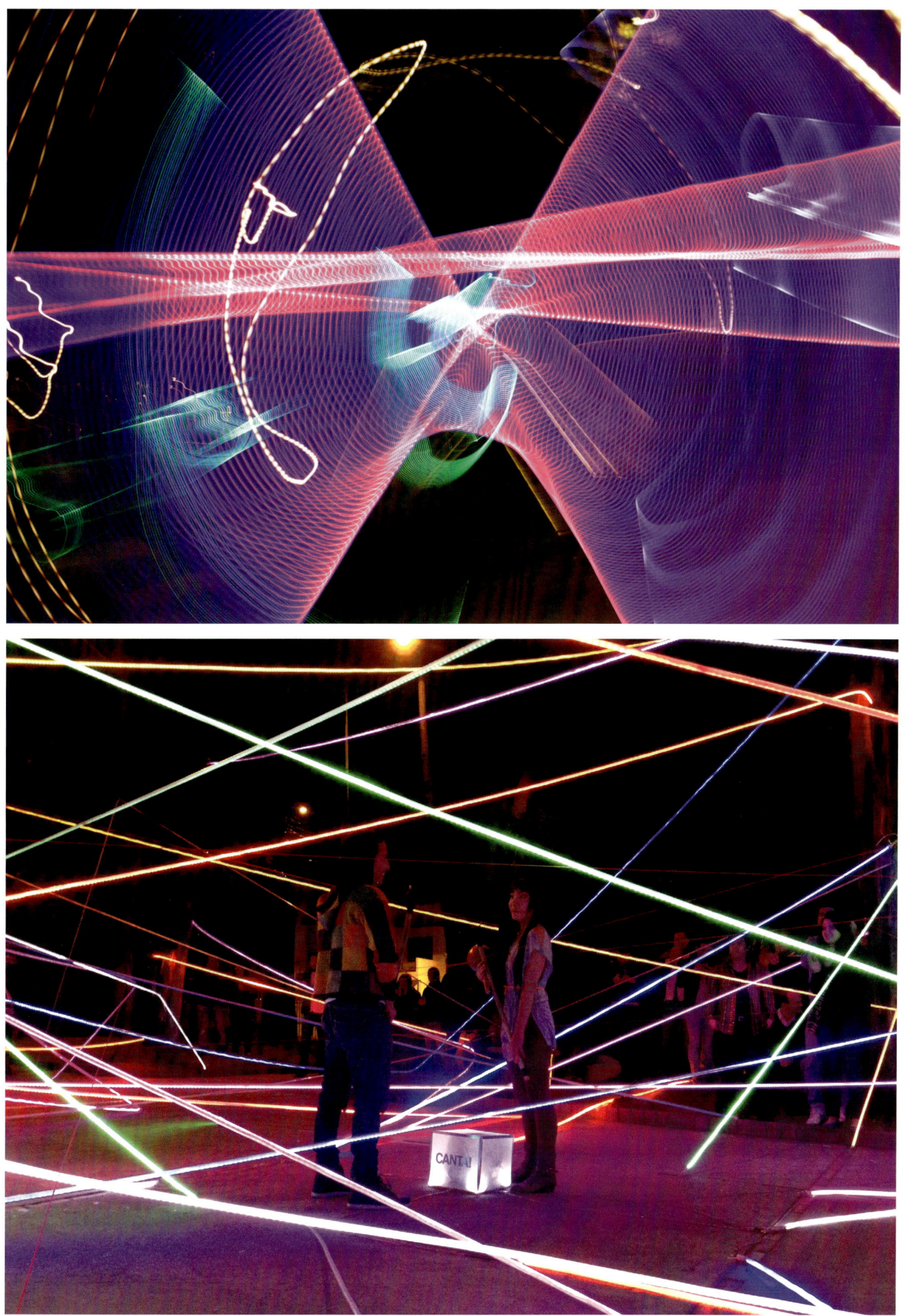

DIGITAL WATER LILIES

Design: **Miguel Chevalier**
Software: **Claude Micheli, Antoine Villeret**

—

Digital Water Lilies is a site-specific virtual interactive garden that comes alive after sunset on the Piazza of the Jing An Kerry Centre, in Shanghai. It's a lush parterre of flowers and different varieties of luminescent plants. In this garden, Chevalier has included some varieties of flowers rich with symbolism and good auspices during the spring in China, such as African lilies, orchids, camellias, and peach blossoms. Flowers appear randomly, come to full blossom and fade away, only to be reborn again. The garden renews itself time after time, constantly changing and flourishing into its summer glory.

As visitors walk around the 600 square-meter flower carpet, the garden senses them and shifts around them with the flowers opening up paths of discovery. In this new form of "digital impressionism," the title and the cosmic sensibility of the work pay homage to Monet and his research on light, seasons, and nature.

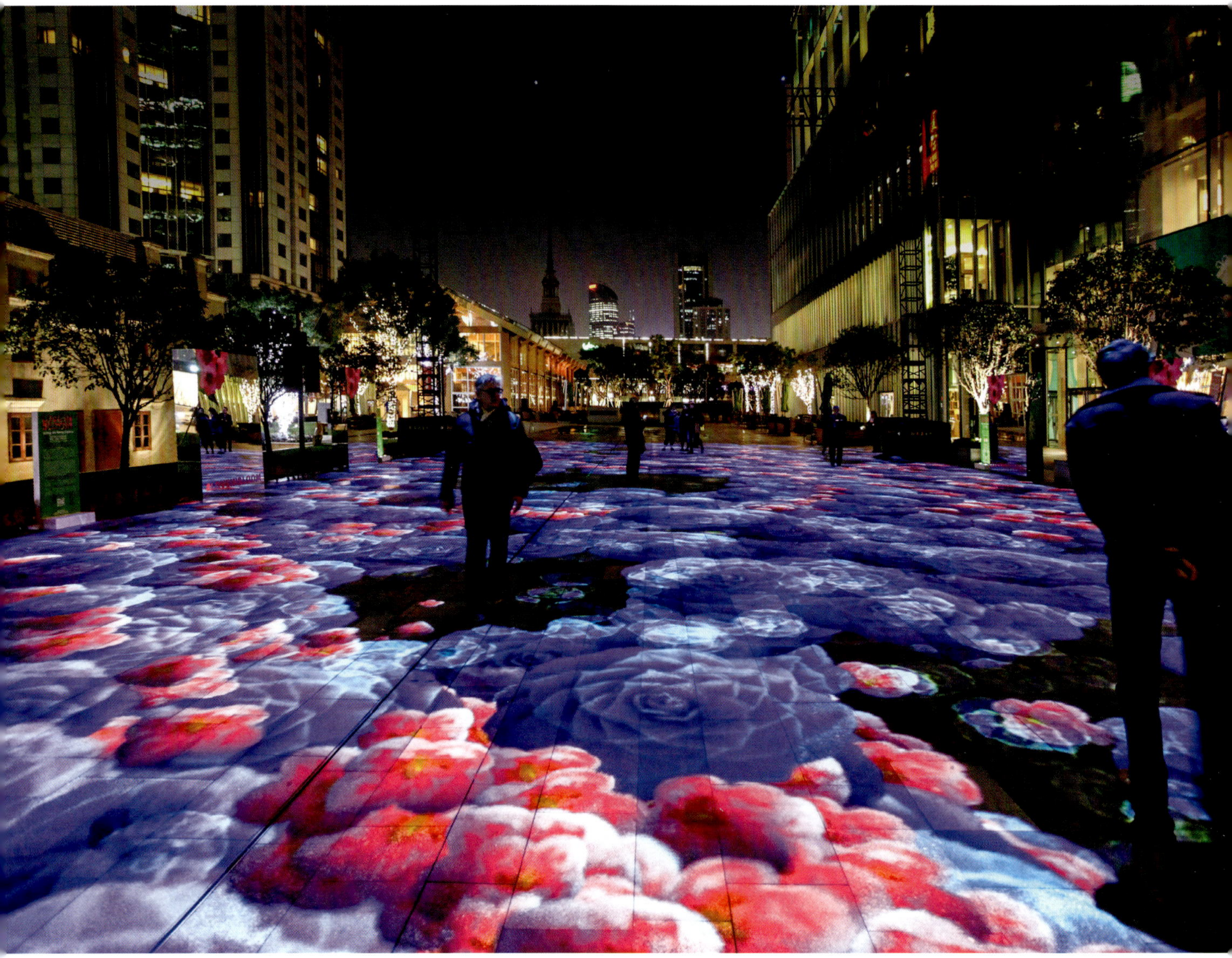

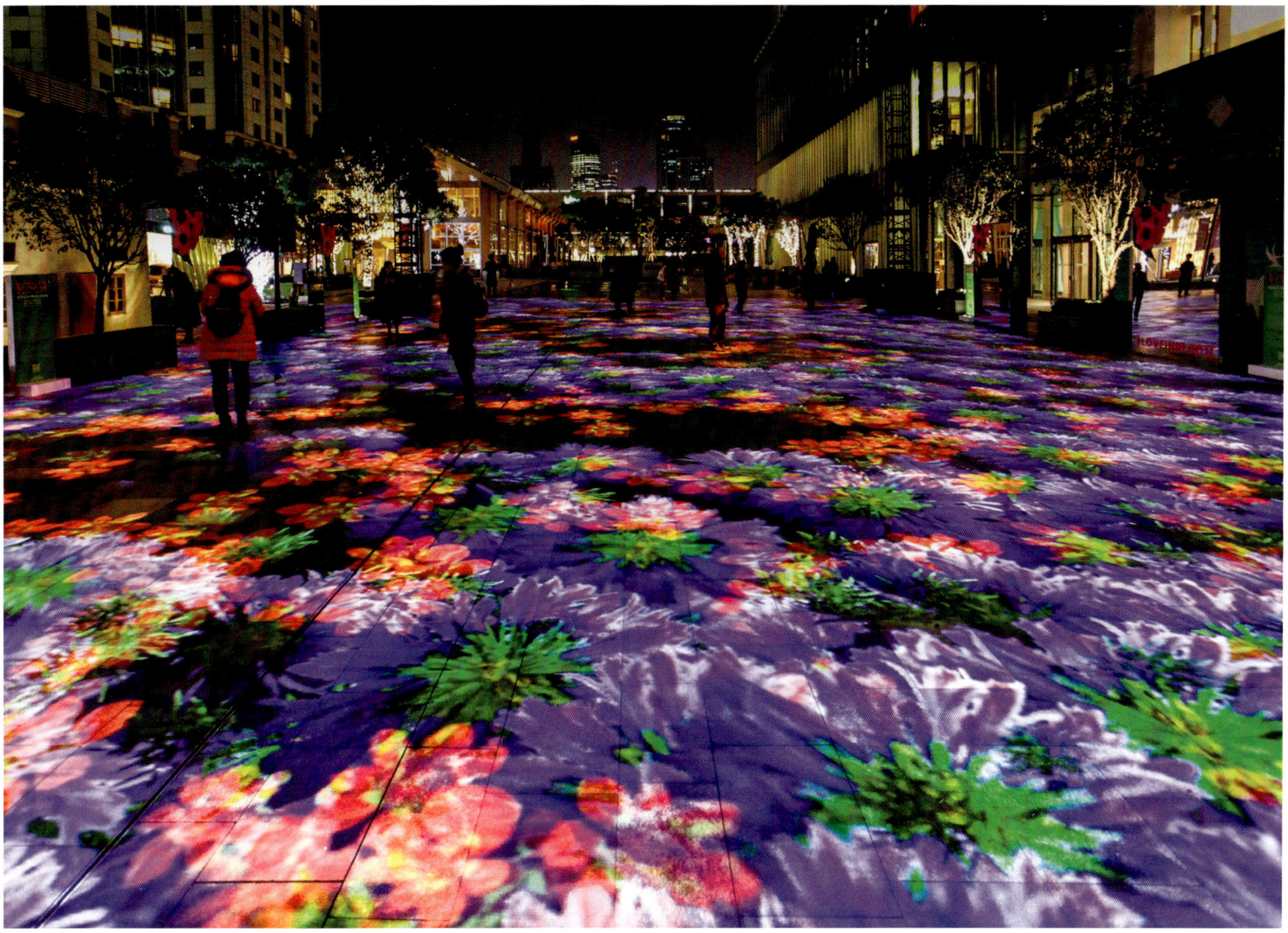

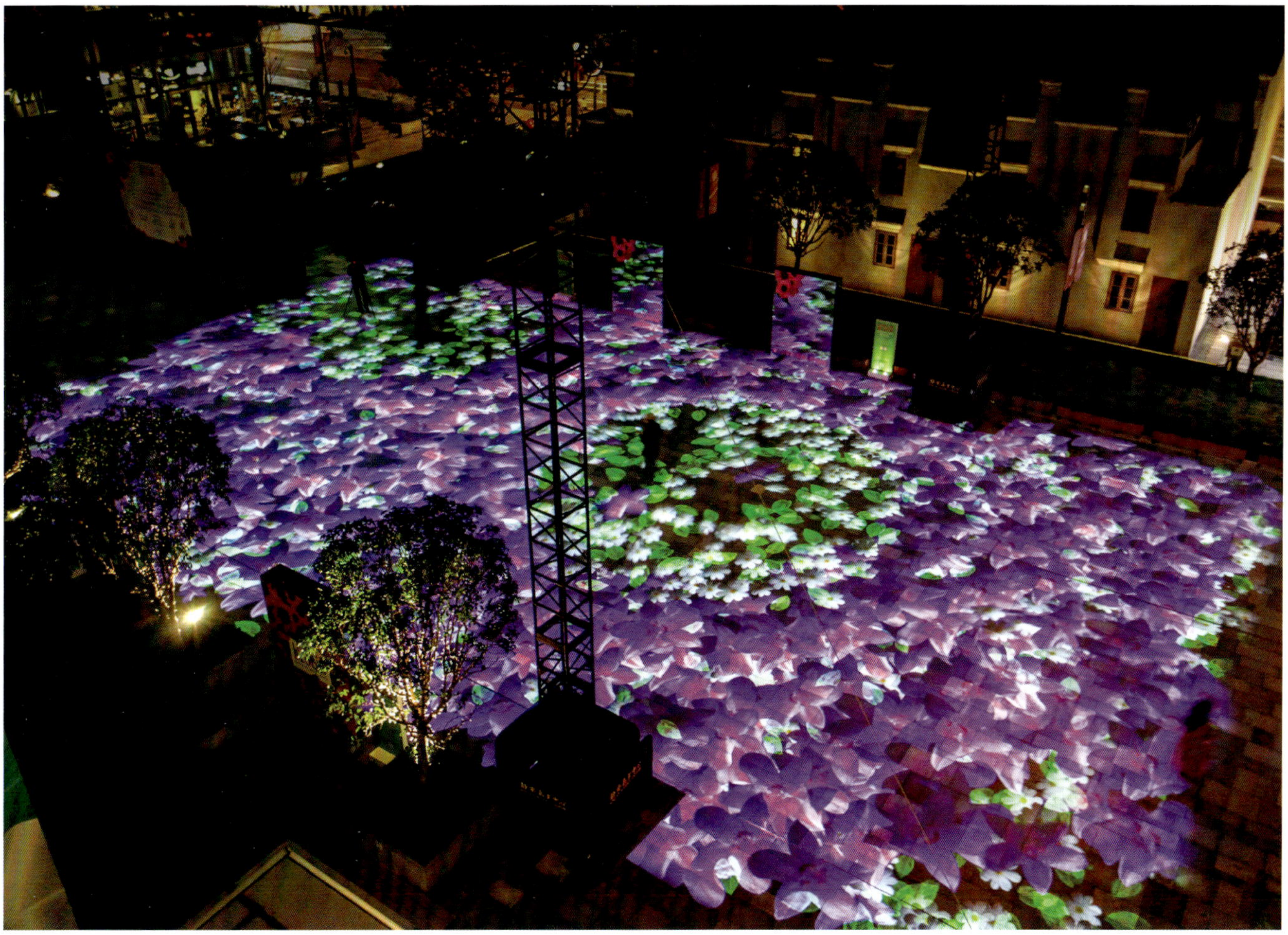

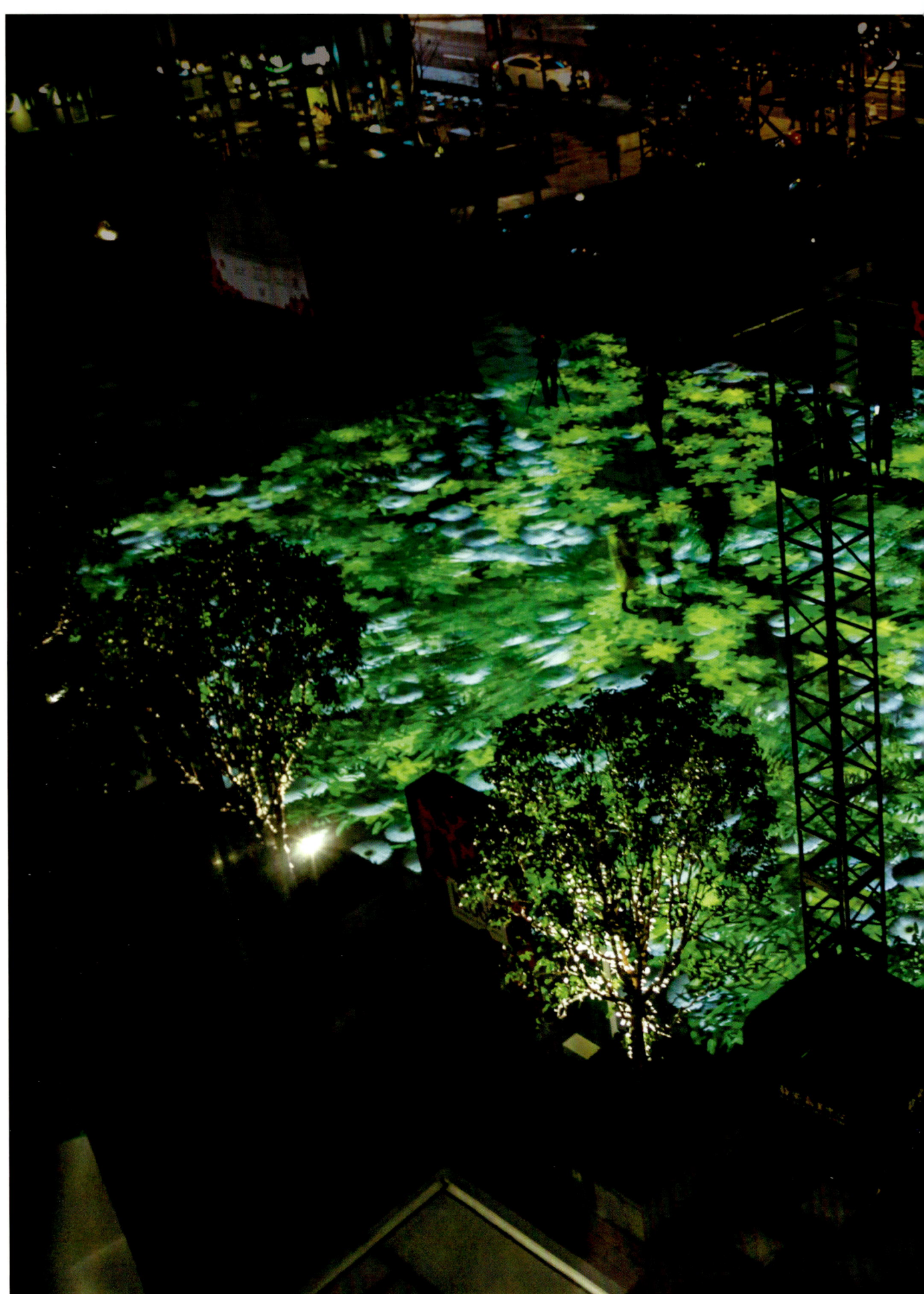

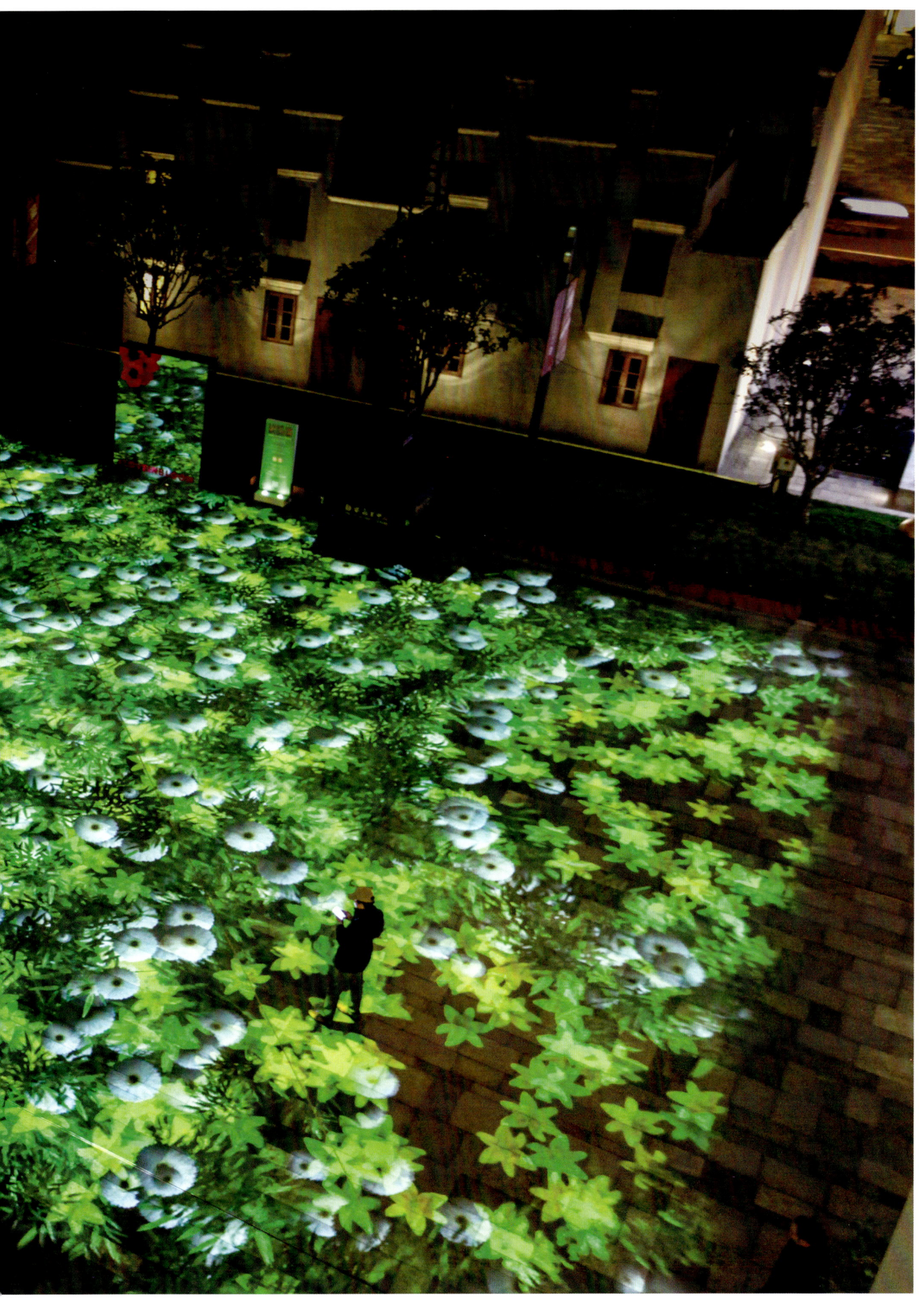

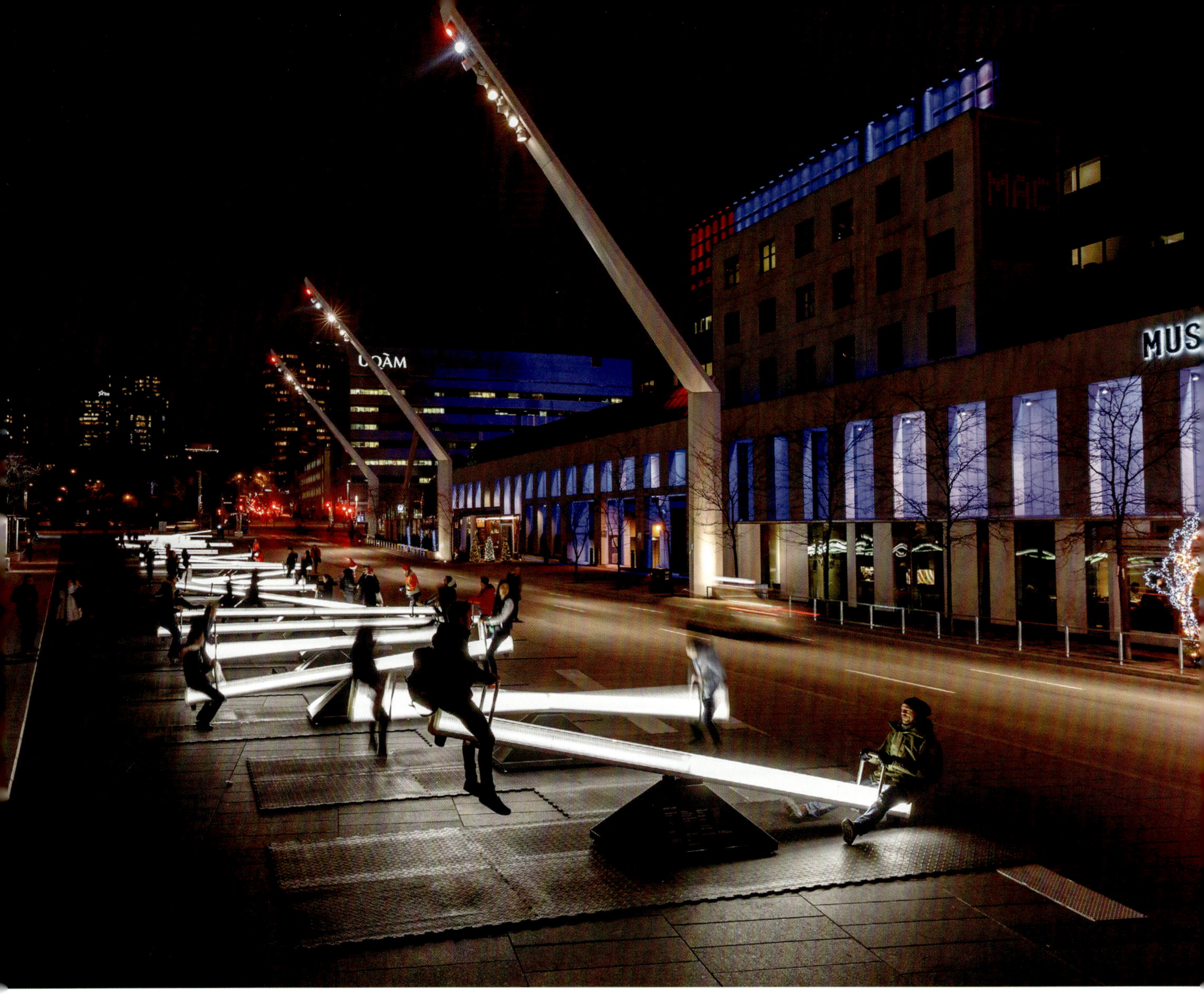

IMPULSE

—

Design: **Lateral Office, CS Design**
Sound Design: **Mitchell Akiyama**
Video Design: **Maotik, Iregular**
Photography: **Martin Doyon, Ulysse Lemerise**

—

The area of Quartier des Spectacles is Montreal's main arts district, with dozens of theatres, performing arts venues, and museums. It is also the home of multiple annual festivals. Yet despite the cultural activity, there remain many vacant, under-utilized lots in the area. There have also been issues with attracting people to the arts district when events were not taking place. The programming of the Quartier des Spectacles aims to bring in and keep visitors in the neighborhood. The *Luminotherapie* event, and the *Impulse* installation in particular, aspire to be inclusive and engaging to a wide-ranging public and to activate public space all year round, both summer and winter months, by engaging ideas of urban play.

Inspired by the iconic cover of the Joy Division album "Unknown Pleasures," as well as Steve Reich's minimalist music, which plays with repetition, rhythm and syncopation, *Impulse* explores how architecture can visualize sound. The Place des Festival in Quartier des Spectacle is transformed into a space of urban play through a series of thirty interactive, acoustic, illuminated see-saws that respond and transform when in motion. The seesaws, of two different lengths, form units of light and sound that can be activated and played by the public to create a temporal, ever-changing event. *Impulse* embodies ideas of serialism, repetition, and variation to produce zones of intensity and calm within a large public space.

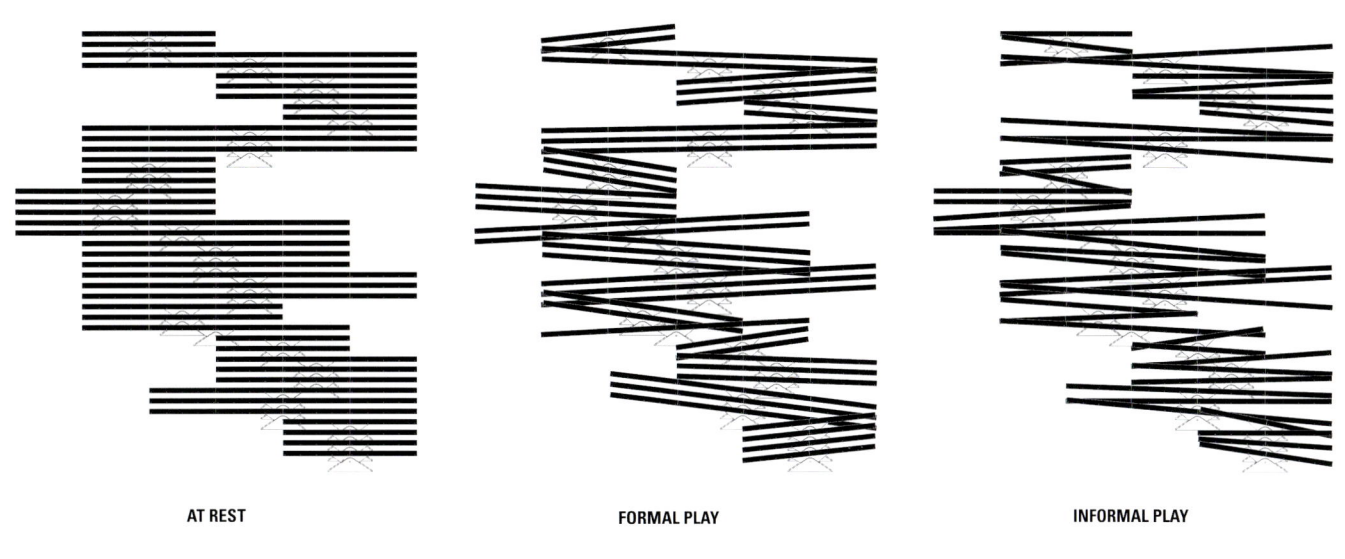

AT REST   FORMAL PLAY   INFORMAL PLAY

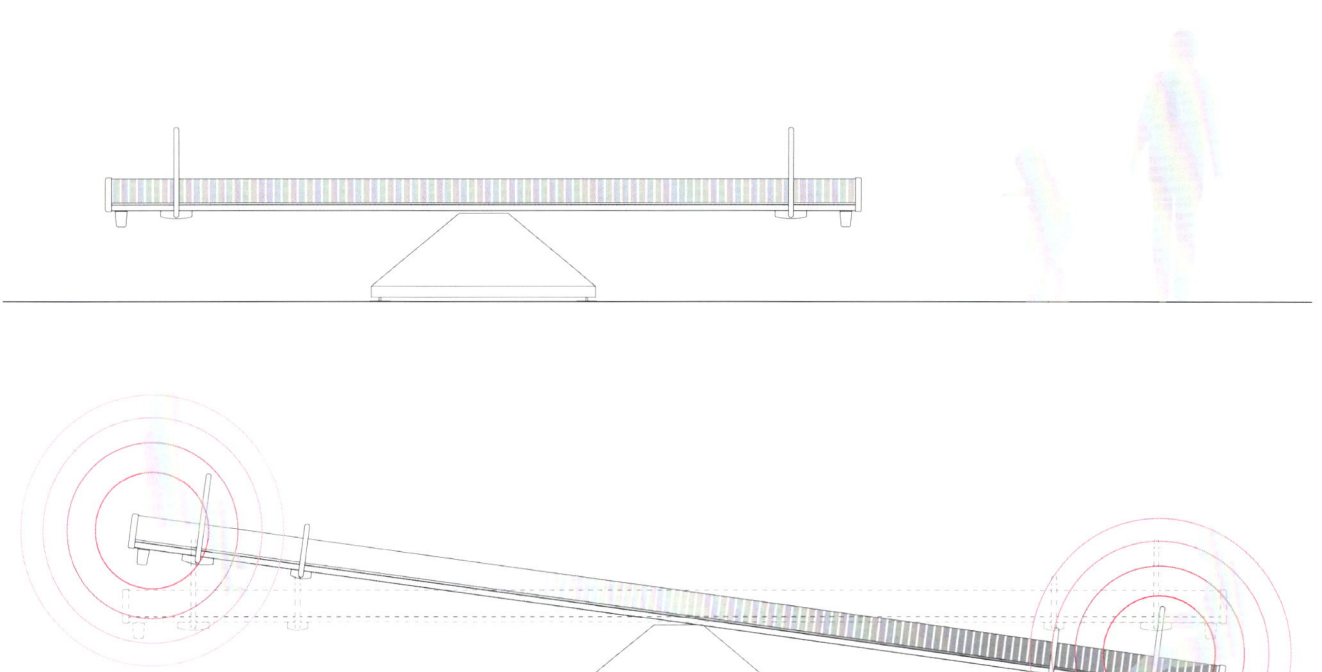

LIGHT AND SOUND ACTIVATION   The speed and rhythm of the see-saw's motion generates light intensity and triggers a series of tones

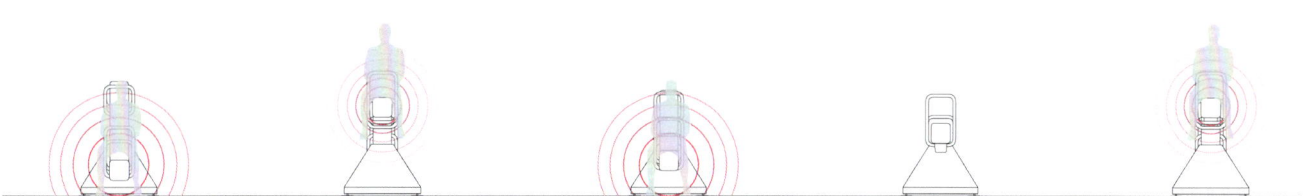

URBAN INSTRUMENT   Each see-saw has a unique set of tones; when played together, they create a dynamic acoustic field

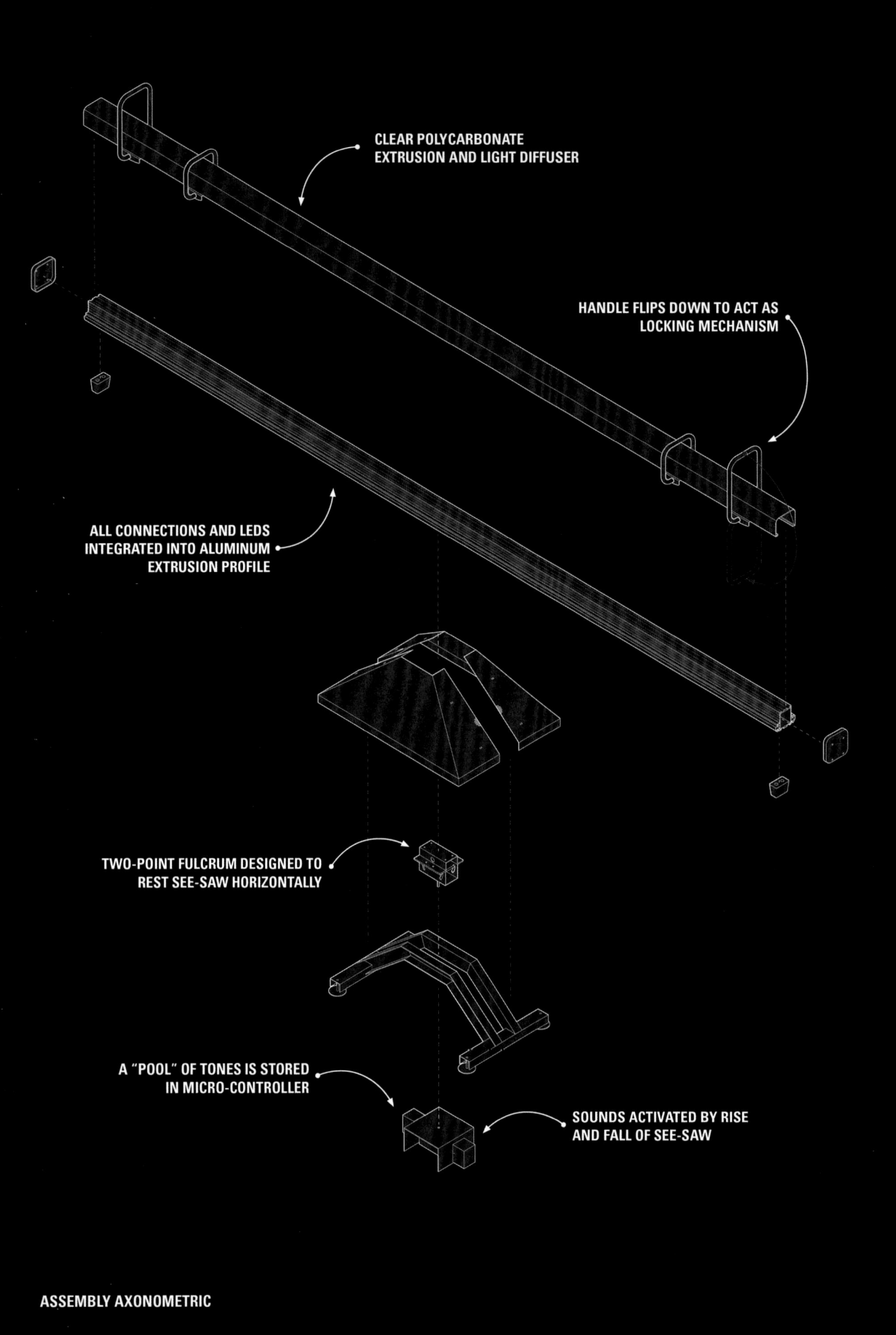

CLEAR POLYCARBONATE
EXTRUSION AND LIGHT DIFFUSER

HANDLE FLIPS DOWN TO ACT AS
LOCKING MECHANISM

ALL CONNECTIONS AND LEDS
INTEGRATED INTO ALUMINUM
EXTRUSION PROFILE

TWO-POINT FULCRUM DESIGNED TO
REST SEE-SAW HORIZONTALLY

A "POOL" OF TONES IS STORED
IN MICRO-CONTROLLER

SOUNDS ACTIVATED BY RISE
AND FALL OF SEE-SAW

ASSEMBLY AXONOMETRIC

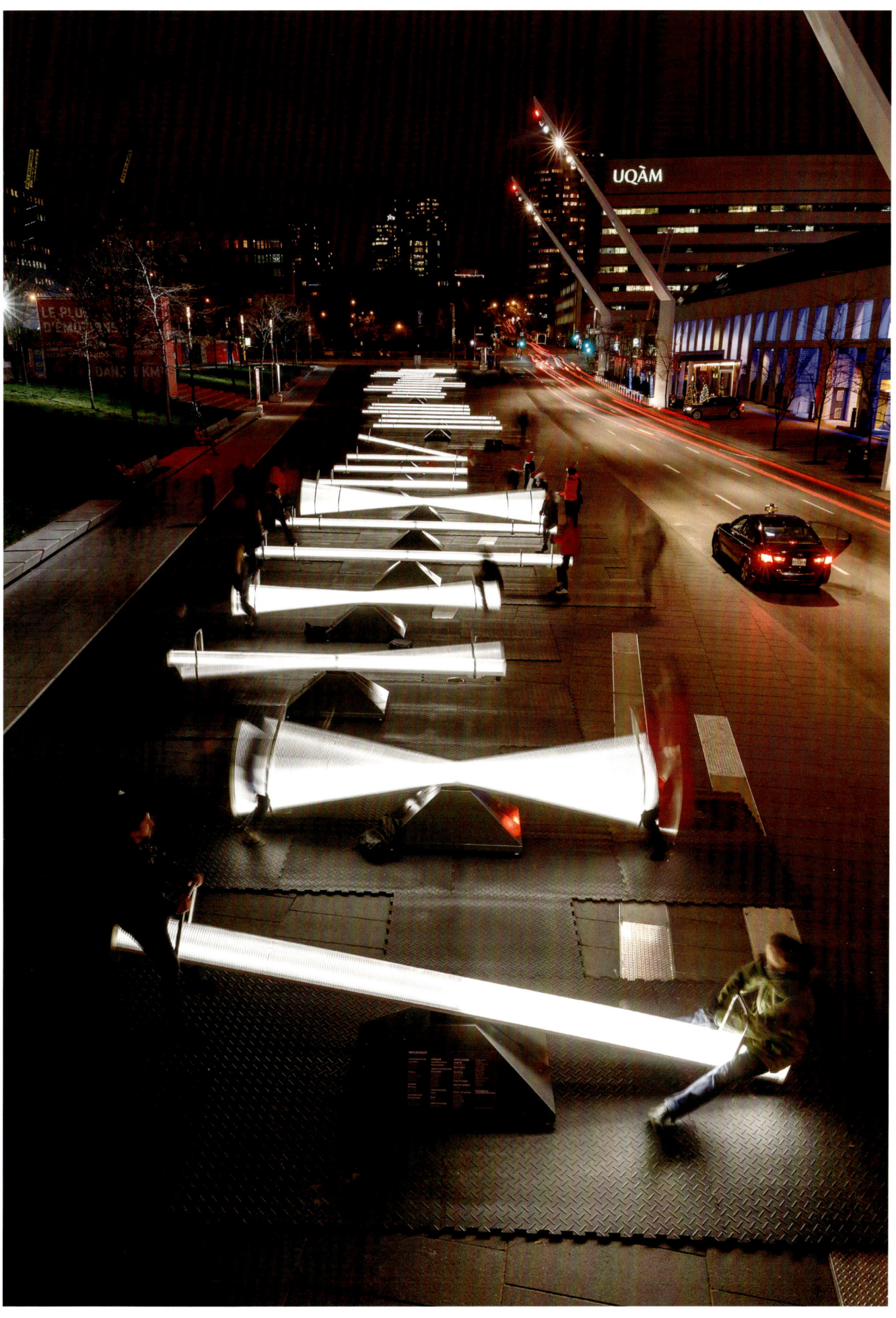

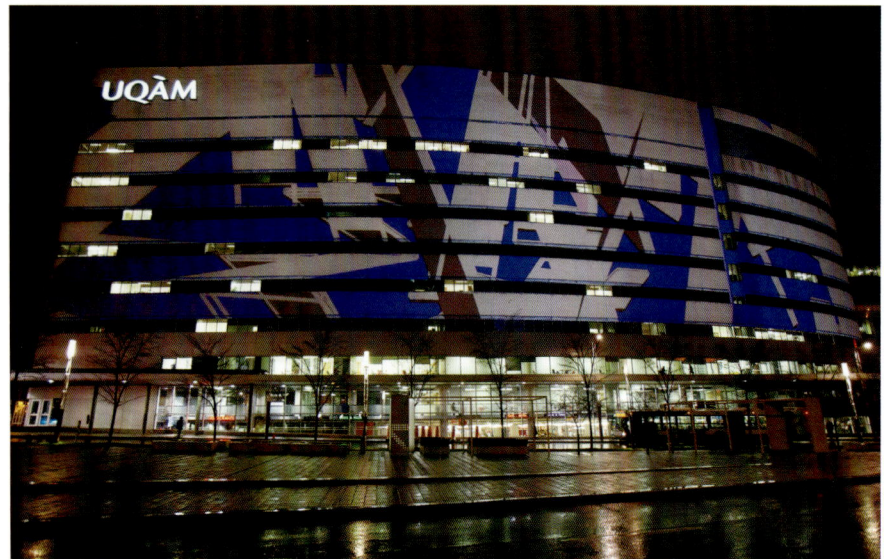

When not in use, the see-saws stabilize to the horizontal and remain at a lower glowing level. When activated by users and inclined, the see-saws, wired to LED lights and a speaker, will grow brighter and emit a sound sequence. The 30 see-saws shift along the length of the Place des Festival, while their vertical motion creates a dynamic light and sound wave. *Impulse* is an ever-changing urban instrument.

Impulse also includes nine commissioned videos, projected on key buildings in the area of Quartier des Spectacles. Some videos highlight and activate important civic buildings, while others serve to activate vacant lots. Each video is finely calibrated to the geometry and architecture of the surface on which it is projected. Like the Place des Festival installation, the videos represent experiments in sound visualization through geometric serial patterns, fields, waves, and plays of dissonance.

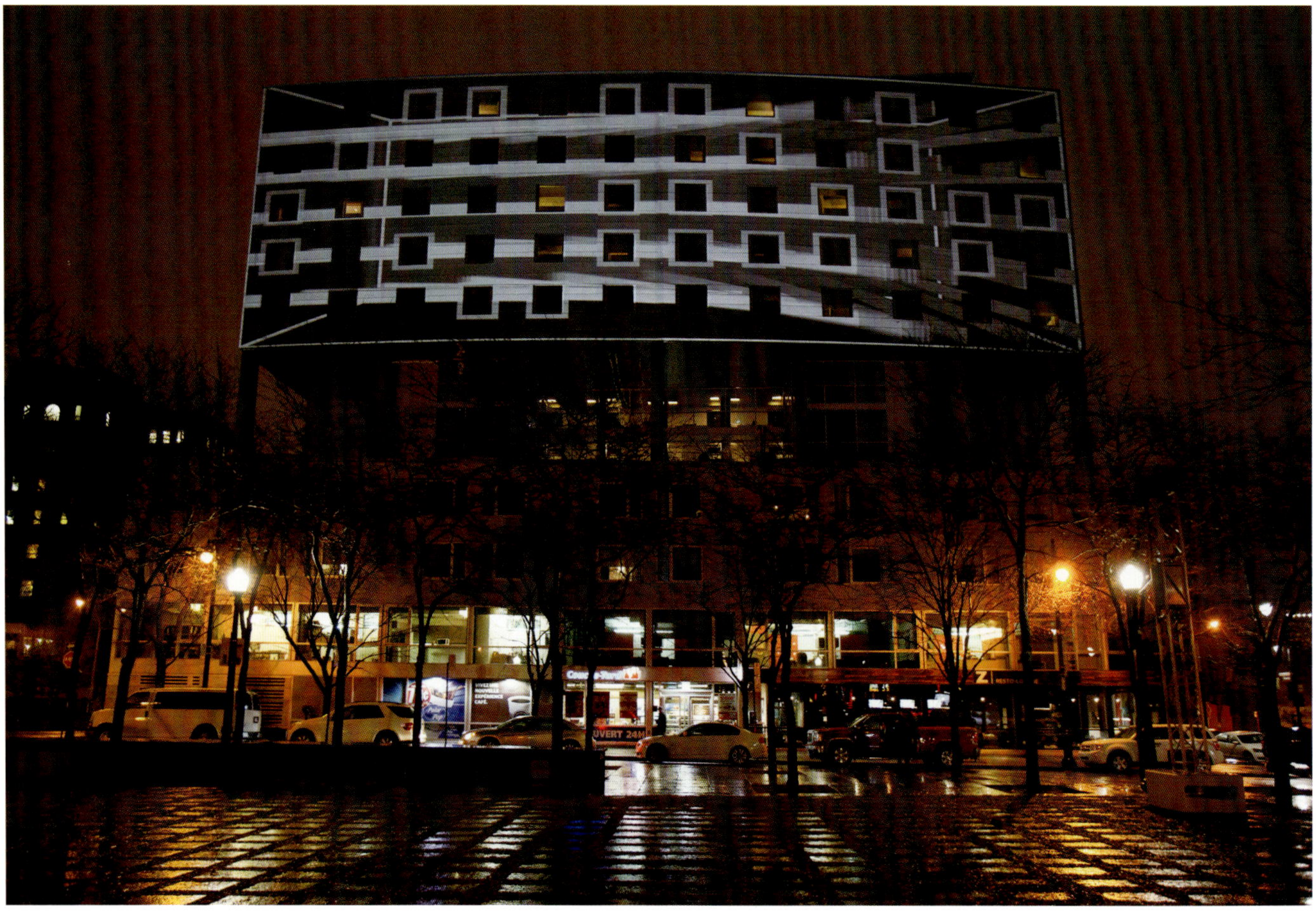

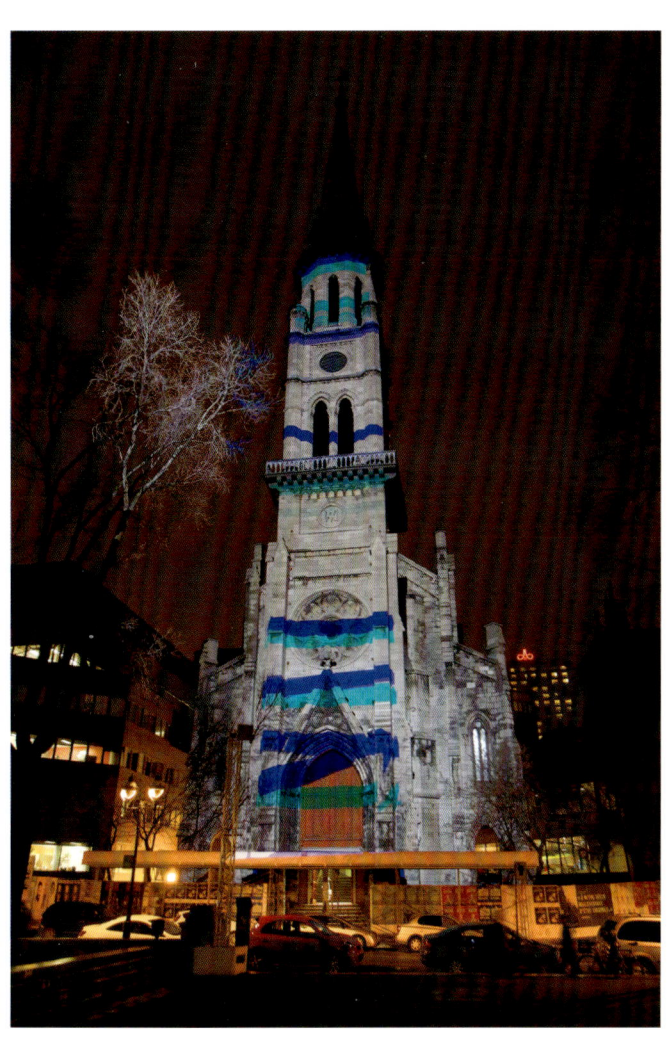

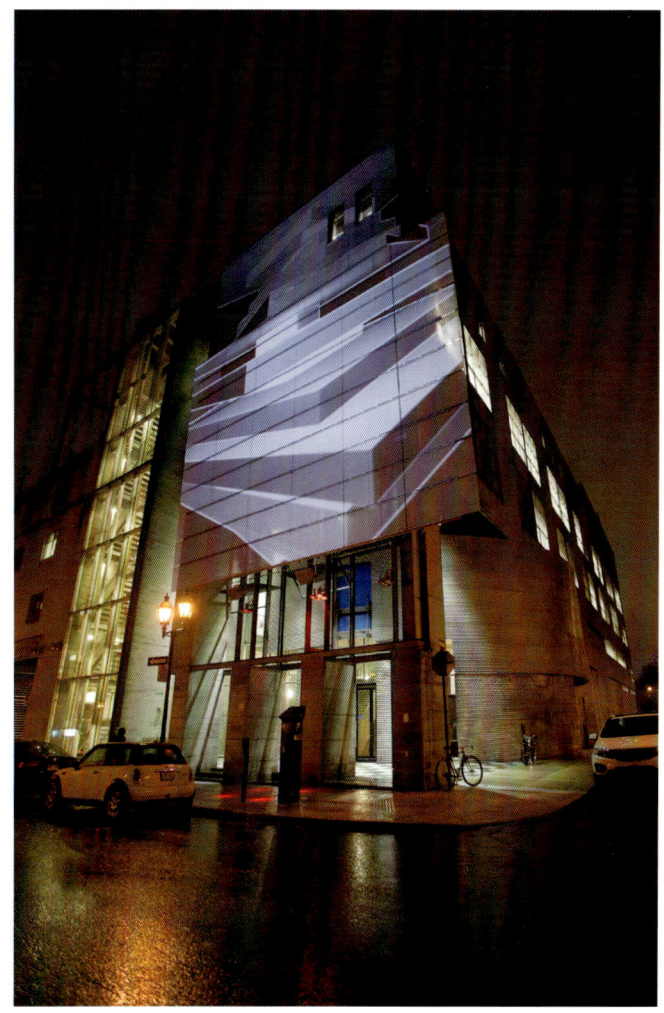

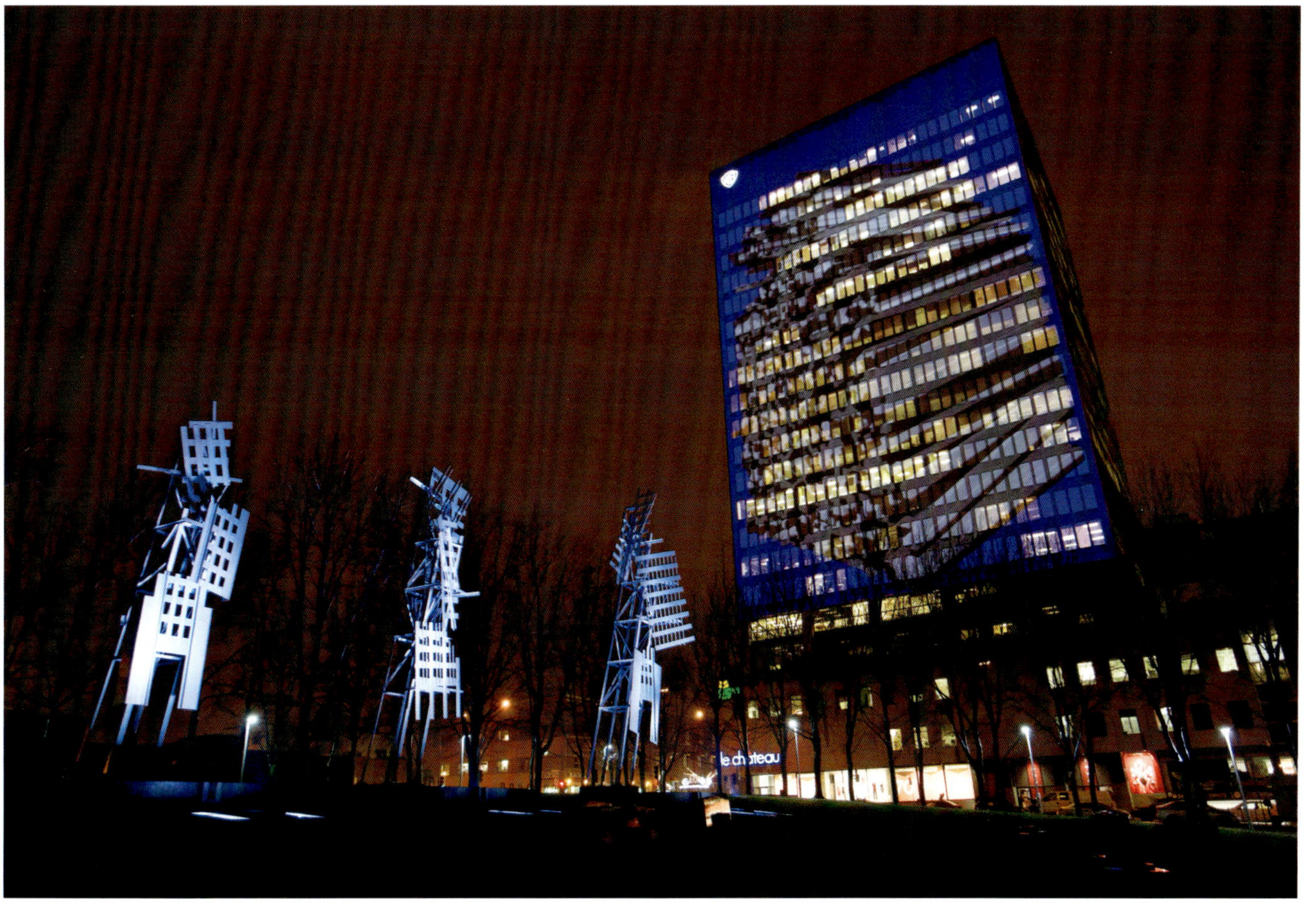

S.A.T

—

Design: **Romain Tardy**

—

S.A.T is a large-scale visual, light and sound installation. It is composed of a total of 72 networked modules, which have two different functions depending on whether it's daytime or night time:

• During the day, they look like mirrors reflecting the sky, poetically merging the terrestrial and the cosmos above.
• At night, the modules light up to create visual patterns. The installation works as a huge but minimalist display which provides an intense and immersive audio-visual experience, visible from far away.

Visitors are invited to connect to a local wifi network with their phones, which automatically display a reinterpretation of 3 messages sent to outer space in the 70's. Each visitor's phone IP is displayed on the installation for a few seconds when he connects to it (visible from far, far above), before turning into a light sequence which encodes the data exchanged between the local server and his phone in order to display the 3 animated messages.

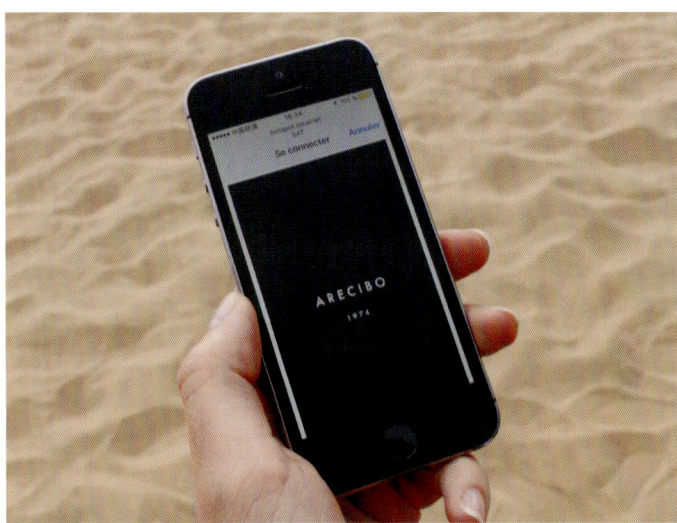

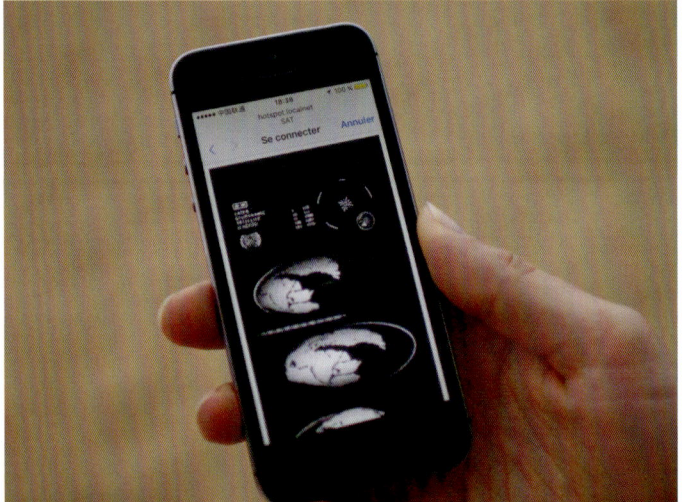

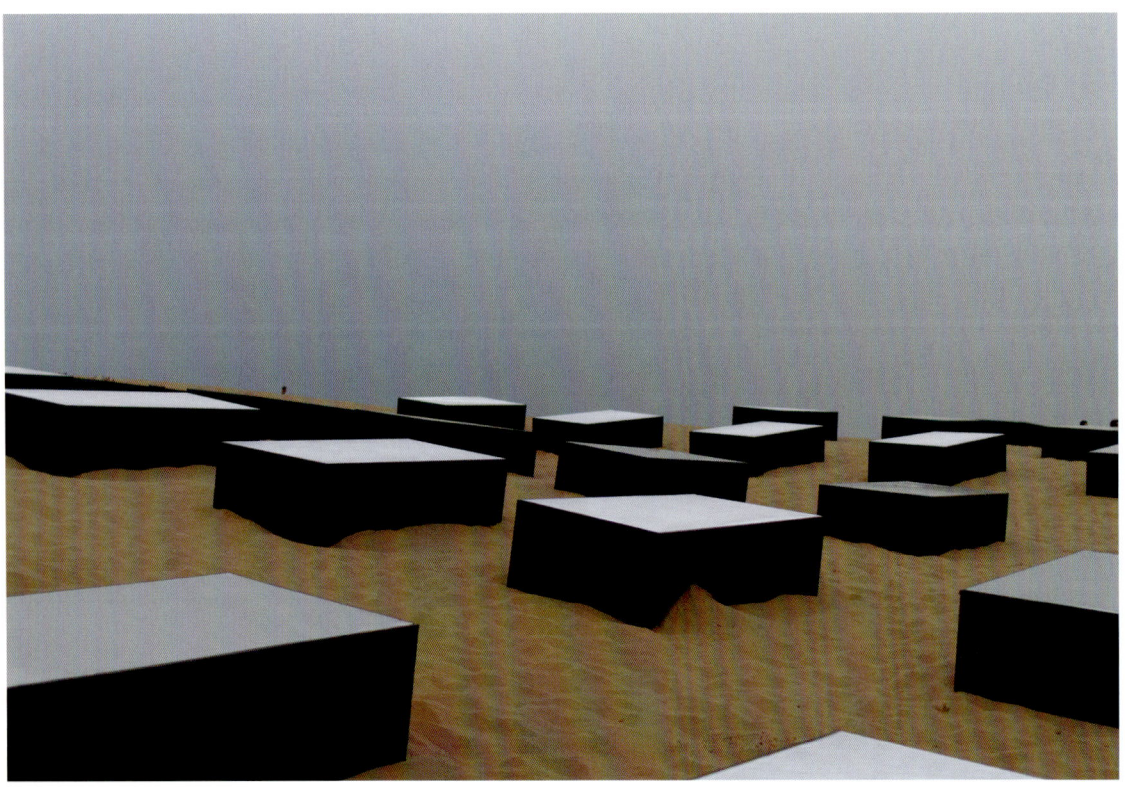

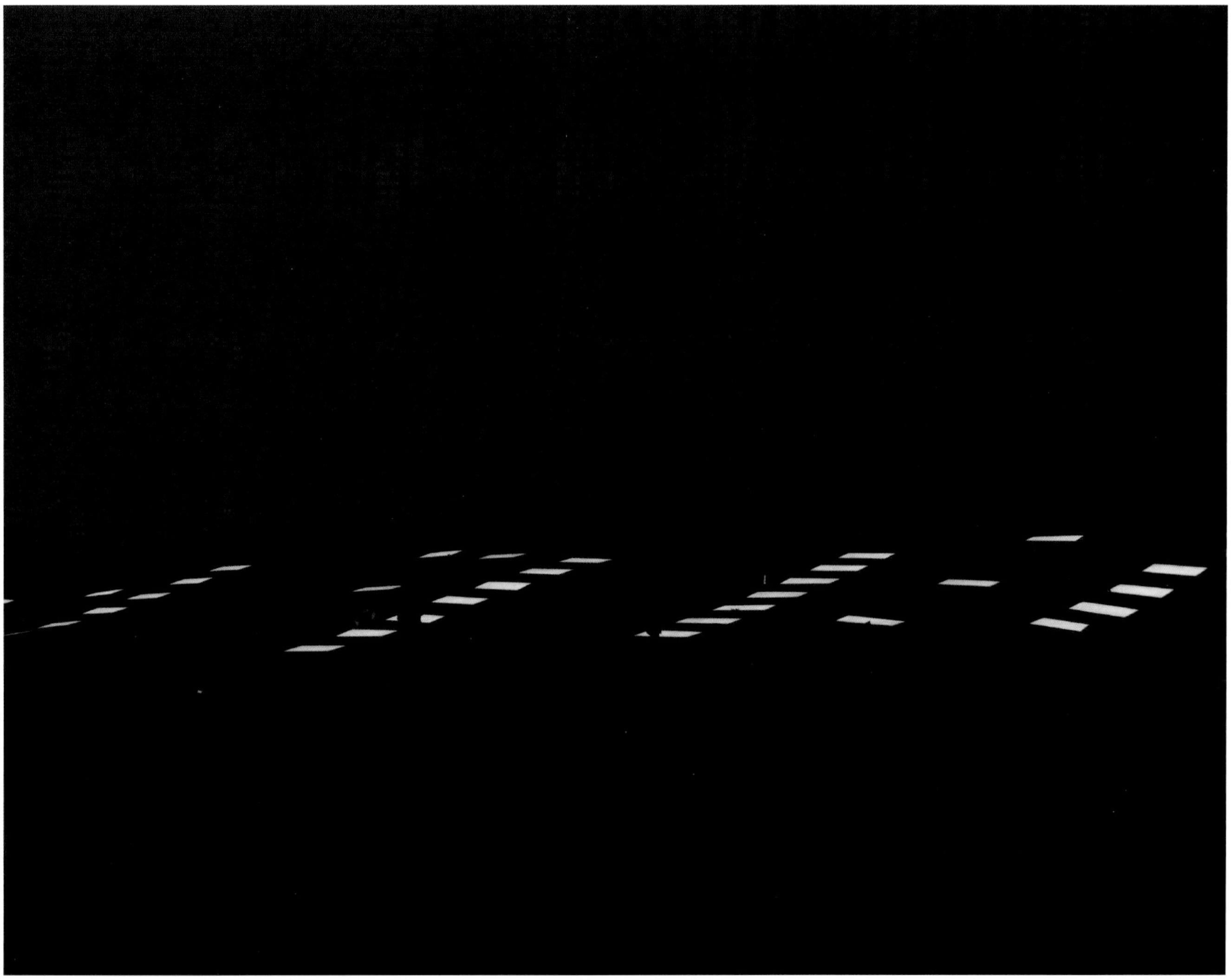

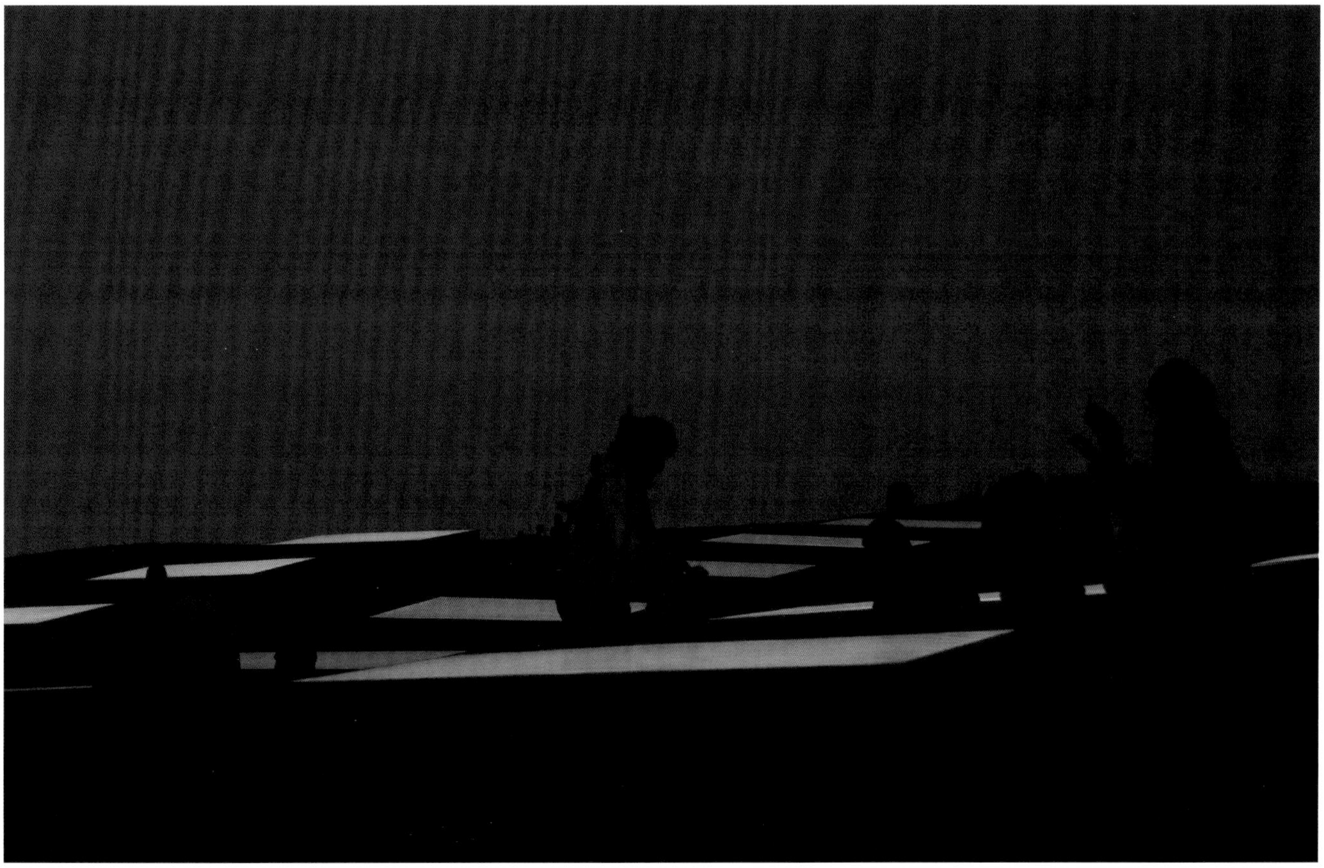

SONIC LIGHT BUBBLE

—

Design: **ENESS**

—

Sonic Light Bubble is a lighted, colored dome that responds to closeness and touch with light and sound. This six-meter wide sculpture radiates a warm glow through 236 programmable LEDs, orchestrated to mesmerize and invite you closer to engage with its beauty. The Bubble evolves its own patterns and visuals with a generative soundtrack, which renews the experience with each moment.

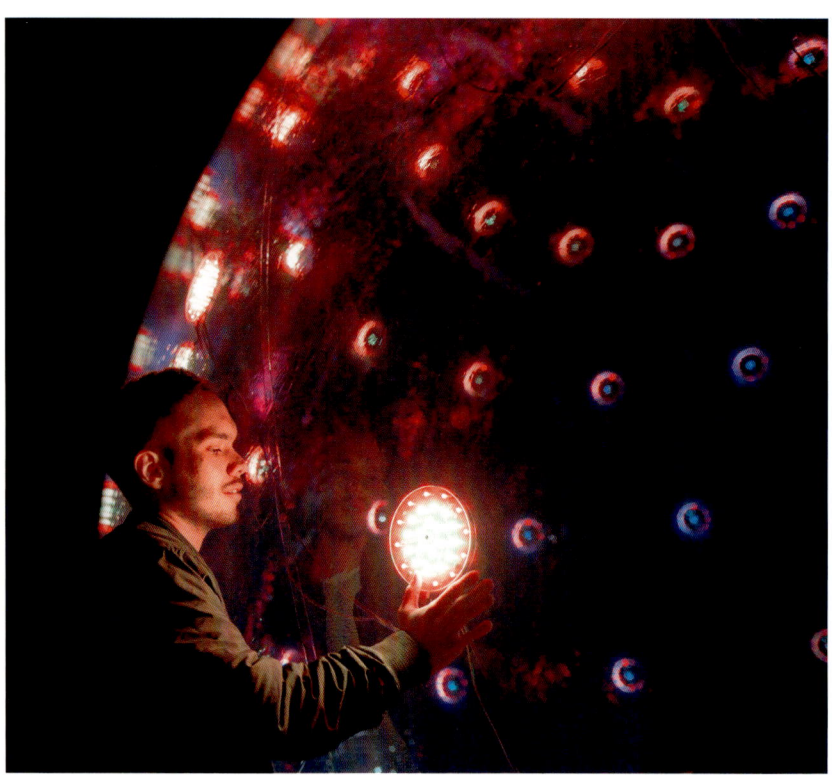

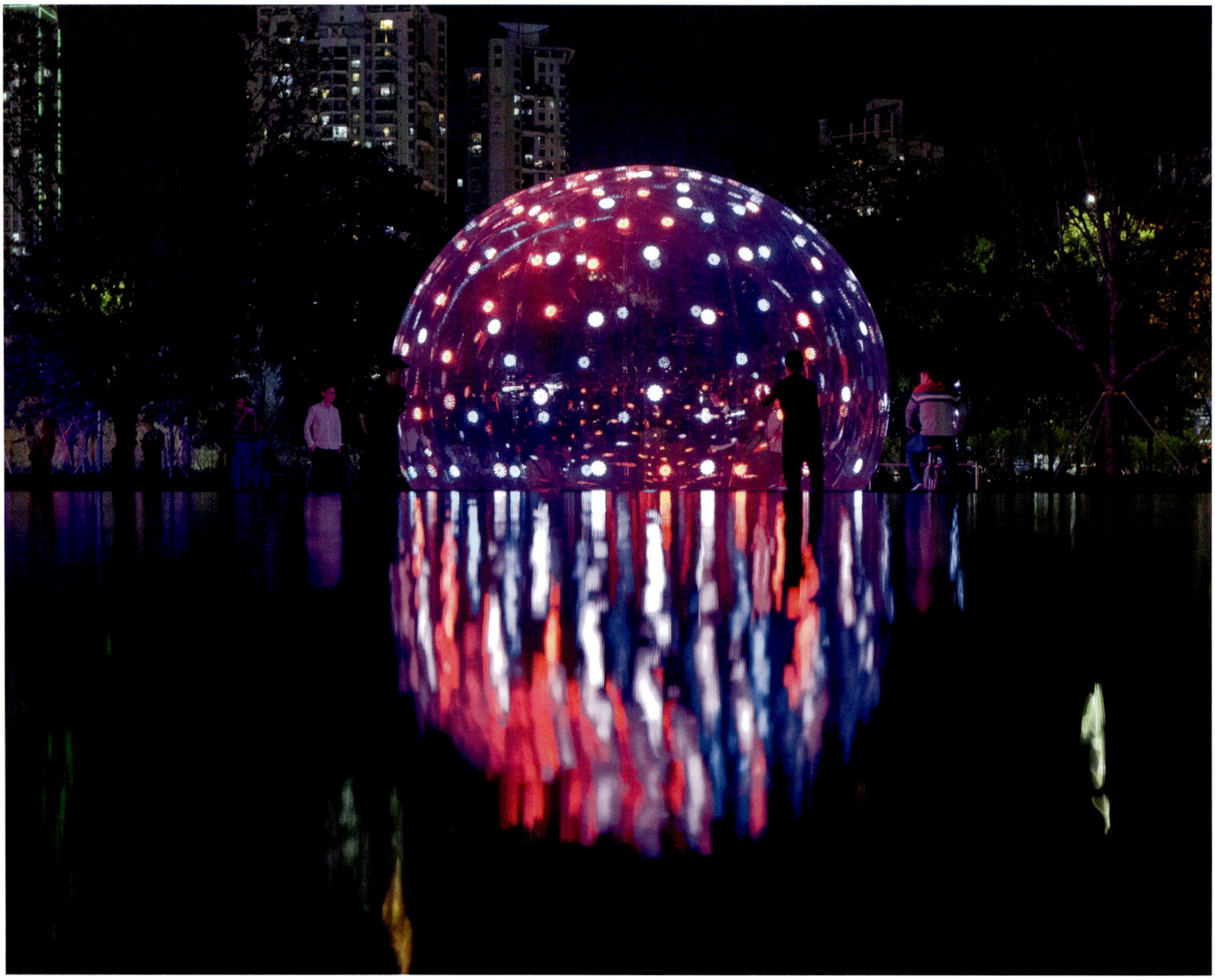

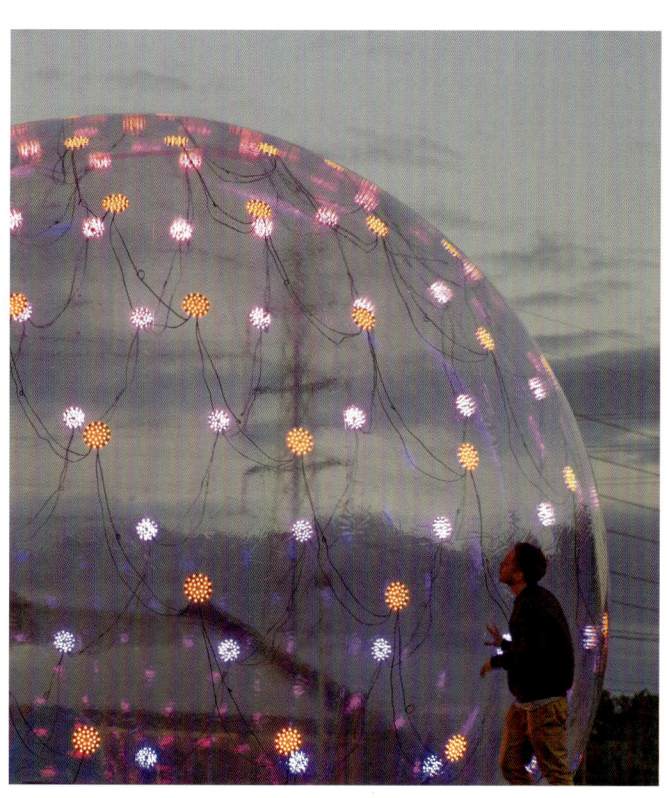
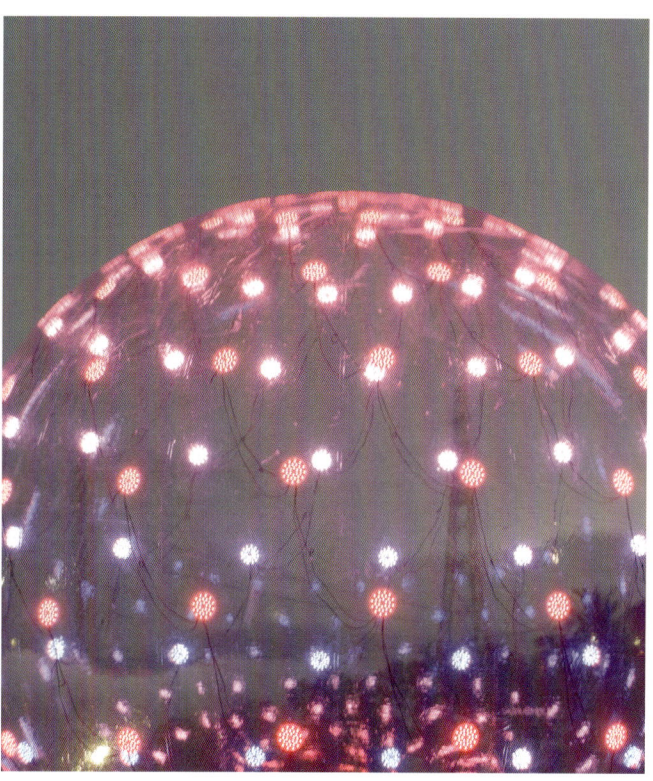

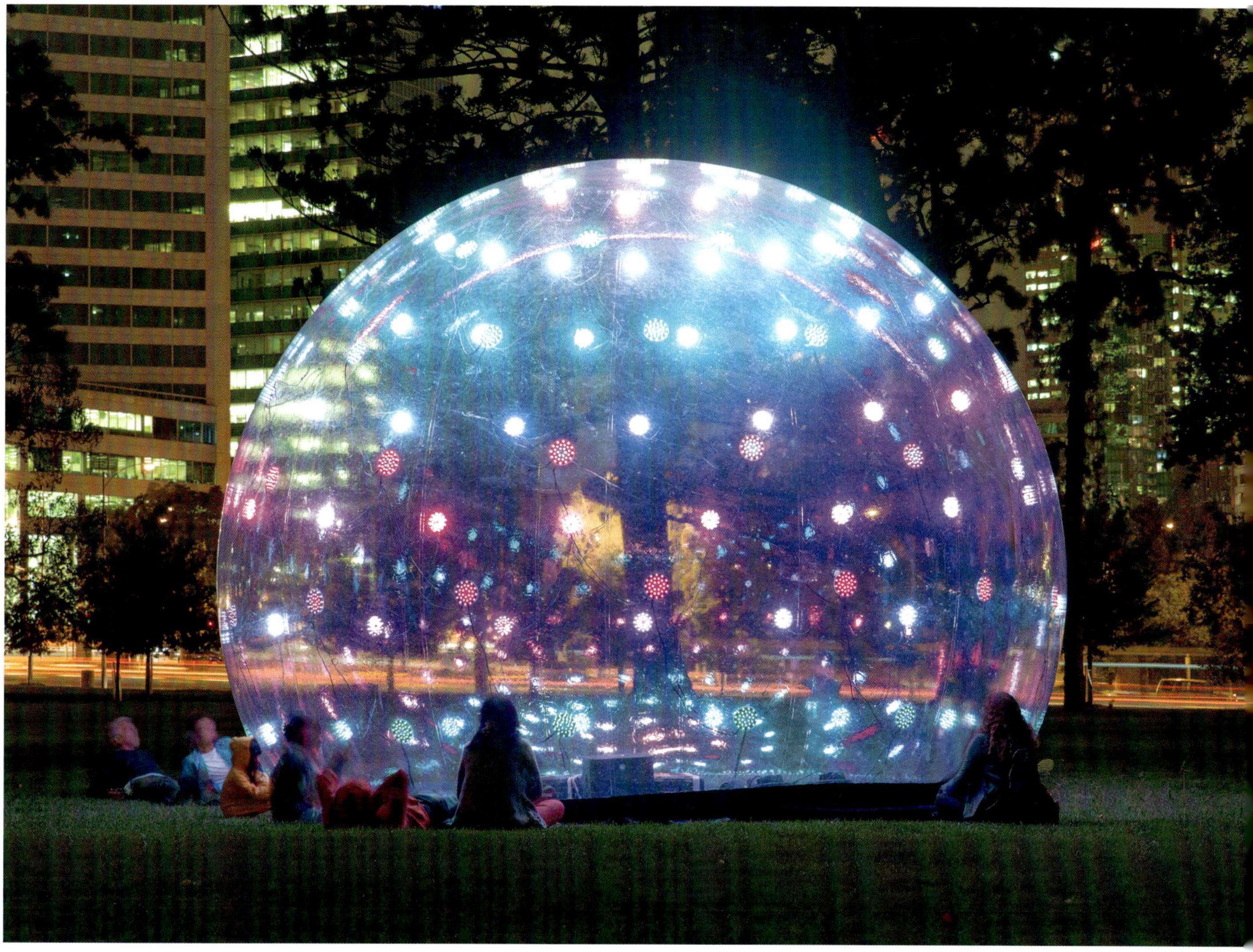

PIXEL FLOW

—

Agency: **Claudia Paz Lighting Studio**
Concept Design & Art Direction: **Claudia Paz**
Technology Design: **Cesar Castro**
Interactive Programming: **Chris Plant**
Sound Design: **Neil Spragg**

—

Pixel Flow is an immersive permanent interactive installation created to transport the participant to a virtual world of light and sound. A spiraling array of linear lights gently encompasses the participant, immersing them in an audiovisual landscape in which even the slightest movement generates ripples of color and sound across the space. The installation switches between energy states and calmer states in response to the user's degree of movement and participation.

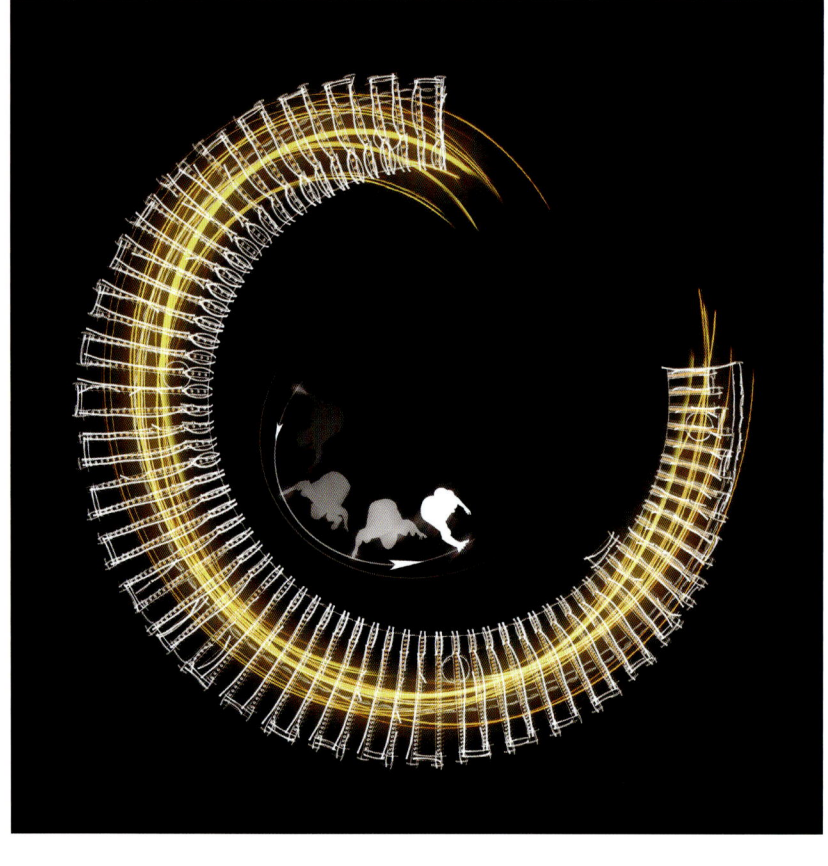

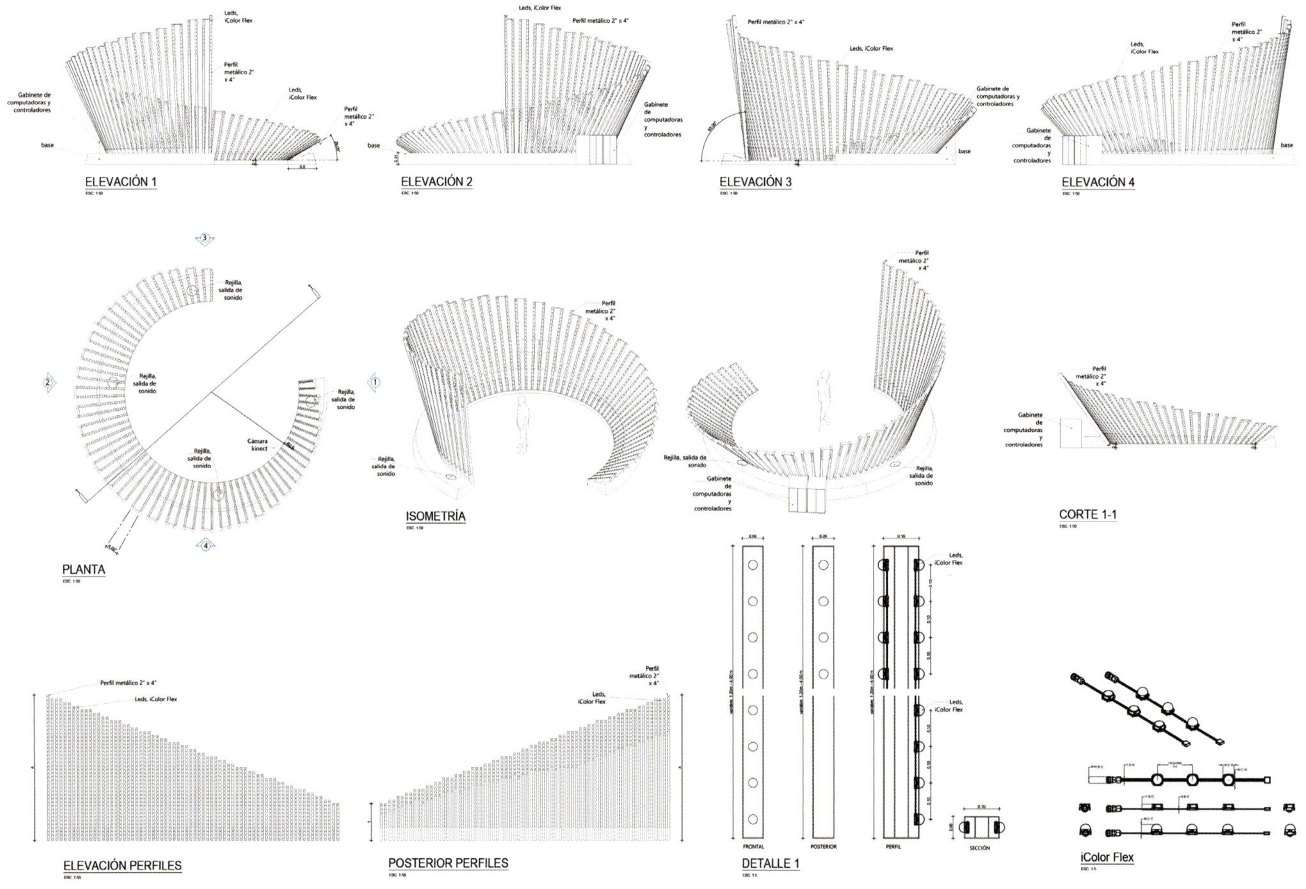

ELEVACIÓN 1

ELEVACIÓN 2

ELEVACIÓN 3

ELEVACIÓN 4

PLANTA

ISOMETRÍA

CORTE 1-1

ELEVACIÓN PERFILES

POSTERIOR PERFILES

DETALLE 1

iColor Flex

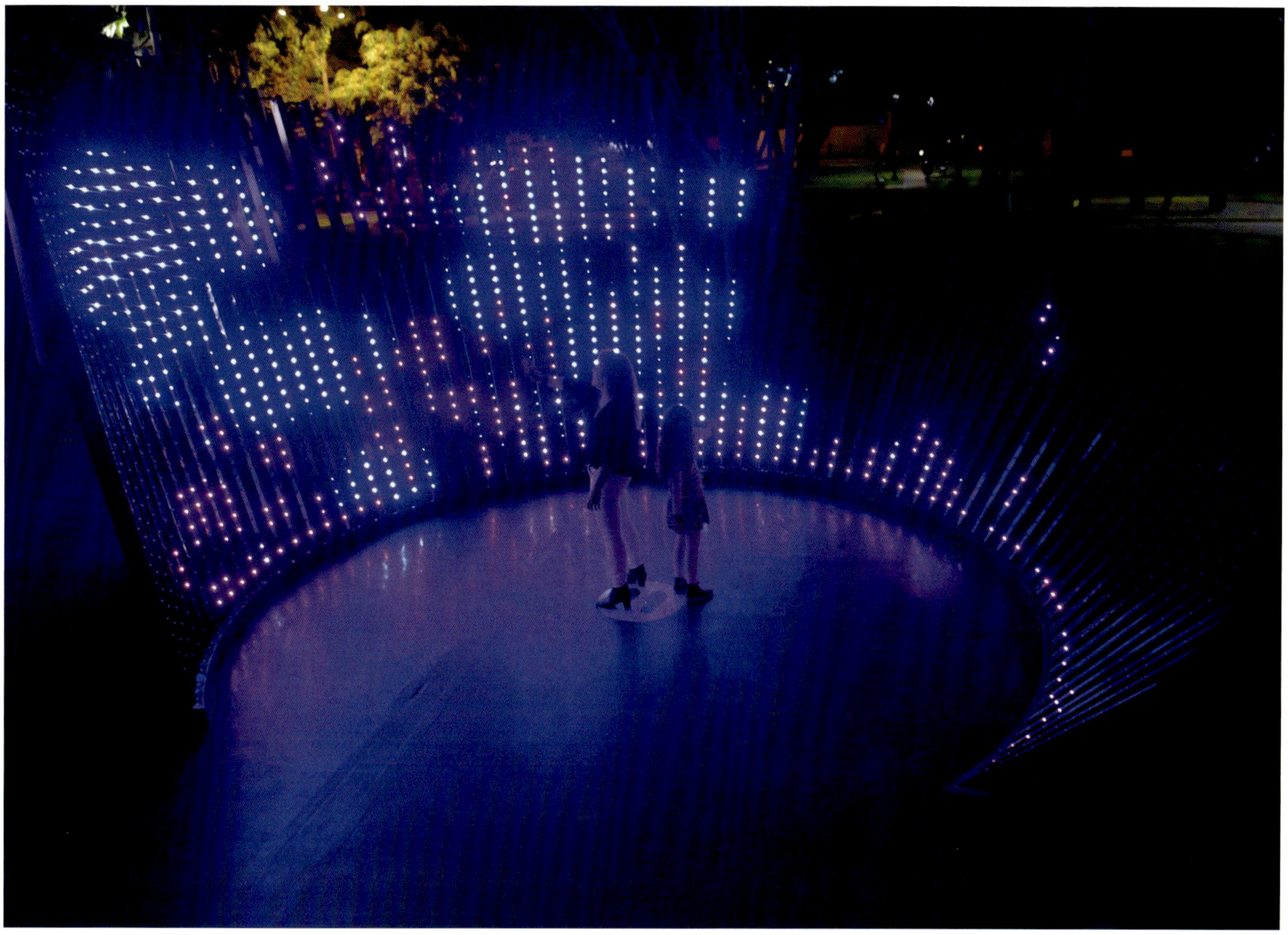

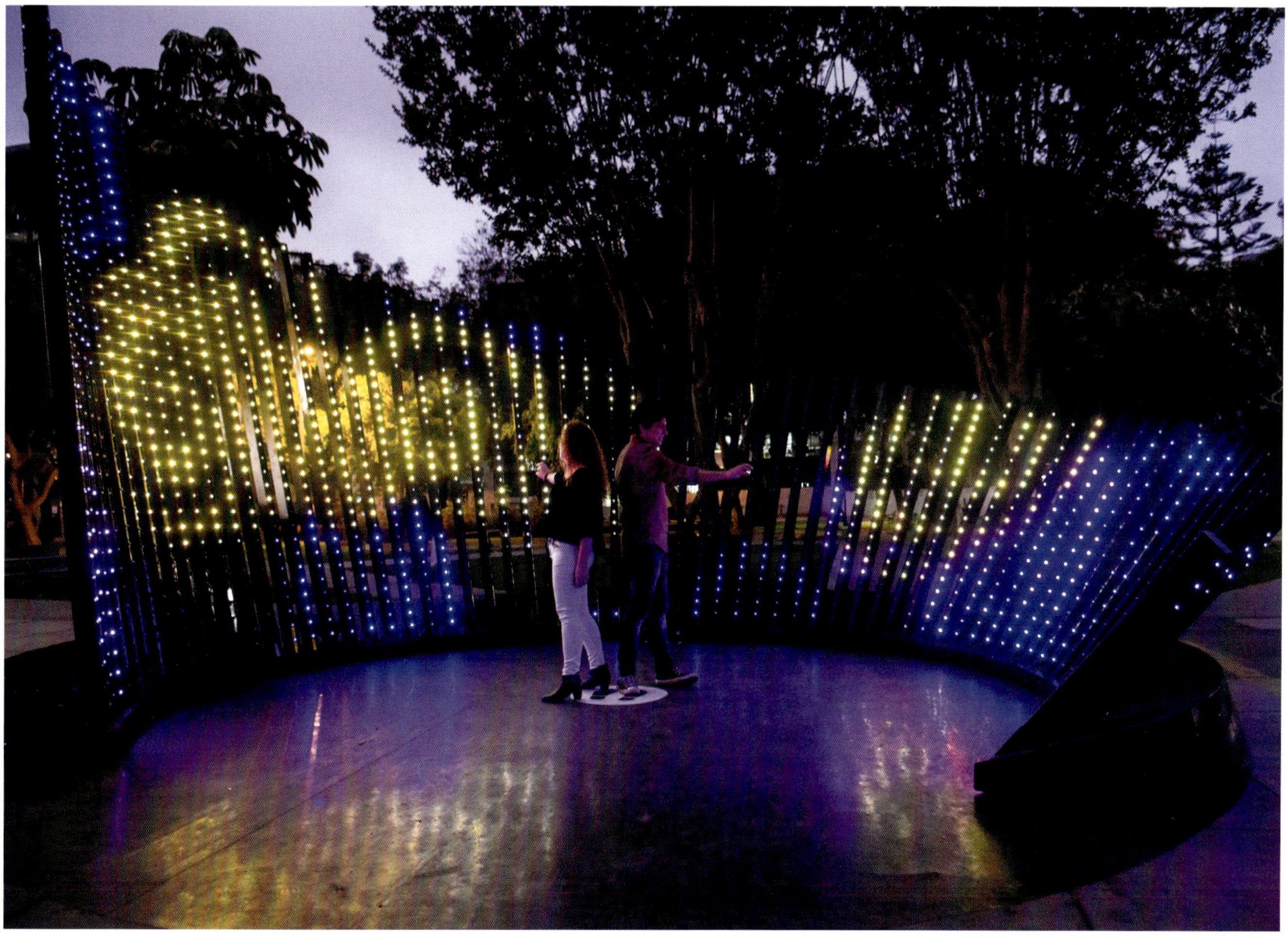

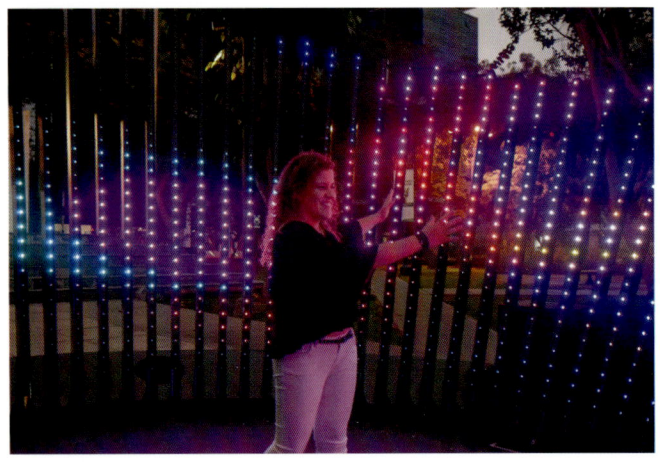
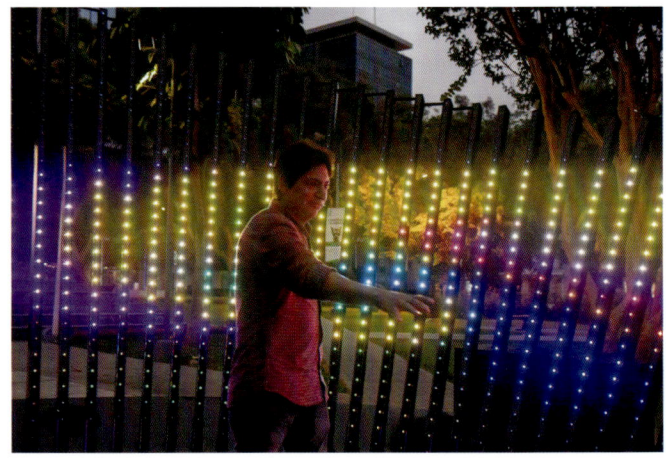
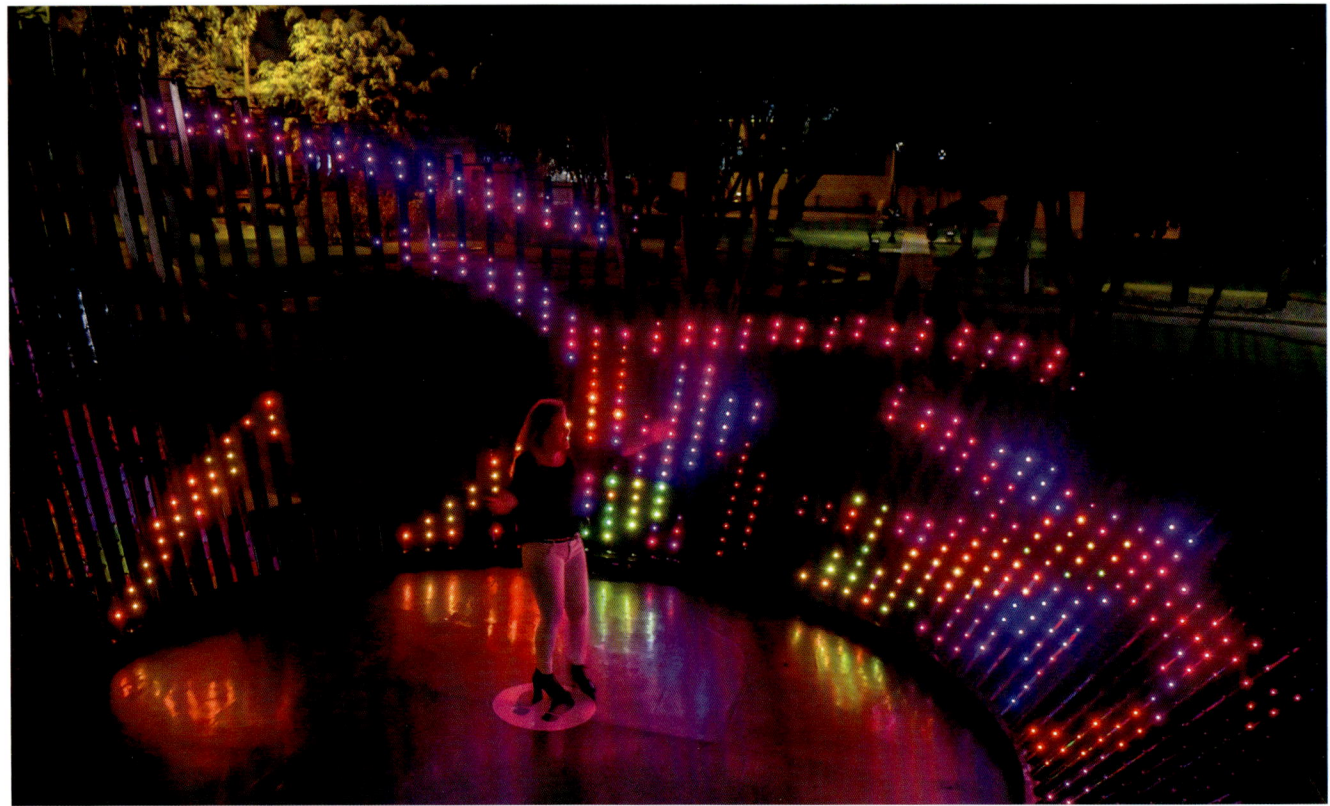
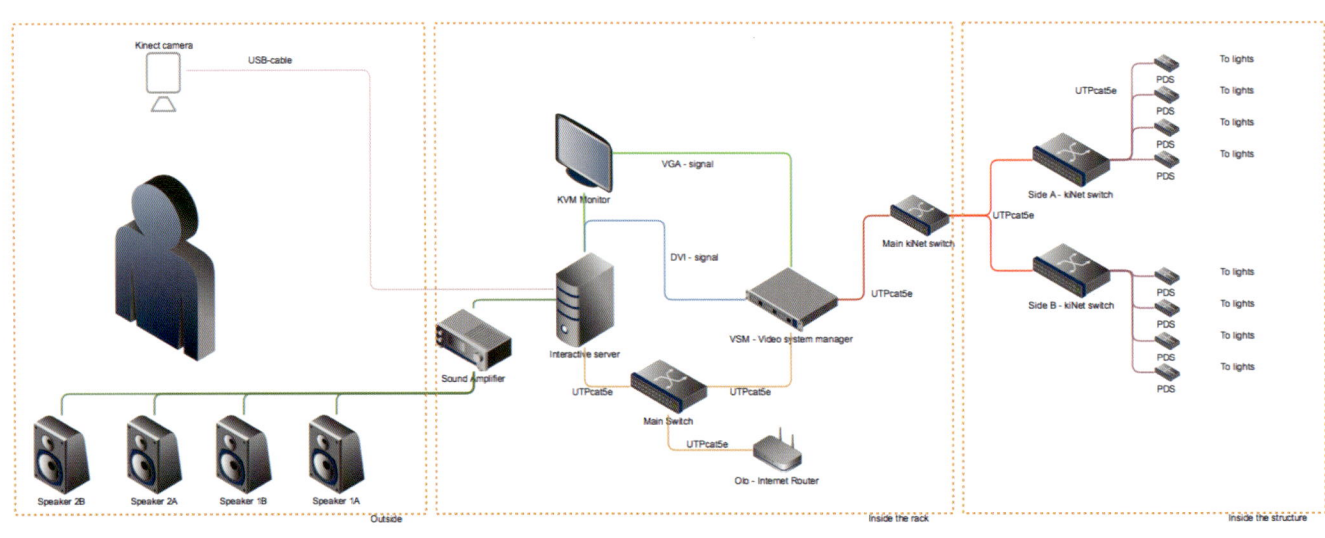

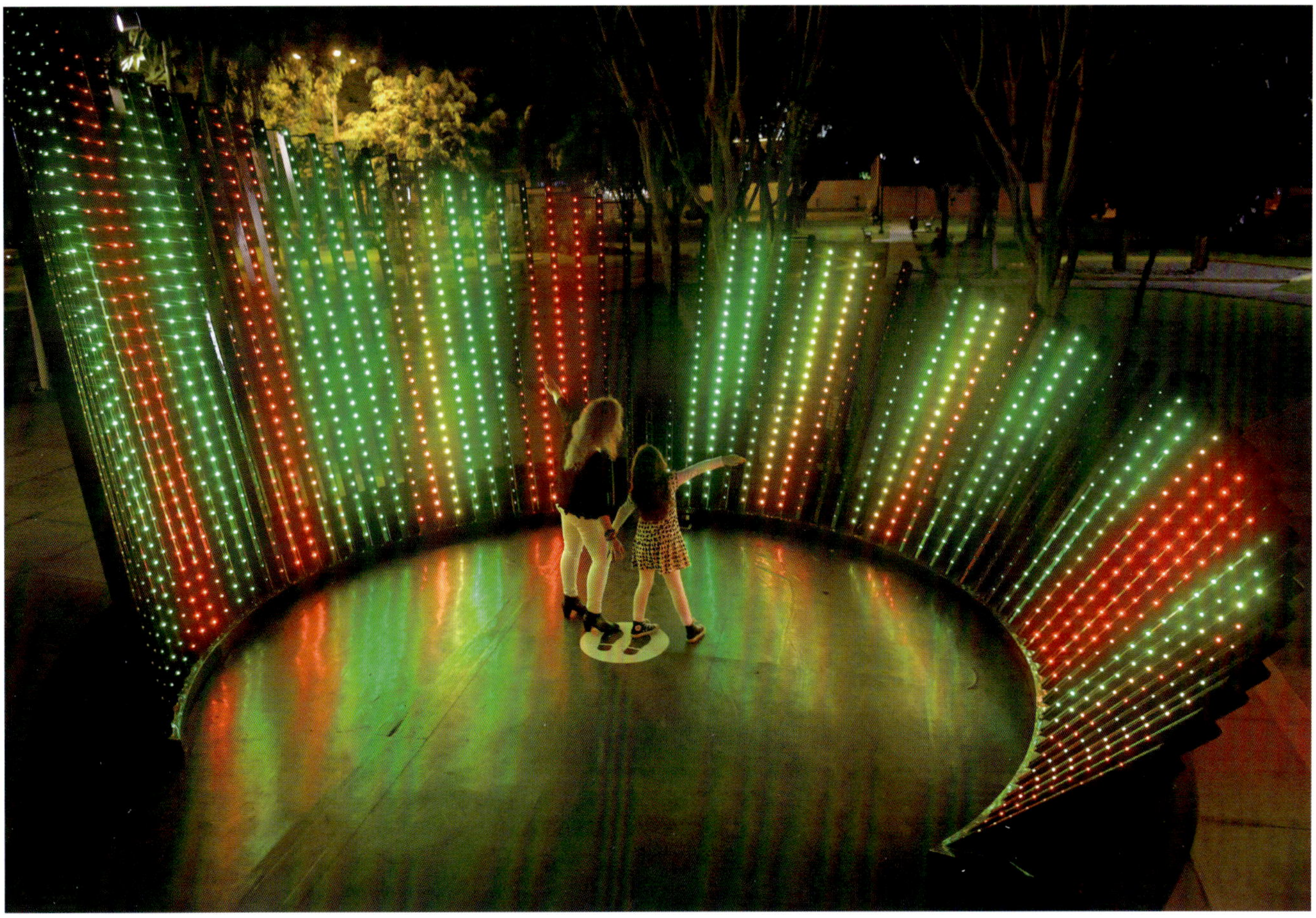

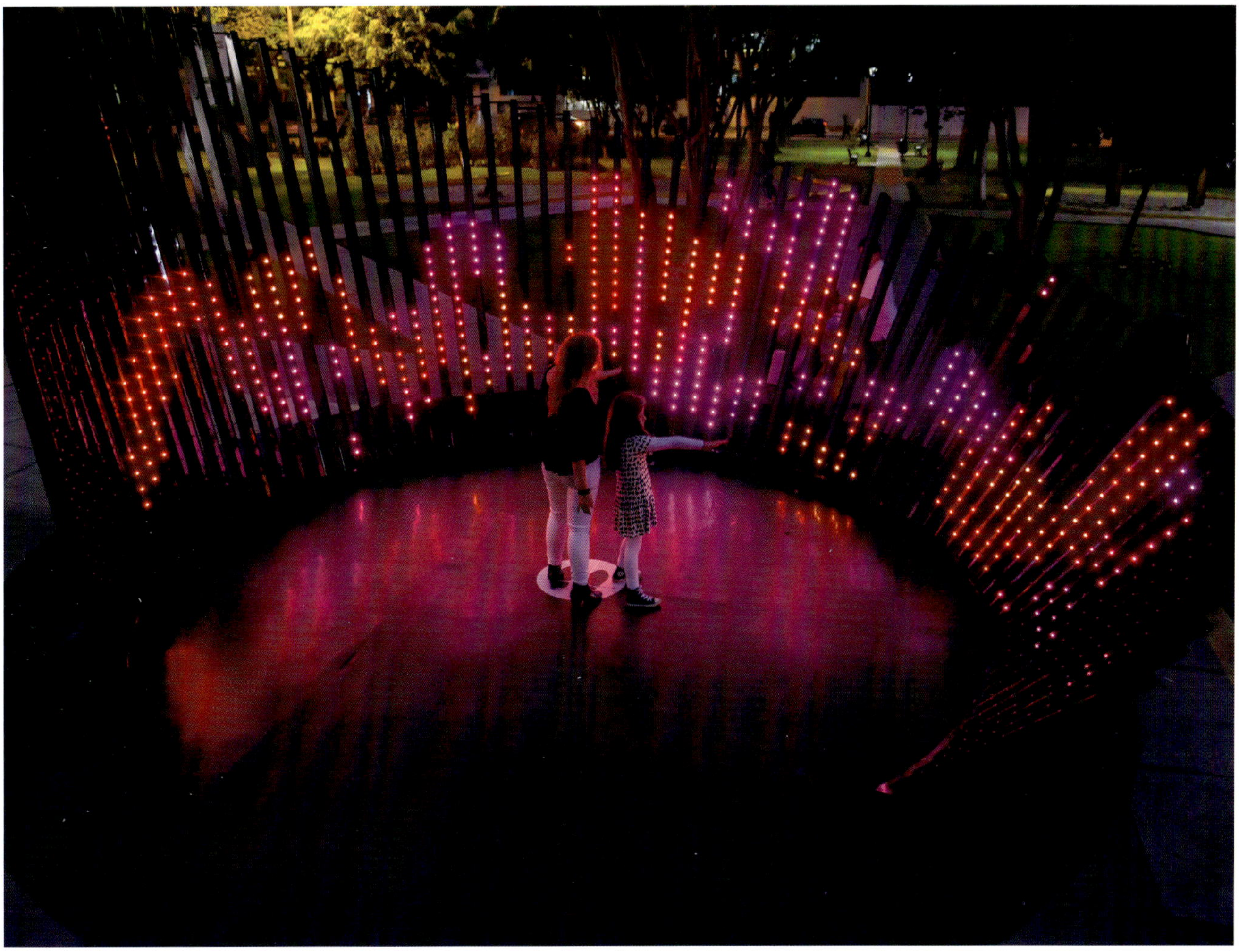

BRUUMRUUM!

—

Design: **David Torrents, artec3 Studio**

—

BruumRuum! is an installation that interacts with shouts from passers-by near the piece and with ambient noise in the city, changing shape and color according to the intensity of this noise. In this way, *BruumRuum!* establishes a dialogue between the visitor and the public space through noise and light, in a square that listens and reacts to words like a huge ear—a public space that can hear.

BruumRuum! combines color and sound through 9,396 LEDs embedded in a 3,300-square-meter area. People stop, shout, smile, sing, become emotional and hug each other. The colors, which are in constant motion beneath their feet, react to the level of ambient noise and the intensity of shouts. Louder, sudden sounds cause radical changes, while softer sounds create more sinuous movements.

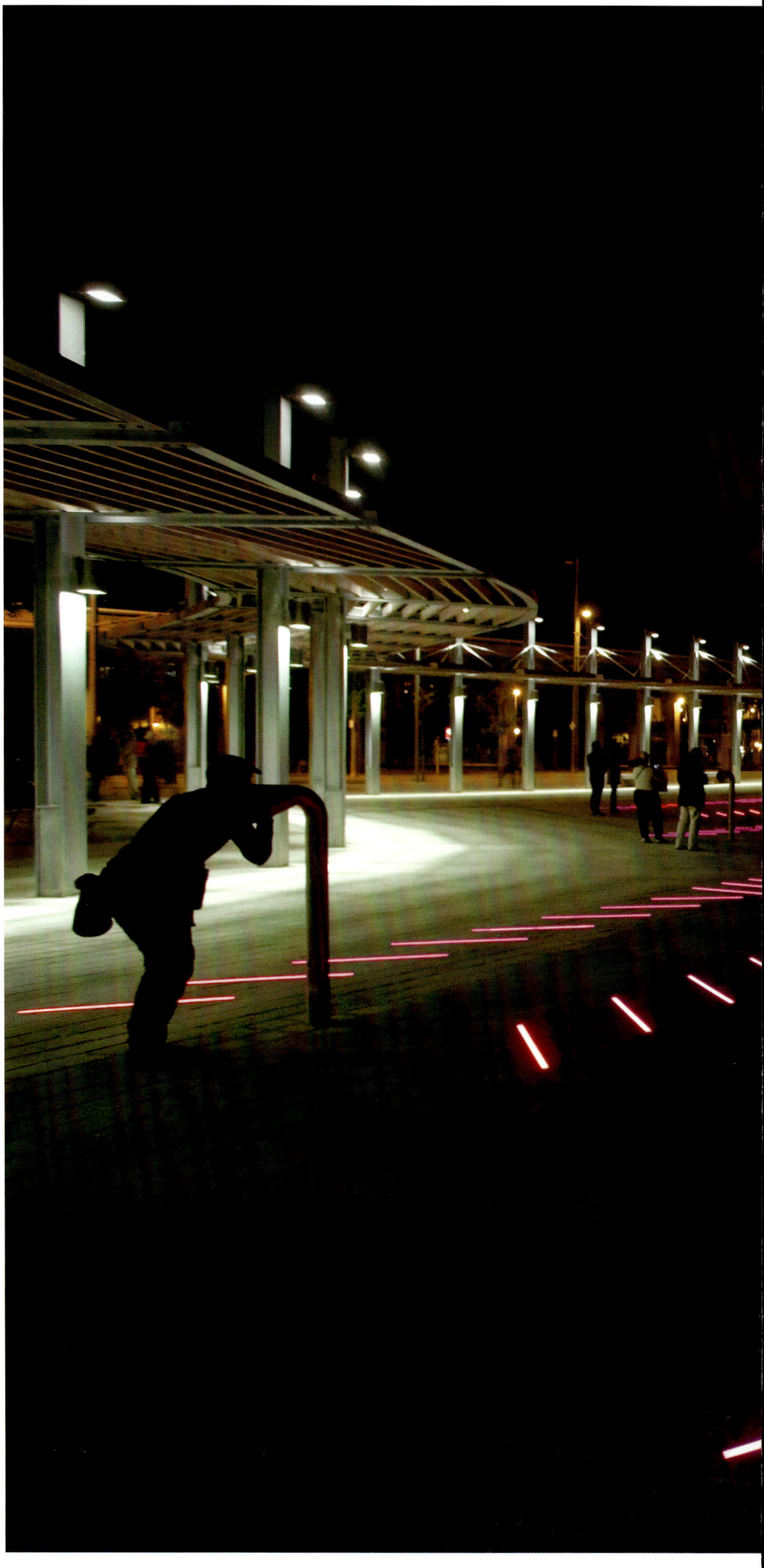

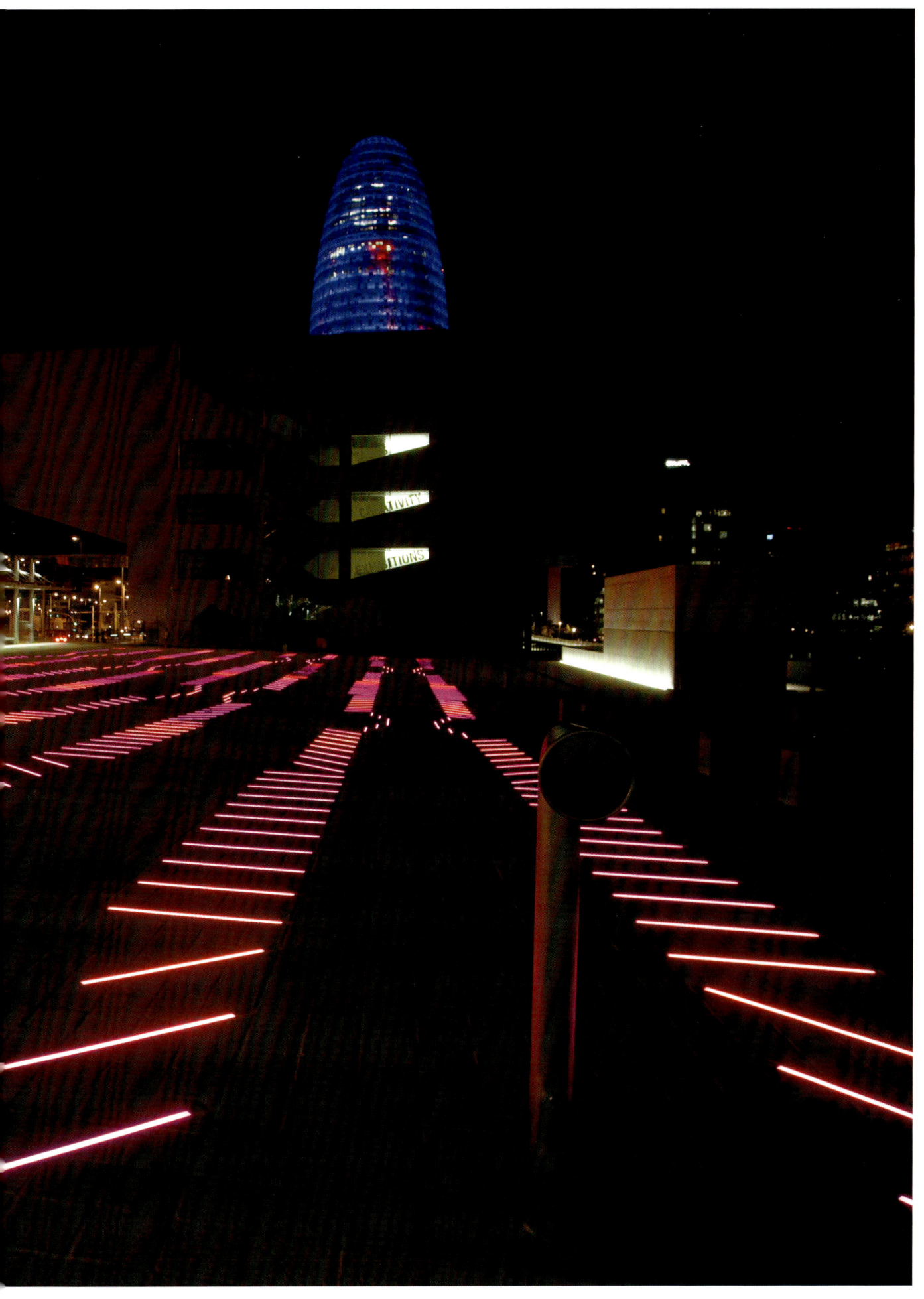

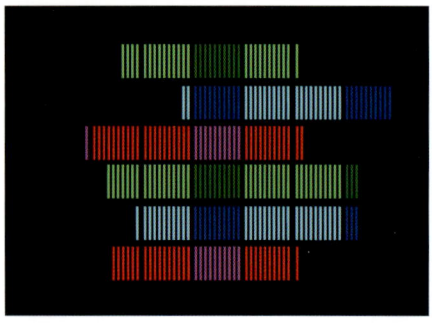

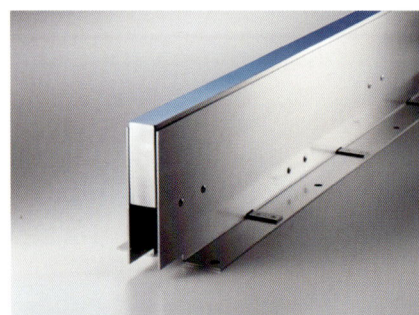

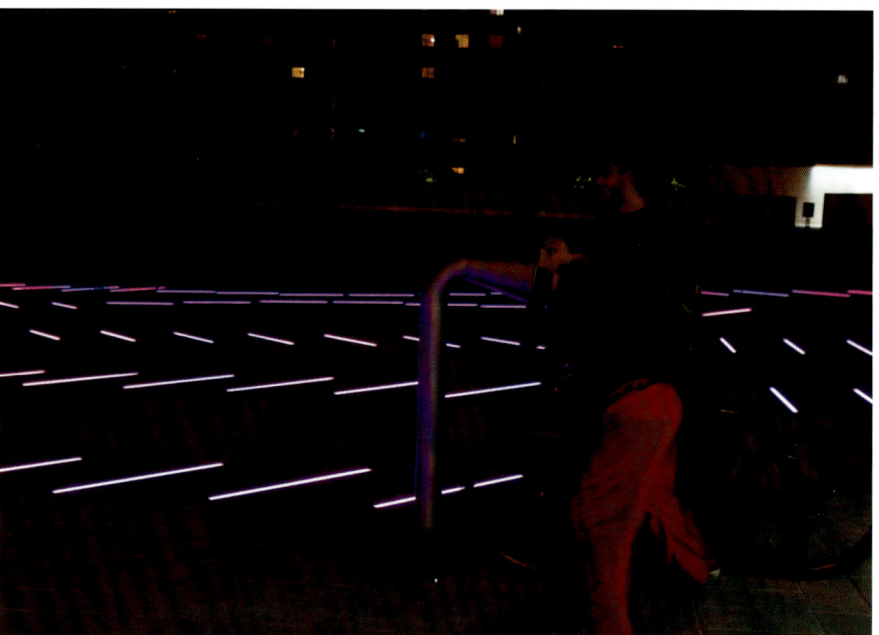

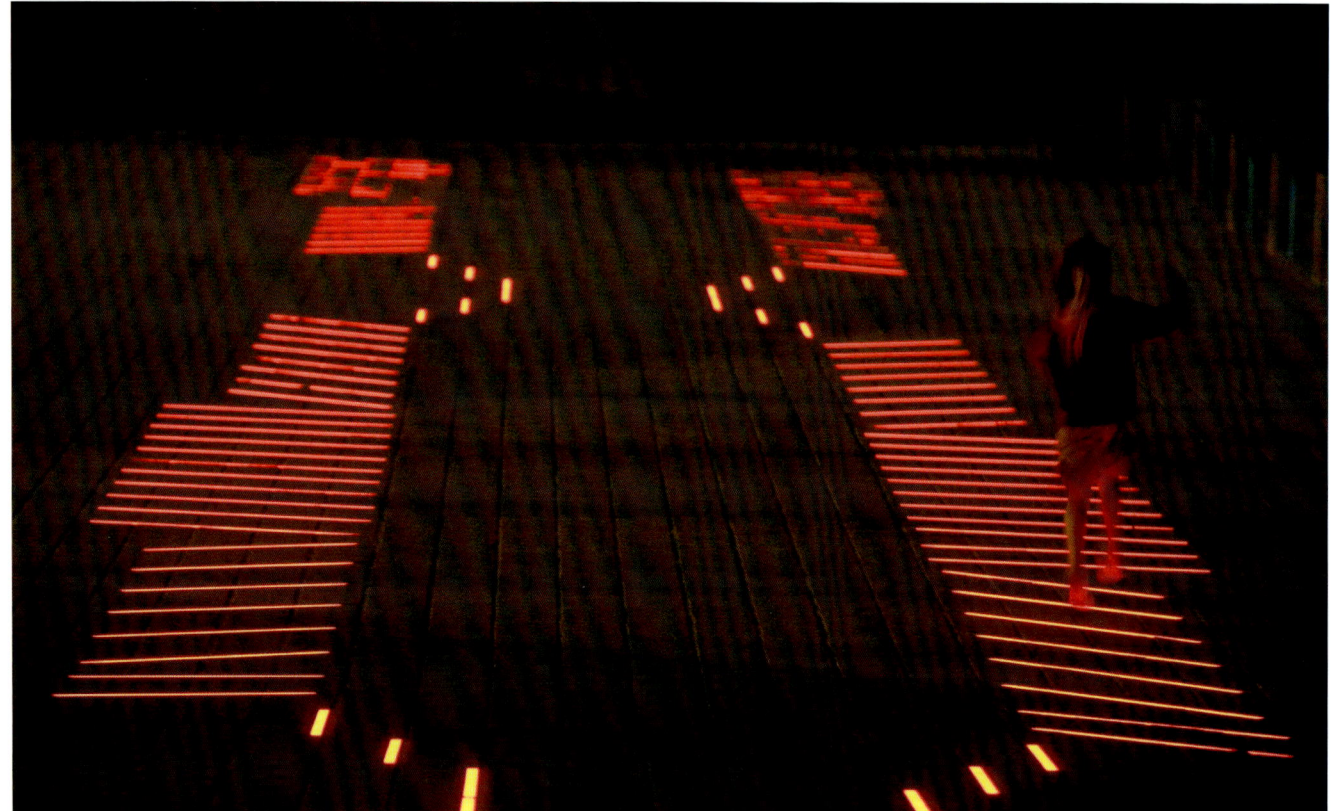

XIUXIU

—

Design: **David Torrents, Maurici Ginés**

—

XiuXiu is a dialogue between people and the public space, conducted through an interactive mapping projection of noise and light. It is a creation that transforms the façade of the Disseny Hub Barcelona building into a huge speaker that listens and reacts to words.

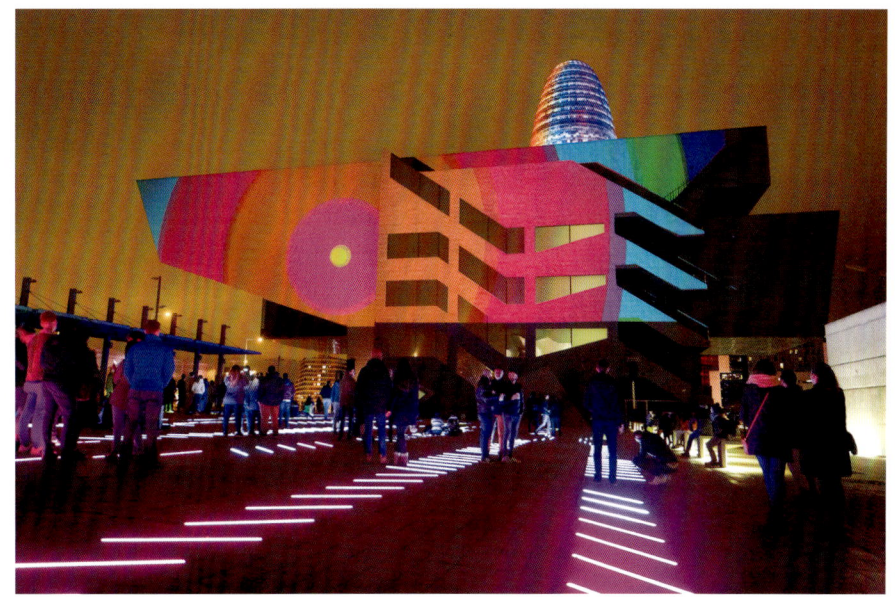

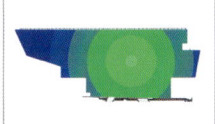 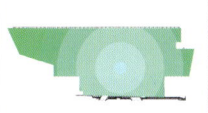 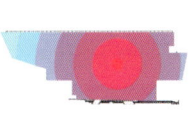 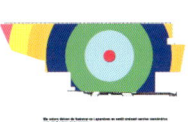 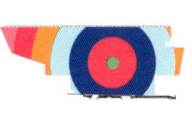 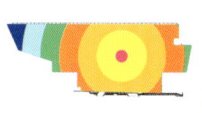

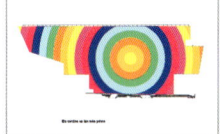 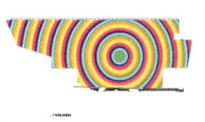 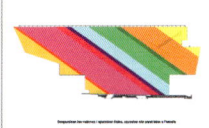   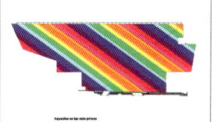

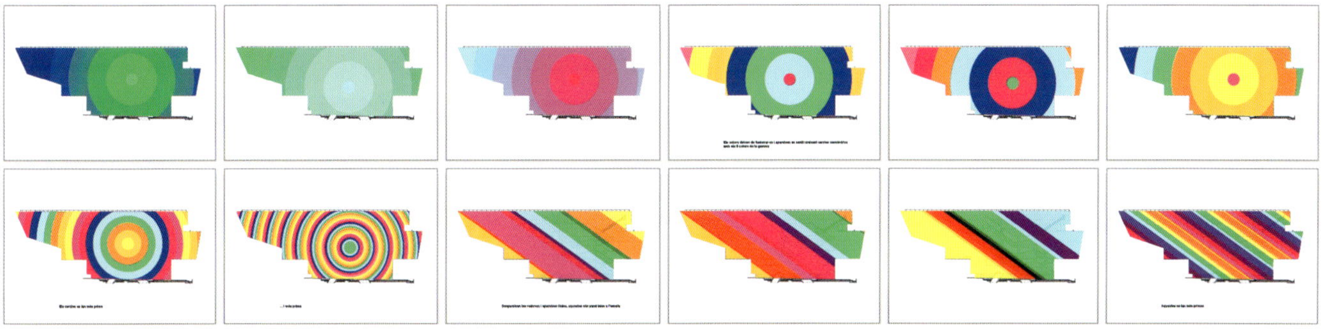

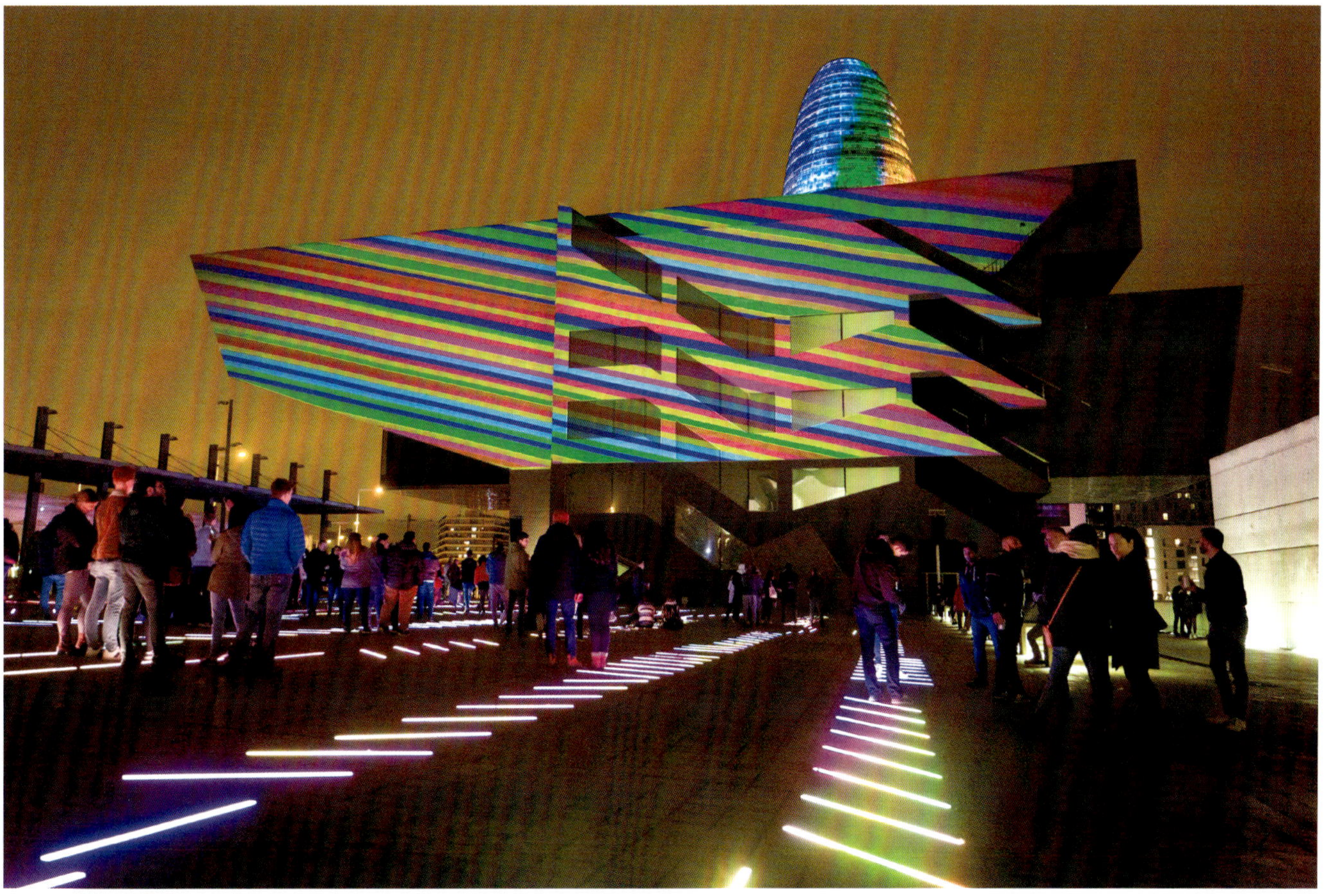

THE POOL

Design: **Jen Lewin Studio**

Photography: **The Sight And Sounds Media House, Brendan Burkett, Aaron Rogosin**

The Pool, by Jen Lewin, has traveled worldwide, with over 60 major exhibitions in over 20 different countries. *The Pool* was created to be a temporary traveling work, designed to activate public space with light and interactive play.

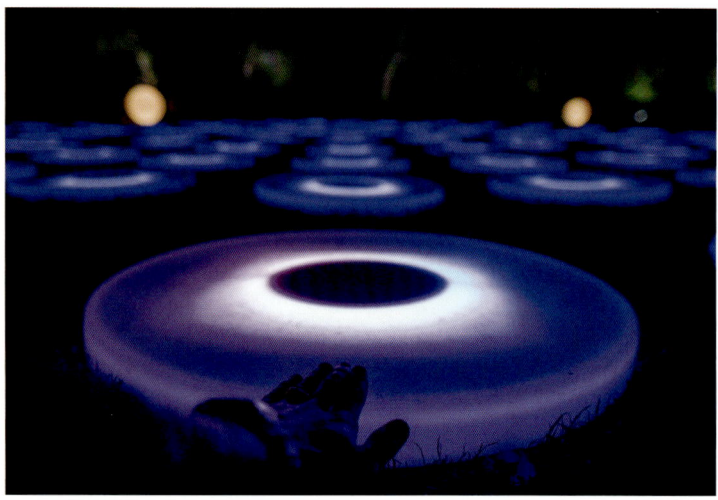

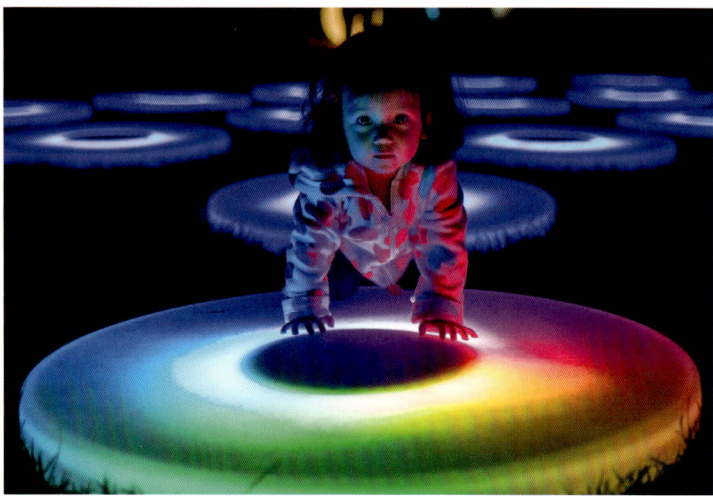

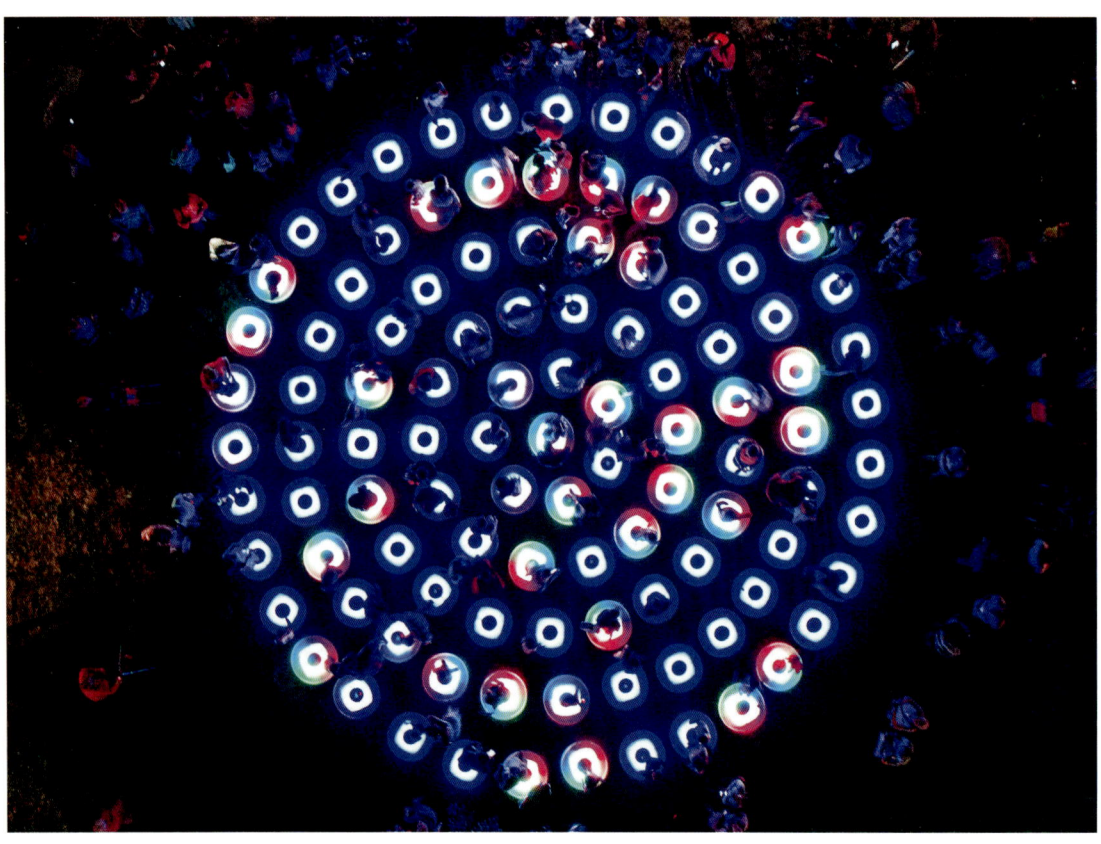

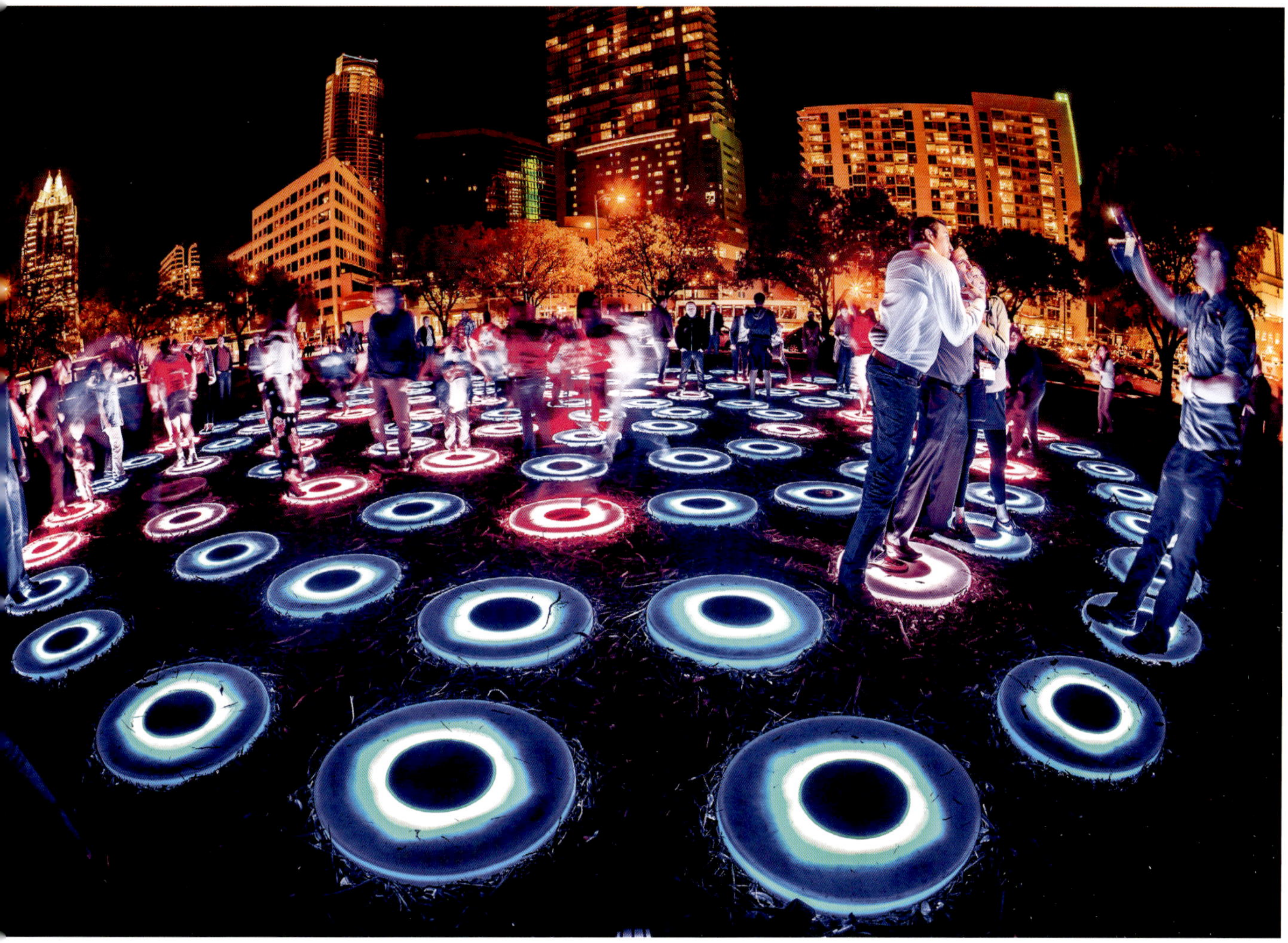

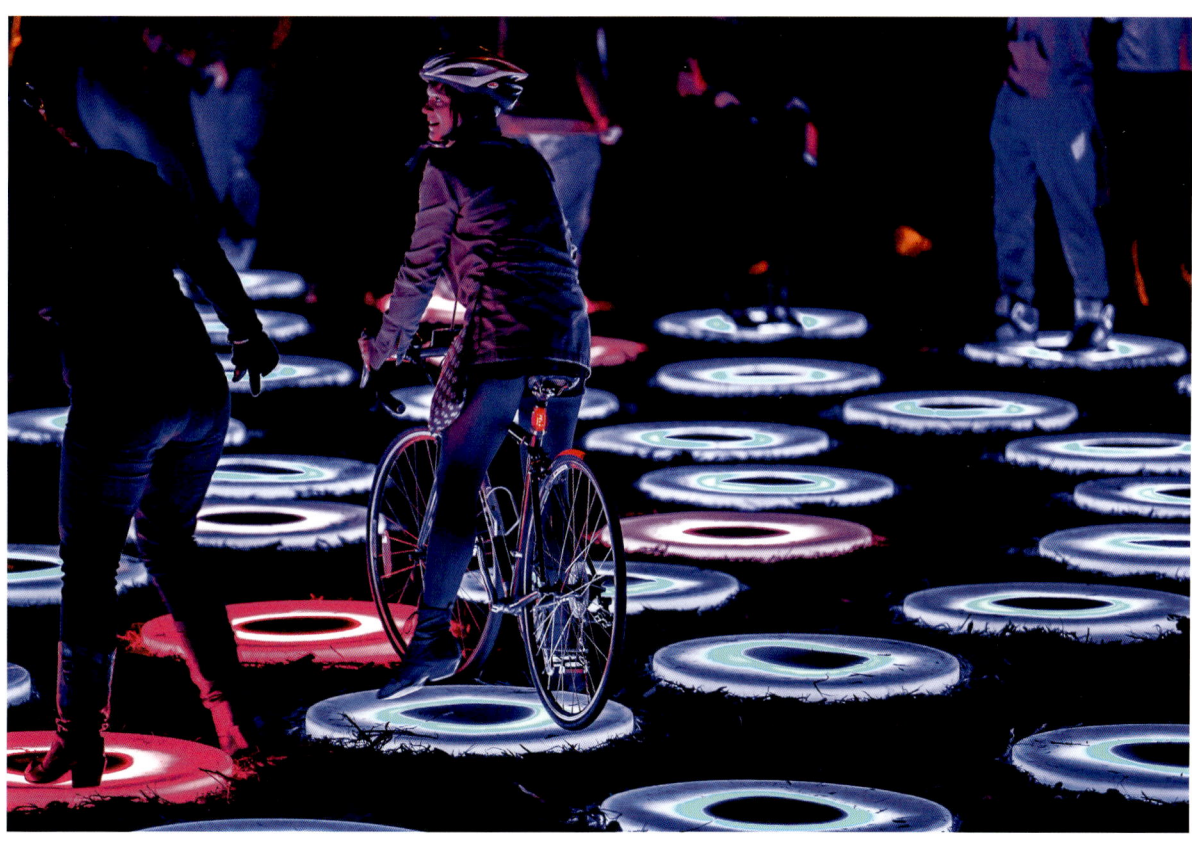

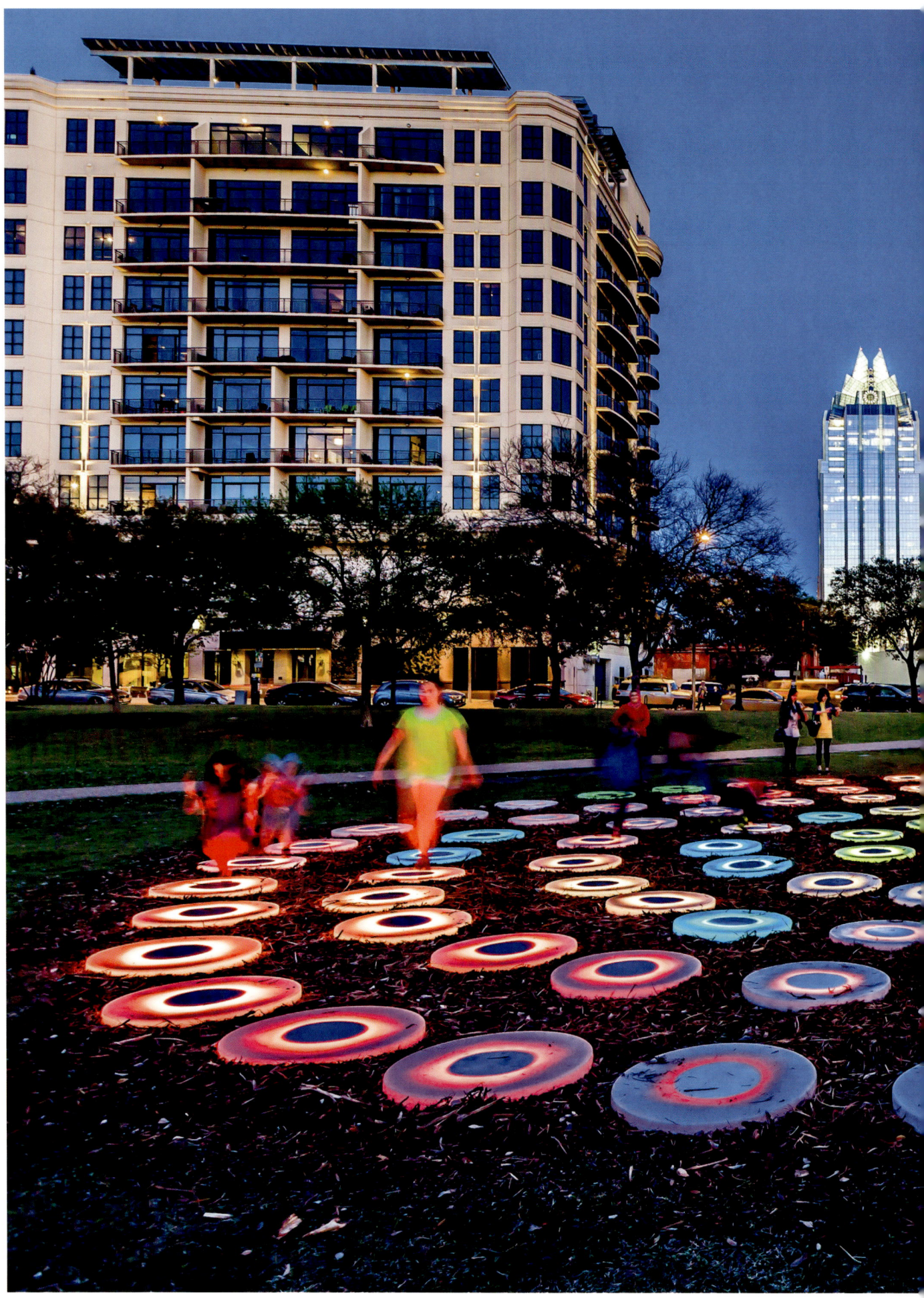

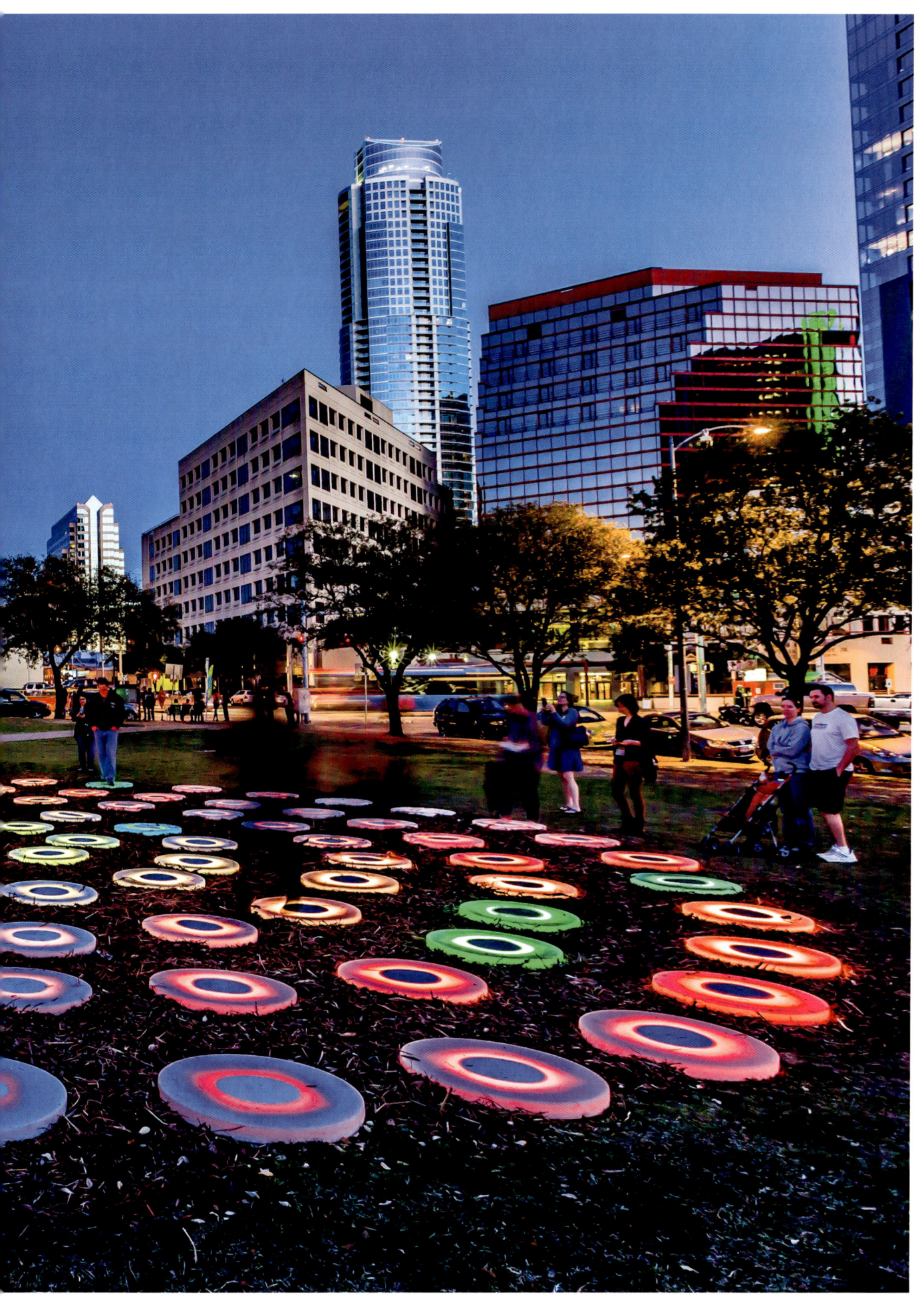

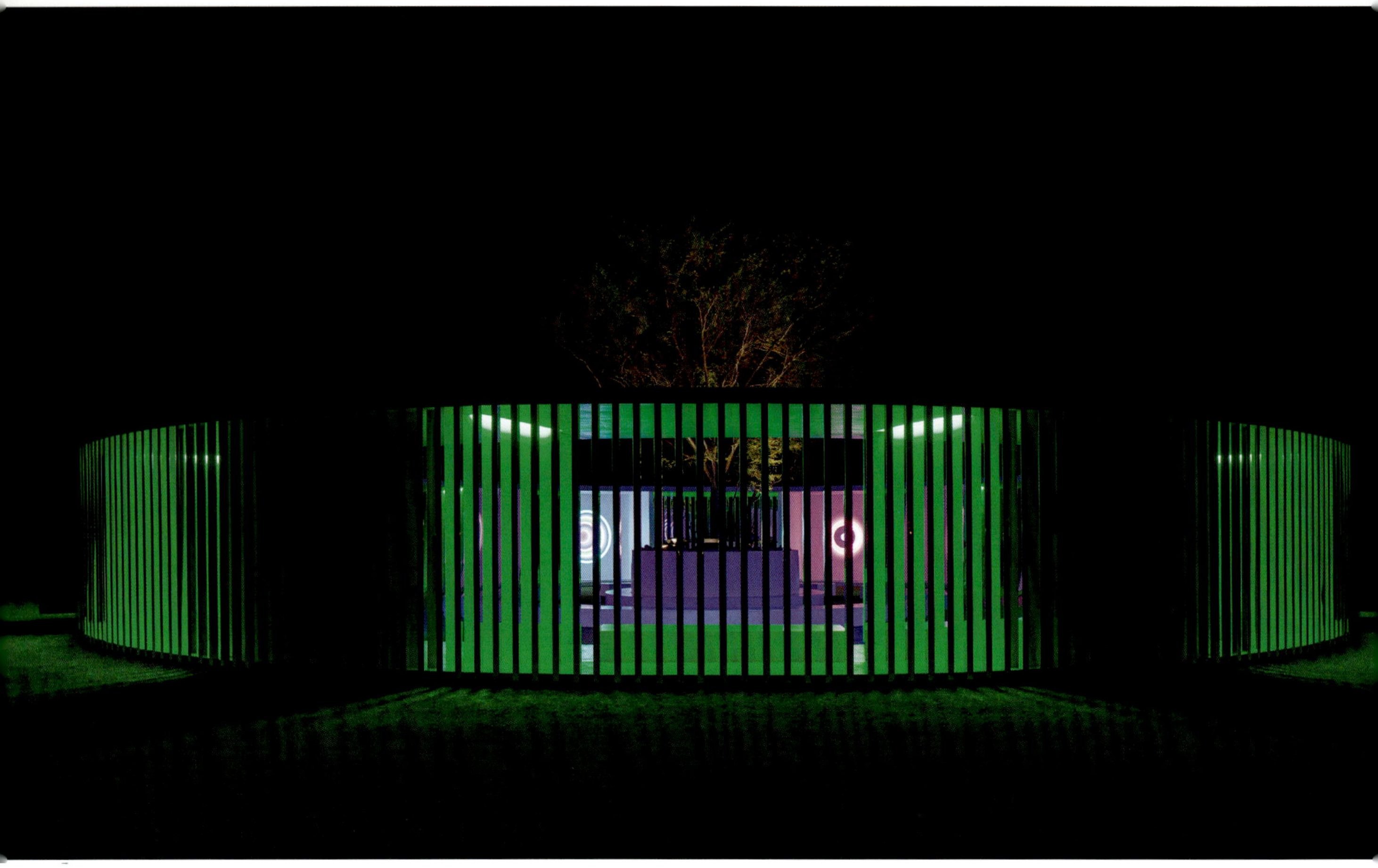

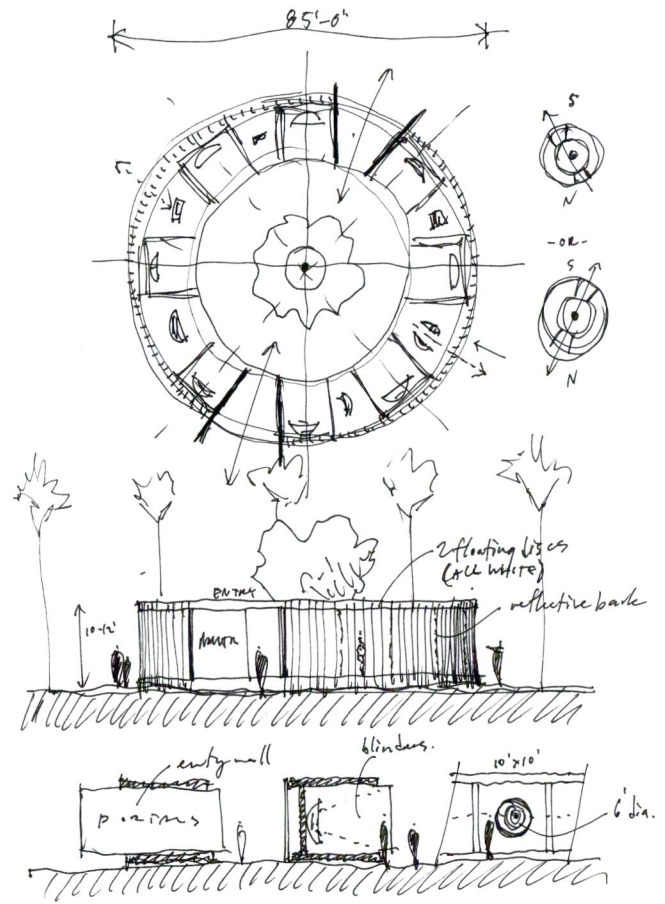

PORTALS

—

Design: **Phillip K. Smith, III**

—

The *Portals* pavilion defines a space for light, while carving out a meditative space for calm amongst the intensity of the Coachella music festival. At 85 feet in diameter, the pavilion's reflective exterior skin dances with the pace of the show and fans, while the interior quietly opens to the sky, pierced by a 35' high mesquite tree. A spatial rhythm of shifting color separated by intermediate reflective public spaces rings the circular structure. Contained within its own open white cube, each light-shifting sculpture projects its color and pace inward where people gather to be bathed in light and sky. As the visitor steps up to the edge of each Portal, the adjacent walls allow the 99,999 other people to fade away, opening the viewer to their own unique, individual experiences with color and light.

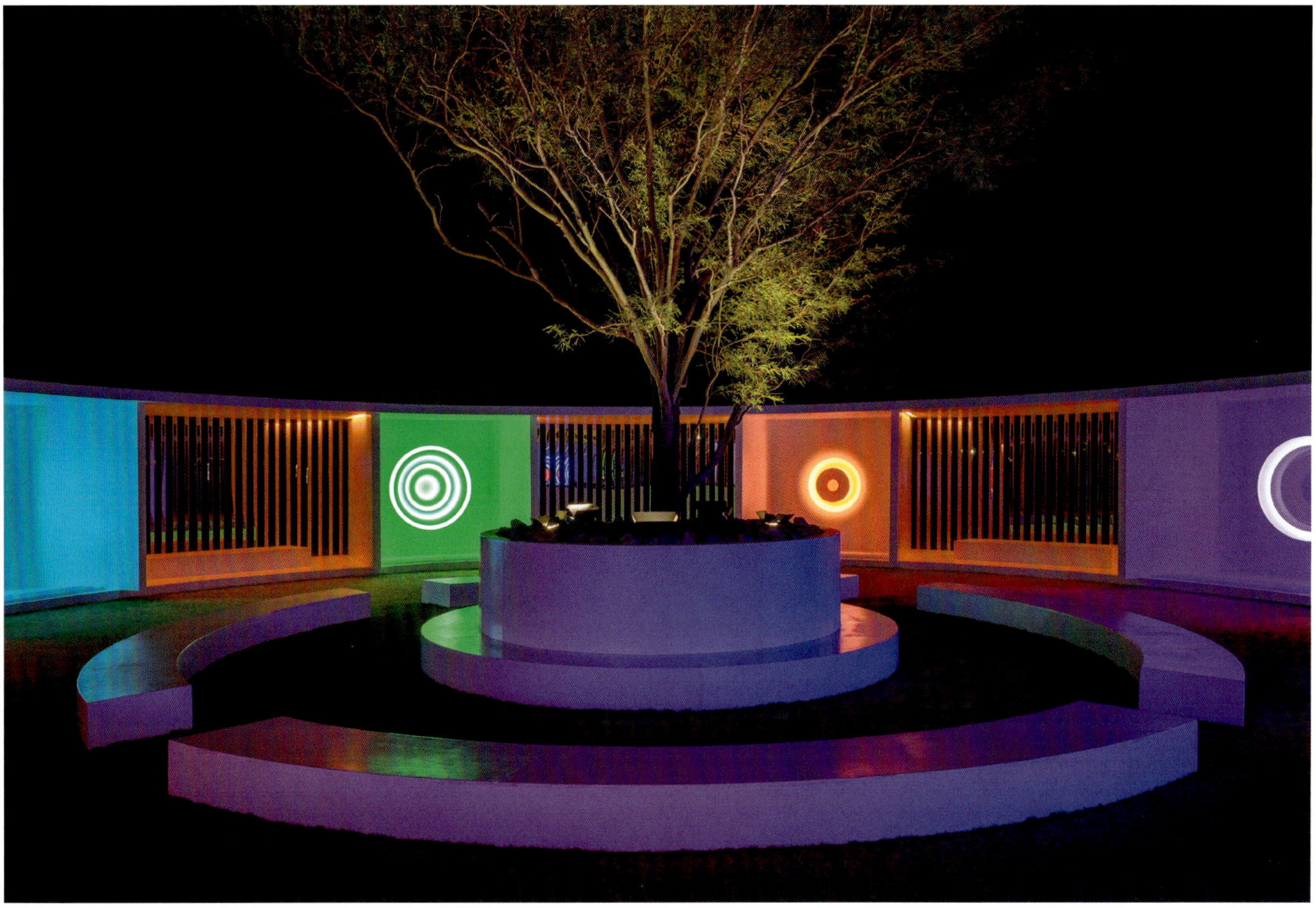

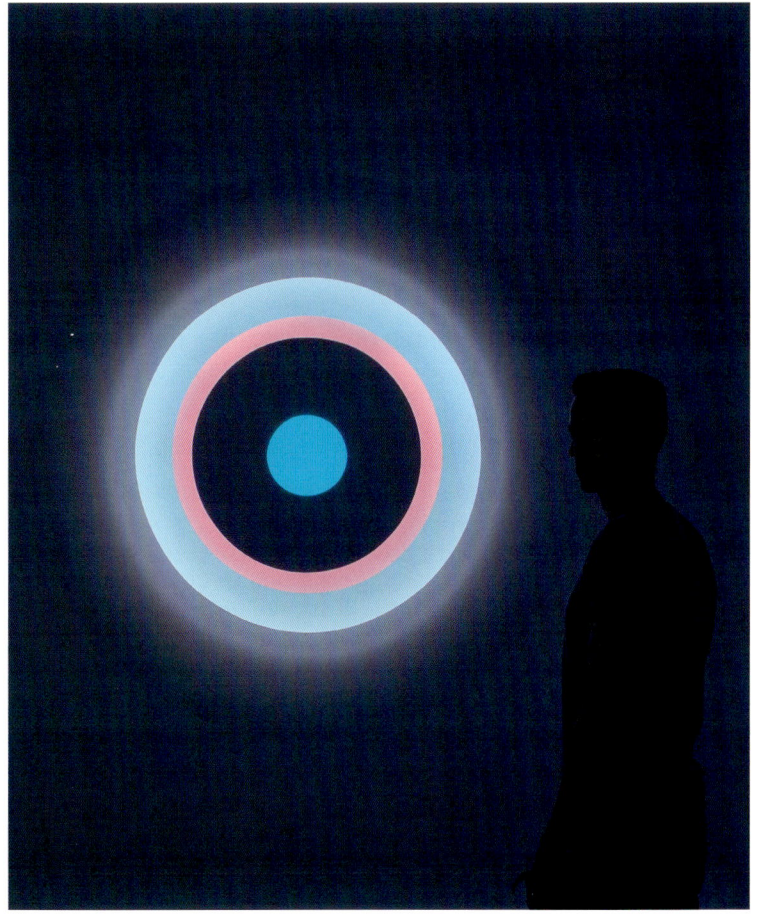

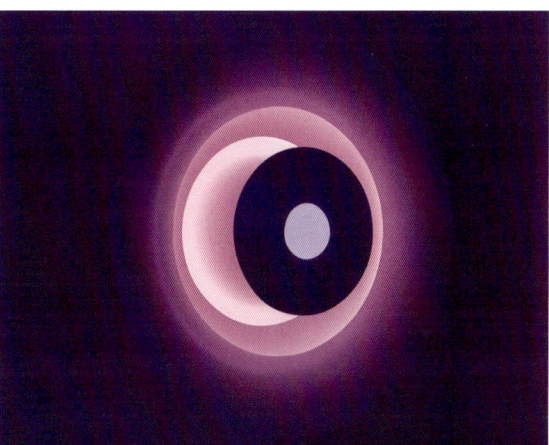

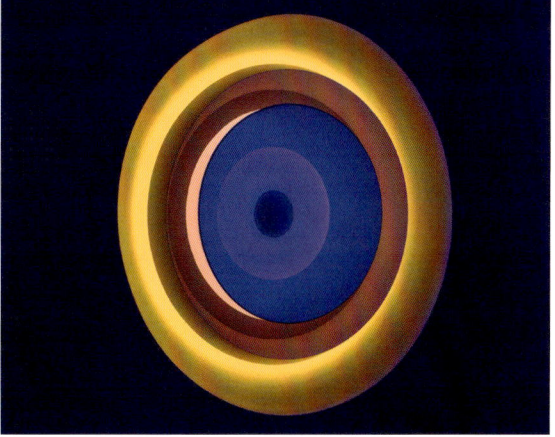

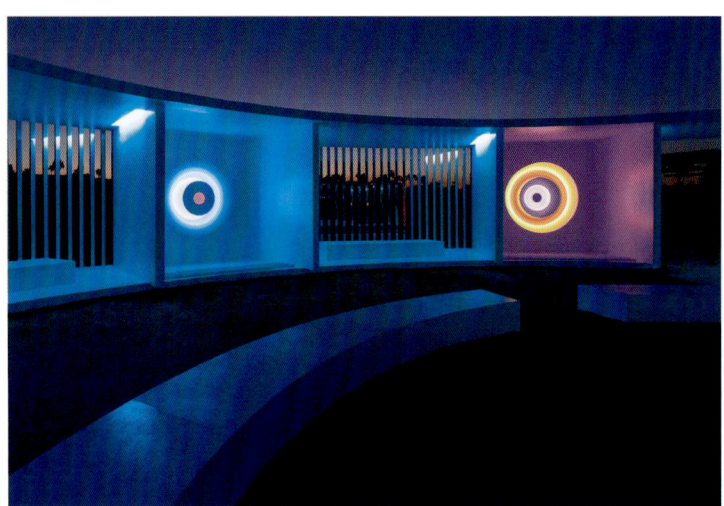
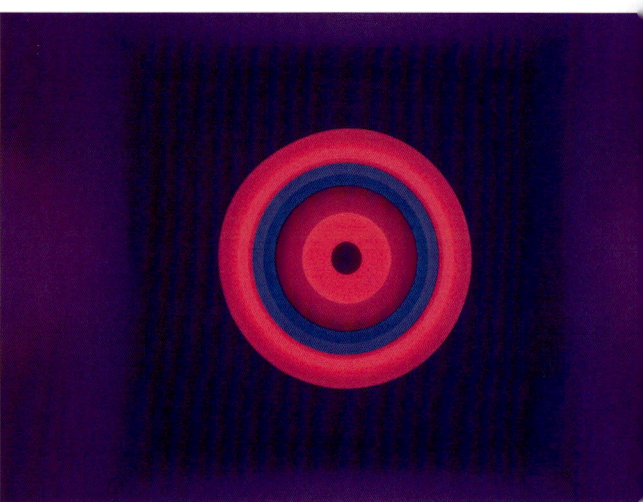

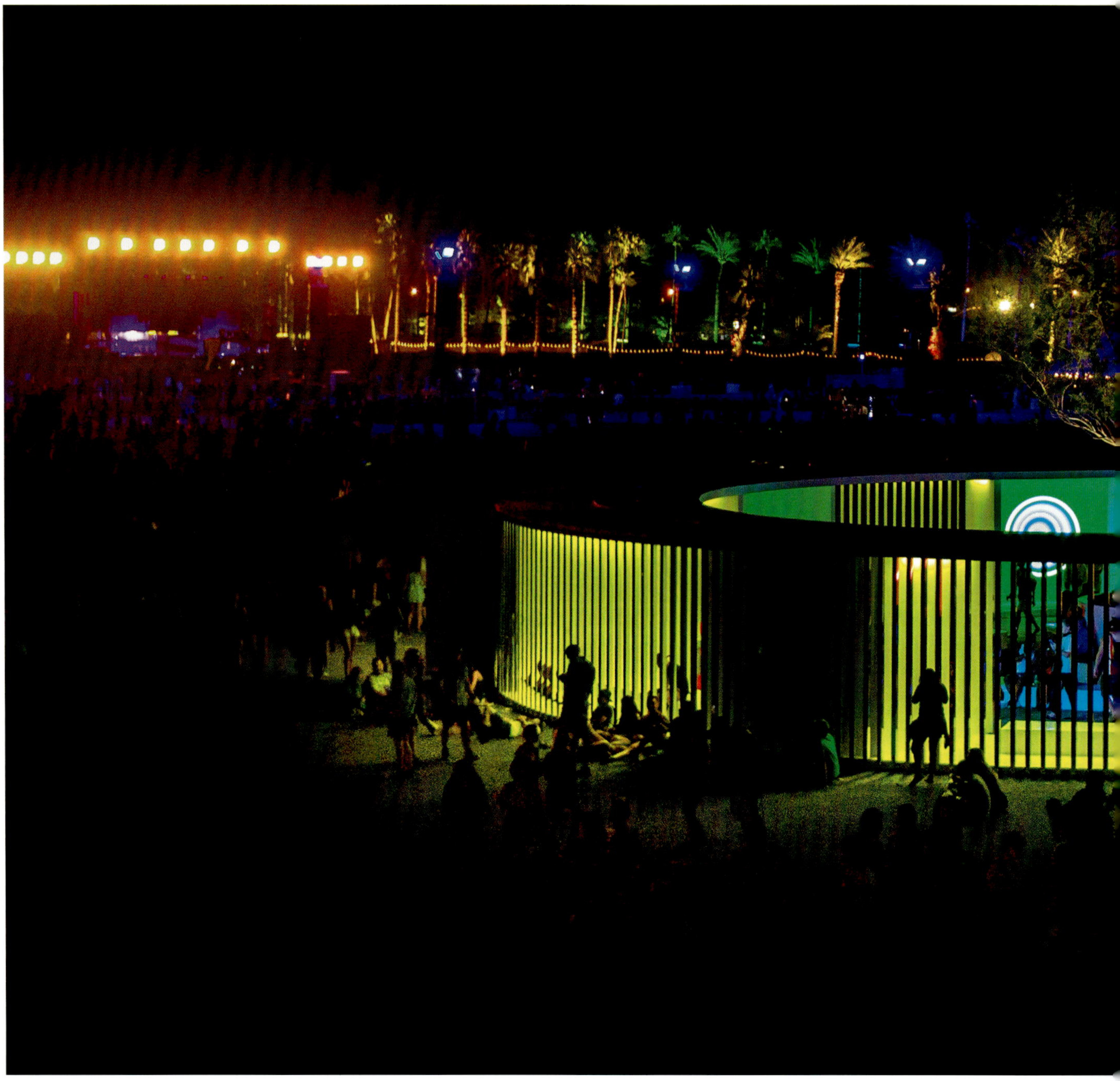

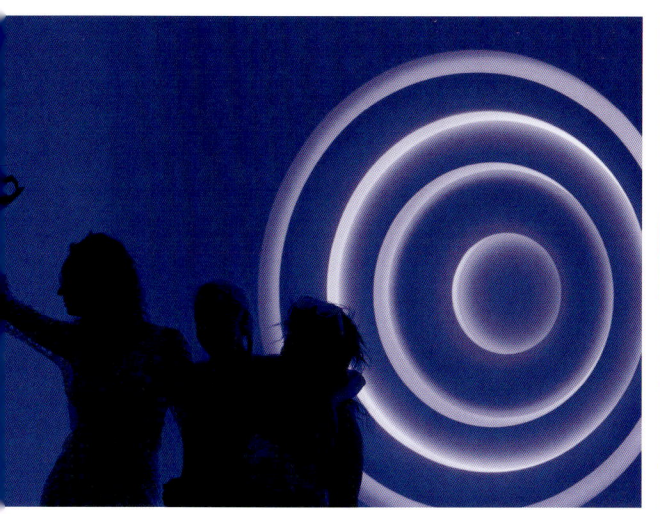
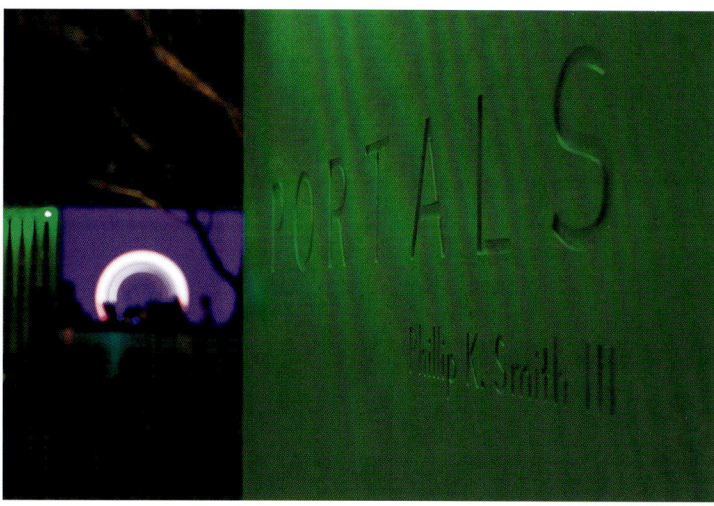

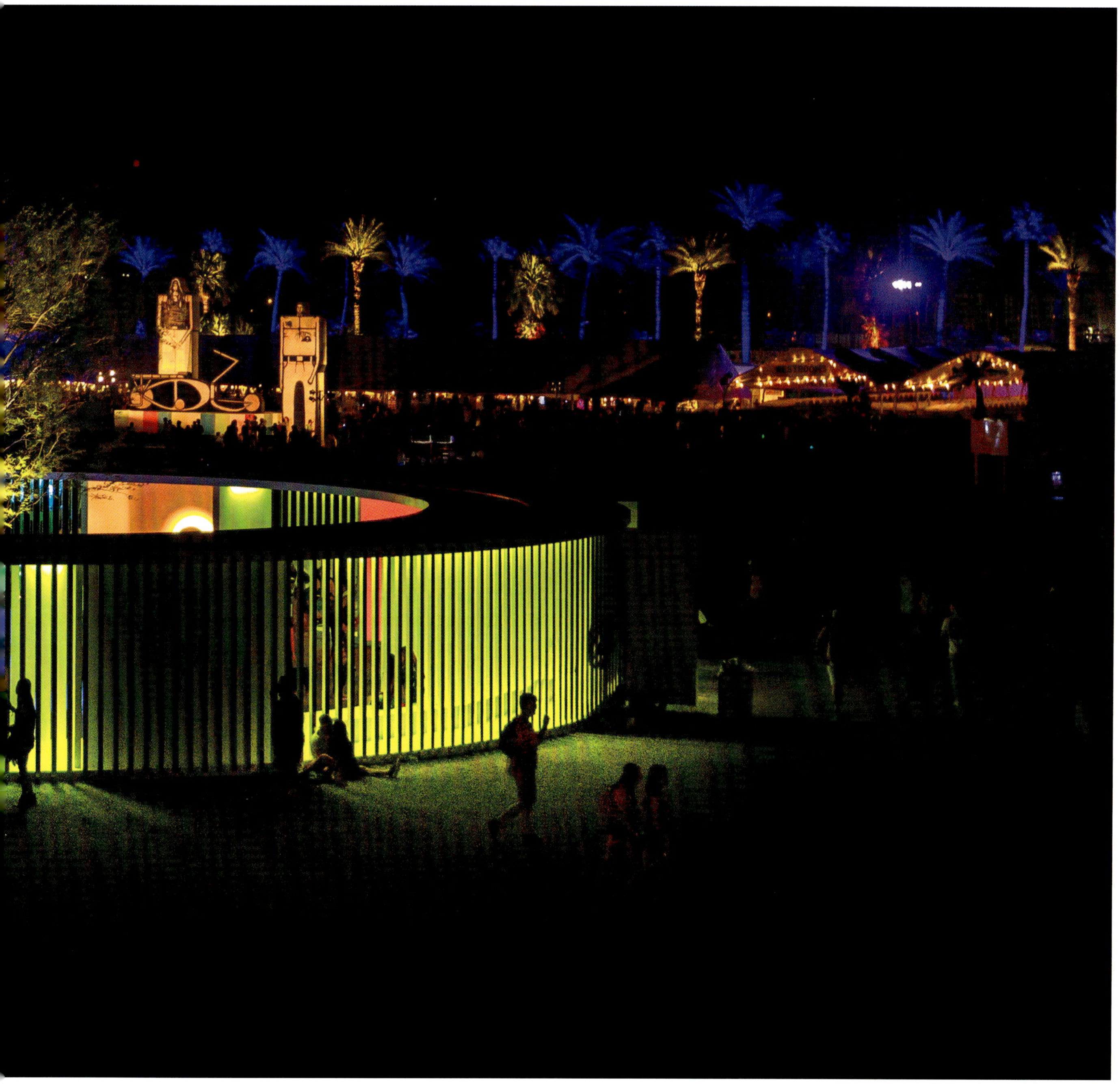

SWING TIME

—

Design: **Höweler + Yoon Architecture**
Photography: **John Horner**

—

The *Swing Time* project, consisting of a custom-fabricated steel frame, solar canopy, and 20 oversized illuminated swings, creates a playful and immersive environment.

The project aims to capture and promote playfulness. The vision was to create a field or a vineyard full of swings hanging from a canopy, resulting in a contemporary take on the classic swing set and the iconic, beloved tire swing.

Each custom-fabricated swing incorporates LED lighting and an accelerometer to change its colors as the swing is used. When the swings are still, they emit soft white lights. As the swings increase in momentum, a microcontroller adjusts the LED output through a gradient scale from white to the programmed color or colors. The integrated functional and aesthetic properties of *Swing Time* highlight energy use and play, while raising awareness of energy production, consumption, and conservation. This direct feedback loop and highly interactive aspect of the swings make this an engaging and popular site.

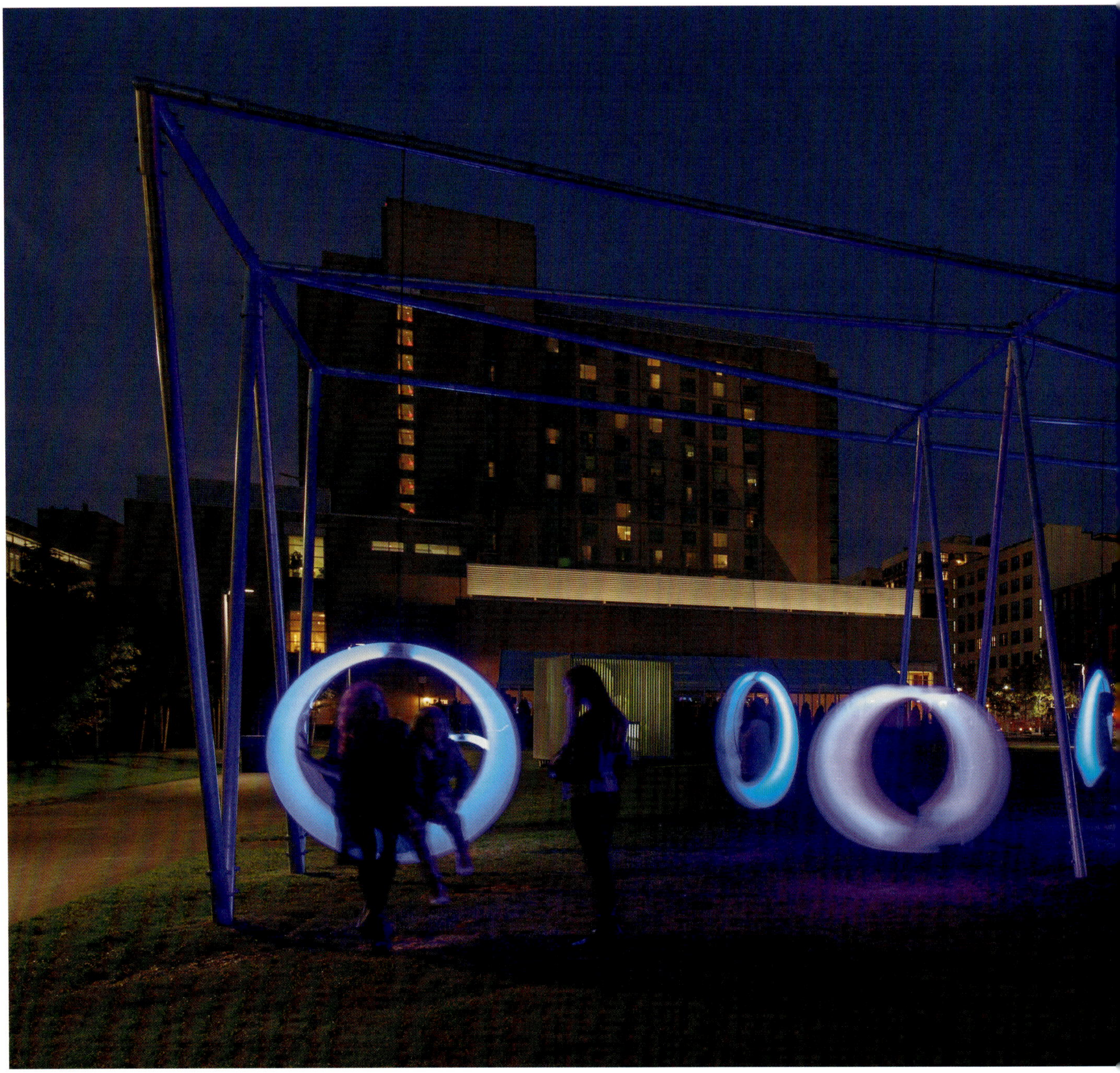

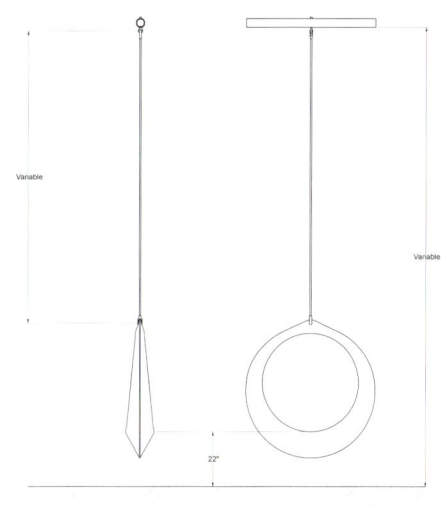

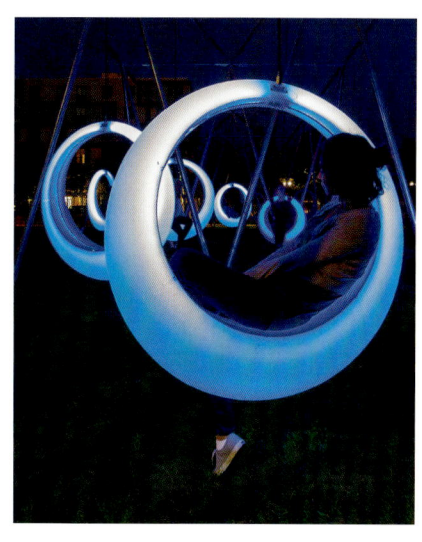

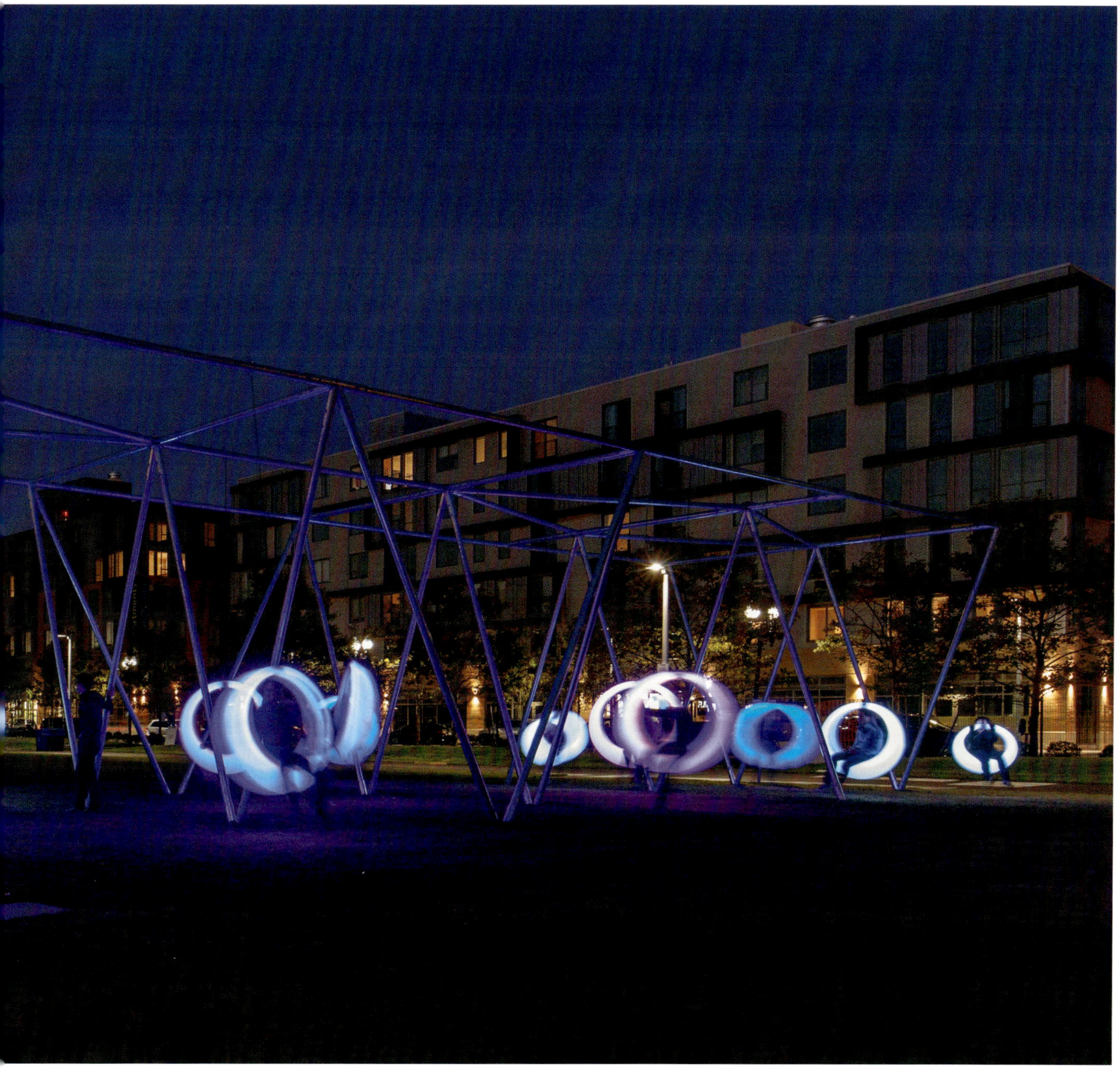

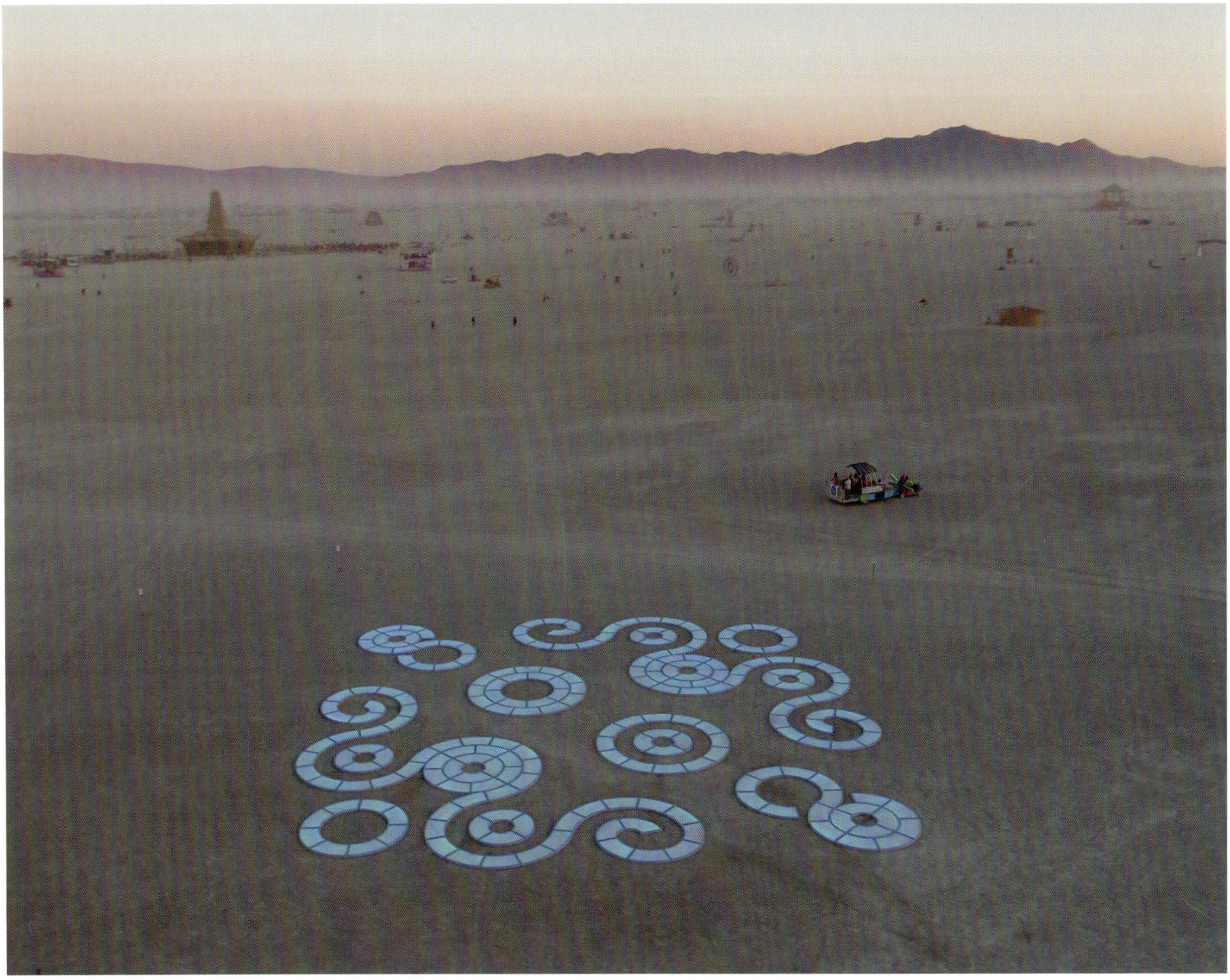

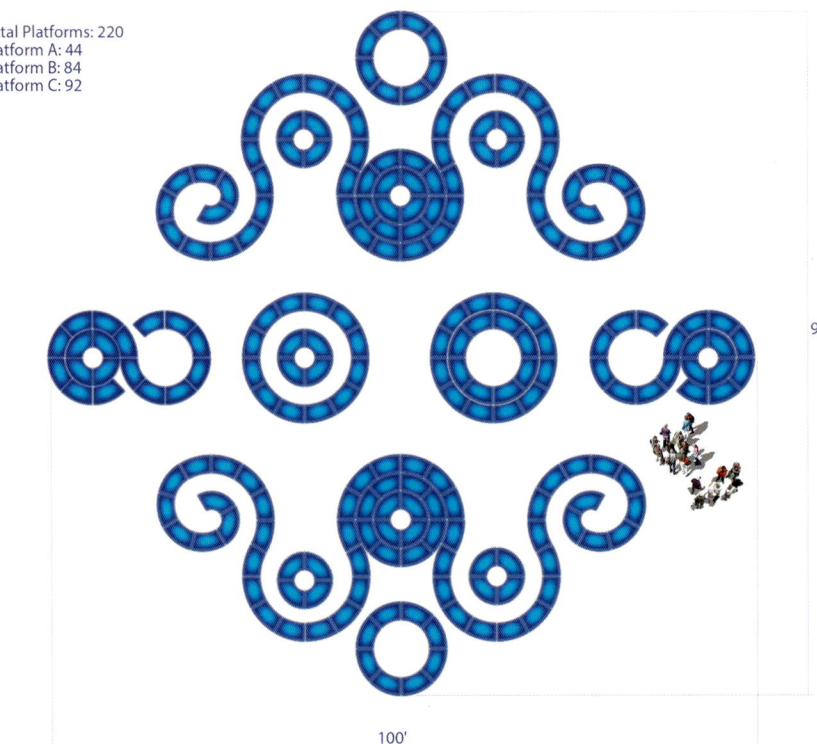

AQUEOUS

—

Design: **Jen Lewin Studio**
Photography: **Matt Emmi, Jen Lewin Studio**

—

Aqueous is an interactive landscape of meandering pathways of light. During the day, *Aqueous* shifts in color and reflection, mirroring the sky within a walkable dichroic surface. At night, *Aqueous* flows and glows in full illuminated interactivity, engaging large groups in collaborative play.

Total Platforms: 220
Platform A: 44
Platform B: 84
Platform C: 92

95'

100'

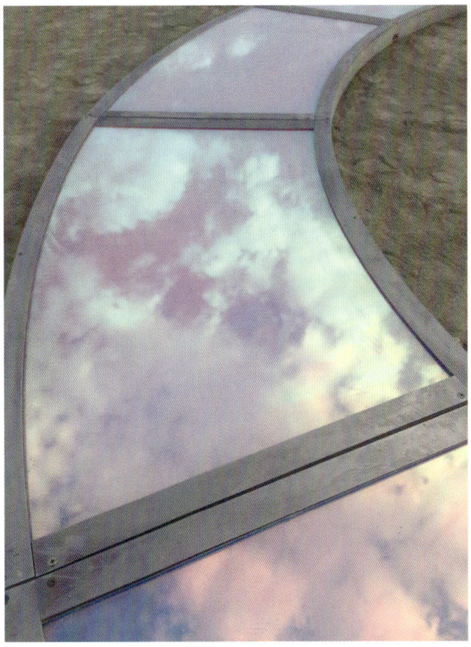

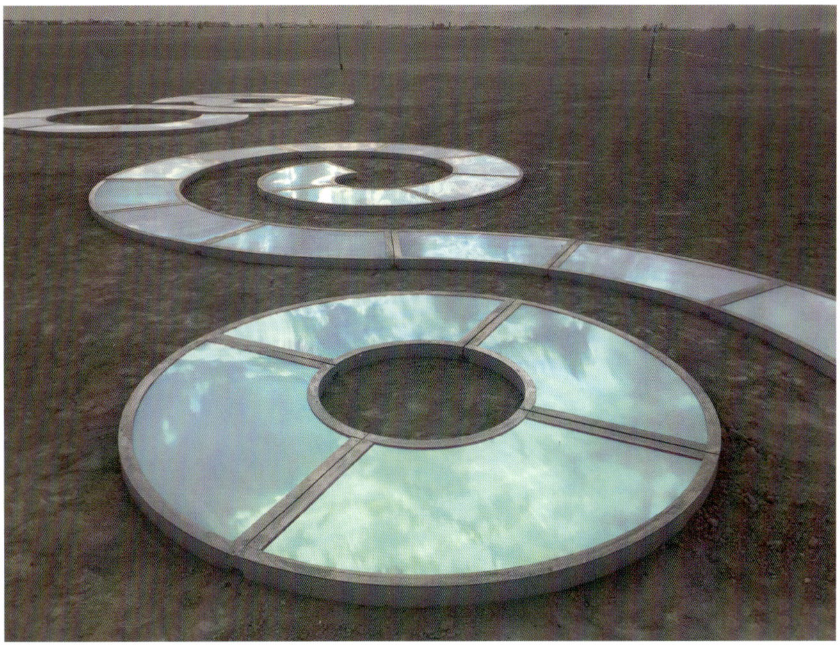

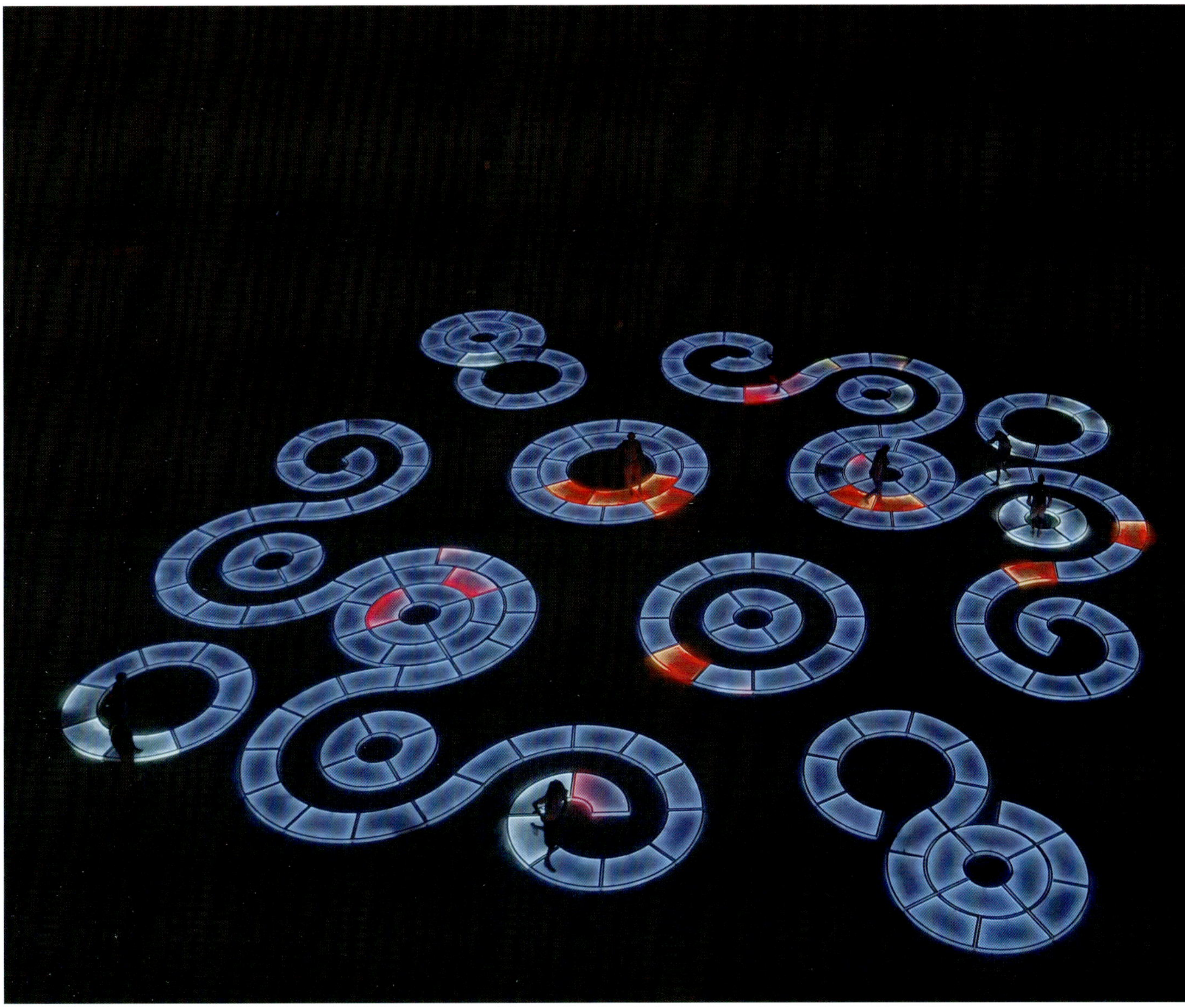

LED FOREST

—

Design: **bildspur**

—

Immerse yourself in a forest of light and magic created by the gentle movement of hands over a control panel—this is made possible by the interactive installation *LED Forest*.

The *LED Forest* consists of 16-24 fluorescent tubes, each of which consists of several LED pixels. These are controlled by the movement of the hands via a control panel. With the position of the hand it is possible to control the colors and patterns on the bars.

Custom software and specially designed, jointed stands enable the installation to adapt to each new exhibition location.

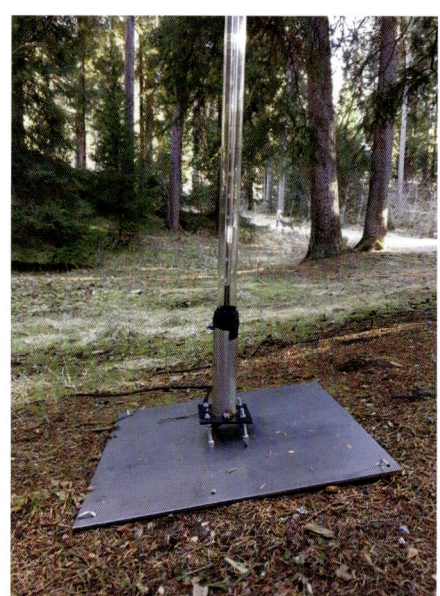

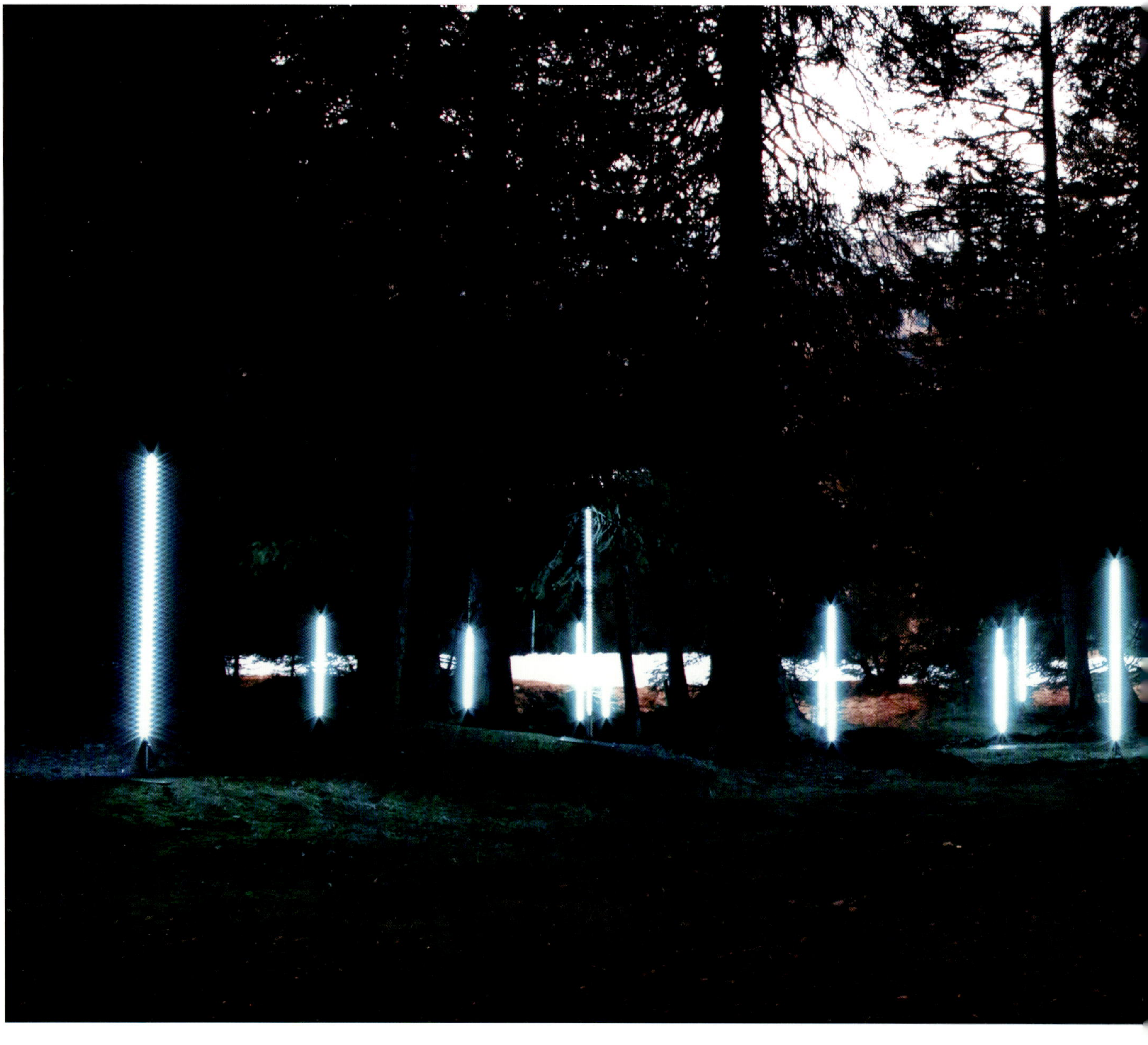

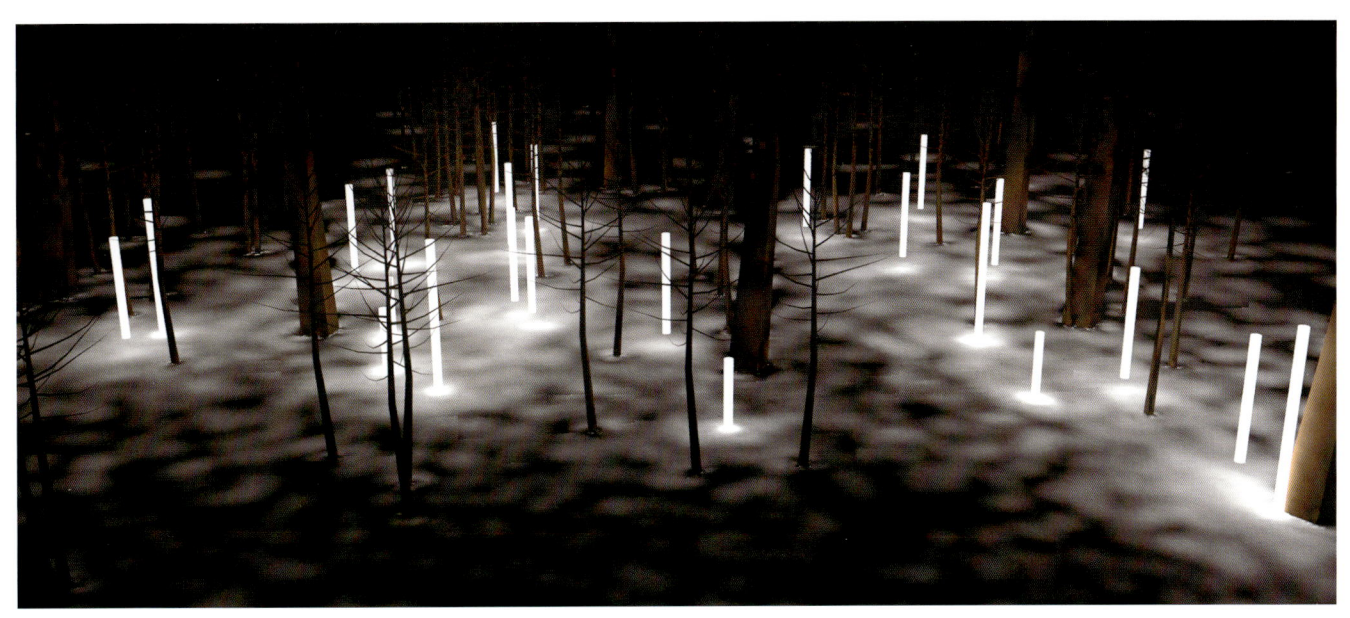

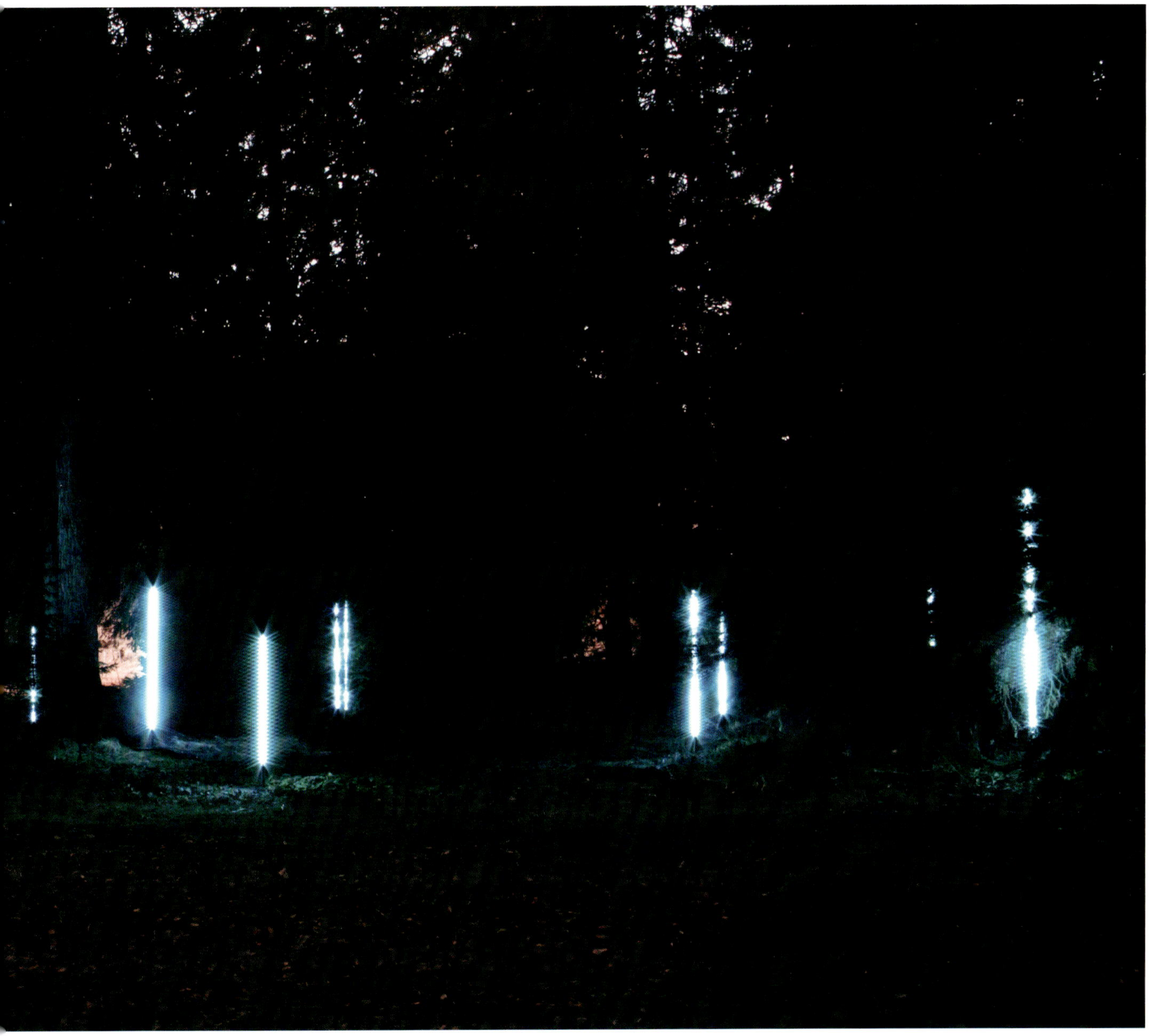

I SAW MY BIRTH, LOVE, AND DEATH IN THE SKY

—

Author: **Maja Petric**
Photography: **Arturo Ortiz**

—

I Saw My Birth, Love, and Death in the Sky is an interactive light art installation of projected stars in the forest in Redmond, Washington, US. Visitors passing through the fog-filled forest glance up and find themselves immersed in a constellation of projected stars that equal the US population. Whenever a baby is born somewhere in the country, a burst of red light appears. Whenever someone dies, a blue star explodes and disappears into space.

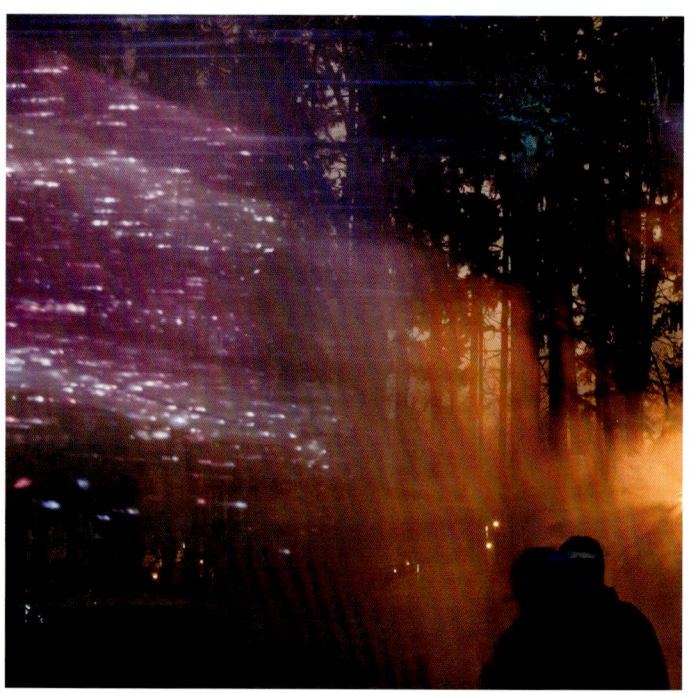

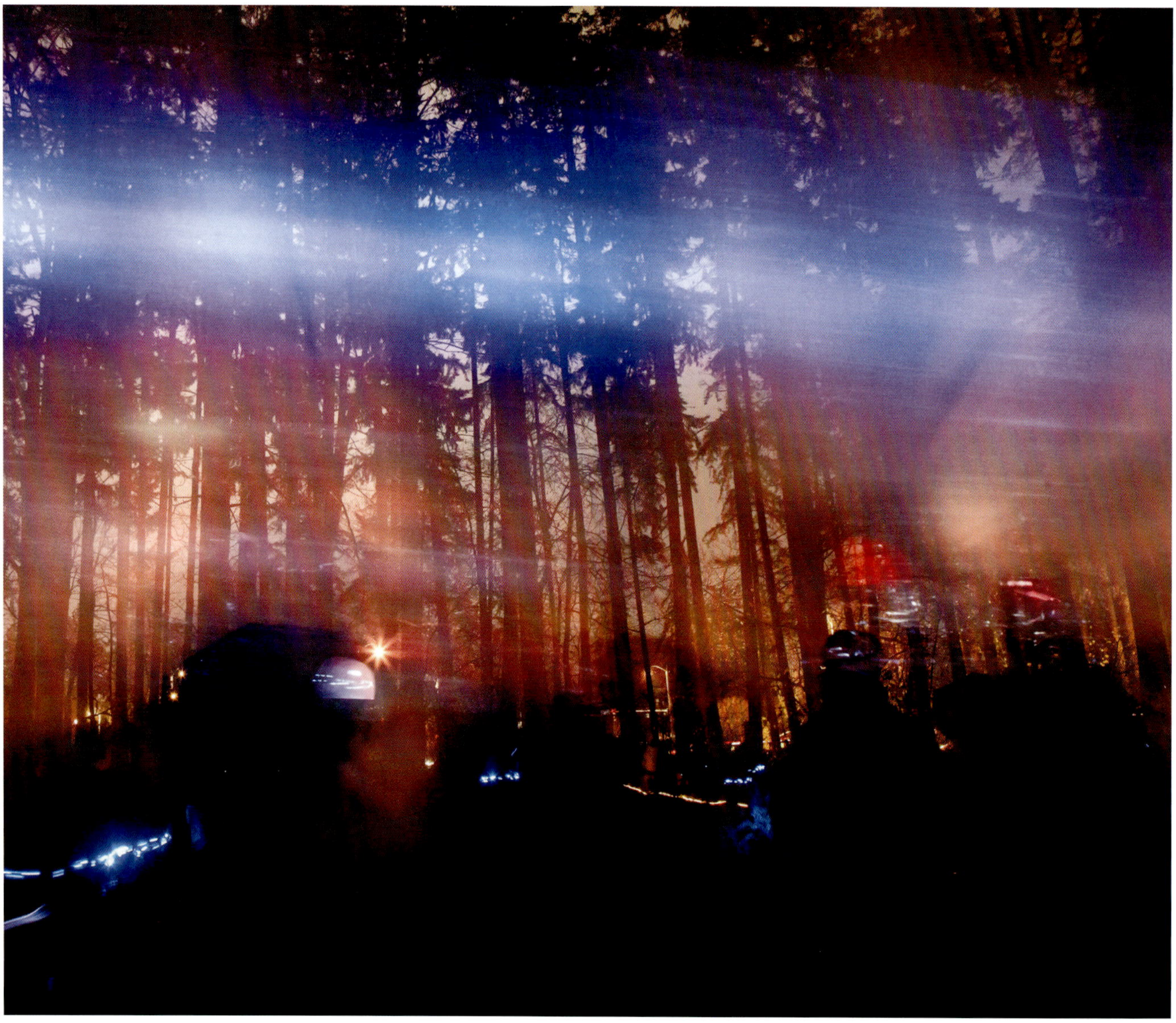

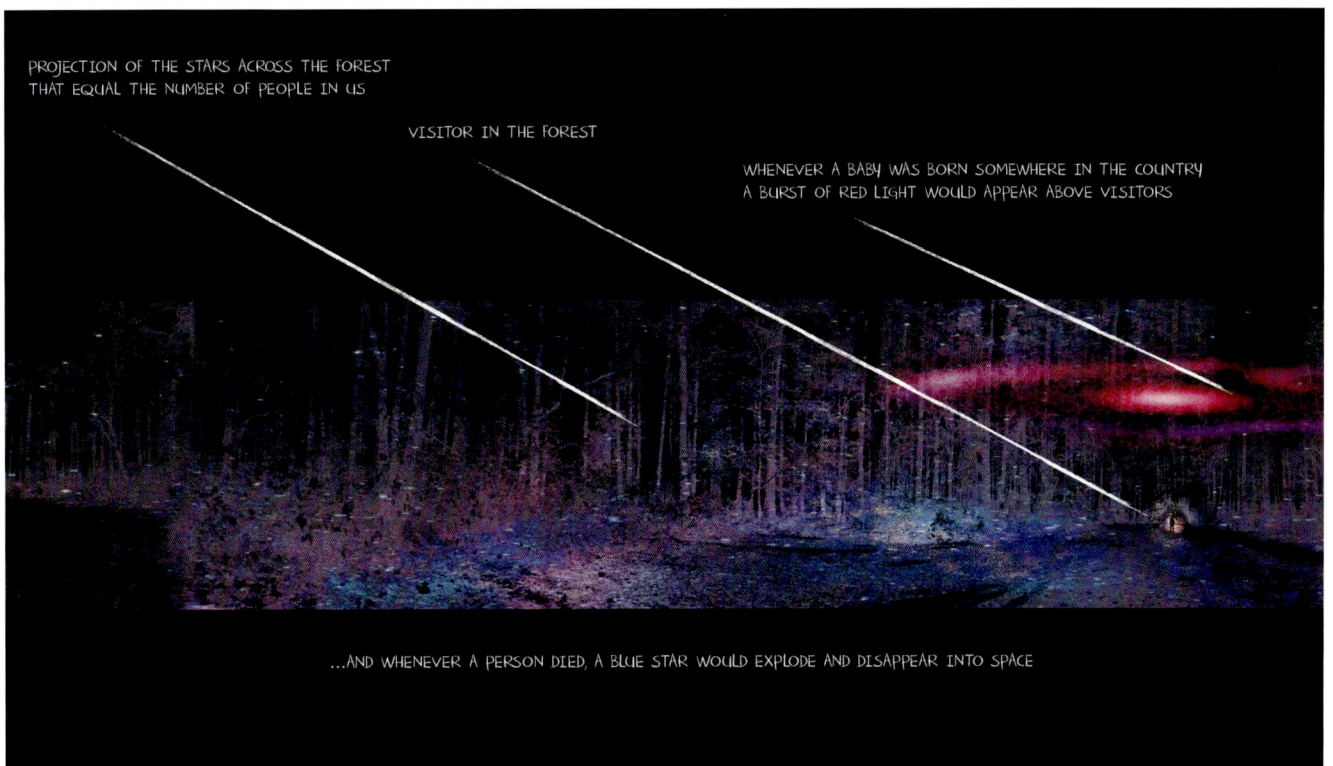

PROJECTION OF THE STARS ACROSS THE FOREST
THAT EQUAL THE NUMBER OF PEOPLE IN US

VISITOR IN THE FOREST

WHENEVER A BABY WAS BORN SOMEWHERE IN THE COUNTRY
A BURST OF RED LIGHT WOULD APPEAR ABOVE VISITORS

...AND WHENEVER A PERSON DIED, A BLUE STAR WOULD EXPLODE AND DISAPPEAR INTO SPACE

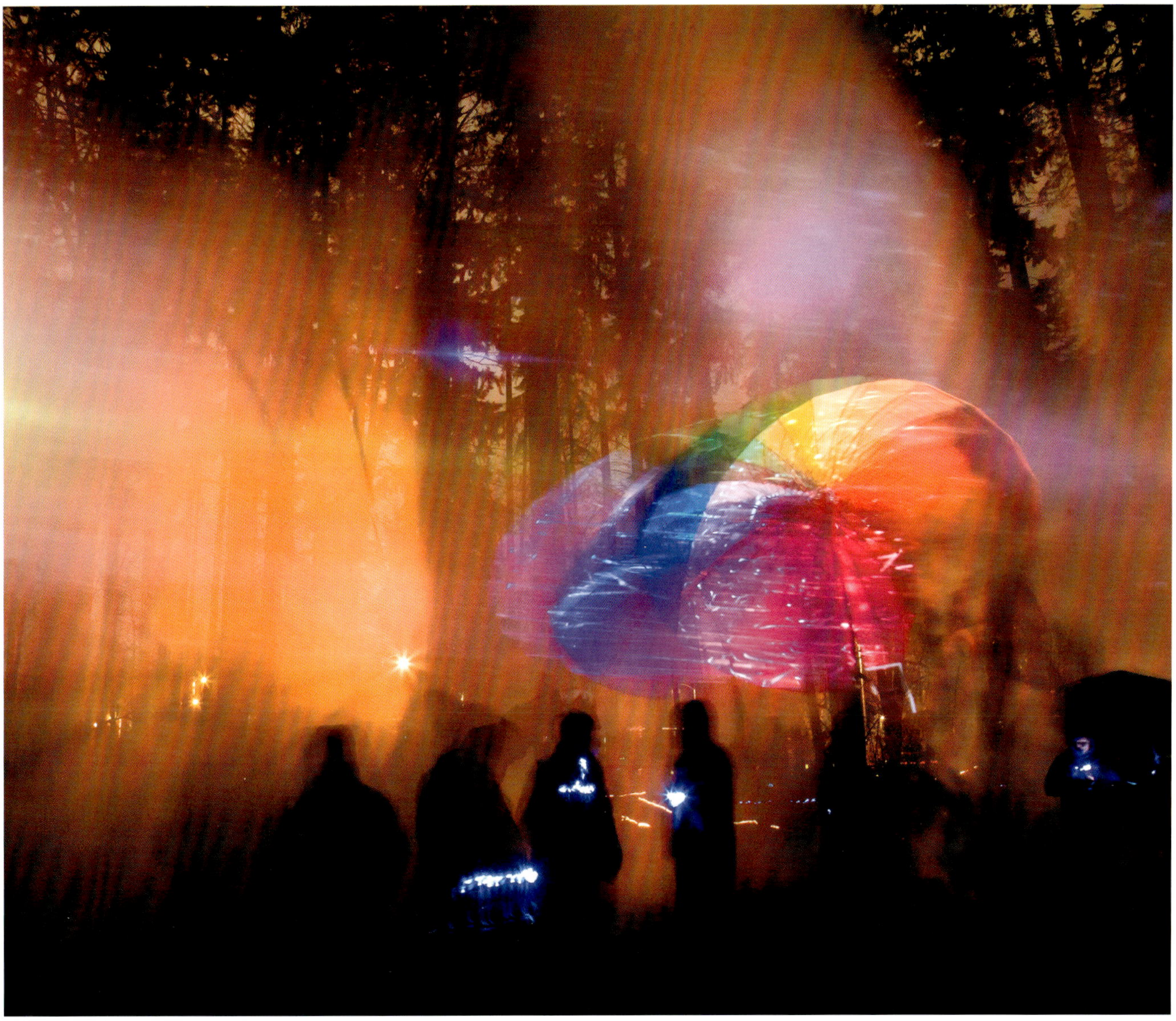

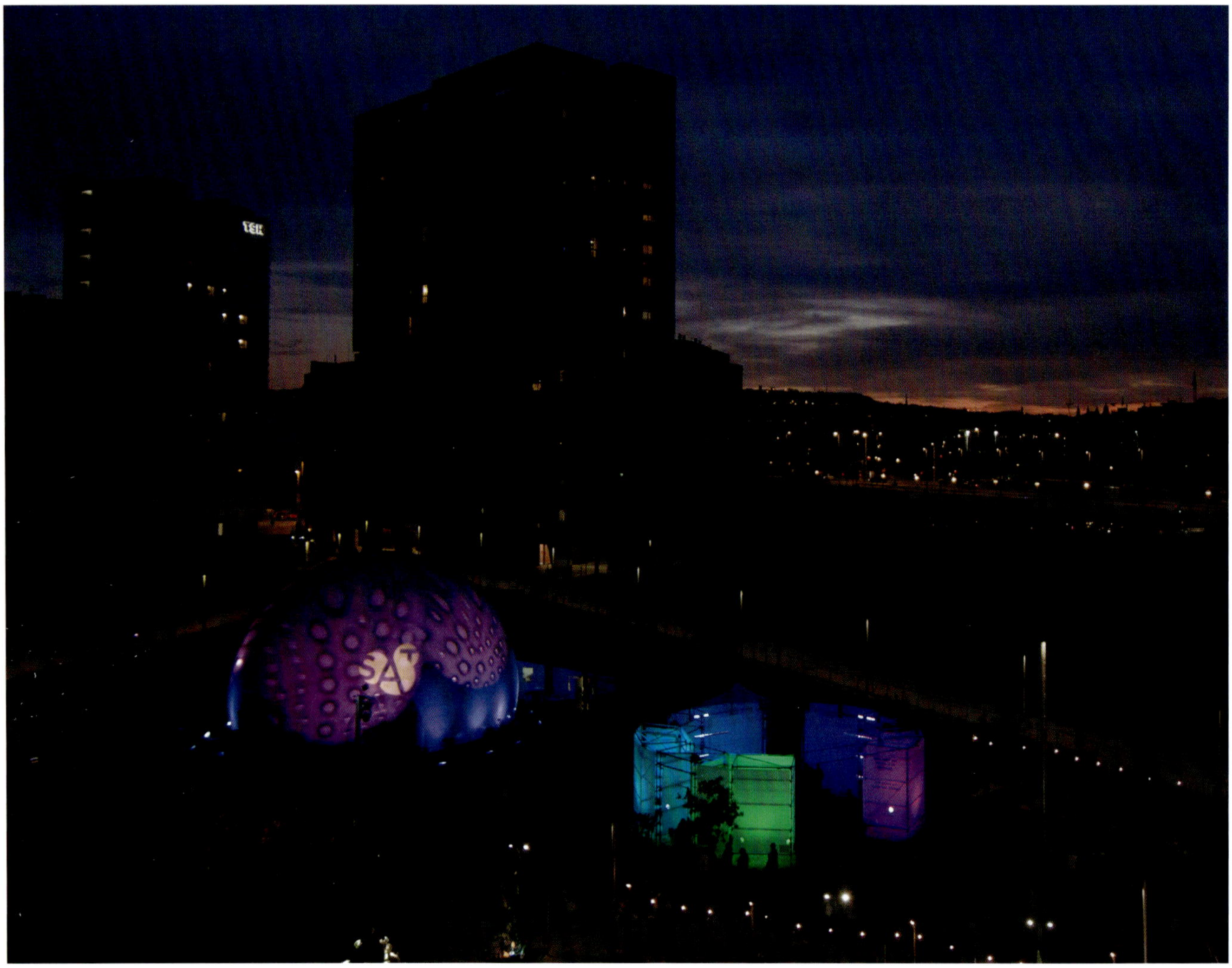

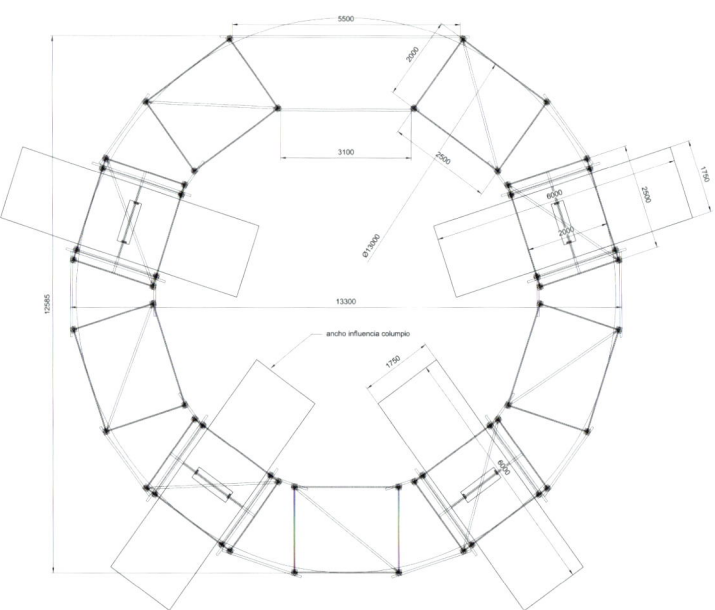

HERE:
THE SQUARE OF
THE FUTURE

—

Design: **Col·lec Studio**

—

Here represents the square of the future, with a set of interactive swings that brings the place back to life with the light and sound produced by the movement and play of people. It suggests a personal immersion, born from the childhood memory of playing on swings. Each swing has a different type of sound, which responds to a specific instrument group, combining harmonically with the rest of the set. It's a collective experience created from interaction and observation.

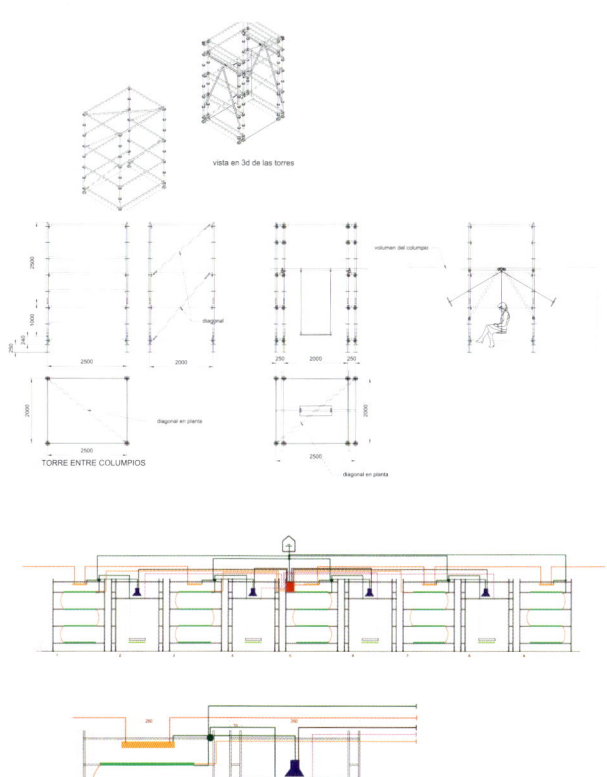

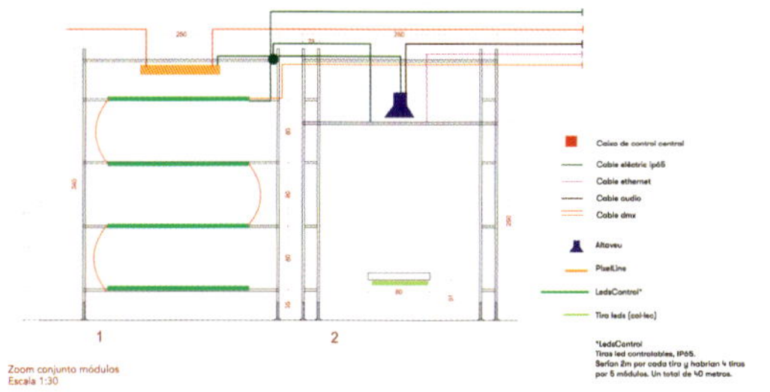

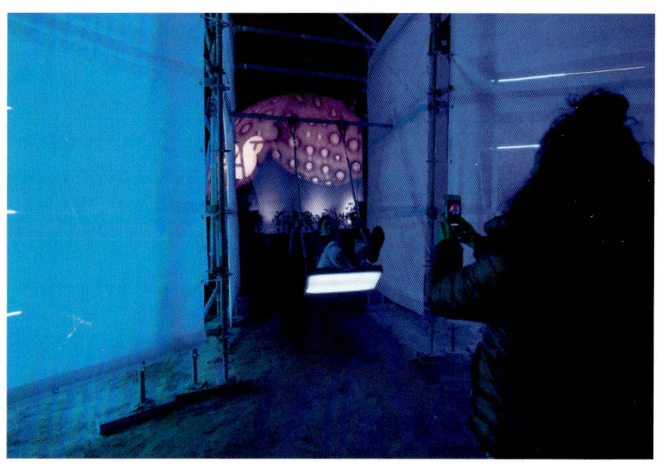

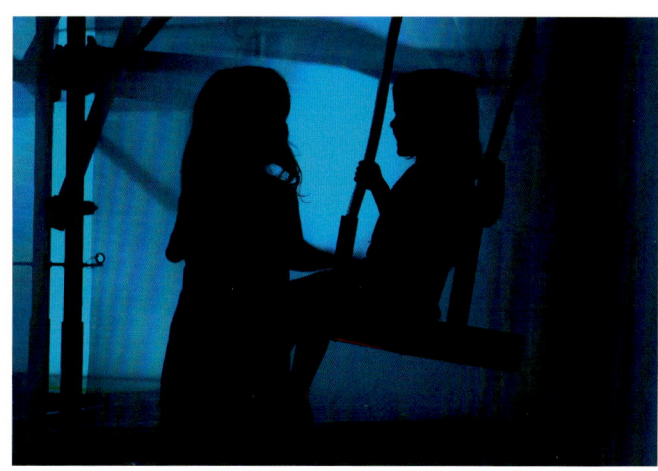

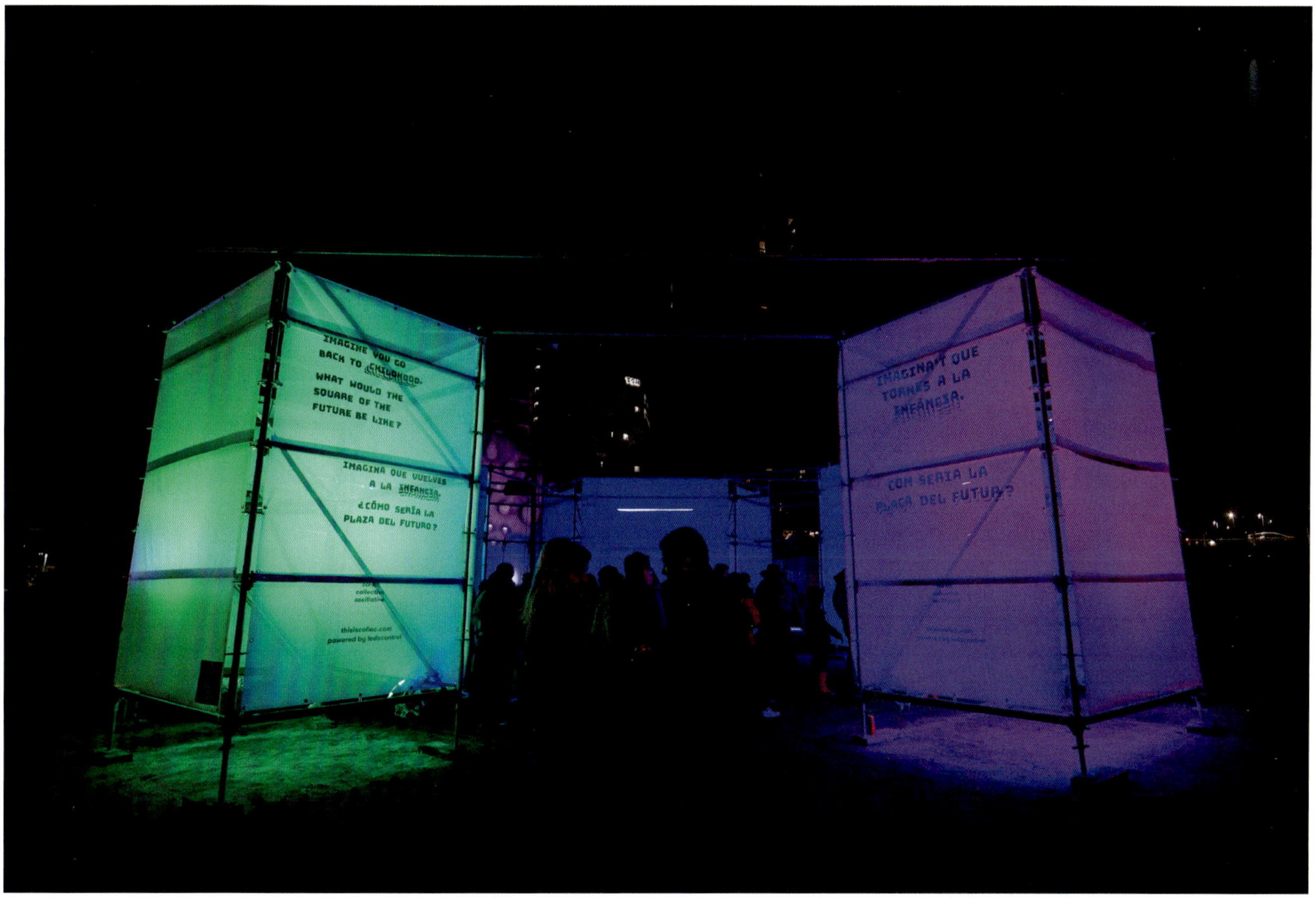

HYDROZOME

—

Design: **Tom Dekyvere**
Photography: **Quays Culture**

—

Hydrozome is a multimedia installation that translates soundwaves into lightwaves. An underwater microphone called "a hydrophone" is placed in the River Irwell at Salford Quays, capturing the sounds underneath the surface. The detected sounds are then transformed by a synthesizer and played live at the steps of Media City UK, where the work is situated. While walking through the work, the visitors can manipulate the sound by generating contact sounds on the floor and railings, sending waves to the hydrophone in the water. The live digital soundscape of the work also connects with several LEDs, making the whole installation an interactive experience of light, sound and material.

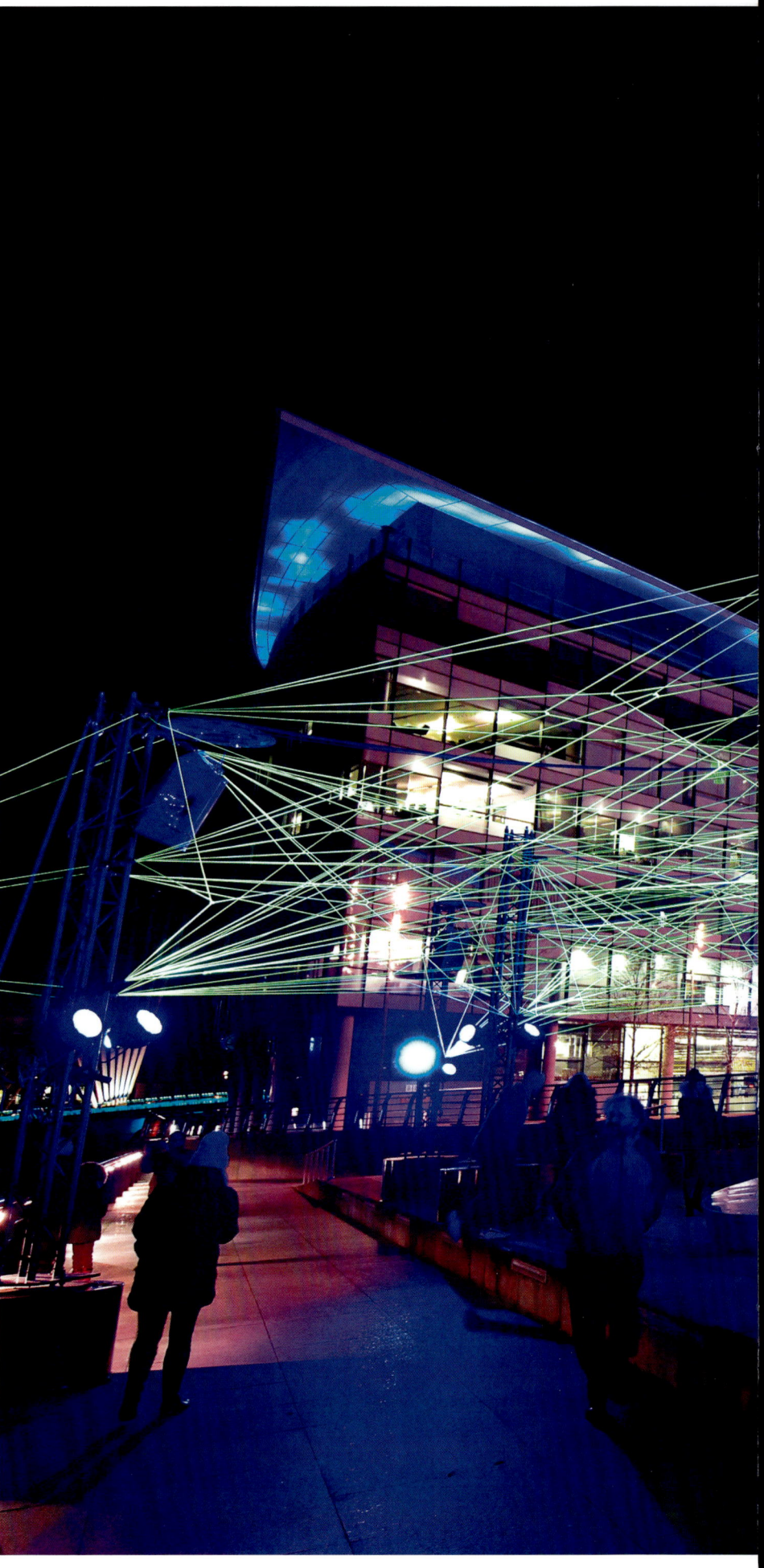

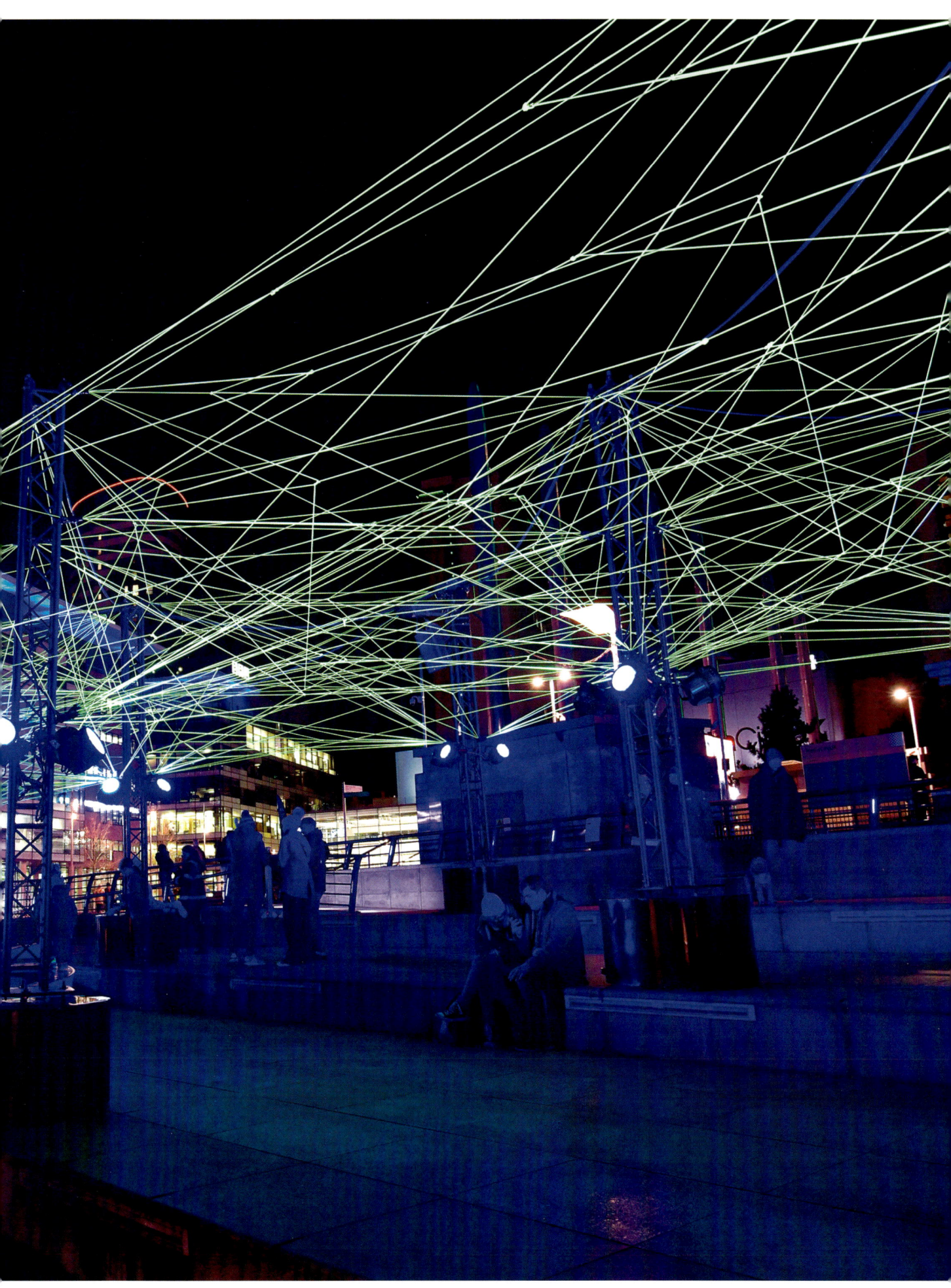

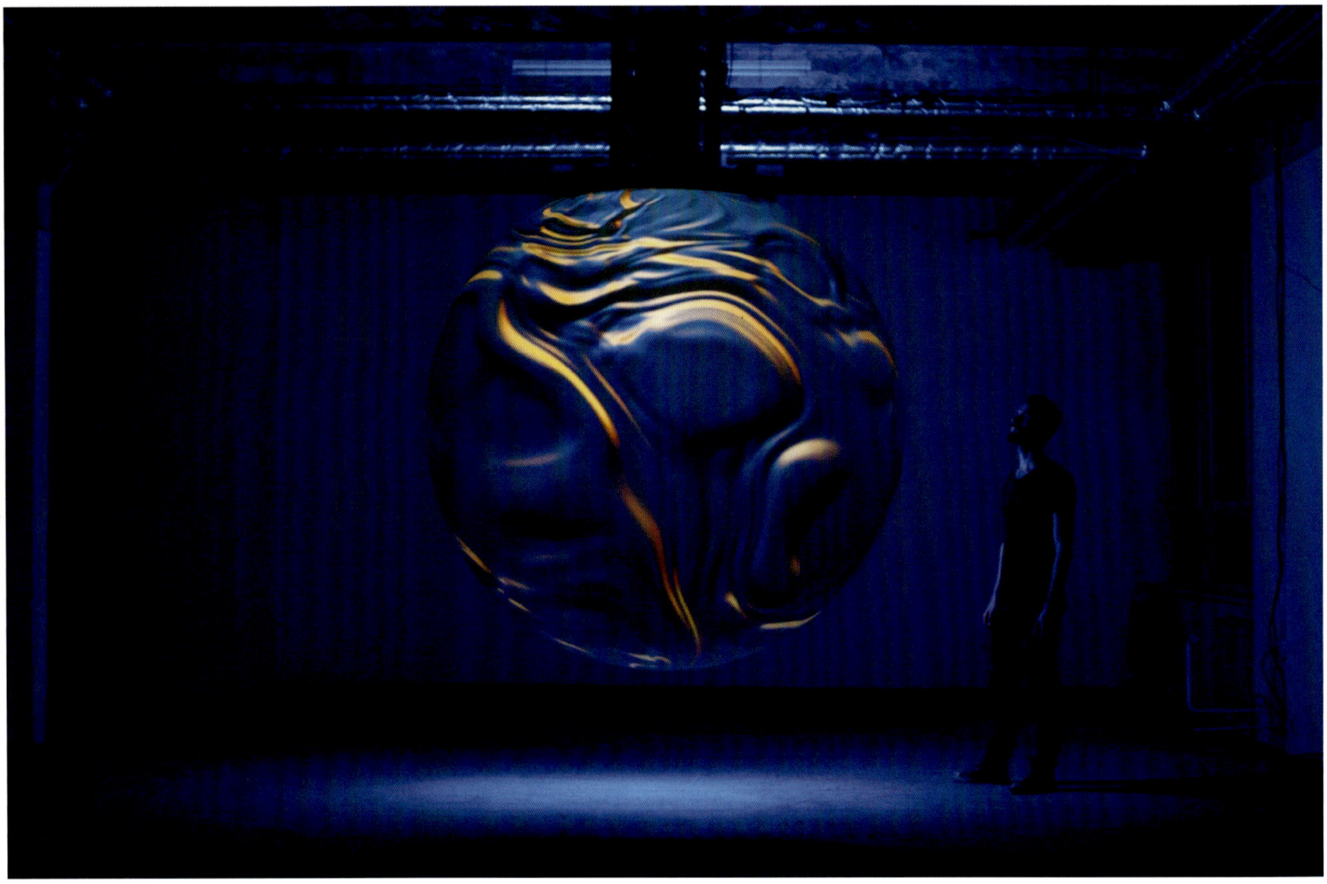

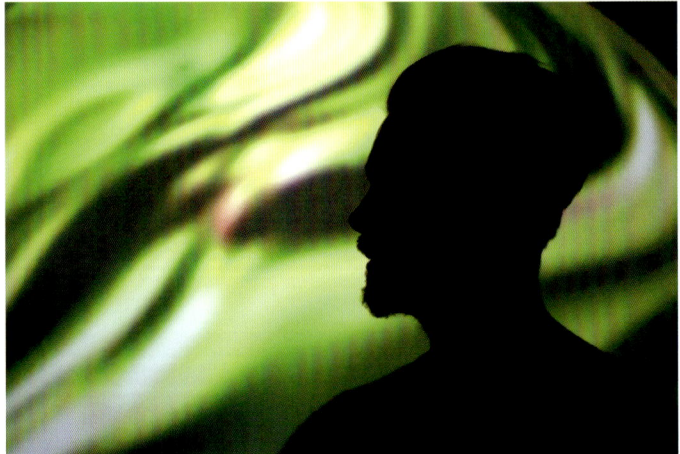

ANIMA

—

Design: **onformative, Studio Nick Verstand**

—

ANIMA is a sculptural installation developed to explore the relationship between itself and its surroundings through the use of movement, texture, light and sound. The installation consists of a giant glowing sphere measuring two meters in diameter. This larger-than-life entity is suspended from the ceiling, as if in mid-air, in a darkened room. The luminescent sculpture acts as the sole light source for the space, drawing viewers in as it reacts to their presence. Visuals of a viscous metallic fluid envelop the globe's surface, creating an intriguing and mysterious ambiance as textures distort and flow around the shape. The reaction of the programmed light formations is a remediation of the surroundings, feasting on its environment to create an immersive and interactive experience of light and sound.

Through this process of refining behavior and visual complexity, *ANIMA* becomes life-like and impressive. Installed in the round, the piece is experienced from all sides. In a unique way, *ANIMA* creates an intelligent reactive dialogue with all bodies within its surroundings.

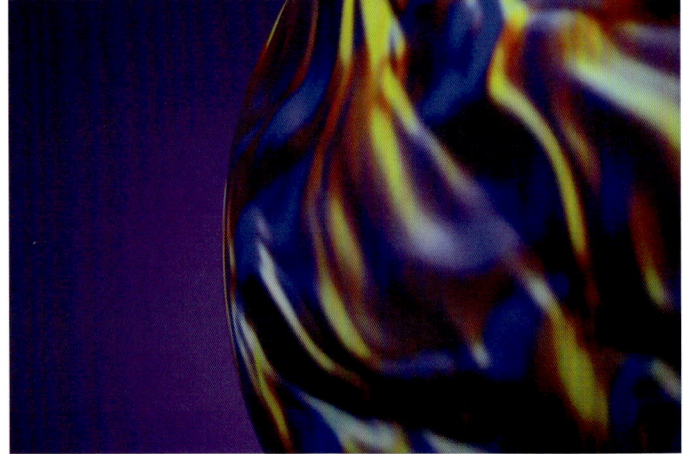

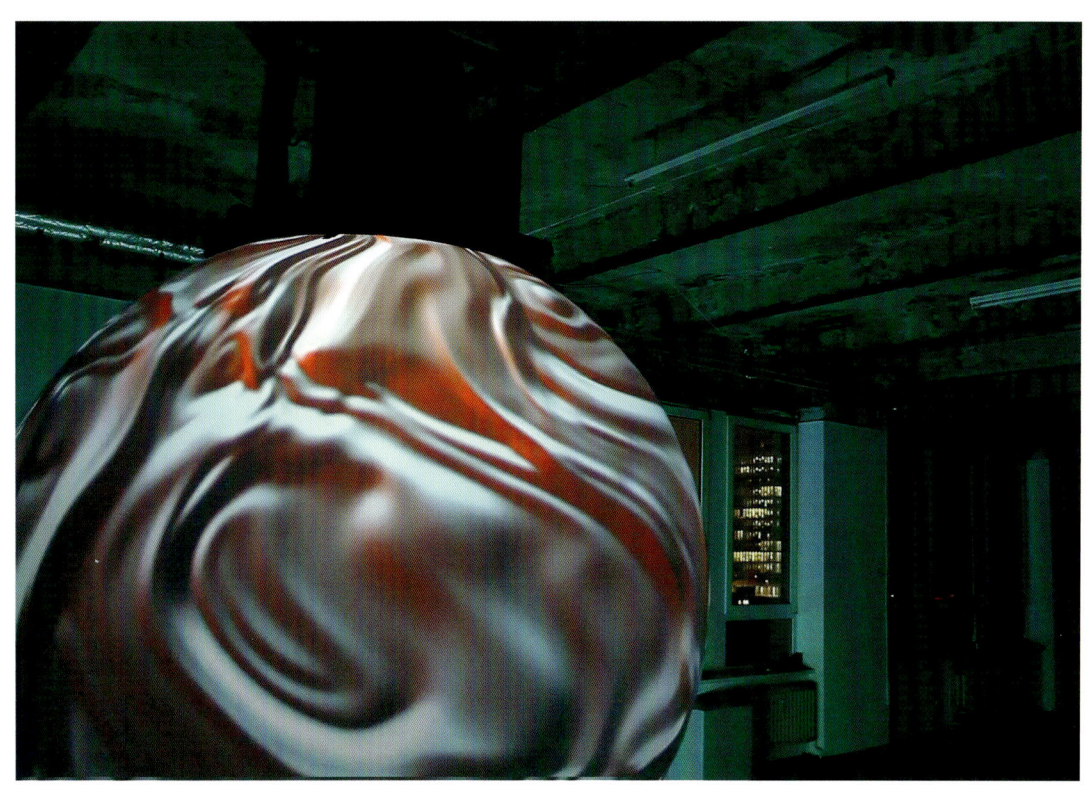

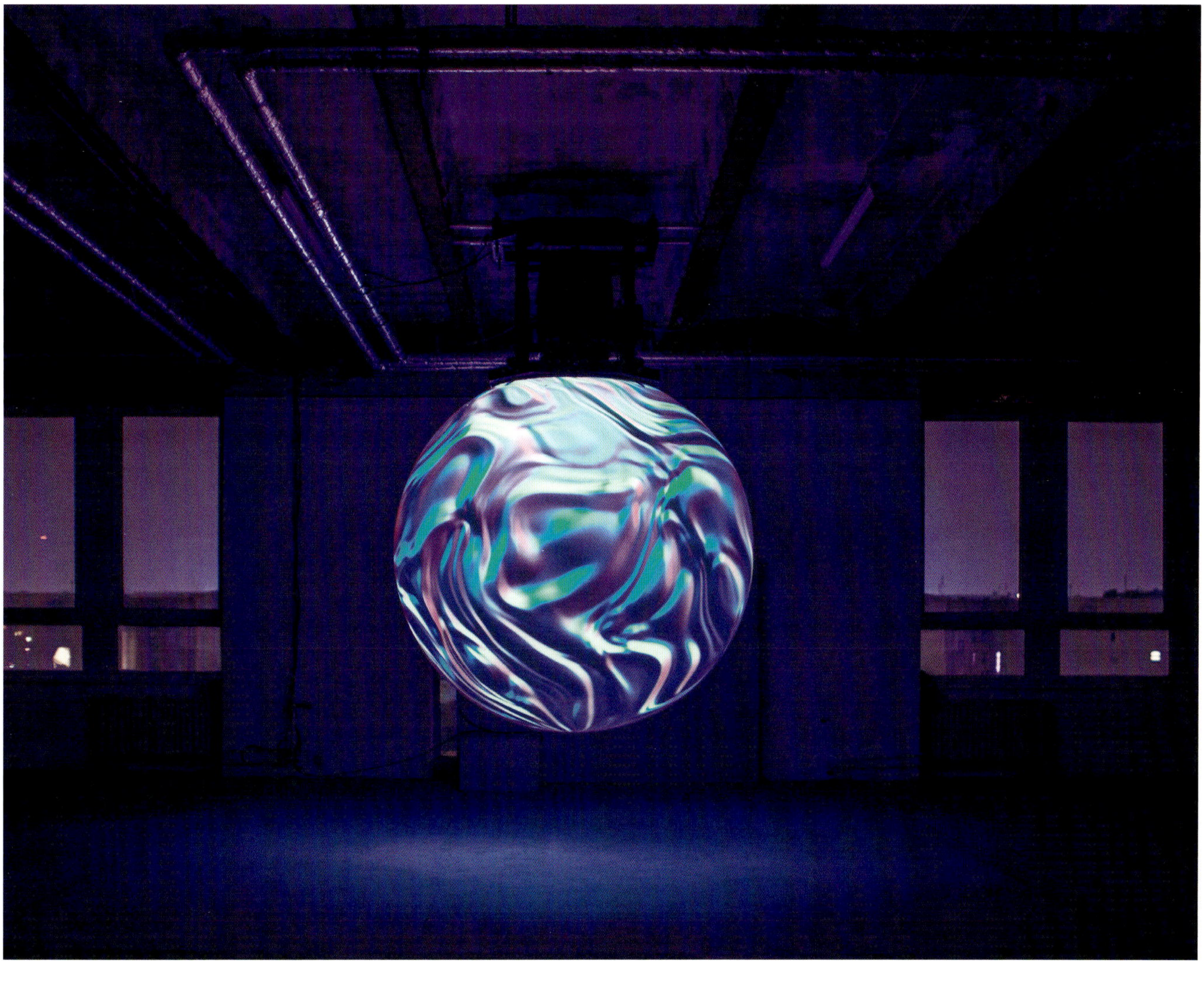

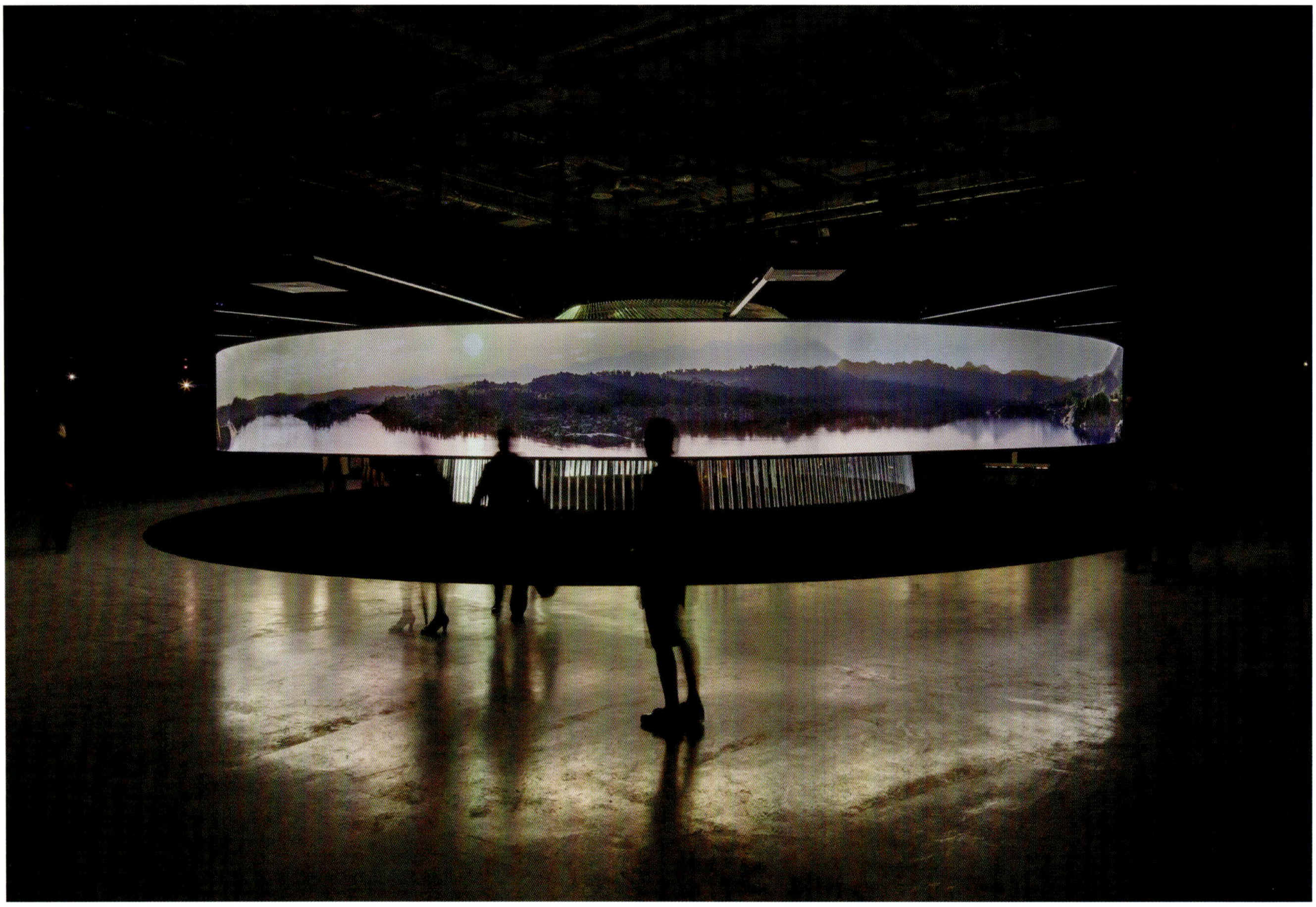

UK PAVILION

—

Design: **Asif Khan**
Photography: **Luke Hayes**

—

The *UK Pavilion* explores the origins of energy. It begins with the birth of the universe, and takes visitors on the journey of energy from the sun through to the earth's landscape, its climate, human civilization and innovation. The *UK Pavilion* is a multi-sensory experience involving film, technology, sound, and computer-generated animation.

At the heart of the *UK Pavilion* is a stunning sixty-meter panorama depicting a living, universal landscape generated entirely by computer. At forty-thousand pixels wide, it is the largest project of its kind ever undertaken.

The panorama surrounds a striking centerpiece structure inspired by the architecture of yurts, representing the timeless connection between human civilization and environment. Its transparent spokes respond to human touch with illumination, which in turn influences the landscape around it, gently altering its weather in reaction to visitor activity. An original score by musician Brian Eno unfolds in parallel with this journey.

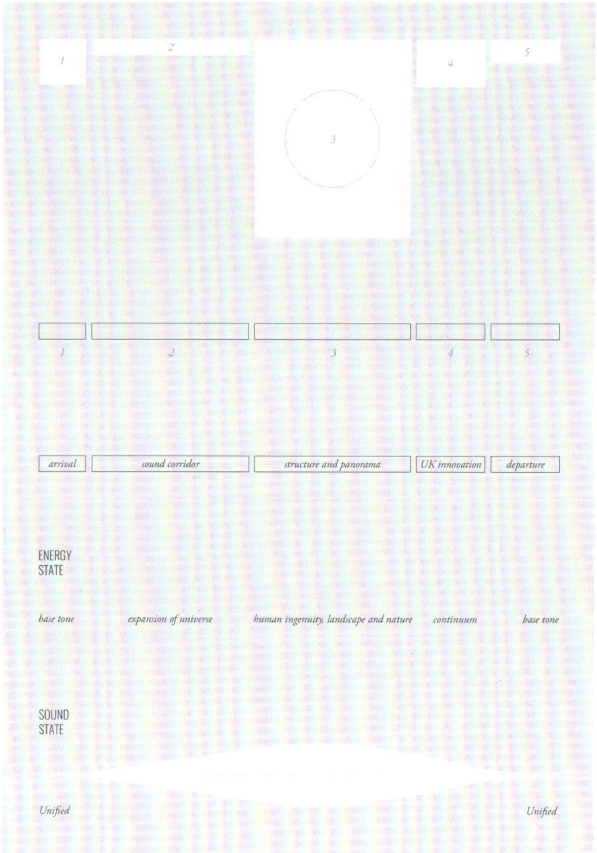

arrival	*sound corridor*	*structure and panorama*	*UK innovation*	*departure*	

ENERGY
STATE

base tone	*expansion of universe*	*human ingenuity, landscape and nature*	*continuum*	*base tone*

SOUND
STATE

Unified   *Unified*

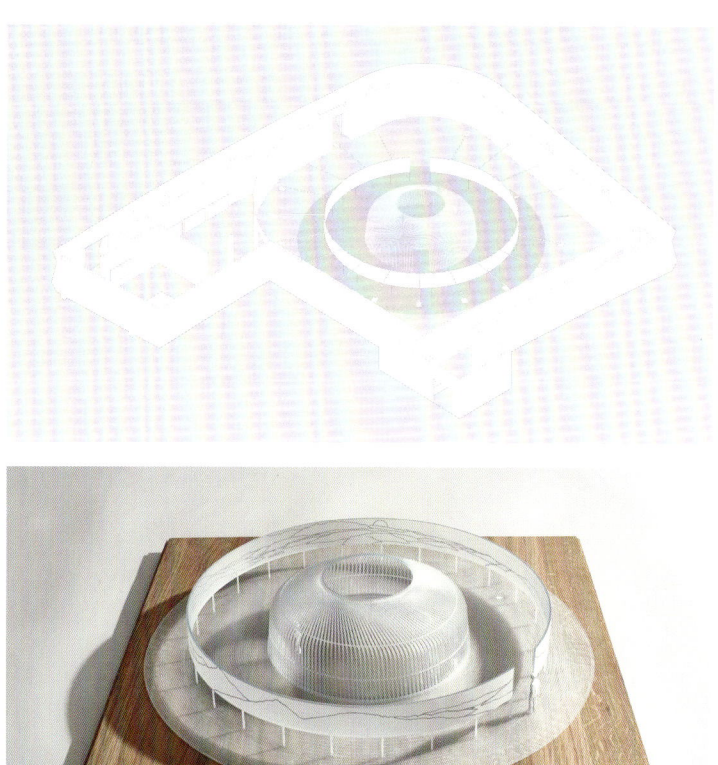

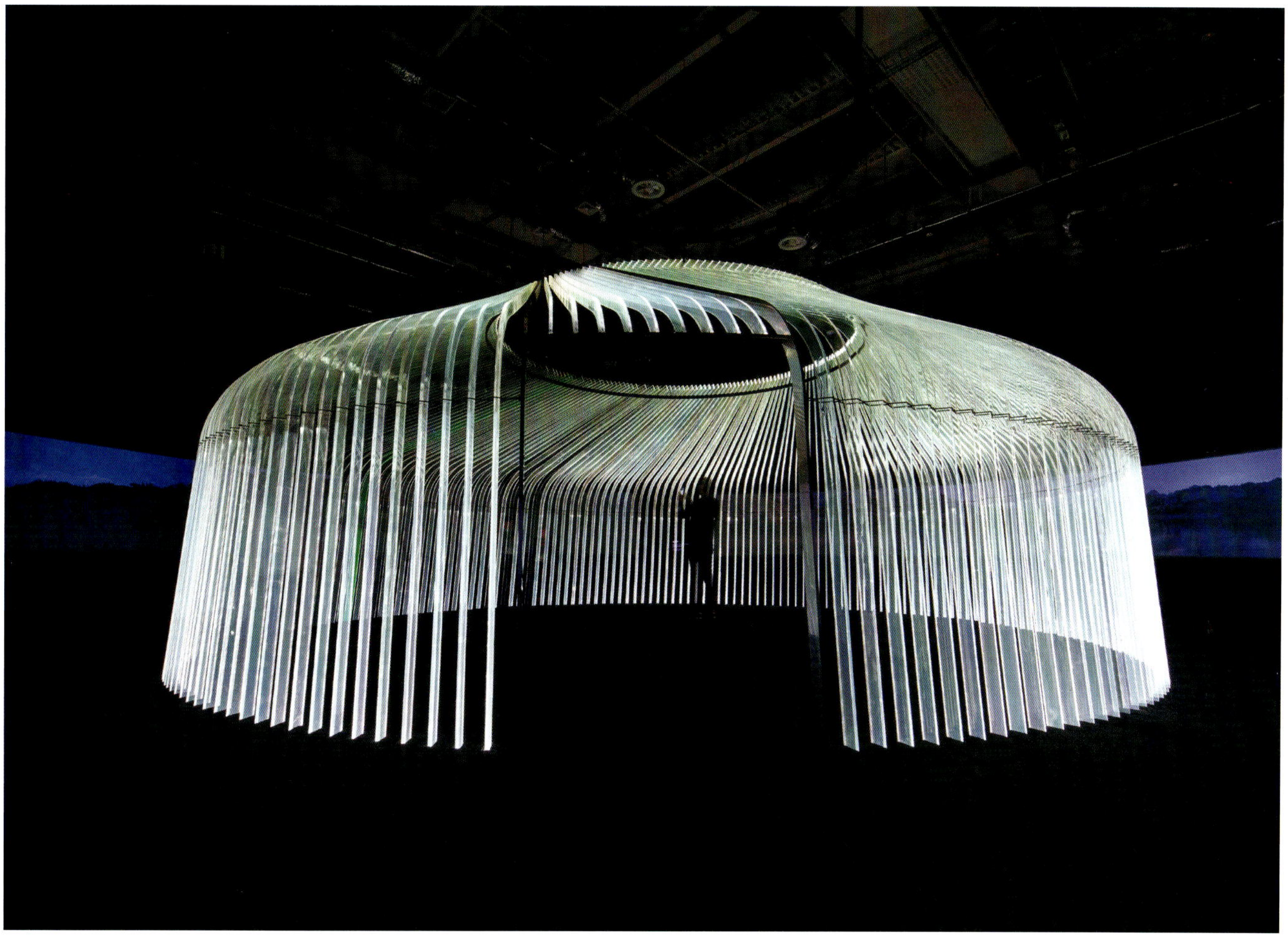

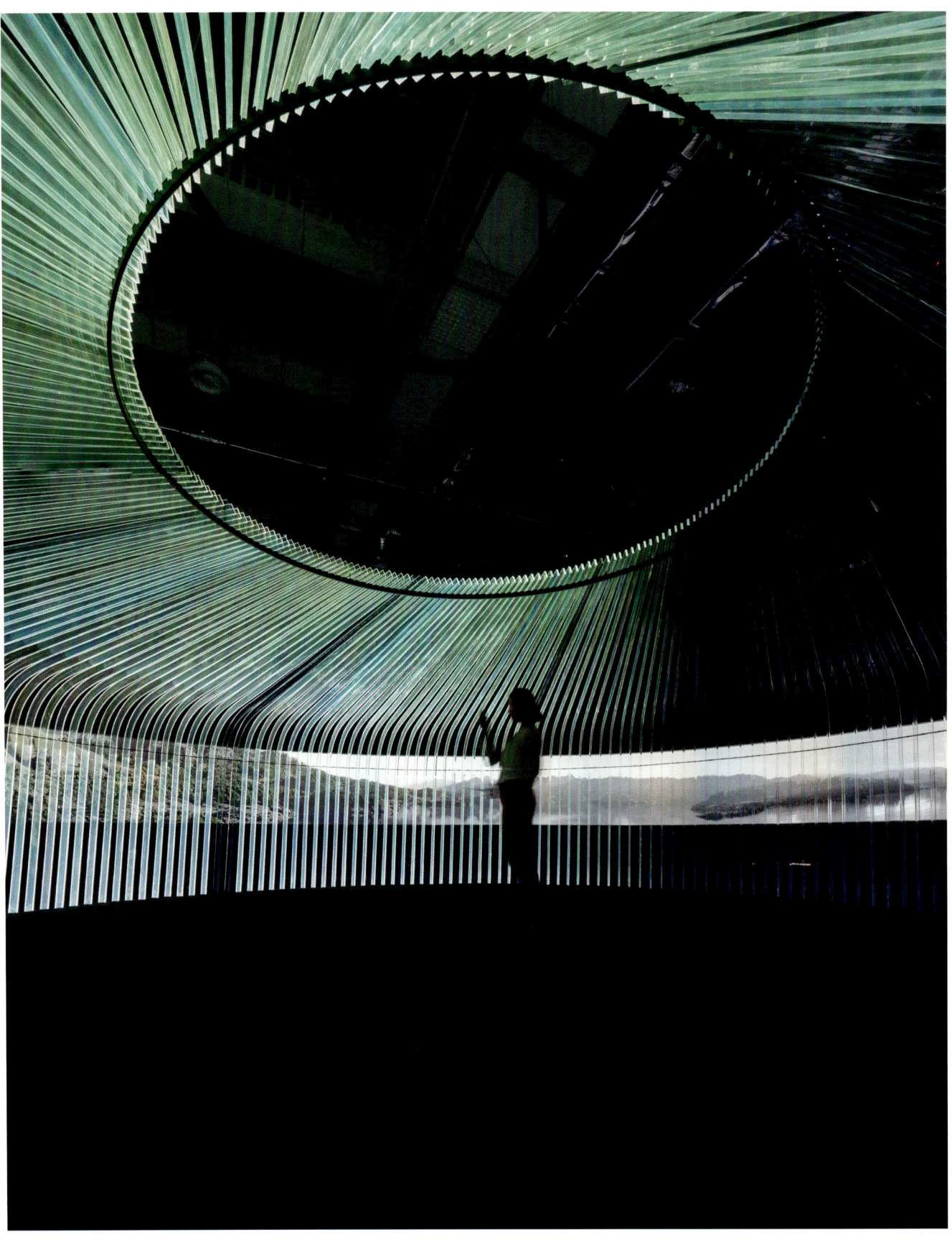

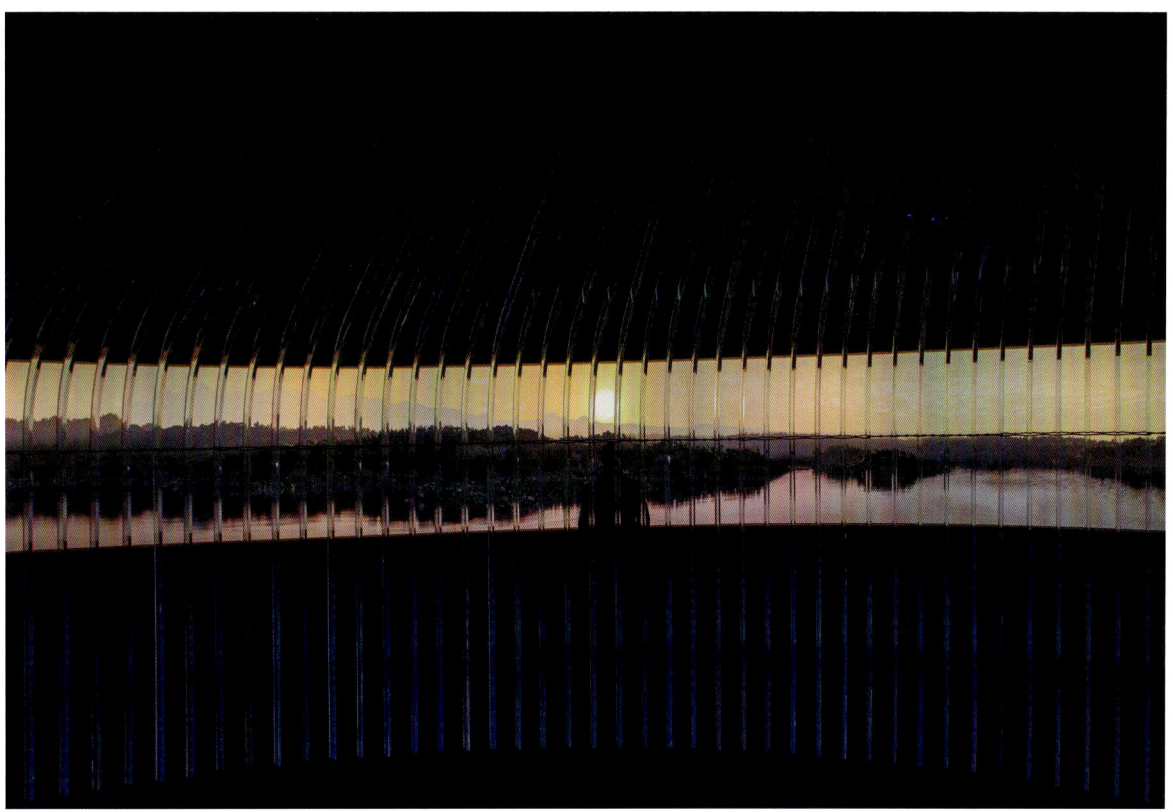

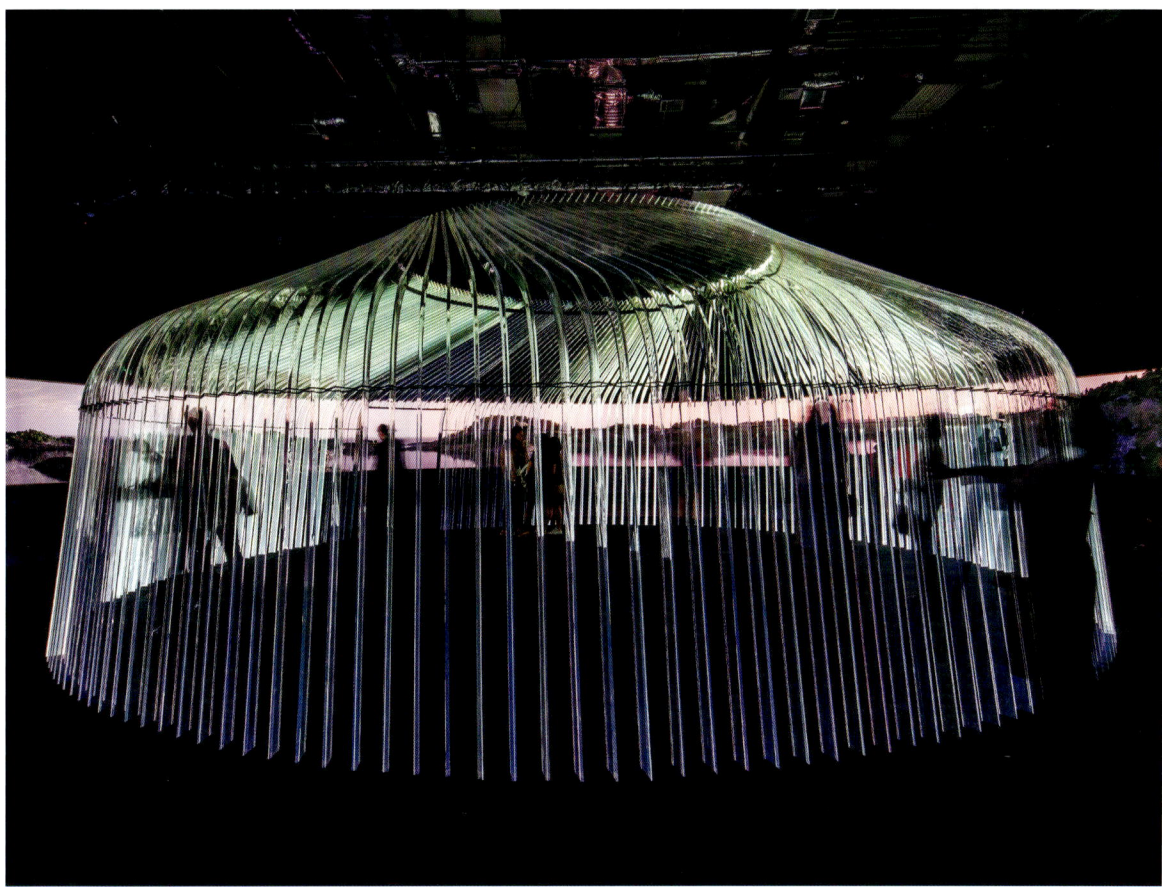

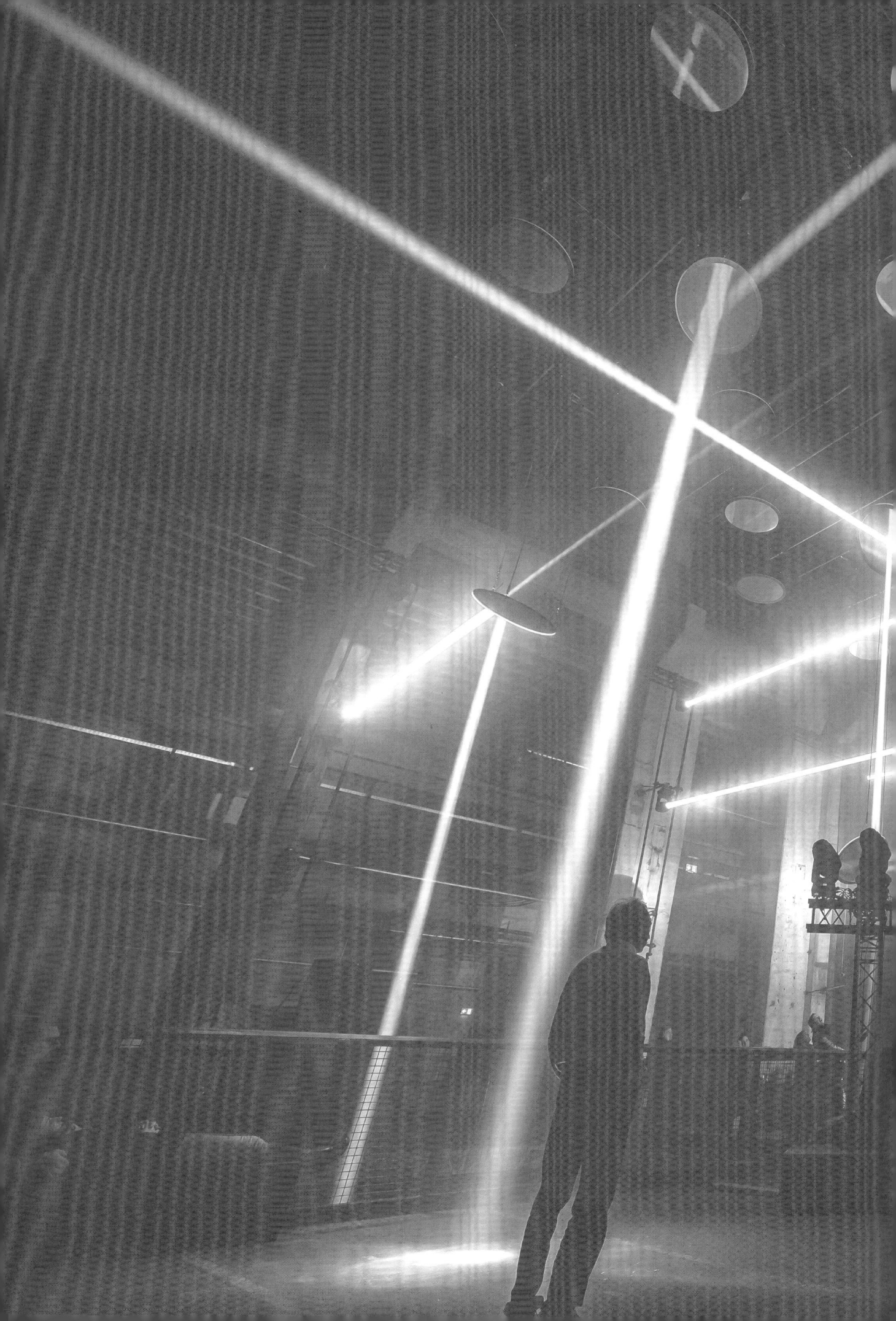

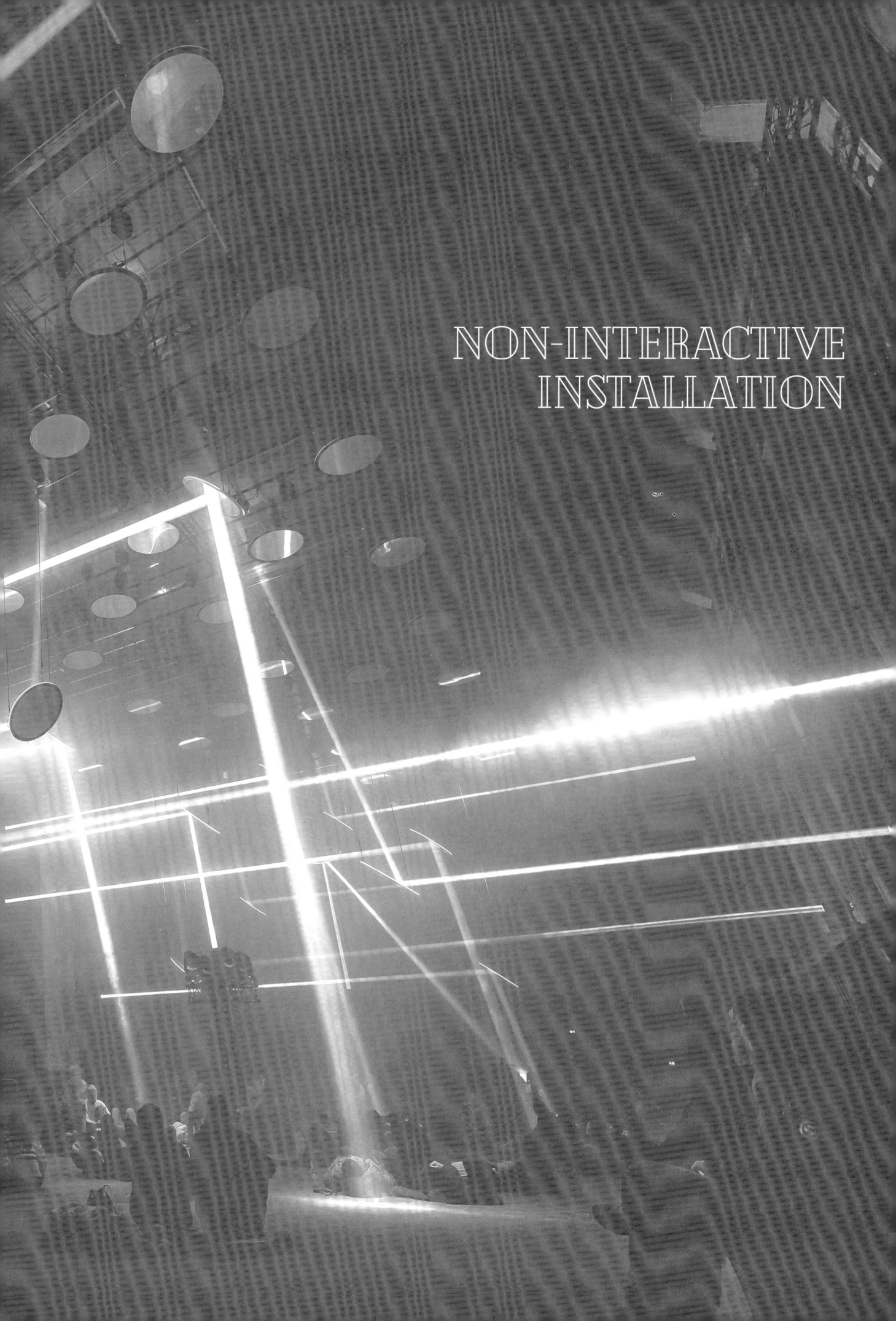

NON-INTERACTIVE
INSTALLATION

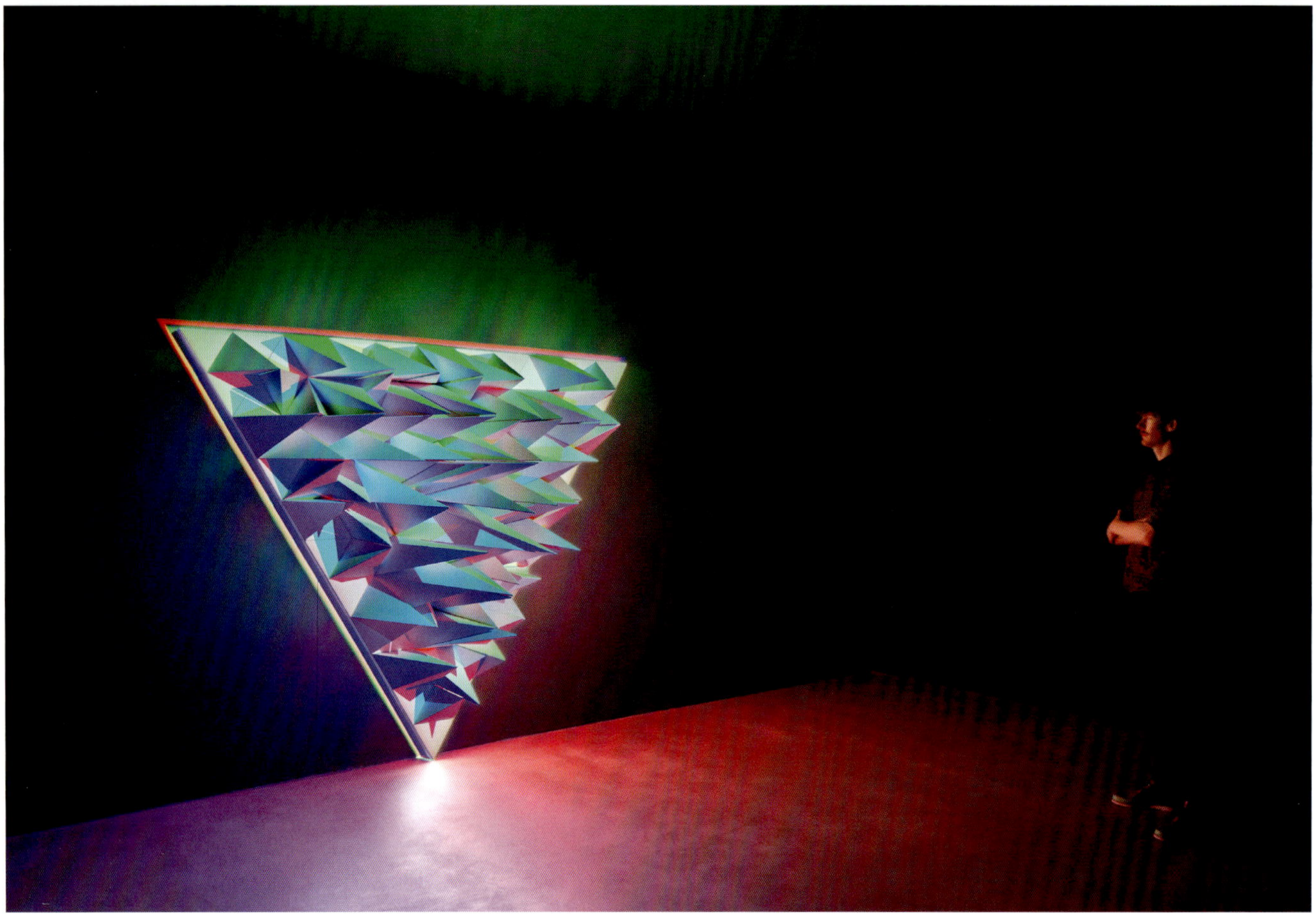

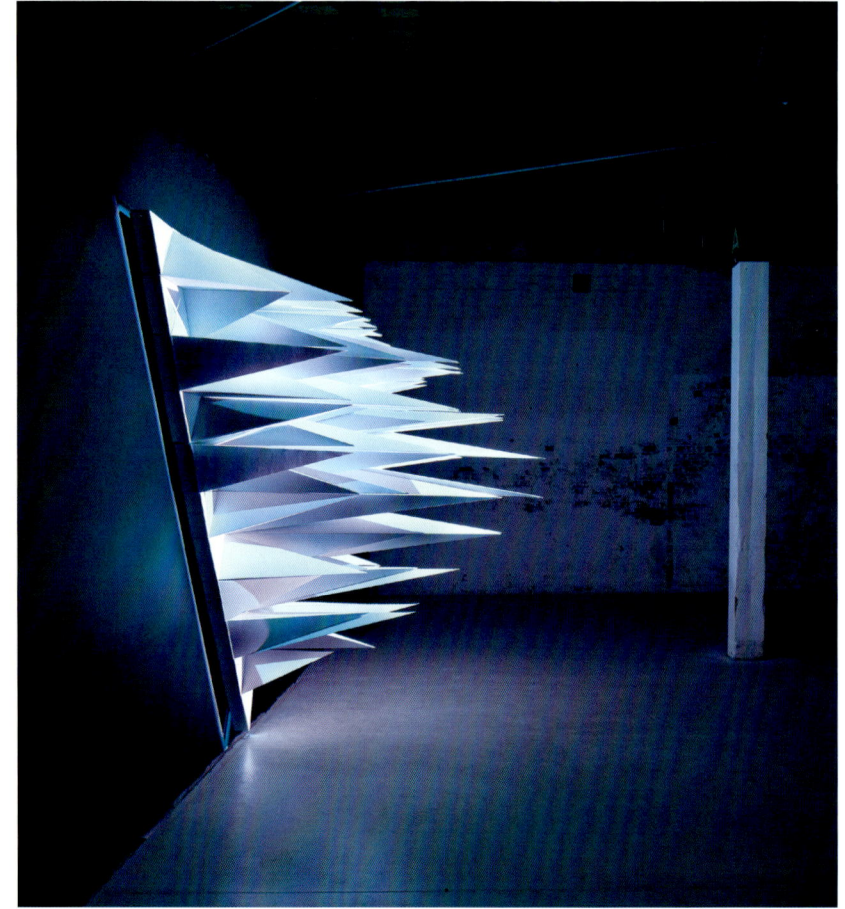

PRIMARY

—

Design: **Flynn Talbot**

—

A new exploration in color and light, *Primary* is a three-sided wall installation which is illuminated by three LED light sources. This is a reference to the primary colors of light: red, green, and blue (RGB). These base colors of light define the quantity of light sources and the use of triangles—everything in threes. The cardboard structure is designed to fragment the light and show how colored light is mixed. Light and object are intrinsically connected.

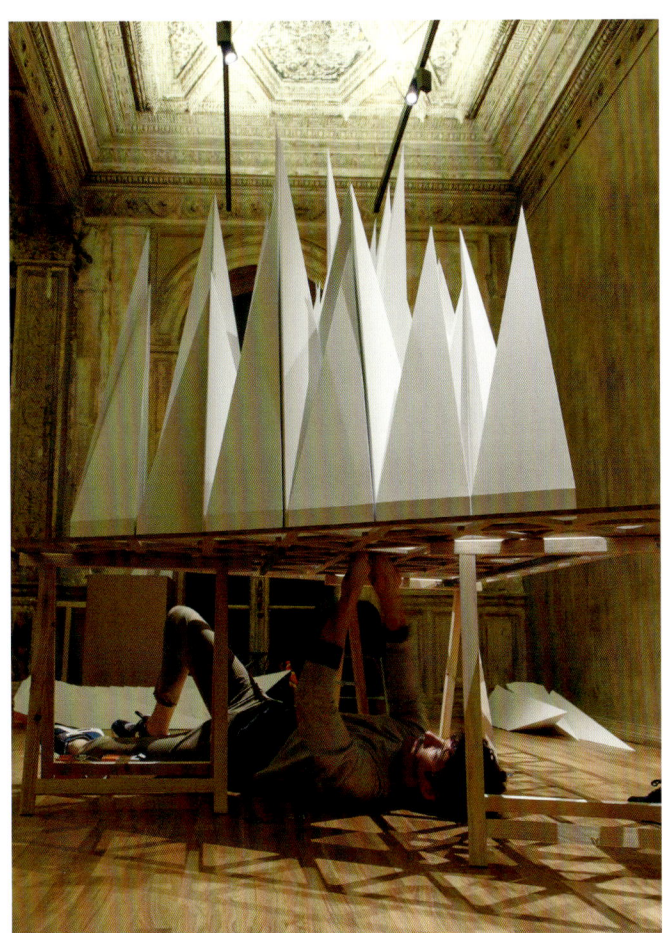

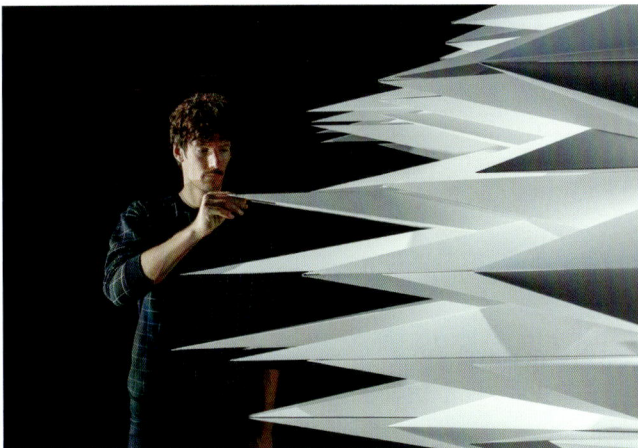

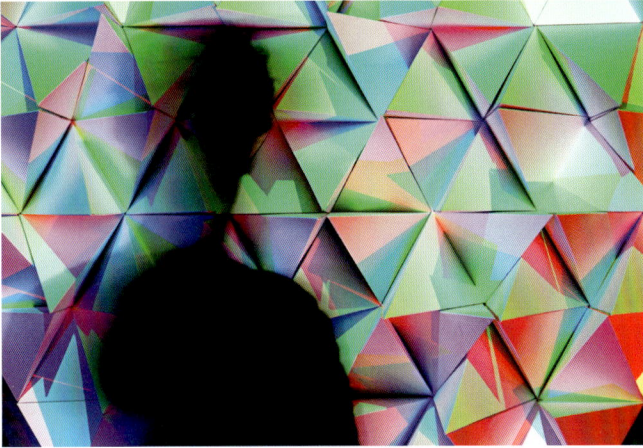

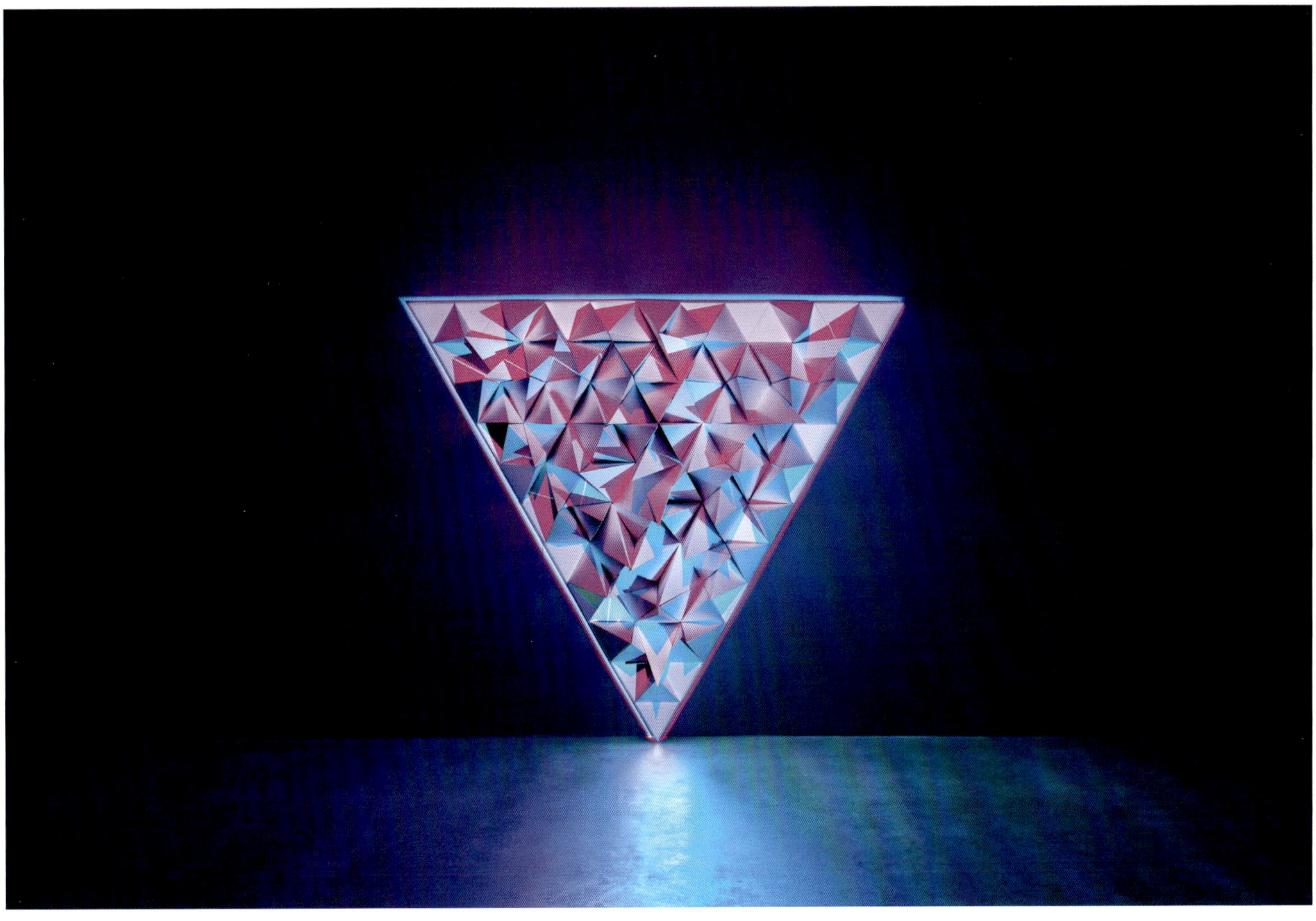

A PANORAMA OF THE SKIES

Author: **Maja Petric**
Photography: **Arturo Ortiz**

A Panorama of the Skies is an art installation that utilizes immersive projection technologies to transform the experience of an ordinary conference room into an ever-changing sky. The audio-visual experience was developed to immerse visitors into an elevated emotional space.

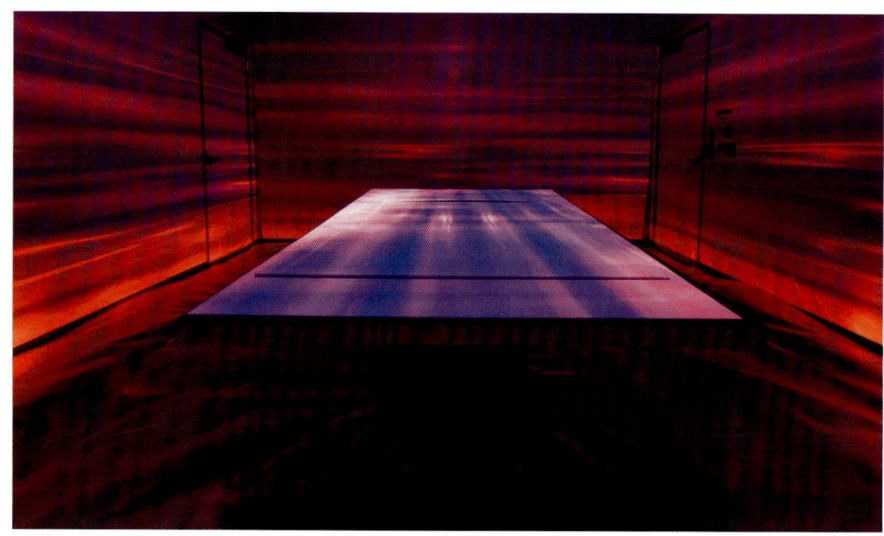

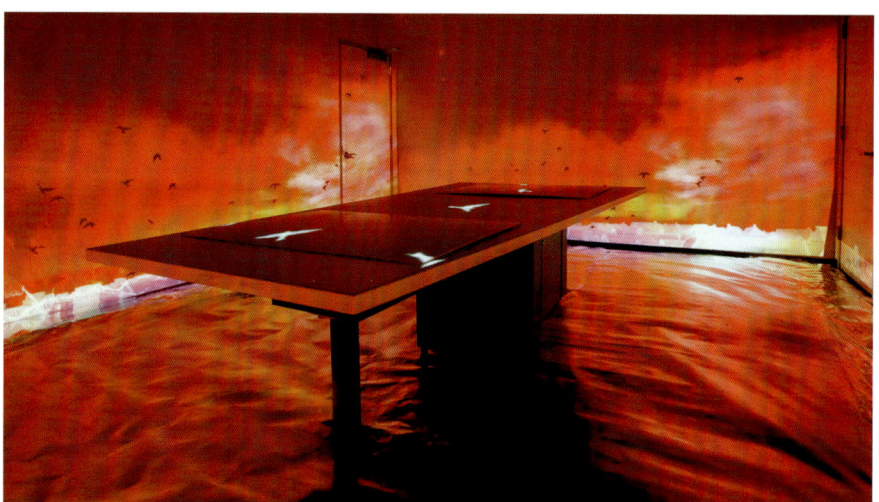

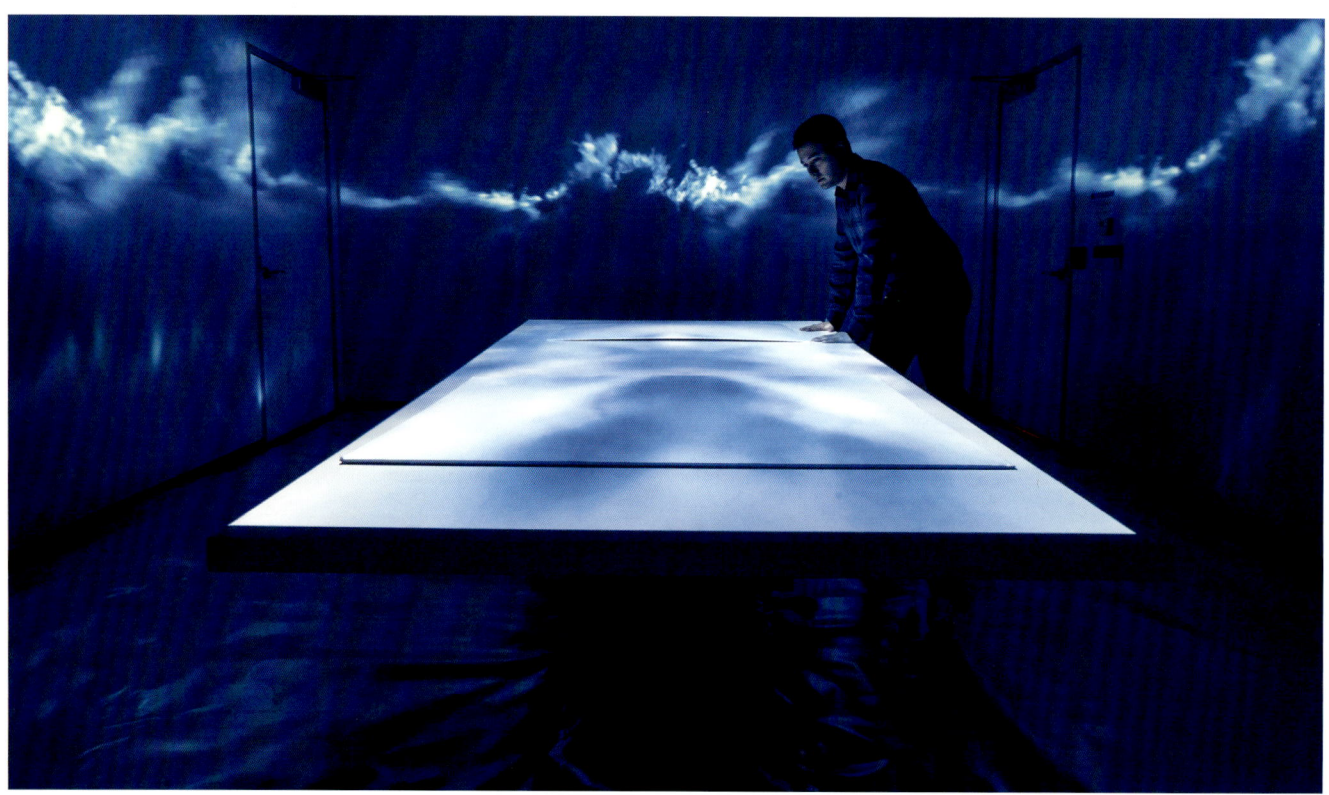

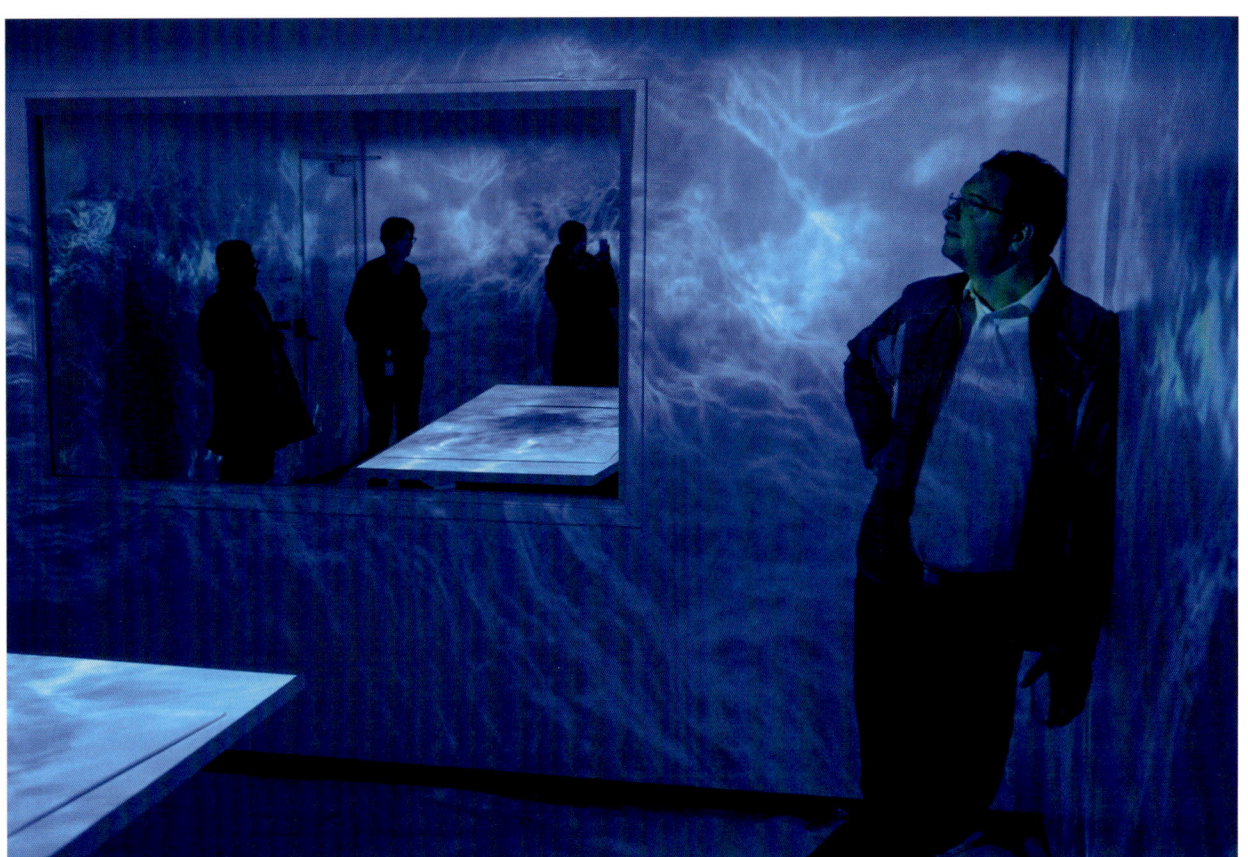

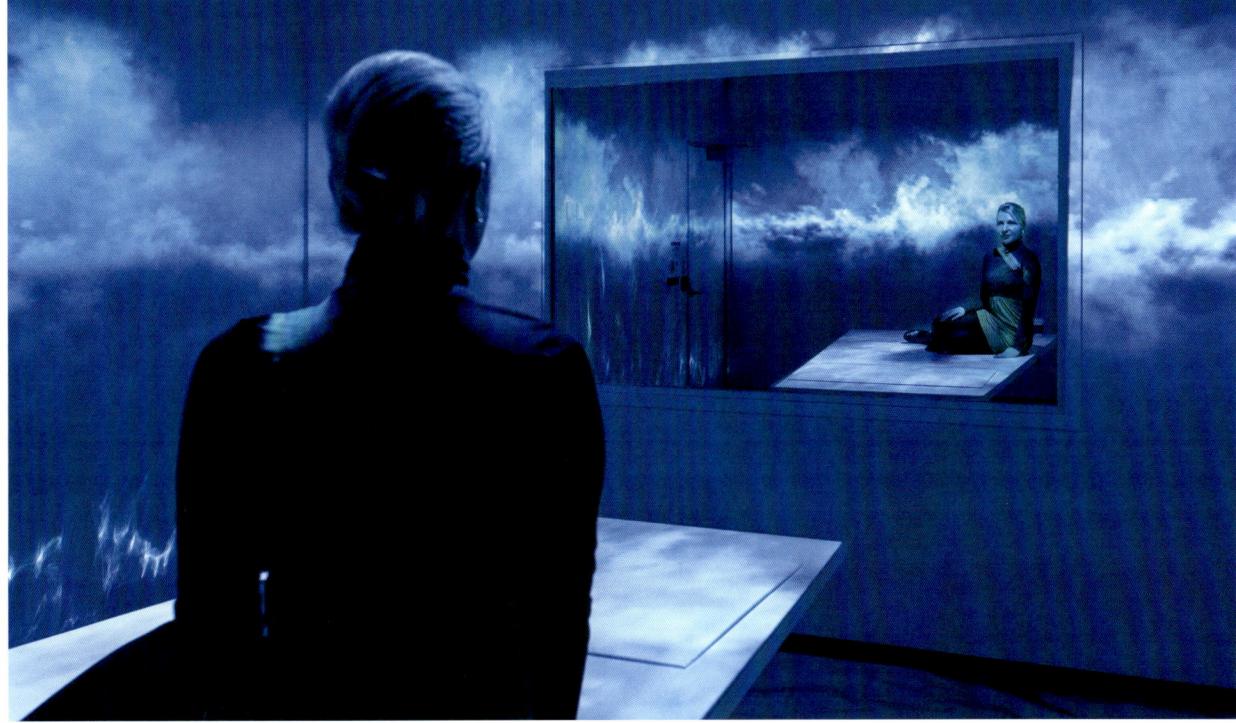

SLICES

—

Design: **URBANSCREEN**
Photography: **Thorsten Bauer**

—

SLICES is a creative study on the capabilities of the next generation of video projectors and the aesthetics of advanced imaging technologies, developed for the ISE fair-booth of NEC. Five semitranslucent plexiglass panels are arranged in a row, enabling the visitors to move around in between them and take different perspectives.

Five individual projectors play the same video loop, each on a slight delay from the next, creating the impression of a continuous light impulse moving from one slice to the next.

The abstract graphic animations are inspired by and created for the technology they are projected with. By challenging its contrast values, resolution and shutter speed, they illustrate the projectors' key qualities.

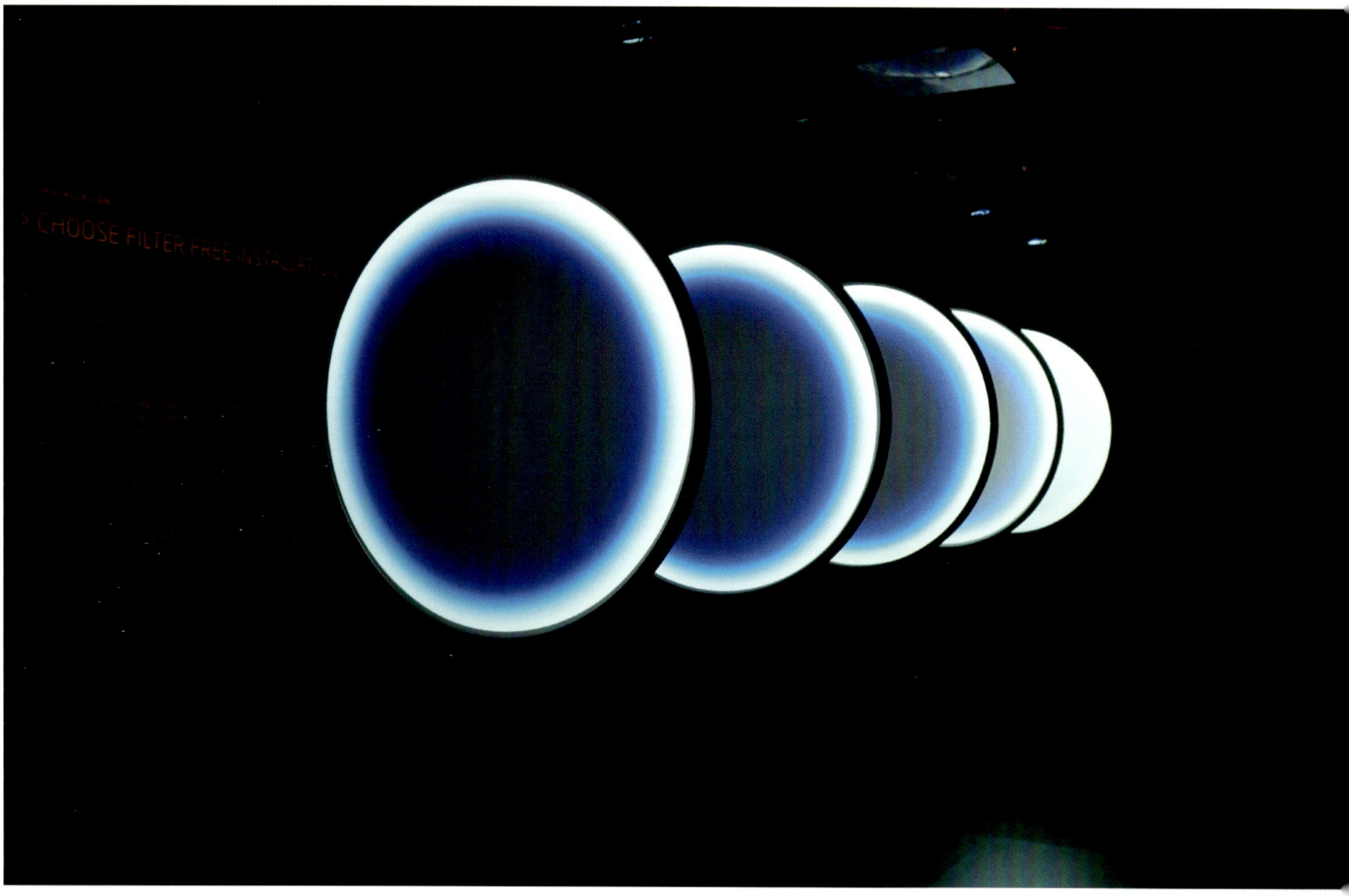

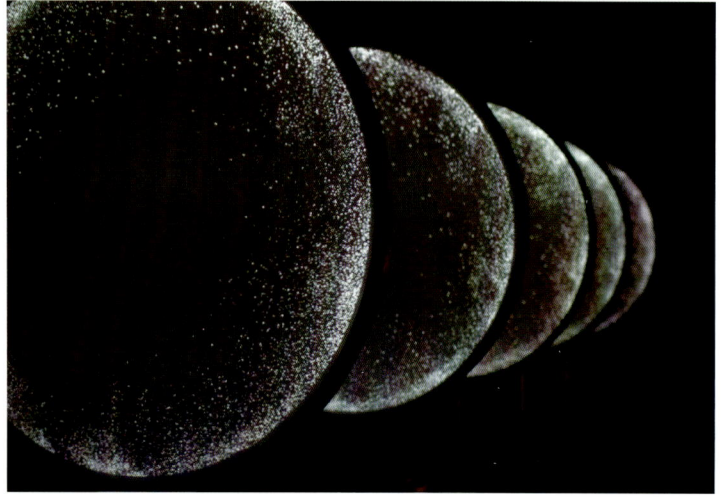

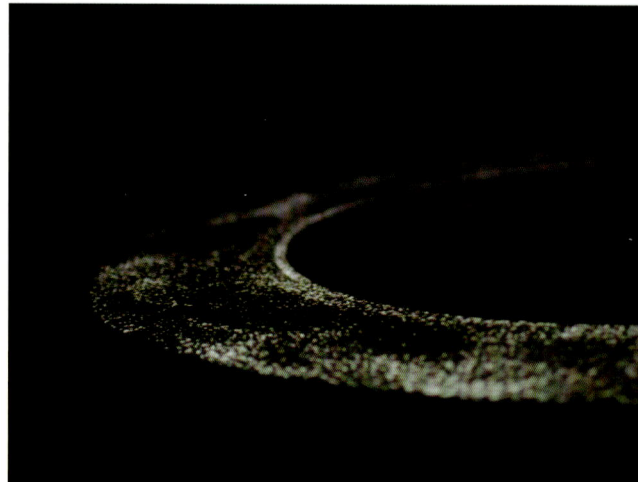

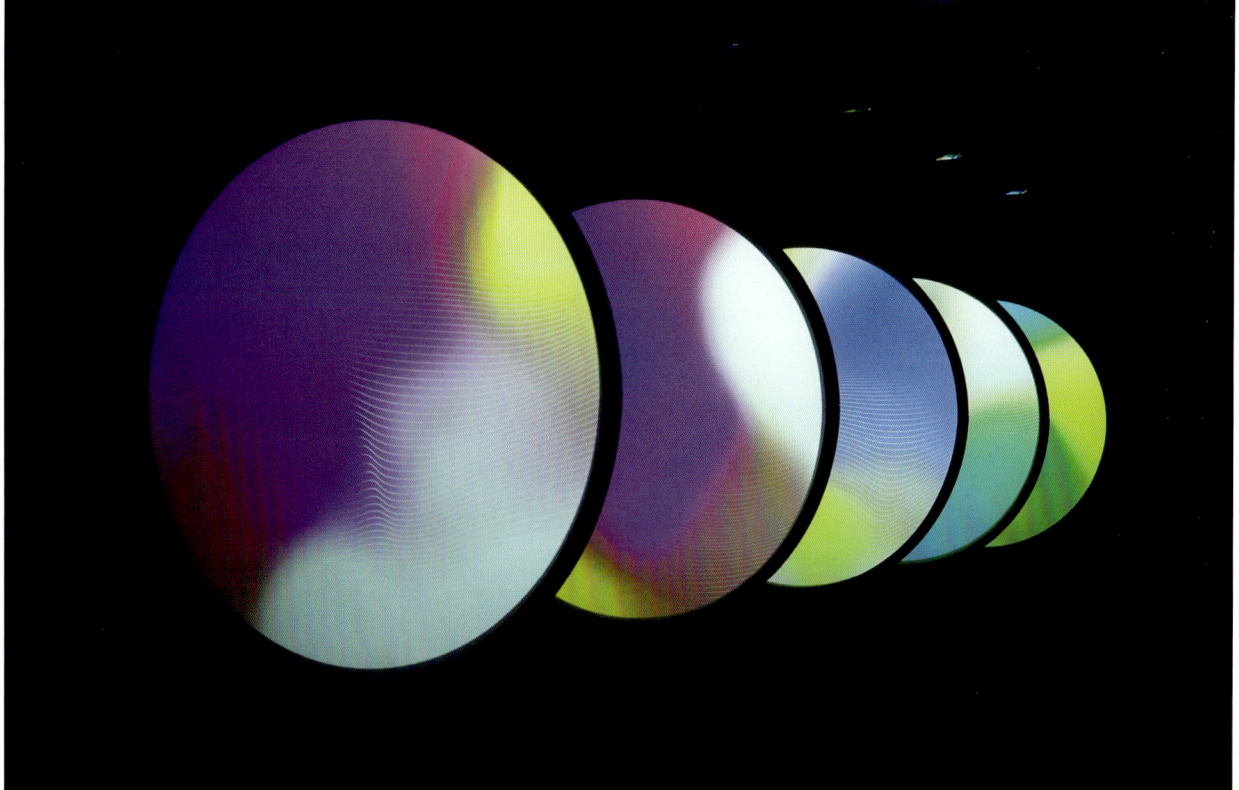

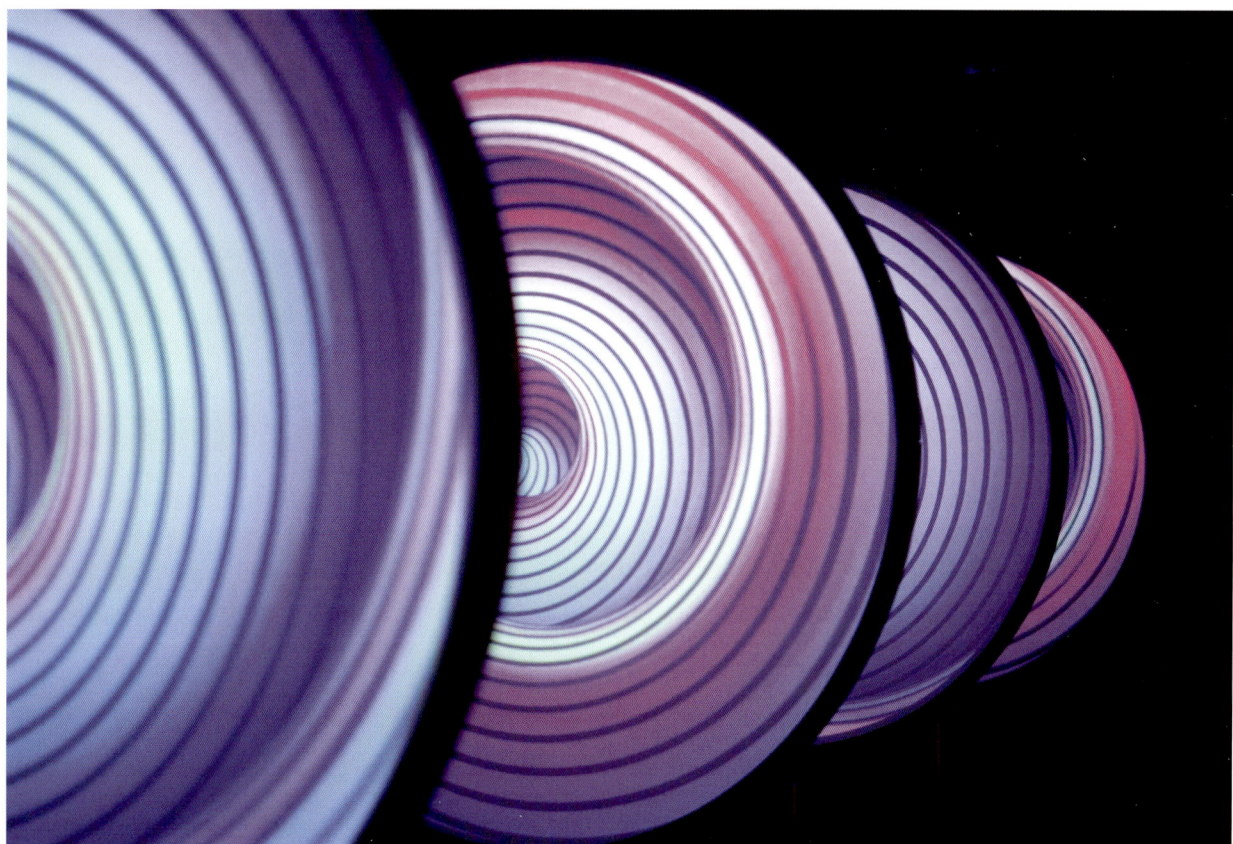

DELTA

—

Concept Design & Art direction: **Olivier Ratsi**
Sound Design: **Thomas Vaquié**

—

Since ancient times, delta, the fourth letter of the Greek alphabet, has been represented by a triangle pointing upwards. Originating from the equivalent letter of the Phoenician alphabet, it is based on a hieroglyph initially representing a door.

Delta, an installation and part of the *Echolyse* project, is a work on the perception of space that explores, through a dematerialised door, the possibility of a fictional three-dimensional space. It uses the different surfaces of a space (walls, ceiling, floor) as a projection canvas.

Making use of the anamorphosis technique, the piece is based on the position of the spectator, predetermined by the artist, from which the audience will be able to visually reconstitute the geometrical symbol and discover the "pelures" (peelings) emitting from the very center of its gravity.

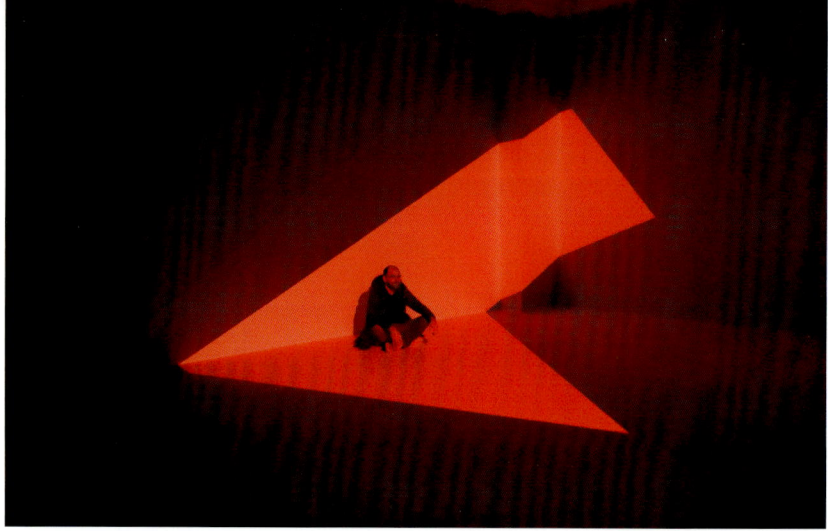

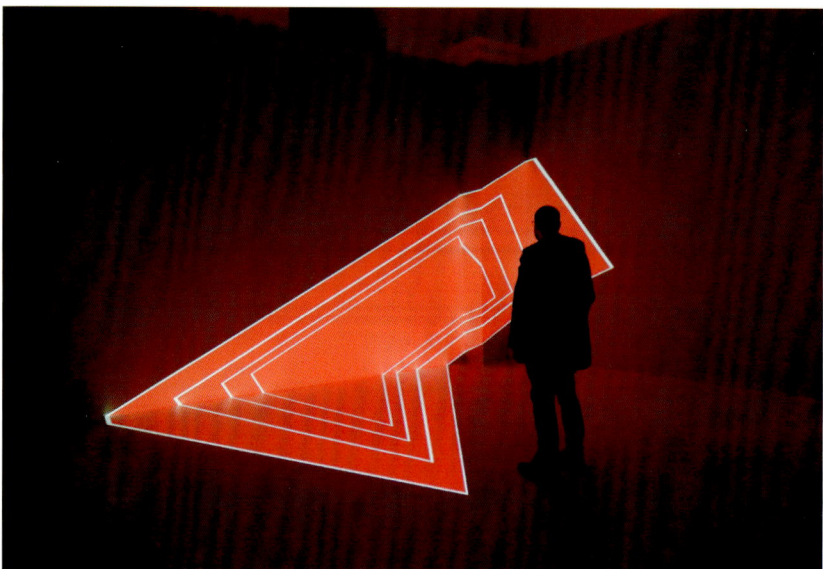

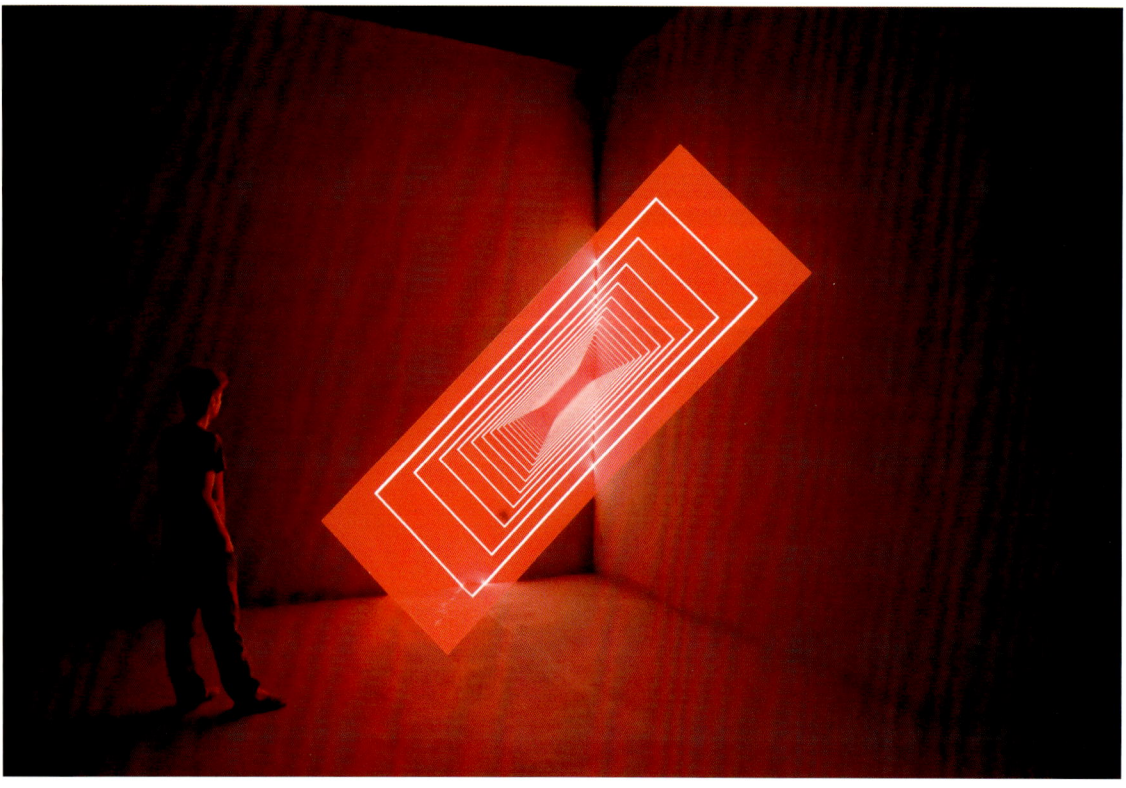

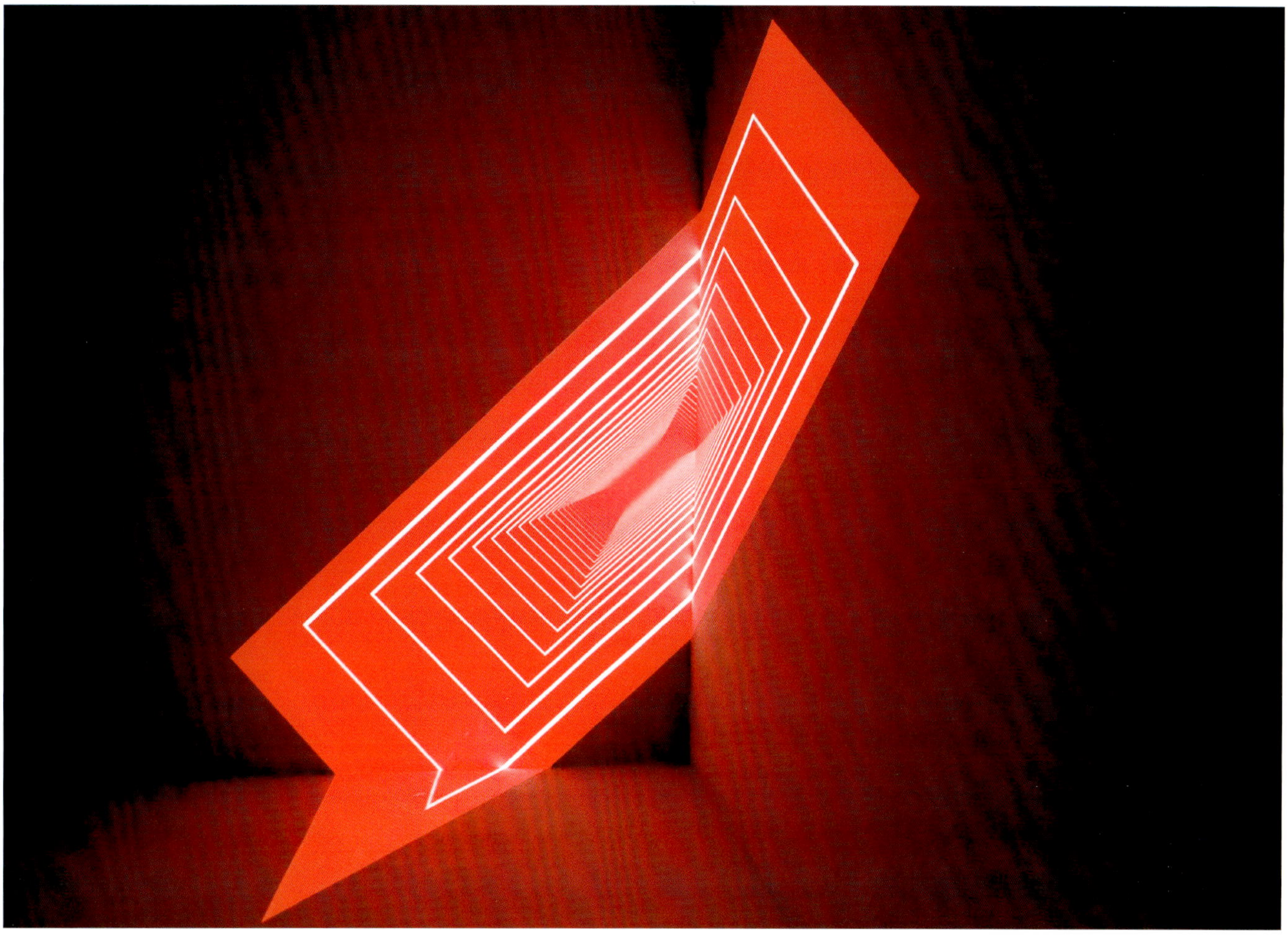

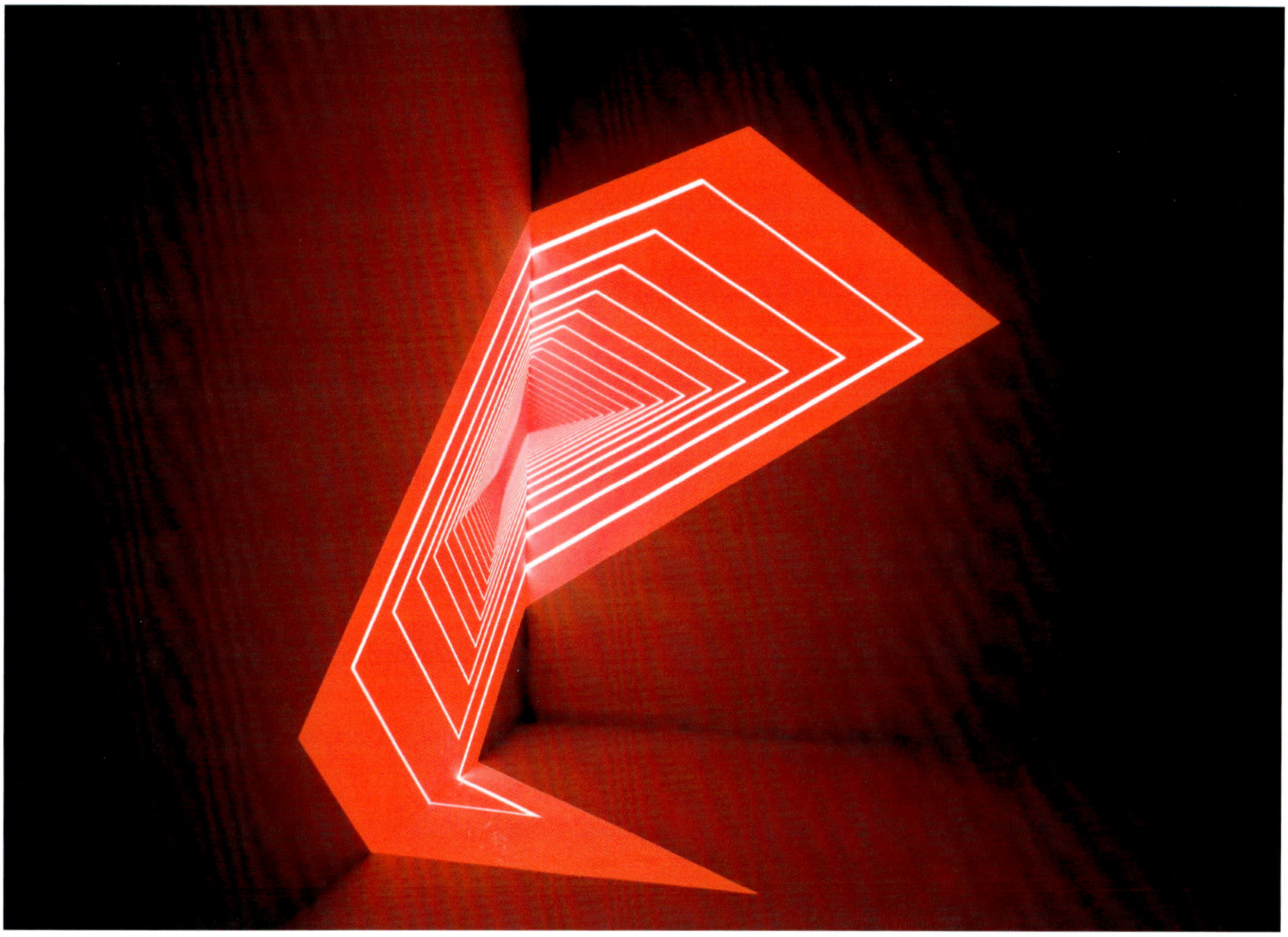

ONION SKIN

—

Concept Design & Art Direction:
Olivier Ratsi
Sound Design: **Thomas Vaquié**
Production: **Nicolas Boritch**

—

This is an audiovisual installation made up of a physical dimension—a module of two walls, positioned at right angles—augmented by a projector and a surround-sound score.

Onion Skin is a graphical work about the re-composition of time and space through a game of perspectives, both of the exhibition space itself and that of the projection canvas. Built around a progressive structure, made up of 4 parts lasting 14 minutes in total, the piece plays on the principle of repetition and scale to create a physical and hypnotic experience that opens doors onto the hidden and untouchable.

The whole experience of the installation is based on a very specific point of view, a precise position from which a new dimension is revealed to the audience by anamorphosis. The simple geometric elements ("peelings") that seemed to be flat at first suddenly start delineating a new space. The illusion of this new dimension within the installation slowly appears as the "onion skins" seem to be leaving their physical surface behind.

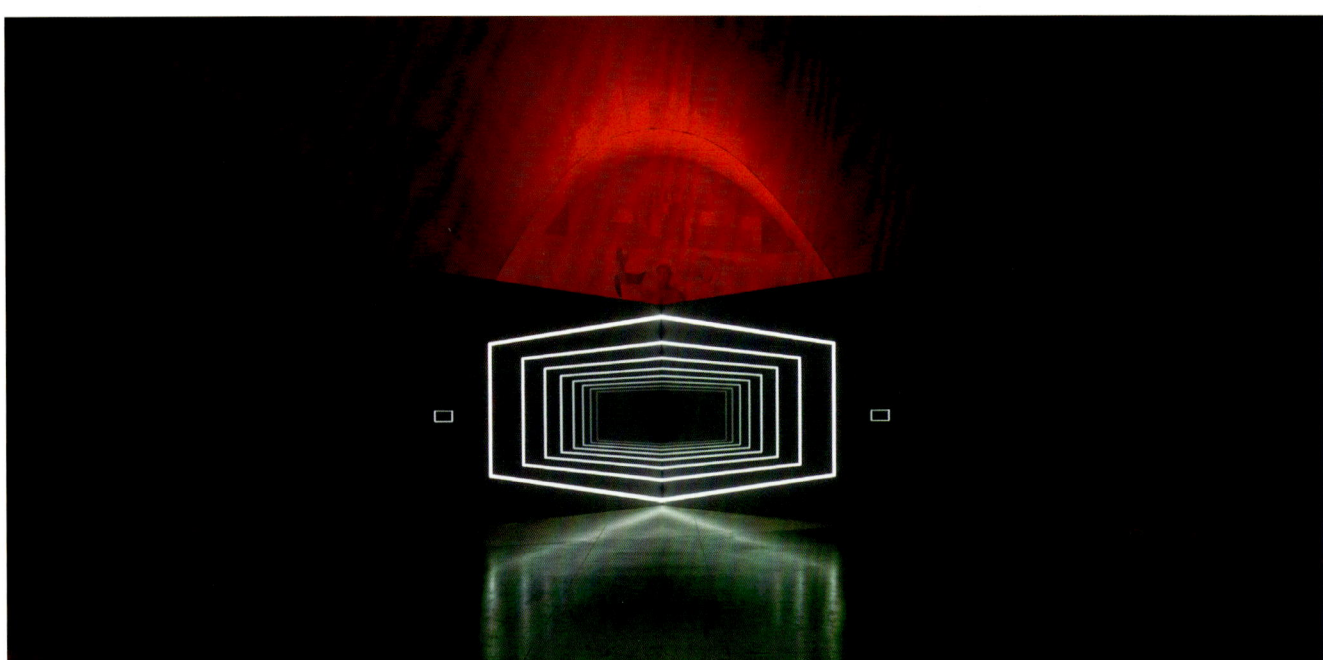

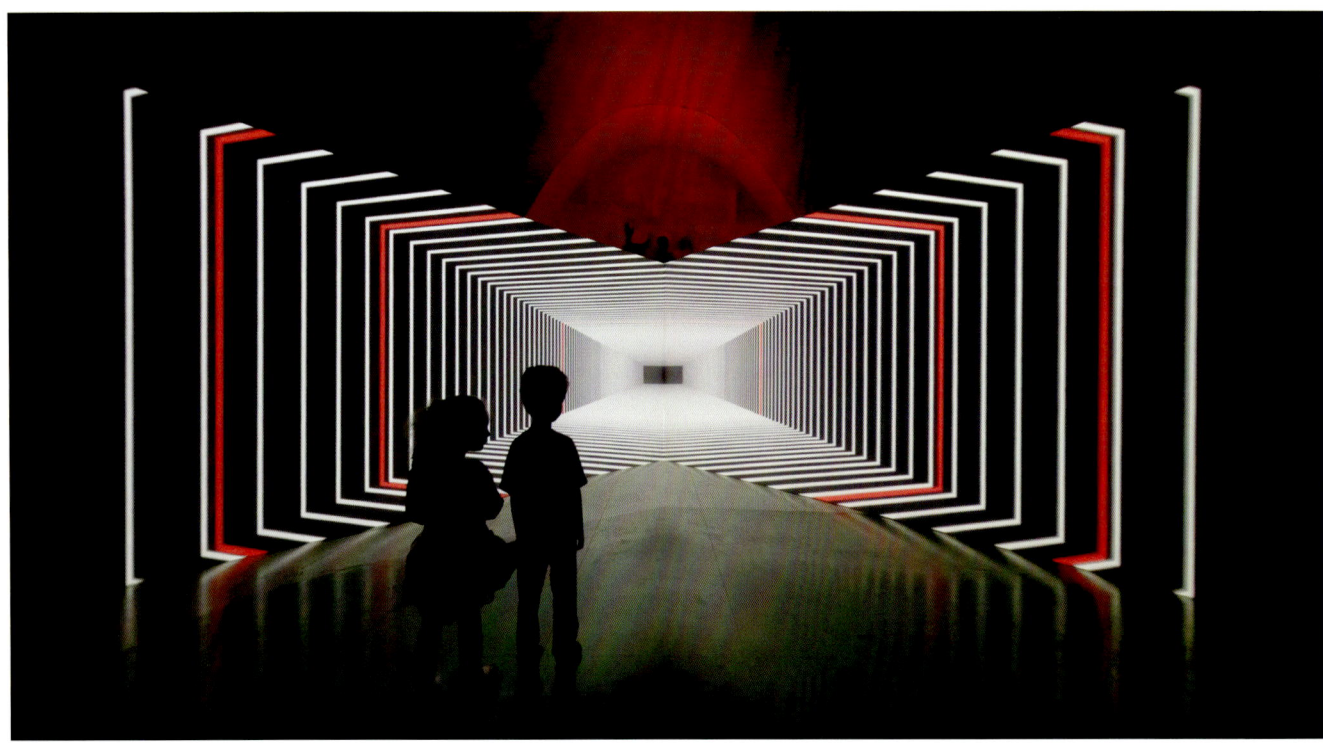

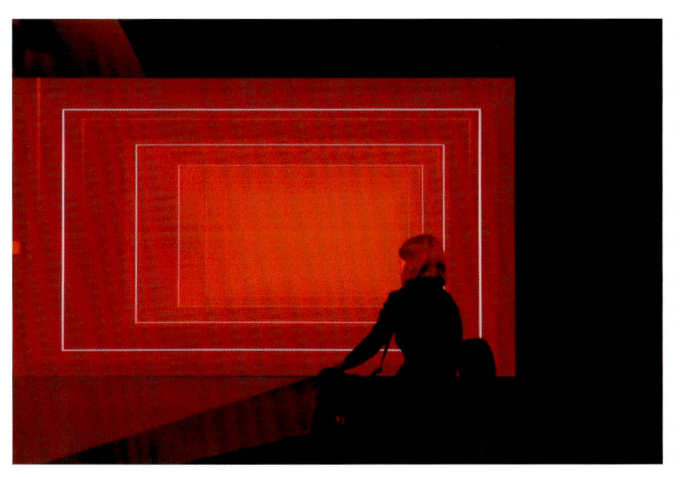

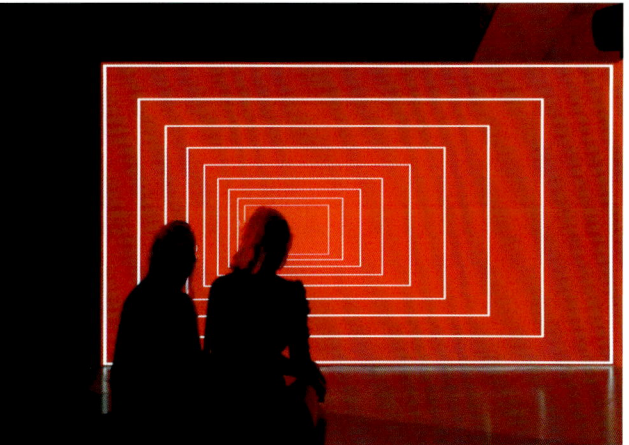

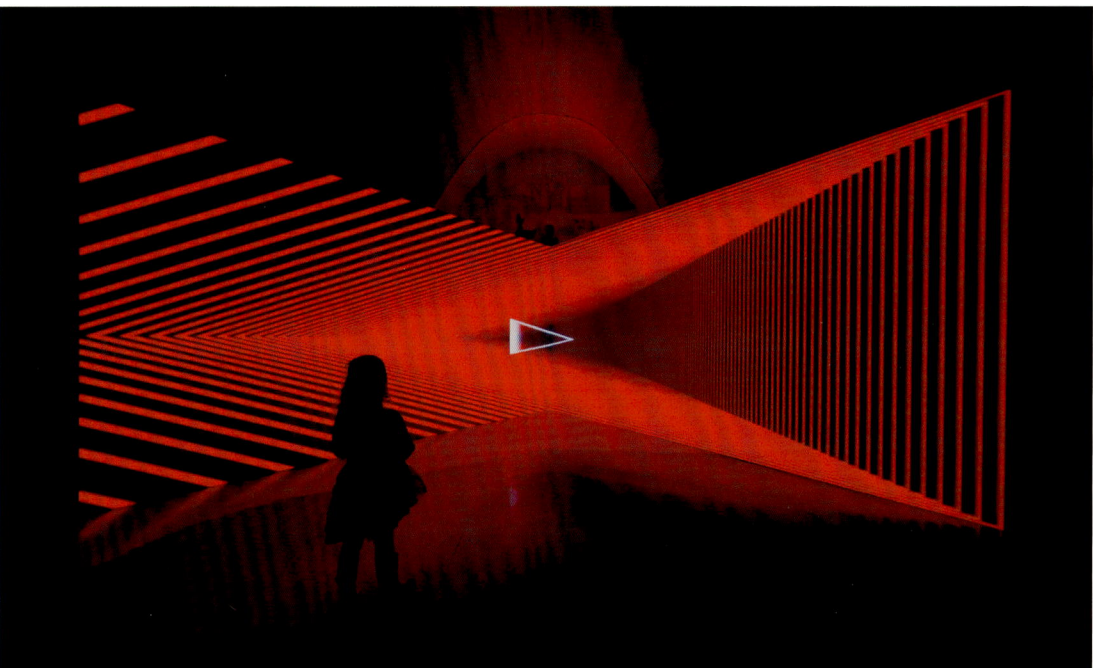

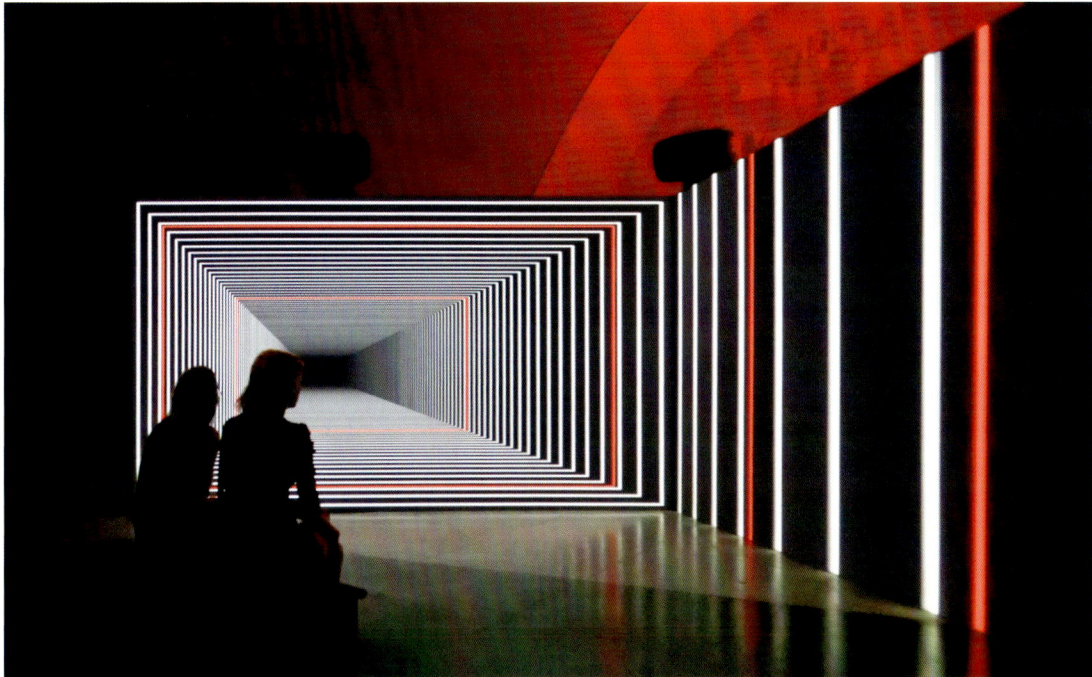

PÊLE-MÊLE

—

Concept Design & Art Direction: **Olivier Ratsi**
Sound Design: **Thomas Vaquié, Olivier Ratsi**

—

Pêle-Mêle uses a double anamorphosis effect, visible from one sole and unique viewpoint. Upon entering the room, the viewer finds himself at equal distance between two transparent modules in the form of right angles, situated on either side of the space, which superimpose themselves on the existing environment.

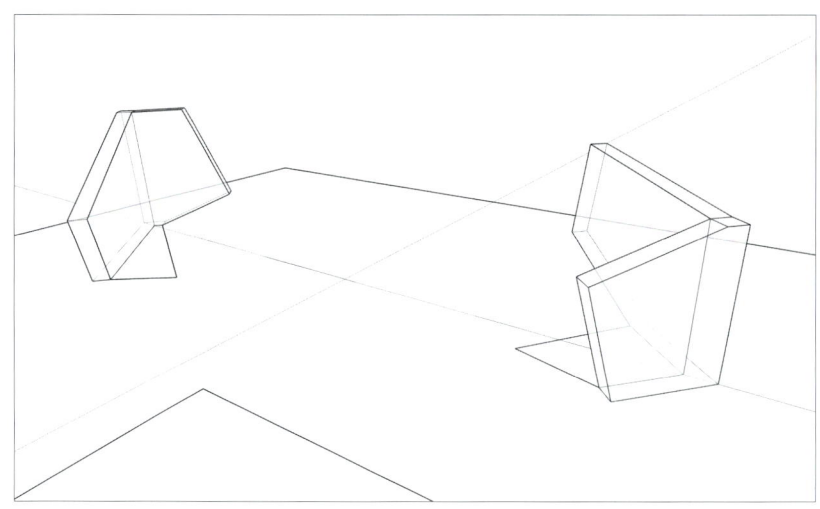

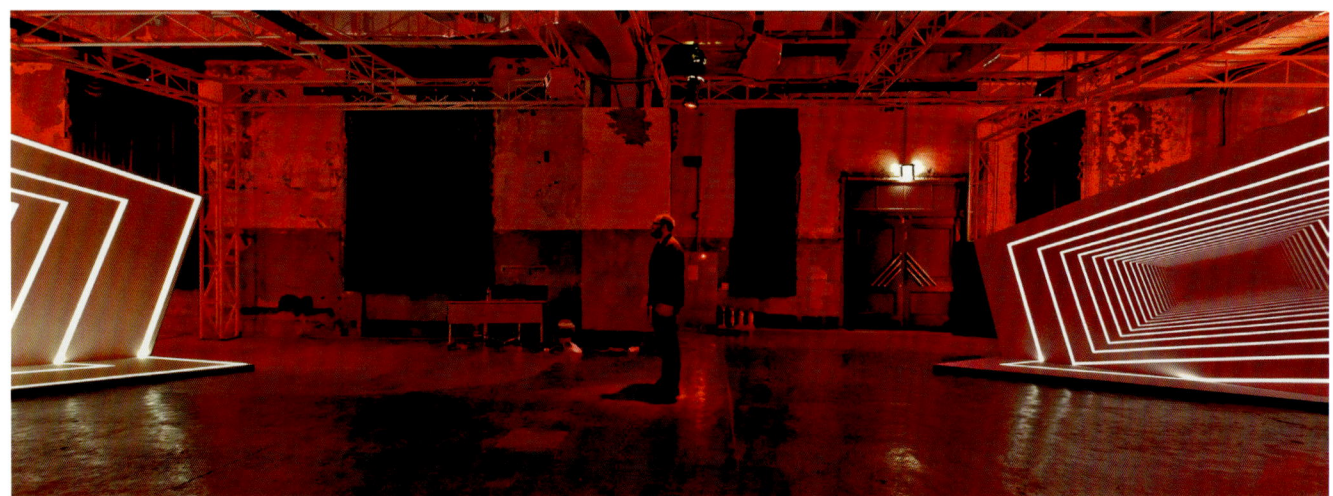

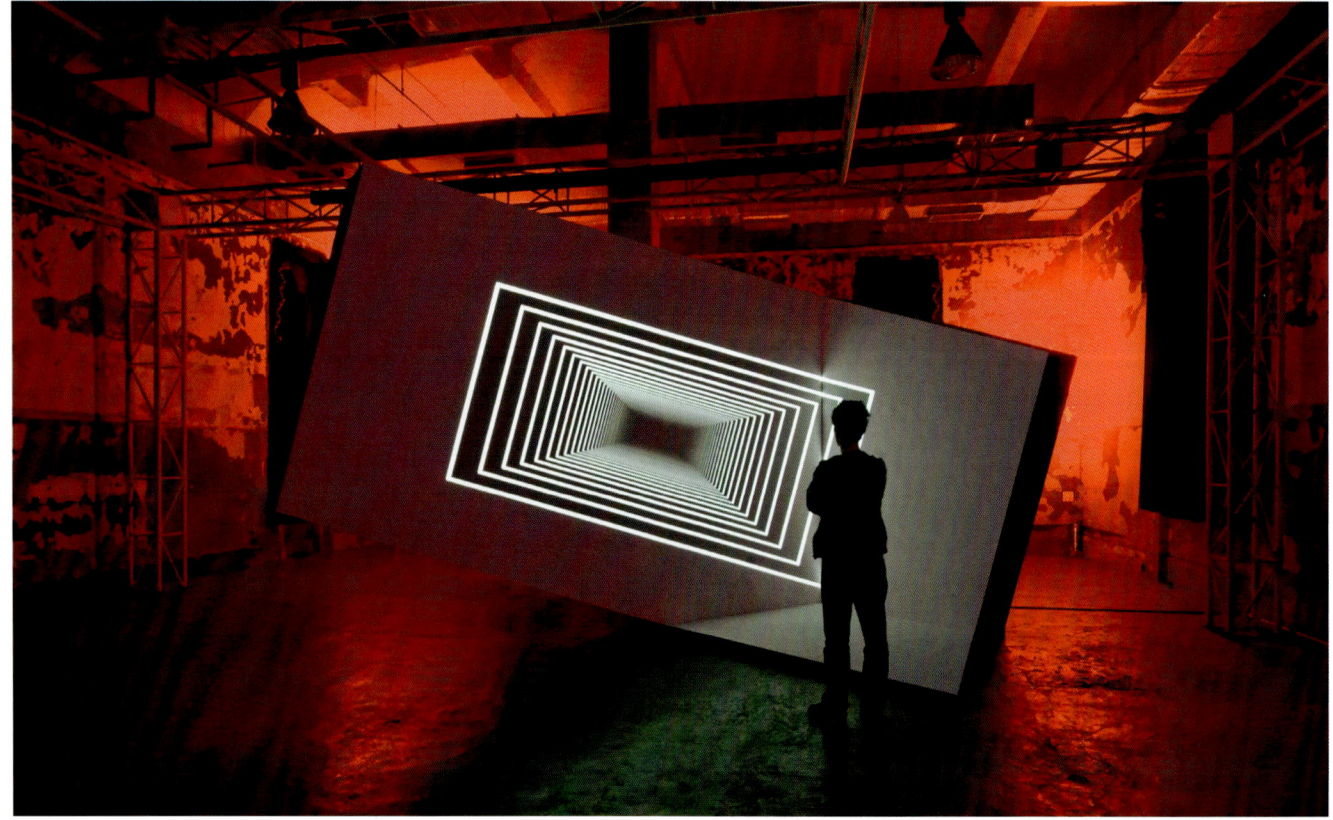

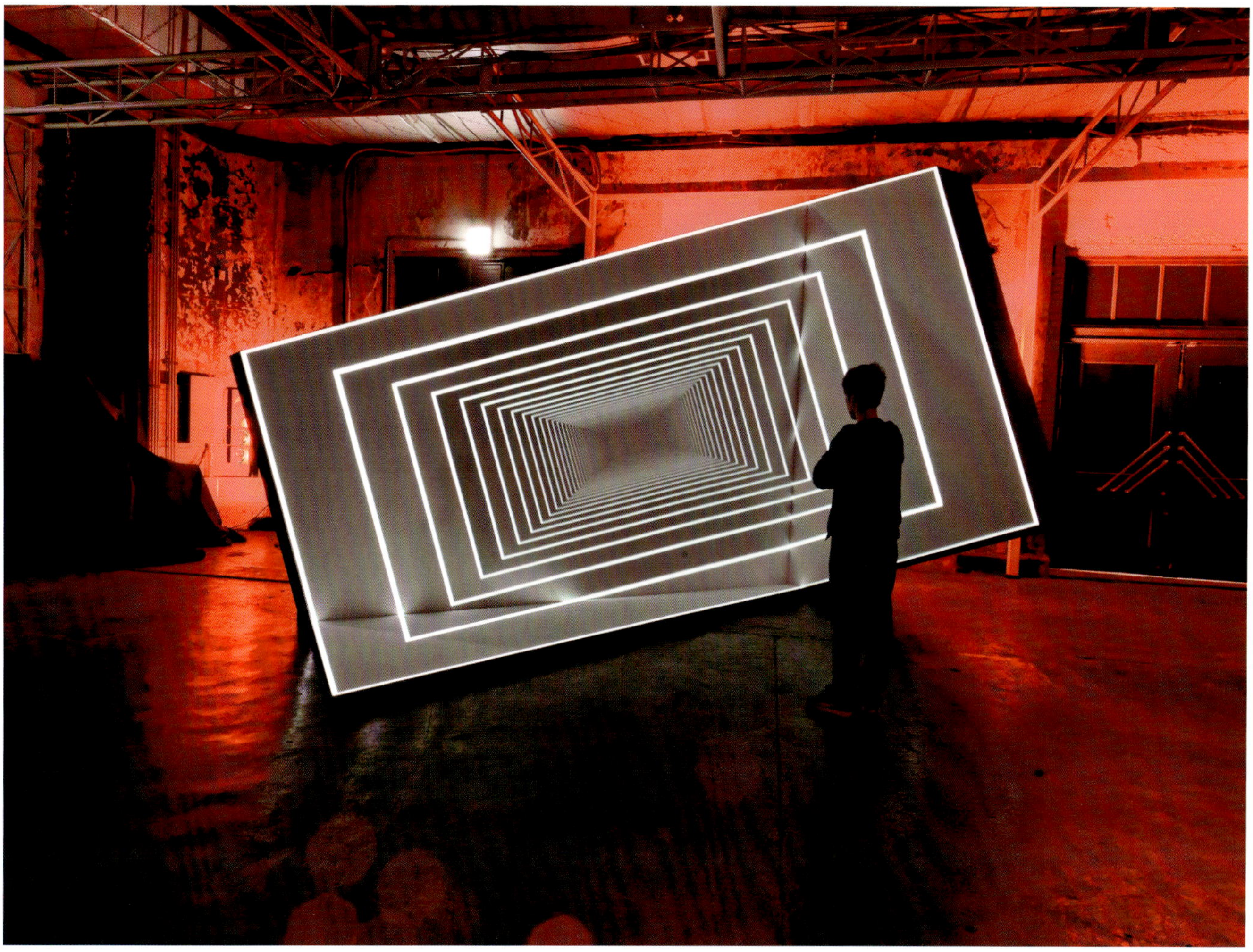

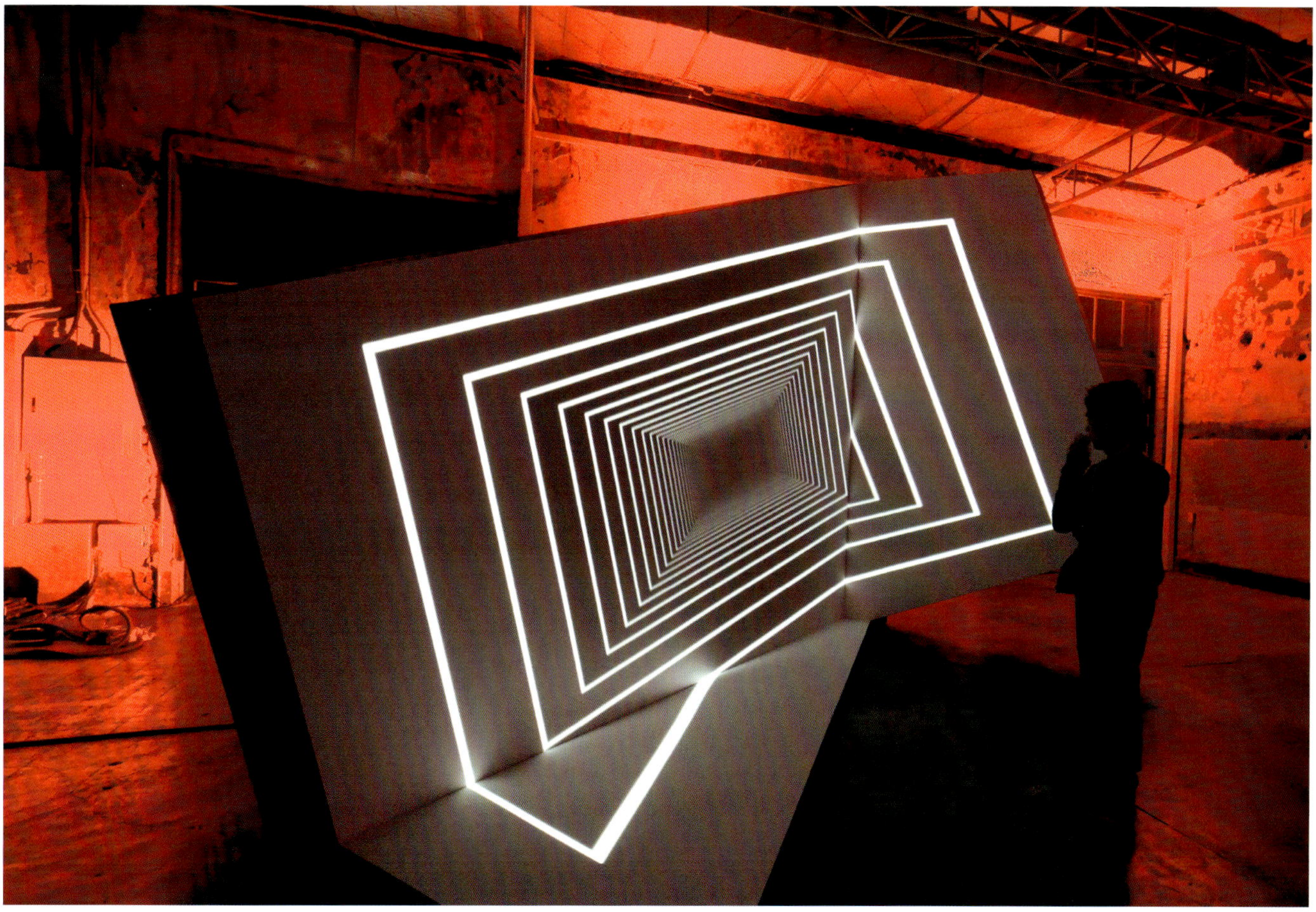

FALLEN WATER

—

Design: **Kevin Cooley**

—

Fallen Water brings its audience's attention to the worsening global freshwater crisis through an exploration of waterfalls and waterways flowing towards Lake Ontario. Shot on location at individual waterfalls along the geologic formation known as the Niagara Escarpment, each of the thirty-one monitors displays a unique video vignette. Imagery from Eugenia, Webster, Decew, Niagara Falls, and many others coalesce into this towering video and sound installation, exemplifying the widespread origin of Ontario's water, which makes up one-fifth of the world's remaining fresh water.

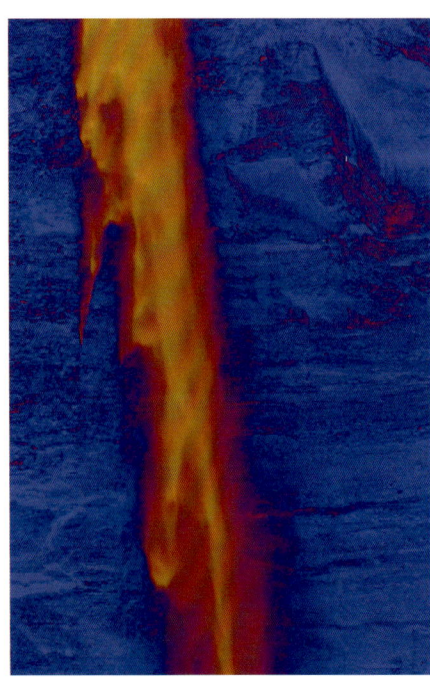

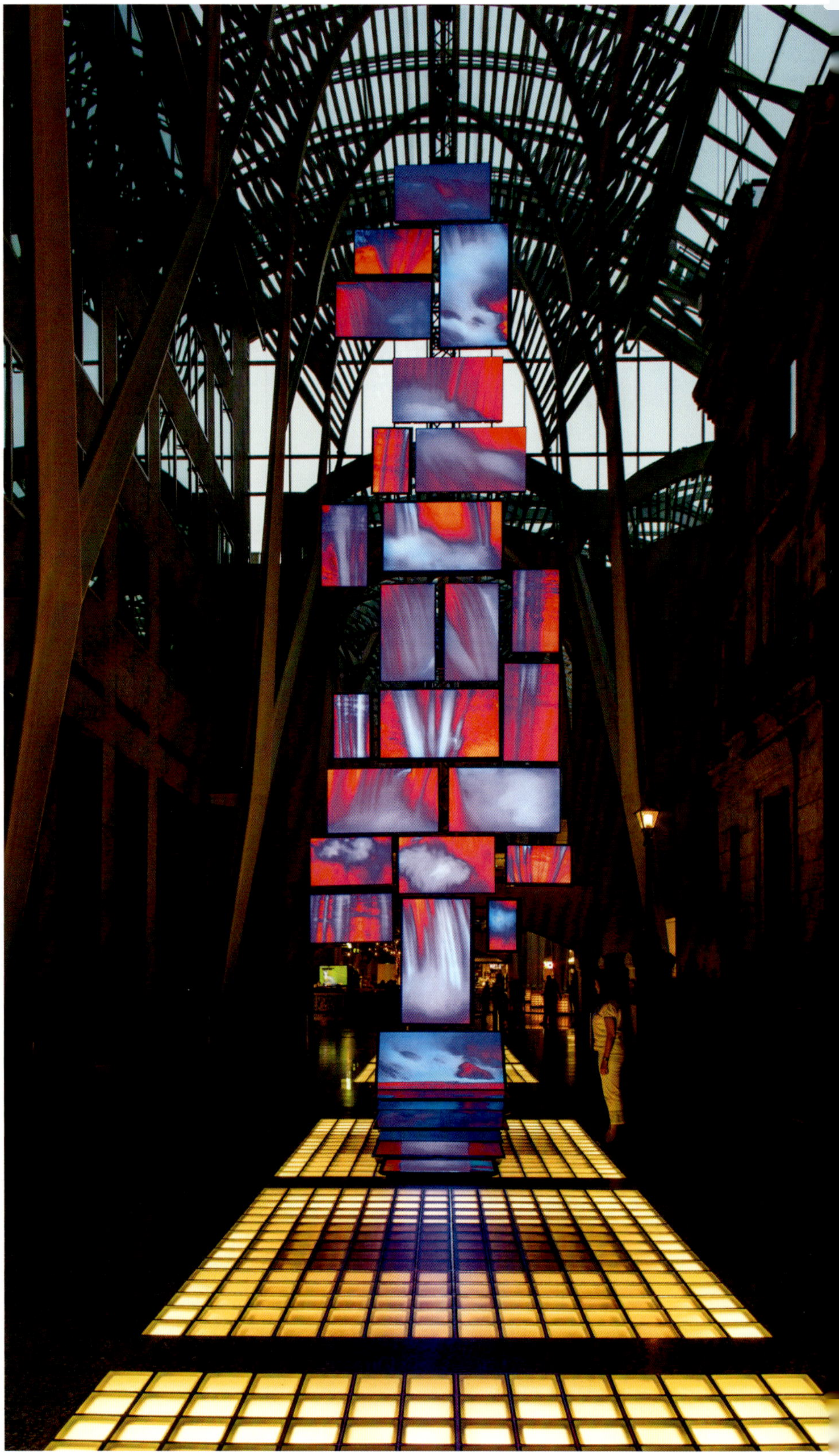

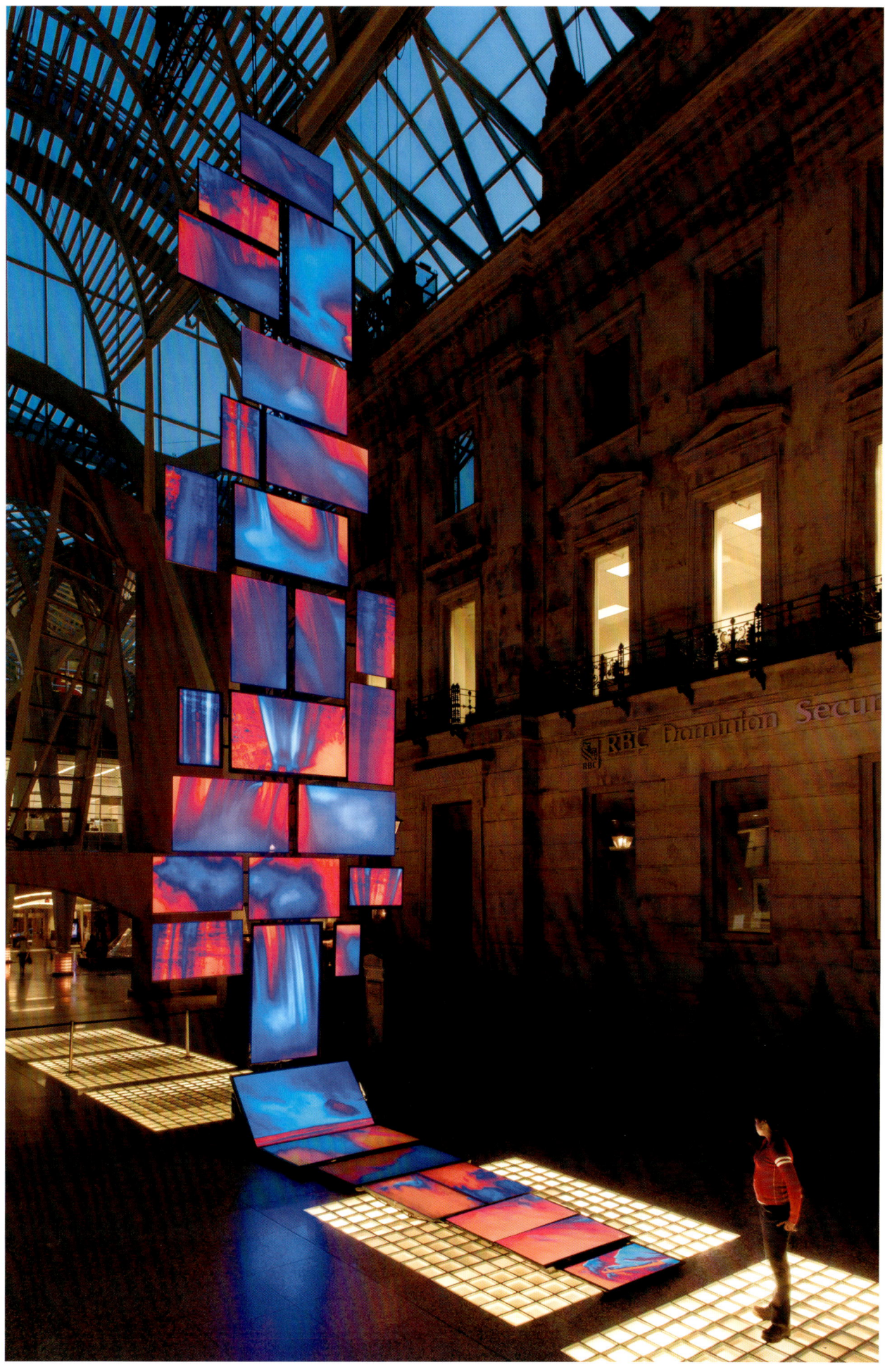

INFINITY ROOM

Design: **Refik Anadol**

—

Infinity Room is a project in immersive environments that attempts to deconstruct the framework of illusory space and to transgress the normal boundaries of the viewing experience. The installation strives to transform the conventional, flat, cinema projection screen into a three-dimensional kinetic and architectural space of visualization.

Light is the major element in the experiment, used to blur the boundaries and interconnect the realms of the actual/fictional and the physical/virtual. It signifies the threshold between the simulated space created by the projection technology and the physical space where the viewer stands. The installation addresses the inherent spatial qualities of immersive virtual environments and their effects on the embodied person. Through the presented framework, the installation questions the relativity of perception and how it informs the apprehension of our surroundings.

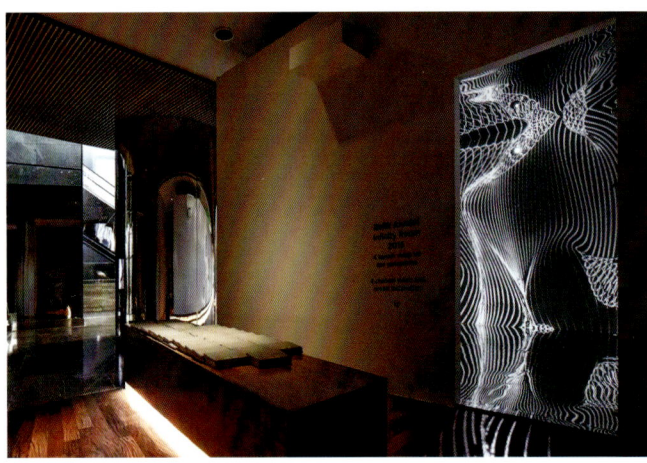
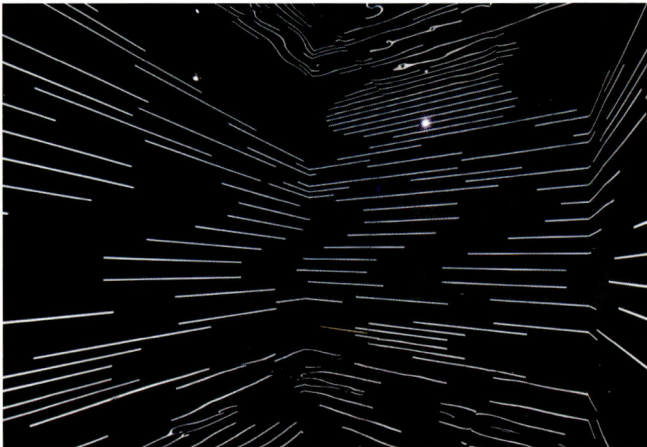

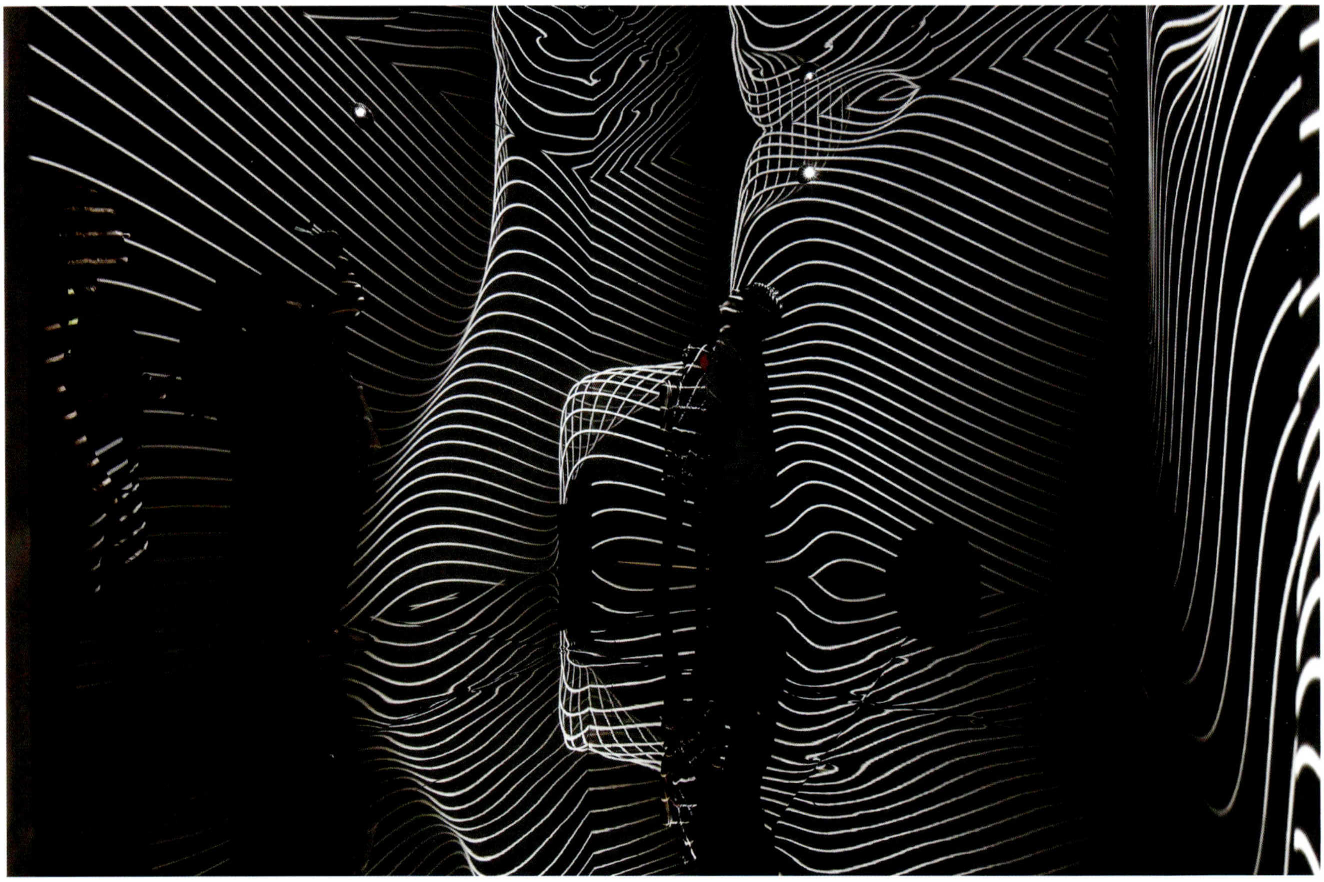

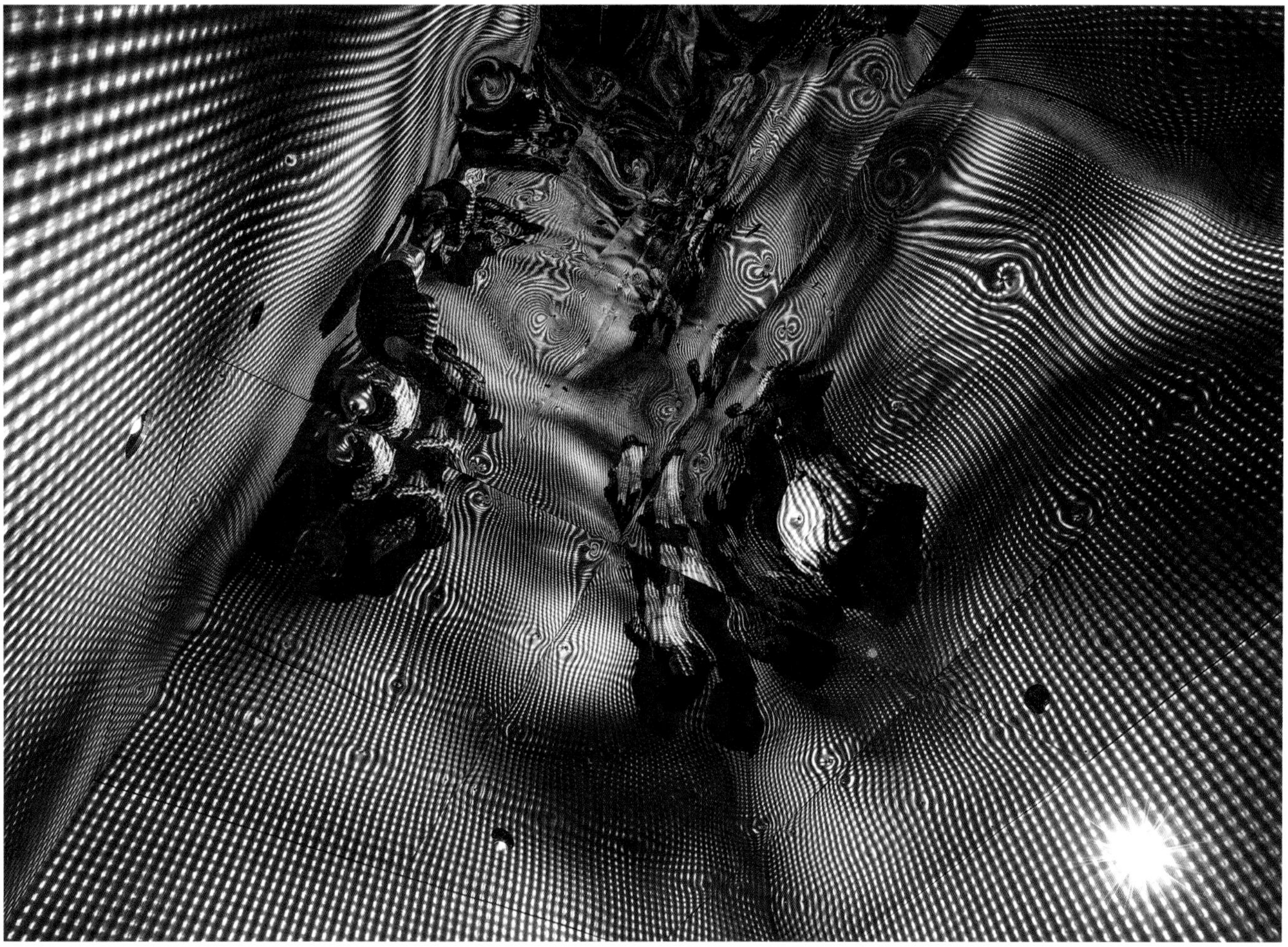

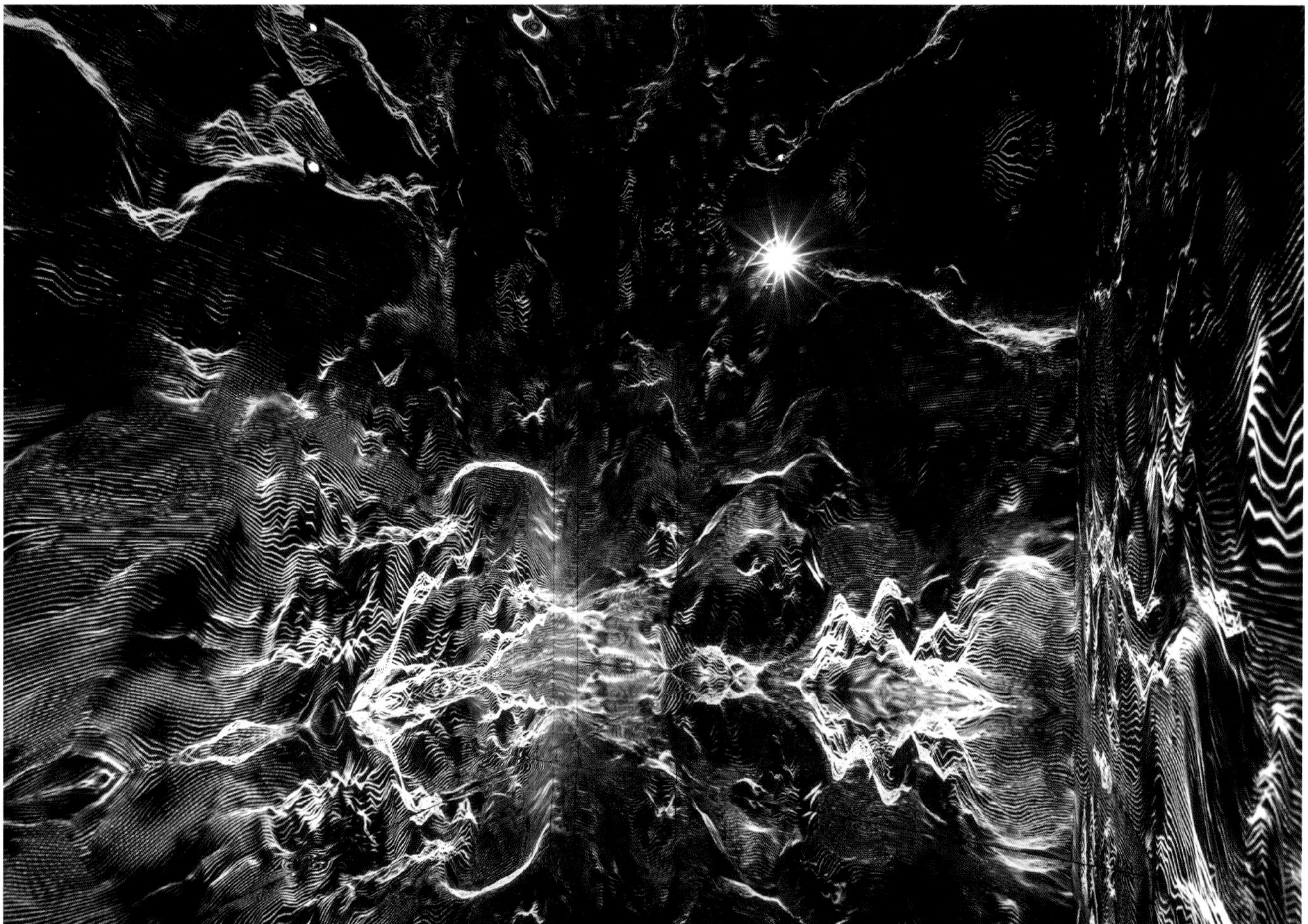

SIKKA INGENTIUM

Design: **Daniel Canogar**
Sound Design: **Alexander MacSween**
Artistic Engineering: **Diego Mellado**
Photography: **Jorge Mirón, Sofía Montenegro**

—

Sikka Ingentium is a sculptural video installation made with 2,400 recycled DVDs. This multi-thematic piece was inspired by "sikka," the gold coins sewn to clothing dating back to Babylonic times that eventually became the shiny plastic objects known today as sequins. They were worn to remind onlookers of the wealth and power of those wearing them while also evoking the light of the divine. Similarly, the surfaces of the DVDs flash back to audiences a series of images born from the glamorous world of Hollywood where image is converted to a kind of currency.

By projecting the contents of the DVDs back onto their surfaces the artist continues to investigate both new uses for discarded objects as well as his interest in combining the phantasmagorical properties of cinema with its physical elements. In this case, film segments were selected from each of the DVDs for their color, shape and movement value, forming a digital palette from which the final projected loops were constructed. The accompanying soundtrack is the resulting composition created by layering the soundtracks from the actual segments being projected. The final effect is an audiovisual mosaic that reflects on our culture, the technologies that we use to store information and their survival in today's world.

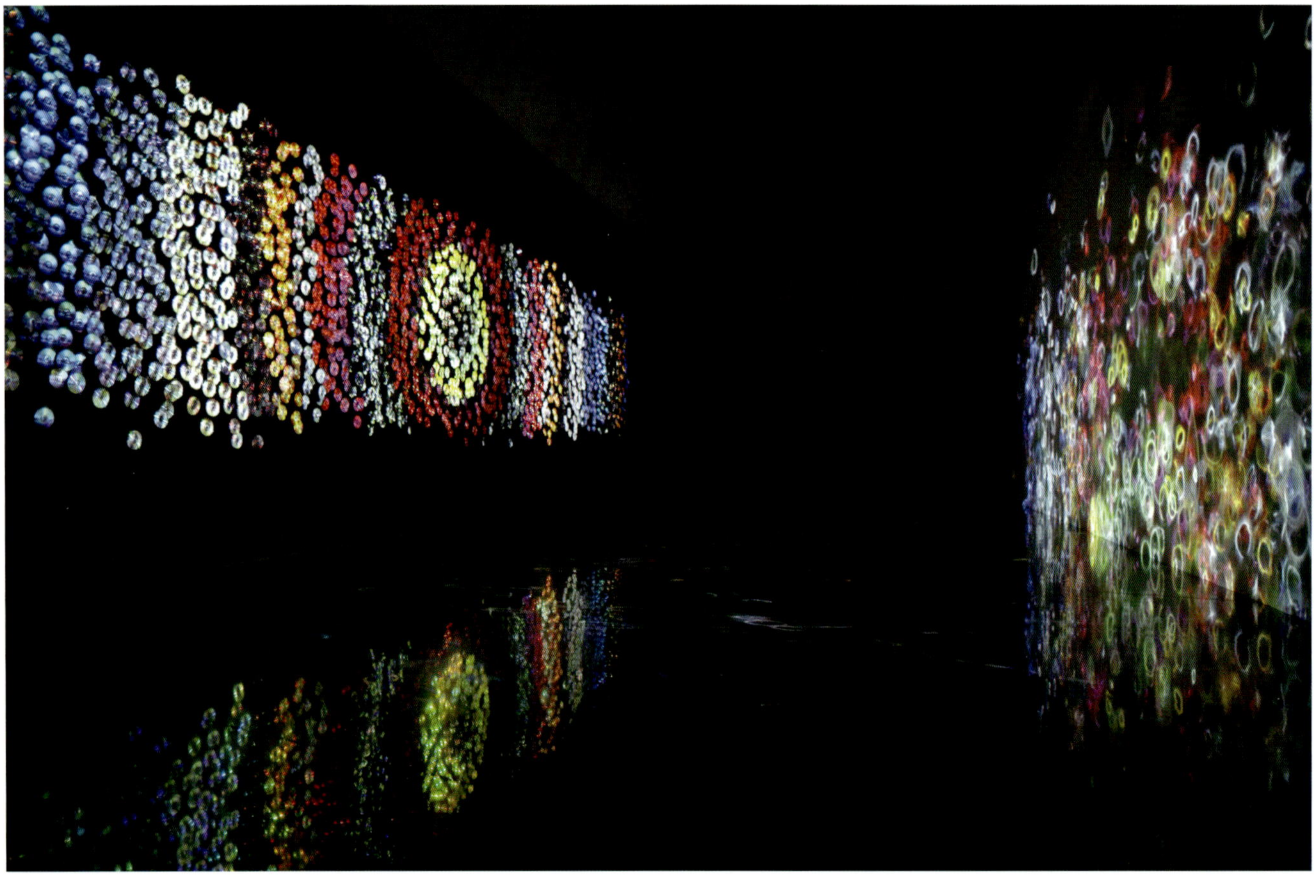

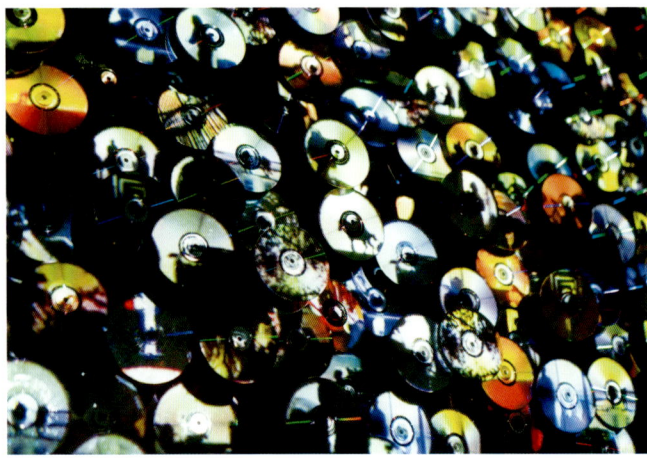

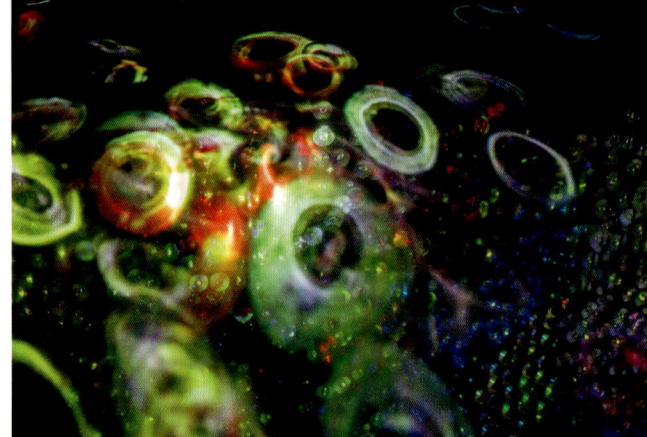

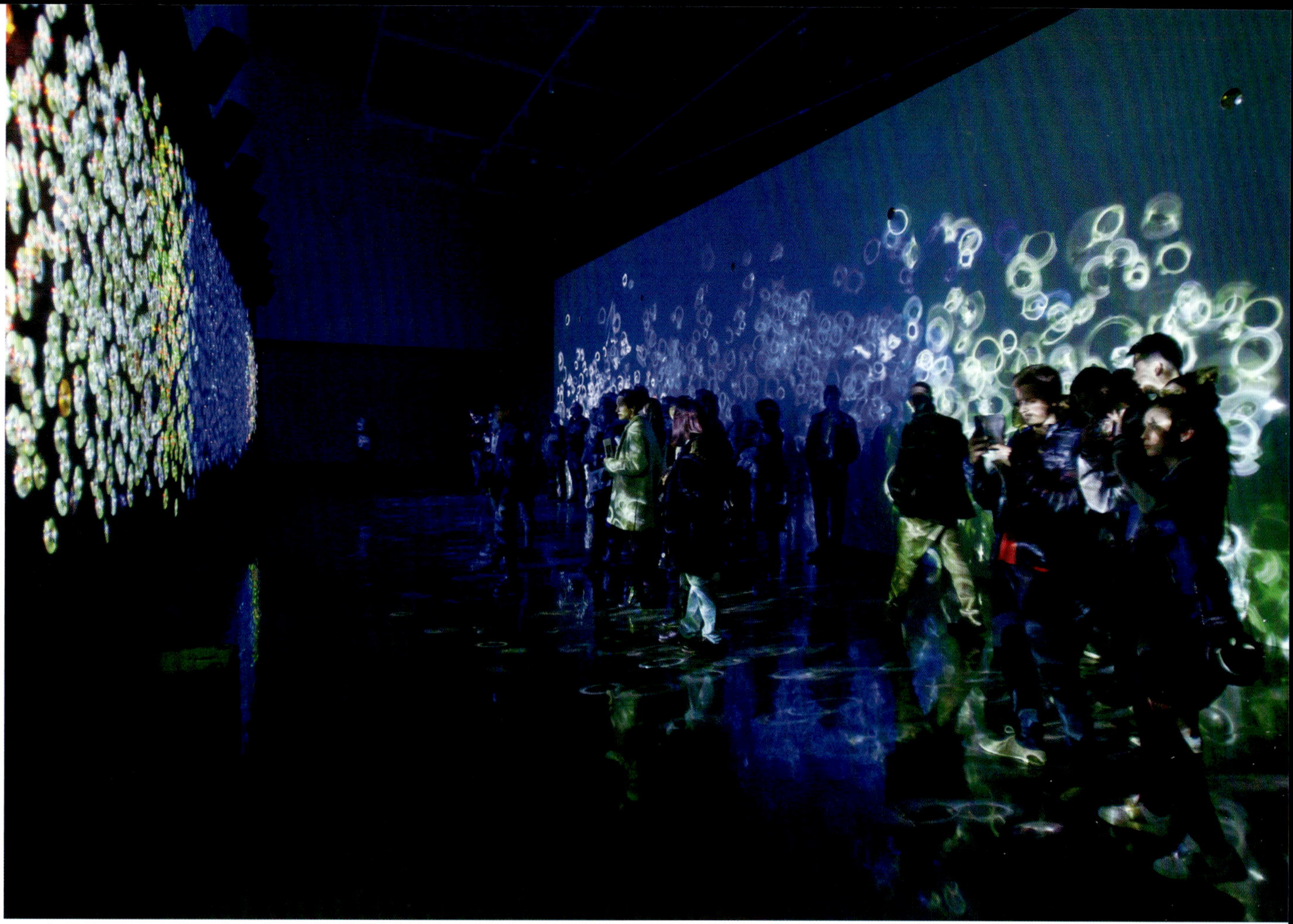

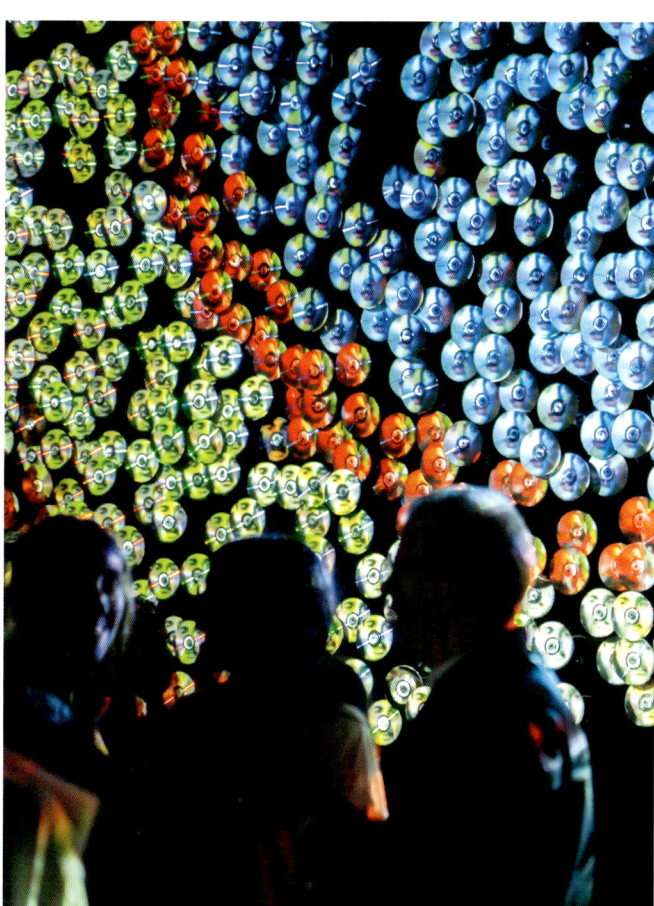

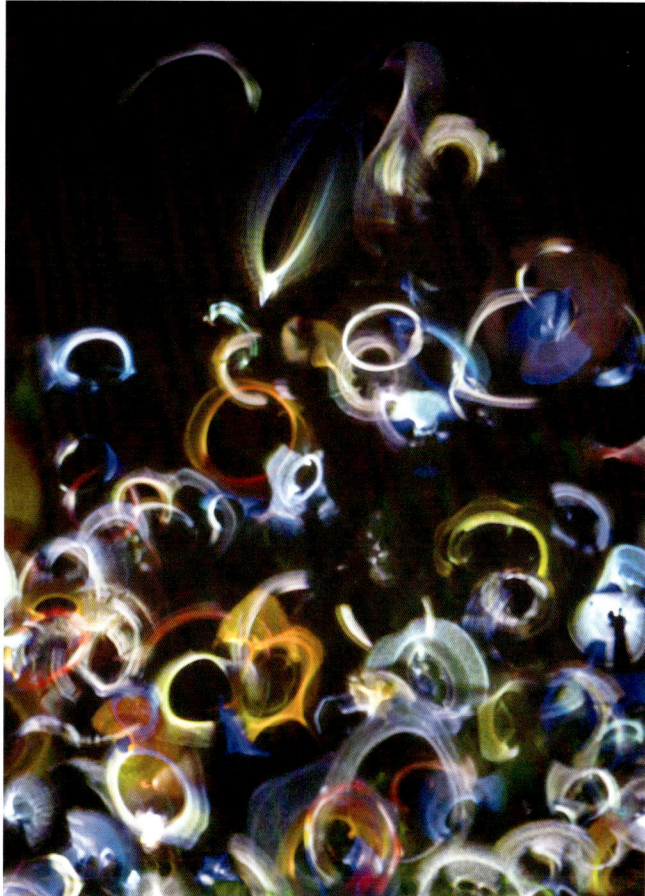

DEAR WORLD... YOURS, CAMBRIDGE

—

Design: **Miguel Chevalier**
Curators: **Helen Marriage, Bill Gee, Artichoke Trust**
Software: **Cyrille Henry, Antoine Villeret**

—

On the occasion of a fundraising campaign organized by the University of Cambridge in King's College Chapel, Miguel Chevalier was invited by Artichoke to create a series of immersive projections to accompany the speeches of renowned professors and alumni.

He imagined a number of different graphic universes, each of which is generated in real-time and uses its own "digital" language to illustrate and interpret a wide variety of subjects including biology, neurosciences, physics, and biotechnology.

To illustrate Stephen Hawking's research about black holes, for instance, Miguel Chevalier imagined an immersive environment made up of thousands of constellations that plunges the guests into the mystery of the universe. In the same spirit, each of the projections entices the audience into a magical and poetic atmosphere where science meets spirituality.

This site-specific installation highlights the cathedral's architecture and the technical achievement of its fan vaults, one of the finest examples of late Perpendicular Gothic English architecture.

The soft light and the wealth of colors from the digital installation also resonates with the light from the stained glass windows.

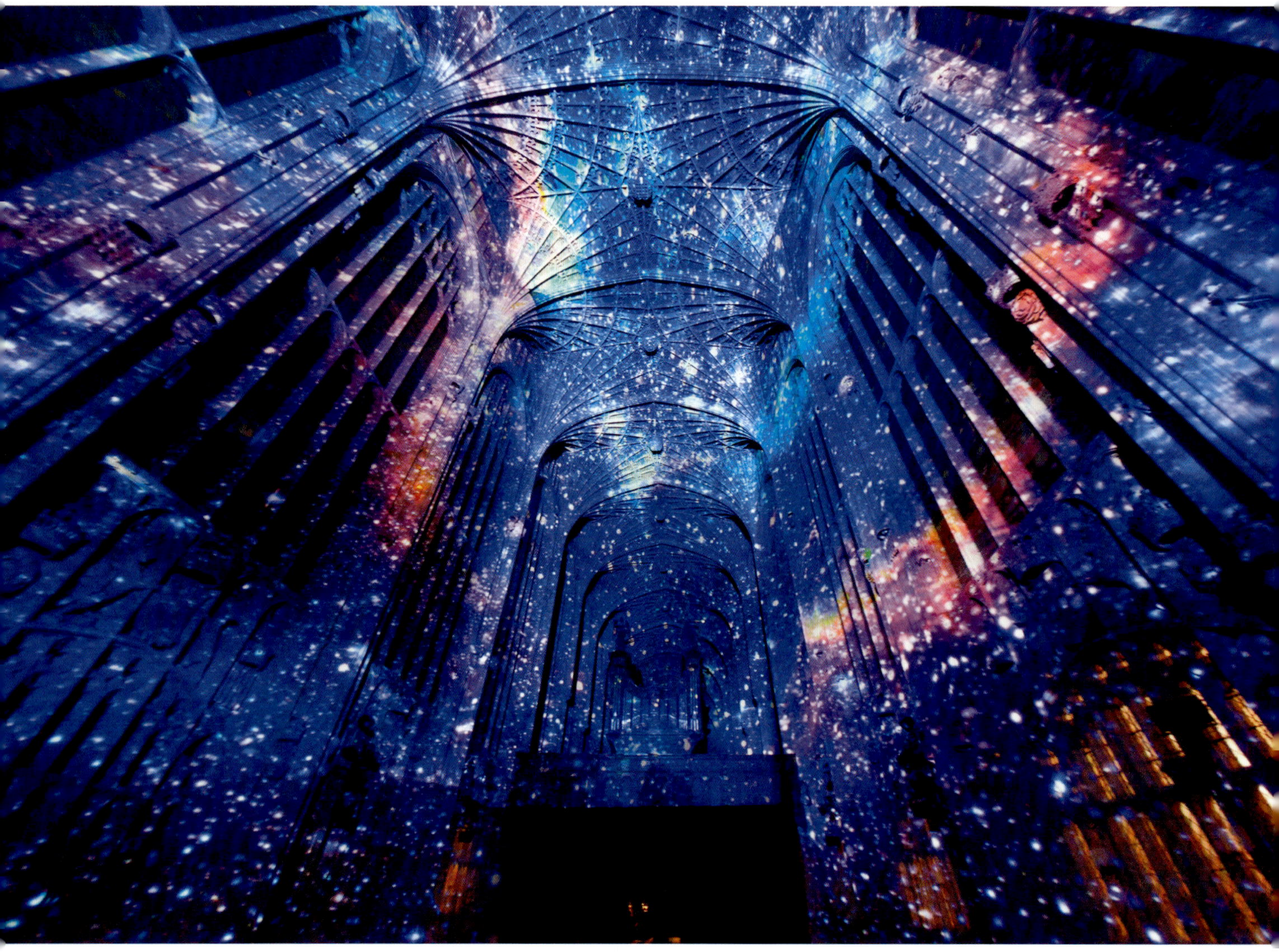

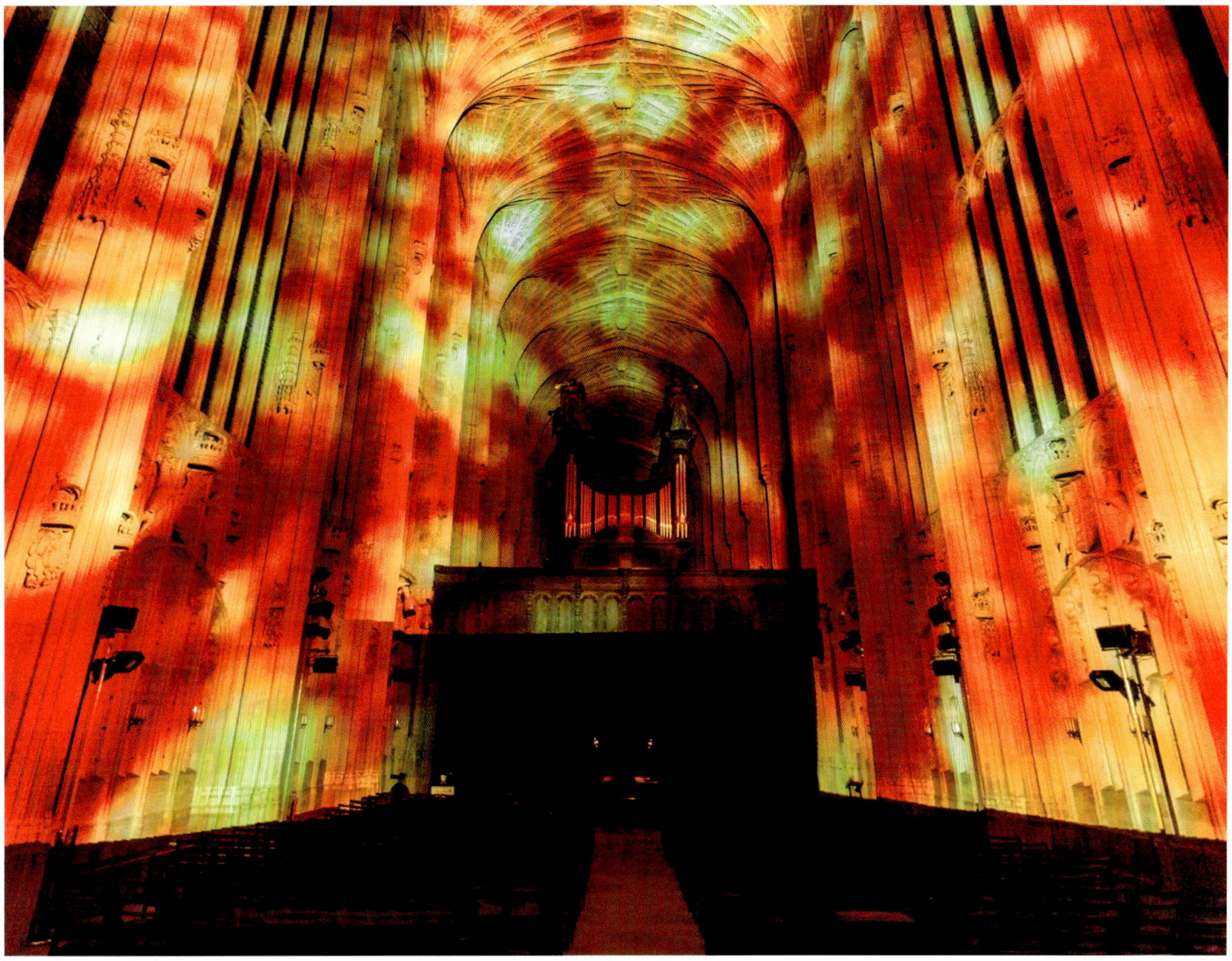

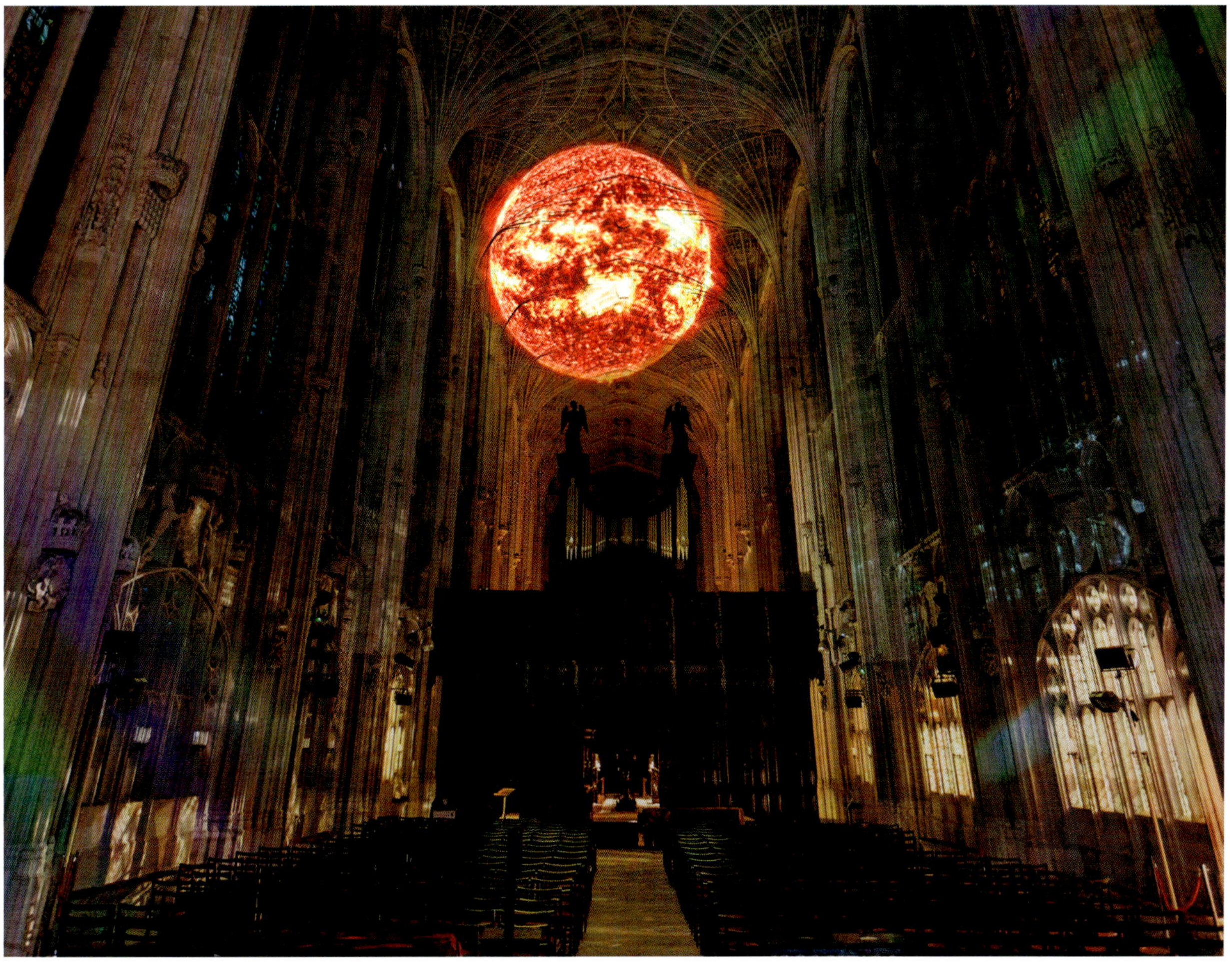

DEEPDREAM

—

Design: **Kit Webster**

—

DeepDream transports its audience into a lush infinite multiverse of light and sound. The vessel is an octagon of mirrors and LED screens producing light sequences that pulse around the audience in 360 degrees.

The video movements work in coherence with the reflective properties of the room, and a quadraphonic soundscape enhances the visuals. The audiovisual composition ebbs and flows through a wide gamut of environmental states, from calm and meditative to more powerful and hypnotic crescendos.

This engaging, immersive experience encourages self-reflection through its exploration of light/data and the sensory effects of enveloping, audiovisual stimuli.

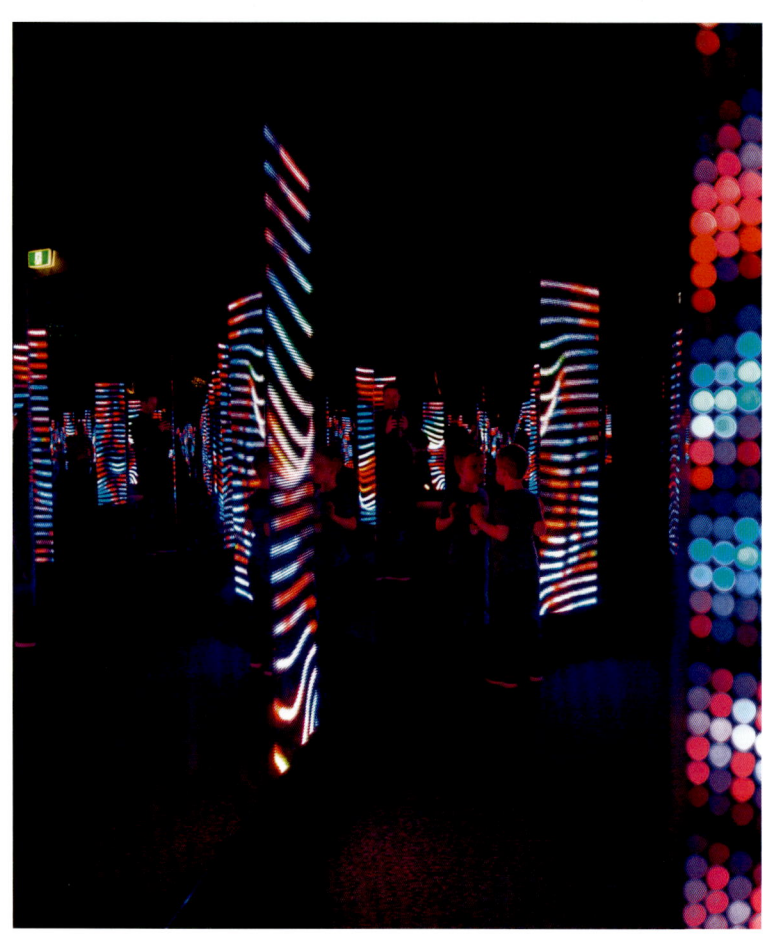

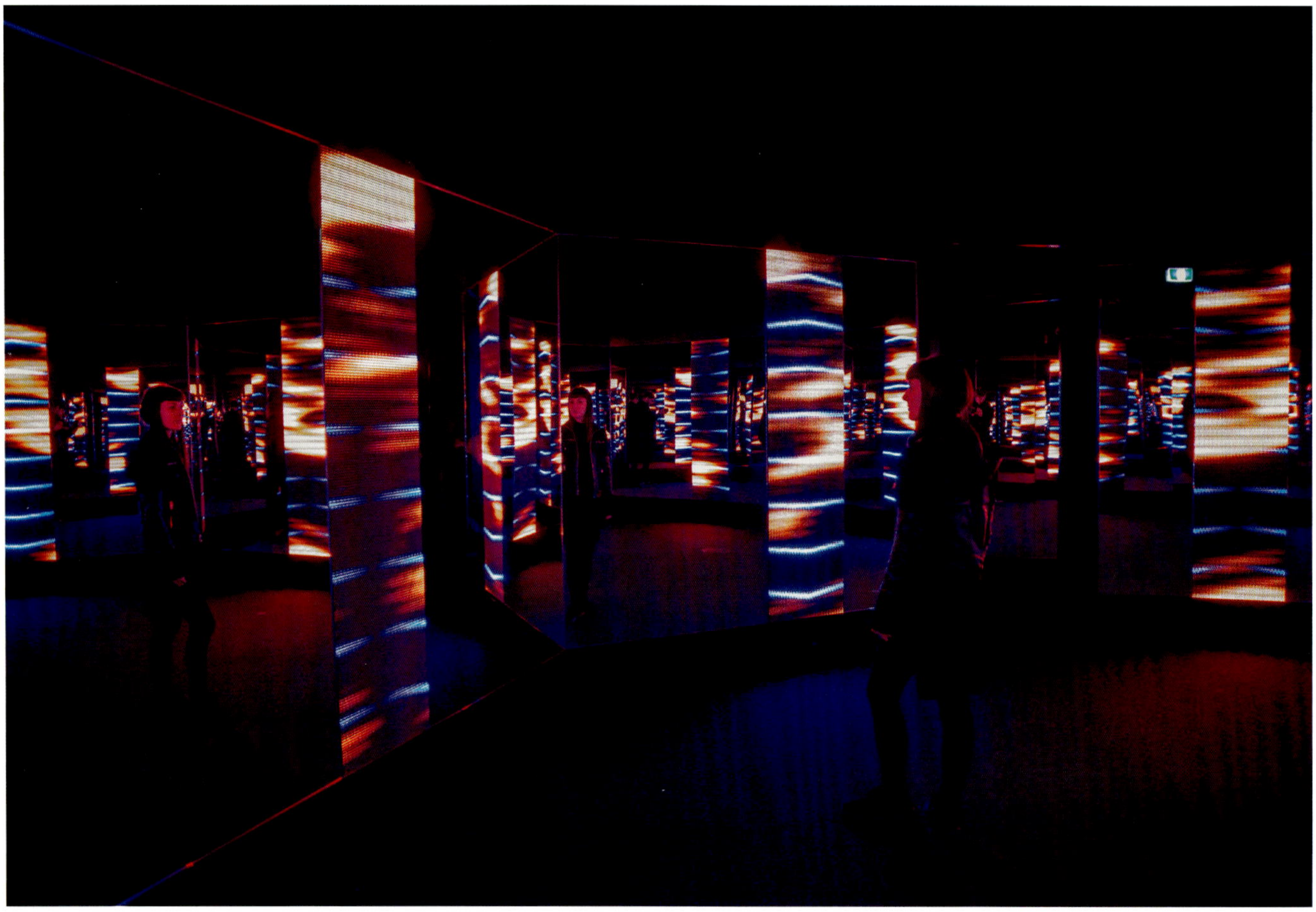

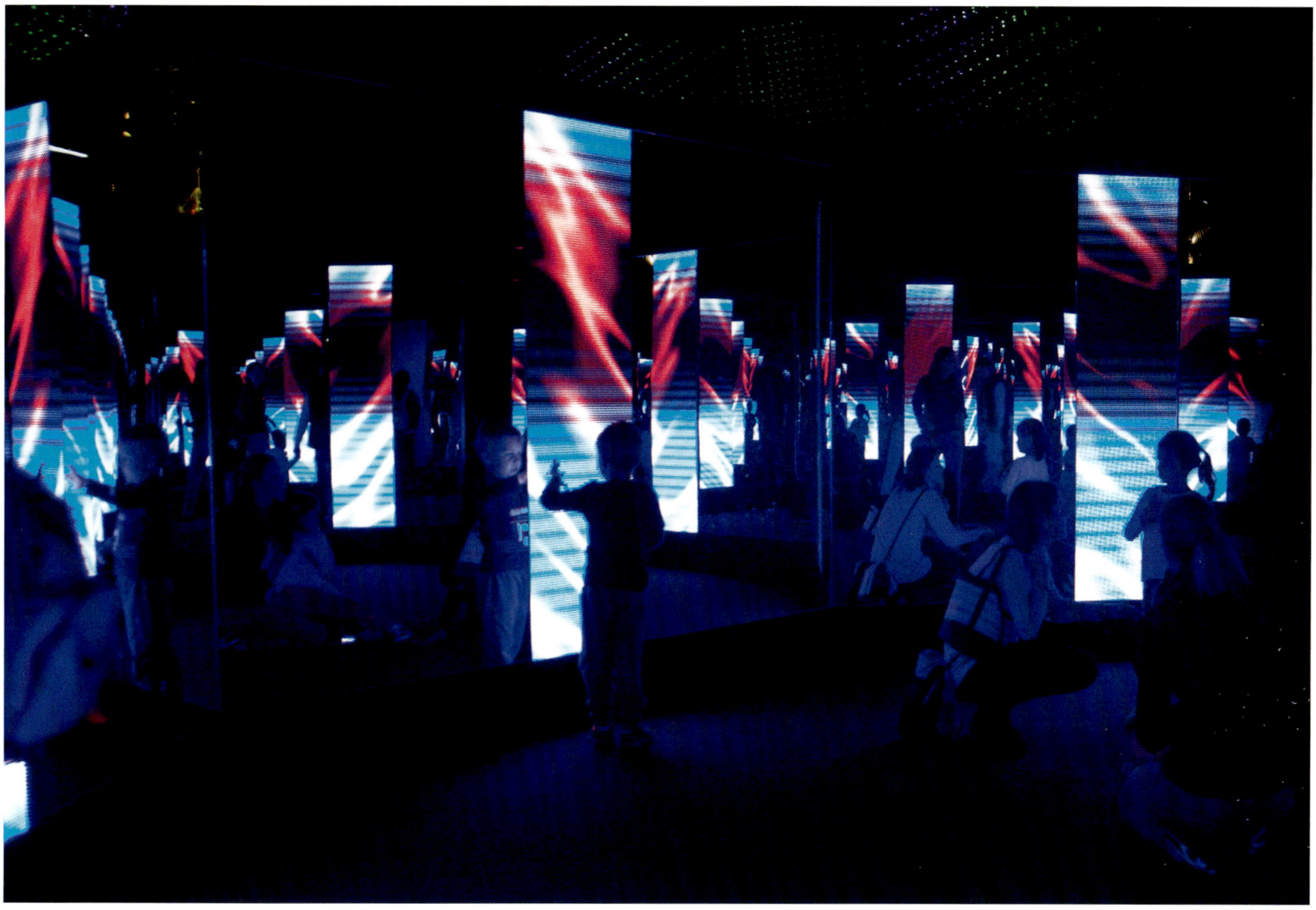

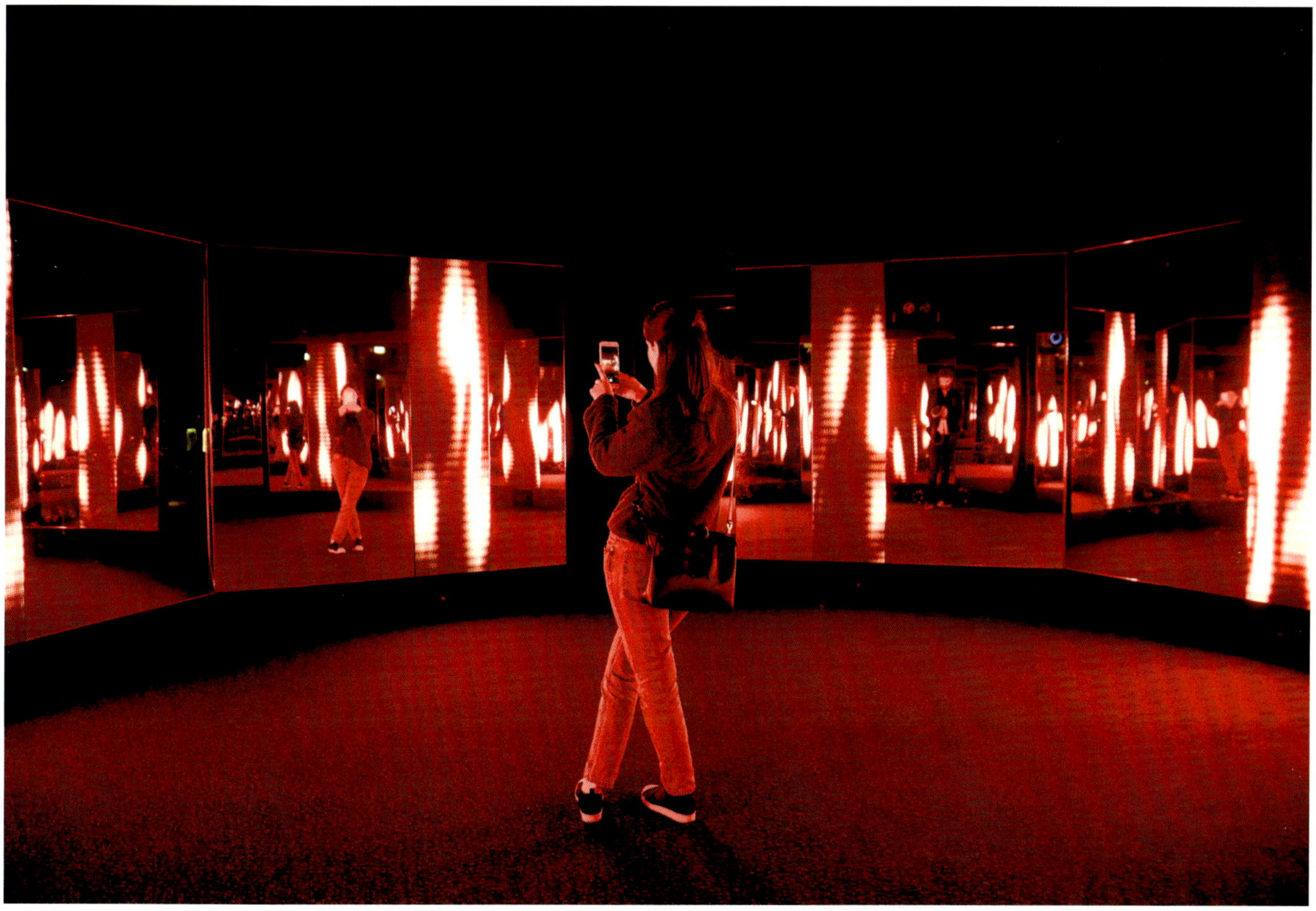

YŬZHÒU LIGHT MAZE

—

Design: **Brut Deluxe**
Photography: **Miguel de Guzmán**

—

yŭzhòu is an immersive light installation that was commissioned for the newly created Luneng Sanya Bay Light and Art Festival in Hainan, China. The installation consists of a maze based on a triangular geometry and built with 2.5-meter-high panels of acrylic glass. A dichroic film glued to one side of the acrylic glass makes the panels semi-transparent and reflects or shifts the light rays along the entire color range of a rainbow while the spectator moves in the installation. On the other side of each acrylic glass sheet, a specifically created pattern of grooves is mechanically carved in.

The grooves are illuminated by powerful LED rails with subtly shifting colors. The panels on the outer perimeter are coated with a mirror film that converts the interior into an infinity room—a unique cosmos of overlapping light patterns and constantly changing colors.

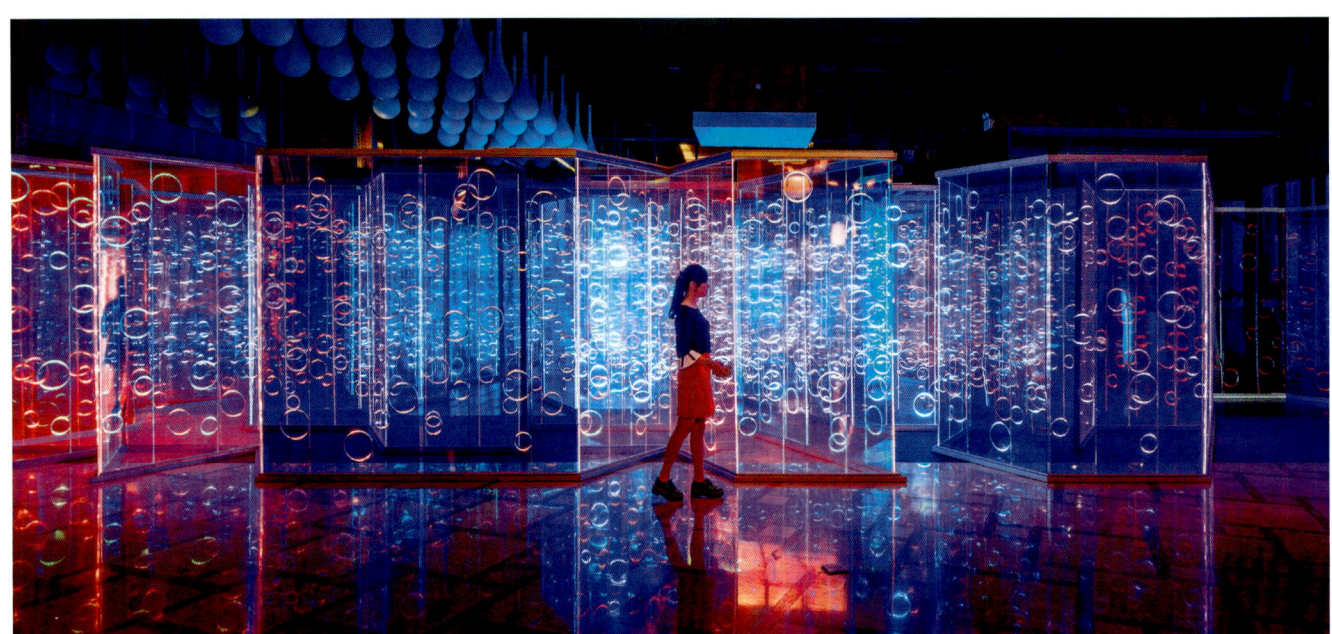

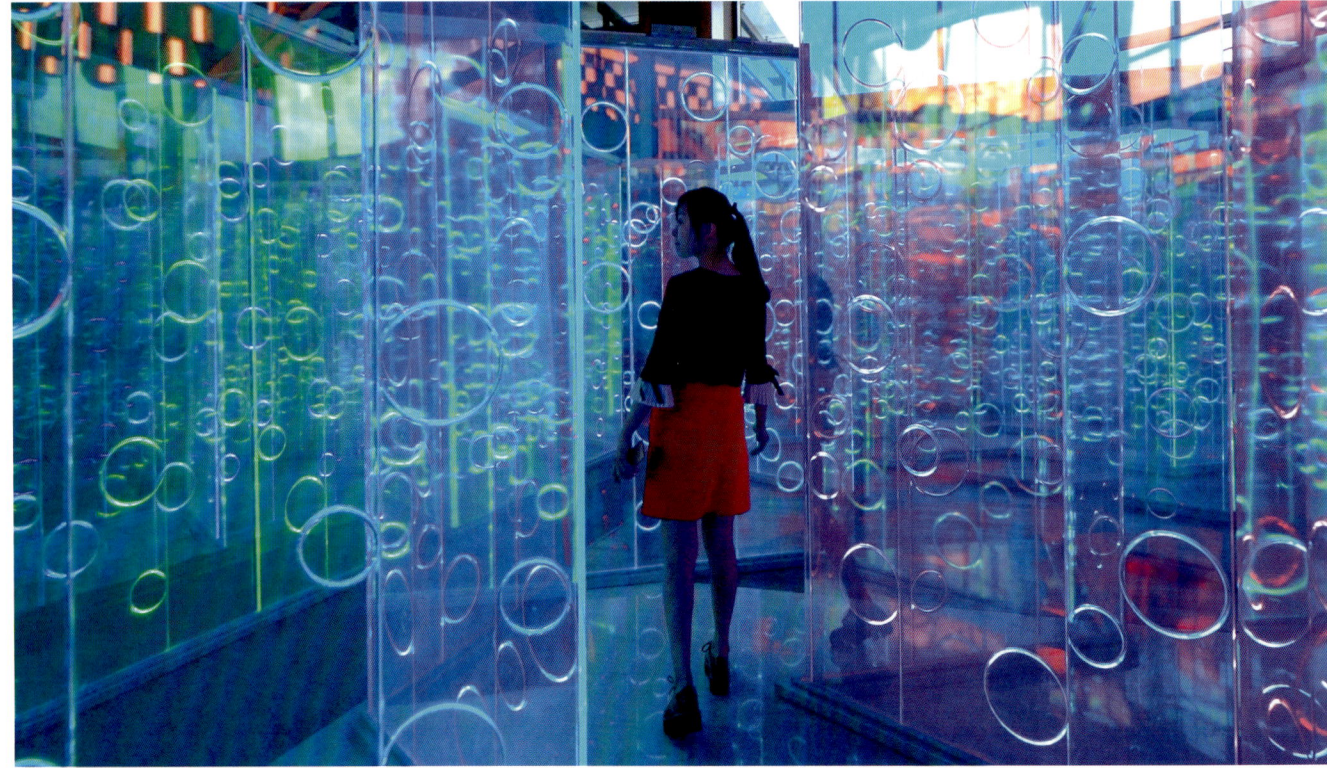

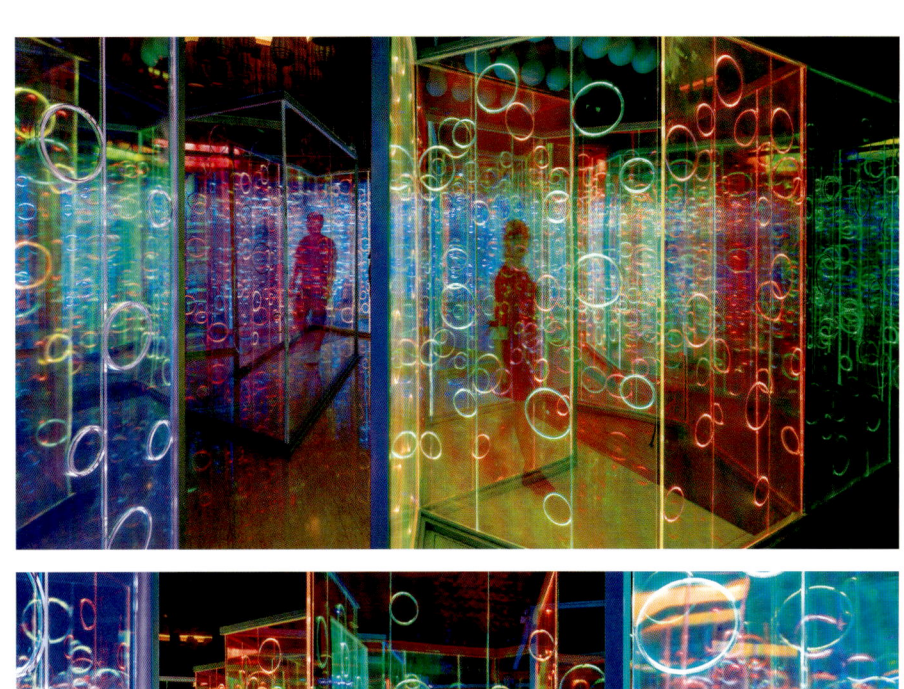

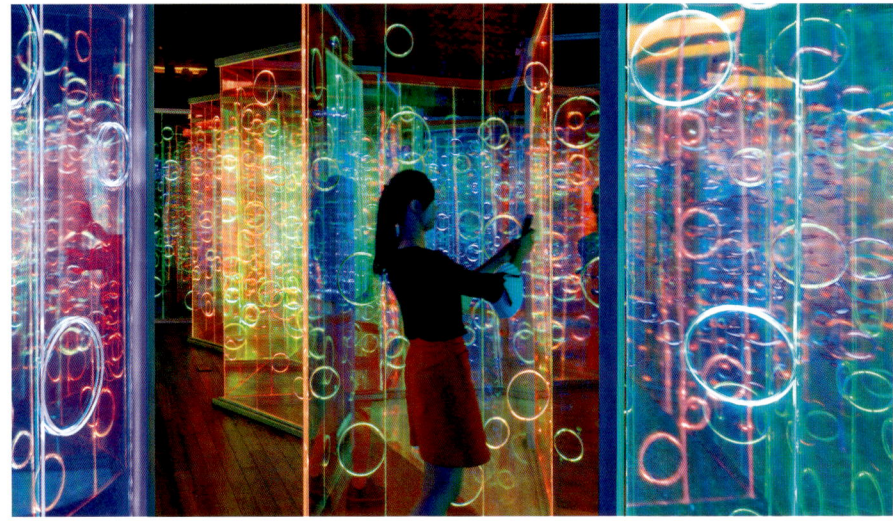

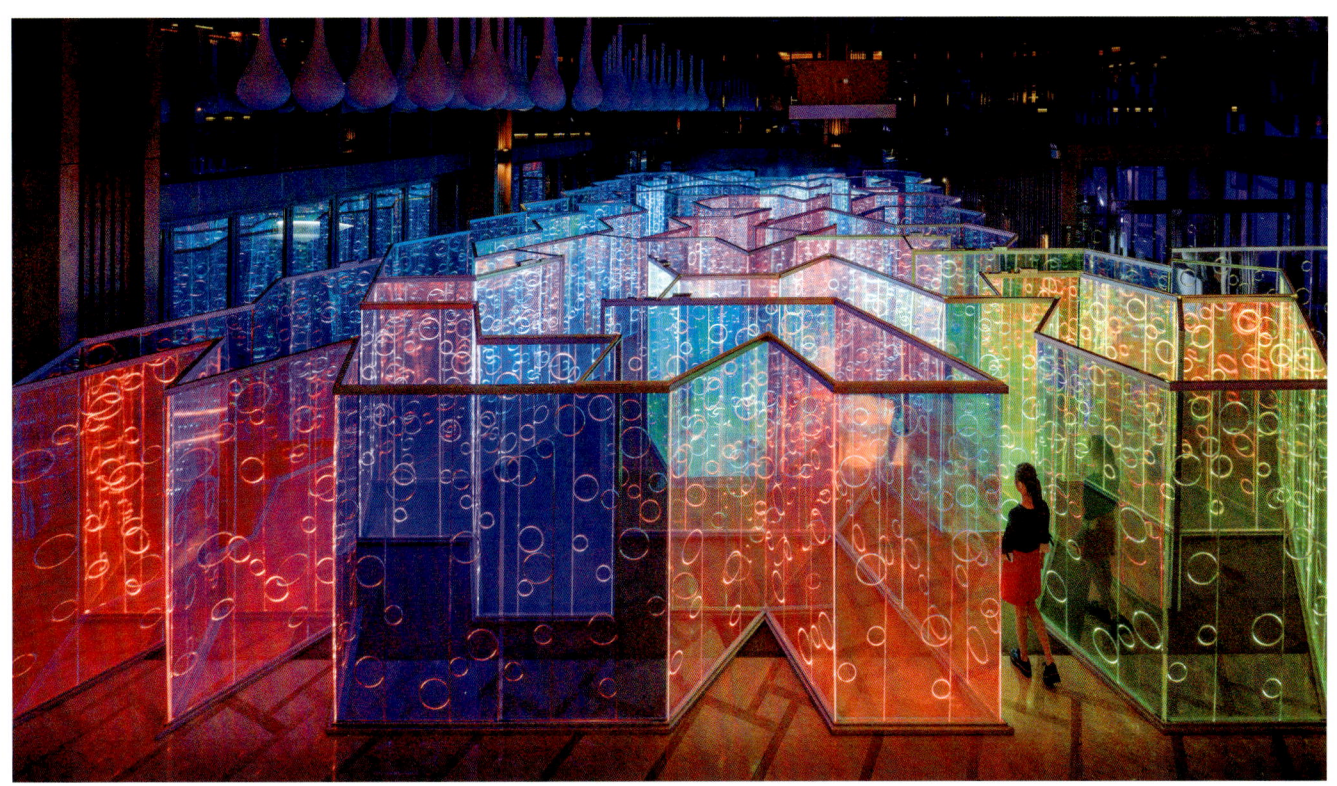

THE MIDNIGHT SPECIAL

—

Design: **ENESS**

—

From the outside, *The Midnight Special* has the appearance of a retro Australian school bus, but step inside and audiences are sucked into a futuristic gravitational vortex of choreographed light and sound. Color shatters in hypnotizing patterns across viewers who lie on the bus floor, soaking up the meditative ambience from the LED light show.

The light vortex calms and speeds up, playing visual tricks on viewers, who forget the structures are there between the illusive, floating light formations. The installation structure is an array of addressable LEDs designed by ENESS—each light is carefully mapped with specific content in collaboration with Hyper Reelist (Jobe Williams), then synchronised to react to a soundtrack composed for this experience by Mark Williams.

The Midnight Special evokes nostalgic feelings mixed with the unseen, unfamiliar and unexperienced.

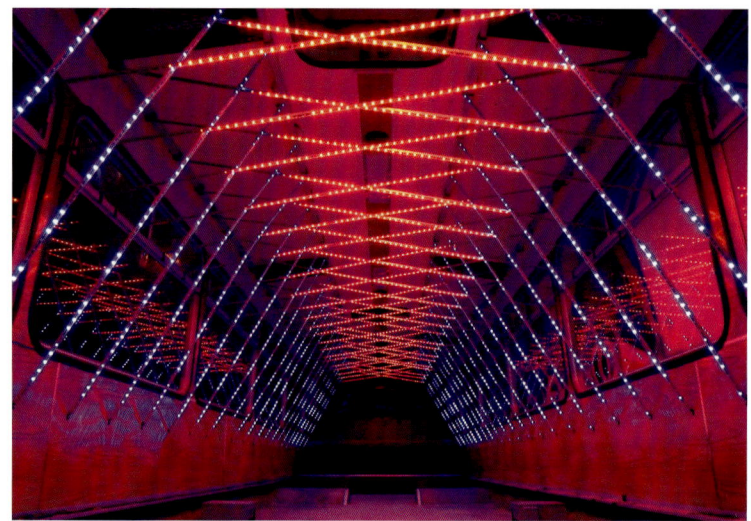

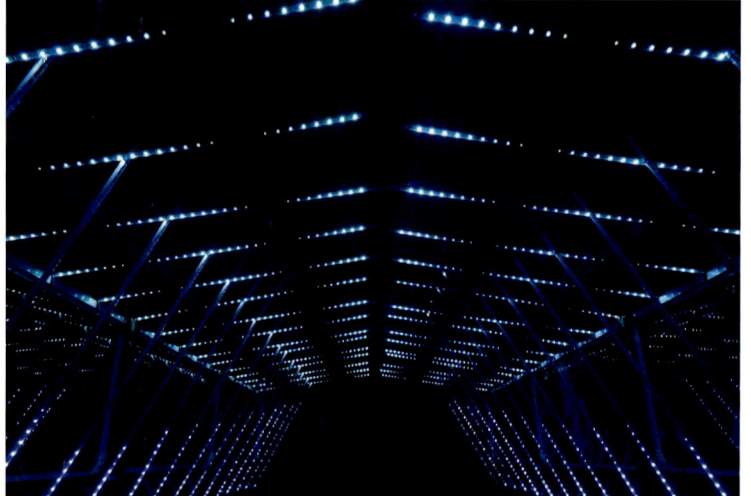

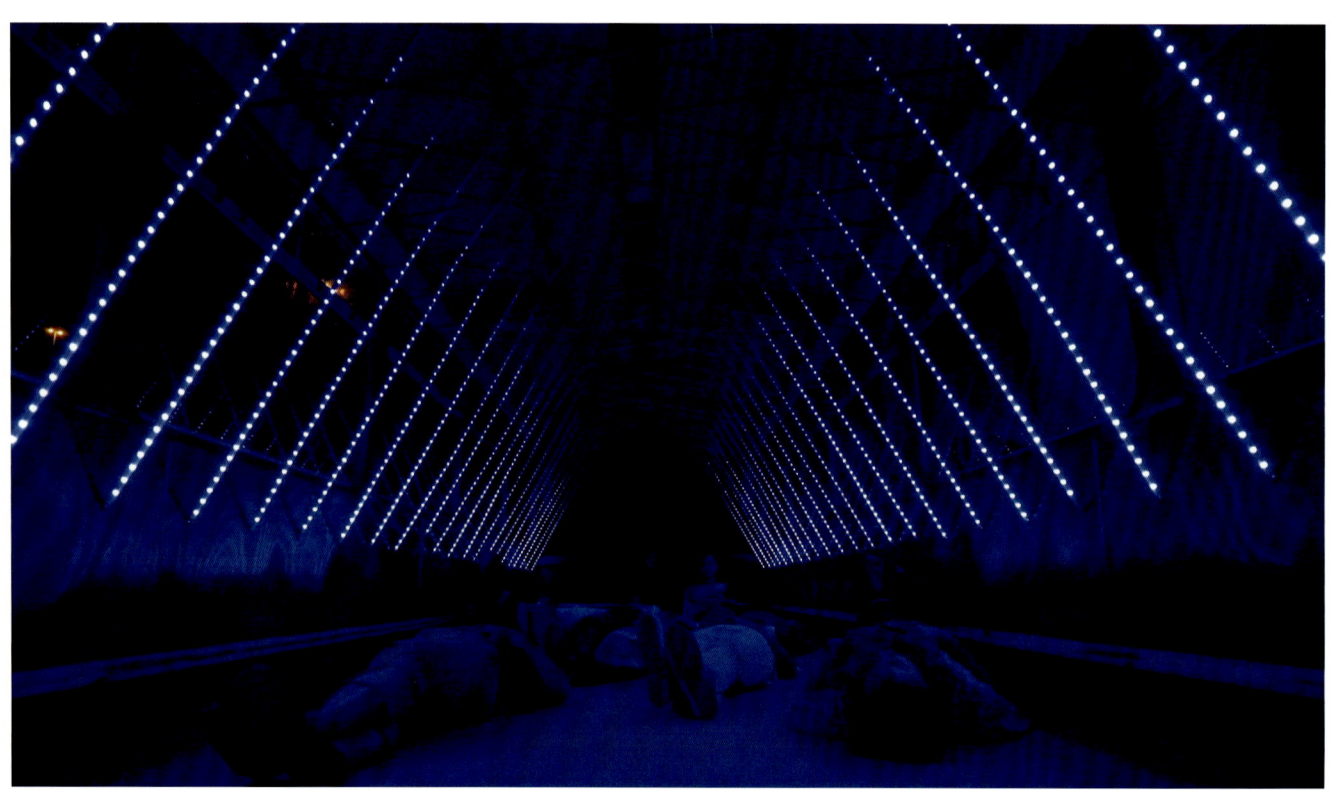

AN ADDITIVE MIX

—
Design: **Liz West**
Photography: **Stephen Iles**
—

Liz West's light installation *An Additive Mix* took center stage in the exhibition "Light Fantastic" at the National Science and Media Museum in England, celebrating the UNESCO International Year of Light. The work comprises a purpose-built 10m x 5m room containing 250 colored fluorescent tubes combined with infinity mirrors. The title *An Additive Mix* comes from the principle that white light is composed of different colors of the spectrum (additive colors). The installation places visitors in the center of the phenomenon, saturating them in individual hues that collectively create an intense white glow in a seemingly endless space. *An Additive Mix* turns this occurrence in natural science on its head, reassembling the diffracted colors of the rainbow and projecting them to "infinity" as visitors explore.

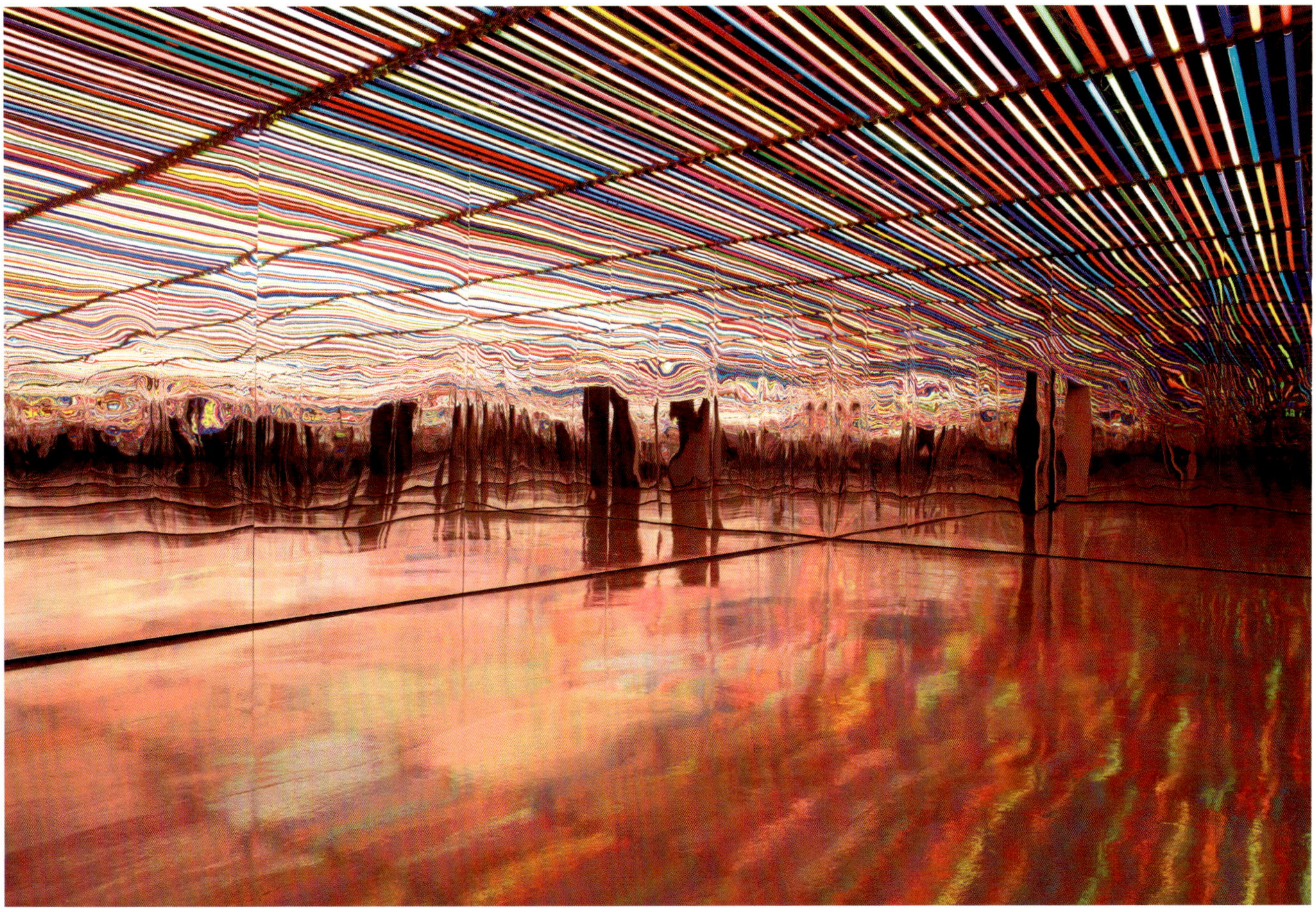

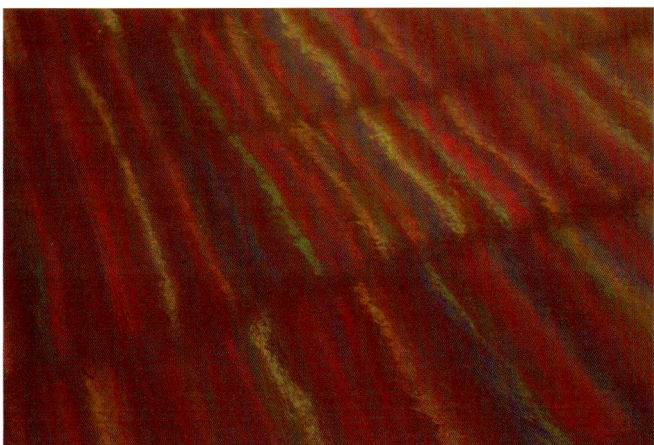

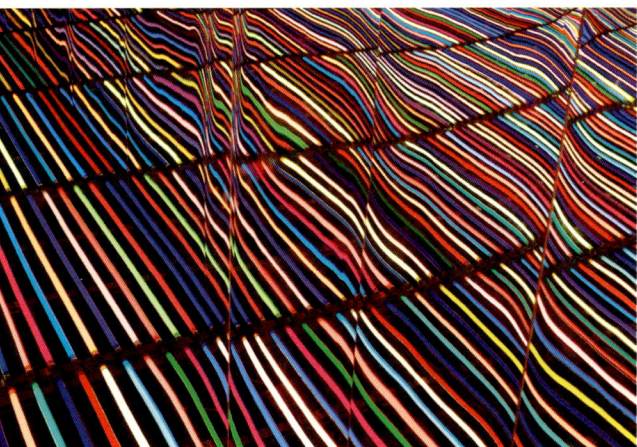

THE DAY
WE LEFT FIELD

—

Design: **TUNDRA**

—

This installation was inspired by the natural environment and its place in the landscape of modern cities. In *The Day We Left Field*, blades of grass play a central role. As in a surrealist painting, the blades of grass hang upside-down, rhythmically waving in a floating meadow amid loops of sound and visual effects. Visitors find themselves fully immersed inside the eerie space of a dream, feeling vulnerable and at the same time aware of the symbolism of experiencing nature from within a building, a closed urban landscape.

This dissonant concurrence evokes a long list of binary oppositions, such as synthetic vs. natural, real vs. virtual, human vs. machine and so on. Viewers cannot help feeling that they are part of both elements in these combinations.

The Day We Left Field uses the force of digitized nature to reflect on the delicate balance between the human and the inhuman. The authors of this installation, the Russian TUNDRA collective, belong to that typology of artists whose works cannot be reduced to narrative patterns. Their works can be seen as the contemporary evolution of the "happening," in which attending the art event is in itself part of the artwork.

Site-specific installations demand direct experience in the place where they are shown. Ultimately, TUNDRA's installation is a sensory experience that has to be felt.

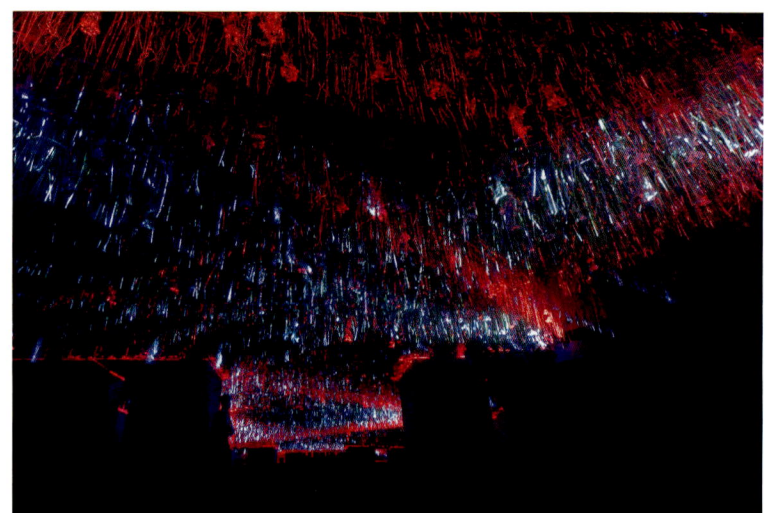

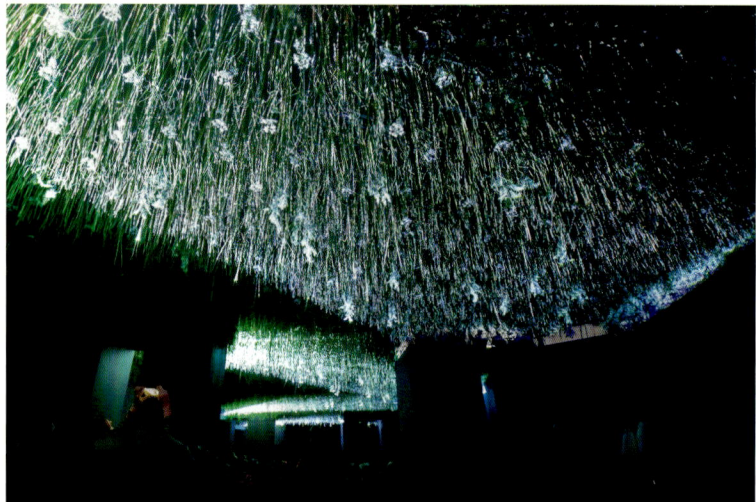

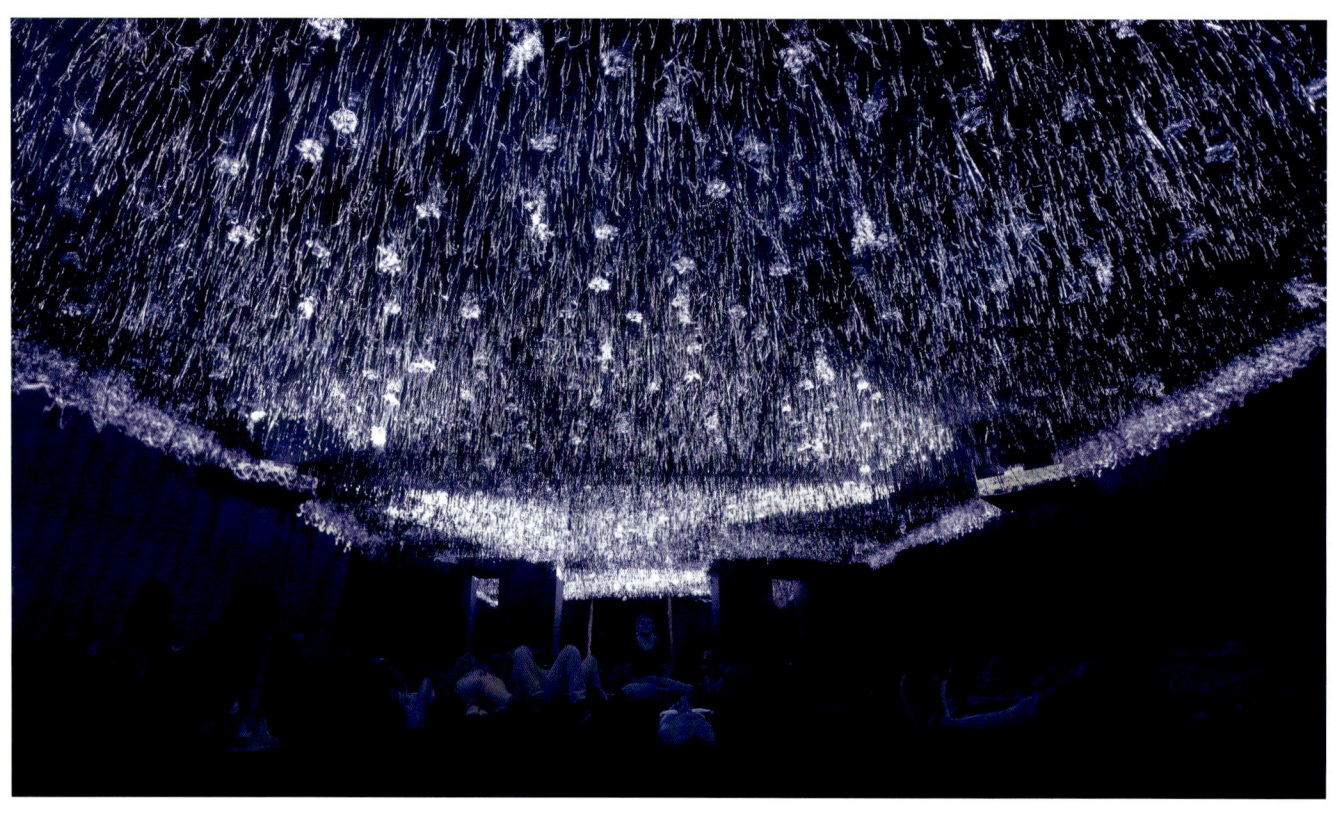

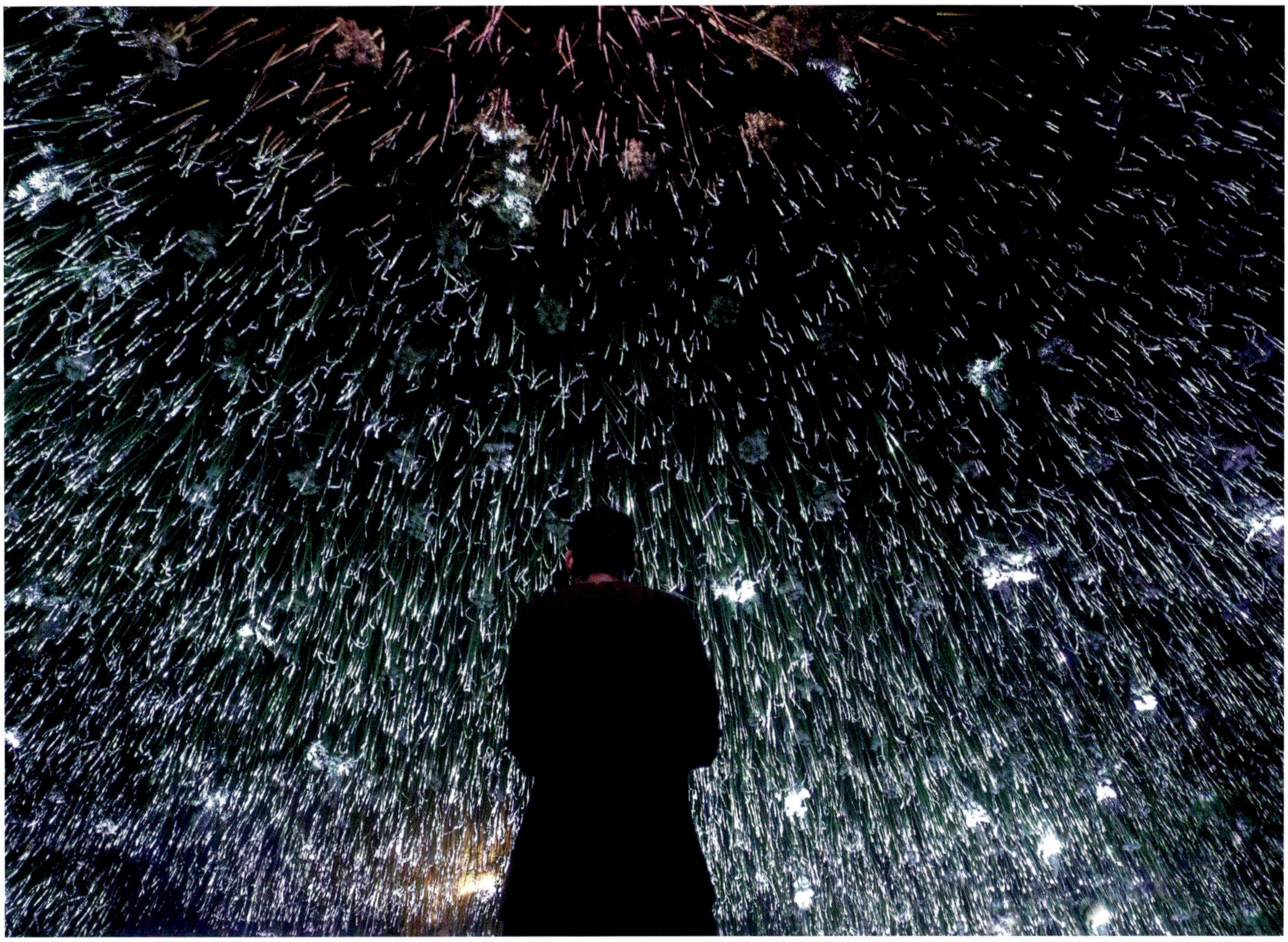

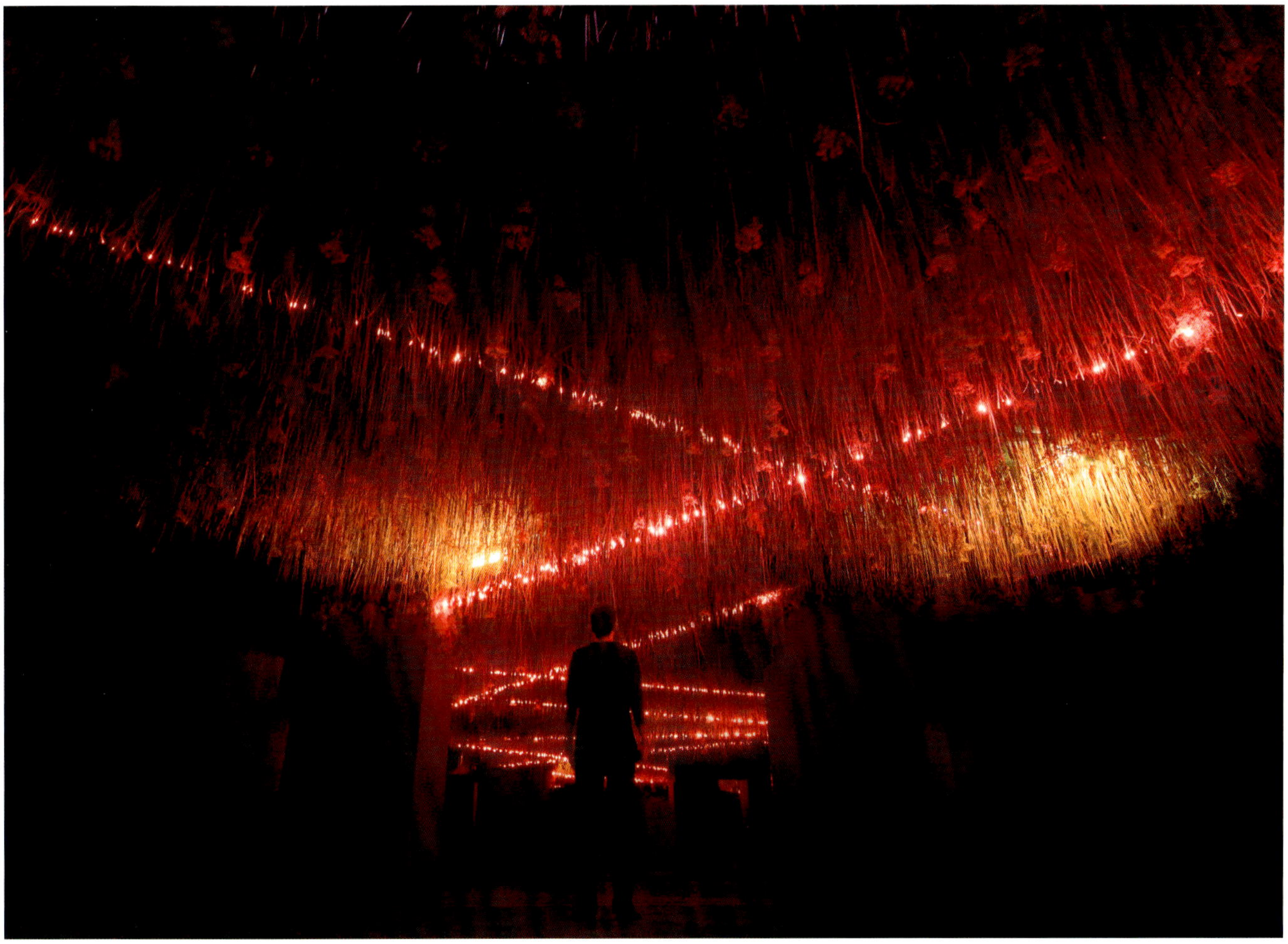

MORPHOGENESIS

—

Concept Design & Art Direction: **Can Büyükberber**
Sound Design: **Yagmur Uyanik**

—

Morphogenesis (from the Greek morphê ("shape") and genesis ("creation"); literally, "beginning of the shape") is the biological process that causes an organism to develop its shape. As a full dome and virtual-reality piece inspired by the phenomenon of emergence in self-organized systems, *Morphogenesis* consists of the continuous transformation of fundamental geometrical patterns and uses them as the building blocks of immersive spaces.

During the audiovisual journey through different planes of the digital and physical universe, *Morphogenesis* embodies the systems producing the complexity we encounter in the living world. By emphasizing the common characteristics of emergence, the installation highlights the systemic interconnectedness of all natural dynamics and demonstrates how these dynamics create novelty in micro and macro scales.

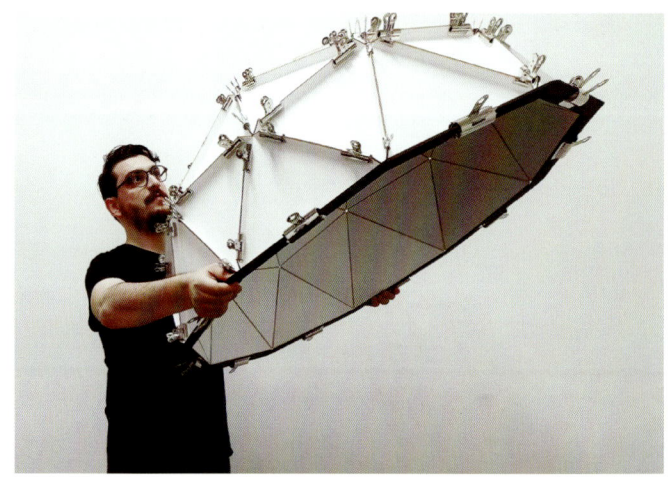

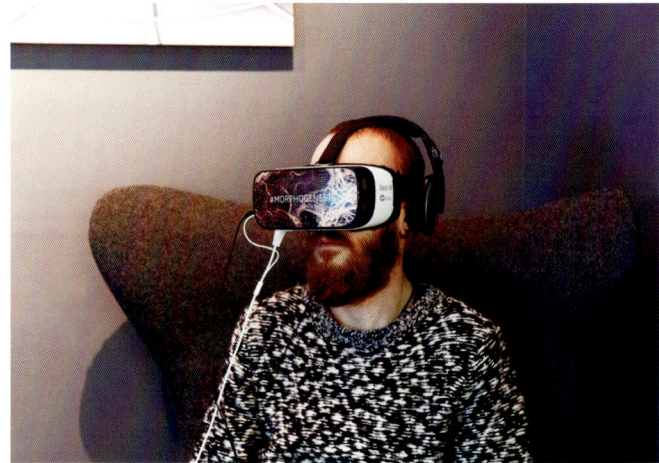

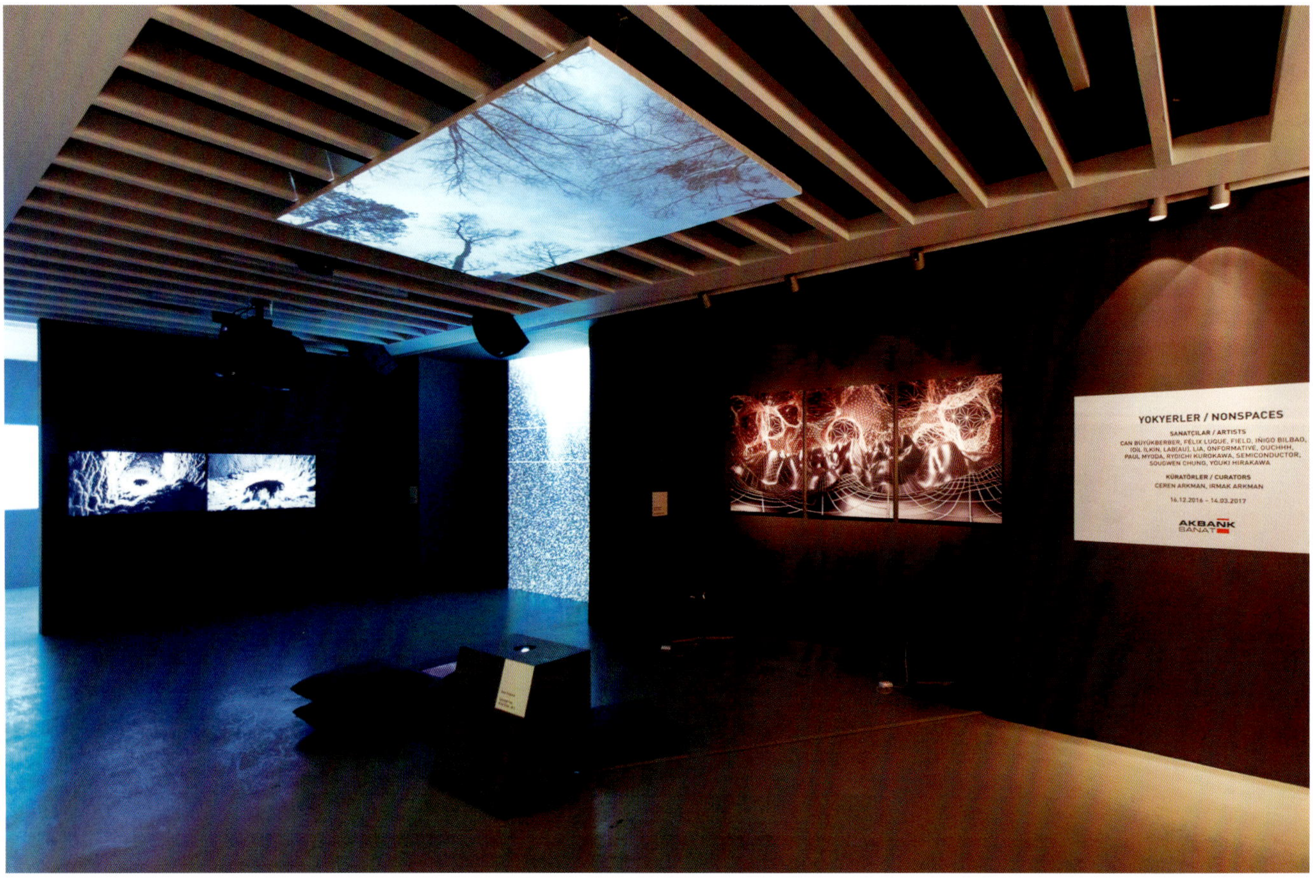

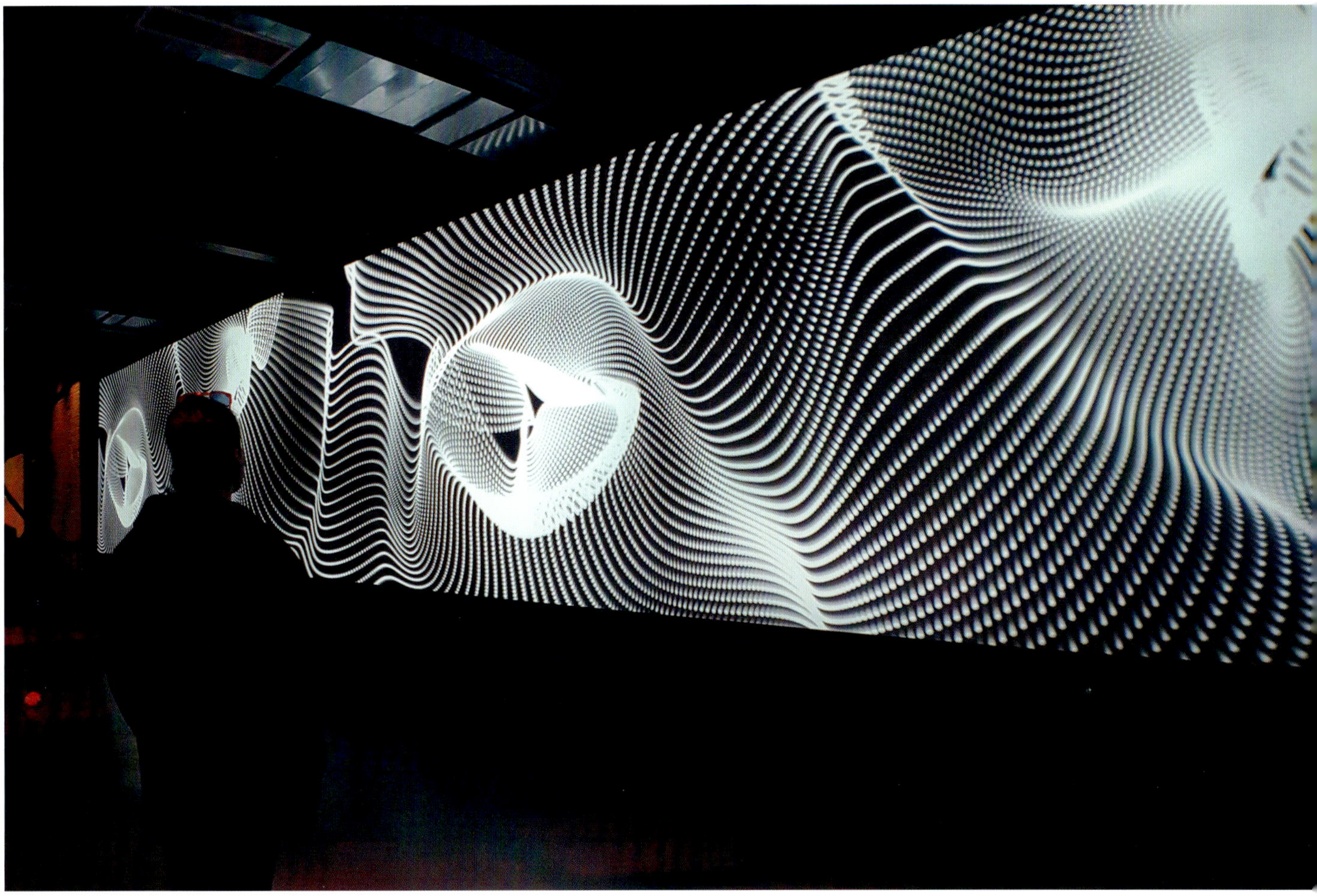

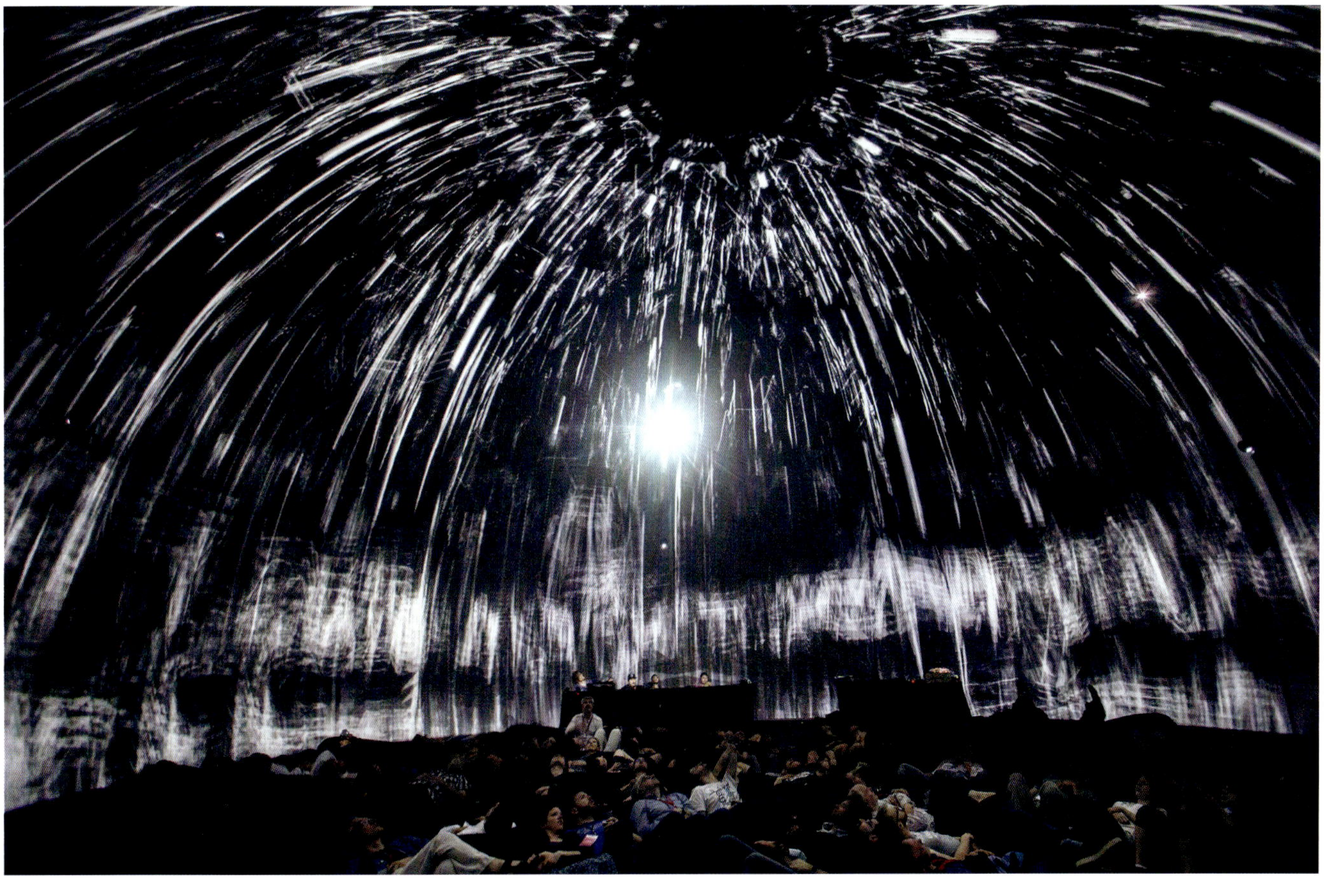

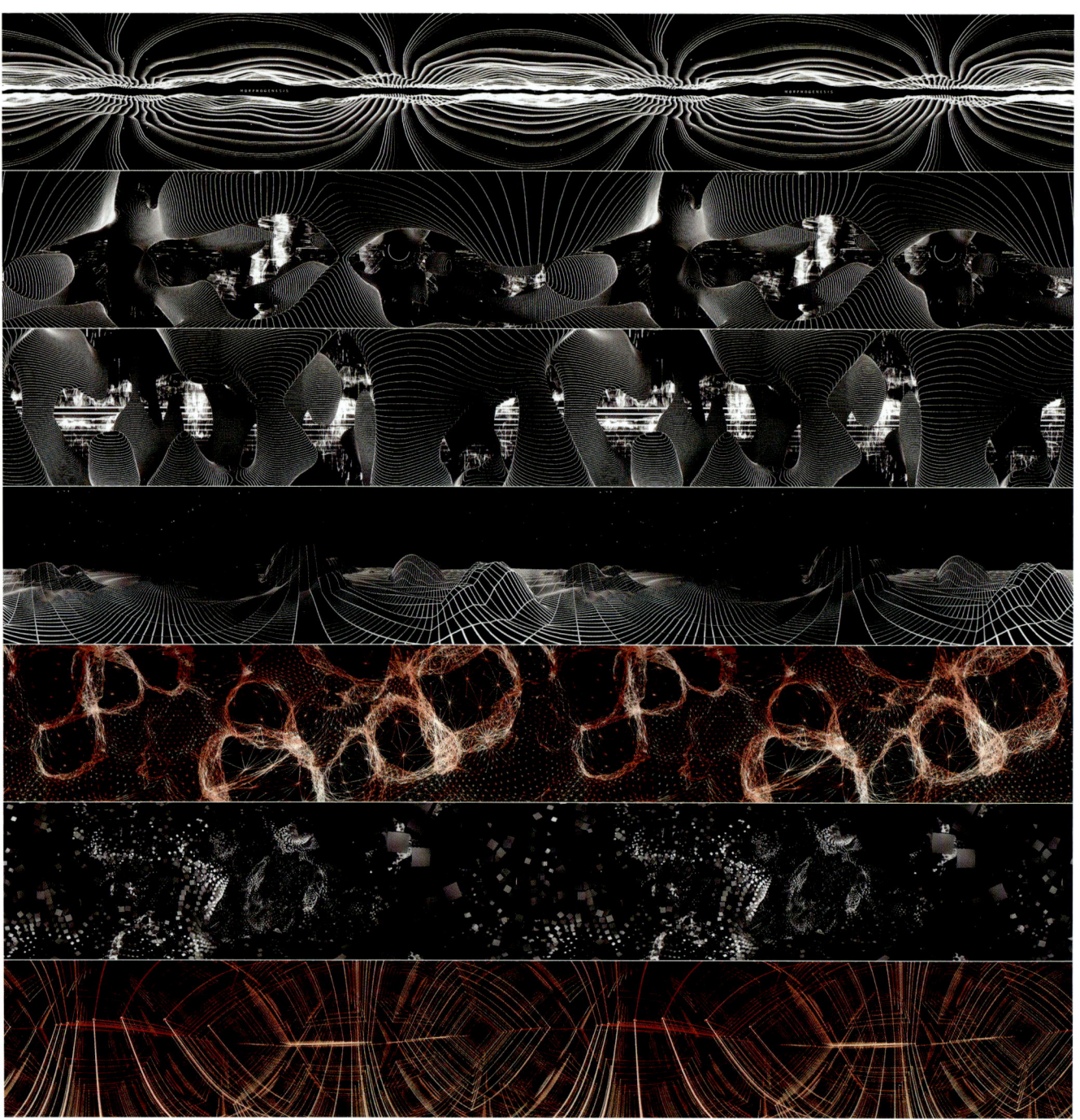

Exploring ideas such as geomorphology, mathematics, and perception, *Morphogenesis* requires the audience to be sentient, not just receivers. It invites the viewer to a poetic and sensational world, where space becomes infinite, and where he can experience a primal sense of the immaterial world and reevaluate the process of creation.

Exhibiting *Morphogenesis* in different places around the world, with different display formats and spatial settings, allows the artists to meet many brilliant individuals from numerous fields and opens up inspiring dialogues on the topics of motion and space, immersion and invisibility,

mythicality and symbolic expressions, and the future of human perception. Using the unrestrained nature of virtual reality, they aim to create a new visual and auditory vocabulary for this new and unique medium.

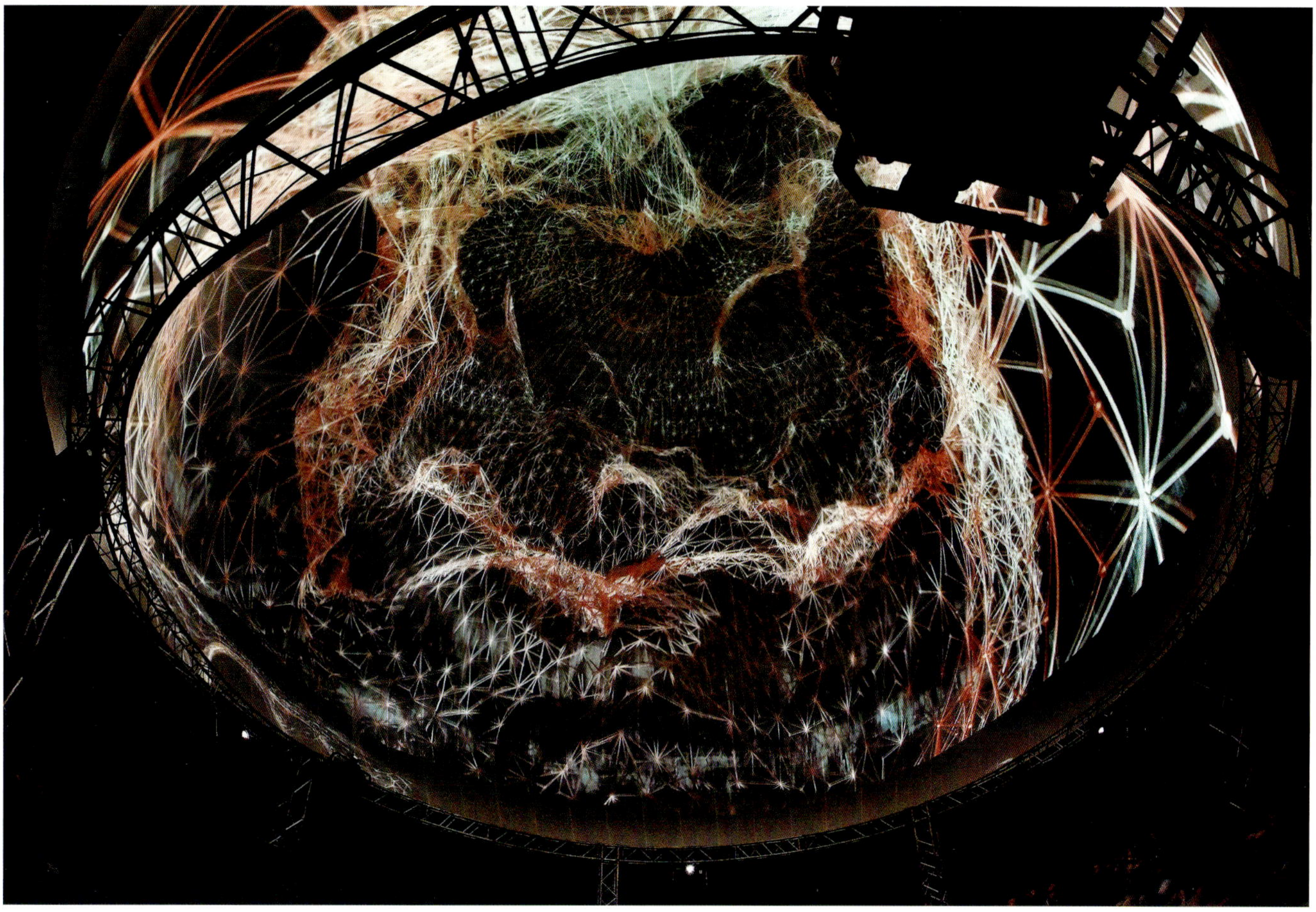

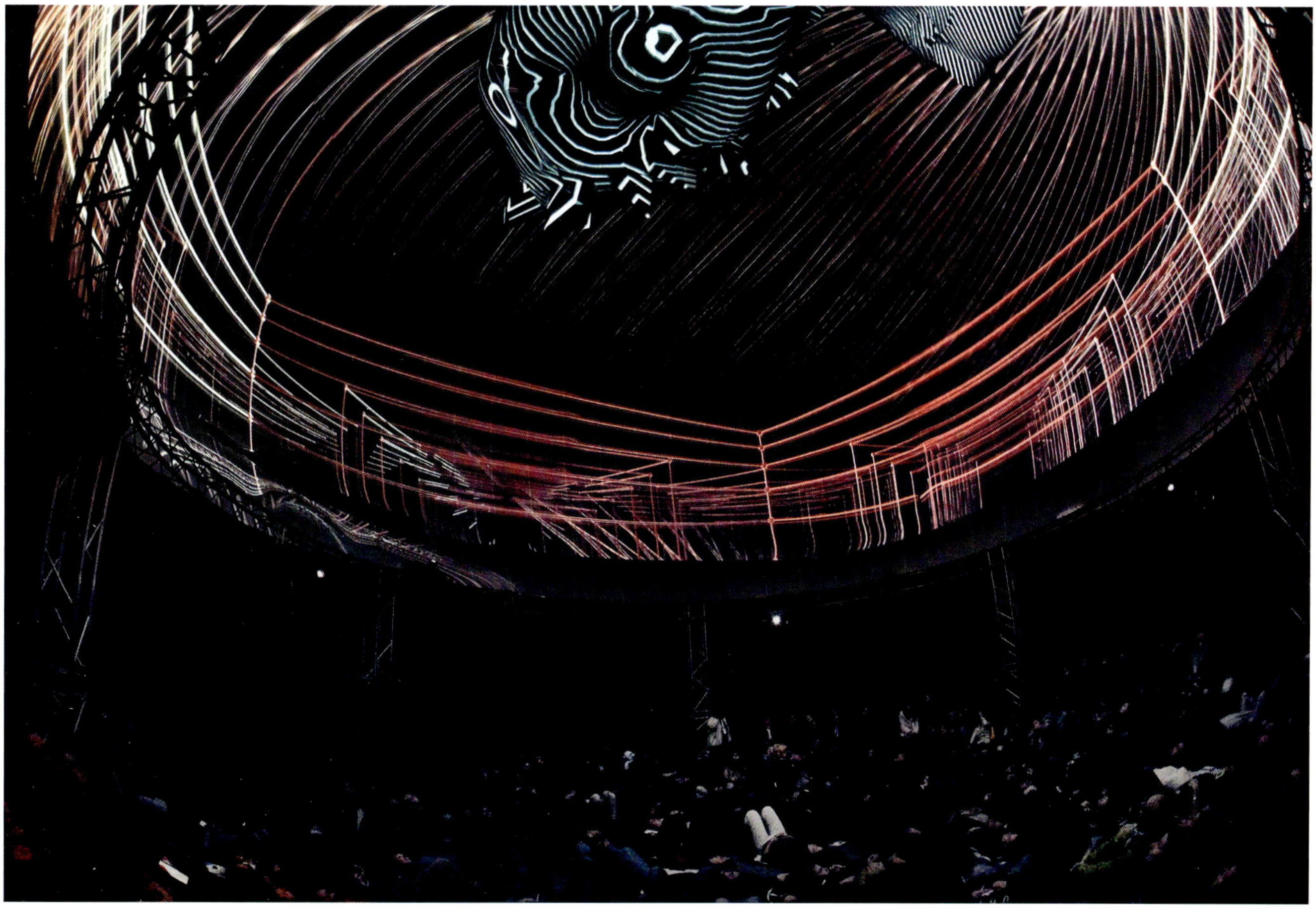

COGNITION

—

Design: **Radugadesign**

—

In the Stockholm City Hall, Radugadesign
presents the audiovisual performance
Cognition in collaboration with the composer
and pianist Nikola Melnikov, specially for the
brand Asko. The installation is an expression
of the act of striving for the perfect shape.
Everything can be perfect—whether it is a
geometric figure or a person. The experience
of perfection exists where people open
themselves to external icons.

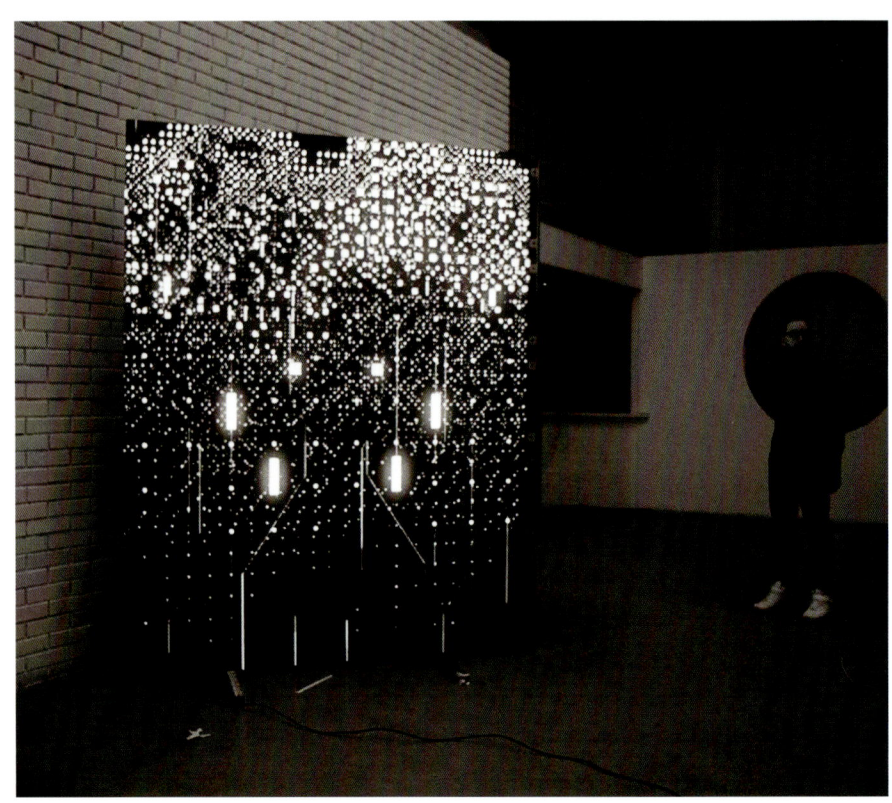

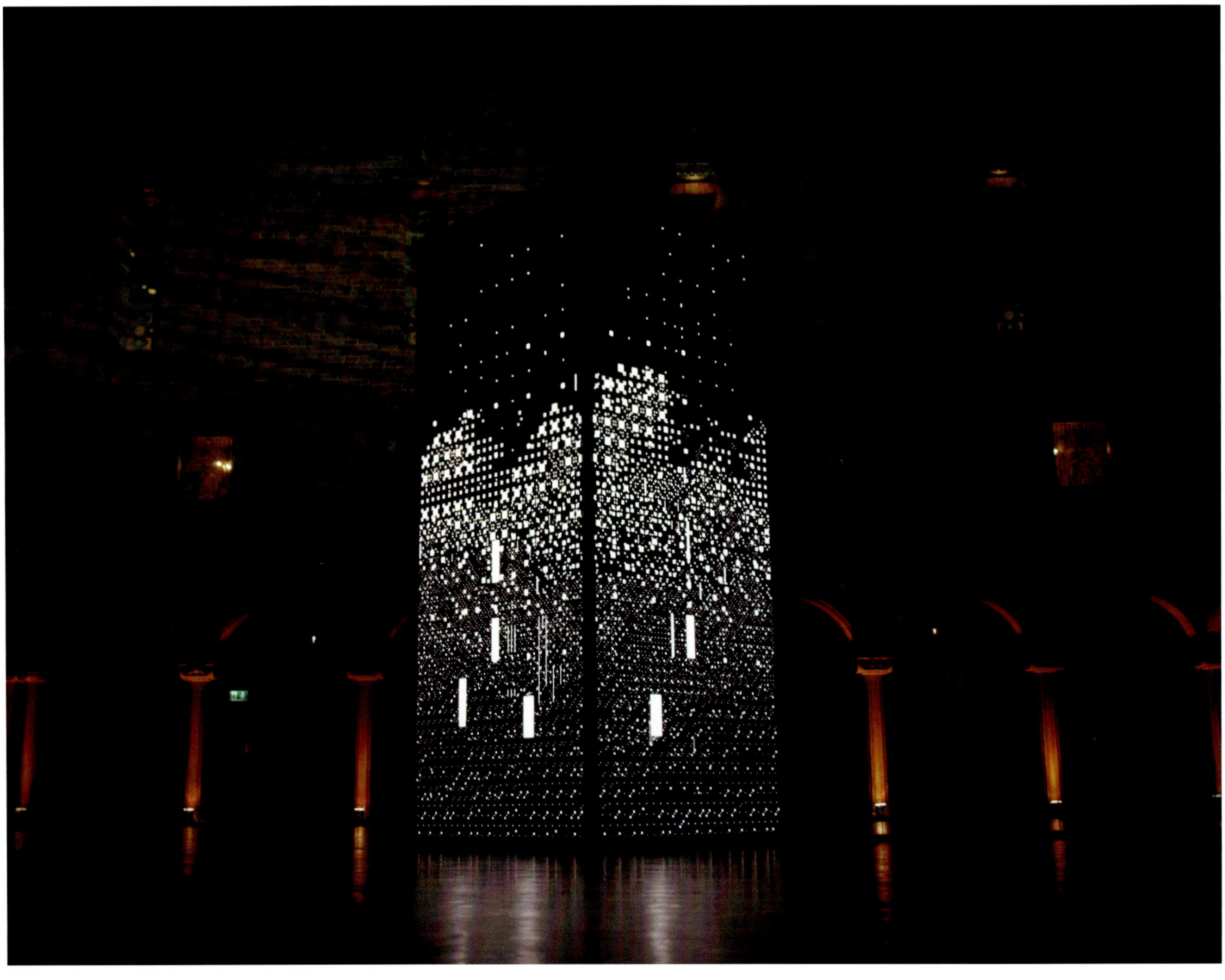

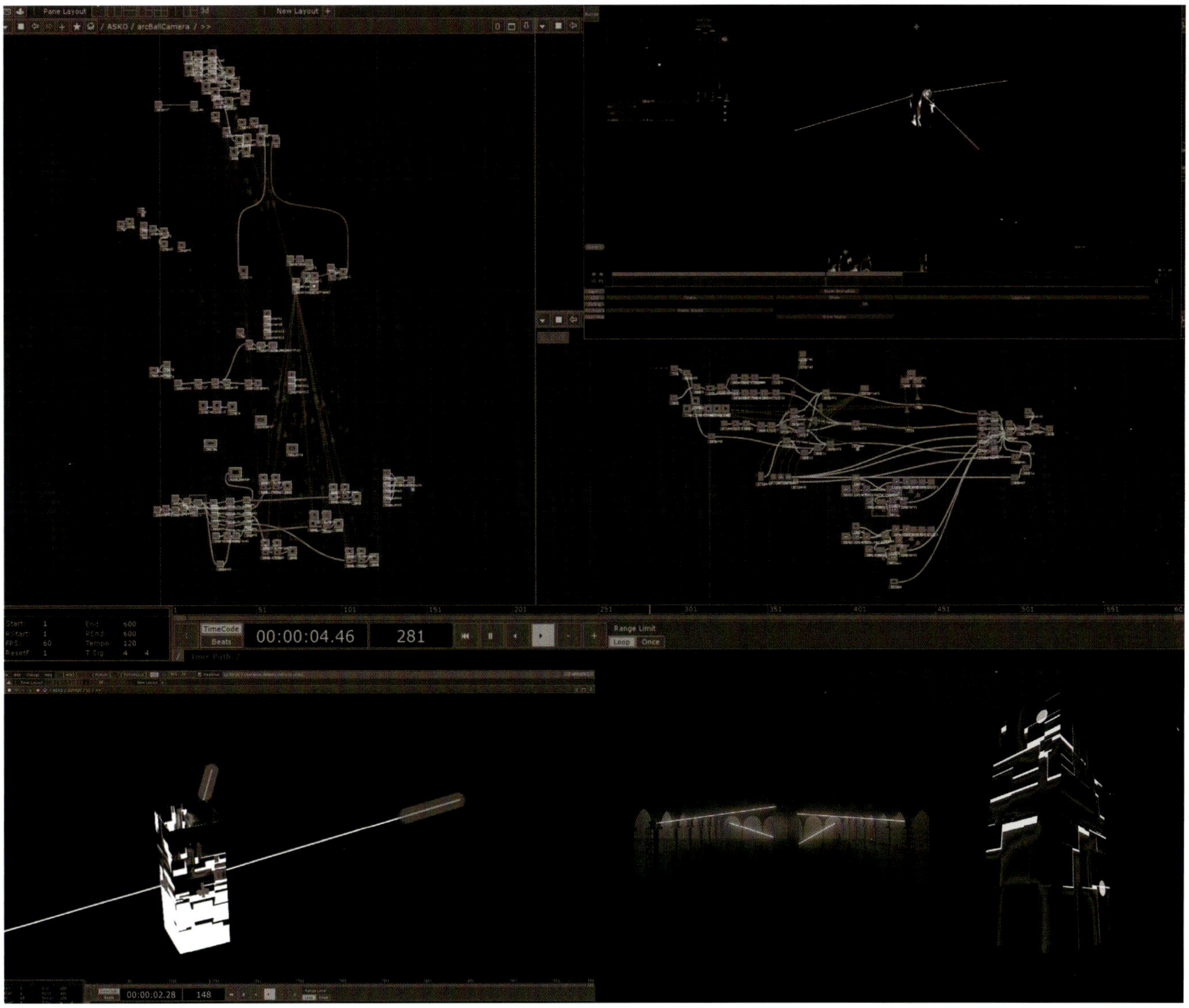

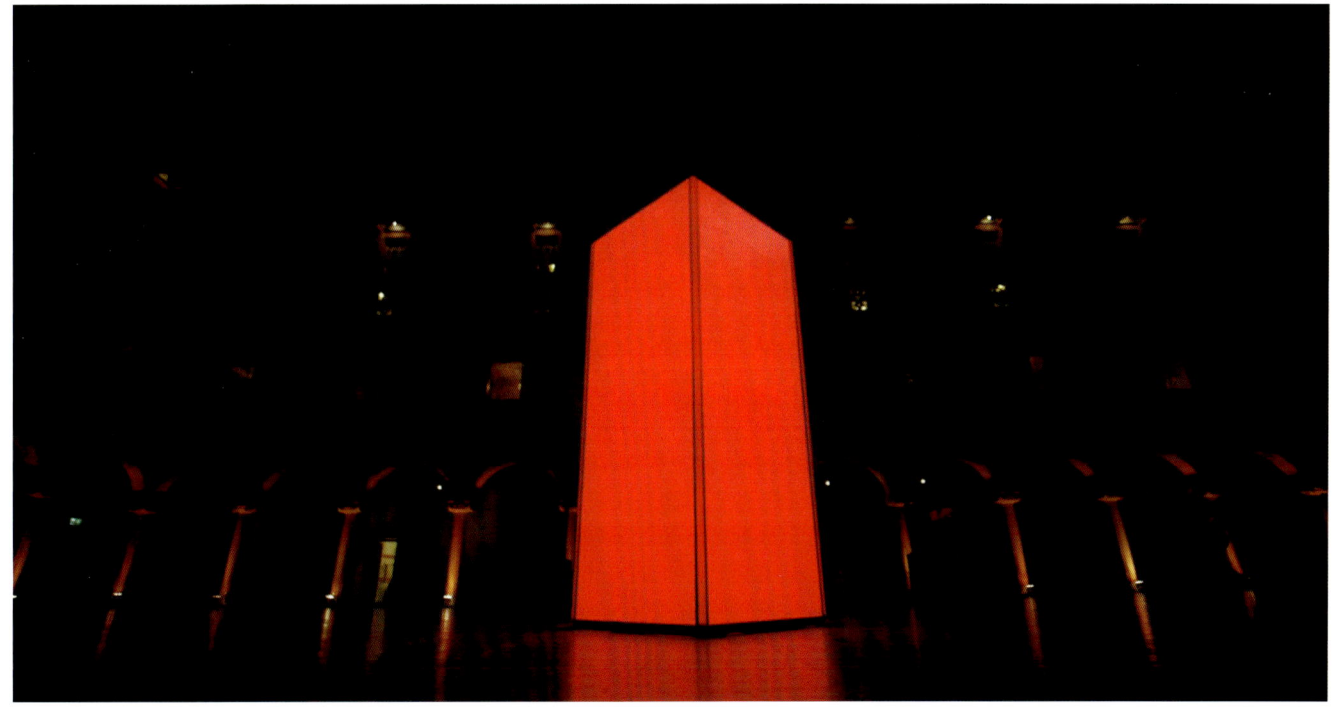

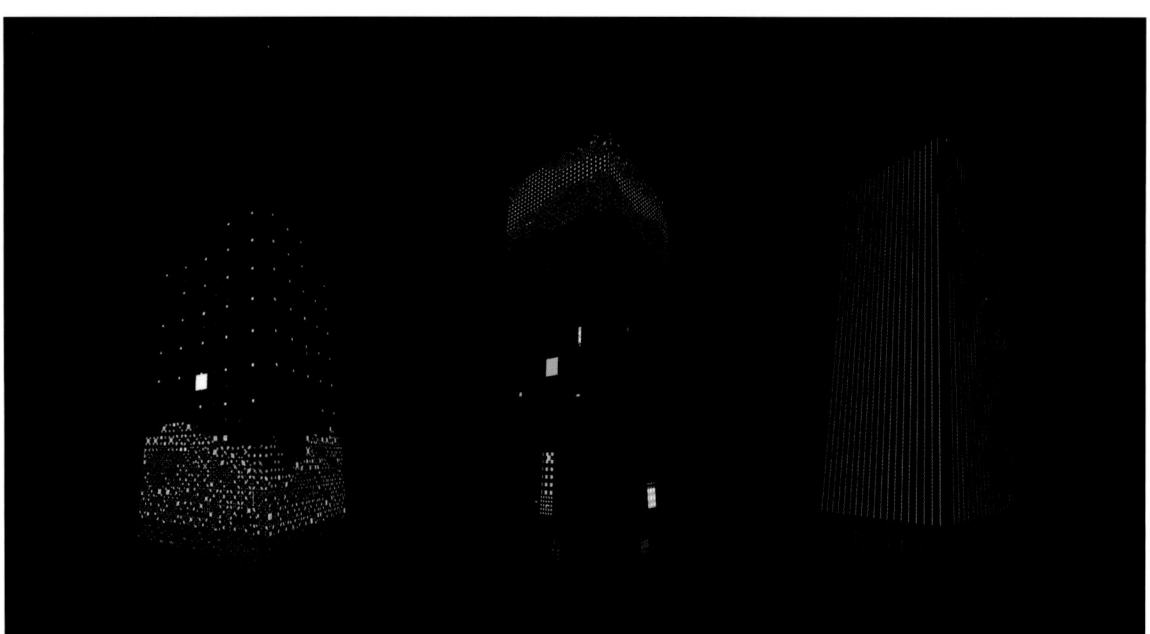

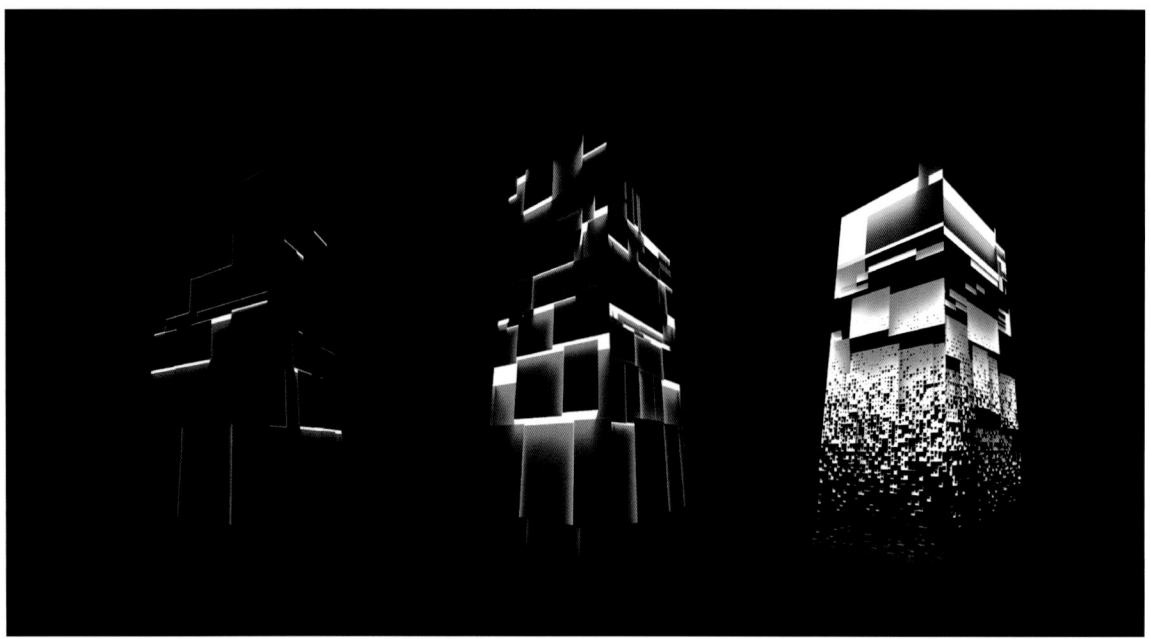

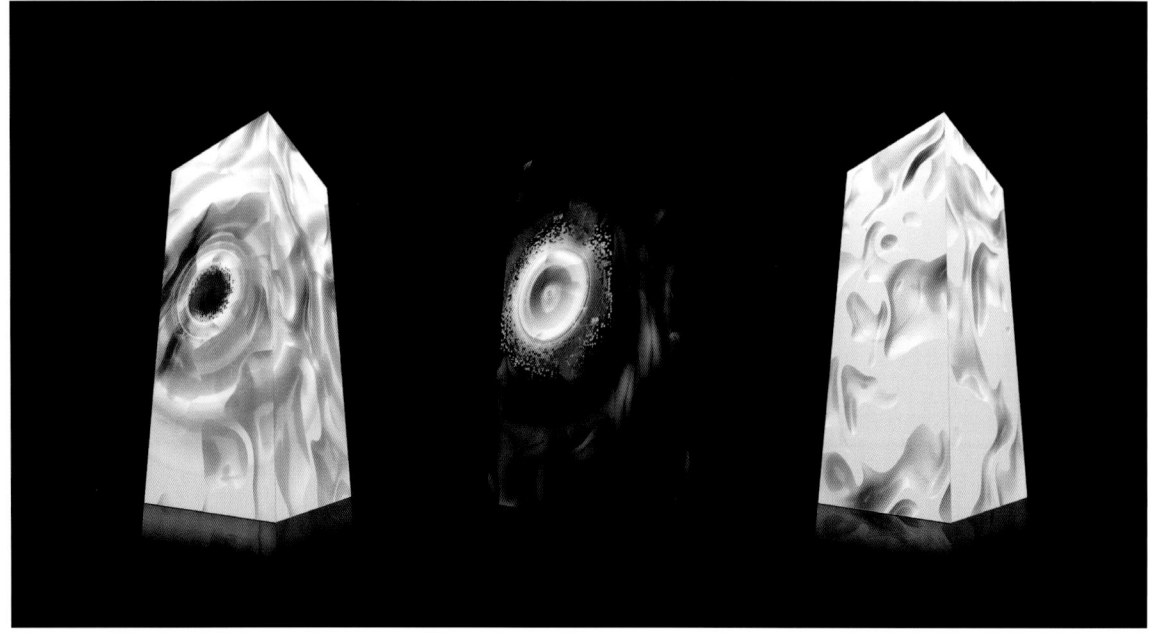

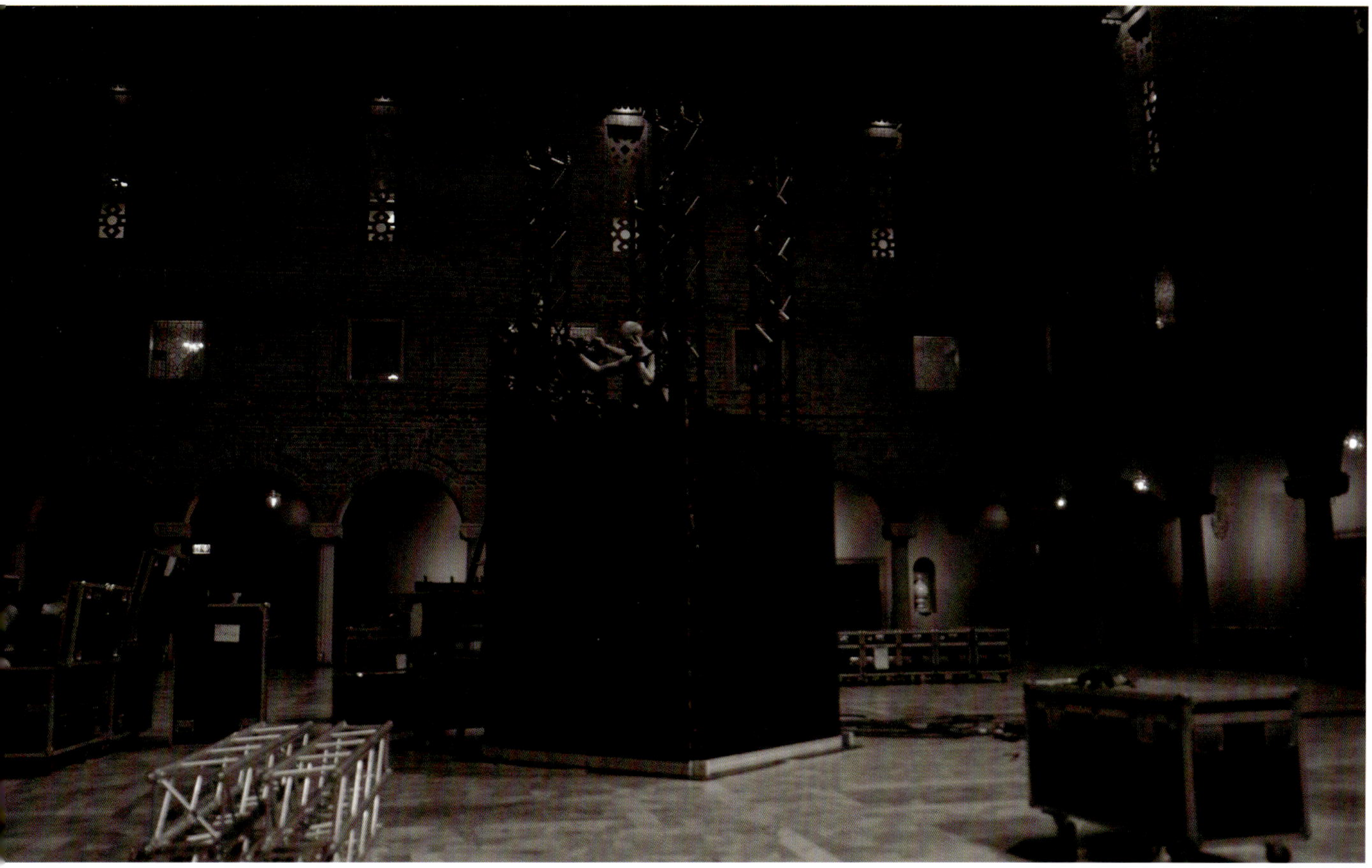

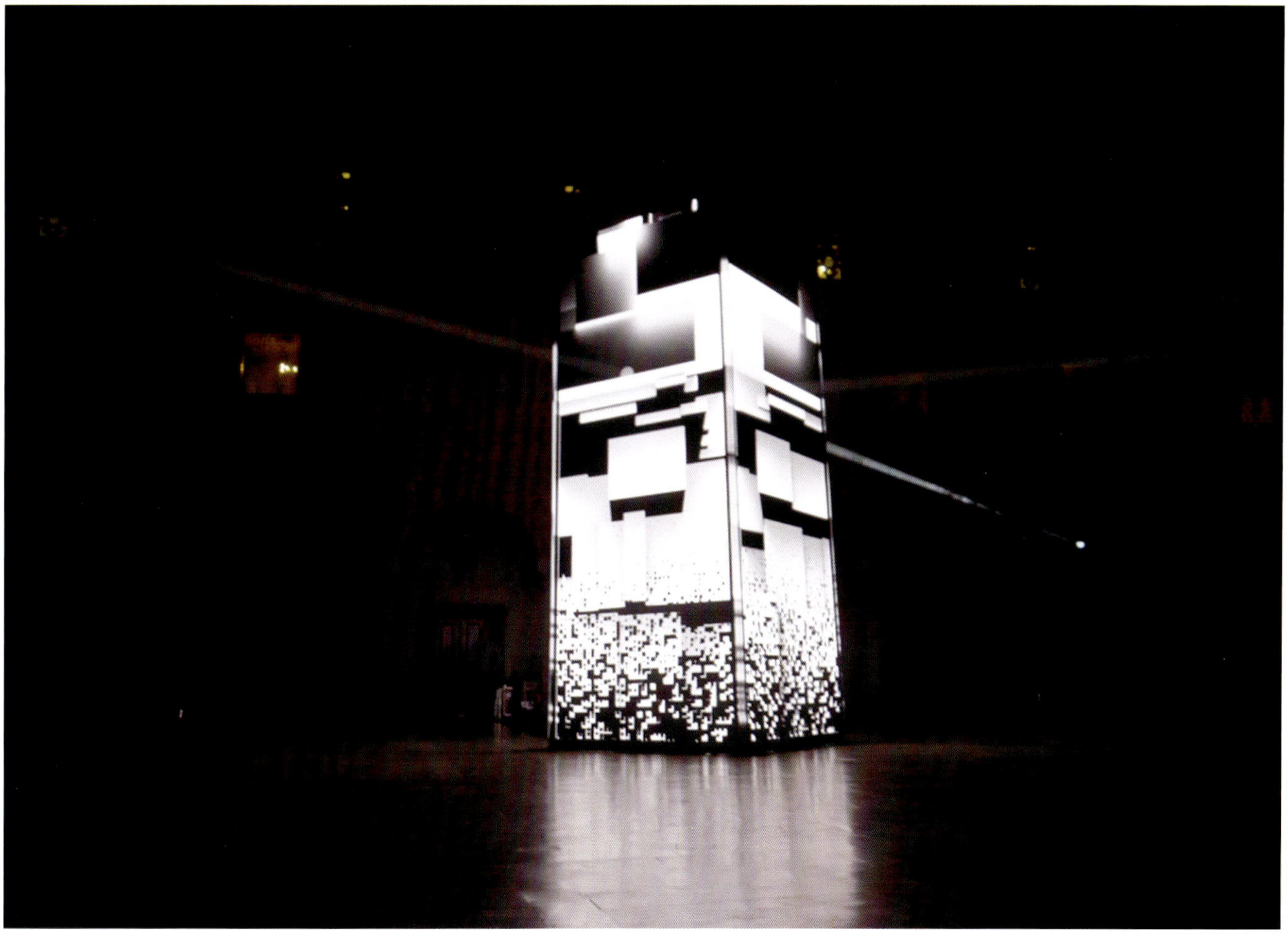

AXIOM

—

Design: **Kit Webster**

—

Axiom is an edifice of light, sculpted from a matrix of more than 700,000 LEDs. Emerging as three symmetrically aligned archways, the installation presents a canvas for a series of video animations designed to embody and envelop its surfaces and contours. Within *Axiom* exists a transition between form and illumination, intending to cause the observer to reconsider what is virtual and what is actual. The animations and synchronized soundscapes provide an evolving syncopated framework, moving from meditative pulsations to rapid percussions, enhanced by hypnotic musical overtones. As these audiovisual arrangements gradually unfold throughout the work, the elements of light, sound, space and time are explored, manifested, and re-invented. This contortion of multiple compositional and choreographic techniques illustrates a consideration and deconstruction of materiality, with the objective of rebuilding it in an alternate mode. *Axiom* breaks conventions by harnessing and re-appropriating the power of cutting-edge event technologies, software systems and construction techniques to evoke a new form of non-linear experiential response.

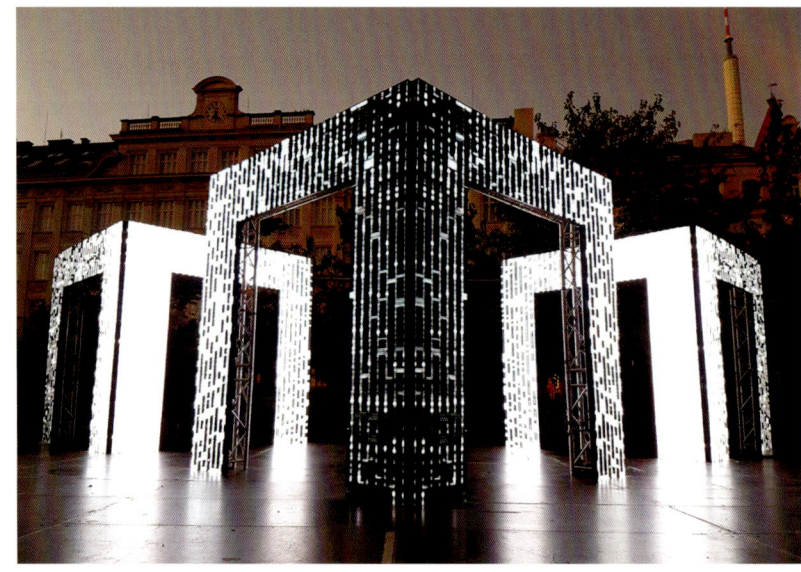

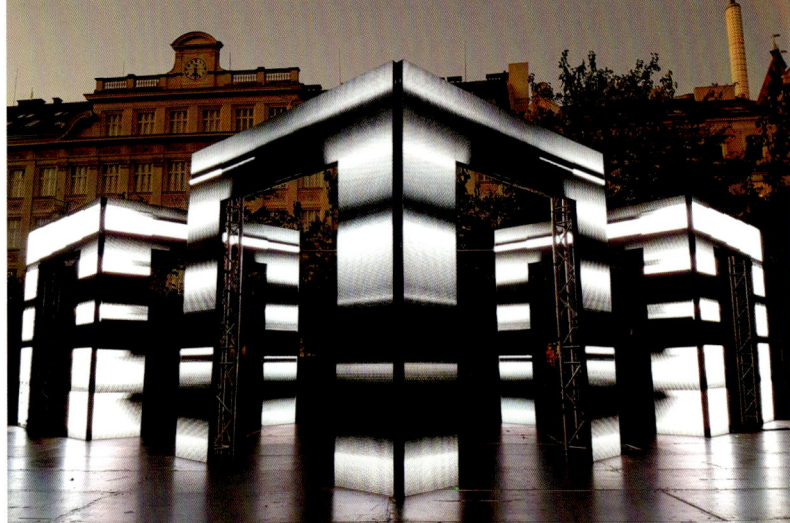

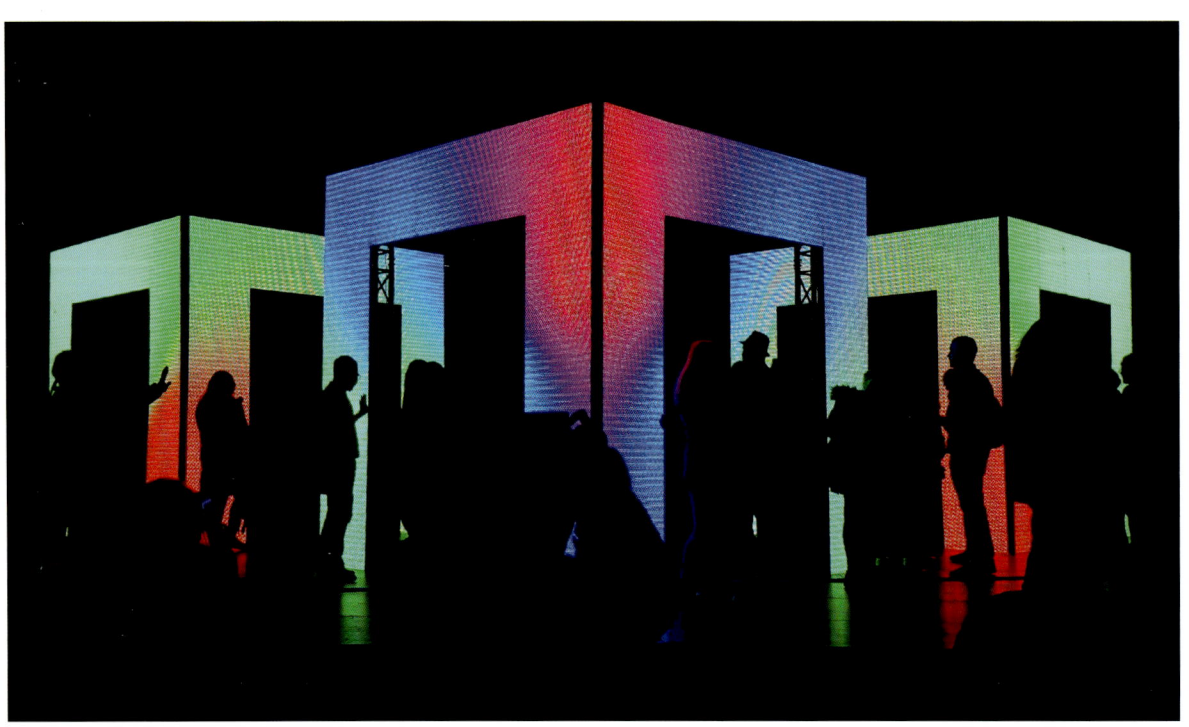

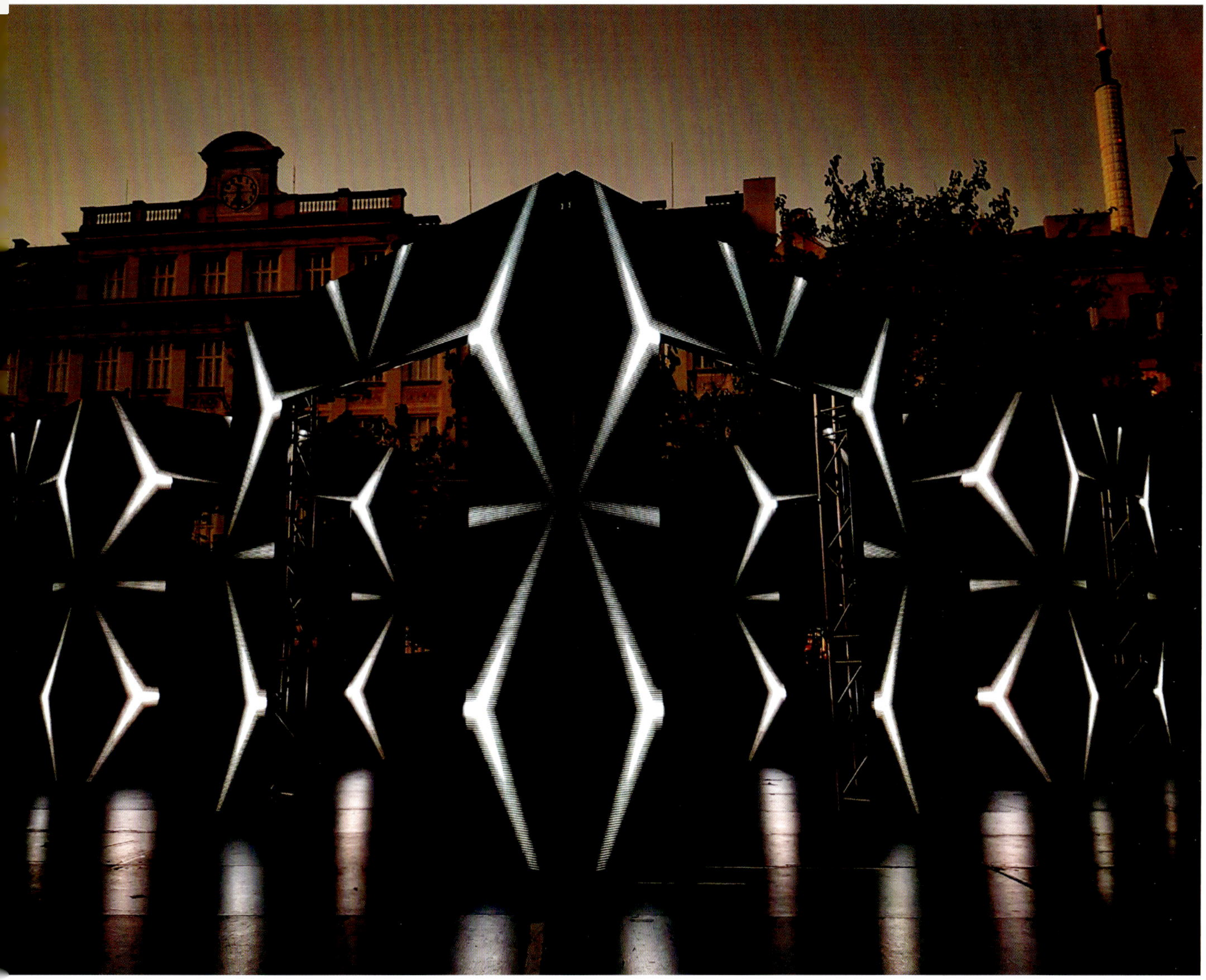

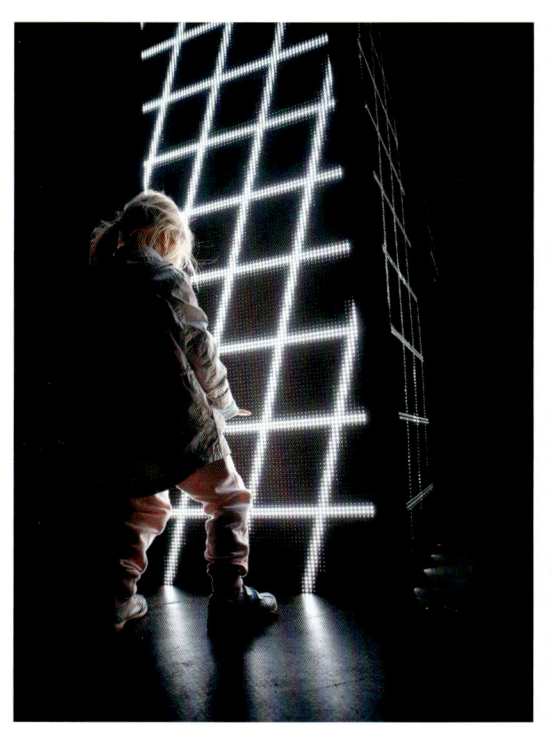

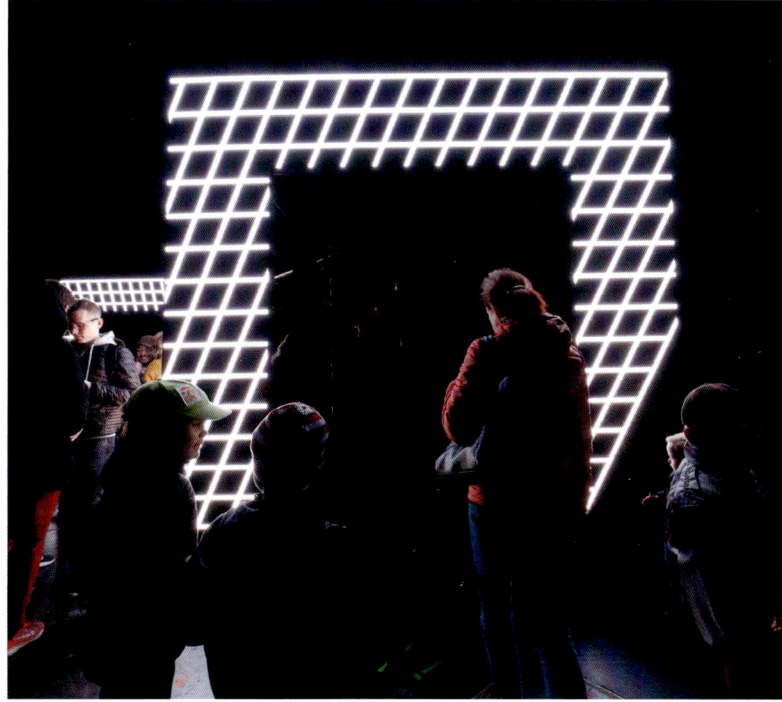

COLORAMA

—

Design: **Playmodes Studio**

—

This installation transforms the serious, boring, geometric and synthetic façade of Barcelona's City Hall into a lively, colorful work of art, full of optical illusions, during the city's annual "La Mercè" celebration, the most joyous festival on the calendar. The choice of venues and the effect have been likened to a small revolution, using color and movement to challenge order and the establishment.

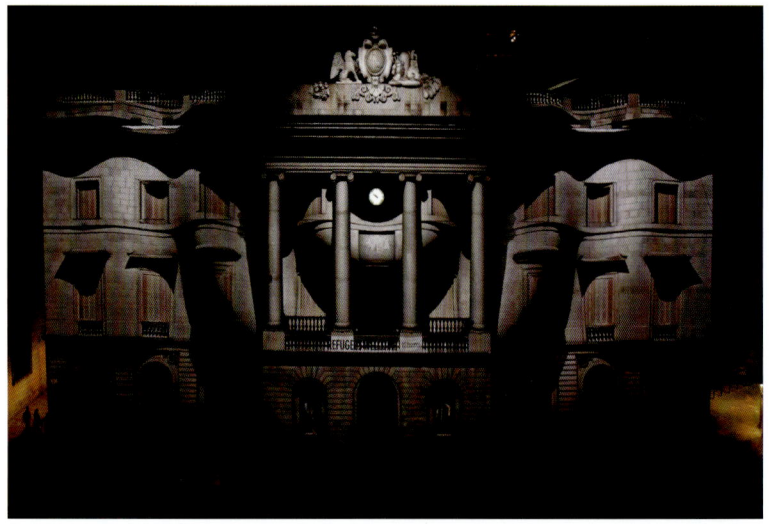

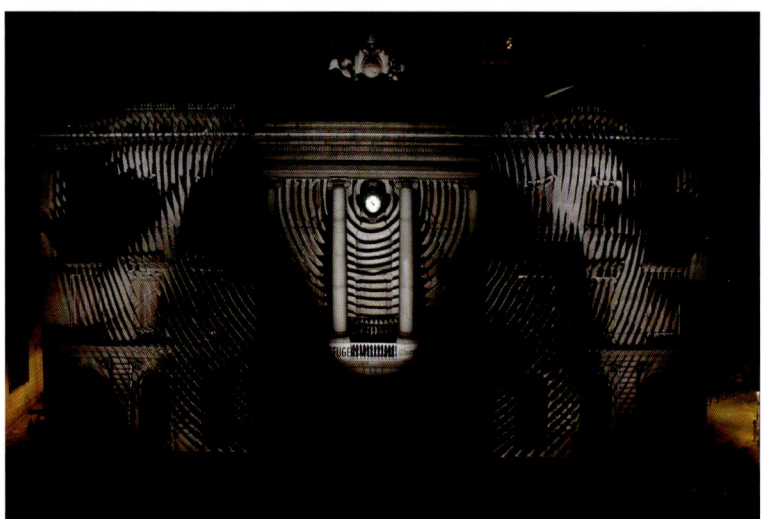

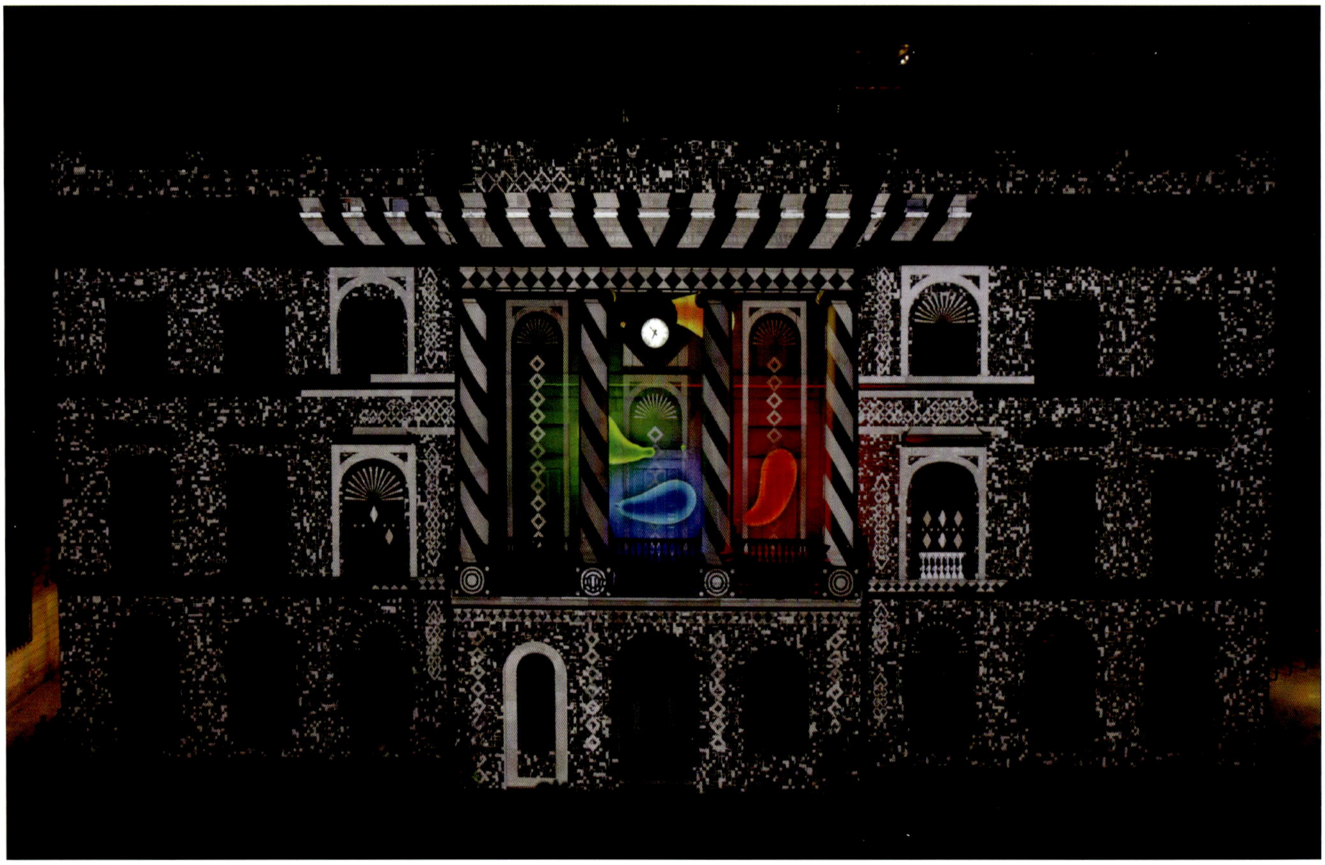

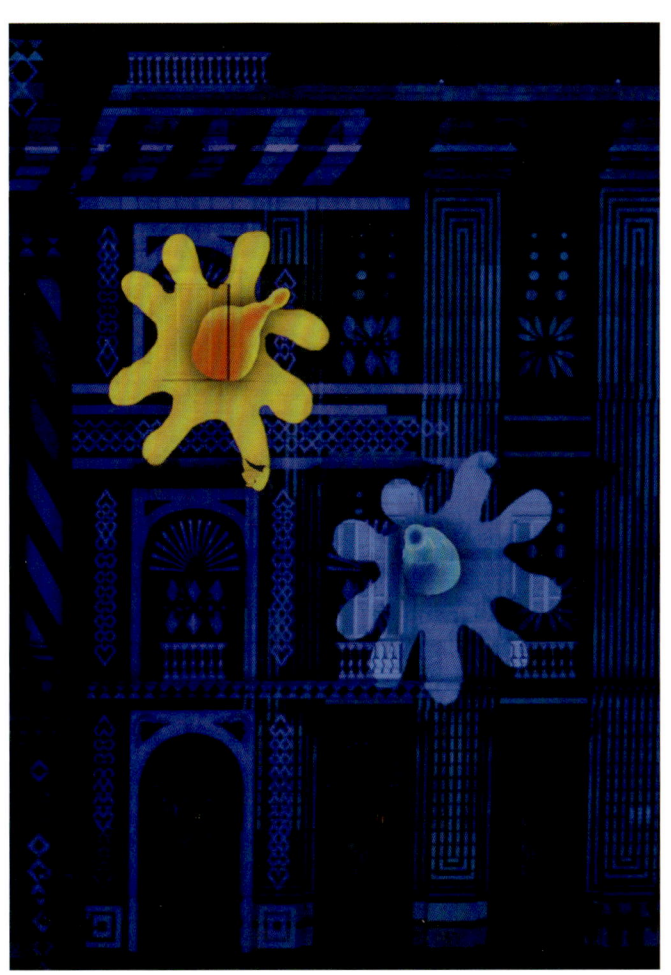
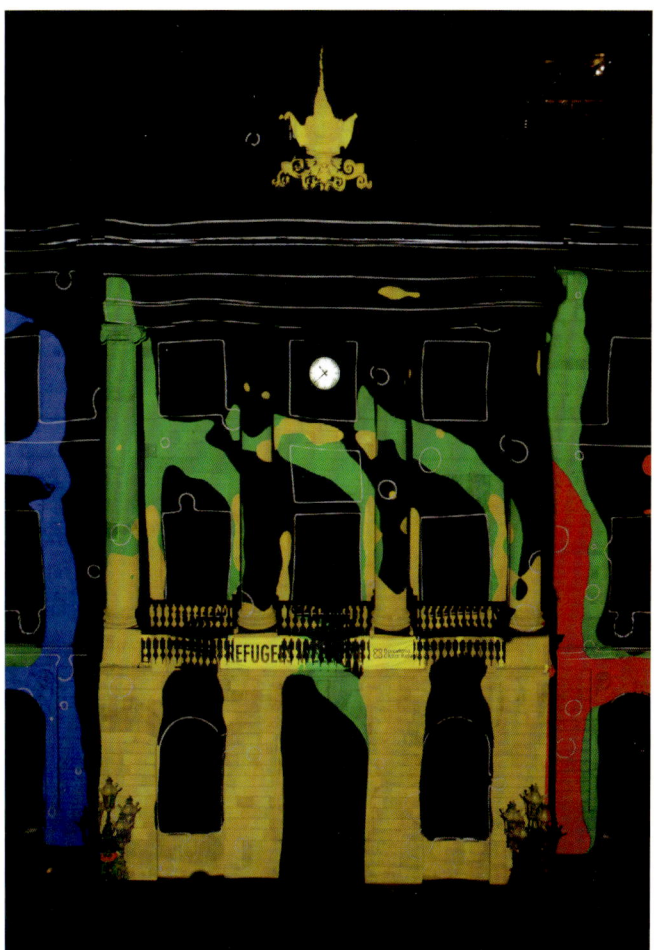

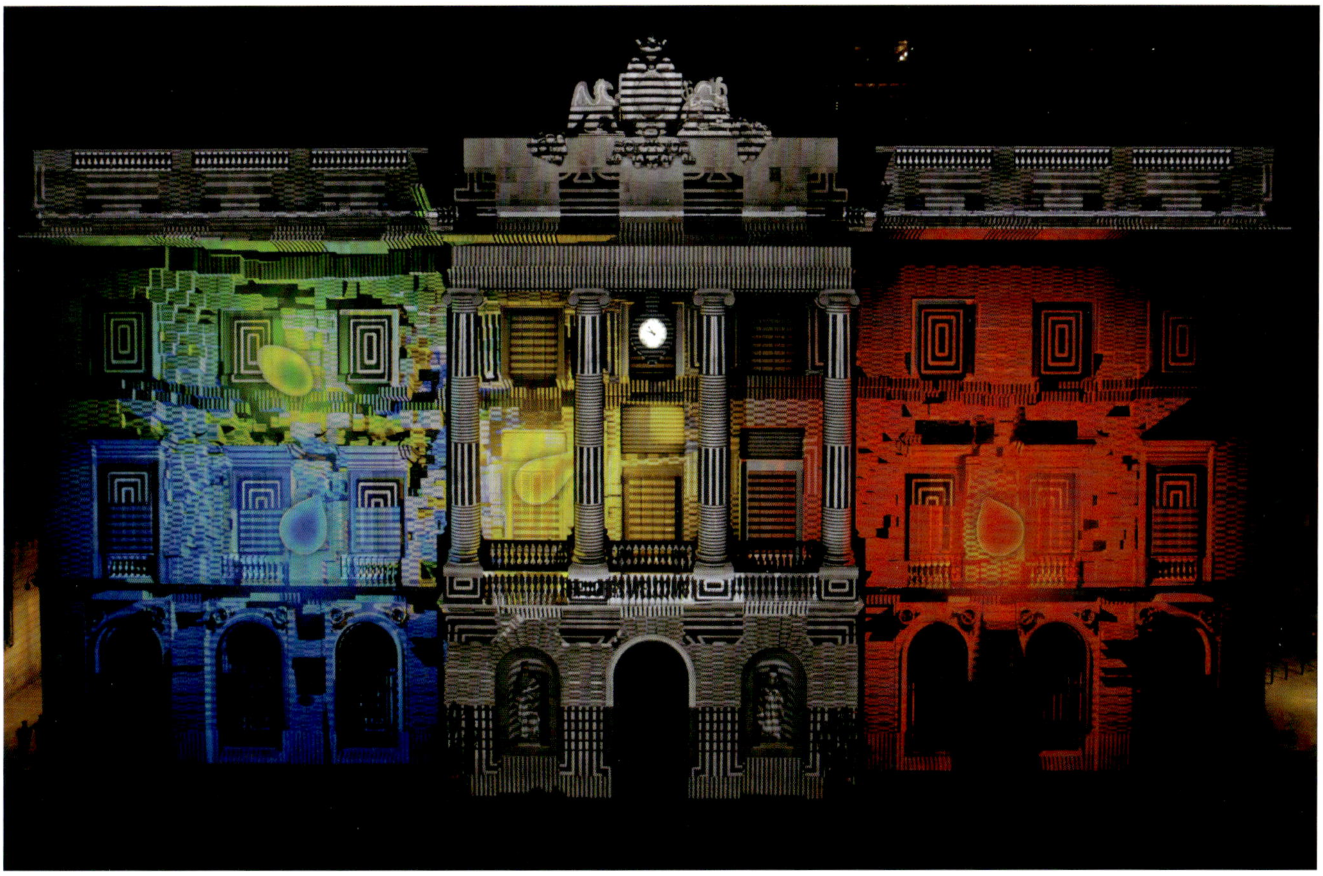

LUMINOUS FIELD

—

Design: **Luftwerk**
Photography: **Peter Tsai**

—

Luminous Field transforms Millennium Park, in Chicago, into a digital canvas of motion, light, and geometrical form as the first site-specific video and sound installation in the park. The ten-day installation illuminated Anish Kapoor's *Cloud Gate* and the AT&T Plaza, with dramatic images and colors set to music composed by Owen Clayton Condon.

The work consisted of projections that video-mapped the tiles of the plaza, creating a digital mosaic. Inspired by the tessellation patterns of Italian marble floors, the digital mosaic added a new, contemporary layer to the work. Animation of the video composition became an informal hopscotch as visitors tried to anticipate the movement and follow along. The projections interacted with the reflective surface of *Cloud Gate* in a new, altered state. The piece, a digital playground for the public, attracted over 65,000 visitors to the park.

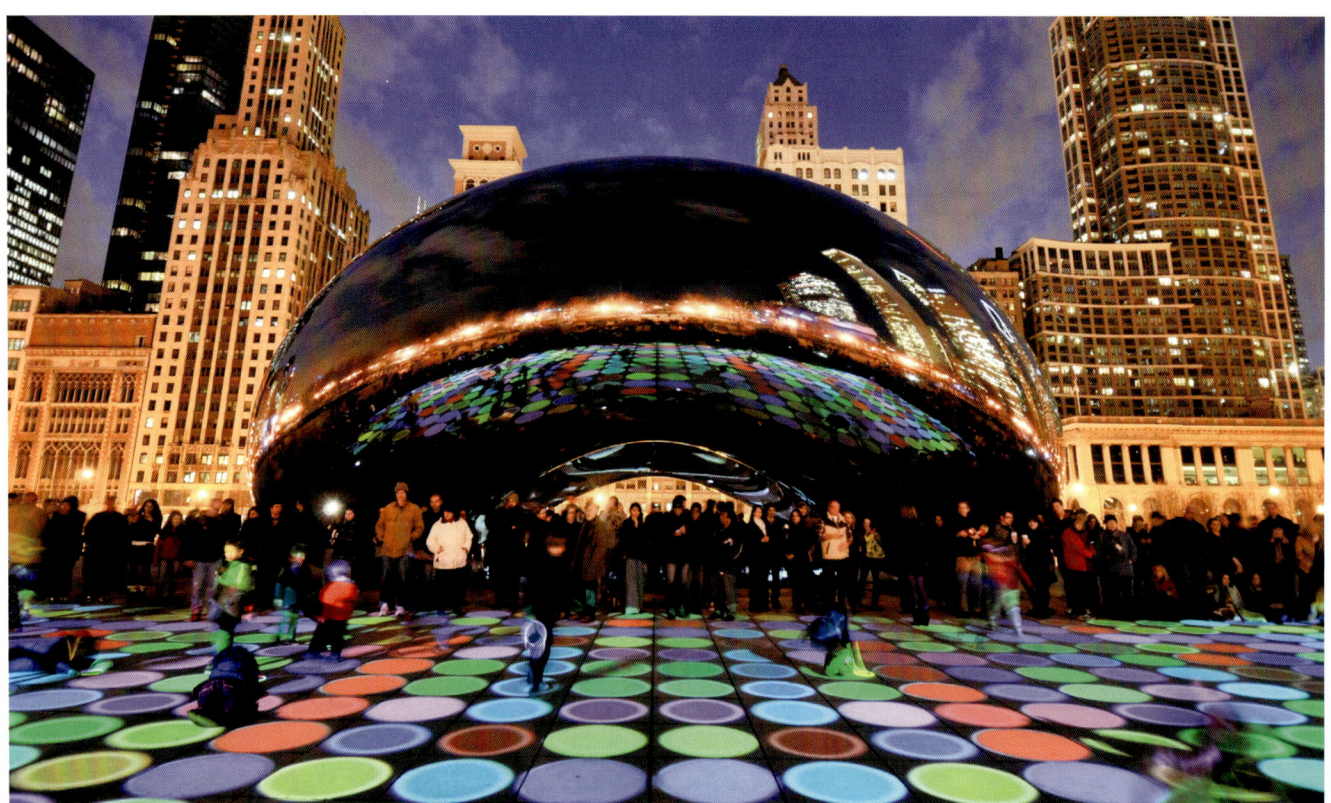

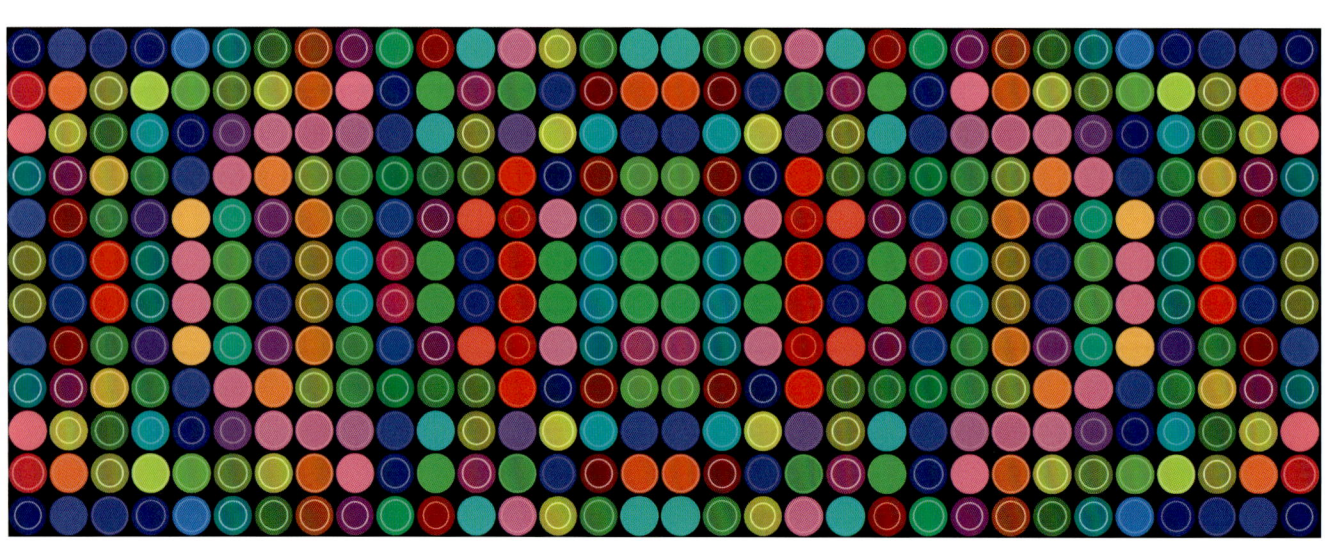

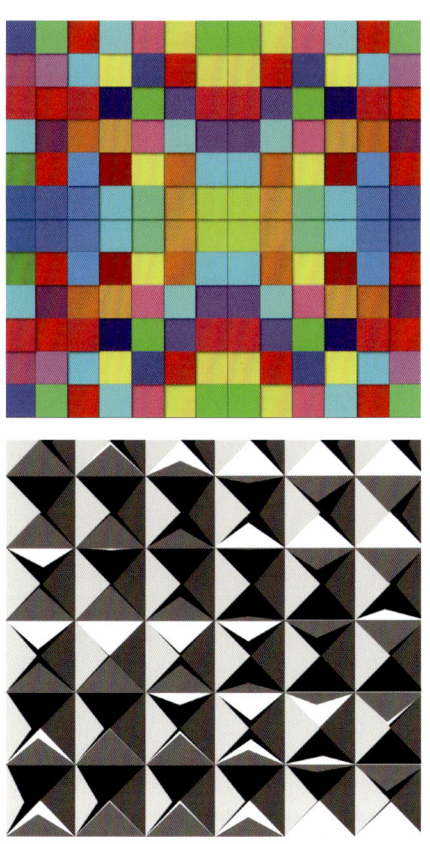

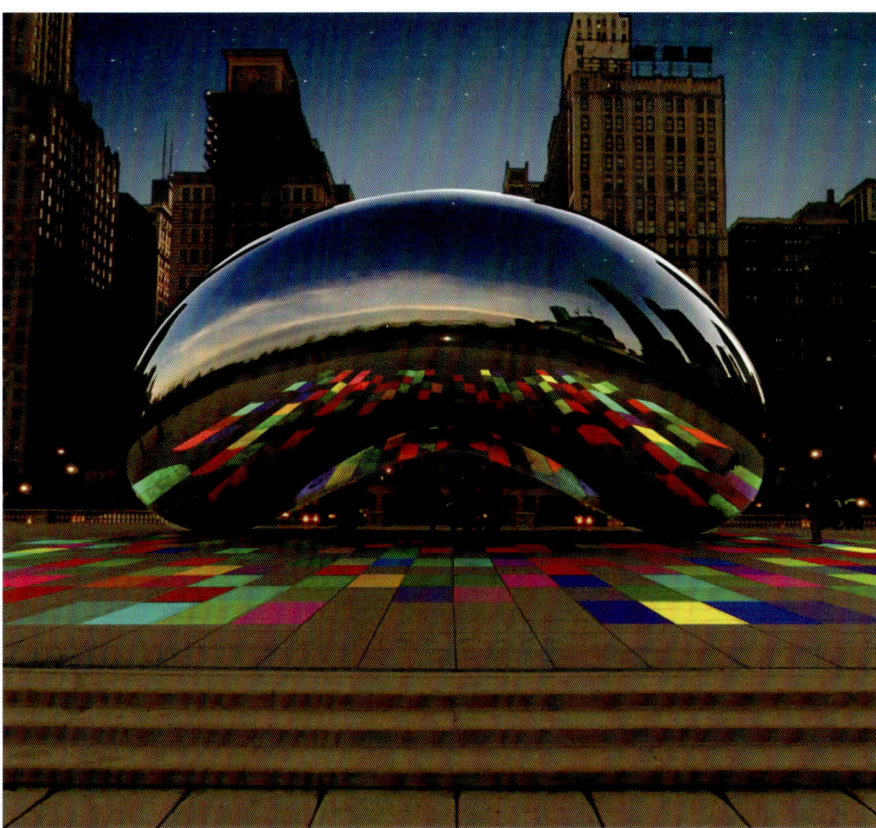

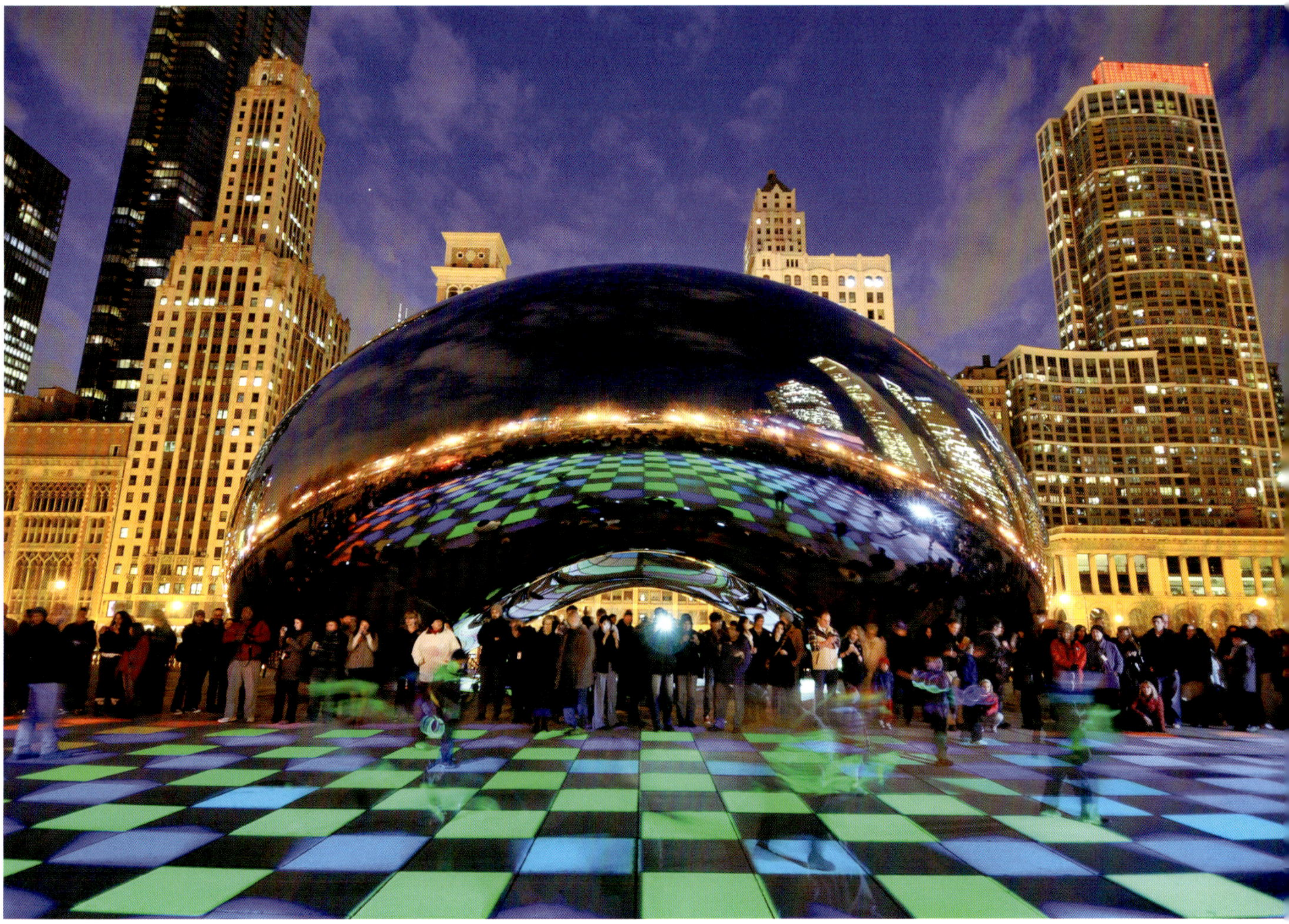

IN-OUT/ ARTIFICIAL PARADISES

—

Design: **Miguel Chevalier**
Music Design: **Jacopo Baboni Schilingi**
Software: **Claude Micheli**

—

IN-OUT/Artificial Paradises is an exclusive multi-sensory work of installation by Miguel Chevalier.

A half-elliptical structure made out of wood and covered by holographic films shines under the sun like a twelve-meter-long beetle. The glimmer of the film reflects all the colors of the light spectrum, attracting everyone who comes within view.

The visitor is welcomed into the geodesic dome where he discovers in a second eight-meter-diameter dome a digital garden, projected in 360°. The public leaves reality and enjoys this unique immersive experience that explores the link between nature and artifice.

The visuals mix different trees, foliage, and flower species against the undergrowth vegetation. Nature sometimes takes realist forms and sometimes takes abstract forms, generating itself indefinitely.

Plants arise randomly, growing before disappearing before the public's eyes. The garden renews itself and permanently transforms itself, reinforced by Jacopo Baboni Schilingi's music.

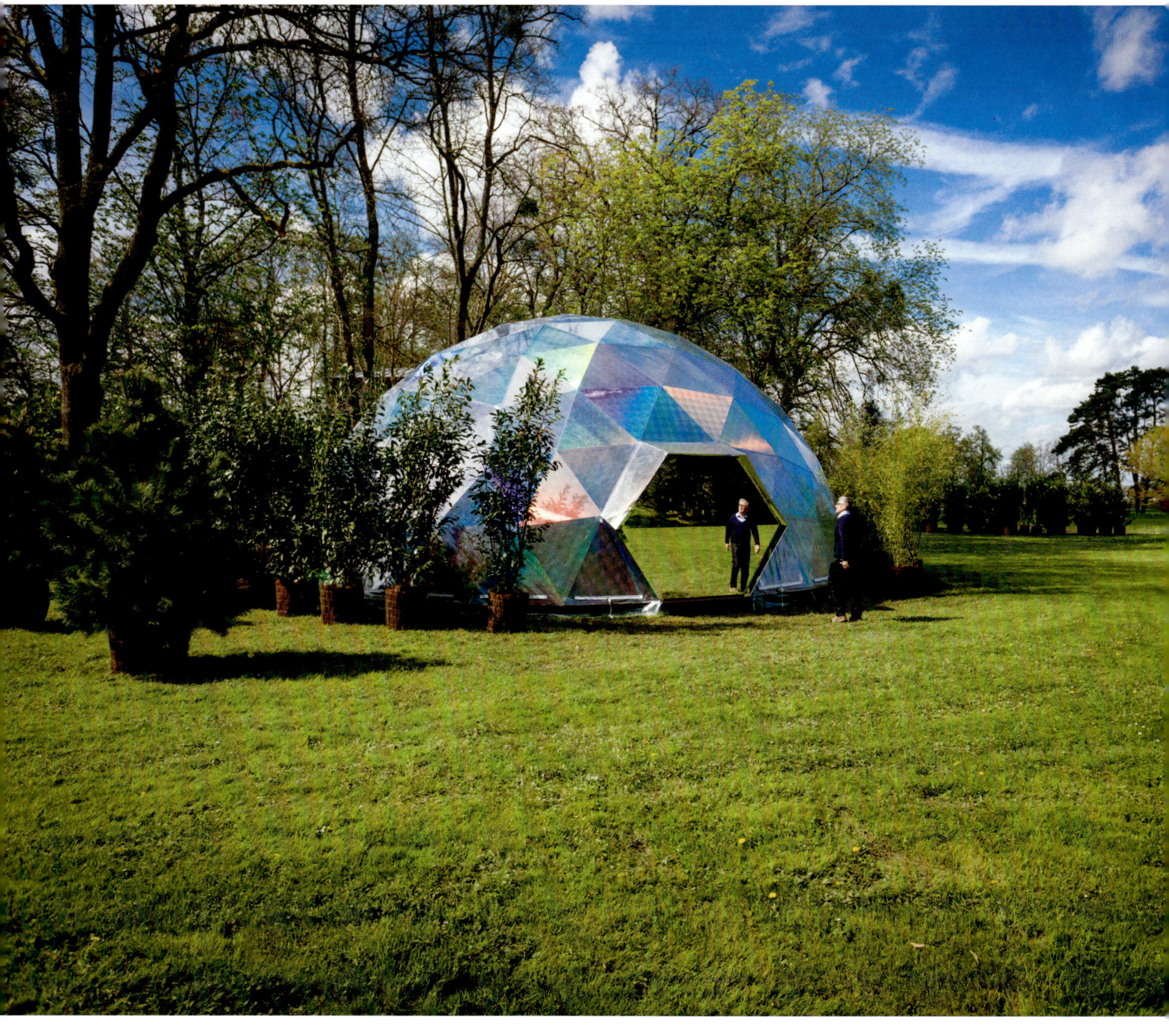

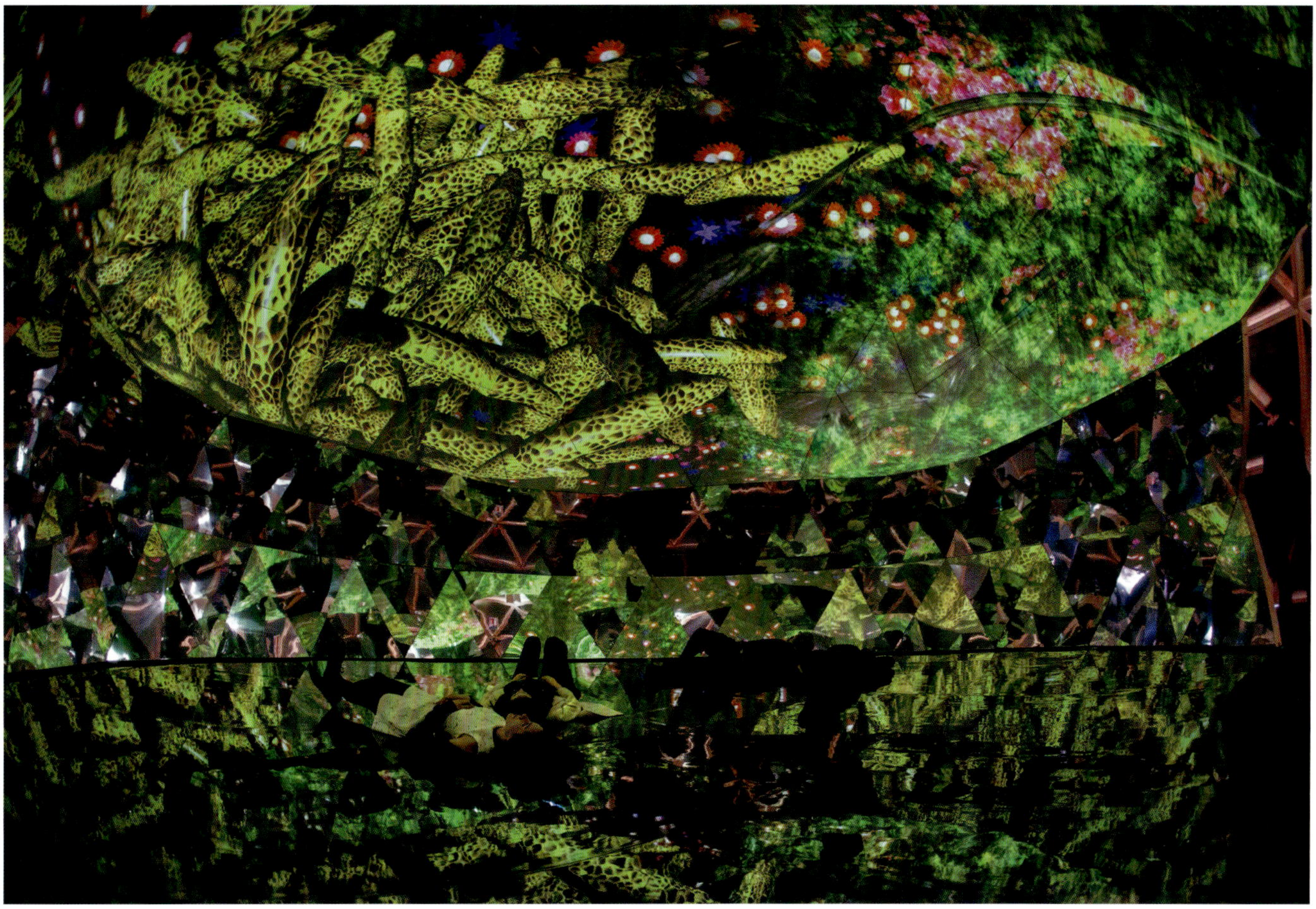

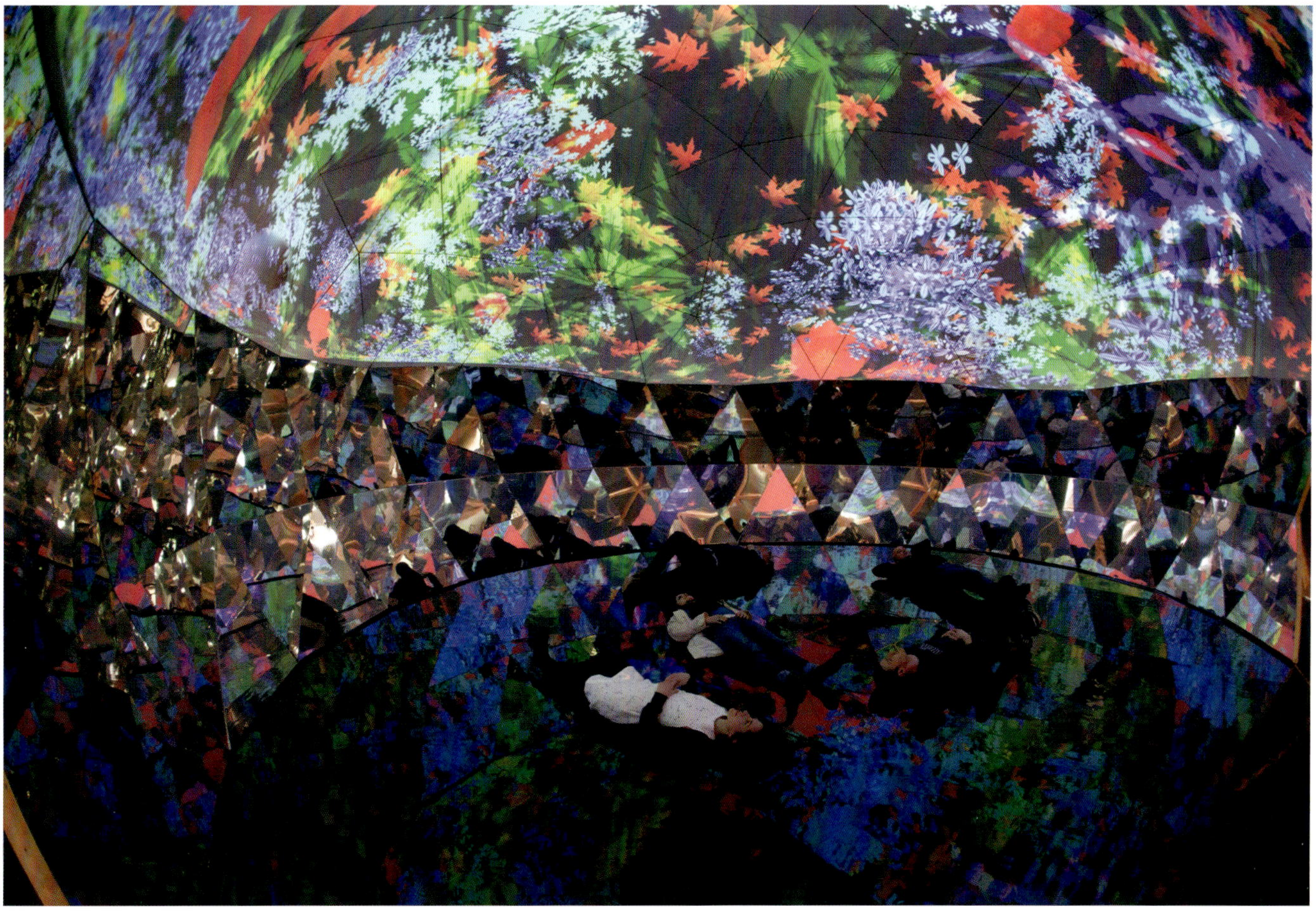

PORTA ESTEL·LAR

—

Design: **Playmodes Studio, MID**

—

Porta Estel·lar (Catalan for "Star Gate") is an immersive light and sound installation inside a plane. It invites the audience to embark on a captivating, perceptively intense cosmic journey.

Through the creation of visual and sound sequences that suggest the idea of interstellar travel, the experience takes the audience to outer space in an intense six-minute trip, from departure and takeoff to the sighting of comets, planets, galaxies, crossing nebulae and visiting alien worlds, until finally returning safely to Earth.

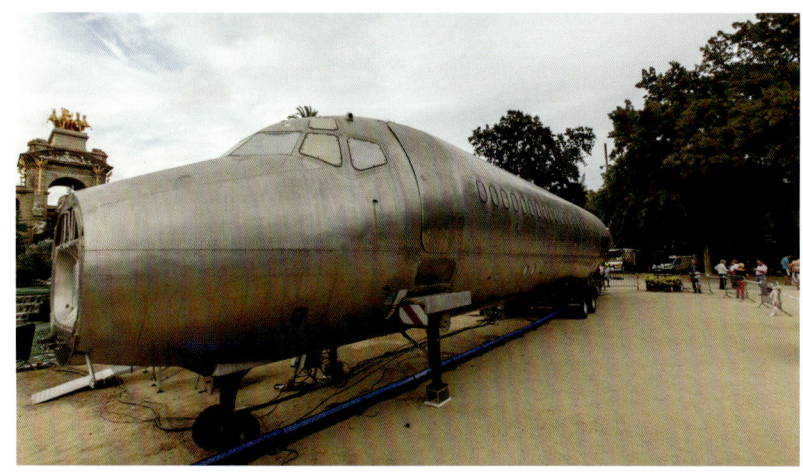

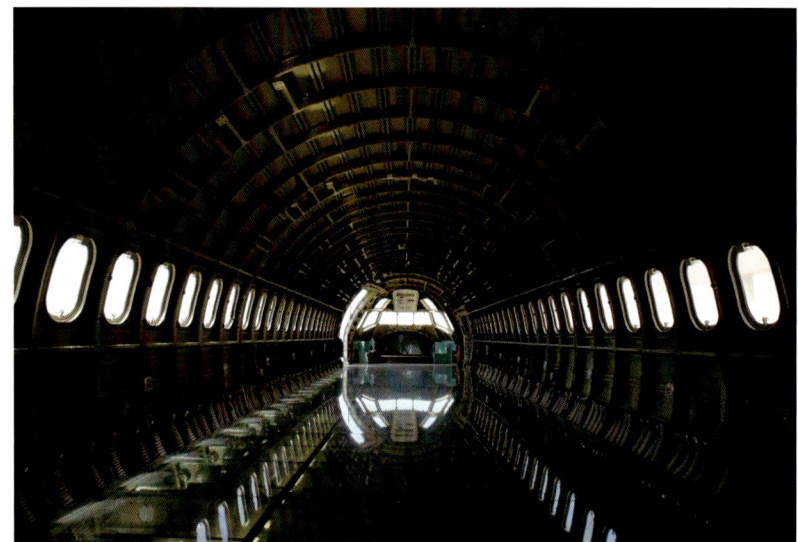

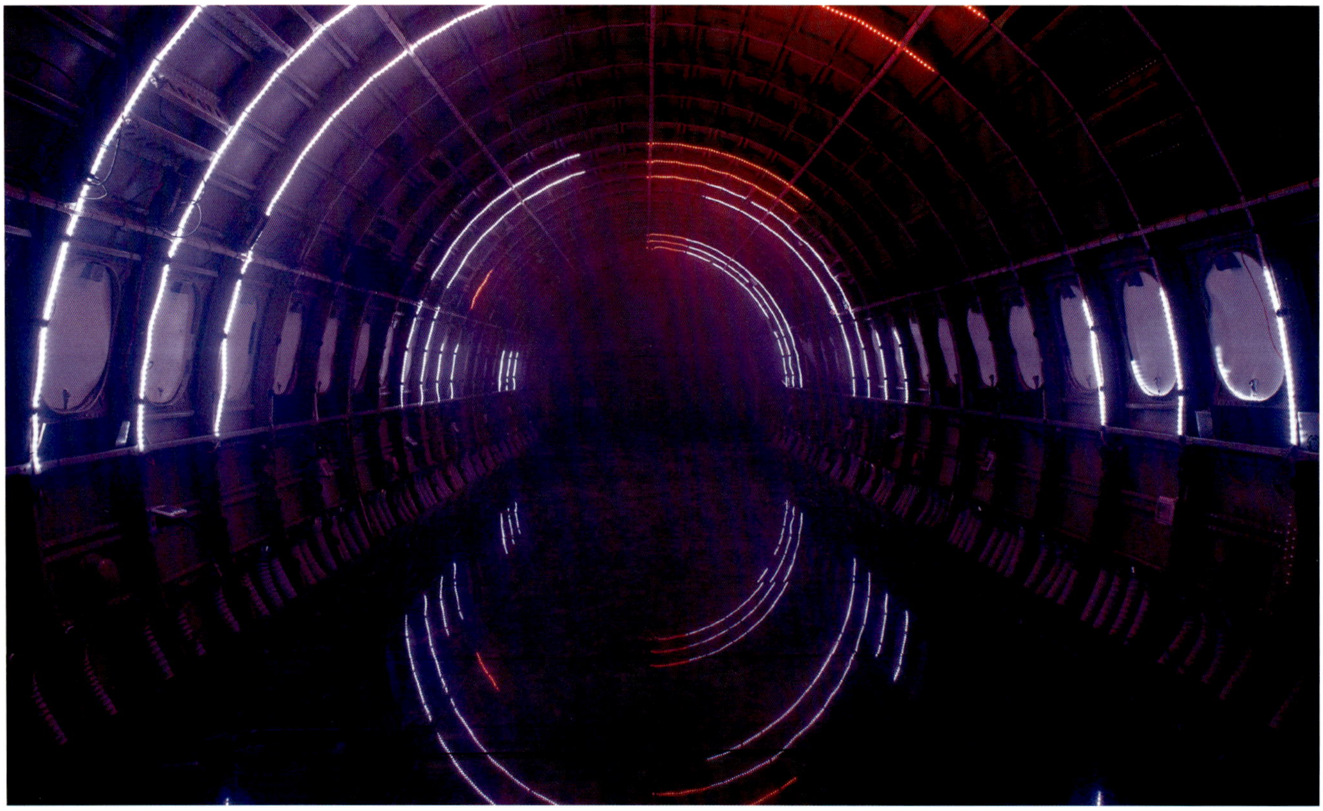

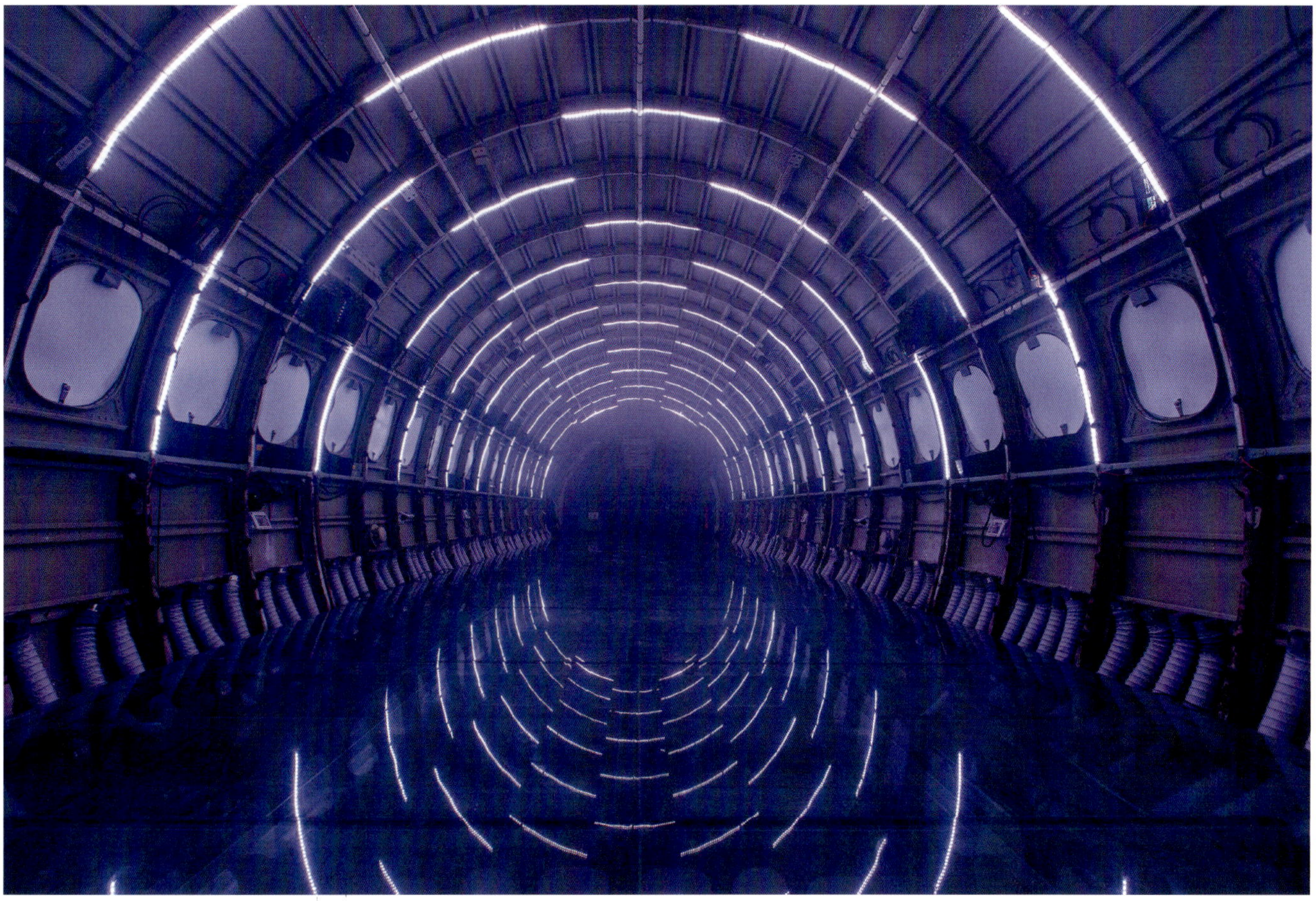

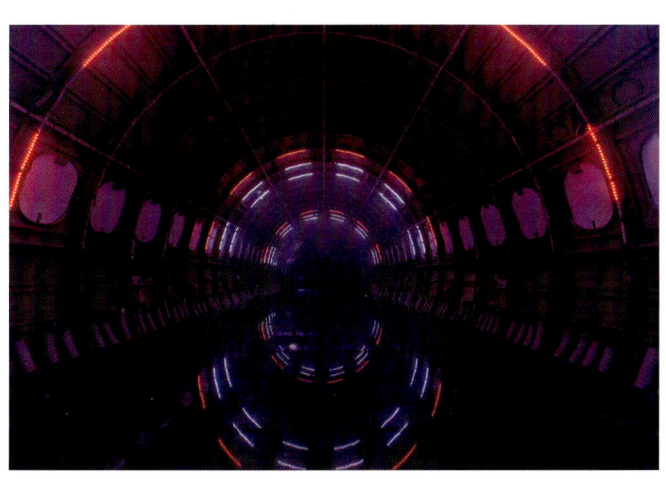

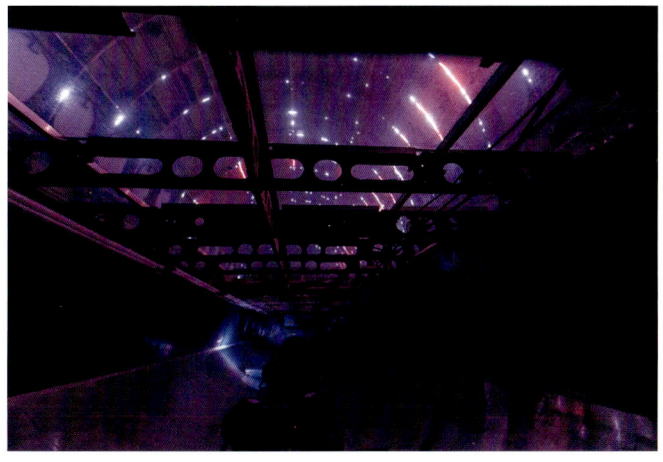

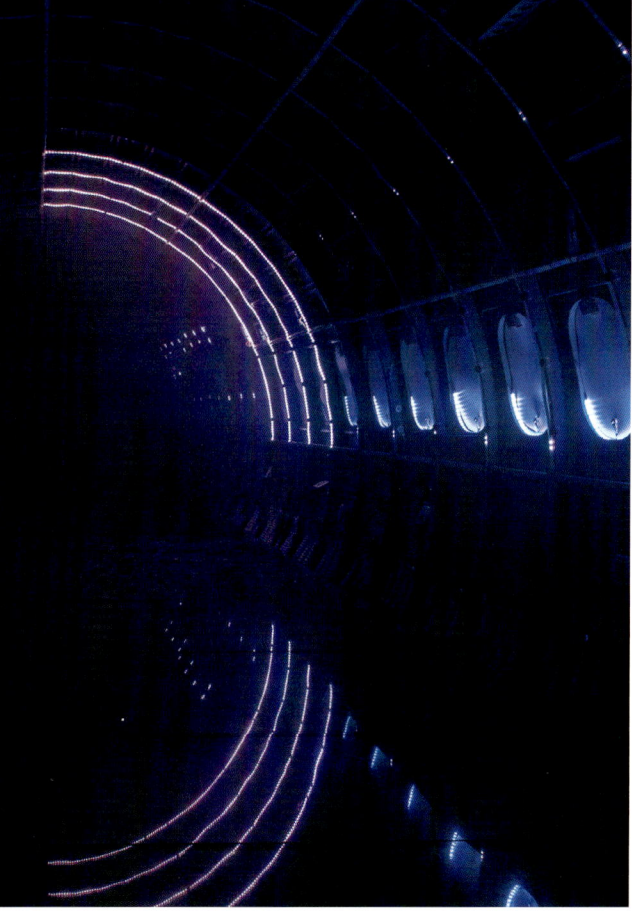

DEEP WEB

—

Design: **Christopher Bauder**
Music Design: **Robert Henke**
Photography: **Ralph Larmann**

—

Deep Web is a monumental immersive audiovisual installation created by light artist Christopher Bauder and composer and musician Robert Henke. The generative, luminous architectural structure weaves 175 motorized spheres and 12 high-power laser systems into a 25-meter-wide by 10-meter-high superstructure, bringing to life a luminous analogy to the nodes and connections of digital networks. Moving up and down, and choreographed and synchronized to an original multi-channel musical score, the spheres are illuminated by blasts of colorful laser beams resulting in three-dimensional sculptural light drawings and arrangements in Kraftwerk Berlin's cavernous darkness.

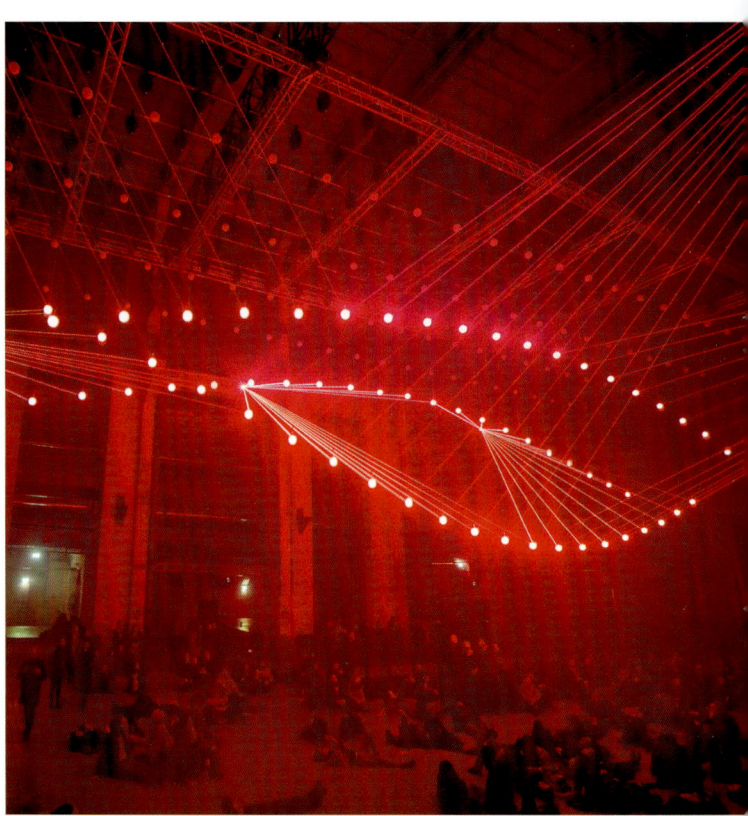

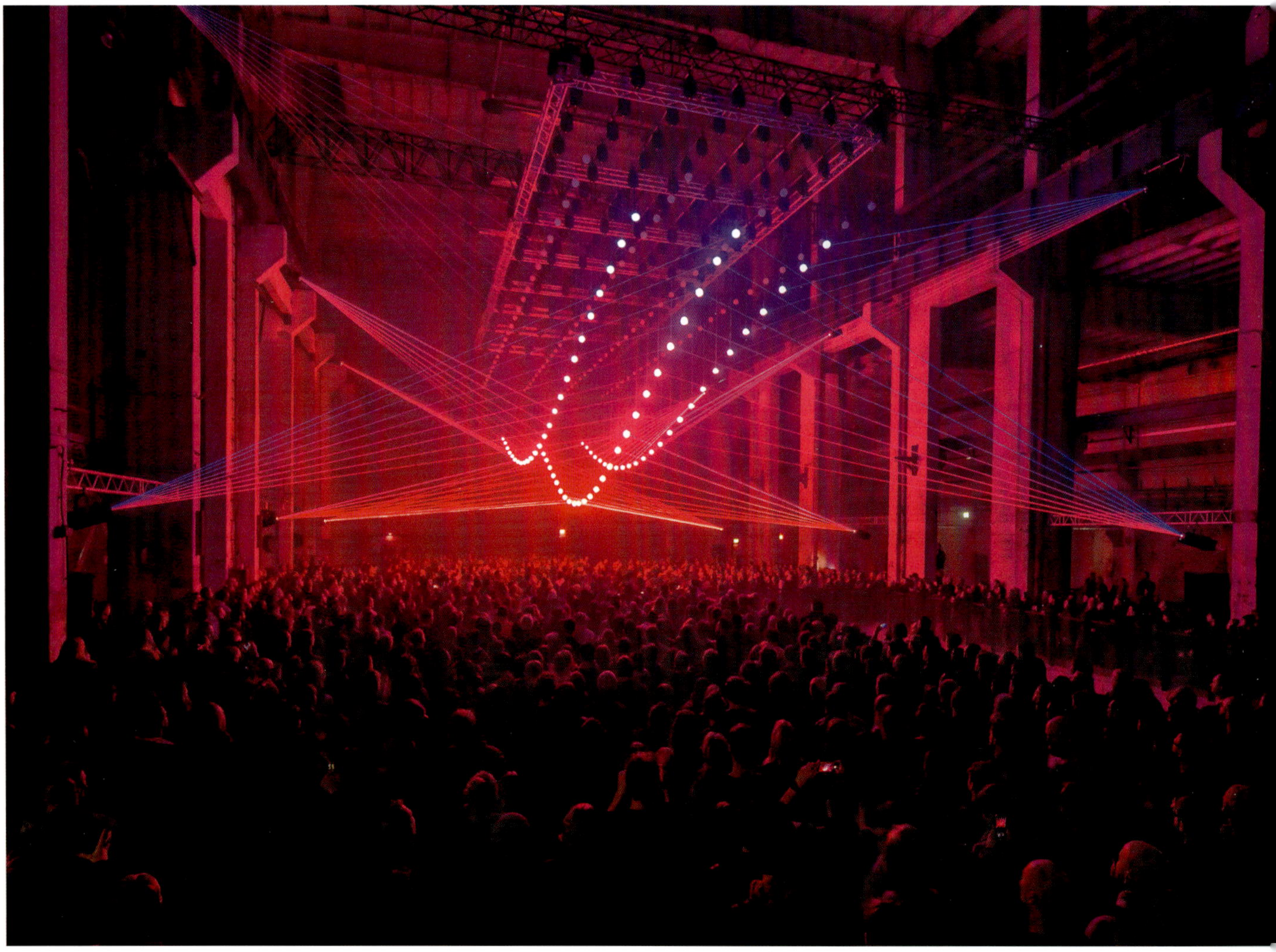

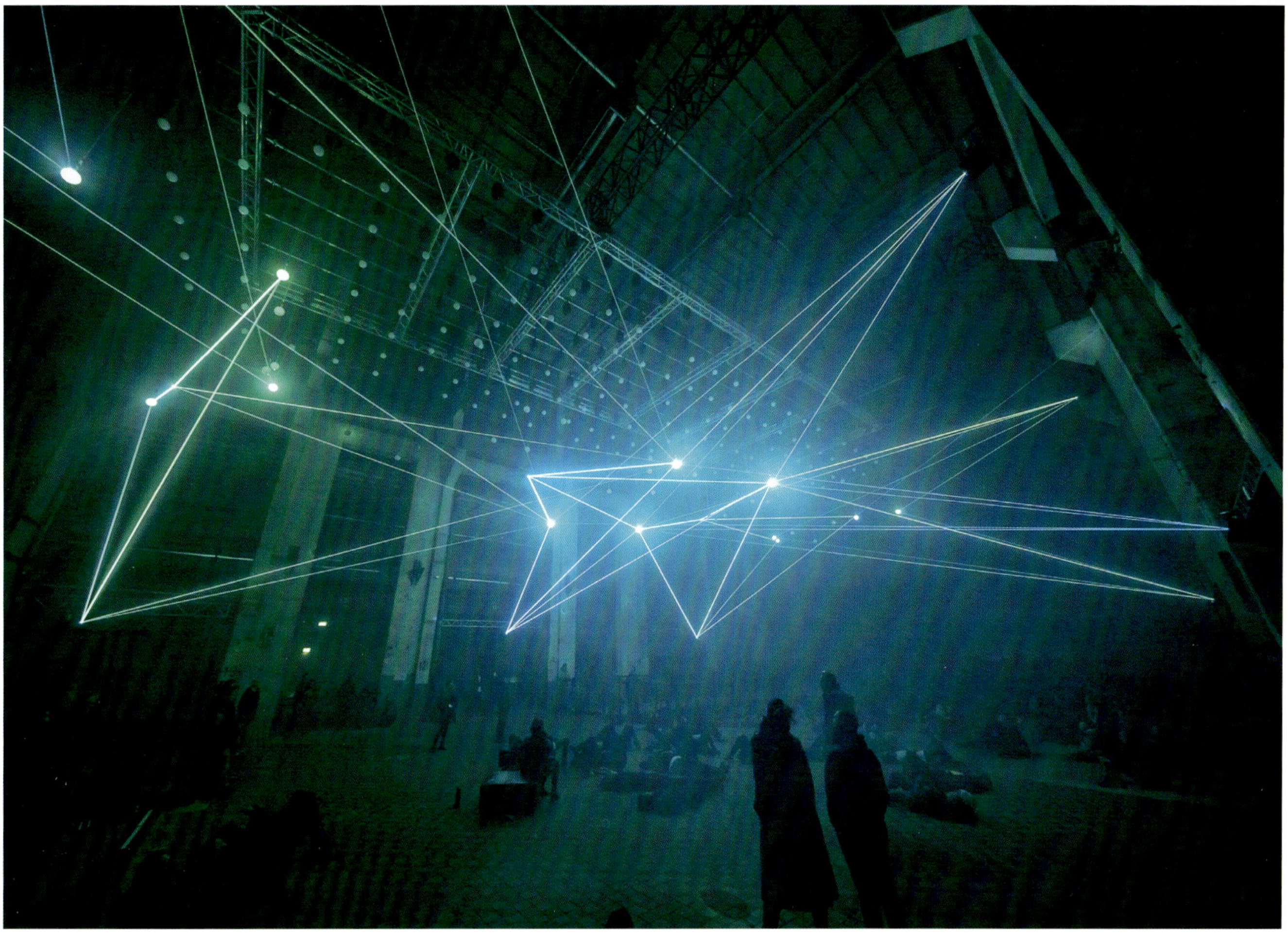

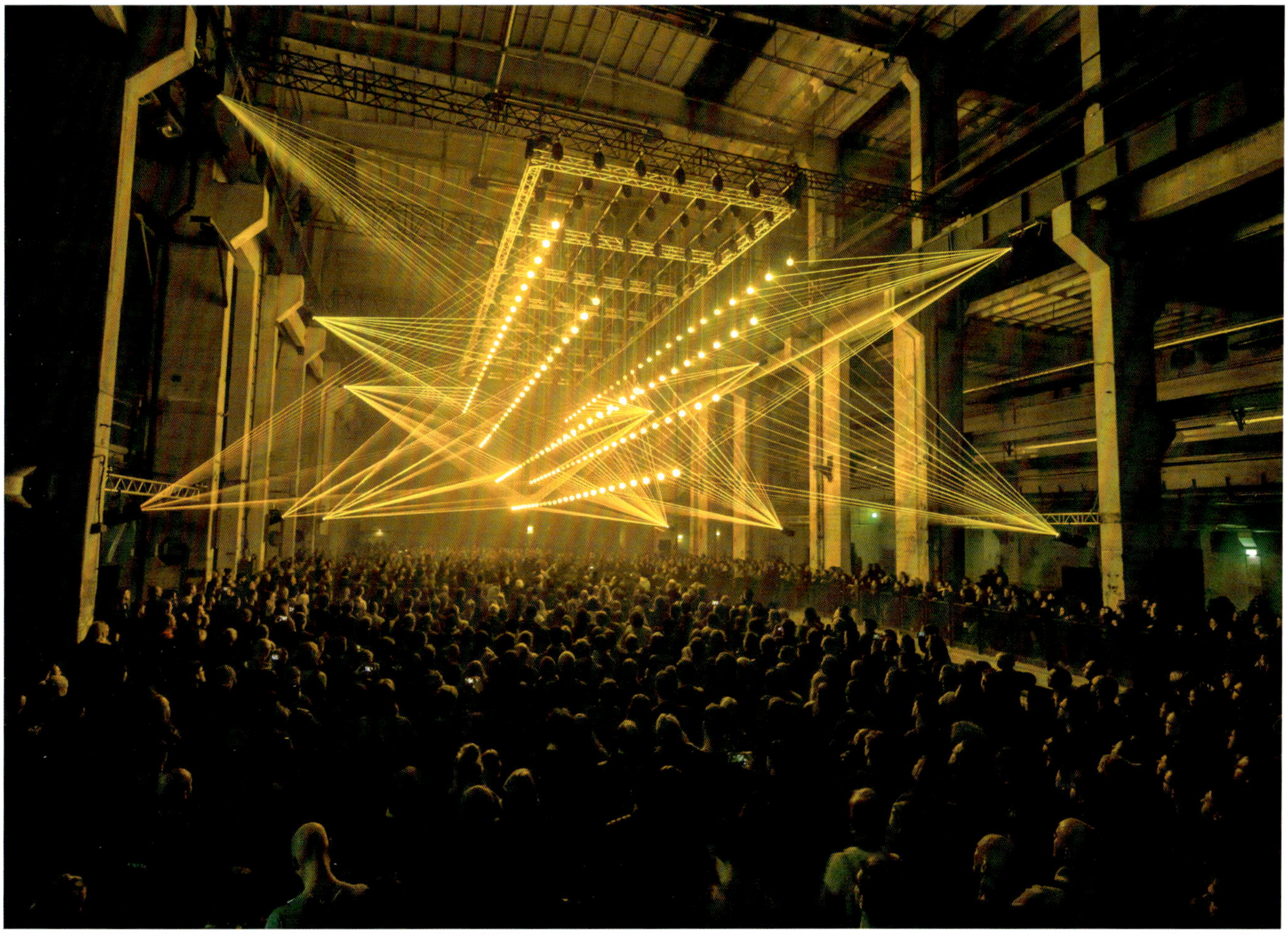

SKALAR

—

Design: **Christopher Bauder**
Music Design: **Kangding Ray**
Photography: **Ralph Larmann**

—

SKALAR is a large-scale art installation that explores the complex impact of light and sound on human perception. By combining a vast array of kinetic mirrors, perfectly synchronized moving lights and a sophisticated multi-channel sound system, *SKALAR* reflects on the fundamental nature and essence of human emotions.

SKALAR is an intense journey through the cycle of the human emotional experience. The full spectrum of emotional experiences is triggered by ever-changing tonalities in light, sound, and motion. Feelings of awe, surprise, exhilaration, anticipation, and overwhelm are created, explored, and repeated in cycles throughout the piece, providing a collective and yet highly individual emotional experience.

SKALAR is a central piece within light artist Christopher Bauder's body of work, reflecting his deep fascination with light. Light and darkness as endless cycles of day and night define people's perception of time and influence their emotions. In *SKALAR*, light is treated as a solid material that can be sculpted and shaped to architectural dimensions, evoking abstract emotional associations. Intertwined with musician and composer Kangding Ray's tireless exploration of textures, rhythm, and sound design, the silence of darkness is filled with iridescent formations of spatial light and sound. Measuring 45m in length, 20m in width, and 10m in height, the generative luminous structure encompasses a perfectly synchronous interplay of 65 motorized mirrors, 90 moving lights, and multichannel sound.

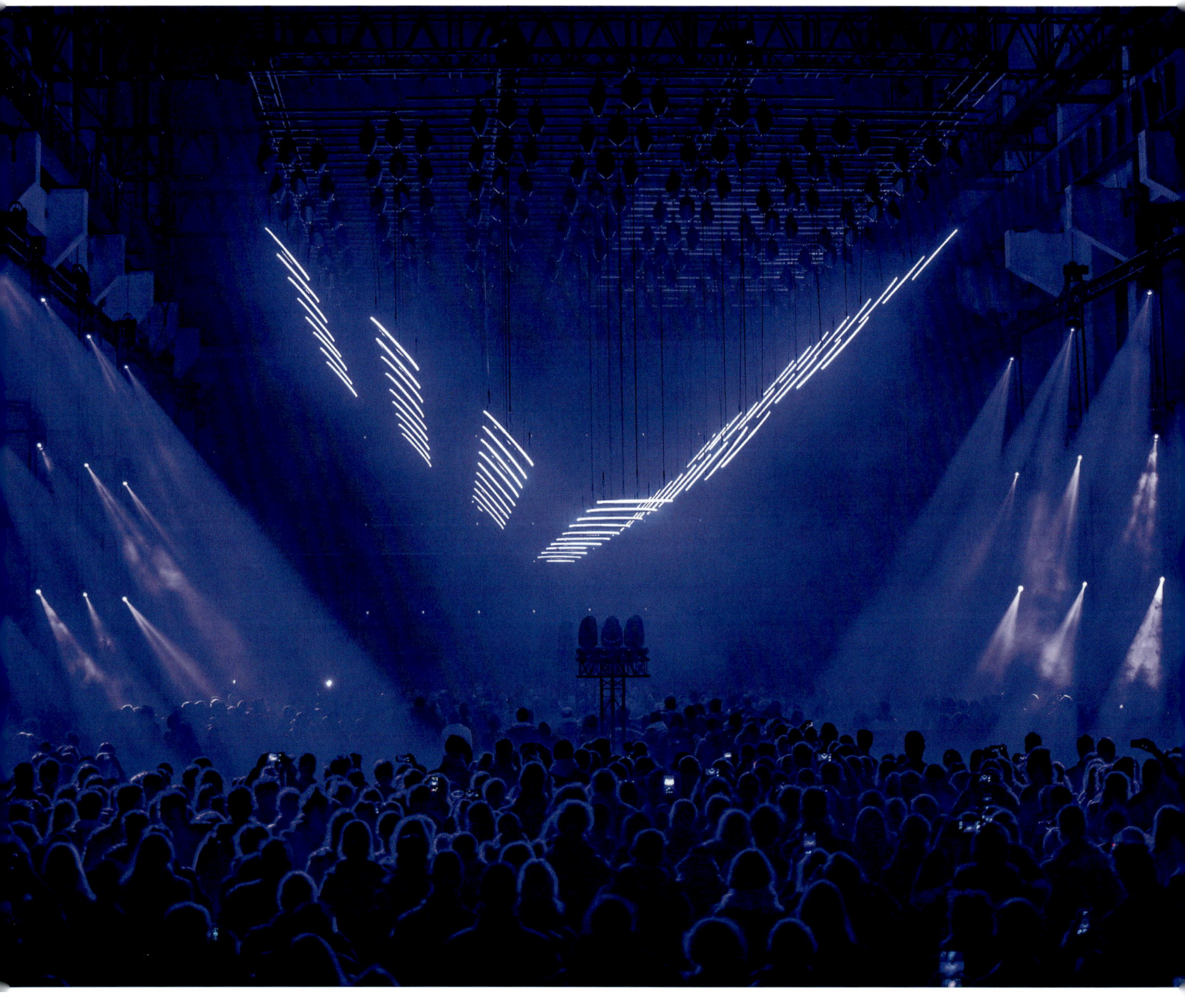

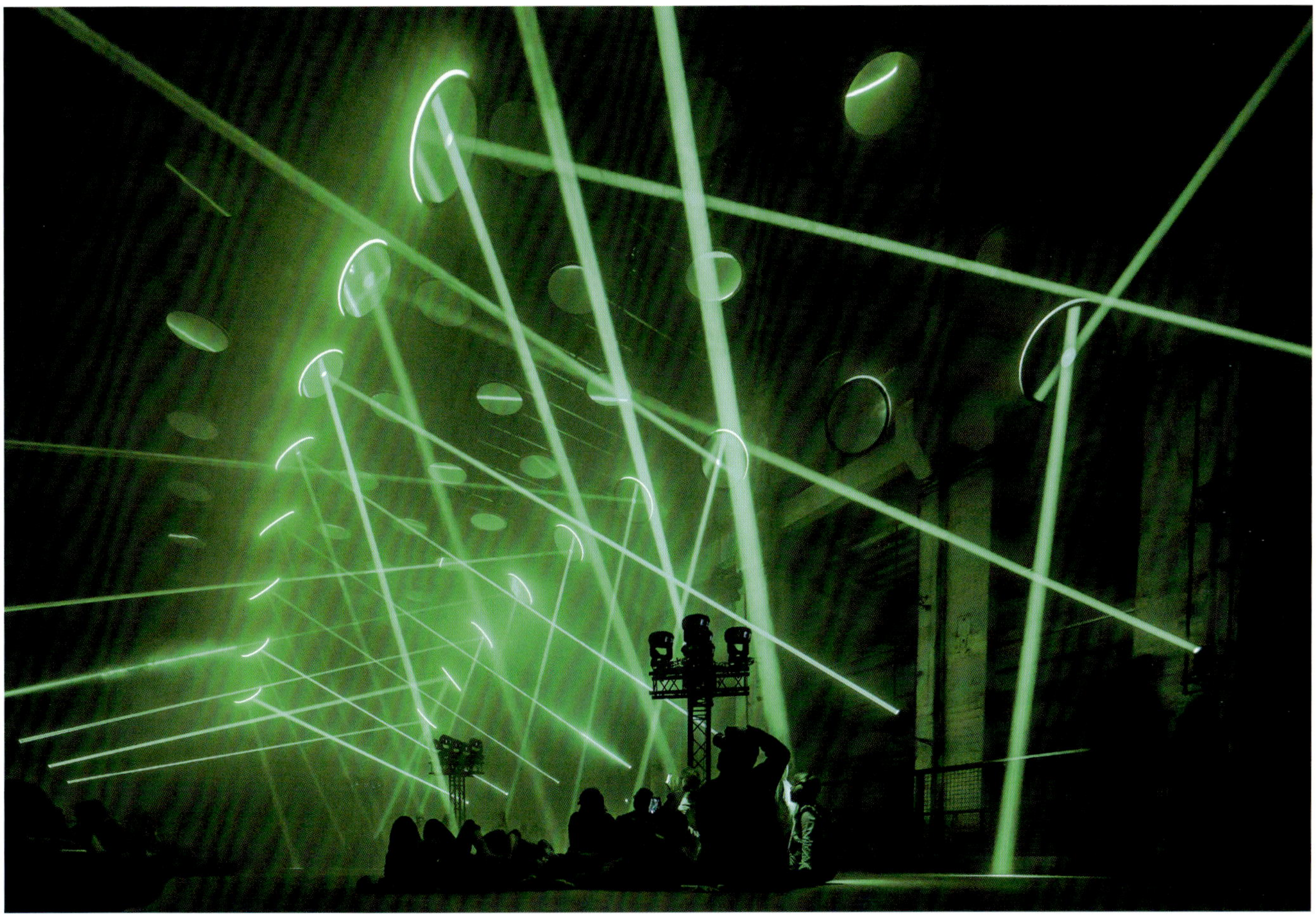

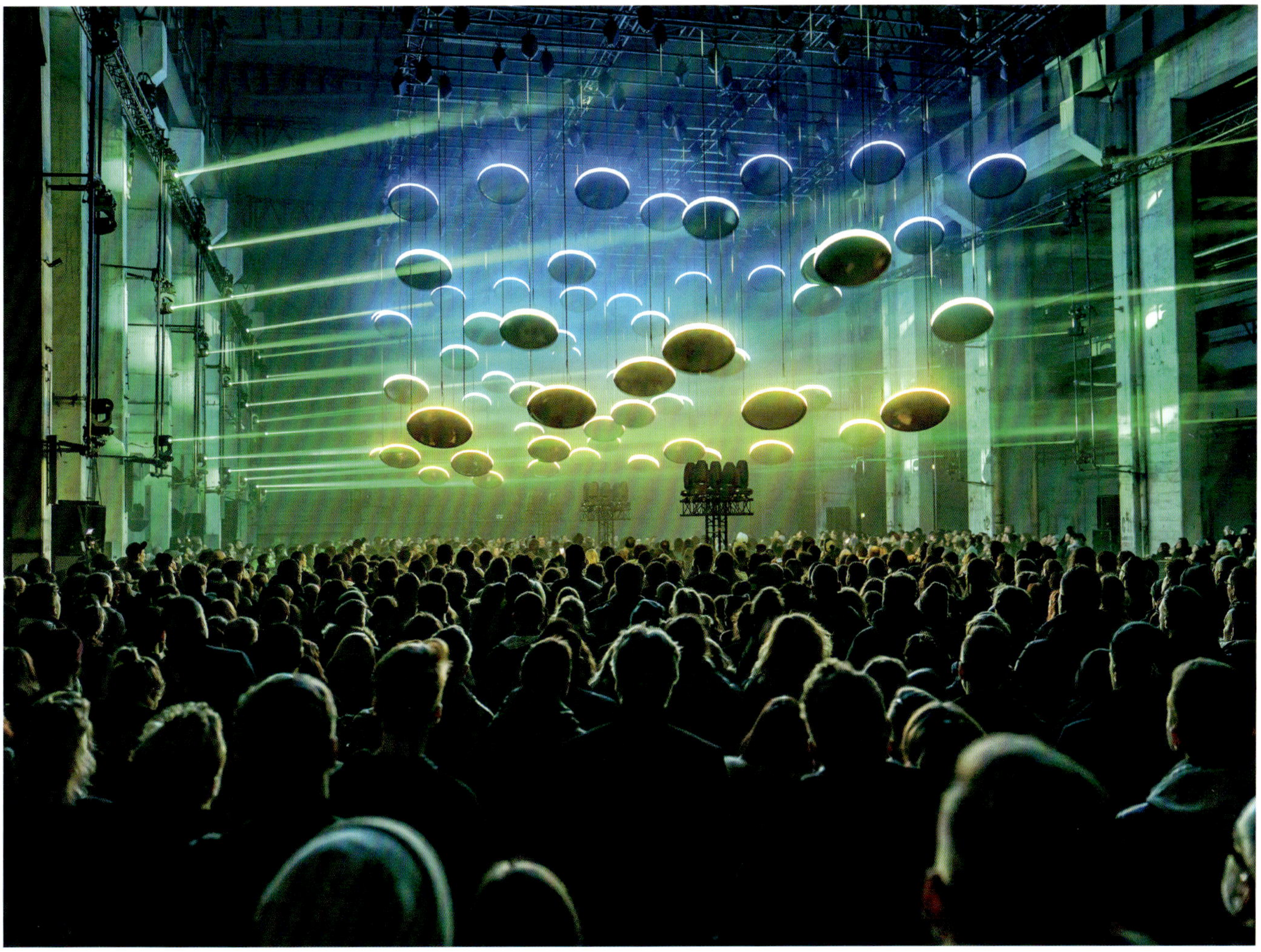

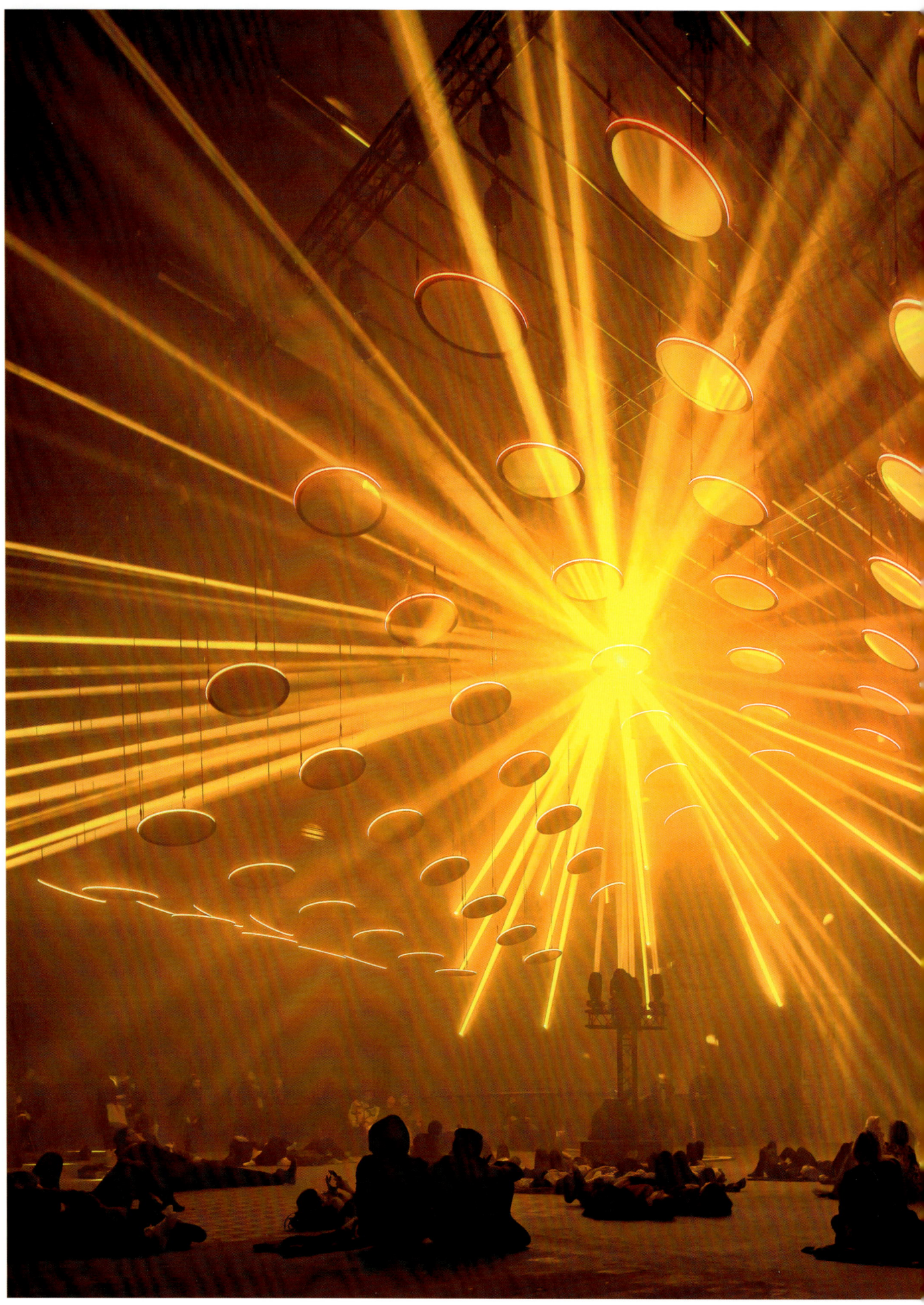

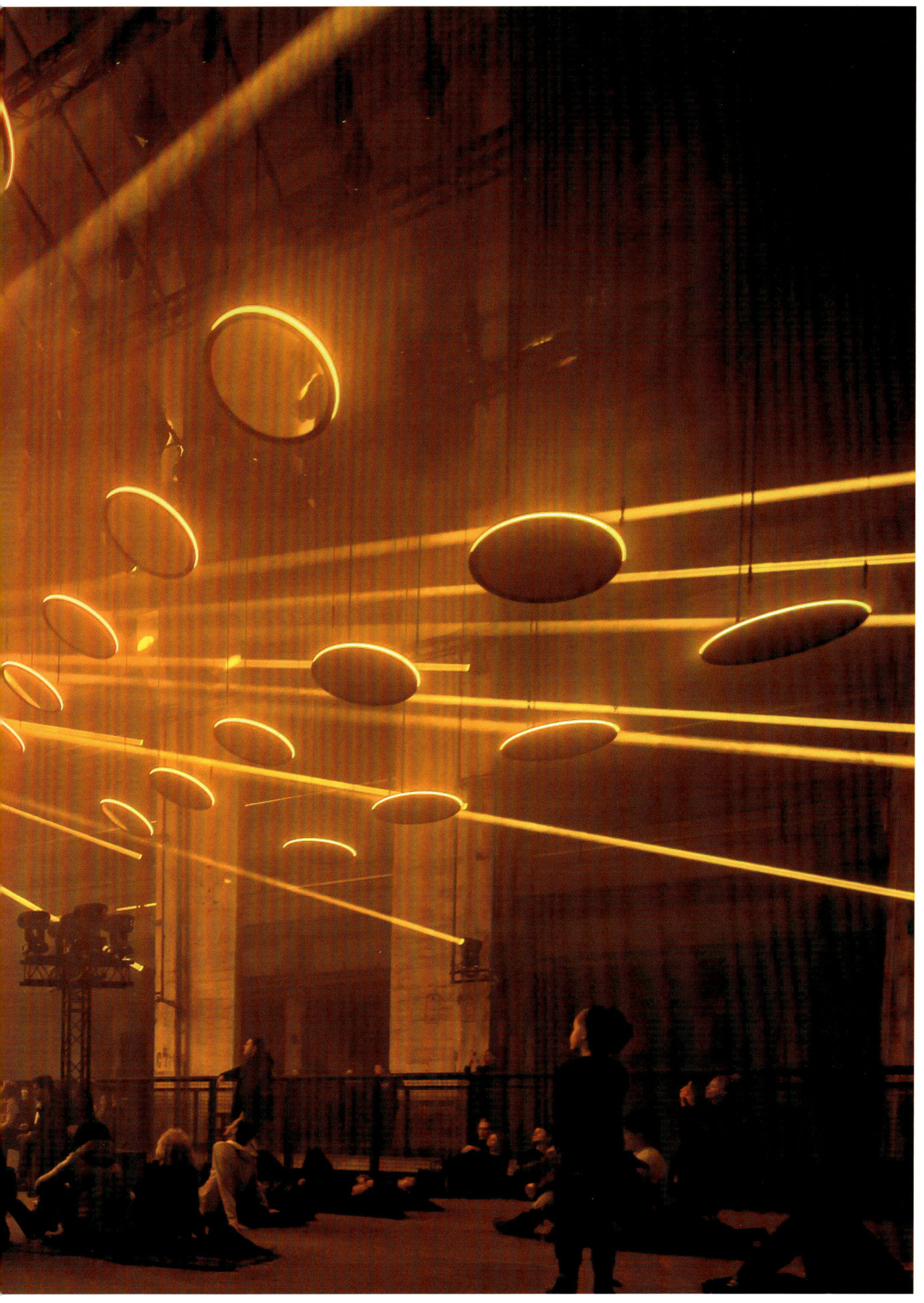

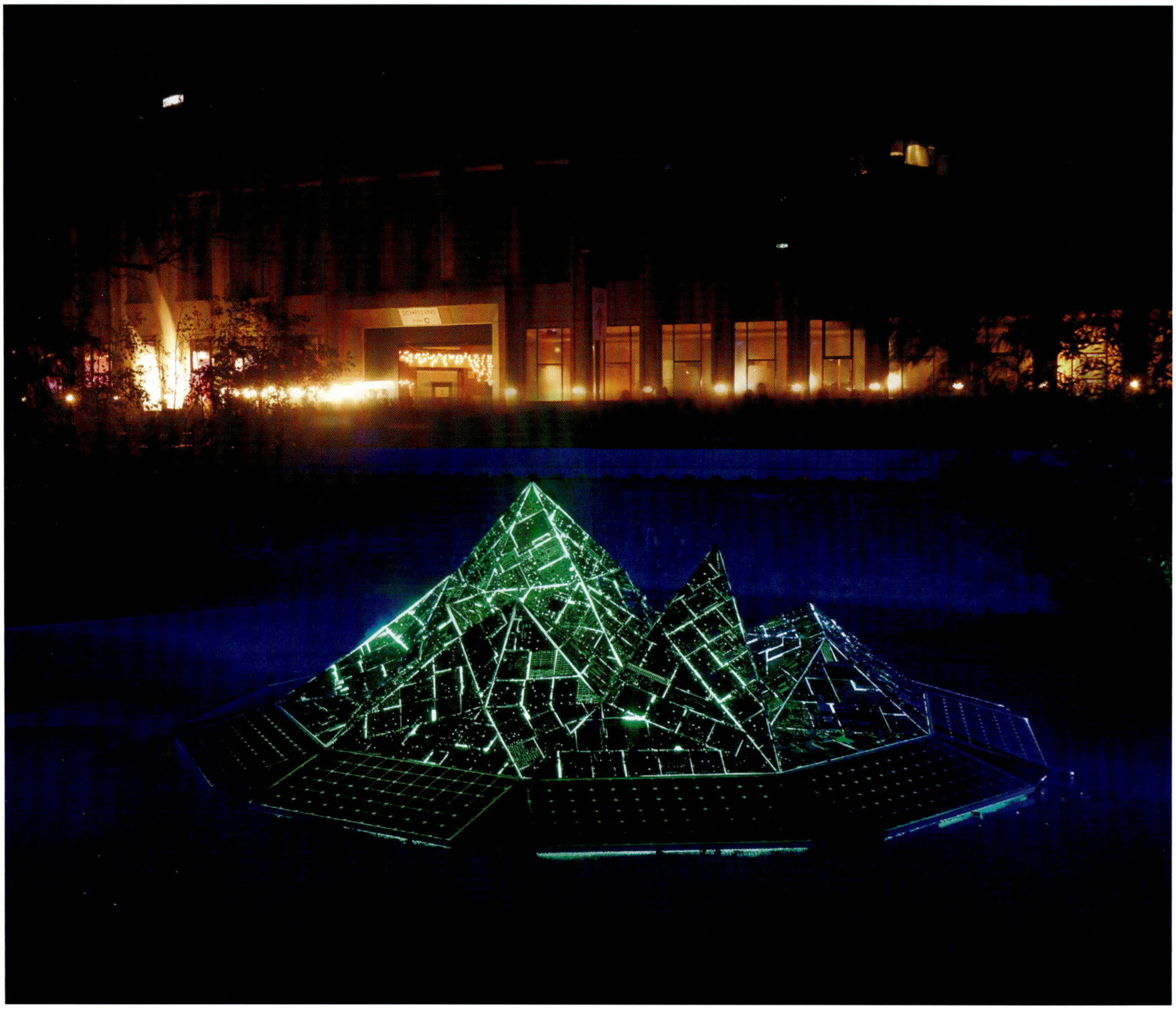

ELANTICA

—

Design: **TOM DEKYVERE**
Photography: **VALERY BELLENGIER**

—

"Our world creates a digital version of reality. And beyond the rather computerized aspect, an effective materialization takes place. Natural rock formations are turning into virtual material, the human mind and body get hardwired extensions... Fauna and flora are replaced by artificial artifacts. In this stadium the visuals remain as we have imagined them, but slowly they evolve into nature-based forms. A replica of our world, camouflaged with conventional skin, designed by a digital source... *Elantica* raises questions about our fractalized acts, in search of a balance that suits both man and robot. The island of *Elantica* is a scale model of this new zone we are looking at from a distance..." — Frank Despriet

Elantica is made of discarded computer circuit boards and e-waste materials. These images show the work at Glow Eindhoven (NL) 2017, where it was first exhibited. Nowadays it travels the world, appearing at various museums and in public spaces.

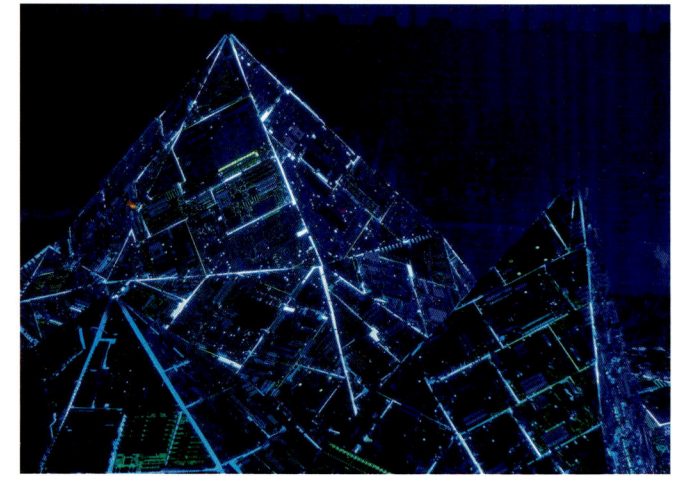

OUR HOUSE

—

Design: **Tom Dekyvere**
Photography: **Jon Bilous**

—

"*Our House* stands for togetherness, happiness, and joyfulness, but also for danger, friction and tension... Tom Dekyvere explores the ideas behind individualism, groups of people living together, which all illustrate togetherness and collaboration in contrast with nature and technology through the metaphoric symbols of sound and vision. The (dis)connections made between people can be displayed as a web. The work mirrors this web idea, as hundreds of meters of light-emitting rope are tied together to form a network. This network is the reflection of our current society, that merges with nature and where people express themselves." — Frank Despriet

Our house has been exhibited in several forms, always site-specific—Dekyvere and his team build each installation from scratch into an existing location. Here it is pictured in Baltimore, Maryland (USA) in 2017, in front of the National Aquarium during the annual event Light City Baltimore.

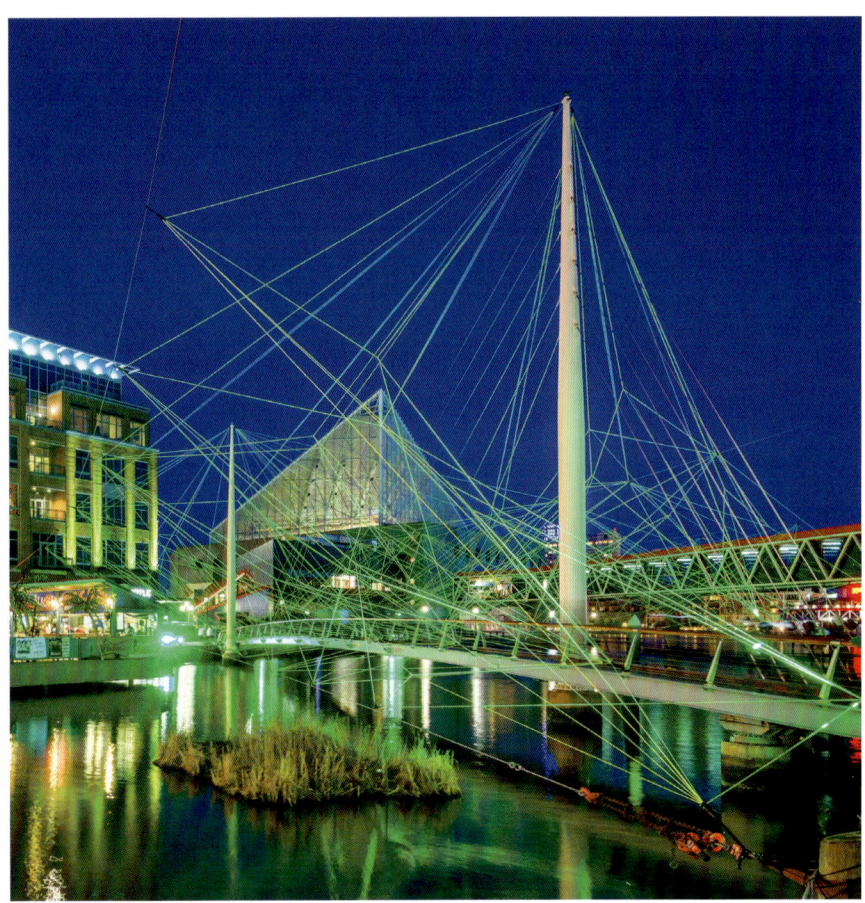

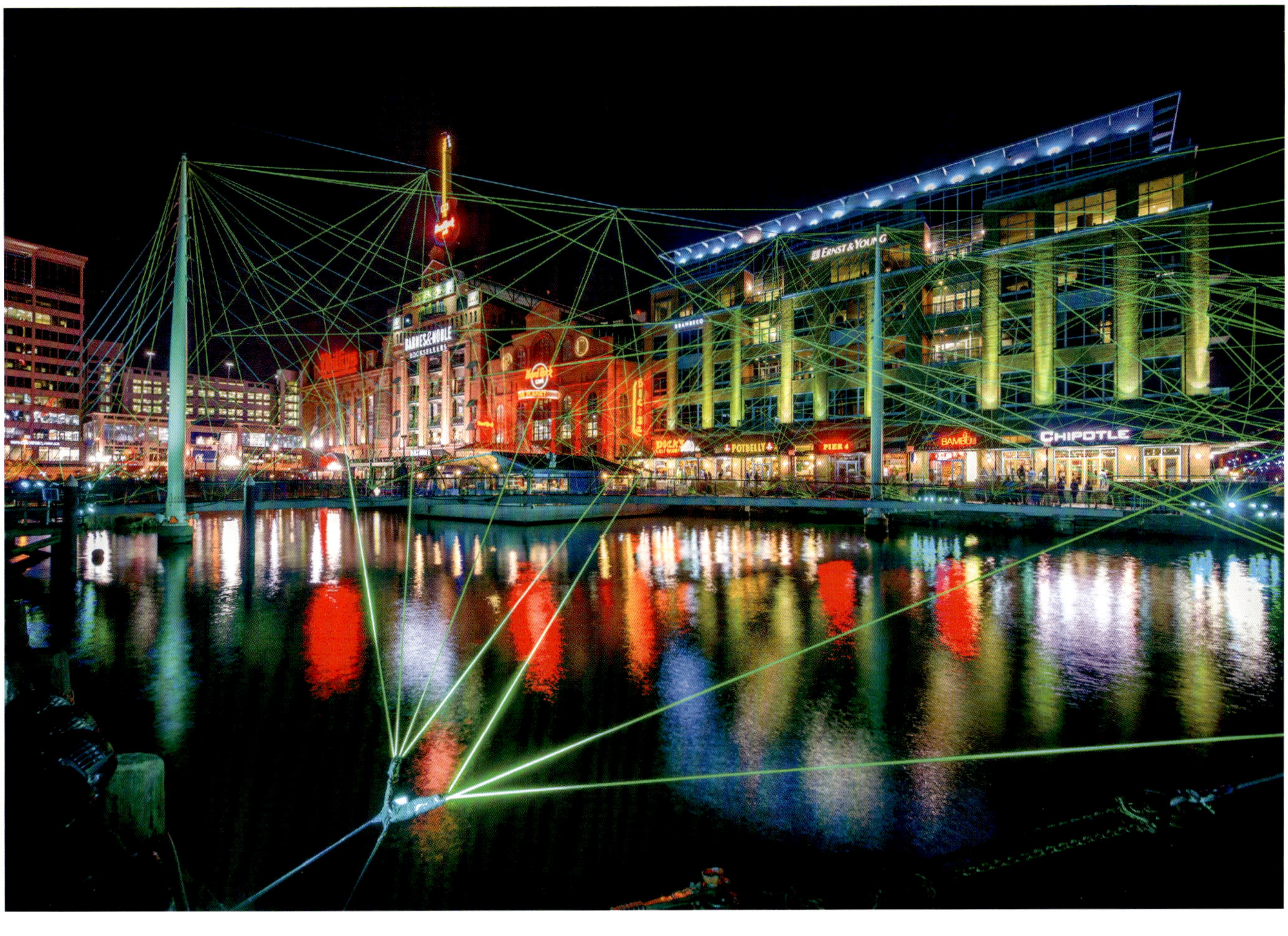

WAVEFRAME

—

Design: **Playmodes Studio**

—

Installed for the DGTL festival in Barcelona, *WaveFrame* is a public sculpture formed by square arches for a total length of around 70 meters, creating a light tunnel where people can stand or walk.

Using oscillator-generated pixel textures, wave forms fill the LED tubes with pulsating light. When delayed from one arch to the other, light creates perspective and time effects, reinforcing the idea of traveling inside a tunnel.

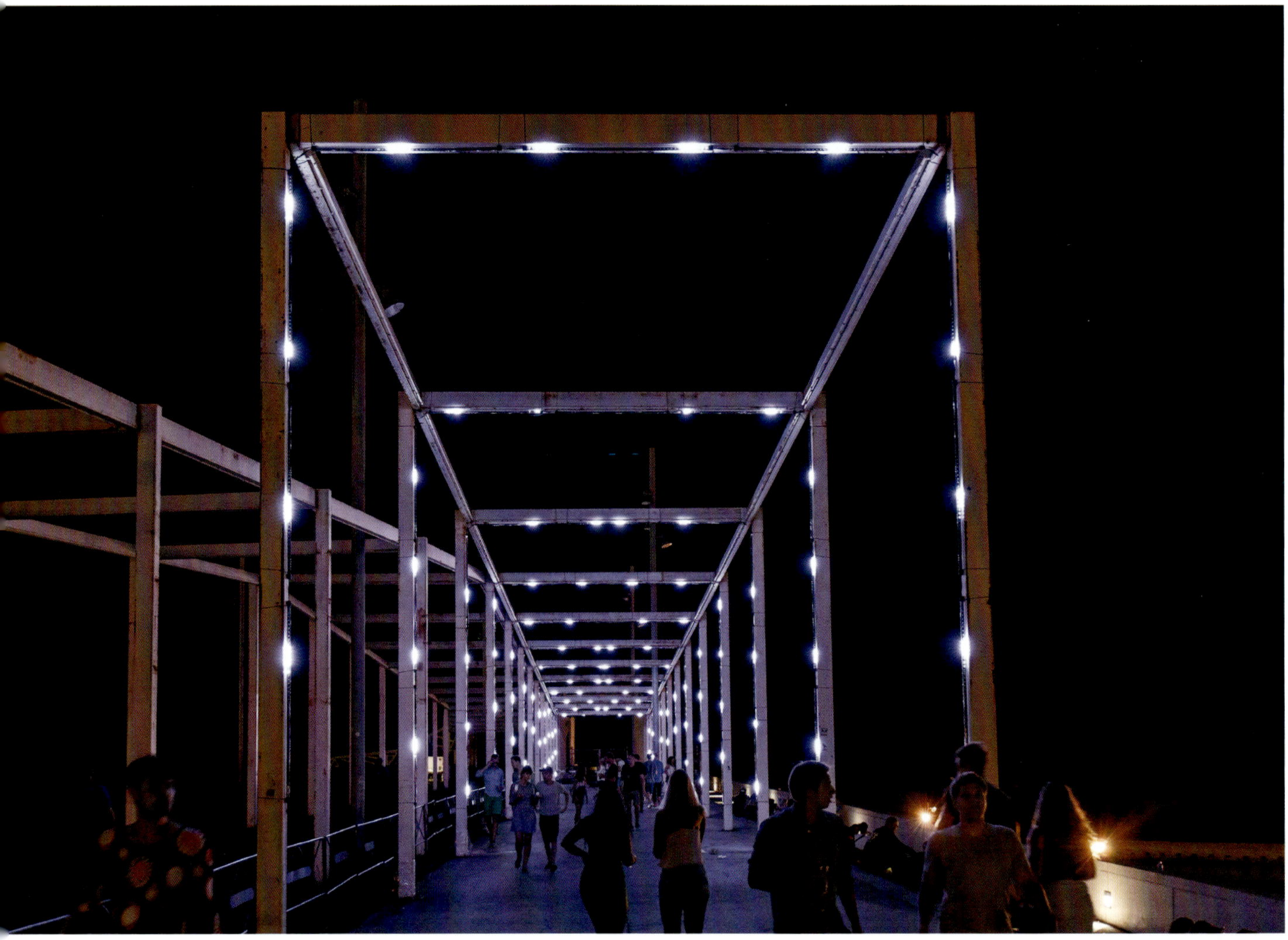

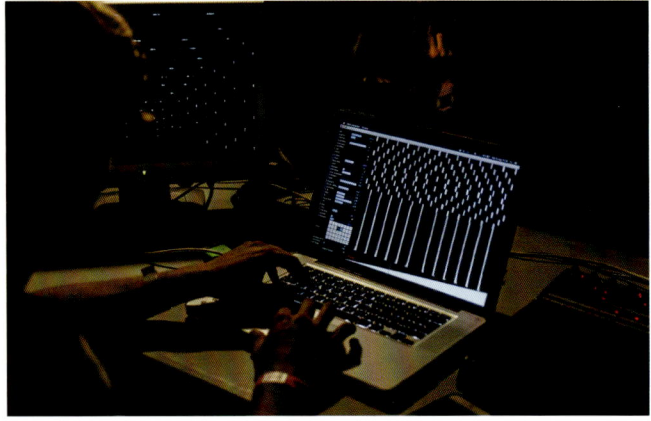

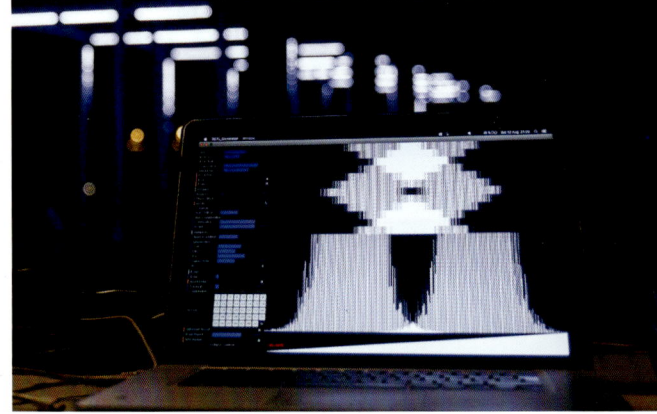

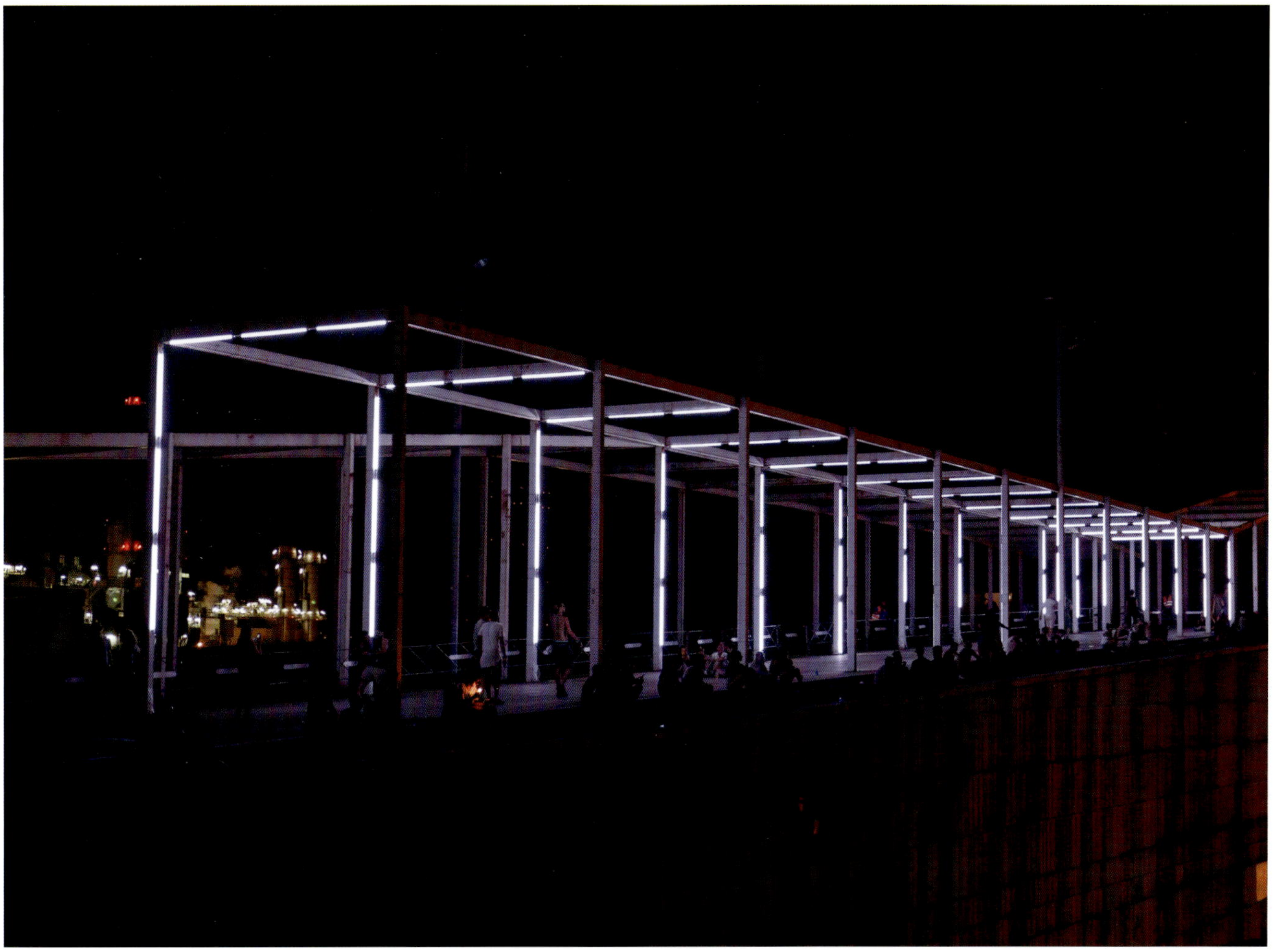

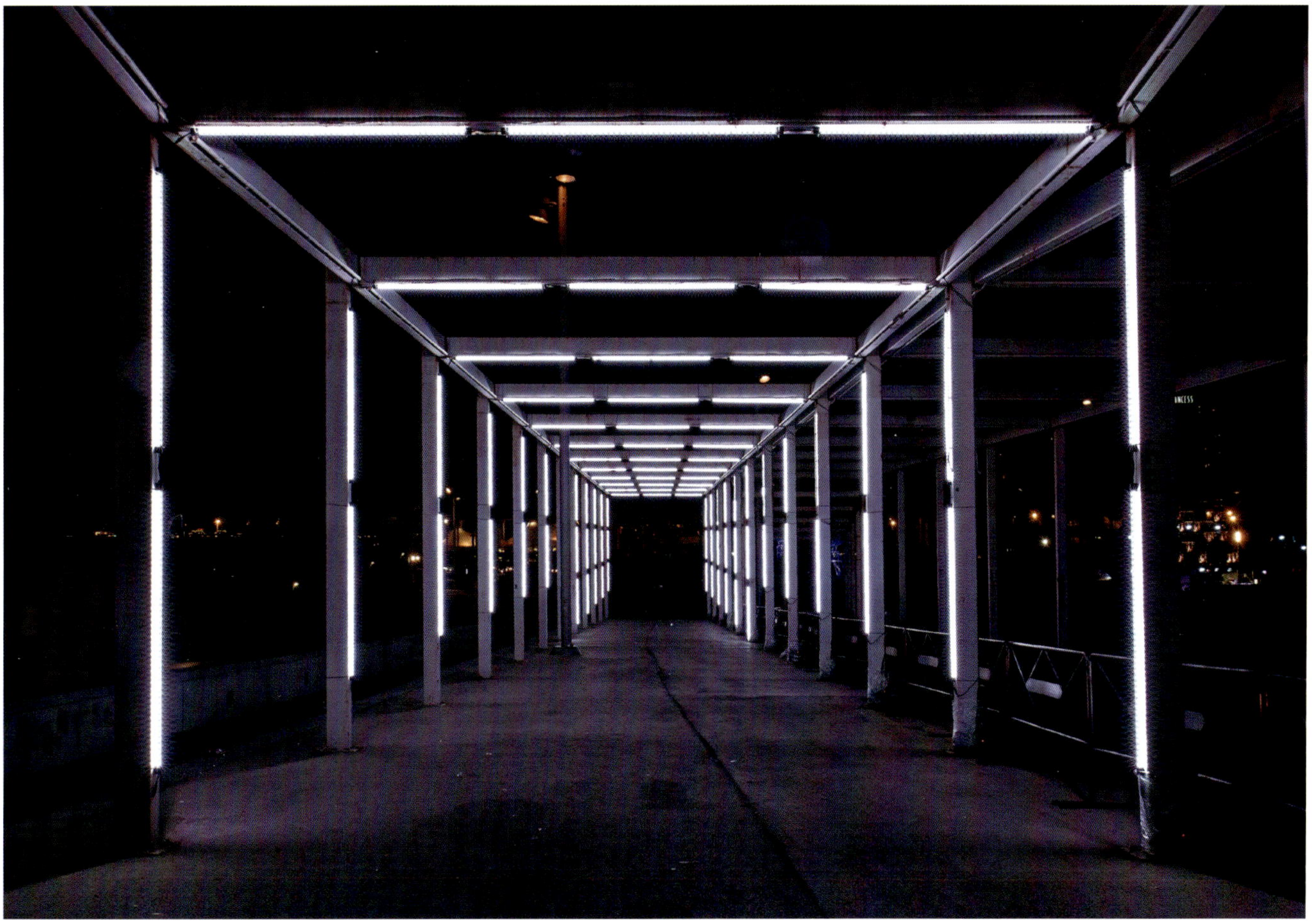

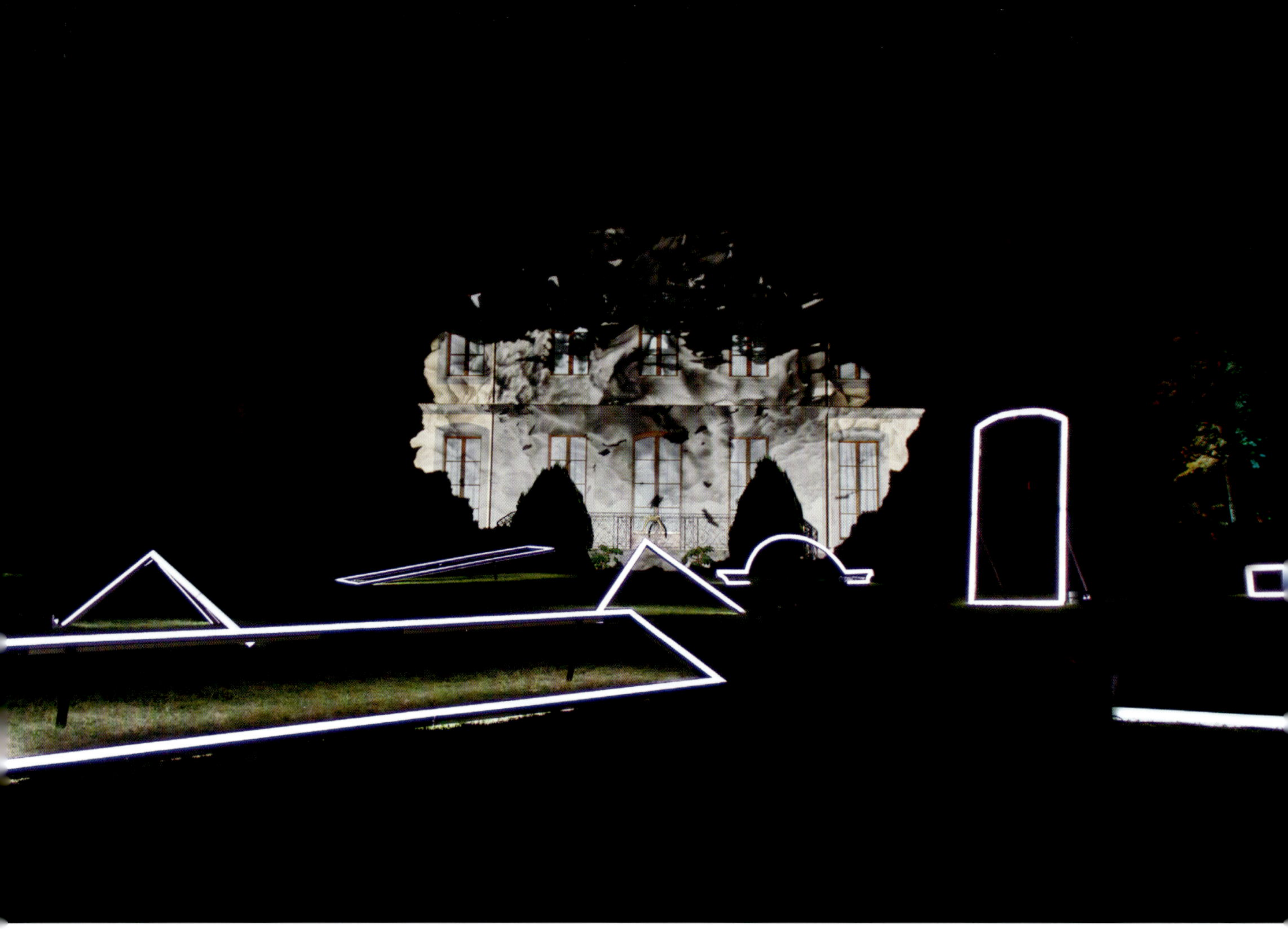

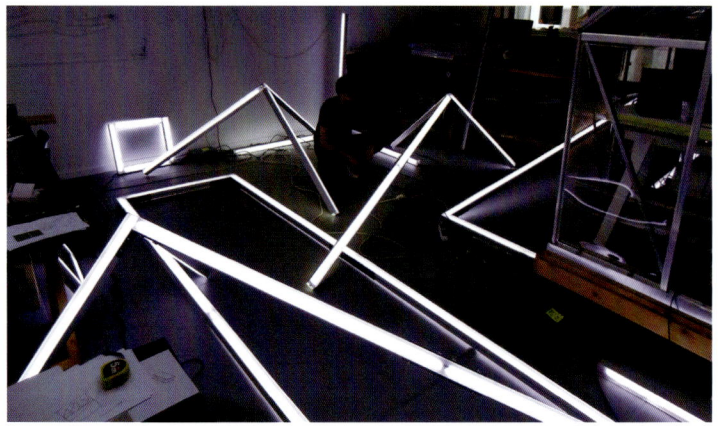

FUTURE RUINS

—

Design: **Romain Tardy**

—

Future Ruins is a site-specific installation designed for
the garden of the Musée de l'Elysée in Lausanne. The
installation combines digital projection on the main
facade of the museum with 12 illuminated aluminum
structures in the shape of architectural elements from
the building at full-scale size, spread on the ground
in a random order. The installation also features an
8-channel soundtrack.

Evoking both technology and neoclassicism, these
structures are the potential remains of our world,
suspended in time. Though they have collapsed, they
still light up the night.

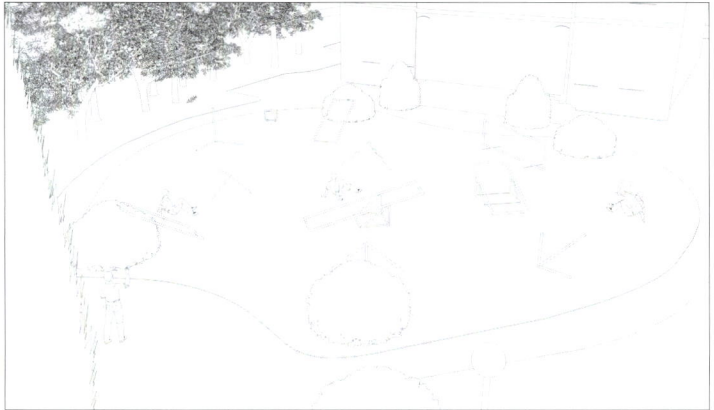

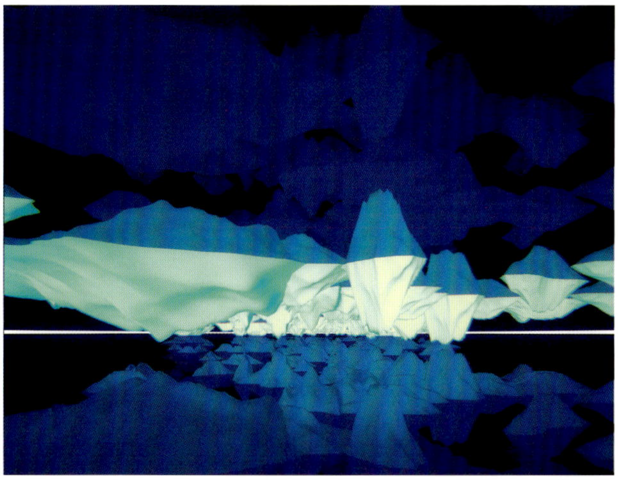

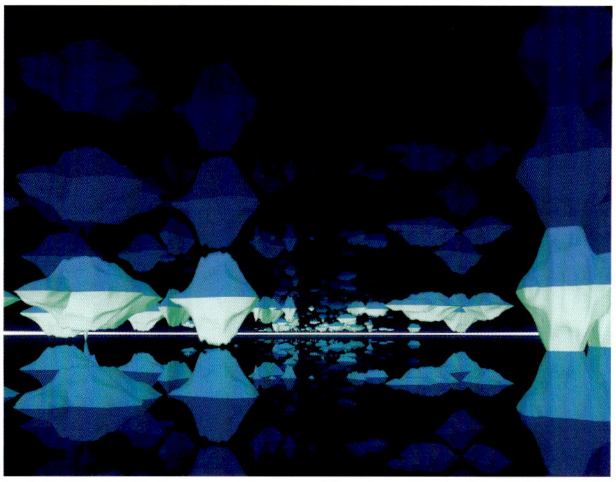

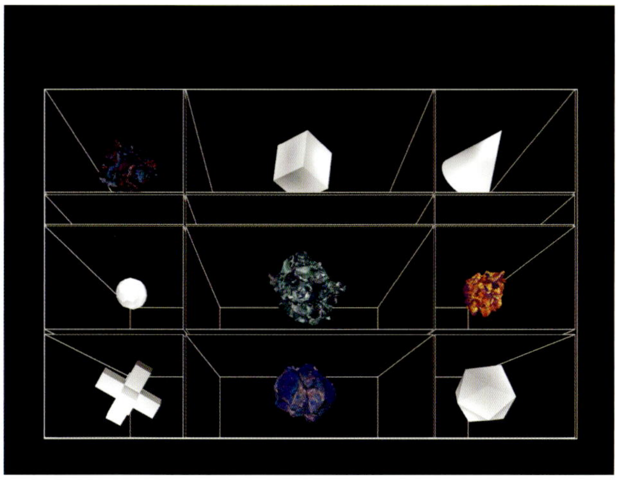

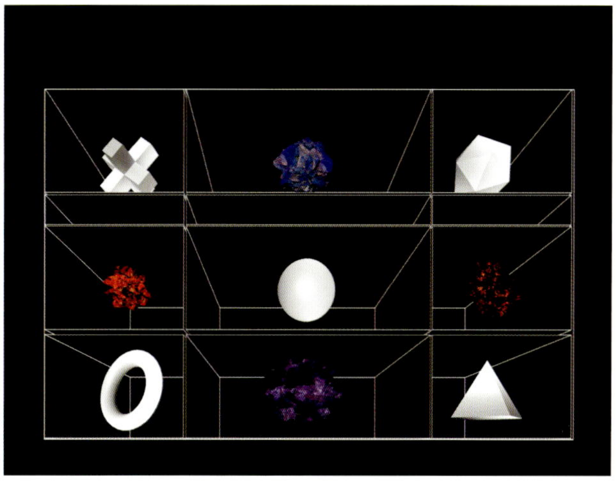

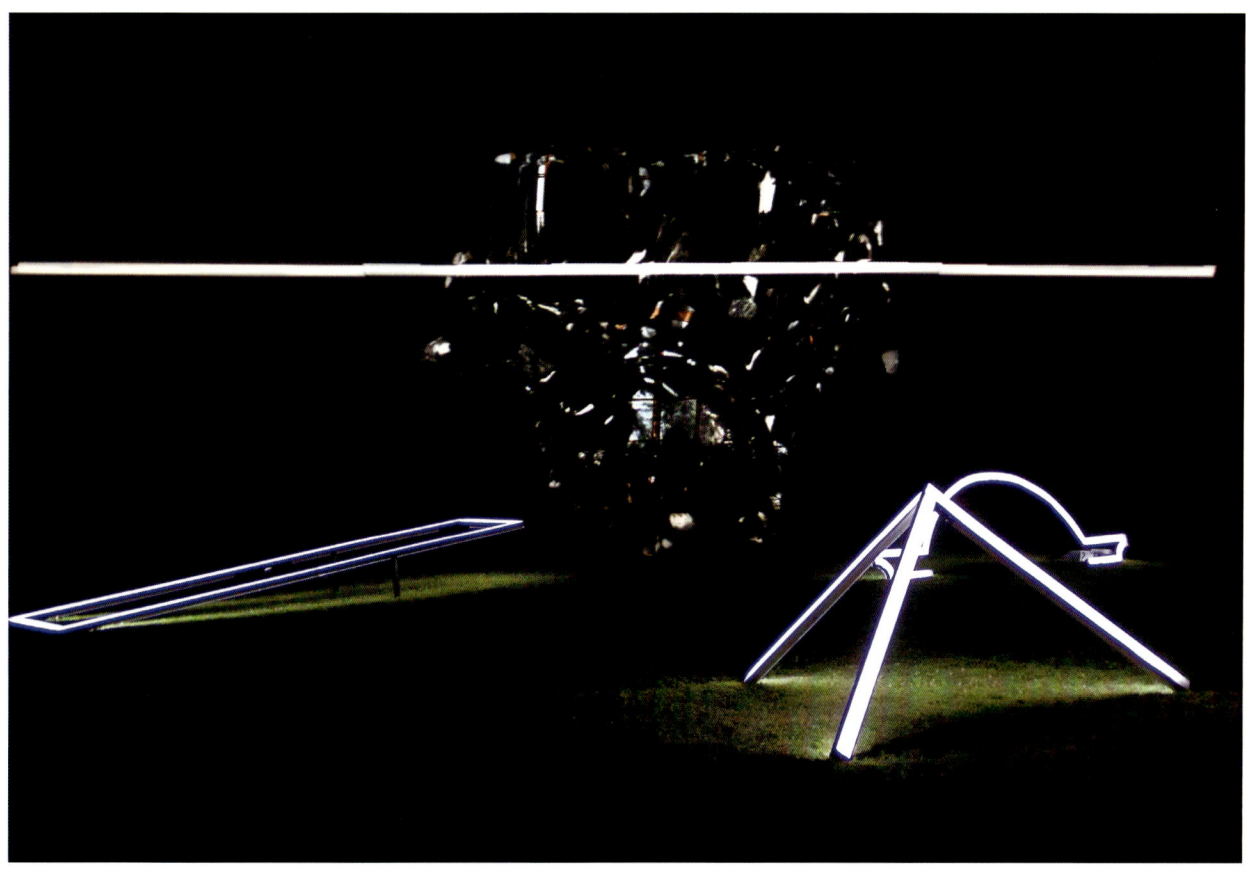

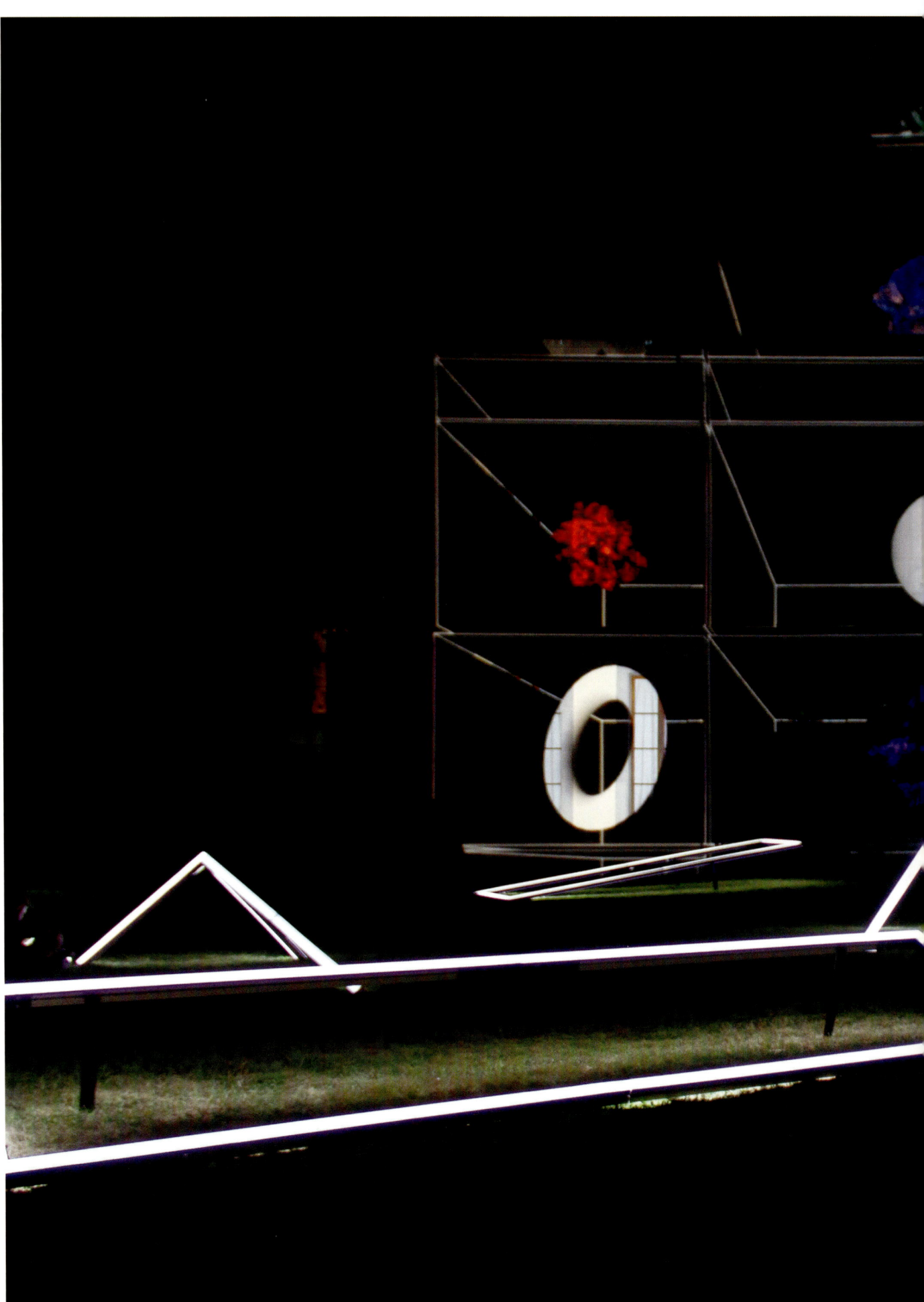

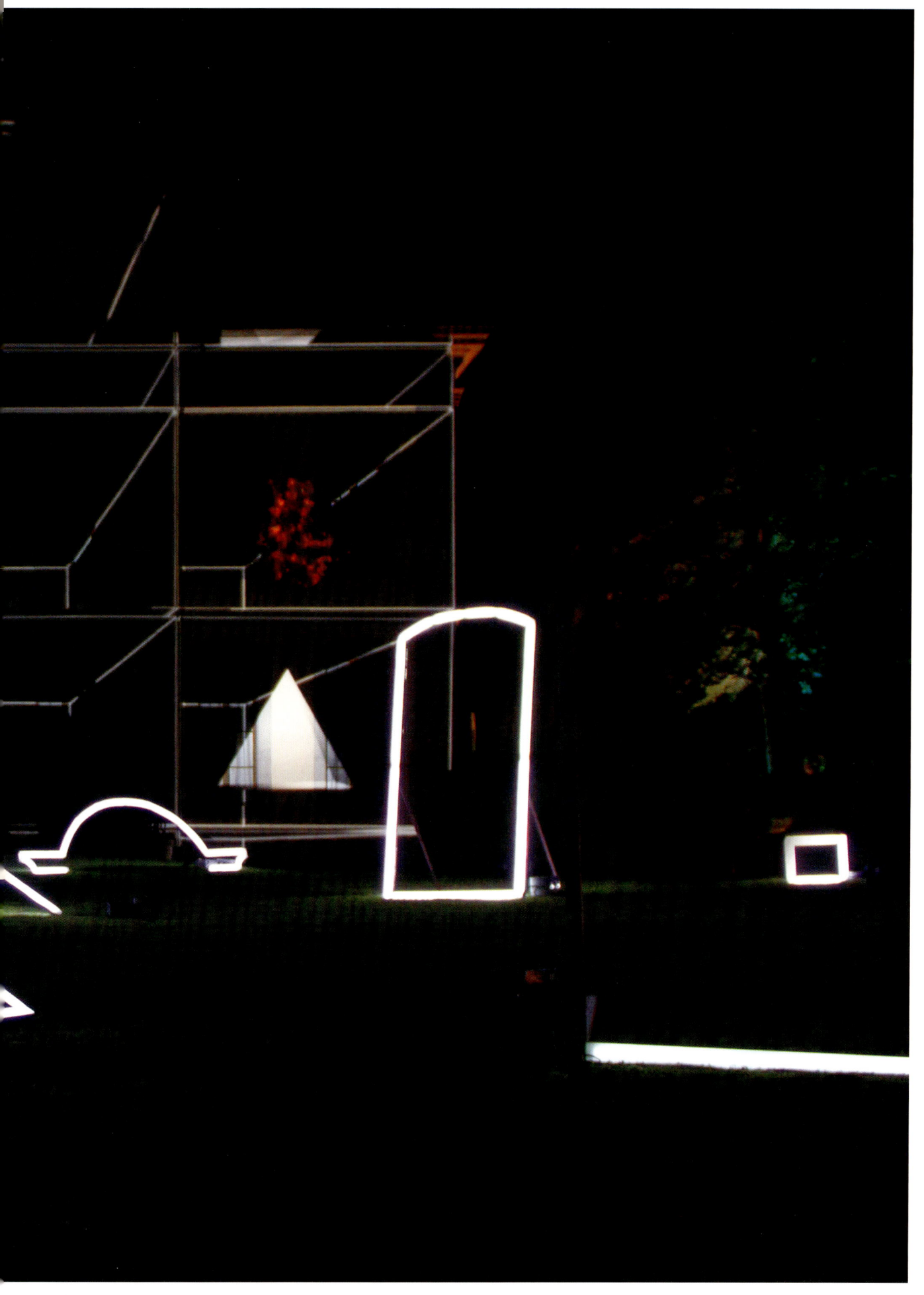

GLOWSCAPE

—

Design: **Praxis Landscape and Urban Design**
Photography: **Enise Burcu Derinbogaz**

—

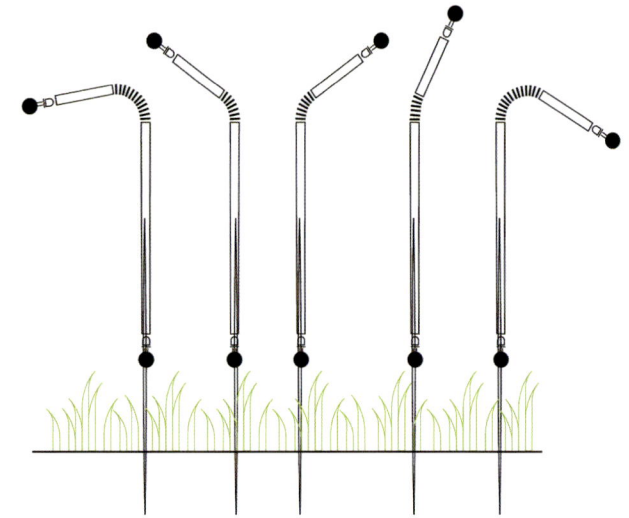

The *Glowscape* installation is the result of a workshop with architectural students of MEF University, in Istanbul. The workshop consisted of a series of experiments between the lighting elements and the daily materials that students brought. Within these experiments students discovered how light and materials can merge and create an atmosphere.

At the end of the workshop students built a kinetic installation at the garden of the university. Every piece is unique and handmade, glowing and moving with the wind.

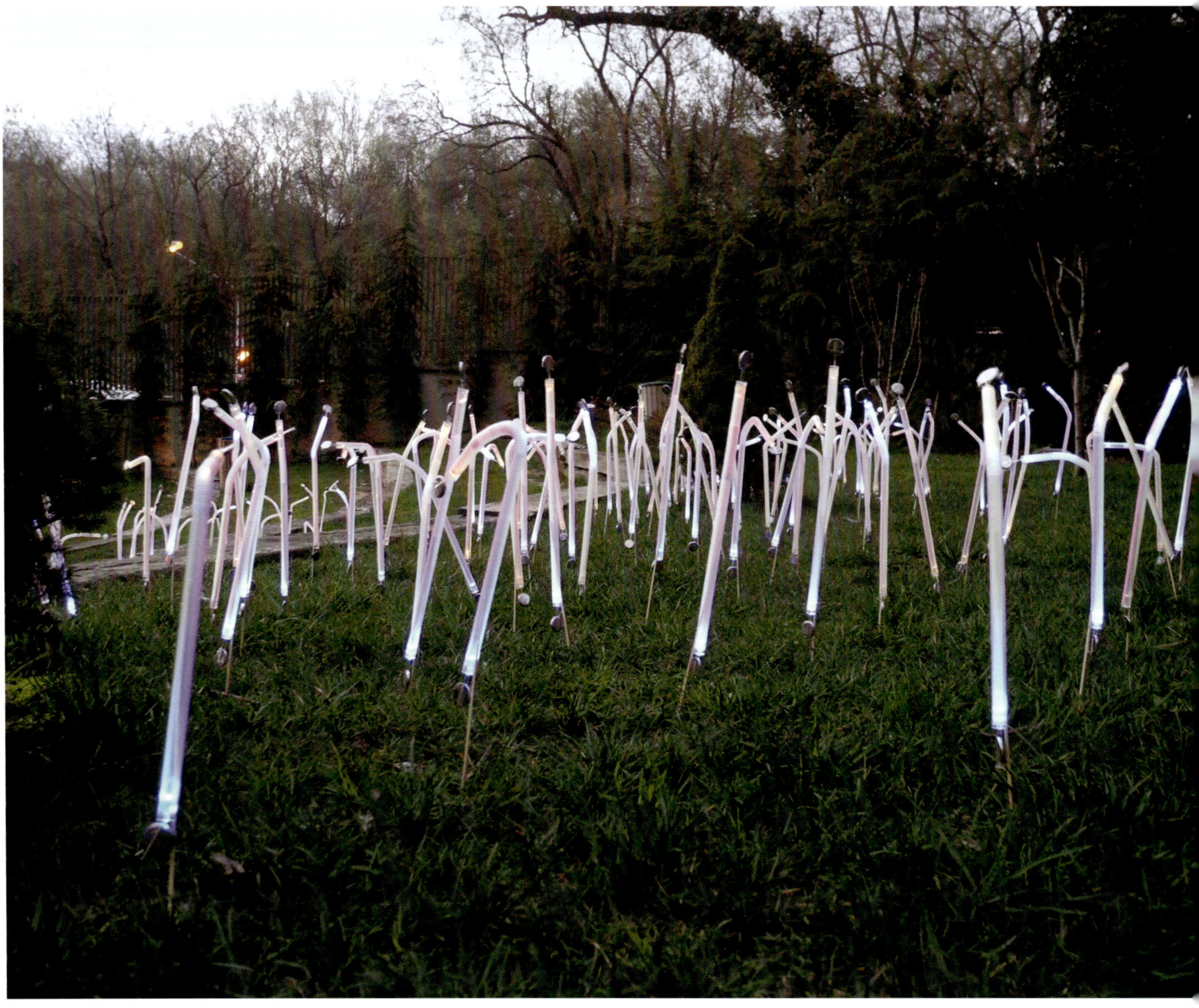

Team:
Barkın Enes Makara, Gökçe Demiral, Damla Çalış, Burak Özcan, Zeki Küçüksarı, Süleyman Aras, Zeynep Akyol, Tunahan Çelen, Emre Yavuz, Jülide Gökçe Ağu, Merve Sandıkçı, Ezgi Herdem, Nur Begüm Acar, Resul Emre Kaba, Gamze Varol, Büşra Yılmaz Şirin

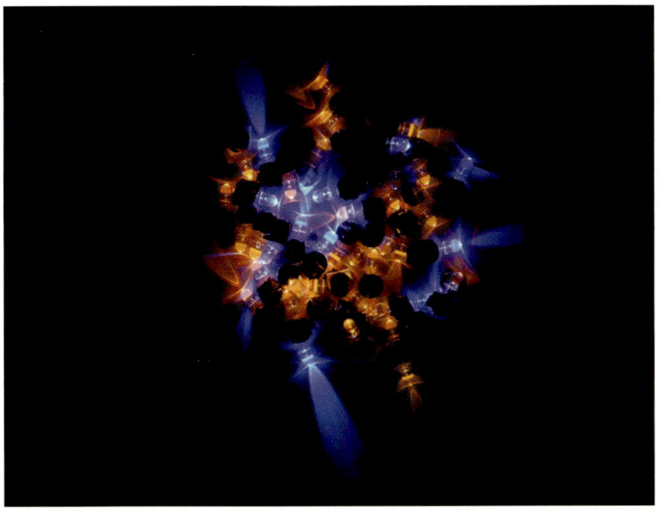

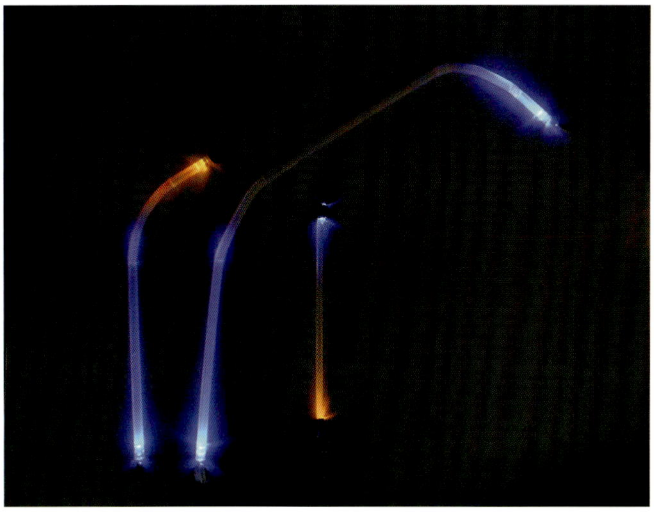

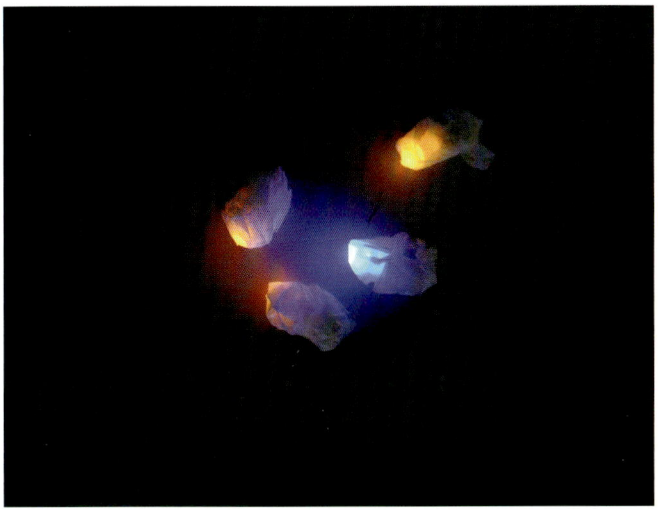

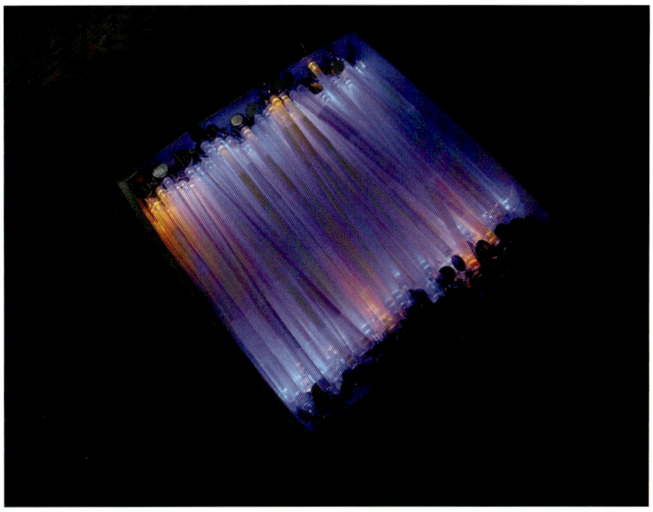

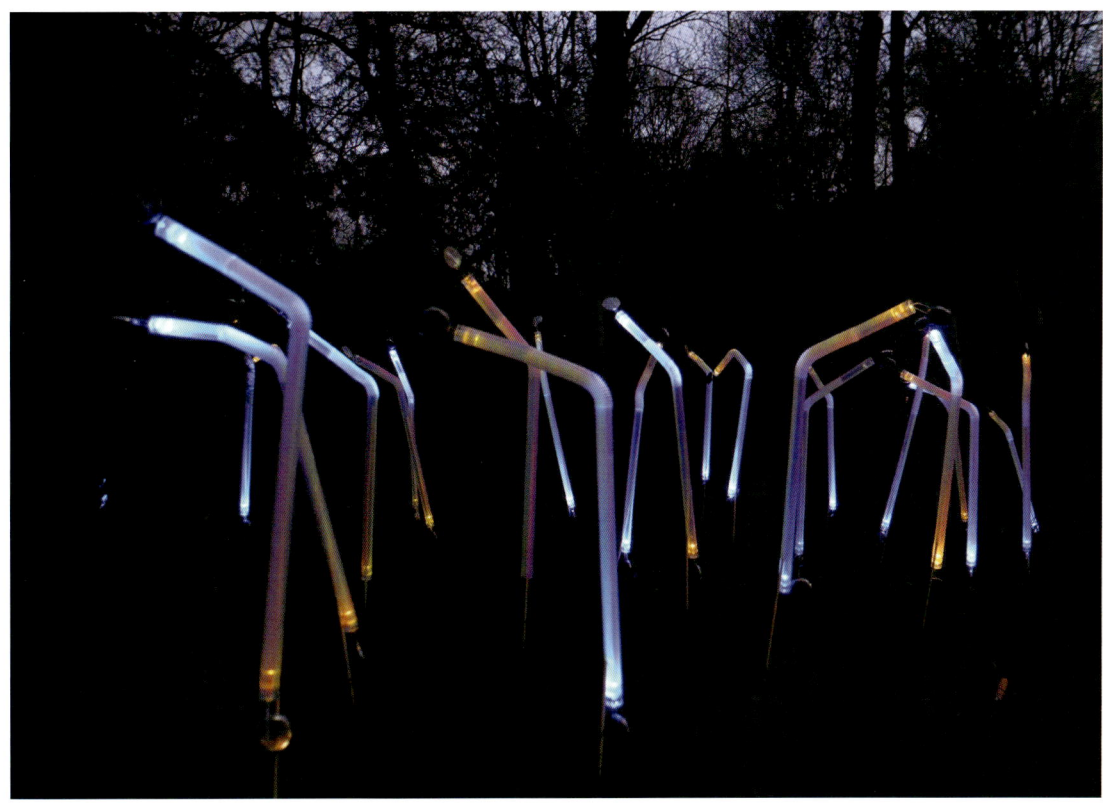

LIGHT FIELD

—

Design: **Praxis Landscape and Urban Design**

Photography: **Kubra Karacizmeli**

—

Light Field is a public installation designed by Praxis Landscape, located in the Sairler Parkı ("Park of Poets") in the Besiktas district of Istanbul. Located at the heart of Istanbul, this 5300-square-meter park was built in the 90s to commemorate the heritage of great poets who used to live in this region.

Park of Poets is open to visitors during the night. Compared to the majority of public parks of Istanbul, this is a unique situation which allows the park to attract even more visitors. The park is not an isolated public space. Instead, it is alive all night. *Light Field* was inspired by the features that coexist harmoniously in the park: the poems, and the fascinating view of the night.

The installation was designed to be an abstract reflection of the verses of poems that obtain a whole new identity in the visitor flow. The rejuvenated verses, and the richness of emotions they evoke in visitors, are transformed into lighting objects that were placed in the most visible corner of the park.

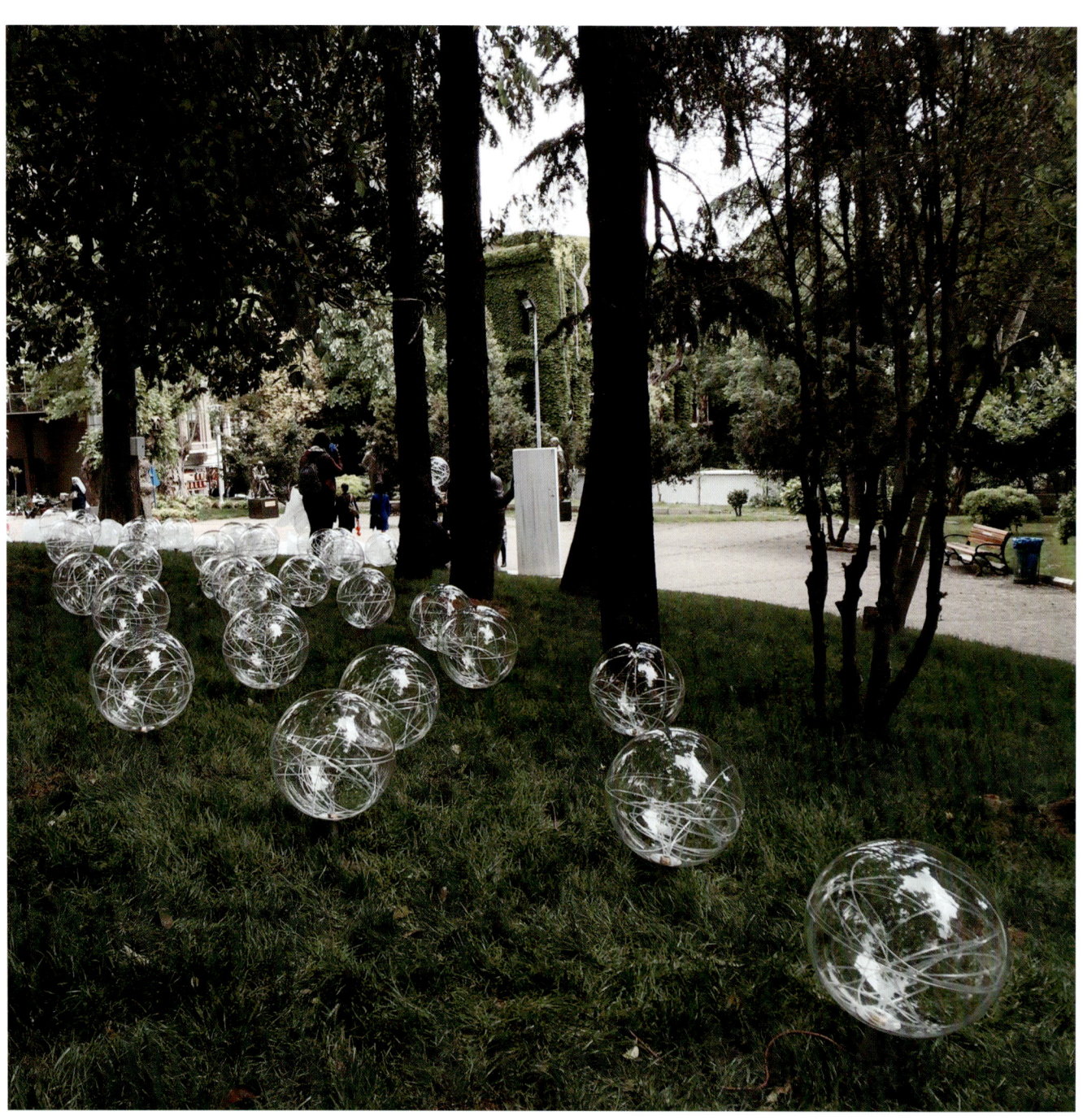

Team:
Enise Burcu Derinboğaz, Büşra Yılmaz Şirin, Nilüfer Çalışkan, Esma Aydın, Merve Mehan, Betül Sisdağ, Ezgi Dinç, Ezgi Sakızcı, Gizem Öğüt

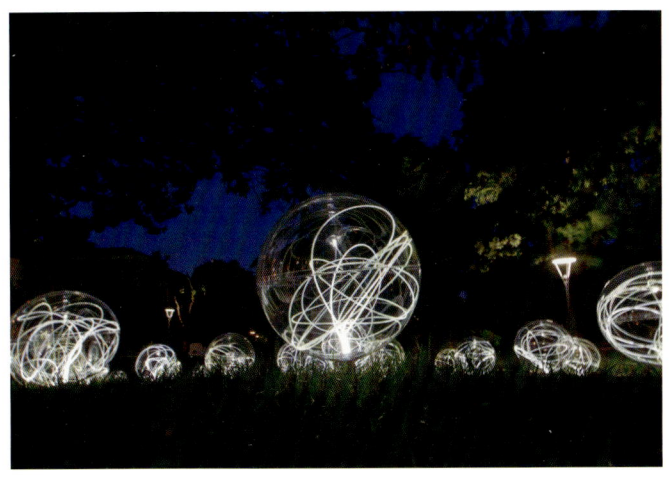
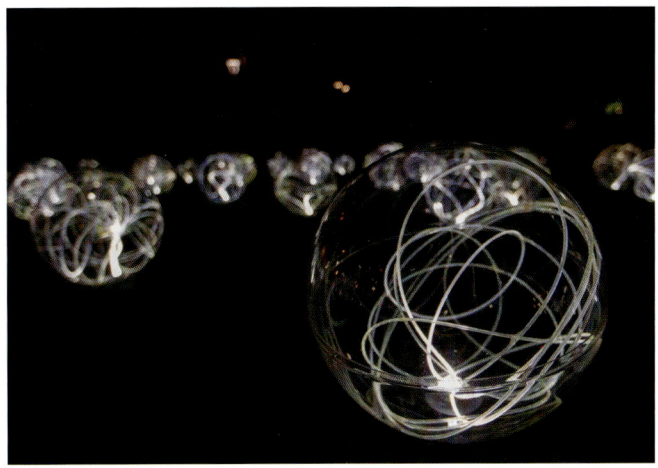

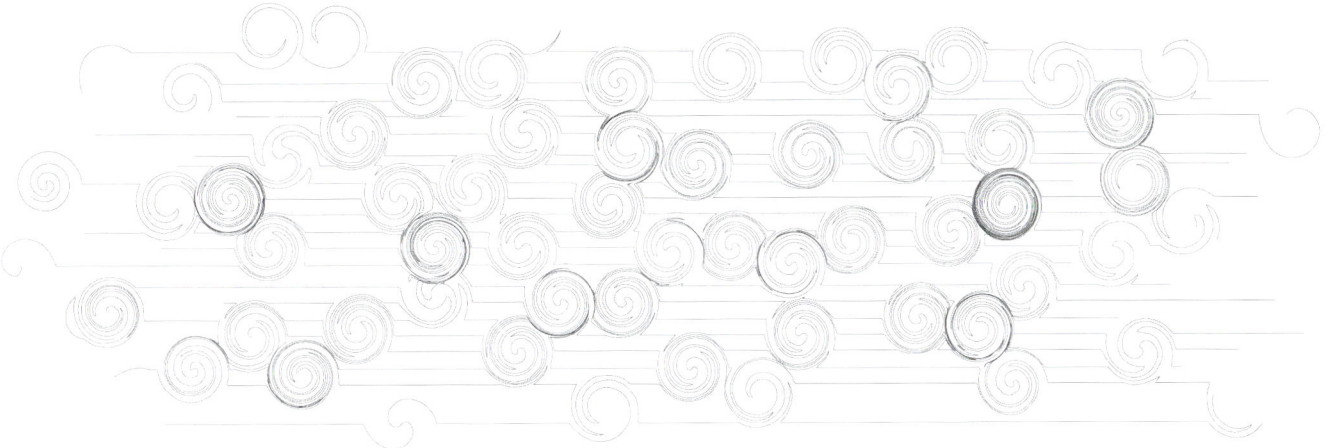

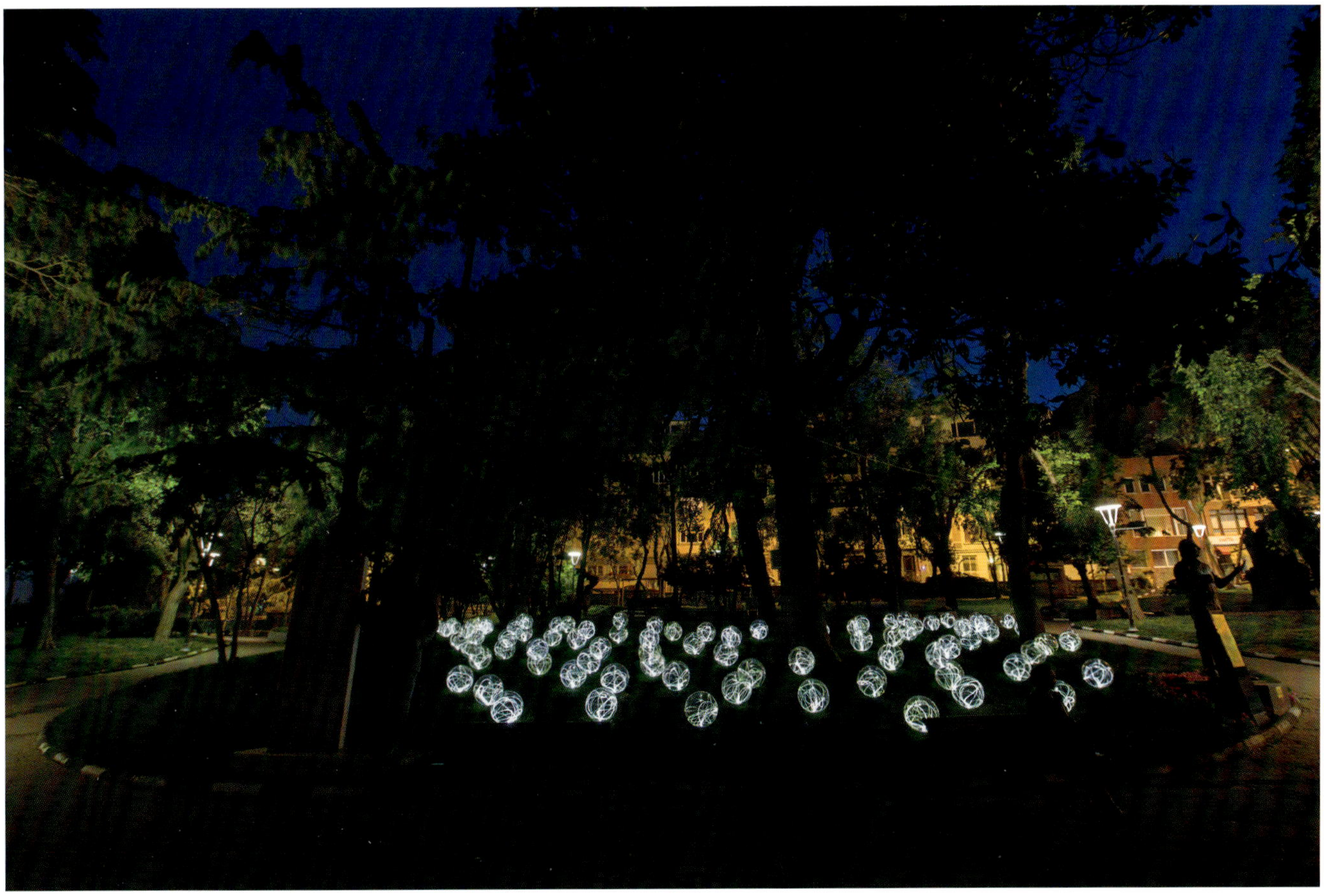

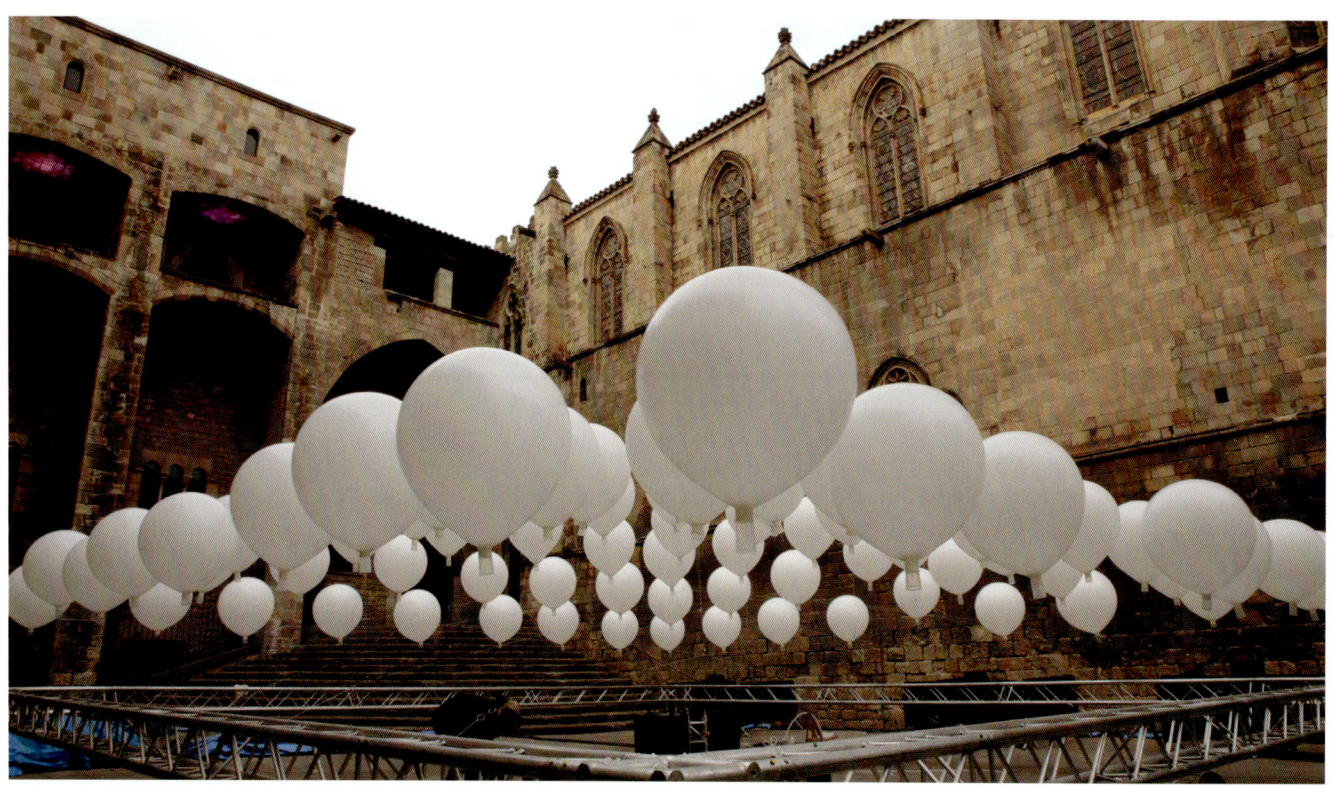

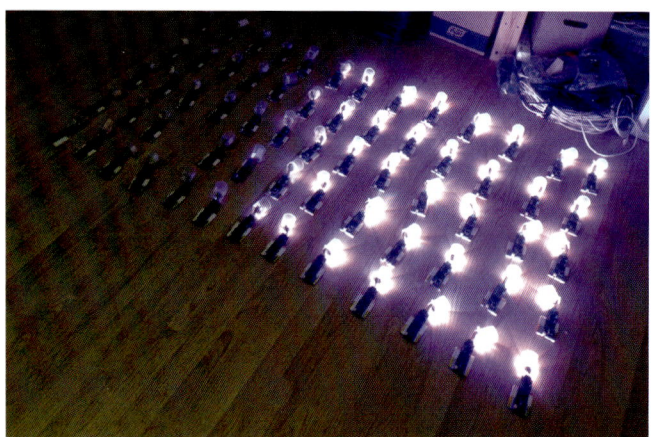

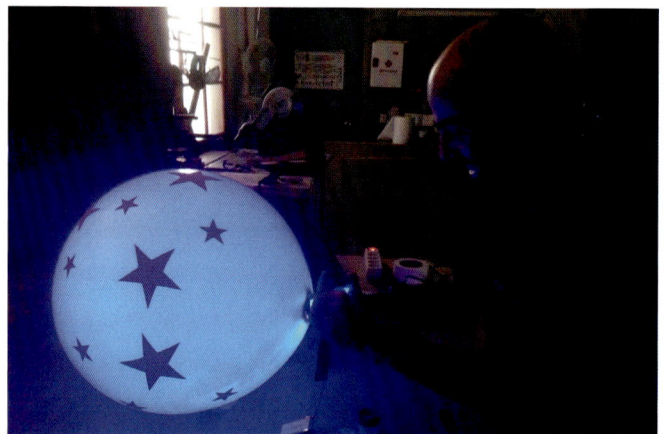

SUSPÈS

—

Design: **Playmodes Studio, MID, David Sarsanedas**

—

Suspès was designed to remind us of the night sky—a spectacle we think of less and less as artificial light grows more and more prevalent and light pollution blocks out much of what we could see a hundred years ago. The installation suspends a matrix of a hundred 90-cm-diameter balloons to a height of 20 to 40 meters. Each balloon has an LED and a control system that allows it to light up individually. Programmers use pixel mapping to create patterns and "constellations," which appear and change with the music. The matrix itself is made of string,

which enables operators to morph the structure dynamically, surprising the audience with new and unexpected forms.

The installation can be held outdoors or indoors, and it includes architectural lighting for the surrounding buildings, which also synchronizes with the balloon matrix.

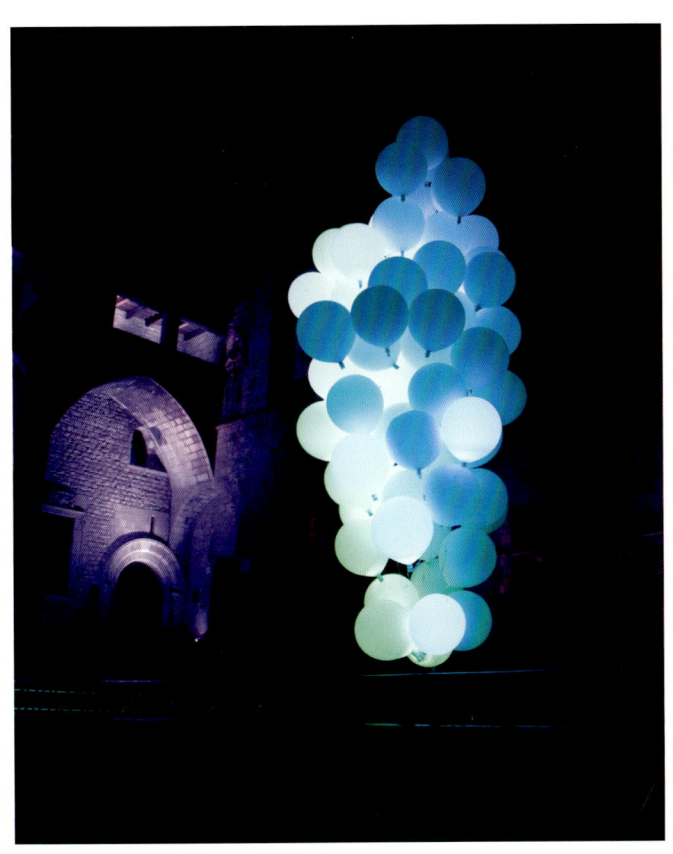
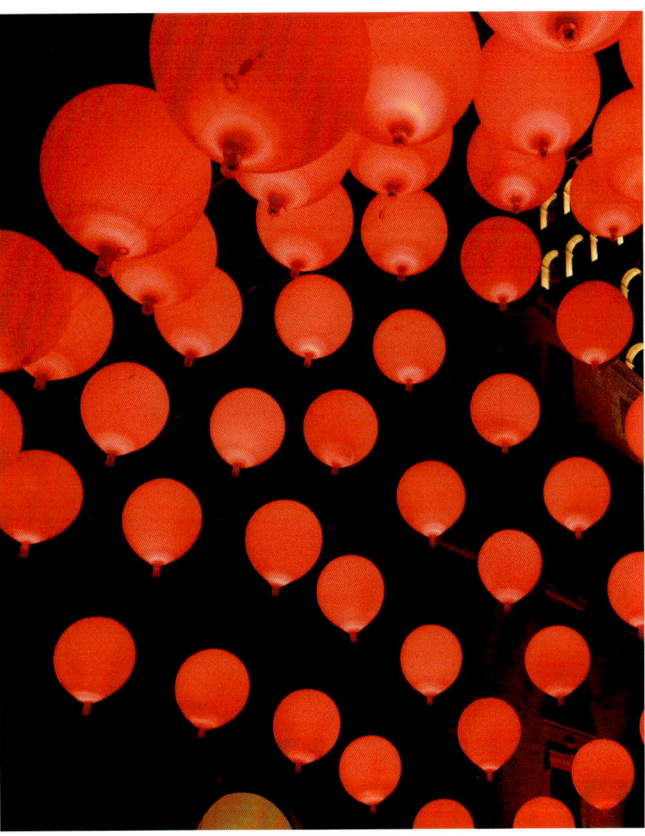

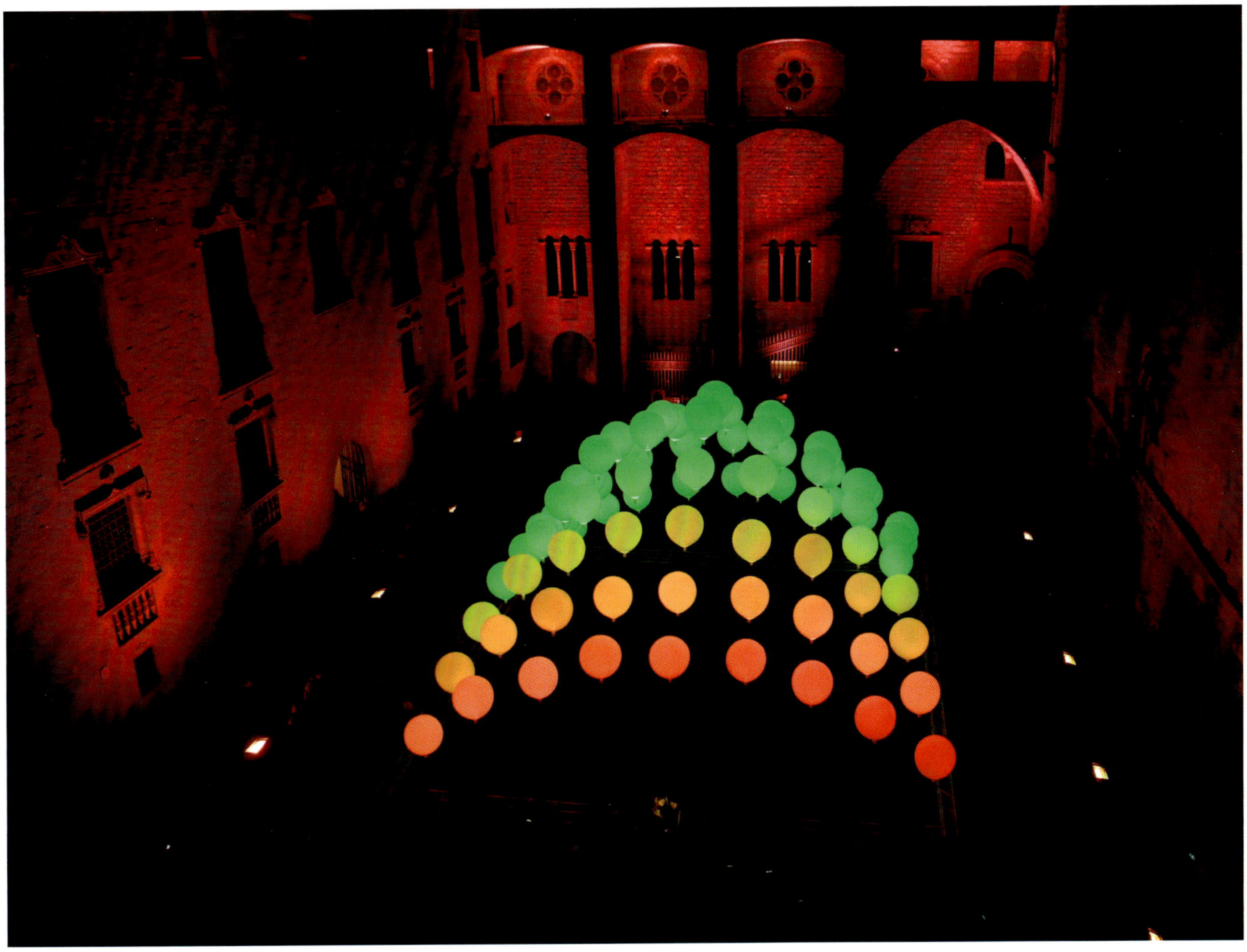

WATERLICHT

—

Design: **Studio Roosegaarde**

—

WATERLICHT is a dream landscape about the power and poetry of water. As a virtual flood, it shows how high the water could reach without human intervention and raises awareness around rising water levels caused by global warming.

This project pays homage to the innovative Dutch water program and the creation of dikes, which keep the sea from flooding the land. Originally created for the Dutch District Water Board, subsequent site-specific installations of *WATERLICHT* were created for the Museumplein in Amsterdam, which attracted more than 60,000 visitors in 1 night, Lumiere London, with saw 1.5 million visits, Nuit Blanche in Paris, UNESCO Schokland, and the Afsluitdijk in the Netherlands.

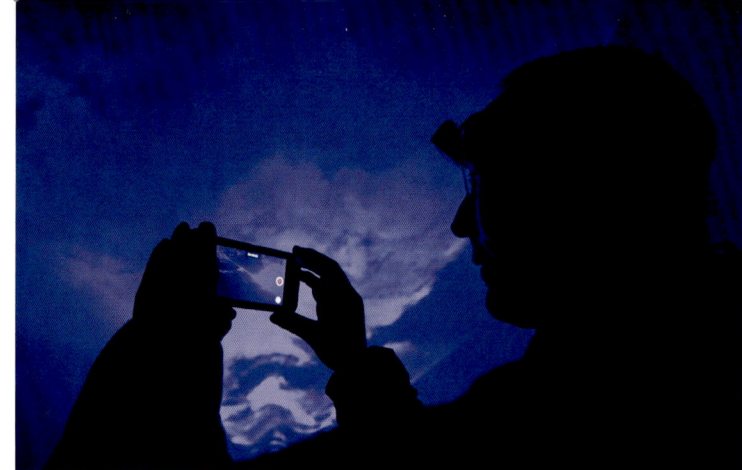

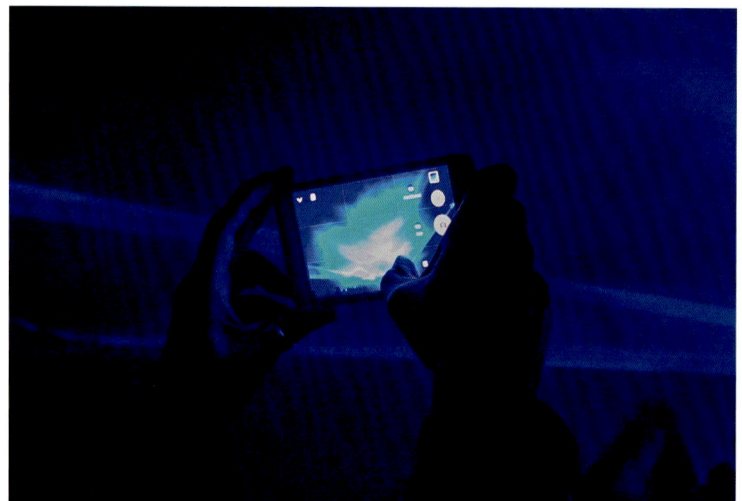

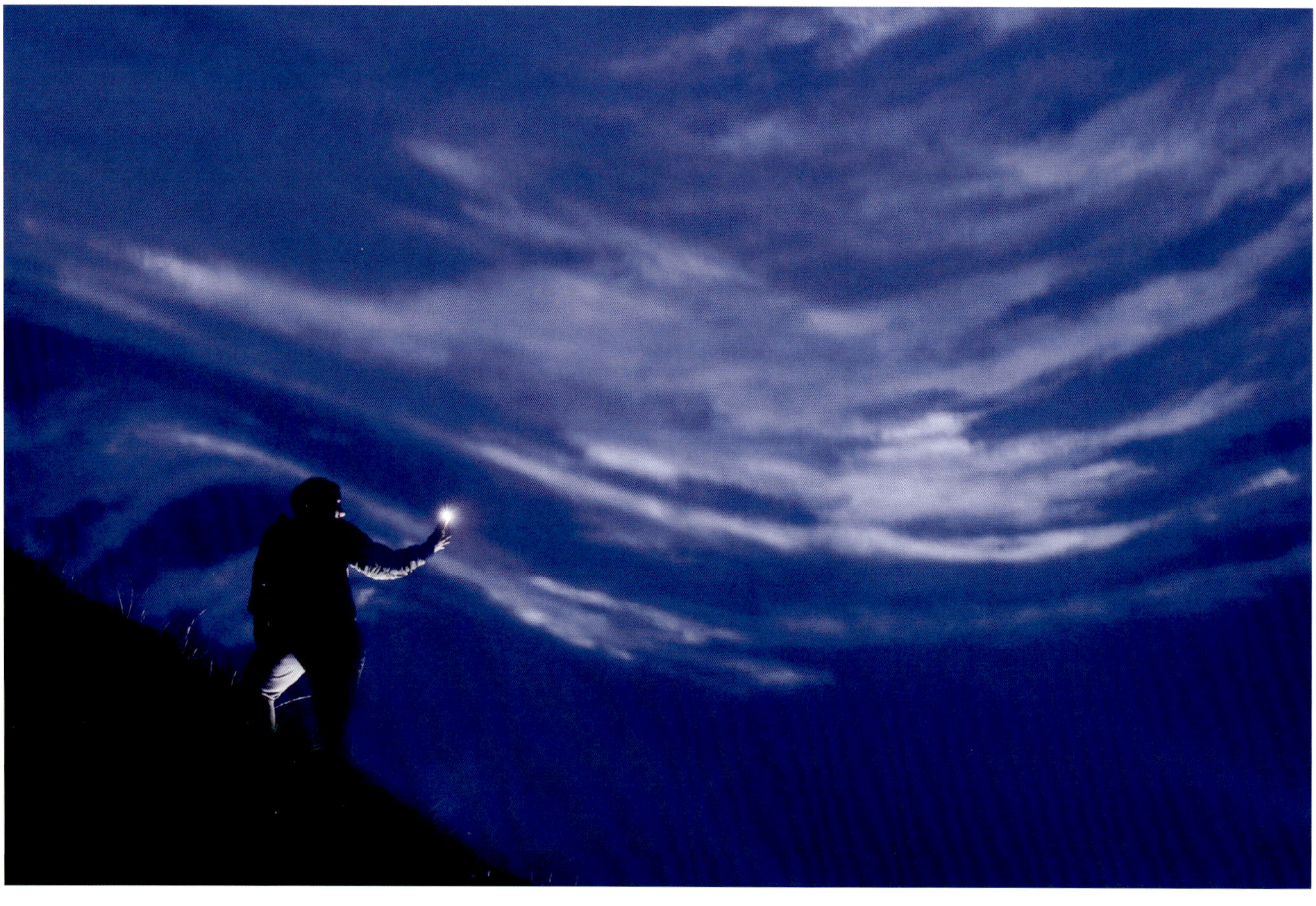

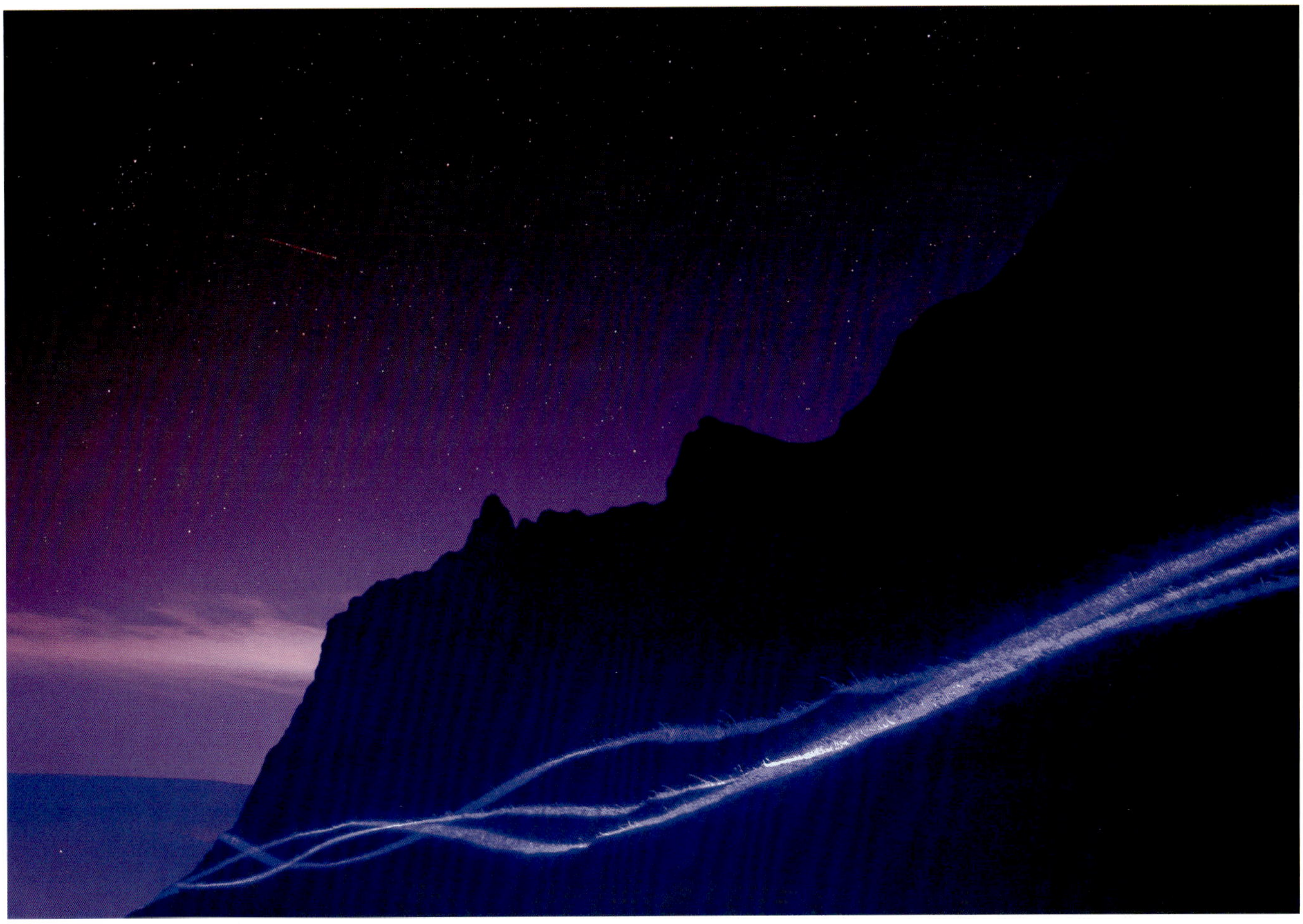

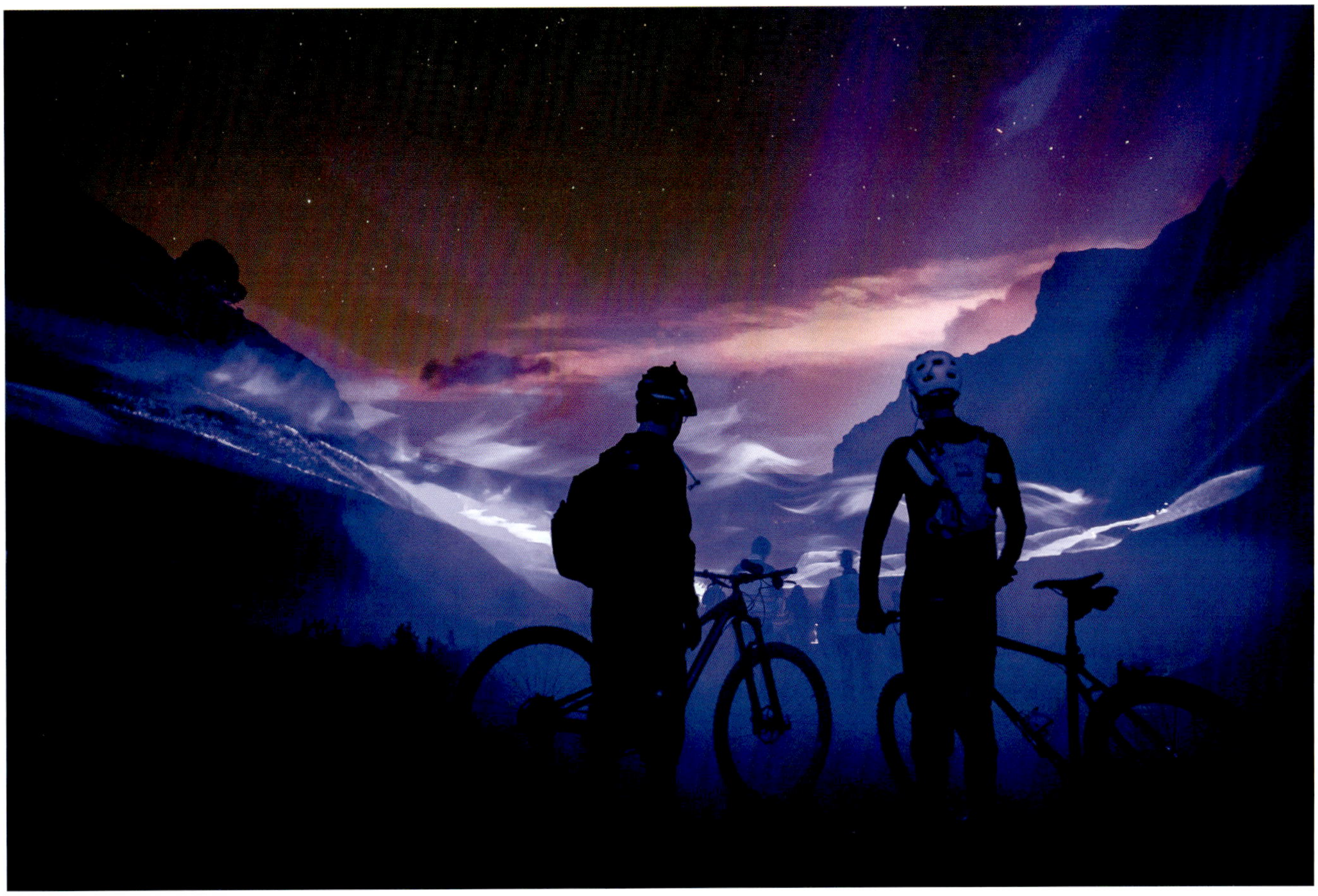

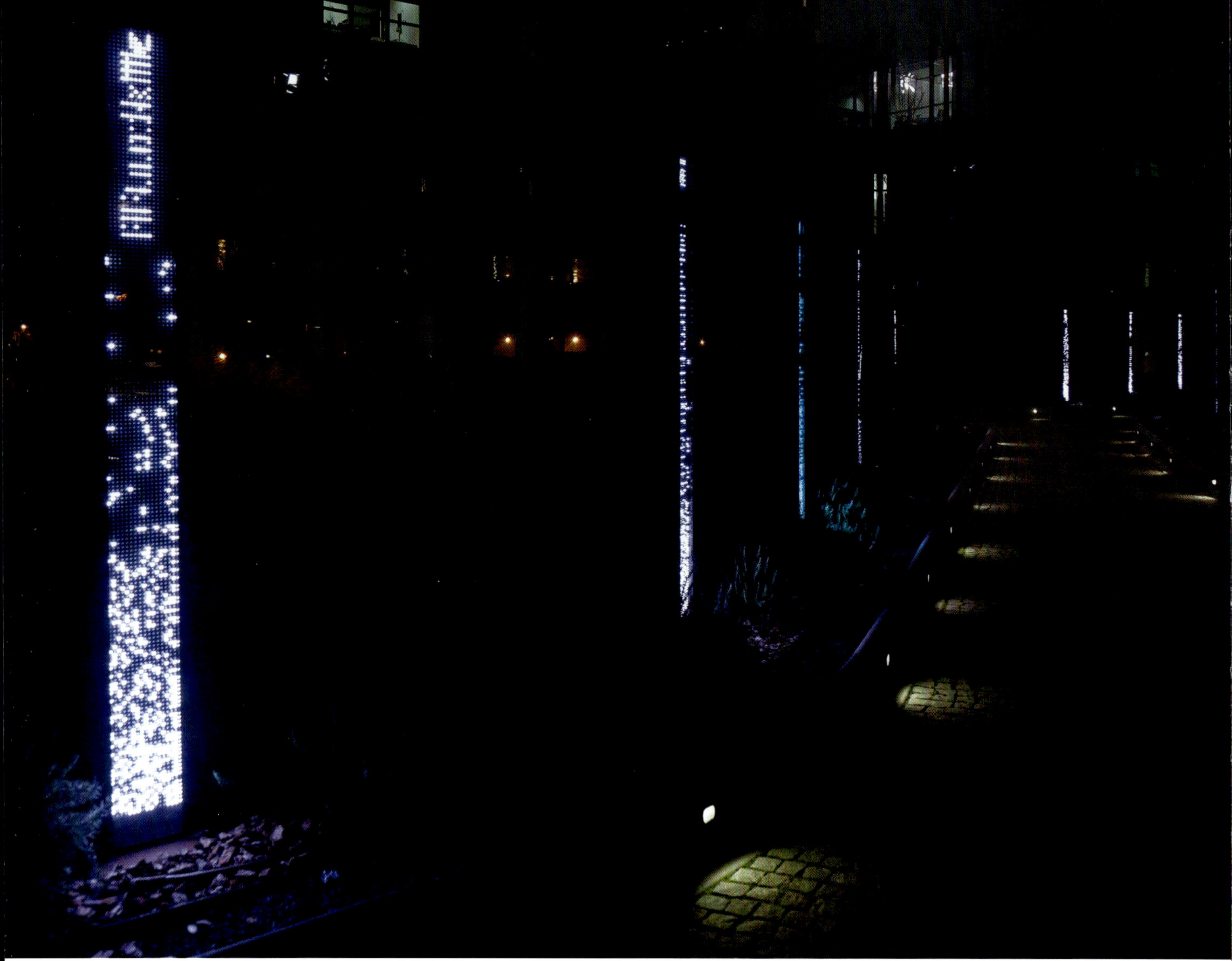

AMYGDALA

—

Design: **fuse***

—

AMYGDALA listens to shared thoughts, interprets states of mind and translates the data gathered into an audiovisual installation capable of representing the collective emotional state of the net and its changes on the basis of events that take place around the world. The aim is to make visible the flow of data and information that is constantly being created by users, and that may be heard and interpreted by anyone, in the attempt to stimulate a reflection on the opportunities and dangers of the digital revolution that we are currently going through. The project was developed in two areas of CUBO, the community center and

multimedia documentation center designed by FUSE*ARCHITECTURE that the UnipolSai Group created in Bologna, Italy, to recount its heritage and identity. In the Media Garden, 125,952 LEDs mounted on 41 columns represent the processes of analysis and emotional recognition while the evolution of the global emotional state is visualized on the 12 videowalls of the Mediateca. In order to keep track of the evolution of the emotional state of the network, every 10 minutes the data gathered and analysed in the Media Garden is sent to the Mediateca to be "archived" on the videowalls in the form of generative emotional graphics.

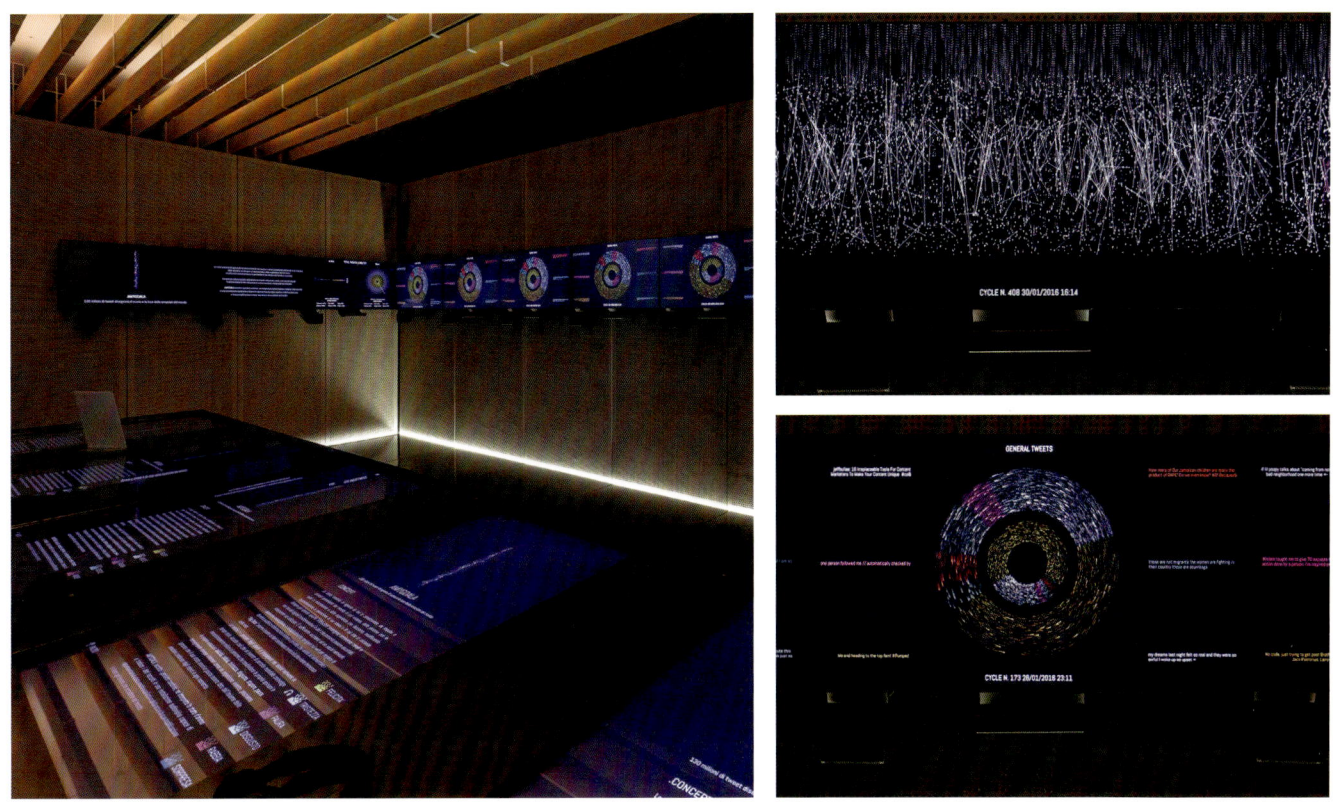

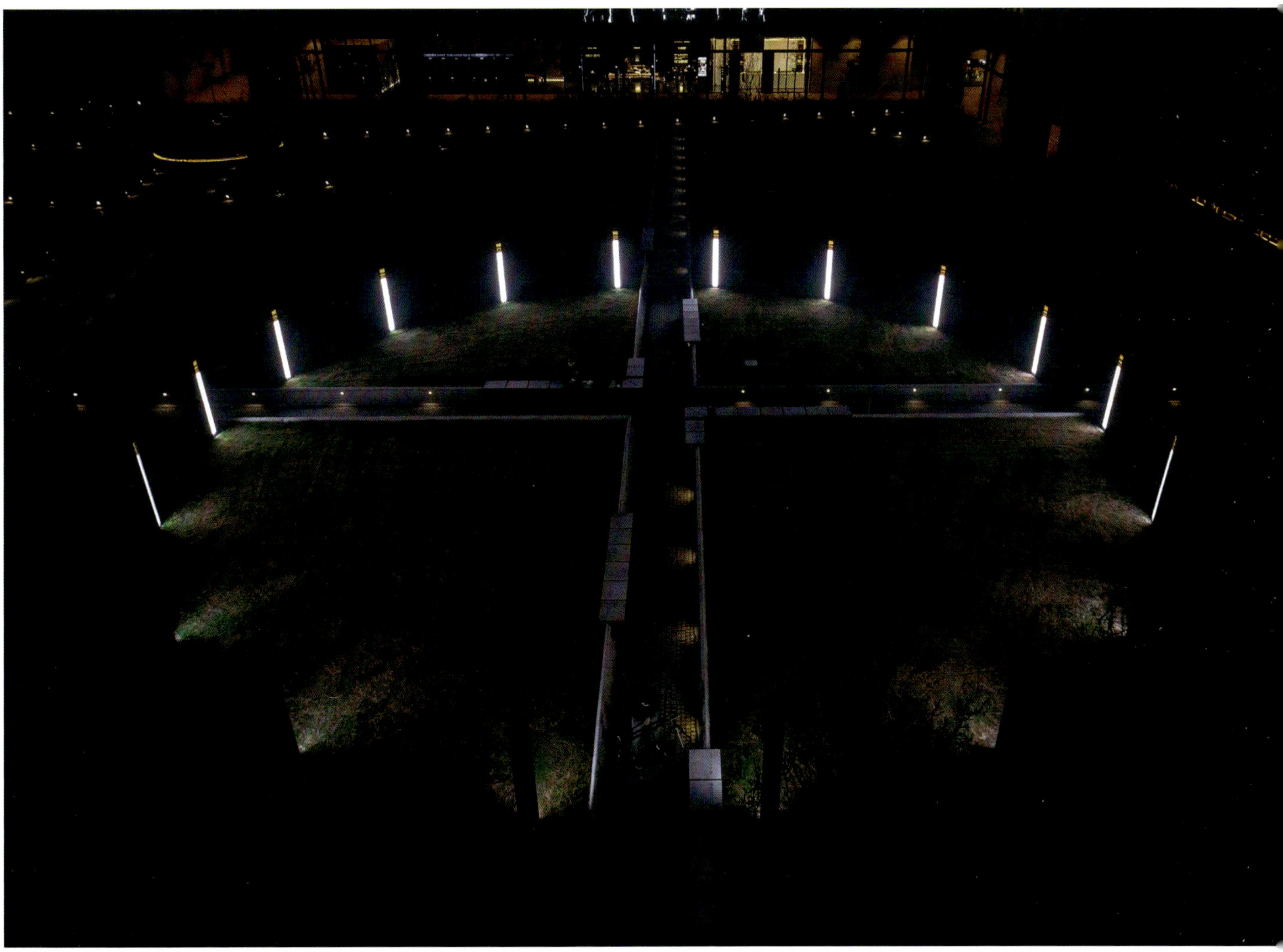

LUMINOUS MEMENTO

—

Design: **Antonin Fourneau**

—

Luminous Memento is a memorial in homage to the citizens of Poitiers who have died in various conflicts since the First World War. The names of the deceased appear and pass through translucent concrete to digitally engrave for a moment their memory in the stone. Every day, the memorial repeatedly displays the names of those who died on that date, commemorating beyond their deaths all those citizens who defended France.

A website (Luminousmemento.fr) connected to the memorial allows visitors to consult the names and birth and death dates for those memorialized. Some of the names carry the epitaph "Death for France."

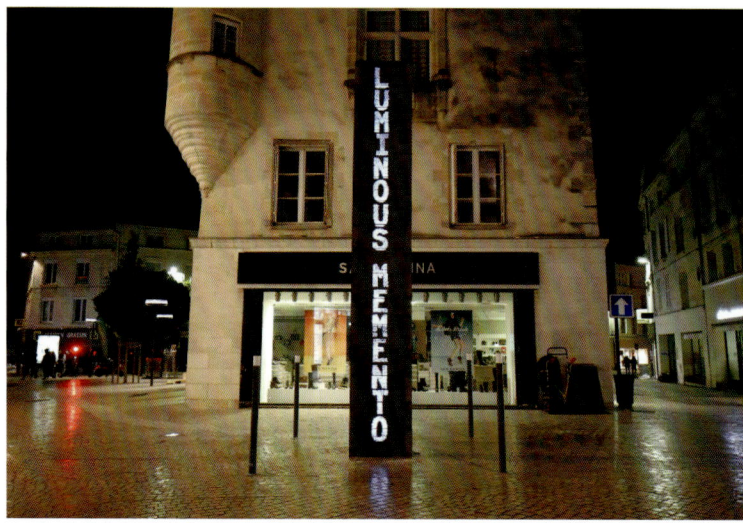

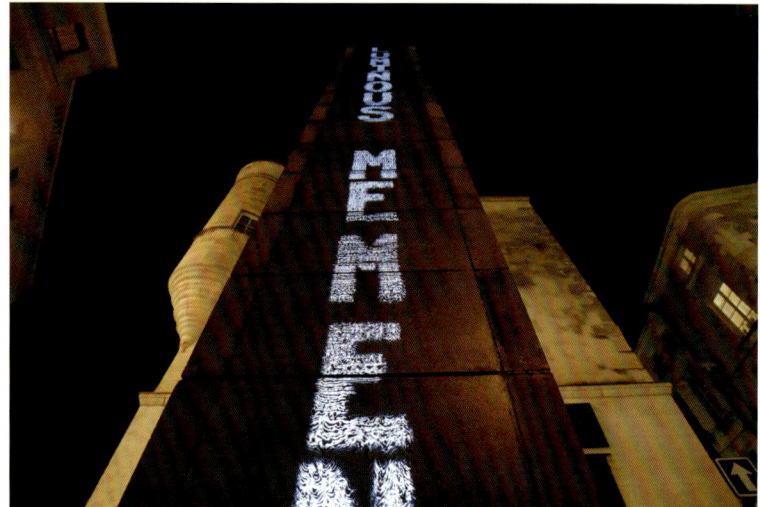

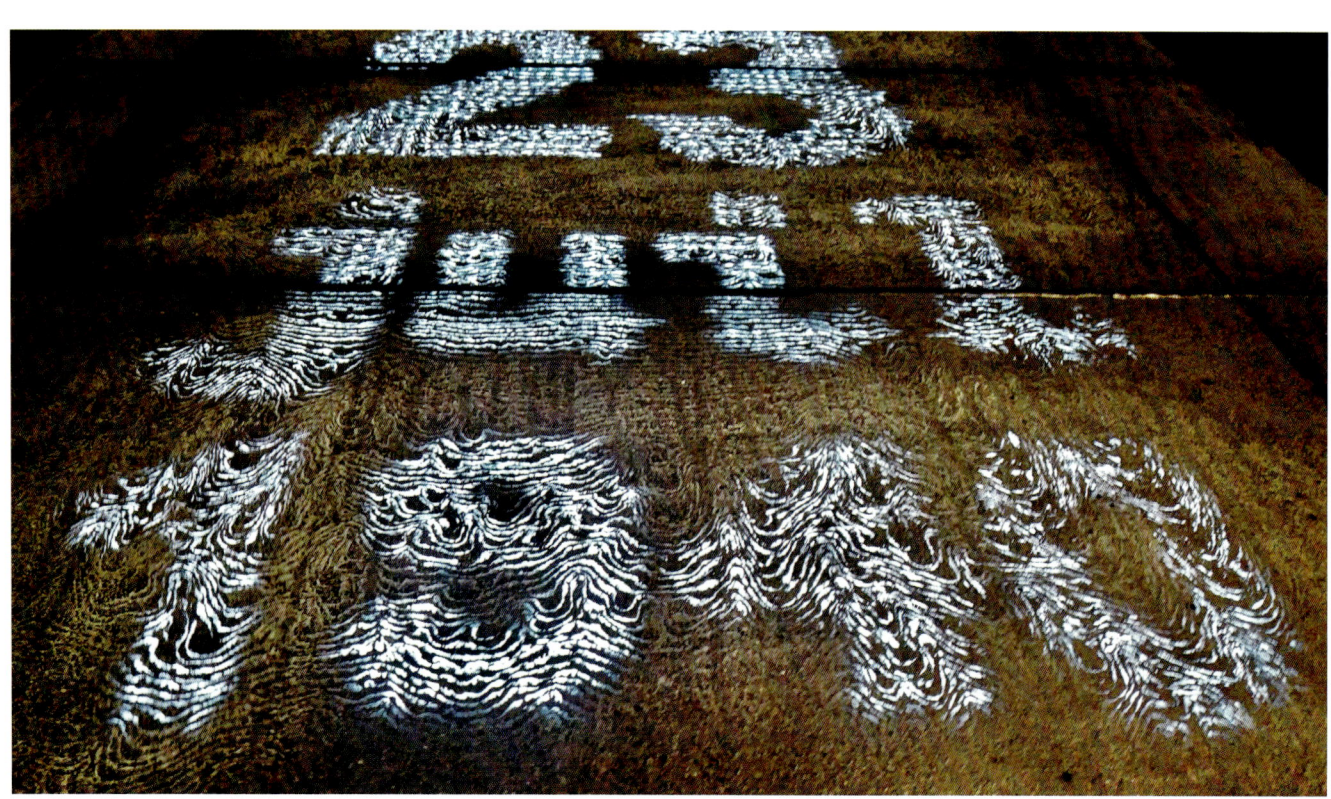

INDEX

Antonin Fourneau

www.antoninfourneau.com

Antonin Fourneau is a French artist and designer living in Paris who has focused on interactive art and popular culture. He created a collaborative project about innovation and a new form of funfair named *Eniarof*. Most of his research focuses on creative interactions in large groups of people. He has taken part in various exhibitions related to digital arts. His *Waterlight Graffiti* has received a lot of acclaim and is still exhibited around the world today. He is currently a professor in new media design at EnsAD, where he leads the research group GoD|Art. He is a guest lecturer and leads workshops in several schools.

P090-091, P232

Asif Khan

www.asif-khan.com

Asif Khan Limited is an award-winning architecture studio based in London and established in 2007. The team of twenty is led by Asif Khan, who was born in London and studied at UCL and the AA School. The success of the studio's projects is due to the unique depth of creative thought and the determination and experience brought to each project, no matter the location or budget. The main focus of the studio is public projects, such as the design of cultural buildings and museums, exhibitions, installations, masterplans, and landscapes. The studio has particularly strong experience in research and experimentation through design utilizing local conditions and cultures.

P156-159

Bertrand Lanthiez

www.bertrandlanthiez.com

Bertrand Lanthiez is a French visual artist who graduated from ESAG Penninghen School in Paris. He chooses to communicate ideas through interactive installations, focusing on a dialogue by letting the audience members become actors rather than merely passive observers.

P020-021

bildspur

www.bildspur.ch

A workspace for communication, bildspur creates immersive experiences by combining design and technology. This collective consists of several young artists from Switzerland who deal mainly with new media and audiovisual works.

P146-147

Bonjour, interactive Lab

www.bonjour-lab.com

Bonjour is a creative studio based in Paris, specializing in projects at the intersection of artistic installation, technological innovation and interactivity. The team focuses most of its efforts on generative design (both graphic and sound), human/machine interaction, and tangible media, which lead Bonjour to create cross-domain experiences and interactions.

P068-069

Brut Deluxe

www.brutdeluxe.com

Brut Deluxe is an architecture and design studio headed by Ben Busche. Founded in 2004, Brut Deluxe operates today from two platforms in Madrid and Munich. Brut Deluxe is focused on the investigation and creation of space and its atmospheric qualities. Projects oscillate between different scales of urban intervention: from ephemeral artistic installations to industrial design, construction design and urbanism. Brut Deluxe is oriented towards the social, economic and aesthetic qualities of the projects and combines both scientific strategies and artistic approximations in the creative process.

P184-185

Can Büyükberber

www.canbuyukberber.com

Born in Turkey and based in San Francisco, Can Büyükberber (b. 1987) creates immersive audiovisual experiences in both physical and digital spaces. His practice experiments with various media such as virtual/augmented reality, projection mapping, geodesic domes, large-scale displays and digital fabrication. Büyükberber studied Physics and Visual Communication Design in Istanbul and received an MFA in Art and Technology from the San Francisco Art Institute. This interdisciplinary education informs his practice, which connects art, design and science. His work often focuses on human perception, exploring new methods for non-linear narratives and emergent forms which blur the sense of scale and presence in physical and digital environments.

P190-193

Chevalvert

www.chevalvert.fr

Chevalvert is a visual design studio co-founded by Patrick Paleta and Stéphane Buellet in 2007. Based on an open, multidisciplinary approach to design, Chevalvert's projects place form in service of ideas. The studio's work is divided across institutional, cultural and industrial orders and self-initiated projects. The studio's knowledge and extensive expertise brings varied perspective to its projects, leading to relevant and coherent answers in each area of graphic design.

P036-039

Christopher Bauder

www.whitevoid.com

Christopher Bauder is an artist and designer working in the fields of light and installation art, media design and scenography. He focuses on the translation of bits and bytes into objects and environments, and vice versa. Space, objects, sound, light and interaction are the key elements of his work. In 2004 he founded the multidisciplinary art and design studio WHITEvoid, which specializes in interactivity, media, interior architecture, and electronic engineering. Bauder has brought his installations and performances to events and spaces around the world, including Centre Pompidou Paris, MUTEK Montreal, Fete des Lumieres Lyon, The National Museum of Fine Arts Taiwan and the National Centre for the Performing Arts in Beijing.

P208-213

Cinimod Studio

cinimodstudio.com

Cinimod Studio is a cutting-edge experiential agency, a boutique lighting company and a multidisciplinary production house. Driven by wild and untamed creativity, exquisite design and an obstinate need to innovate, the studio transforms space and experience through the use and misuse of technology.

P102-105

Claudia Paz Lighting Studio

www.claudiapaz.com

Claudia Paz Lighting Studio is a design practice based in Lima, Peru, specializing in lighting design. Their vision is to link art, technology and architecture through light, and their innovative designs combine the use of the latest technology with a concern for energy efficiency. Their constant search to achieve unique solutions for each client that integrate architectural lighting design, technology and art, has brought their projects international recognition. As a fundamental principle, they believe that the most important part of lighting design is in the emotions and effects that light causes.

P100-101, P126-129

Col·lec Studio

thisiscollec.com

Col·lec was founded in 2017 with the aim of creating significant experiences for people through immersive installations. They work in a multi-disciplinary team that includes engineers, visual, space, and product designers. Their diverse backgrounds, nationalities, and cultures add a transversal vision and approach to their concepts and work method.

P150-151

Daniel Canogar

www.danielcanogar.com

Most of Daniel's recent sculptural installations are constructed with discarded electronic materials: computer, telephone and electric cables, thousands of burnt-out bulbs, meters of videotape, old slot machines, celluloid, DVDs, etc. The installations explore the short life expectancy of the technologies people cast off and their relationship to organic mortality. These installations also seek to reanimate the lifeless. Light animations projected onto the installations appear to free the energy stored in the electronic waste, awakening in it memories of its past. Through his work he tries to bring dead materials back to life, reveal their secrets, and revive the collective memory they contain to construct an accurate portrait of a society and an age.

P178-179

Daria Jelonek

www.dariajelonek.com

Daria Jelonek is a digital artist, designer and researcher who lives and works in London. Her work is situated in the field of interaction design and immersive art installations, with a focus on the relationship between nature and technology. She is currently focusing on augmented reality's positive uses for our environment and consumer behaviors. Her artworks have been exhibited and screened at cultural institutes. She has given talks about the intersection of art and technology at cultural and tech institutes, such as V&A London, ICA London and Microsoft Research Cambridge.

P028-029

David Torrents

www.torrents.info

David Torrents (Barcelona, 1971) is a multidisciplinary designer with expertise in commercial and non-commercial projects which are often closely aligned with culture. David has received several design awards and he has often been invited to sit on international award juries. Furthermore, he teaches at Bau Design College of Barcelona and IDEP Barcelona,

leads workshops and gives lectures. He has also curated exhibitions at the Disseny Hub Barcelona. Although the radius of action of his projects is wide, he likes to define himself as an urban designer because he believes that the city agglutinates most of his wits.

P130-133

Design I/O

design-io.com

Design I/O is a small studio that is passionate about creating immersive interactive environments, new forms of storytelling, and developing prototypes that lead toward a more magical future. Design I/O was founded by Emily Gobeille and Theodore Watson, who have been working together on interactive projects for the past thirteen years. Emily's passion for animation and storytelling, and her interest in creating shared interactive experiences where people can tell their own stories, combined with Theodore's interest in developing custom tools and techniques for real-time interaction, allow Design I/O to conceive and build cutting-edge projects that push the boundaries of what is possible.

P042-045

ecco screen

eccoscreen.xyz

ecco screen is a San Francisco-based experimental art practice created by American artist Jeffrey Bryant in 2015. ecco screen explores human emotion and interaction through the use of light, sound, and technology. The works range from interactive installations and immersive experiences to audiovisual performances, designed to evoke crowd participation. ecco screen has exhibited at festivals and galleries across North America and Europe including the Brooklyn Academy of Music (New York), Igloofest (Montreal), ArtFutura (Rome), Mirus Gallery (San Francisco), and Stanford University (Stanford). Collaborations with established brands, agencies, and figures include Dolby, NASA, Acura, Tool of NA, MullenLowe, Google, ASAP Rocky, and A-Trak.

P070-075

ENESS

eness.com

ENESS is a multimedia design studio that works at the intersection of art and technology. Combining varying disciplines including lighting, software, interaction design, product design, sculpture and architecture, the outcomes are often unique and unexpected. Founded in 1997, ENESS has pioneered the art of 3D-projection mapping and interactive real-time motion-tracking in theater and extreme sports. Their work has been exhibited worldwide in museums of modern art to the streets of Mumbai.

P124-125, P186

ESI Design

www.esidesign.com

Founded by interactive pioneer Edwin Schlossberg, ESI Design is an experienced design studio that transforms places into experiences. From its roots reinventing the Brooklyn Children's Museum into one of the country's first interactive museums, ESI Design has defined the field of experience design for over forty years, fundamentally changing how people connect with brands, organizations, cultural institutions and, most importantly, each other. A collaborative, in-house team of designers, strategists, storytellers, technologists, artists, and problem-solvers work with clients from day one, until it's done. ESI Design seamlessly weaves the physical and digital worlds together to create immersive experiences with enduring impact. Recent clients include eBay, the Ellis Island National Museum of Immigration, Comcast, PNC Bank, Beacon Capital, and the Edward M. Kennedy Institute for the U.S. Senate.

P058-059

Flynn Talbot

www.flynntalbot.com

Flynn Talbot is an Australian lighting artist and designer based in London, UK. Talbot creates lighting installations and commissioned pieces for galleries and unique buildings along with innovative lighting products for serial production. Talbot's starting point is always the same for each project. He begins with considering the "light effect" and constructs each project around it. Every decision and detail is made with the quality of light and user connection in mind. Talbot does not believe in being bound by style, material or form. This method creates a timeless quality and a strong point of difference in his work.

P162-163

fuse*

fuseworks.it

fuse* is a studio and a production company founded in 2007 that operates at the intersection between art and science, with the aim of exploring the expressive potential offered by the creative use of emerging digital technologies. Ever since the outset, the studio's research has focused primarily on the production of installations and live-media performances capable of profound audience engagement, amplifying the emotional impact of the narration. Over the course of years, the studio has evolved, developing a more holistic approach to the creation of new projects. Adopting a modus operandi which valorizes pure experimentation, the goal is to create works that inspire people, push back the limits and seek out new interplay between light, space, sound, and movement. fuse* has always linked its activity and development to that of the community in which it operates, supporting, promoting and developing projects aimed at spreading culture and knowledge. For this purpose, it has co-produced NODE, an electronic music and digital arts festival, since 2016.

P230-231

Höweler + Yoon Architecture

www.howeleryoon.com

Höweler + Yoon Architecture LLP is an award-winning international design firm recognized for innovative work across the domains of architecture, urban design, public space, immersive experience, and design strategy. Founded in 2005, Höweler + Yoon has earned a reputation as a pioneering design practice, integrating emerging technologies into both architecture design and building construction. HYA is as much a laboratory as a studio, transforming speculative ideas into built realities across scales ranging from residential builds to public space and installations, to new cultural institutions to campuses and masterplans.

P142-143

Iregular

www.iregular.io

Iregular is a Montreal-based studio founded in 2010. Working at the intersection of art and technology, the studio approaches design using a code-driven and real-time mindset. A creator of audiovisual experiences for installations and websites, its work combines geometry, typography, light and sound with software, mathematics and algorithms. The results are systems with infinite possibilities, making every instance of its projects unique.

P082-087, P092-093

Jen Lewin Studio

jenlewinstudio.com

For the last 15 years, Jen Lewin has been creating large, immersive, interactive art pieces for the public, such as interactive sound and light sculptures that inspire people to play, woven fiber video curtains that reflect movement, and giant, robotic, ethereal moths that dance based on human touch. Lewin's ability to utilize technology as a medium is rare and unprecedented. She brings an organic, feminine quality to her electronic work that leaves viewers enchanted and surprised.

P134-137, P144-145

Karina Smigla-Bobinski

www.smigla-bobinski.com

Karina Smigla-Bobinski lives and works as a freelance artist in Munich. She studied art and visual communication at the Academy of Fine Arts in Krakow, Poland and Munich, Germany. She works as an intermedia artist with analog and digital media and moves between science, intuition, expression and cognition. She produces and collaborates on projects ranging such as kinetic sculptures, interactive installations, and art interventions, featuring mixed-reality objects, multimedia physical theater performances and online projects. Karina's works bridge kinetic art, drawing, video, installation, painting, performance and sculpture. Her works contain the method of their making—they are direct art, which foregrounds the material, movement through time and impact on results.

P024-027

Kevin Cooley

www.kevincooley.net

In his multidisciplinary art practice, Cooley works with elemental forces of nature to question systems of knowledge as they relate to our perceptions and experience of everyday life. Using photography, video, and installation, his phenomenon/systems-based inquiries aim to decipher our complex, evolving relationships to nature, to technology, and ultimately to each other.

P174-175

Kit Webster

www.kitwebster.com

Kit Webster's multidisciplinary practice transverses sculpture, installation and new technologies, creating works for festivals and exhibitions, performance pieces, and architectural and commercial projects. At the forefront of digital and spatial experimentation, he has become known for his hybrid sculptural forms and immersive environments that enthrall through the vivid play of audiovisual space. His contortion of multiple compositional and choreographic techniques illustrates a consideration and deconstruction of materiality. He brings a new thinking and novel approach to digital/physical hybridization. Webster sees his artistic practice as a way of articulating in physical form the intricacies and dimensionality of abstract states of consciousness and matter.

P182-183, P198-199

Kuflex

kuflex.com

Kuflex is a studio of interactive design and audiovisual art. It was founded in 2012 by video artist Igor Tatarnikov, programmer and scientist Denis Perevalov and producer Ksenia. The installations by Kuflex are represented in numerous museums in Russia and abroad, and have been shown at festivals and exhibitions. Kuflex works on the border between visual arts and cutting-edge technologies, inspired by the latest scientific discoveries. The team explores the newest ways of using video, sound and light, while tracking technology and generative graphics allow viewers to dive into that digital space and feel it to the fullest.

P046-050, P054-055

Lateral Office

lateraloffice.com

Lateral Office, founded in 2003 by Mason White and Lola Sheppard, is an experimental design practice that operates at the intersection of architecture, landscape, and urbanism. The studio describes its practice process as a commitment to "design as a research vehicle to pose and respond to complex, urgent questions in the built environment," engaging in the "wider context and climate of a project— social, ecological, or political." Lateral Office is committed to an architecture that responds directly to the demands of the 21st century—and the subsequent new typologies made possible by an architecture that brazenly confronts today. Recent work and research focus on powerful design relationships between public realm, infrastructure, and the environment.

P116-121

Liz West

www.liz-west.com

Liz West creates vivid environments that mix luminous color and radiant light. Working across a variety of mediums, West aims to provoke a heightened sensory awareness in the viewer through her works. She is interested in exploring how sensory phenomena can invoke

psychological and physical responses that tap into our own deeply entrenched relationships to color.

P187

LUCENT

www.lucent-design.co.jp

LUCENT, by Takahiro Matsuo, creates emotional light artworks and design items, using diverse technologies and aesthetic expressions, that fuse with lighting, spaces, human beings, and interaction.

P030-031

Luftwerk

luftwerk.net

Luftwerk explores light, color, and perception in immersive, experience-based installations. Focusing on the context of a site for each project, Luftwerk applies their own interpretive layer, integrating the physical structure, historical context, and embedded information into each piece. Light and color are primary elements in works by Luftwerk. Their interest lies in the power of light as a crucial element to sight, exploring its dynamic relationship with the perception of color. Using various modalities— projecting videos, casting shadows, creating custom sculptures—they integrate light into every project to explore its ephemeral and shifting nature.

P202-203

Maja Petric

www.majapetric.com

Maja Petric is an artist working with cutting-edge technology to create transformative spatial experiences. She received a doctorate degree from University of Washington and a master's from New York University on the topic of transforming the poetic experience of space through the experimental use of technology. Her training at pioneering institutions gave her an opportunity to explore various artistic methods to manipulate people's senses, through which they experience space cognitively and emotionally. During her studies, Maja discovered that lighting is one of the most potent tools to shape experience. Since the year 2000, she has been researching, practicing, and teaching about the complementary potential of light and art to create transformative human experiences.

P148-149, P164-165

Malin Bobeck Tadaa
www.malinbobeck.se

Malin Bobeck Tadaa is a textile artist and designer working with smart textiles, combining traditional textile materials with optical fiber, LEDs and new technology. With her revolutionary textiles she creates spatial installations that invite the audience to interact with the art. She is fascinated by the worlds that are hidden to us— worlds in the deep sea, outer space or inside our imagination. By creating spaces with inspiration from these worlds she gives the viewer an experience of shifted perspectives.

P012-017

Maurici Ginés
www.artec3.com

Maurici Ginés (Barcelona, 1970), founder and creative director of artec3 Studio, which is based in Barcelona and Mexico City, has more than 20 years of experience working with light in different fields. He has done interactive light art projects in urban public spaces, both ephemeral and permanent. His artwork evolves from his persistent investigations during all his years dedicated to light. He was the president of the Professional Lighting Designers Association of Spain (APDI) from 2008 to 2014 and is a professional member of the International Association of Lighting Designers (IALD). Ginés has been awarded several national and international awards.

P133

Miguel Chevalier
www.miguel-chevalier.com

Since 1978, Miguel Chevalier has focused

exclusively on computers as an artistic means of expression. He is a pioneer of virtual and digital art. His oeuvre is experimental and multidisciplinary. Taking references from the history of art and reformulating them using computer tools, his works investigate and explore recurrent themes such as nature and artifice, flows and networks, and virtual cities. His images are a rich source of insights into ourselves and our relationship with the world.

P112-115, P180-181, P204-205

NutBrother
www.weibo.com/p/1005051781910610/home?from=pa ge_100505&mod=TAB&is_hot=1#1512026732662

NutBrother is an installation artist. He has participated in various events, like Jeonbuk Museum of Art's "ASIA YOUNG 36," the Nanjing International Art Festival, the Bi-City Biennale of Urbanism/Architecture, etc. He has won the Academic Award of the Nanjing International Art Festival, and has been honored by Jiemian News as Chinese Annual First Ten Man of the Year. He describes his own works as "a joke, a ridiculous mistake."

P076-079

Olivier Ratsi
www.ratsi.com

Olivier Ratsi's work presents objective reality, time, space and matter as a series of intangible informative notions. Focusing on the experience of reality and its representations as well as the perception of space, he conceives works that encourage the viewer to question his or her own interpretation of what is real. Making a break with objective reality, Olivier Ratsi's works are not specifically aimed to unleash emotions or to perturb the senses, but rather to work as a catalyst for different points of view and cultural and psychological references. As such, the viewer is not deprived of his own subjective capacity to reconstruct/reconstitute reality. Instead, he is invited to make up his own mind and to experience the works through his own personal reactions.

P168-173

onformative
www.onformative.com

onformative is a studio for digital art and design. Guided by an emotional approach and experimental practice, the studio creates meaningful works to challenge the boundaries between art, design and technology. Projects take on varying forms across media through self-initiated and commissioned works that range from interactive media installations, generative design and dynamic visuals to data-driven narratives. Observations of surroundings provide inspiration to explore the possibilities between analog and digital fields to examine the relationship of humans and technology. Founded by Julia Laub and Cedric Kiefer, onformative has been evolving and refining its interdisciplinary collaborative practice since 2010.

P056-057, P154-155

Oslo School of Architecture and Design
www.behance.net/ariadneandr

The whole team includes: Amalie Skrede, Ole-Birger Neergård, Diana Jamoido, Michelle Chow, Jialing Li, Martin Brændhaugen, Xuan Guo, Shirui Zhuang, Anniken Sunde Frich, Ariadne Androulaki, Caroline Guilvard, Christopher Pearsell-Ross, Irén Skjelbostad Andresen, Ivy Ferguson, Izelin Tujunen, Laura Purlytė, Ragnhild Frøyen Milter, and Thea Tollefsbøl Jegerud.

P108-109

Phillip K. Smith, III
www.pks3.com

From his Palm Desert, CA studio, Phillip K. Smith, III creates light-based work that draws upon ideas of space, form, color, light + shadow, environment, and change. Smith continually distills his concepts to create intensely physical, seemingly ephemeral, and highly meditative works that affect perception, breath, and pace of experience. Incorporating a sense of change in his work through shifting color or the movement of the sun, Smith challenges us to slow down and align ourselves with his work so that we can better see and hear the beauty that is in front of us.

P138-141

Playmodes Studio

www.playmodes.com

Playmodes is an audiovisual research studio that works with custom technologies. Their mixture of creativity, software and hardware gives birth to immersive installations, projection mapping, lighting for buildings, digital scenography, audiovisual instruments and sound design. Their innovative approach, attention to detail and a craving for storytelling make them consider projects from all points of view, delivering intensely unique works that translate across cultures.

P200-201, P206-207, P216-217, P226-227

Praxis Landscape and Urban Design

www.praxislandscape.com

Landscape is an interface that connects the physical space between people and their living environment. This interface takes different shapes while transforming in time. It is these shapes, their transformations and stories that Praxis Landscape is mostly interested in. Founded by Enise Burcu Derinboğaz in 2013, the office has been working at these transformational phases while pursuing possible relationships between architecture and environment. In this scope it provides services for landscape architecture and urban design at a wide range of scales.

P222-225

Punto.Lab

www.behance.net/puntolab

Horizontal and collaborative work is a challenge that, as a group, Punto.Lab decided to face in order to recognize how these alternative organizational structures could transform both the creative processes and the spaces people inhabit. Interactive installations became for them a call to action, to movement, a way of taking part in making decisions in their surroundings.

Following these ideas, the group Punto.Lab designed and built several large-scale urban interactive installations.

P110-111

Radugadesign

www.radugadesign.com

The portfolio of Radugadesign studio includes several hundred projects realized in Russia, Europe, the United States, China, and even the North Pole. In every project the studio strives to interconnect artistic vision and modern technologies. The studio participates often in Russian and international art projects, such as the festivals of light in Berlin, Bucharest, Prague, and Moscow; the largest Russian and European festival of landscape art objects "Arhstoyanie"; the show by Chinese director Zhang Yimou "2047 Apologue" and many others. The studio pays special attention to the search for new visual techniques and strives to offer viewers an experience they never had before.

P194-197

Refik Anadol

www.refikanadol.com

Refik Anadol works in the fields of site-specific public art with a parametric data sculpture approach and live audio/visual performance with an immersive installation approach. In particular, his works explore the space among digital and physical entities by creating a hybrid relationship between architecture and media arts with machine intelligence. As a media artist, designer and spatial thinker, Refik Anadol is intrigued by the ways in which the transformation of the subject of contemporary culture requires rethinking the new aesthetic and techniques, as well as the dynamic perception of space.

P032-035, P176-177

Romain Tardy

romaintardy.com

Romain's primary focus is to create tangible, offline art installations. He does creative and

art direction, as well as art consulting. He also designs still and animated things. He co-founded the European visual label ANTIVJ, and was active as an artist in this group from 2008 until late 2013.

P122-123, P218-221

Scenocosme

www.scenocosme.com

The couple artists Gregory Lasserre and Anais met den Ancxt work under the name Scenocosme. These French artists overturn various technologies in order to create contemporary artworks. Their works come from possible hybridizations between the technology and living world (plants, stones, water, wood, humans...). Their artworks are exhibited in numerous museums, contemporary art centers and digital art festivals around the world: ZKM (Karlsruhe), NCCA (Moscow), NAMOC (Beijing), Future Sonic (UK), Biennial Experimenta (Australia), Gaîté Lyrique (Paris), ISEA (Belfast, Istanbul, Albuquerque, Sydney, Hong Kong), FILE (São Paulo), and the Museum of Art (Daejeon).

P040-041, P051-053

Studio Nick Verstand

www.nickverstand.com

Nick Verstand is a contemporary artist researching human behavior and perception by composing with light and sound in spatial dimensions. The resulting intuitive experiences, co-creations of artist and audience, generate a meditative environment for the subconscious mind. Nick's work is created through collaborative design processes, transcending disciplines.

P096-097, P154-155

Studio Roosegaarde

www.studioroosegaarde.net

Studio Roosegaarde is the social design lab of Dutch artist and innovator Daan Roosegaarde. Together with his team of designers and engineers Roosegaarde creates landscapes of the future for a better world. The studio connects people, technology and space to improve daily life in urban environments and spark imagination. Studio Roosegaarde is located in a former glass factory, also known as the Dream Factory, in the harbor of Rotterdam. Here new innovations are developed into smart prototypes for the landscapes of tomorrow.

P022-023, P228-229

Tom Dekyvere

www.tomdekyvere.com

Tom Dekyvere explores the deeper layers of reality and mind, just as the alchemists of former times probed for unexpected connections. Dekyvere searches the boundaries between nature and technology, between man and robot, between dead and living matter.

P152-153, P214-215

TUNDRA

www.facebook.com/tunddra

TUNDRA is a St.Petersburg-based collaborative artist collective focused on creating spaces and experiences by exploring facets of interaction between audio and visuals and human emotions. TUNDRA specializes in multimedia performances and immersive audio-visual installations. Its multidisciplinary team involves musicians, sound engineers, programmers and visual artists. The team is known for works presented at multimedia festivals in the USA, Europe, Asia, and Russia.

P080-081, P188-189

UniversalAssemblyUnit

www.universalassemblyunit.com

UniversalAssemblyUnit is a London-based art practice that creates installations using light and media. Founded in 2013, they have been commissioned to create interactive and multi-sensory installations for performance, exhibition, and outdoor festival venues across the UK and Europe. These include the Roundhouse, Barbican, Royal Festival Hall, Sonar+D Barcelona, London Design Festival, AND Festival, and

FOTODOK Utrecht.

P018-019

Universal Everything

www.universaleverything.com

Universal Everything is a global collective of digital artists, designers, animators, musicians, and developers. They create video artworks for iconic architecture, invent immersive multi-sensory experiences, and direct new forms of moving images for the screens of the future. Their work explores the future of human expression and collaboration, brought to life using emerging display technologies. Their work has played a central role in bold launch events for pioneering brands and in exhibitions at leading cultural institutions around the world.

P060-063

URBANSCREEN

www.urbanscreen.com

URBANSCREEN is an artist collective and creative company based in Bremen, Germany. They develop site-specific media installations for public spaces, including architectural projections, augmented sculptures, media façade concepts, and virtual theater. Their work tackles the countless questions surrounding the new principles of communication, lifestyle and art that have emerged in the afterglow of the digital revolution. They investigate the phenomena that occur when the material world is superimposed with the digital, and inversely, when the digital overlaps with reality.

P106-107, P166-167

Vincent Houzé

www.foliativ.net

Vincent Houzé uses modern computer graphics techniques to create interactive art, performances, and large-scale multimedia installations. His practice centers on dynamic simulations and systems in which simple rules give rise to complexity and realistic motion in his work. Houzé was born and raised in Paris, where

he studied computer science and graphic design. Before embracing interactive art he worked in Paris and London as a visual effects designer for films and video games. He now lives and works in New York, where he was previously a member at NEW INC, the New Museum incubator for art and technology.

P064-067

YOKE

www.yoke.dk

YOKE is a digital design agency with a particular focus on interaction design, experience and exhibition design as well as software development. Working in the intersection between digital and analog techniques, they use the latest technology to move, engage and communicate with visitors. YOKE's portfolio ranges from interactive installations for museums and visitor centers to engaging brand experiences and events.

P088-089

YPL

www.yp-lab.com

YPL is a digital art and design practice founded by Yves Peitzner. They create sensual, poetic, interactive art installations that build strong emotional connections with the audience and form meaningful brand experiences. Their work explores the fusion of art, design and technology through continuous investigation, experimentation and purification of ideas. YPL has conceived numerous successful projects for international clients and cultural institutions in the fields of art, architecture, branding and performance.

P094-095, P098-099

ACKNOWLEDGEMENTS

We would like to thank all of the artists involved for granting us permission to publish their works, as well as the photographers who have generously allowed us to use their images. We are also very grateful to many other people whose names do not appear in the credits but who made specific contributions and provided support. Without these people, we would not have been able to share these beautiful works with readers around the world. Our editorial team includes editor Zhang Zhonghui and book designer Wu Yanting, to whom we are truly grateful.